COLLEGE READING
PURPOSES AND STRATEGIES

NANCY V. WOOD

With chapters taken from:

Psychology, Fifth Edition
by Stephen F. Davis and Joseph J. Palladino

Biology: Life on Earth, Eighth Edition
by Teresa Audesirk, Gerald Audesirk, and Bruce E. Byers

PEARSON
Custom
Publishing

PEARSON
Prentice
Hall

PEARSON CUSTOM PUBLISHING
75 Arlington Street, Suite 300, Boston, MA 02116
A Pearson Education Company

Contents

Part III Critical Reading and Thinking: Reading to Analyze, Evaluate, Think 257

Chapter 11 Develop Media Literacy 365

Chapter 12 Use Reading to Help You Think 407

Preface

Purpose and Scope

College Reading: Purposes and Strategies provides instruction and practice for two major purposes for college-level reading: (1) **study reading,** which focuses on understanding and learning information, and (2) **critical reading and thinking,** which focuses on analyzing and evaluating ideas and, as a further step, on thinking beyond these ideas to create new or related ideas. Study reading and critical reading are separated in this book for purposes of instruction but are then integrated for use in other classes through the reading questions in each chapter and in a practice exam at the end of the book.

The reading process is also emphasized in this textbook. Students analyze their present reading process and learn how to adapt it for study reading and for critical reading and thinking. Active reading strategies are taught in each chapter to help students understand exactly what to do to improve their academic reading process.

Instruction and practice in *College Reading: Purposes and Strategies* are based on psycholinguistic theory that recognizes that students use what they already know to help them read. Consistent with this theory, students are taught to access and use their prior knowledge to predict, understand, and evaluate what they read. Students are also taught to understand the conventions of writing to improve their reading. The links between reading and writing are made explicitly and frequently throughout the book.

Reading practice is provided in every chapter. In fact, roughly half of the book is made up of readings that are drawn from various types of college-level sources. A set of three to four related readings that are organized by a common topic appears at the end of every chapter (except Chapter 7). Readings for these sets are drawn from college textbooks as well as from current and historical essays. They demonstrate that textbook topics are by no means limited to textbooks, and that, indeed, they often become the topics of various types of personal and argumentative writings. The 53 readings in *College Reading* cover a broad range of subjects and help students develop useful background for their reading in other classes. The readings vary in length from 2 to 8 pages. Two-thirds of them, however, are short, usually less than 1,000 words. Others are longer and provide opportunities for more sustained reading practice.

Writing is taught as an integral part of the reading process in this book. Students learn to use writing to help them concentrate, understand, think, and remember. To facilitate study reading, students are taught to write survey maps, vocabulary sheets, outlines, marginal annotations, and summaries. To facilitate critical reading and thinking, students are taught to brainstorm lists of ideas, to freewrite in response to reading material, and to write summary responses and reactions. In addition, students are taught to write study sheets and exam answers in response to both study reading and critical reading exam questions. To effectively display on exams what one has learned and thought as a result of reading is a major final goal of college reading.

Content and Organization

The twelve chapters in this book are arranged in a three-part structure. **Part I, Some Ways to Get Started,** is composed of three chapters that describe college reading; teach methods for increasing reading speed and surveying textbooks; and provide suggestions for vocabulary improvement. **Part II, Study Reading: Reading to Learn,** is composed of four chapters that teach students to recognize the organization of ideas; to understand the main ideas and details in sentences, paragraphs, and longer sections of material and take reading notes; to understand visual material; and to organize a study reading process and use it to prepare for and take an exam on part of a chapter from a history textbook. **Part III, Critical Reading and Thinking: Reading to Analyze, Evaluate, Think,** is composed of five chapters that teach students to understand the author's purpose and point of view; to evaluate support, reasoning, and conclusions; to make inferences and analyze values and beliefs; to develop media literacy; and to use reading as a springboard for critical and creative thinking. Students take a second exam at the end of the book on four readings about the environment that requires them to integrate what they have learned about study reading and critical reading and critical thinking.

Special Features

- **Chapter goals** help students focus their attention and plan their reading of each chapter.

- **Boxed chapter practice exercises** encourage student interaction and immediate application of chapter explanations.

- **Five reading strategies in each chapter** show students specifically what to do to improve their reading and thinking. Each set of strategies includes one writing strategy to help students learn and think.

- **Collaborative reading exercises** at the end of every chapter make reading sociable for reluctant readers and provide opportunities for productive class participation and discussion.

- **Application exercises** in every chapter invite students to use and apply what they have learned from this book in their other classes.

- **Review and evaluation** of the strategies taught in each chapter invite students to look back and decide on the reading strategies they want to continue to use.

- **Fifty-three practice readings** represent many different types of academic sources, including textbooks, personal and argumentative essays, a few historical writings, and articles from current magazines and newspapers.

- **Strategy questions, study reading questions, and critical reading and thinking questions** accompany each of the readings, which are organized around a common topic, at the end of each chapter.

- **The essays in each set of common topic readings are related** and comment on each other, and students are invited to make connections and see relationships among them.

- **Textbook chapters followed by practice exams,** with instructions for scoring and evaluation, appear at the end of Part II, Study Reading, and Part III, Critical Reading and Thinking.

- **Study skills that facilitate college reading and exam taking** appear throughout and include strategies for time management, for taking reading and lecture notes, for writing summaries, as well as for studying for and taking exams.

- **Checks on reading speed can be conducted repeatedly** as students work their way through the text. The number of words in each practice reading is provided at the end of each selection. Students are shown in Chapter 2 how to use this information to compute their reading speed in words per minute for any of the selections.

New to This Revision

- New **Chapter 11, "Develop Media Literacy,"** teaches students to recognize, analyze, and evaluate many types of media, with special emphasis on Websites and Web-based materials and visual images that make arguments. Students are also taught to recognize misleading evidence, faulty reasoning, and the common fallacies. **Twelve photographs, drawings, and advertisements for student analysis. One Website for analysis.**

- Fifty-five percent (29) of the 53 practice readings are new.

- New information on the following topics:

  - **Taking reading notes** in three formats: outlines, the Cornell method, and the UAS method (underlining, annotating, and summarizing) in the book itself.

  - **Taking research notes,** with examples of a quote, a paraphrase, a summary, and an idea note.

  - **Writing summaries.**

  - **Analyzing refutation and conclusions.**

- New vocabulary exercises that teach suffixes, the most common prefixes, and 96 common roots.

- One new and one revised exam.

- **Revised Chapter 6 on visuals.** New emphasis on visuals that present information and appeal mainly to logic and reason: charts, graphs, tables of figures, geographical maps, and diagrams. **All new exercises. Fifteen (85%) of the 18 examples of visuals are now embedded in the accompanying text where they first appeared.**

- **New essays grouped under new or revised themes** that include: Ethics, Modern Computers, Learning and Memory, Fast Food, and the Media.

- **Other themes that continue in book:** Readers Learning to Read; People Who Made It in Spite of the Odds; The Punishment of Criminals; Change; Medical Marijuana; Language and Culture; and the Environment.

Acknowledgments

No college textbook goes to press without the expert advice of many capable teacher-critics who know what they want in a textbook and are willing to say so. I was particularly fortunate this time to have unusually astute and thorough critics who generously provided many excellent suggestions for improving this book. I hope they will be pleased when they see how much of their advice I followed.

I am especially grateful for the helpful suggestions and ideas of our reviewers. For this revision I received outstanding suggestions from the reading faculty at Central New Mexico Community College: Andrew Tibble, Larry Johnson, Nora Nixon, Nina Dorrance, Theresa Sullo, Elizabeth McDermott, Kenneth Chavez, Mary Rupe, Peggy Homan, Robin Ramsey, Jocelyn Mims, Roberta Ataman, and Gigi Bayley all participated in many planning meetings, including a day-long session with me. Their suggestions for revision were insightful and practical, and I was able to use almost all of them in revising this book. I am especially grateful to Larry Johnson and Andrew Tibble who contributed material on media literacy, Websites and Web-based materials, and some of the exercises and readings for the new Chapter 11.

I remain grateful for the helpful suggestions and ideas of the reviewers who worked on the earlier version of this book: Sue McGown Hightower, Tallahassee Community College; Nancy Meyer, DeVry Institute of Technology; Dennis Keen, Spokane Community College; Theresa Sullo, Albuquerque TVI; Roberta Panish, Rockland Community College; Judy Dzarnowski, J. Sargeant Reynolds Community College; Elaine Chakonas, Rosary College; Barbara Henry, West Virginia State College; John R. Wolfe, Wright State University; Elizabeth Semtner, Rose State College; Barbara Fowler, Longview Community College; and Ann Faulkner, Brookhaven Community College.

I am also indebted to Beth Brunk who helped me locate some of the readings for this book and who also drafted many of the questions on the articles. She had a major hand in writing the Instructor's Manual as well. I am grateful for her capable, creative, and consistently reliable work.

At Prentice Hall, I feel fortunate to have worked with Leah Jewell, English Editor-in-Chief, Craig Campanella, Editor for Developmental English, and Joan Polk, Editorial Assistant. These individuals always responded quickly with excellent help and advice whenever I needed it. I owe a special debt to Shelly Kupperman, Senior Project Manager, who took immense care in seeing this book through all the phases of production. She and proofreader Diane Garvey Nesin worked tirelessly to make this book attractive, readable, and accurate. They are both outstanding professionals. Fred Courtright did a fine job of obtaining permissions for this book. I also thank Brandy Dawson, Marketing Manager, for her interest and support at various stages of the project. At Pearson Custom Publishing Brian Kracke and Erin Murray have guided this revision through all the phases of production.

Finally, I thank all of you who use this book. I would like to hear about your experiences with it, and I am especially interested in your ideas for improving the chapters and readings. My e-mail address is ⟨woodnv@uta.edu⟩.

Nancy V. Wood

PART I

Some Ways to Get Started

Develop Purposes, Processes, and Strategies for College Reading

CHAPTER GOALS:

1. **To explain what happens when you read.**

2. **To describe two major purposes for college reading: study reading and critical reading and thinking.**

3. **To provide insight into your reading process and suggest ways to improve it.**

4. **To teach you five powerful prereading strategies to get you started.**

College Reading: What Is Involved?

College textbooks are better than ever. They are big, beautiful, and reader friendly. You will read many such textbooks while you are at college, but that's not all you will read. You will also read paperback books, library books, and magazine and journal articles. Some will be current; others will have been written in other centuries and may include unfamiliar words and writing styles. You will also read lab manuals, class handouts, syllabi, and test questions. Some of this material will be printed, and some of it will be on the computer screen and will include, among other things, material on the Internet.

Practice will help you read well. In fact, there is plenty of research that suggests college students improve as readers simply because they do so much reading. You can speed up that improvement, however, not only by practicing but also by developing a sense of purpose for reading, by understanding your own reading process, and by adding some new and powerful reading strategies to what you already do. This book provides practice with many types of college reading materials and explains what to do to become a more expert college reader. Working your way through the chapters and exercises in this book will help you acquire expertise much faster than you would ever be able to do on your own, using trial and error methods.

What Happens When You Read?

Reading is a mysterious activity. People who have studied it do not understand exactly how people learn to read or why it is easier for some than for others. In 1997 a long-term study completed by the National Institutes of Health reported that one in five American children has difficulty learning to read. The good news is, however, that the reading ability of 96 percent of these individuals can be improved with help. A description of what good readers do as they read will suggest ways you can improve your own reading. You will need such a description if you are to work efficiently for improvement.

Reading involves getting meaning from written words. We used to think that meaning resided on the page in the words themselves and that it was put there by the author. The information then traveled from the page, through the eyes, and into the brain of the reader so the reader could understand. In reading classes of 30 or 40 years ago, reading teachers tried to help students learn to see the words faster and more accurately in order to improve their understanding. The emphasis in reading was on the words as they appeared on the page.

Words are still regarded as important in reading, but so is another part of the reading process. In the past 25 years or so, reading experts have shifted their focus from a primary interest in the words on the page to an interest in the mind of the reader and what goes on there while he or she is reading. The psycholinguists (*psycho* meaning mind and *lingua* meaning language) emphasize that *both the mind of the reader and the language on the page are what enable people to read and understand.* Here are 10 ideas from **psycholinguistic reading theory** to help you understand what goes on in your mind as you read.[1] Instruction to help you improve in all of these areas appears in future chapters.

Ten Ideas to Help You Understand Yourself as a Reader

1. **Readers think as they read.** Reading is often described as synonymous with thinking. You are reading when you can explain what you have just read, or what it has made you think about. You are *not* reading if you stare at or even say the words, think of something else, and have no ideas about what you have just read. To understand the words on the page, you need to think about them and understand them.

---

[1] The psycholinguistic approach to reading is explained in Frank Smith, *Understanding Reading: A Psycholinguistic Analysis of Reading and Learning to Read*, 5th ed. (Hillsdale: Erlbaum, 1994).

2. **Readers interact with the material they read.** You use what you already know to help you read. Furthermore, you combine what you already know with the new information you read to create new composite meanings. Psycholinguists describe this as "interaction" between the information you know and the information provided by an author. For example, if you read an article about racing motorcycles, you will understand and picture the information in the article better if you have ridden or raced motorcycles yourself. You will add your experience to the information provided by the author to create a unique and personal meaning of your own.

Since no two readers have identical experiences or background information, your understanding of what you read will not be exactly like anyone else's. Thus, a variety of responses to questions about the readings in this book will be acceptable, just so long as they fall within a reasonable range of possibilities and are clearly a result of your mental interaction with the information on the page.

3. **Readers depend on their prior knowledge.** What you already know, your prior knowledge, is really all you have to work with to help you read. Furthermore, the more you learn, the more information you can draw on, and the better you will read. For instance, if you know nothing about motorcycles, reading one article about them will make it easier to read another article about them later. The first article will have supplied you with prior knowledge about motorcycles. Wide reading on a variety of subjects will increase your prior knowledge by improving both your general background knowledge and your vocabulary. The readings at the end of the chapters in this book cover a wide array of topics to help you add to your present store of knowledge and better read your college textbooks.

4. **Readers are constantly predicting as they read.** Readers should anticipate the next subject and think ahead when they read. Notice how this works as you

read the next few lines. Your mind is often reaching for the next idea. For example, you know there are 10 ideas about reading in this section. You have read four. You can anticipate six more. Look back at the reading goals at the beginning of this chapter. They tell you that in the rest of this chapter you can predict information about purposes for college reading, your reading process, and prereading strategies. Use the chapter goals at the beginning of each chapter to help you predict.

5. **Readers ask questions to help them predict.** Learning to ask questions will help you draw on prior knowledge, predict, and understand. All readers may not ask the same questions or even understand the answers to them in exactly the same way. This is to be expected. One reader, reading the title of an article, "Racing Motorcycles," might ask, "Is this about some well-known motorcycle races?" while another might ask, "What does it take to win a motorcycle race?" These are examples of big questions that these readers might expect this article to answer. Ask your own questions as you read the chapters and readings in this book. Questioning is a powerful reading strategy that can aid concentration, understanding, and memory.

6. **Readers use what they know about writing conventions to help them read.** Knowing writing conventions, like how paragraphs are put together or how transitions lead from one idea to another, will help you find your way through written texts. Understanding writing conventions makes you aware of the rules authors follow when they write. Consider this. Most people have been to football games or other sports events. The people in the crowd who know the rules of the game are usually paying attention and concentrating, even predicting what will happen next. Those who do not understand the rules may not be looking at the players and may even be thinking of something else. The same is true of readers. Those who know the rules of writing and the conventions that writers follow are much more likely to concentrate, follow what is going on, and anticipate what might be coming next. According to psycholinguists, writing conventions are the "common currency" of reading and writing.

7. **Readers understand best in a context that makes sense.** Apply what you read to contexts that are meaningful to you. Such contexts might include your other classes, home or work, other reading you have done, or experiences you have had. For example, if you are studying types of rocks in a geology class, compare them with the rocks you collected as a child or go pick up some rocks to make the descriptions in the book more familiar and meaningful to you. Establishing the links between new and already familiar material makes the new ideas easier to understand.

8. **Readers can collaborate to enhance individual understanding.** You may think of reading as something you do on your own. You may also, however, collaborate at times with other readers when you have difficulty understanding. Discussing and comparing your understanding of an essay about ethics and the media with your classmates, for example, encourages cooperative understanding, analy-

sis, and thinking. Reading becomes both more meaningful and more enjoyable for everyone in class.

9. **Readers can be tested on their understanding.** There are two basic types of reading tests: the standardized test and the teacher-made test. Standardized multiple-choice tests are used to measure people's reading ability and sometimes to place them in reading classes. There are limits to what standardized tests can reveal about individual reading ability, however. Think about your own experiences with these tests. At times, when you are answering multiple-choice questions, you will understand meaning in the same way that the author of the test did, and you will answer the questions in the way the test maker has hoped you will. At other times, you will read a passage somewhat differently than the test maker did, and you will have difficulty answering a question. The best reading test, according to the psycholinguists, is the homemade test, constructed on the spot by the reading teacher, that reassures your teacher that you are understanding what you read. A simple test is provided at the end of this section. Complete it from memory or by looking back if you need to. Your answers will reassure you that you have understood what you have just read.

10. **Readers should have a purpose for reading.** Reading is a purposeful activity. If you do not have a purpose for reading, you will not be very successful in creating meaning because you will lack clear reading goals. Possible purposes might include escaping for a while by reading something fun, skimming the first page of the newspaper for the basic news, or reading an essay to get an idea for writing an English paper. The next section introduces you to two major purposes for reading in college, study reading and critical reading and thinking.

Test your understanding.

1. Jot down 10 words or phrases to help you remember the 10 ideas that can help you better understand yourself as a reader. The list is started for you.

   (1) Think while reading

   (2) _____

   (3) _____

   (4) _____

   (5) _____

   (6) evaluate

   (7) predict

   (8) visualize

   (9) _____

   (10) _____

2. Which of these ideas seem most striking and important to you personally?

   _____

   Why? _____

Study Reading and Critical Reading and Thinking: Two Major Purposes for College Reading

You will read for a variety of purposes in college, but the two main purposes will be *study reading*, or reading to understand and learn, and *critical reading and thinking*, or reading to analyze, evaluate, and come up with new ideas of your own. The first question in the previous test is a study reading question. It asks you to recount what you have just understood and learned. The second question is a critical reading and thinking question. It asks you to apply what you have learned to your own reading and to think about the significance of your answer.

Some courses in college require predominantly study reading, like beginning accounting, for example. Others, like philosophy, require predominantly critical reading and thinking. It is difficult to imagine a college course that does not require some of both. Let us look first at what will be required of you as you work to meet each of these purposes. The rest of this book will provide explanations, strategies, and practice to help you pursue both purposes separately and together as required.

Study Reading

Study reading focuses on comprehending, learning, and displaying knowledge on tests and exams or in class discussion. In this and future chapters you will learn to improve your study reading by accessing your prior knowledge, asking big questions that you think will be answered, and making some predictions. You will learn to find the important ideas, understand the vocabulary, take reading notes, write summaries, and put complicated material into your own words so that you can understand it better. You will learn to visualize complicated descriptions and make drawings, diagrams, or flow charts of difficult concepts or complicated processes. You will also learn to organize new information by rearranging it, listing it, or numbering its parts. You will learn to check your comprehension to make certain you are understanding. This is called **comprehension monitoring.** You will learn to memorize by associating new ideas with familiar ideas, by using rhymes or acronyms, by employing recitation (looking away and repeating to yourself what you are learning), and by utilizing review. You will also learn to write answers to exam questions. These are examples of strategies that will help you fix new information in your long-term memory, where it will remain for life; demonstrate that you have learned; and help you understand other related material.

Your college instructors will facilitate study reading by assigning readings, by lecturing, and by assigning textbook exercises, lab sheets, problem sets, and other material to help you learn and understand. Your professors may also conduct review sessions where you and your classmates will recite aloud and discuss information for a coming test. Ultimately, your instructors will test you to measure how well you have learned. As you write the answers to the test questions, your purpose will be to show that you know the material, that you understand and remember it. In fact, you must know quantities of material in order to pursue the second major purpose for college reading, critical reading and thinking. There is another way to put this. If you do not study and learn, you will not have much to think about.

Critical Reading and Thinking

Critical reading and thinking help you to analyze and evaluate the author's ideas and also to think beyond those ideas to come up with new and related ideas of your own. Here are some examples of specific reading strategies that you will practice and learn to use to facilitate critical reading and thinking. You will learn to identify controversial issues and to figure out authors' positions on them. You will also learn to recognize the support and evidence the author provides, and to evaluate their validity. You will develop strategies for analyzing unstated assumptions, and you will learn to make assumptions and inferences of your own. To stimulate productive critical thinking, you will learn to ask the *why* and *how* questions. You will also learn to elaborate on new material, to see new applications to real life, to react to new material by associating and comparing it with familiar material, and to defend your new ideas by providing evidence that makes them clear, vivid, and believable. You will be encouraged to think in new ways and, always, to stay open to new developments that can change the way everyone thinks about a subject.

To help you read and think critically, your instructors may expect you to participate in class discussions that focus on what class members think, or to work collaboratively with other students in groups, where you will discuss your ideas together. You may also be asked to write responses to what you have read, or to participate in other learning activities that require critical or original thinking, such as debates, symposia, and interviews. To test the quality of your analysis and thinking, your instructors may assign essay exams or written assignments that ask you to demonstrate what you think as well as what you know. Notice that the writing that accompanies study reading (notes, summaries, study sheets) is done to help you learn, while the writing that accompanies critical reading and thinking (reactions, original ideas, unique positions, and essay exams) is done to help you think.

Integrating Study Reading and Critical Reading

Study reading and critical reading and thinking are not totally separated in actual college reading practice. They are separated here for the purpose of instruction to make it easier for you to develop strategies to respond to both purposes. In most of your courses you will be expected to study and learn, but also to analyze, evaluate, and come up with new ideas of your own. Each reading selection in this book is followed by questions that require you to use both study reading and critical reading and thinking strategies to answer them. The final reading exercise at the end of the book requires a complete integration of study reading and critical reading and thinking strategies. It represents what you will finally be expected to do as a mature and experienced college reader.

What Is Your Current Reading Process? How Do You Read Right Now?

If you have been in high school during the past 15 to 20 years, you have probably been taught a process for writing. That is, you have worked with ideas for prewriting, for writing the first draft, and for rewriting and revising that draft. Process is central to reading as well. Like the writing process, the **reading process** is often described in terms of prereading, reading, and postreading. You can add new strategies to all the phases of your current reading process to help you meet the demands of difficult college reading assignments.

Think about what you do now when you read a fairly complicated assignment. You probably have some strategies for studying and learning, as well as some strategies for analyzing, evaluating, and thinking in original ways. Furthermore, you probably value your reading process, and you will be reluctant to make changes in it. You will not have to change what you already do, but you can try to improve your process. Most current research indicates that you will be more successful in improving your reading process if you analyze and acknowledge how you read right now so that you can then build on that valuable core.

Analyze your present reading process.

Think about how you would read right now if you were faced with an assignment that requires mostly study reading. You have been asked to read a textbook chapter in psychology about individuals and how they relate to groups, and it is full of new vocabulary and concepts. You will be given a reading quiz in the next class to test whether or not you know the material.

What is your present process for study reading?

Jot down your answers:

1. What would you do *before* reading to prepare yourself to read?

   _____

2. What would you do *while* reading to help you get meaning?

   _____

3. What would you do if the material became *difficult to understand?*

   _____

4. What would you do *after* you finished reading to help you remember it?

   _____

Now think about what you would do in response to this reading assignment if the professor added a critical reading and thinking requirement. You have been asked to read the assignment and, in addition, to write a paper that shows how the ideas apply to an individual close to you. You are to use the ideas in the chapter to help you explain how this individual behaves in a particular group and also to provide possible reasons for this behavior. How would you change the reading process you have just described?

What is your present process for critical reading and thinking?

Jot down your answers:

1. What would you do *before* reading to prepare yourself to read and think about this assignment? _____

2. What would you do *while* reading to help you read and think about this assignment? _____

3. What would you do *if you got stuck* with your reading and thinking?
   _____

4. What would you do as soon as you *finished* reading to help you think and complete the assignment? _____

You have now described your present processes for completing assignments that call for study reading and for critical reading and thinking. You have probably not said that you would "just read" the chapter in psychology in response to either of these assignments. "Just reading" in response to assignments like these would not allow you to understand enough, to take a quiz successfully, or to write a good critical-thinking paper. In describing your current reading processes for study reading and for critical reading and thinking, you have described what you would do in addition to "just reading," when "just reading" clearly is not enough.

Add Reading Strategies to Your Present Reading Process

The two processes you have just described for study reading and critical reading and thinking are made up of reading strategies. Strategies describe what you do when you read to help you meet specific reading goals. You can add to your present strategies to make your reading more powerful. Every chapter in this book will provide you with new strategies, along with the opportunity to practice them. Think of reading strategies as conscious procedures that involve reading, writing, and thinking to help you understand and form ideas. At first, as you practice some of these new ways to read, you will be very conscious of them, and you may even find them distracting because they are different. Later, however, with more practice, many new strategies will become as automatic and unconscious as your present ways of reading. Those that do not become automatic you will probably discard. For now, however, try all of the new strategies. Many will improve your reading almost immediately.

PREREADING: FIVE STRATEGIES

Here are five prereading strategies that you can use both for study reading and for critical reading. Understand them and then practice them on the reading selections at the end of the chapter.

Strategy 1: Get organized; then decide when and where to read.

The purpose of this first strategy is to minimize frustration and keep your concentration and motivation at a high level.

Step 1: Gather your materials and decide where to keep them.

You will need *your own textbooks*, as well as *pencils*, and *paper or note cards* for note making. Make photocopies of other important reading materials and keep them in folders. Write here where you will keep these materials so you can study them later for exams.

_____

Step 2: Decide when to read.

Different individuals experience varying degrees of alertness at different times of the day or night. Discover when you are most alert and set that time aside to do your reading assignments. Complete the Time Analysis Sheet on page 34 to help make decisions about your use of time. Write here the best times for you to read.

_____

Step 3: Decide where to read.

Find a good place to read, free from distractions, where you feel alert and comfortable. Do most of your reading in this place every day. Think of a couple of other places to read in case you can't always get to the best place. Where is your best place? _____ Where also might you read? _____

Strategy 2: Assign a purpose for reading in each of your classes.

List your courses this semester and write next to each of them whether you think it will require primarily study reading, primarily critical reading, or a mix of both.

Course	Primary Purpose for Reading
_____	_____
_____	_____
_____	_____

▶

Course	Primary Purpose for Reading
_____	_____
_____	_____

Strategy 3: Identify the subject, call up your prior knowledge, and make some predictions.

Discover the subject of an essay or chapter by reading the title and the first paragraph. These will introduce the subject and provide you with some preliminary information. Then consider what you already know about the subject. Write down a few items of information. Practice on an example from a chapter in a history book entitled *The Civil Rights Movement, 1945–1966*. Think for a moment about movies and television programs you have seen on this subject as well as material you have read, and jot down what comes to mind. _____

_____

What did you write? Possibilities might include *segregation, sit-ins, Martin Luther King, Birmingham, "We Shall Overcome," Malcolm X, new laws.* You have at this point called up some items from what you already know, and now you can use that information to predict what will be in the chapter. Predict here what you think the chapter on civil rights might be about. _____
Did you predict information on Martin Luther King and Birmingham, or on the murder of NAACP chairman Medgar Evers, or something else? Plan to continue to make predictions as you read.

Strategy 4: Ask a big question that you think will be answered.

Ask one big question that you think will probably be answered while you read. Try it. Write a question about the civil rights movement of 1945 to 1966. _____

_____

What did you ask? Possibilities might include, "What were the major events?" or "What were the major results of the movement?" If you can answer questions like those when you finish reading, you will probably understand many of the most important ideas in the chapter.

Strategy 5: Write at all stages of the reading process.

As you know, you can stare at words without concentrating or understanding. When you do this, you are not thinking, and you are not reading. As soon as you pick up a pencil, however, and start to write ideas as you read, you will change this pattern. You will be reading, and you will be thinking. *Each of the remaining chapters in this book will suggest at least one writing strategy to help you learn or to help you think.* Examples of strategies that will help you learn include making annotations in the margins, taking reading notes, and writing summaries. Examples of strategies that will help you think include writing your reactions and jotting down original ideas as they occur to you. Read from now on with a pencil in your hand and begin to make some reading notes.

▶

The writing strategies that you have learned in this chapter and that you will practice as you read the selections at the end of the chapter are *write the subject, write two predictions based on what you know about the subject, and write one big question that you think will be answered—all before you begin to read* (see p. 13).

EXERCISES AND READINGS

The exercises and readings at the end of each chapter in this book follow a common format and include: (1) collaborative reading exercises that you and your classmates can do together in class to help you understand chapter explanations; (2) practice readings on a common topic, drawn from different types of college reading material, that you can read and answer questions about; (3) application exercises that encourage you to use what you have learned to help you read for your other classes; and (4) a review and your personal evaluation of the strategies taught in each chapter.

THREE COLLABORATIVE CLASS EXERCISES

Exercise 1

Understand purpose in reading. *Groups of students.*

This exercise will help you understand the concept of reading with a purpose. You and your classmates will experience four different purposes for reading the same essay. Form four groups by counting off around the room. All of the "ones" will be leisure readers, the "twos" will be study readers, the "threes" will be critical readers, and the "fours" will be critical thinkers. All groups will read the essay that starts on page 16 and answer the questions below.

Directions for Reading "Las Colonias: America's Third World"[2]

1. **Leisure Readers:** Read the article as though you were at the breakfast table reading the newspaper. What use, if any, would you make of the information? What personal value, if any, does it have for you?

2. **Study Readers:** Read the article as though it were a handout in your political science class. Suppose that this part of America is not explained in the textbook, and your instructor wants you to know about it. You will also

---

[2] My colleague Ann Faulkner and I have used this activity in reading workshops. She shares the credit for the basic idea.

have a test on this article. What do you think the instructor would expect you to understand and remember from your reading? Make notes that you could use to review the article for a test.

3. **Critical Readers:** Read this article as though you were assigned to write an analysis for your political science class. The instructor has provided the following questions to guide your work. Jot down your answers:
    a. What is the problem that is described in this article? How might the recent Census Report have provided motivation for the author to write about this problem?
    b. What do you think the author's purpose is in writing this article?
    c. How do the residents of these border towns regard living in them? How do the Texas officials mentioned in the article regard these towns and their residents? How do you regard them?
    d. What types of evidence are used in this article? Give examples of facts and figures as well as quotations from various individuals. What is the effect of this evidence?
    e. What conclusion does the author seem to draw about "the colonies" and the people who live in them? What do you think he might do, if he could, to solve the problems he identifies?
    f. What is your final reaction to this article?

4. **Critical Thinkers:** Read the article as if your political science professor has assigned you to a group of students to consider the long-term future of these small border towns. Your group is to evaluate current official policy regarding these towns and to make recommendations you consider necessary for their future. Read the article to understand the background information, and answer the following questions:
    a. Evaluate the situation described in the article. Do the colonies represent a problem for the United States, or not? Describe your conclusions.
    b. Evaluate the oversight of these towns provided by the developers and the state officials. Which of their actions do you consider responsible and which do you consider irresponsible?
    c. Write recommendations, which will be forwarded to the governor of Texas, for the future treatment of the colonies. Is all, or is part of the present policy regarding the care and development of these towns acceptable? How? If it is not, what new policies should be put in their place? How should they be implemented?

    All Readers: When you have finished reading and discussing, assign a spokesperson who will share the outcomes of your group's work with the rest of the class. Report what you did. Report what you decided. Finally, describe your emotional reaction to the experience of reading to meet the purpose your group was assigned. How did you feel about reading to meet your purpose?

Las Colonias: "America's Third World"[3]

JOHN J. MACIONIS

What should be the future of these small border towns?

"We wanted to have something for ourselves," explains Olga Ruiz, who has 1
lived in the border community of College Park, Texas, for eleven years. There is
no college in College Park, nor does this dusty stretch of rural land have sewer
lines or even running water. Yet this town is one of some 1,800 settlements that
have sprouted up in southern Texas along the 1,200-mile border from El Paso
down to Brownsville. Together, they are home to perhaps 700,000 people, a number expected to pass 1 million by 2010.

Many people speak of *las colonias* (Spanish for "the colonies") as "America's 2
Third World" because these desperately poor communities look much like their
counterparts in Mexico or many other middle- or low-income nations. But this is
the United States, and almost all of the people living in the *colonias* are Hispanic
Americans, 85 percent of them legal residents and more than half U.S. citizens.

Anastacia Ledsema, now seventy-two years old, moved to a *colonias* called 3
Sparks more than forty years ago. Born in Mexico, Ledsema married a Texas man,
and together they paid $200 for a quarter-acre lot in a new border community. For
months, they camped out on their land. Step by step, they invested their labor and
their money to build a modest house. Not until 1995 did their small community
get running water—a service that had been promised by developers years before.
When the water line finally did arrive, however, things changed more than they expected. "When we got water," recalls Ledsema, "that's when so many people came
in." The population of Sparks quickly doubled to about 3,000, overwhelming the
water supply so that sometimes the faucet does not run at all.

Courtesy of David Butow/Redux Pictures.

[3] John J. Macionis, *Sociology,* 11th ed. (Upper Saddle River: Prentice Hall, 2007) 311.

The residents of all the *colonias* know that they are poor. Indeed, the Census 4
Bureau recently declared the county surrounding one border community to be the
poorest in the entire United States. Concerned over the lack of basic services in so
many of these communities, Texas officials have banned any new settlements. But
most of the people who move here—even those who start off sleeping in their cars
or trucks—see these communities as the first step on the path to the American
Dream. Oscar Solis, a neighborhood leader in Panorama Village, a community
with a population of about 150, is proud to show visitors around the small but
growing town. "All of this work we have done ourselves," he says with a smile, "to
make our dreams come true."

Source: Based on Schaffer (2002).

416 words*

Exercise 2

Test the Idea: Reading is thinking. *Pairs of students.*

This exercise will enable you to experience the idea that reading is thinking. You will
need a partner. Both of you will read the first passage, "Teaching Johnny to Read."
One of you will read silently, and one of you will read and "think aloud" while you
are reading to let the other student know what you think as you read. Speak softly to
your partner so that you do not disturb other pairs of students in the class. Then you
will reverse roles. Both of you will read "My Father, the Graduate." The student who
did the listening the first time will now "think aloud" and reveal the thoughts that
occur as a result of reading. The other student will follow along and read silently. To
help you get started, answer these questions: What do I understand? What do I think?
Here is an example of how this "thinking aloud" might go for "Teaching Johnny to
Read": "It says it has been hard to figure out why some students have trouble learning to read. Why is this so hard? I guess we can't see what students are doing when
they read. This study began in the early 1980s. Did they just finish it? Oh, I see, yes,
they have followed some students for 14 years . . ." That should get you started.
When you have finished reading and thinking aloud, write rapidly for five minutes
about the thoughts that occurred to you as you read your article. Share some of these
thoughts with the class and compare them with the thoughts generated by others
who read the same article. Why might some ideas be different from reader to reader?
   Warm up for this exercise by silently reading the article about *Las Colonias*
on page 16. Class members may volunteer any thoughts that occur to them as
they read. Continue until everyone feels comfortable with reading silently and
thinking aloud.

* The number of words in each article in this book is printed at the end of each of the articles. Follow
the directions on pages 39–40 to calculate how fast you are able to read these articles in words per
minute.

Teaching Johnny to Read[4]

"Johnny" is a generic name for non-readers that comes from the book "Why Johnny Can't Read" by Rudolph Flesch.

1   Americans have been deluged with studies that describe how schools fail. But few if any offer convincing answers to the question of why so many children find reading so difficult that they never learn. Long-term studies begun by the National Institutes of Health in the early 1980's are shedding light on this problem. The studies offer clear strategies for teaching children who struggle to read—and a cautionary tale for schools that would mainstream learning-impaired children without making careful plans for their instruction.

2   Ten years ago, Congress directed the N.I.H. to increase its understanding of learning disabilities and how reading develops. The agency financed a series of studies that have followed about 2,500 young children, some of them for as long as 14 years. The studies, which employ brain imaging and other techniques, are conducted at several universities. The data show that a startling one in five American children have what the research director, G. Reid Lyon, terms "substantial difficulty" learning to read.

3   Contradicting a common stereotype, girls and boys were equally affected. Reading problems are just as common among children of above-average intelligence as among those who are slower. Impairment is found almost as often in children who grew up being read to as in those who grew up without a book in sight. Reading-impaired children are considerably more likely to drop out of school. Of those who graduate, fewer than 2 percent attend a four-year college.

4   The symptoms are varied. Some children labor over words, sounding out syllables and mispronouncing them. Others say the words easily but fail to comprehend them. N.I.H. researchers say the problem lies in the parts of the brain that process the written word. For many children the disorder is hereditary. For others the problem is insufficient exposure to language and reading. Nevertheless, about 96 percent improve after intensive help.

5   American educators recently engaged in a bitter and spurious debate about the relative merits of the "whole-language" approach, which often immerses children in literature at the expense of phonetic drill and practice, and the phonics approach, which provides drill and practice in phonetics and grammar. But the N.I.H. has concluded that both literature and phonics practice are necessary for impaired and unimpaired children alike. The phonics component is vital for the 40 percent of children for whom word recognition is difficult.

6   These findings underscore the need to do a better job of training teachers. The N.I.H. researchers found that fewer than 10 percent of teachers actually know how to teach reading to children who don't get it automatically. This should shock everyone, from the President and Congress to the local school board. The country will need to do better if its children are to have any chance at all.

450 words

[4] *The New York Times* 25 January 1997, A–16.

My Father, the Graduate[5]

AZIZA DAVIS

For this student, watching her own father get a degree was more inspiring than she could have imagined.

1　It was a beautiful day for a graduation. The sun was out and a crowd of happy onlookers flooded the small quad. Cameras clicked and flashed, and video cameras whirred. Binoculars everywhere reflected the sun's glare. I sat looking out at all of the people and thought, "Here comes the big moment." The name I had been waiting to hear would be called next: Edward Davis, Jr. My mom and I stood up. We yelled and cheered as my dad walked across the stage to receive his college diploma, the culmination of a lifetime of hard work and determination both in and out of the classroom.

2　My father grew up as the oldest son in a house of seven children in the inner city. He attended public schools and loved learning, although he didn't receive much encouragement from those around him. In high school, when he asked a guidance counselor if he could take college preparatory courses like his Caucasian counterparts, he was told that those courses were "not suitable" for him. His counselor suggested that he take shop instead.

3　Disappointment doesn't wholly describe what my father felt that day. Not believing there were any options left, he let the matter drop.

4　At seventeen, my father decided that the best way to get out of the environment he was in and get some advanced training was to join the military. He enlisted and became a sailor in the U.S. Navy. While in the service, he received more schooling and began to take classes at colleges and universities near his military base. Eventually, he earned an associate degree in general studies. He also married and started a family.

5　After giving twenty-three years of service to his country, my father retired and began working at a large corporation. He inquired about a program that his company sponsored that helped pay the expenses of employees who wanted to return to school, provided that their major was related in some way to the position they held in the company. My father applied and was accepted to college. He enrolled as a part-time student majoring in business.

6　From that point on my father was a near-perfect student. He devoted himself to whatever courses he was taking and became a master at managing his time. My mother did an excellent job of taking up the slack, but my dad always managed to make some time for us too. With a wife, children, a mortgage, a car, and who knows how many other things on his mind that had nothing to do with college, my dad's courses had to be infinitely more difficult for him than they are for the traditional college student. I can only imagine the amount of stress he was under. Yet he worked until he earned a bachelor of science degree from his university, and I never heard him voice a complaint.

[5] *Tools for Life from Tripod* 1:1 (Fall 1996): 8.

My father's decision to go back to school had a huge impact on how I viewed   7
my education and how I faced problems in my life. Before I had seen education as
merely a means to an end. I enjoyed it because I believed the work I put into it
would eventually pay off. It wasn't until I saw what my father went through that
I realized that education was something valuable in and of itself, something to be
enjoyed and savored, not just treated as a tool. My parents always wanted us to
learn from their experiences as well as from our own, and I learned a lot from my
father's pursuit of knowledge. I came away with three rules to live by:

1. Don't let others discourage you from pursuing your dream.

2. If you are going to accomplish anything, it will take hard work. Nothing is
   achieved without it.

3. Take advantage of any opportunity to learn.

Not only did he realize his own dream, my dad also taught me how to follow   8
mine. But I wondered how he kept from getting discouraged all those years. Then
one day I came home from high school upset about a test grade I had received. I
talked to my parents and they said that next time I would just have to try harder.
My reply was an almost tearful "I can't." My father told me no one could achieve
anything with that kind of attitude. He then took me aside and gave me a small
piece of paper with a quotation on it. "If you live by this quote anything will be
possible for you," he said. "This is what I live by. You should take this into consideration when you feel you can't." Then he walked out. I turned the sheet over
and it read as follows:

Nothing in this world can take the place of persistence. Talent will not;   9
there is nothing more common than unsuccessful men with talent. Education will not; the world is full of educated derelicts. Genius will not;
unrewarded genius is almost a proverb. Persistence and determination
alone are omnipotent. The slogan "press on" has solved and always will
solve the problems of the human race.

—Calvin Coolidge

Need I say more?   10

800 words

**Create a composite class reading process for study reading and critical
reading.** *Whole class.*

This exercise will provide you and your classmates with additional insight into the
study reading and critical reading processes. Put the heading "Study Reading" on
the board and, under it, make four columns headed with the questions, "What do
you do before you read?" "What do you do while you read?" "What do you do
when it is hard to understand?" and "What do you do when you finish reading?"
All class members should contribute answers to the four questions, describing
how they actually read. Then repeat the procedure exactly for "Critical Reading."
Refer back to your answers to these questions on pages 10 and 11. Take a look at

what the class has created. Are the processes for study reading and critical reading complete and useful? Or do one or both of the processes need improvement? Where and how could they be improved? The class may want to repeat this activity at the end of the semester to see how the processes have changed.

THREE READING EXERCISES:
ABOUT READERS LEARNING TO READ

The following three readings are drawn from an autobiography, a scholarly book, and a popular magazine. All are about readers learning to read, a major topic developed in this chapter.

Practice the prereading strategies taught in this chapter before you read each of the three articles printed here.

1. Read the title, the explanatory notes, and the first paragraph of the essay and write down the subject. Access your prior knowledge: What do you know about the subject?

2. Make two predictions about what you think may be discussed in the essay. If your predictions are not accurate, change them as you read.

3. Ask one big question that you think the essay will answer.

When you finish reading each essay, write your answers to the questions that appear at the end of the essay on separate sheets of paper. Notice that some of these questions ask about the prereading strategies you have just used, some ask about study reading, and some ask about critical reading.

Reading I

Learning to Read[6]

MALCOLM X

Explanatory Notes: *Malcolm X was a well-known African-American speaker, writer, and leader during the 1960s. He was a member for a time of the Nation of Islam (also known as the Black Muslims), which was headed by Elijah Muhammad, whom he mentions in this excerpt from his* Autobiography, *coauthored with Alex*

---

[6] Malcolm X with the assistance of Alex Haley, *The Autobiography of Malcolm X* (New York: Random House, 1965).

Haley in 1965. Malcolm X was sent to jail for various illegal street activities when he was fairly young. You can learn more about him by reading his entire autobiography. **Access your prior knowledge: What is the subject? What do you remember about learning to read yourself? Make two predictions. Ask one big question that you think will be answered.**

It was because of my letters that I happened to stumble upon starting to acquire some kind of homemade education. 1

I became increasingly frustrated at not being able to express what I wanted to convey in letters that I wrote, especially those to Mr. Elijah Muhammad. In the street, I had been the most articulate hustler out there—I had commanded attention when I said something. But now, trying to write simple English, I not only wasn't articulate, I wasn't even functional. How would I sound writing in slang, the way I would *say* it, something such as, "Look, daddy, let me pull your coat about a cat, Elijah Muhammad—" 2

. . .

Many who today hear me somewhere in person, or on television, or those who read something I've said, will think I went to school far beyond the eighth grade. This impression is due entirely to my prison studies. 3

It had really begun back in the Charlestown Prison, when Bimbi first made me feel envy of his stock of knowledge. Bimbi had always taken charge of any conversations he was in, and I had tried to emulate him. But every book I picked up had few sentences which didn't contain anywhere from one to nearly all of the words that might as well have been in Chinese. When I just skipped those words, of course, I really ended up with little idea of what the book said. So I had come to the Norfolk Prison Colony still going through only book-reading motions. Pretty soon, I would have quit even these motions, unless I had received the motivation that I did. 4

I saw that the best thing I could do was get hold of a dictionary—to study, to learn some words. I was lucky enough to reason also that I should try to improve my penmanship. It was sad. I couldn't even write in a straight line. It was both ideas together that moved me to request a dictionary along with some tablets and pencils from the Norfolk Prison Colony school. 5

I spent two days just riffling uncertainly through the dictionary's pages. I'd never realized so many words existed! I didn't know *which* words I needed to learn. Finally, just to start some kind of action, I began copying. 6

In my slow, painstaking, ragged handwriting, I copied into my tablet everything printed on that first page, down to the punctuation marks. 7

I believe it took me a day. Then, aloud, I read back, to myself, everything I'd written on the tablet. Over and over, aloud, to myself, I read my own handwriting. 8

I woke up the next morning, thinking about those words—immensely proud to realize that not only had I written so much at one time, but I'd written words that I never knew were in the world. Moreover, with a little effort, I also could remember what many of these words meant. I reviewed the words whose meanings I didn't remember. Funny thing, from the dictionary first page right now, that 9 "aardvark" springs to mind. The dictionary had a picture of it, a long-tailed, long-eared, burrowing African mammal, which lives off termites caught by sticking out its tongue as an anteater does for ants.

I was so fascinated that I went on—I copied the dictionary's next page. And the same experience came when I studied that. With every succeeding page, I also learned of people and places and events from history. Actually the dictionary is like a miniature encyclopedia. Finally the dictionary's A section had filled a whole tablet—and I went on into the B's. That was the way I started copying what eventually became the entire dictionary. It went a lot faster after so much practice helped me to pick up handwriting speed. Between what I wrote in my tablet, and writing letters, during the rest of my time in prison I would guess I wrote a million words. 10

I suppose it was inevitable that as my word-base broadened, I could for the first time pick up a book and read and now begin to understand what the book was saying. Anyone who has read a great deal can imagine the new world that opened. Let me tell you something: from then until I left that prison, in every free moment I had, if I was not reading in the library, I was reading on my bunk. You couldn't have gotten me out of books with a wedge. Between Mr. Muhammad's teachings, my correspondence, my visitors, . . . and my reading of books, months passed without my even thinking about being imprisoned. In fact, up to then, I never had been so truly free in my life. 11

The Norfolk Prison Colony's library was in the school building. A variety of classes was taught there by instructors who came from such places as Harvard and Boston universities. The weekly debates between inmate teams were also held in the school building. You would be astonished to know how worked up convict debaters and audiences would get over subjects like "Should Babies Be Fed Milk?" 12

Available on the prison library's shelves were books on just about every general subject. Much of the big private collection that Parkhurst had willed to the prison was still in crates and boxes in the back of the library—thousands of old books. Some of them looked ancient: covers faded, old-time parchment-looking binding. Parkhurst . . . seemed to have been principally interested in history and religion. He had the money and the special interest to have a lot of books that you wouldn't have in a general circulation. Any college library would have been lucky to get that collection. 13

As you can imagine, especially in a prison where there was heavy emphasis on rehabilitation, an inmate was smiled upon if he demonstrated an unusually intense interest in books. There was a sizable number of well-read inmates, especially the popular debaters. Some were said by many to be practically walking encyclopedias. They were almost celebrities. No university would ask any student to devour literature as I did when this new world opened to me, of being able to read and *understand*. 14

I read more in my room than in the library itself. An inmate who was known to read a lot could check out more than the permitted maximum number of books. I preferred reading in the total isolation of my own room. 15

When I had progressed to really serious reading, every night at about ten P.M. I would be outraged with the "lights out." It always seemed to catch me right in the middle of something engrossing. 16

Fortunately, right outside my door was a corridor light that cast a glow into my room. The glow was enough to read by, once my eyes adjusted to it. So when "lights out" came, I would sit on the floor where I could continue reading in that glow. 17

At one-hour intervals the night guards paced past every room. Each time I heard the approaching footsteps, I jumped into bed and feigned sleep. And as soon as the guard passed, I got back out of bed onto the floor area of that light-glow, where I would read for another fifty-eight minutes—until the guard approached again. That went on until three or four every morning. Three or four hours of sleep a night was enough for me. Often in the years in the streets I had slept less than that. 18

. . .

I have often reflected upon the new vistas that reading opened to me. I knew right there in prison that reading had changed forever the course of my life. As I see it today, the ability to read awoke inside me some long dormant craving to be mentally alive. I certainly wasn't seeking any degree, the way a college confers a status symbol upon its students. My homemade education gave me, with every additional book that I read, a little bit more sensitivity to the deafness, dumbness, and blindness that was afflicting the black race in America. Not long ago, an English writer telephoned me from London, asking questions. One was, "What's your alma mater?" I told him, "Books." You will never catch me with a free fifteen minutes in which I'm not studying something I feel might be able to help the black man. 19

Yesterday I spoke in London, and both ways on the plane across the Atlantic I was studying a document about how the United Nations proposes to insure the human rights of the oppressed minorities of the world. The American black man is the world's most shameful case of minority oppression. What makes the black man think of himself as only an internal United States issue is just a catch-phrase, two words, "civil rights." How is the black man going to get "civil rights" before first he wins his *human* rights? If the American black man will start thinking about his *human* rights, and then start thinking of himself as part of one of the world's great peoples, he will see he has a case for the United Nations. 20

I can't think of a better case! Four hundred years of black blood and sweat invested here in America, and the white man still has the black man begging for what every immigrant fresh off the ship can take for granted the minute he walks down the gangplank. 21

But I'm digressing. I told the Englishman that my alma mater was books, a good library. Every time I catch a plane, I have with me a book that I want to read—and that's a lot of books these days. If I weren't out here every day battling the white man, I could spend the rest of my life reading, just satisfying my curiosity—because you can hardly mention anything I'm not curious about. I don't think anybody ever got more out of going to prison than I did. In fact, prison enabled me to study far more intensively than I would have if my life had gone differently and I had attended some college. I imagine that one of the biggest troubles with colleges is there are too many distractions, too much panty-raiding, fraternities, and boola-boola and all of that. Where else but in a prison could I have attacked my ignorance by being able to study intensely sometimes as much as fifteen hours a day? 22

1450 words

Strategy Questions

Write brief answers to these questions on separate sheets.

1. What did you guess was the subject of the essay? What in the title, explanatory notes, and first paragraph helped you decide on the subject? What did you know about this subject before you began to read?
2. What two predictions did you make about what would be discussed in the essay? Was the essay about what you predicted?
3. What big question did you ask that you thought the essay would answer? How was it answered?

Study Reading Questions

1. Where did Malcolm X achieve his self-education? What motivated him to learn to read and write?
2. Describe the procedure Malcolm X followed to improve his reading.
3. Where did Malcolm X prefer to read while he was in prison?
4. When did he do his reading? How many hours a day did he sometimes spend reading?
5. How many years of formal education did Malcolm X have? What did he claim as his "alma mater" during his phone conversation with an Englishman?

Critical Reading and Thinking Questions

1. Why was prison such an ideal place for Malcolm X to learn to read? Where might you study and read that would be as effective for you?
2. Malcolm X states that "reading had changed forever the course of my life" and that "the ability to read awoke . . . some long dormant craving to be mentally alive." Elaborate on these statements. What did he mean by them?
3. Why did it take jail to make Malcolm learn to read?
4. Why do some people desire to become mentally alive while others do not?
5. Is Malcolm X describing primarily a study reading process or a critical reading process in this essay? Defend your answer with evidence from the essay.

Reading 2

Disliking Books at an Early Age[7]

GERALD GRAFF

Explanatory Notes: *Gerald Graff is an English professor at the University of Chicago. The following is an excerpt from his book* Beyond the Culture Wars: How Teaching the Conflicts Can Revitalize American Education, *published in 1992. He reveals in this excerpt how he finally got over his dislike of reading.* **What is the subject?**

[7] Gerald Graff, *Beyond the Culture Wars: How Teaching the Conflicts Can Revitalize American Education* (New York: W. W. Norton and Company, Inc., 1992). Excerpted and published under the title "Disliking Books at an Early Age" in *Linguafranca* September/October 1992: 45–51.

I like to think I have a certain advantage as a teacher of literature because when 1
I was growing up I disliked and feared books. My youthful aversion to books showed a fine impartiality, extending across the whole spectrum of literature, history, philosophy, science, and what was known by then (the late 1940s) as social studies. But had I been forced to choose, I would have singled out literature and history as the reading I disliked most. Science at least had some discernible practical use, and you could have fun solving the problems in the textbooks with their clear cut answers. Literature and history had no apparent application to my experience, and any boy in my school who had cultivated them—I can't recall one who did—would have marked himself as a sissy.

As a middle-class Jew growing up in an ethnically mixed Chicago neighborhood, 2
I was already in danger of being beaten up daily by rougher working-class boys. Becoming a bookworm would only have given them a decisive reason for beating me up. Reading and studying were more permissible for girls, but they, too, had to be careful not to get too intellectual, lest they acquire the stigma of being "stuck up."

In *Lives on the Boundary,* a remarkable autobiography of the making of 3
an English teacher, Mike Rose describes how the "pain and confusion" of his working-class youth made "school and knowledge" seem a saving alternative. Rose writes of feeling "freed, as if I were untying fetters," by his encounters with certain college teachers, who helped him recognize that "an engagement with ideas could foster competence and lead me out into the world." Coming at things from my middle-class perspective, however, I took for granted a freedom that school, knowledge, and engagement with ideas seemed only to threaten.

My father, a literate man, was frustrated by my refusal to read anything besides 4
comic books, sports magazines, and the John R. Tunis and Clair Bee sports novels. I recall his once confining me to my room until I finished a book on the voyages of Magellan, but try as I might, I could do no better than stare bleakly at the pages. I could not, as we would later say, "relate to" Magellan or to any of the other books my father brought home—detective stories, tales of war and heroism, adventure stories with adolescent heroes (the Hardy Boys, *Hans Brinker, or The Silver Skates*), stories of scientific discovery (Paul de Kruif's *The Microbe Hunters*), books on current events. Nothing worked.

It was understood, however, that boys of my background would go to college 5
and that once there we would get serious and buckle down. For some, "getting serious" meant prelaw, premed, or a major in business to prepare for taking over the family business. My family did not own a business, and law and medicine did not interest me, so I drifted by default into the nebulous but conveniently noncommittal territory of the liberal arts. I majored in English.

At this point the fear of being beaten up if I were caught having anything to do 6
with books was replaced by the fear of flunking out of college if I did not learn to deal with them. But though I dutifully did my homework and made good grades (first at the University of Illinois, Chicago branch, then at the University of Chicago, from which I graduated in 1959), I continued to find "serious" reading

painfully difficult and alien. My most vivid recollections of college reading are of assigned classics I failed to finish: *The Iliad* (in the Richmond Lattimore translation); *The Autobiography of Benvenuto Cellini*, a major disappointment after the paperback jacket's promise of "a lusty classic of Renaissance ribaldry"; E.M. Forster's *A Passage to India*, sixty agonizing pages of which I managed to slog through before giving up. Even Hemingway, Steinbeck, and Fitzgerald, whose contemporary world was said to be "close to my own experience," left me cold. I saw little there that did resemble my experience.

Even when I had done the assigned reading, I was often tongue-tied and embarrassed when called on. What was unclear to me was what I was supposed to *say* about literary works, and why. Had I been born a decade or two earlier, I might have come to college with the rudiments of a literate vocabulary for talking about culture that some people older than I acquired through family, high school, or church. As it was, "cultured" phrases seemed effete and sterile to me. When I was able to produce the kind of talk that was required in class, the intellectualism of it came out sounding stilted and hollow in my mouth. If *Cliffs Notes* and other such crib sheets for the distressed had yet come into existence, with their ready-to-copy summaries of widely taught literary works, I would have been an excellent customer. (As it was, I did avail myself of the primitive version then in existence called *Masterplots*.) 7

What first made literature, history, and other intellectual pursuits seem attractive to me was exposure to critical debates. There was no single conversion experience, but a gradual transformation over several years, extending into my first teaching positions, at the University of New Mexico and then Northwestern University. But one of the first sparks I remember was a controversy over *The Adventures of Huckleberry Finn* that arose in a course during my junior year in college. On first attempt, Twain's novel was just another assigned classic that I was too bored to finish. I could see little connection between my Chicago upbringing and Huck's pre–Civil War adventures with a runaway slave on a raft up the Mississippi. 8

My interest was aroused, however, when our instructor mentioned that the critics had disagreed over the merits of the last part of the novel. He quoted Ernest Hemingway's remark that "if you read [the novel] you must stop where the nigger Jim is stolen by the boys. This is the real end. The rest is cheating." According to this school of thought, the remainder of the book trivializes the quest for Jim's freedom that has motivated the story up to that point. This happens first when Jim becomes an object of Tom Sawyer's slapstick humor, then when it is revealed that unbeknownst to Huck, the reader, and himself, Jim has already been freed by his benevolent owner, so that the risk we have assumed Jim and Huck to be under all along has really been no risk at all. 9

Like the critics, our class divided over the question: Did Twain's ending vitiate the book's profound critique of racism, as Hemingway's charge of cheating implied? Cheating in my experience up to then was something students did, an unthinkable act for a famous author. It was a revelation to me that famous authors were capable not only of mistakes but of ones that even lowly undergraduates might be able to point out. When I chose to write my term paper on the dispute over the ending, my instructor suggested I look at several critics on the opposing sides—T.S. Eliot and Lionel Trilling, who defended the ending, and Leo Marx, who sided with Hemingway. 10

Reading the critics was like picking up where the class discussion had left off, and I gained confidence from recognizing that my classmates and I had had 11 thoughts that, however stumbling our expression of them, were not too far from the thoughts of famous published critics. I went back to the novel again and to my surprise found myself rereading it with an excitement I had never felt before with a serious book. Having the controversy over the ending in mind, I now had some issues *to watch out for* as I read, issues that reshaped the way I read the earlier chapters as well as the later ones and focused my attention. And having issues to watch out for made it possible not only to concentrate, as I had not been able to do earlier, but to put myself into the text—to read with a sense of personal engagement that I had not felt before. Reading the novel with the voices of the critics running through my mind, I found myself thinking things that I might say about what I was reading, things that may have belonged partly to the critics but also now belonged to me. It was as if having a stock of things to look for and to say about a literary work had somehow made it possible for me to read one.

[. . .] Reading books with comprehension, making arguments, writing papers, 12 and making comments in a class discussion are *social* activities. They involve entering into a cultural or disciplinary conversation, a process not unlike initiation into a social club. We obscure this social dimension when we conceive of education as if it were a process of contemplating important truths, values, and "cultural literacy" information in a vacuum and consequently treat such student tasks as reading assignments, making arguments, writing papers, and entering class discussions as if they were a matter of performing abstract procedures in a social void. Choose a topic that interests you, freshman writers are told; organize your paper logically around a central idea, and remember to support your thesis with specific illustration and evidence. Such advice is usually more paralyzing than helpful because it factors out the social conversation that reading, writing, and arguing must be part of in order to become personally meaningful.

Choosing a topic that interests you or making an effective argument depends 13 on having a sense of what *other people* are saying, of what the state of the discussion is. Before my exposure to the critical debate on *Huckleberry Finn,* I had been trying to generate that discussion out of myself, something I did not know how to do. Exposure to the debate made me less of an outsider, provided me with a social community that gave my reading stimulus and direction. I could now discover what my teachers meant by "enjoying literature" because this had ceased to be a matter of vainly struggling to achieve some mysterious and rarefied experience. Relation to a community made the intimacy of literary experience possible.

1700 words

Strategy Questions

1. What did you guess was the subject of this essay? What helped you figure it out? What did you already think or know about the subject before you began to read?
2. What two predictions did you make about what would be discussed? Describe how your predictions were or were not accurate.
3. What big question did you ask? How was it answered?

Study Reading Questions

1. Why did Graff hate to read when he was young?
2. What did his father try to do about it?
3. What was the effect of his father's efforts?
4. Describe Graff as a college reader before his junior year when he read *The Adventures of Huckleberry Finn*. What changed for him when he read this novel in his junior English class?
5. Look back at the last two paragraphs. What kind of activity does Graff say reading is?

Critical Reading and Thinking Questions

1. Is there still a stigma attached to being a bookworm or being "stuck up" because one does well in school, as there was for Graff when he was young? If so, how have you and your friends responded to this stereotyping?
2. Why do you think Graff's father's efforts to turn him into a reader did not work? What might have worked better?
3. How do you feel about becoming part of a larger community and conversation in college?
4. How do you react to those who challenge your thinking?
5. Is Graff describing primarily a study reading process or a critical reading process in this essay? Defend your answer with evidence from the essay.

Reading 3

Join the Incredible Reading Rally[8]

MICHAEL RYAN

Explanatory Notes: *The author wrote the following article for* Parade *magazine early in 1997. Tara Holland was Miss America for that year, and this describes her efforts in helping people learn to read. The Incredible Reading Rally referred to in the title took place in February 1997. For two weeks thousands of volunteers across the nation worked to help 44 million adult Americans learn to read.* **What is the subject? Access your prior knowledge: Do you know any adults who can't read? What efforts to improve people's reading ability do you know about? Make two predictions. Ask one big question that you think will be answered.**

For Tara Holland, the literacy crisis in America struck home when she was still a little girl. "I was a strong student in school," she told me. "I always enjoyed   1

---

[8] Michael Ryan, "Join the Incredible Reading Rally," *Parade* 5 January 1997: 4–6.

reading, and I took it for granted that everybody could read." But Holland, 24, the Southern schoolgirl who grew up to be crowned Miss America last September, soon discovered that a reading problem existed in her own family.

"I realized that somebody very close to me was not able to read," Tara said. "She never seemed to have her glasses when she needed them. She never read her own mail. When she went to the doctor, she made sure she had verbal instructions on how to use medicine. She cooked wonderfully and sewed beautifully, but she never used recipes or sewing patterns. I thought she was the only one in the world who couldn't read."

Tara doesn't say publicly who this loved one is, for fear of embarrassing her. "To this day, she believes that none of us know," Tara said. But the realization that the problem could strike so close to home changed the young girl's life. "I started tutoring when I was 17 years old," she said. "I was a freshman at Florida State University, and I went to work for the Campus Alliance for Literacy. It astounded me to learn that there were about 40 million Americans who can't read." Today, the number is closer to 44 million.

This year, Tara Holland will be joining thousands of other volunteers throughout the country in the second annual Incredible Reading Rally, an event developed by Literacy Volunteers of America (LVA) to help Americans understand the extent of the literacy problem and to begin to solve it. All over the country, adults, teenagers and younger children will come together to read books and enlist sponsors who will match their reading with donations to LVA and its affiliates. *Parade* and its sister publication, *react*, the official media sponsors of the event, will donate $100 for every book Tara reads—either alone or to children—during the two-week rally beginning Feb. 22. . . .

Tara Holland spent years working with people who couldn't read before she was crowned Miss America; she will devote this year to barnstorming the country promoting literacy. As I discovered when we sat down in her suite in a Manhattan hotel, she has learned a great deal about the problems of people who can't read.

"The biggest misconception is that people who can't read are dumb," she explained. "That's just not true. Oftentimes, they're very smart. They're smart enough to get that facade by people." Tara pointed out that many people who can't read actually get by in school, excelling in art or other courses that require little reading and pretending to be unable to find their glasses or books when called upon to read in other classes. "Often, there's a learning disability that's not diagnosed," she said.

Tara told me the moving story of a man named William Frets, who started out as her student and has become her friend. Born with cerebral palsy, Frets, now 50, was considered ineducable—even though only his body, not his mind, was impaired. Now he is well on his way to a GED and his dream of a job in the computer field. "Tara never accepted the words 'I can't,'" Frets told the Miss America organization. "She is a strict tutor but is also a lot of fun."

Tara Holland earned her undergraduate degree in music education at Florida State and will return to graduate school at the University of Missouri at Kansas City when her reign as Miss America is over. She is a professional educator, and she is using her newfound visibility to teach her fellow Americans about one of the greatest problems in education today.

"One person out of every 10 who graduates from high school cannot read his or her diploma," said Tara. "I've worked with people from ages 18 to 75 who can't read." 9

When she launched her Miss America campaign for literacy last year, Tara appeared at an adult center called the Academy of Hope in Washington, D.C., which runs a program that has helped more than 1000 adults gain literacy in the last decade. There, Tara met Mary Harshaw, who was a 25-year-old mother of three when she decided to learn to read. "I didn't want my kids to go through life having to ask the neighbors for help with their homework," Harshaw explained. "I didn't want them being asked, 'Why can't your mother help you?' and have to say, 'She can't read.'" 10

Some people might feel self-conscious about going back to school in adulthood, but both Bill Frets and Mary Harshaw demonstrate that the experience is far from humiliating. "I never looked at it like that," Harshaw said. "There were other grown-ups there. I wasn't alone. Age didn't make a difference to me." 11

Learning to read can be a difficult choice for a grown-up. "It's hard for an adult to say, 'I don't have the skills,'" Tara Holland explained. "They're embarrassed. But the message I'm trying to get across this year is: You're not alone. You're not the only one out there, and there's nothing to be ashamed of." 12

The problems that result from an inability to read are obvious: Blue-collar jobs that require no reading skills are fast disappearing. According to *Nation's Business* magazine, an estimated 15 million adults holding jobs today are functionally illiterate. The worker of tomorrow will have to be faster, smarter, brighter and, most of all, literate. Mary Harshaw already has used her abilities to pass examinations and become a personal care aide, and she intends to keep on learning. Bill Frets plans to find that computer job soon. 13

Tara Holland told me about other lives she had seen transformed through the magic of the printed word. "I worked with one woman who was a grandmother," she recalled. "She had never wanted to read for herself, but the time came when she wanted to be able to read to her grandchildren. She worked very hard, and now those grandchildren sit on her lap and learn the magic of reading from her." 14

The Incredible Reading Rally aims to spread the advantages of literacy to every American, no matter how poor or rich, old or young. "Remember that magic moment in childhood when you looked at a book or a sign or even a cereal box and realized you could read it?" asked Beverly Miller of Literacy Volunteers. "In a real sense, you joined the human tribe that day. We want every American to experience that feeling." 15

With her background in education, Tara Holland has learned that failing to read can often be traced to a learning disability—or, as she likes to say, "a teaching disability." In earlier generations, especially, many teachers were not trained to understand that some students had different needs, as well as visual or aural problems that kept them from learning to read as quickly as their peers. "If a student is not completing homework or coming to class, then the educator needs to recognize that there might be some disability that should be dealt with," Tara said. 16

What has cheered her immeasurably is the zest that her adult students bring to learning. "It's never too late to learn," she told me. "I've worked with people who 17 are 70 and above. Even if you're going to live just one more year, it's better to live that year able to read. If you're not perfectly happy with yourself, there's no reason to deny a chance to improve your life."

In fact, Tara pointed out, adults often learn to read much more quickly than children. "They already know the language, because they speak it all the time," she explained. "They recognize words more readily. A child might not know a word like 'iridescence,' but an adult will. They have the ability to accelerate much faster." 18

Although the Incredible Reading Rally lasts just two weeks, its purpose is to raise consciousness about reading year-round. The rally's founding sponsor—Ferrero USA, the makers of Tic Tac breath mints—is providing funding for programs across the country that will try to prove to adults that reading can be fun and that learning to read can be easier than they think. Every year, hundreds of thousands of adults in America swallow their pride and their fear and enroll in literacy programs. 19

There are some scary statistics about the lack of reading skills in this country: 60 percent of prison inmates can't read; one-third of mothers who received Aid to Families With Dependent Children grants cannot functionally read. But, as Tara Holland pointed out, the reason to learn to read is positive, not negative. It's not just to cut down on crime and welfare dependency but to make America a better, richer society. "If we give people the ability to read," she said, "we give them the tools they need for a better life." 20

1550 words

Strategy Questions

1. What is the subject of the essay? What helped you figure it out? What did you already know about teaching people to read?
2. What predictions did you make about the essay? Were they or were they not discussed? If they were misleading, how did you change them as you read?
3. What big question did you ask? How was it answered?

Study Reading Questions

1. What happened in Tara Holland's life that motivated her to want to teach people to read?
2. What is a common mistaken idea that people often have about why some people don't learn to read? What is often the real reason for the problem?
3. What is the percentage of people who graduate from high school who cannot read their diplomas? What percent of prison inmates cannot read? What percent of mothers on welfare cannot read? What are some of the ways mentioned in the article that people use to disguise their inability to read?
4. What are some of the reasons mentioned in the article for learning to read, even when one has been unsuccessful in the past?
5. What methods for teaching people to read are mentioned in the article?

REVIEW AND EVALUATE THE STRATEGIES

The following is a review of the five strategies you learned in this chapter:

1. Get organized; then decide when and where to read.
2. Assign a purpose for reading in each of your classes.
3. Identify the subject, call up your prior knowledge, and make some predictions.
4. Ask a big question that you think will be answered.
5. Write at all stages of the reading process.

Make a personal evaluation of these strategies:

1. Underline your favorite strategies in the list above.
2. Make a check mark by those you want to continue to use.
3. Cross out any you probably will not continue to use. What are your reasons for rejecting them?

Improve Your Reading Efficiency and Focus

CHAPTER GOALS:

1. **To explain when to read slowly and when to speed up.**

2. **To describe surveying, skimming, scanning, and reading selected parts.**

3. **To demonstrate how to take reading notes in the form of a map, an outline, or Cornell reading notes.**

4. **To provide five strategies for reading more efficiently.**

The Importance of Purpose and Level of Difficulty

You were invited in the last chapter to think about the courses you are taking this semester and to assign purposes for reading in each of them. As you contemplated your reading assignments, you may have concluded that you will be doing a lot of reading during the coming months. Most students need some instruction right away on how to read more efficiently if they are going to get all of it done.

You will not finish your reading assignments if you read everything in the same way and at the same speed. There is no one speed appropriate for every kind of reading. You will need to develop a range of reading speeds and a variety of reading strategies to help you move through your assignments in the time you have set aside to read them. Your **purpose for reading** and the **level of difficulty** of the reading material will largely determine how fast you will read. Your **purpose** will vary with specific reading assignments. At times, for example, your purpose may be to learn and remember a reading assignment in detail so that you can take a test on it. Then you will read slowly. At other times, your purpose may be to understand some of the main ideas so that you can think about them for class discussion. In this case you may read more rapidly and spend the rest of your study time thinking, taking notes, and writing out your ideas.

The **level of difficulty**, or how hard the material is for you to read, will also determine how fast you are able to read an assignment. In future chapters you will be provided with many strategies to help you slow down and do close and detailed reading. The rest of this chapter, however, teaches you how to speed up when that is appropriate. The assumption is that you are now in the mainstream of college reading, that there will be a lot of reading, and that you will need some strategies to help you move through some of this reading quickly at times. You may not achieve perfect comprehension using the strategies in this chapter—none of them are a substitute for careful reading. Still, when pressed for time, using them will guarantee that you will learn much more than if you had not looked at an assignment at all. This chapter will help you adapt to the volume of reading that college students often face.

You can speed up your reading in one of two ways, either by using a speed-reading method or by skipping and reading only the selected parts of a text that are likely to contain the information you need most. This chapter will teach you how to do both. But first, learn to analyze the level of difficulty of texts so you will know which you can read rapidly and which you need to read more slowly.

When to Read Slowly, When to Speed Up

Most of your professors will want you to read slowly most of the time, requiring you to pay attention to detail and to think about the ideas. Some professors will assign you modern and ancient classics to read, and most people agree that you will be rewarded as a reader if you read these works slowly. The same is true of your textbooks, particularly if the material is new to you and seems hard. You can, however, also speed up when some of this material seems easier. How will you decide if reading material will be easy or difficult for you? Some of the answers have to do with you and what you already know, and others have to do with the nature of the reading material itself.

Research into how difficult a specific reading assignment will be for an individual student identifies the following factors as important considerations.

Identify How Difficult a Reading Assignment Will Be for You

1. **How much prior knowledge do you already possess about the subject?** When the subject is familiar, you can relate it to what you already know, predict what will come next, and read and remember it more easily. When the subject is unfamiliar, you will need to slow down and build some background for reading.

2. **What is your attitude? Are you motivated and concentrating?** You can read faster when you are interested in the subject and are motivated to read about it and when you feel alert. You can often read faster, for example, if you are trying to learn how to do something, or you need to find specific information, or you are eager to see what happens at the end of a story. On the other hand, if the subject is new to you, and you have not figured out a good reason for reading it, then it will seem harder to read and you will slow down.

3. **Is the organization of ideas obvious and easy to follow?** In Chapter 4 you will learn to recognize the organization of ideas in the material you read. Authors

can make ideas and their organization obvious and easy to recognize by using headings and other obvious transitions like numbering, as is done here, and that can help you read faster. Or, they can eliminate these aids to understanding and make it harder to recognize the main ideas. Then you will need to read more slowly.

4.   **How many connective words are there?** In Chapter 5 you will learn to recognize how authors repeat key words and use transitions to connect the ideas from sentence to sentence and paragraph to paragraph. This helps you read and follow along, the material seems easier, and you can read more rapidly. When few such connections are provided, the material is harder to understand and you will need to slow down.

5.   **How dense is the material?** You will find yourself slowing down when many new ideas are explained in a relatively small space. When explanations, examples, and illustrations are provided for each new idea, the material will seem easier and you will be able to read more rapidly.

6.   **How many different words are there in a passage?** Passages that contain relatively few different words can be read more rapidly than those that contain many different words.

7.   **How well can you understand the words?** Passages that contain familiar words that yield instant and rich meaning for you are much easier to read than materials that contain many words that are new and unfamiliar to you.

You can usually read a few sentences of an assignment and know right away if it is difficult and you will have to read it slowly or if it is fairly easy and you will be able to move through it comparatively rapidly.

Stop and reflect.

How difficult are your reading assignments this semester? Which are:

Easy?   Medium Difficult?   Difficult?

_____   _____   _____

_____   _____   _____

Why are the readings in your "difficult" column difficult for you? _____

_____

Why are the "easy" readings easy for you? _____

Now think about one of your fairly easy reading assignments, which you think you will be able to read more rapidly than some of the others. Adequate understanding of such an assignment is always the goal. You do not want to train your eyes to move so rapidly across the page that your mind cannot keep up and understand. Then you would only be seeing words. Let your reading purpose help you decide how much information you need to understand. Then, as you experiment with some of the methods described in this chapter, monitor your comprehension and insist on adequate understanding that is consistent with your purpose. To monitor your comprehension, stop reading, look away, and see if you can complete these statements: "This is about . . ." and, "Some of the topics it covers are . . ." If you cannot remember enough to respond to these statements, you are not understanding the reading, and you will need to slow down and read more thoroughly.

How Fast Do You Read? How Can You Improve Your Speed?

Generally, beginning college students read most material somewhere in the range of 150 to 220 words per minute. There is a reason for this. This is the range at which people read aloud. Since we spend considerable time as children reading aloud, many of us continue to read at this rate, even when reading silently as adults. A reasonable goal is to develop a more extensive range of reading rates—for example, from 150–400 words per minute—and then to use a speed that is appropriate for a particular text.

PRACTICE. Research has shown that most college students automatically improve their reading speeds while they are at college as a result of all the reading they do. If you want to accelerate this process, refer to Strategy 1 on pages 43–44 for specific procedures for increasing your beginning reading speed and developing a broader range of speeds.

Make an estimate.

If you like, you can get an idea about how fast you read right now. The number of words in each article in this book is printed at the end of each of the articles. Here is how you can check your present reading rate. Turn to Reading 3, "We've Overlooked One of Our Greatest Assets," page 66, and read this article at your normal rate of speed. Use a stopwatch or a watch with a sweep second hand to time your reading. Put the watch in front of you and jot down the time that you begin reading. Look at the watch again when you finish, and write down the ending time. Now subtract the beginning from the ending time to discover how many minutes and seconds you took to read the article. Next, calculate your speed in words per minute. There are 760 words in this article. Divide 760 words by the minutes and fraction of a minute you spent reading. Round off the seconds to 15, 30, or 45 seconds, and convert the seconds to fractions as follows: 15 seconds = 0.25 of a minute, 30 seconds = 0.5, and 45 seconds = 0.75.

Example: If it took 3 minutes and 15 seconds to read the article, convert 15 seconds to 0.25 and divide as follows:

$$
\begin{array}{r}
2\ 34 \quad \text{w.p.m.} \\
3.25\,)\overline{760.00} \\
650 \\
\hline
1100 \\
975 \\
\hline
1250 \\
1300
\end{array}
$$

Make your calculation and record your speed: _____ w.p.m.

Do you consider yourself (check one): a fast reader? _____ an average reader? _____ a slow reader? _____

How would you rate your comprehension of this article? (check one) I understood it well _____ I understood only parts of it _____ I didn't understand very much of it _____

This quick assessment will give you an idea of your present reading speed and comprehension. Because you will read so much while you are working your way through this book, you may be able to increase your present speed by 50–100 words per minute by the end of the semester. You will also increase your comprehension if you complete most of the exercises and readings at the end of the chapters.

You can use this method to check your speed at any time. Simply time your reading of any article in this book and divide the number of words listed at the end of the article by the time you spent reading it. Not all of the readings in this book are at the same level of difficulty. You will be able to read faster when you already know something about the subject of the article. You will read more slowly when an article is difficult for you. Remember that understanding what you read is always more important than speed.

Surveying, Skimming, Scanning, and Reading Selected Parts

Besides increasing your range of reading speeds, you can also move through a lot of reading material more rapidly by learning to read only parts of a text. But you must know which parts to read so that you will locate the information you need. Here is a description of four strategies for reading only selected parts instead of the entire text. Strategies 2 to 5, which begin on page 44 will teach you exactly how to use each of them.

1. **Surveying** can be done either on an entire book or on a chapter. Surveying enables you to identify the subject of a book or chapter, to find some of the main ideas, to study how the ideas are organized, and to locate some of the key terms or vocabulary words. Surveying a book can help you learn about the author, the text itself, and how you will need to read it. Answering the questions in Figure 2-1 can yield useful information that will introduce you to a book and teach you a great deal about it. Obtaining such information through a quick survey can also motivate you to read and learn more about the book later.

When you survey a book, notice the front matter, which comes at the beginning of the book before the first chapter and may include a table of contents and a preface. Notice also the back matter, which follows the last chapter, and may include the index and possibly a glossary as well. The author places this information in the front and back of a book to help readers find the information they need.

Surveying a chapter can help you see the big picture at that level as well. You will learn to recognize the subject of the chapter as well as most of the main ideas and how they are organized, and you will learn which special features the author has included to help you learn and think about the material. These might include, for example, vocabulary in boldface type; learning goals; summaries of important ideas; or special exercises, activities, or word lists at the end of the chapter.

When you survey at the chapter level, look at the beginning and end of two or three chapters to see if they are set up in the same way. All of the chapters in this book, for example, begin with chapter goals and end with strategies, exercises, and readings. When you fix this pattern in your mind, you will find it easier to survey and read.

Use surveying for a variety of reading purposes. Surveying is useful, for instance, before you begin to read to get the lay of the land, so to speak. Besides introducing you to the subject and main ideas, surveying before you read can help you plan your

FIGURE 2-1 *Questions to Ask When Surveying a Book*

strategies for reading later. Surveying is also an excellent way to review material that you have already read and that you need to have clear in your mind for an exam or a class discussion. You can also survey when you have finished reading an assignment that you found difficult or which you did not quite understand. Surveying a difficult chapter after reading allows you to get a better idea of the parts and how they fit together to make up the whole. Finally, surveying a book instead of reading it is sometimes useful. You can learn quite a bit about a book or chapter with this strategy. Surveying instead of reading is especially useful when you intend to take research materials from a book without reading all of it. Surveying in this case helps you represent the context for your quotes accurately. Or, you may be wondering whether to read or even buy a new book. A quick survey will help you decide.

2. **Skimming** is a bit more thorough than surveying. Your objective in skimming is to locate the subject, the most important ideas, and enough of the details so that you can identify the subject and describe, in general, what the author says about it. You will use skimming techniques when you want to get the gist of something, but you do not want to slow down and read all of it. Skimming involves reading only the opening and closing paragraphs and the intervening sentences and words that carry most of the meaning. Many of the words you will skip over. You might skim a chapter or an article just before a class discussion when you do not have the time to read it in detail. You might also skim a letter, a newsmagazine, a newspaper, or a supplemental article for a class that the professor has recommended but that will not be on the test. You can sometimes save time by skimming an entire selection and then going back to read thoroughly the parts that meet your immediate reading purpose. Skimming can also help you understand a difficult reading that you have already read to help you review the main ideas.

3. **Scanning** is looking through reading material for a specific bit of information that you think is likely to be there because you have checked it in the index, because someone has told you it is there, or because you think you remember seeing it there. Scanning can help you locate particular bits of information very quickly. Finding a service and a telephone number in the yellow pages of the telephone book is an example of scanning.

4. **Reading selected parts for research** is useful when you are reading to answer research questions or to locate information on specific topics that you have found in the index at the back of the book. You will need to use this strategy when you write research papers for some of your classes.

If you are preparing to write a research paper, you will also want to take some research notes as you read. These notes will either be direct quotes, paraphrases, or summaries. Direct quotes require quotation marks since you are using the author's exact words. Paraphrases and summaries do not require quotation marks since you are putting the author's ideas into your own words. The cardinal principle in taking all three types of research notes is that you must clearly indicate on every note that the words in direct quotes and the ideas in paraphrases and summaries belong to someone else. Make a complete record of your sources on a separate sheet of paper. You will need it later when you write. Include the author, title, place of publication, publisher, date, and page number(s) for every source you use. Write briefer information on the notes themselves: author, source, and page number.

You will often get original ideas of your own as you read. Write idea notes and label them "mine" to keep them separate from the ideas that belong to others. Keep your idea notes with your other reading notes. Strategy 5 on page 51 provides examples of these different types of research notes.

Make Some Reading Notes When You Survey a Chapter

When you finish surveying a chapter or article, take a few minutes to make some notes on what you have learned. Survey notes identify the main ideas in a chapter or article and help you visualize their order and how they are related to each other. You can expand and add to your survey notes later when you go back and read for more detail. Format your survey notes in a way that is comfortable for you. You may decide that you like survey maps best, or that you prefer outlines or Cornell reading notes. Strategy 4 on page 46 provides examples of each of these types of notes and gives instructions for writing each of them.

EFFICIENT READING: FIVE STRATEGIES

These five reading strategies will teach you exactly what to do when you want to speed up your reading or read only parts of a text to get information you need. *Remember that none of these will substitute for close, thorough reading.*

Strategy 1: Develop a range of reading speeds.

Determine your purpose, sample the reading material for level of difficulty, and figure out how fast you will be able to read and still meet your purpose. Select one of the following methods to help you read faster when that is appropriate.

Use a pacing device.

Increase your reading speed by moving a 3" × 5" or 4" × 6" index card down the page at a rate that pushes you to keep ahead of it. Or use your finger or a pencil, without marking the page, to quickly underscore each line as you read. Another pacing method is to place your open hand on the page and drag it down the page as you read. You will discover that you will read faster to keep up with the card, your finger, or your hand. Experiment to see which is best for you.

Set time limits and meet them.

To increase your reading speed in a particular book, begin by reading for 15 minutes to see how many pages you can read in that time period. Now count off that many additional pages *plus one more*, use a pacing device, and finish reading those pages in the next 15 minutes. Use a timer that will signal the end of 15 minutes. As soon as you can, add one more page and later another to the total you are able to

▶

read in 15 minutes. Continue to pace yourself and time yourself. Monitor your comprehension by stopping at times to mentally rehearse what you have understood. If you are not understanding enough, slow down.

Practice by doing leisure reading.

Find books or magazines that you really want to read and that are fairly easy to read and think of them not only as rewards at the end of a busy day of study but also as an opportunity to practice reading faster. Try to read for 15 to 30 minutes each day. Use pacing devices and set time limits initially to practice reading this material more rapidly. Later, just push yourself to read faster than you do now. Your speed will improve as you continue to practice, and as you learn to read one type of material more rapidly, the speed at which you read other types of material will also improve. Are you reading something for fun right now? What is the title?

Strategy 2: Survey books.

Here are the steps for surveying a book. Use them to learn a great deal about a book in about 15 to 30 minutes.

Step 1: Read the title.

Focus on the subject as indicated by the title. What do you already know about it? Make two predictions. Ask a big question to spark your interest.

Step 2: Read the title page and introduction or preface.

Check the copyright date to see when the book was written. Read for information about the author and the book that will help you understand why it was written, how it has been put together, and how you can best read it.

Step 3: Read the table of contents.

This is the list of the main topics in the book. What are these topics? Why do you think they have been put in this order?

Step 4: Examine the special features.

Look at the material (the front matter) in the front of the book, before the first chapter, and look at the material (the back matter) in the back of the book, after the last chapter. What is included to help you read the book? Now, look at one chapter. What has the author included to help you read the chapters? How will you use these special features?

▶

Step 5: **Look at the** *first and last chapters* **in the book.**

Read the titles and the first and last paragraphs of these chapters to get a sense of what they are about. Why do you think the author has begun and ended with these subjects?

Step 6: **Look at the** *other chapters* **in the book.**

Read the title and first paragraph of each of the other chapters. Get a sense of the progression of ideas in the book. Identify some of the key vocabulary terms, either as they appear in chapter titles or in boldface type.

Step 7. **Reflect** *on what you have learned and write a few notes.*

Complete this statement, "This book is about . . . and it covers the topics. . . ." To motivate yourself to read more of the book, write a sentence or two about what seems valuable or interesting in the book at this point. This will help you read in more detail later.

Strategy 3: Survey chapters and articles.

Here are the steps for surveying a chapter or an article. Use them to learn a great deal about a chapter or article in about 5 to 10 minutes.

Step 1: **Focus on the subject as indicated by the title.**

What do you already know about the subject? Make two predictions. Ask a big question to spark your interest.

Step 2: **Read the** *introduction.*

Find out what the chapter or article is about. Read the chapter goals or any other explanatory material that appears before the first paragraph. Read the first paragraph.

Step 3: **Read the** *summary.*

Find out how the chapter or article ends. Read material marked "summary" or read the last paragraph. Look for a restatement of main ideas or a particular idea that is emphasized at the end. Look for any other material at the end of the chapter or article (exercises, bibliography, word lists, reviews, etc.) to see what else the author wants to emphasize.

▶

***Step 4: Read the* headings.**

Read the **headings** and **subheadings** that appear in boldface or italics to get a sense of the progression of ideas. If there are no headings, read the first sentence of each paragraph to accomplish the same purpose.

***Step 5: Look at the* visuals.**

Look at all the pictures, graphs, charts, and diagrams and read their captions. This will also help you become acquainted with the major ideas.

***Step 6: Circle the* key words or terms.**

These may appear in italics, in the margins, or in the title, headings, or introduction. You will need to understand them when you read.

***Step 7: Reflect* on what you have learned.**

Complete this statement, "This chapter (or article) is about . . . , and it covers the topics. . . ." To motivate yourself to read more, write a sentence or two about what seems valuable or interesting at this point.

Strategy 4: Take reading notes after you survey: write a survey map, an outline, or Cornell reading notes.

Option 1: Write a survey map. (These maps are sometimes called mind maps to distinguish them from geographical maps.)

A survey map is a picture of the most obvious main ideas in a book, chapter, or article that surveying has helped you locate. See Figures 2-2 and 2-3 for examples. Survey maps show the basic shape of the material: the main ideas that are emphasized in headings or first sentences in paragraphs, the order in which they are presented, and how they relate to each other. Here are three steps for making a survey map.

***Step 1. Write the* subject.**

Write the subject of the chapter as stated by the title at the top or in the middle of a page and draw a box or circle around it.

Step 2. Write the* main ideas *that stand out.

Attach lines to the circle or box and write briefer versions of the headings in boldface type on the lines. If there are no headings, read the first and last paragraphs and the first sentence of each paragraph. Write the ideas that stand out from this reading on the attached lines.

▶

Step 3. Attach other ideas to the main ideas.

Attach ideas about the main ideas that are printed in boldface or italics. Attach them to the main headings that they support.

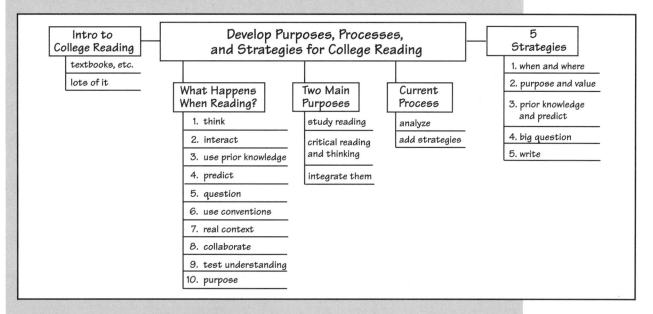

FIGURE 2-2 *A Survey Map of Chapter 1*

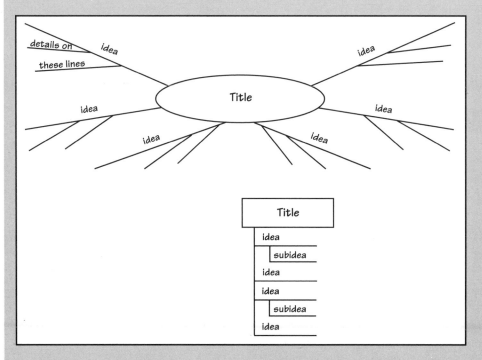

FIGURE 2-3 *Other Ways to Draw Survey Maps*
Use the one that is easiest for you, or make up your own.

Option 2: Write an outline.

An outline, like a map, lays out ideas in a visual form and shows how ideas are related to each other. Here are four steps for making an outline.

Step 1. Write a title.

Step 2. Write the most general main ideas, those that appear in the largest boldface type, at the left-hand margin.

Step 3. Indent the sub-ideas.

Skim the material under each heading and add one or two ideas about each of the general ideas to your outline. Some of these ideas may appear in smaller boldface type under a main idea.

Step 4. Add specific facts, opinions, examples, illustrations, other data, and statistics later when you read.

Indent this material under the sub-ideas.

An outline of Chapter 1 appears in Figure 2-4. It contains main ideas and sub-ideas.

CHAPTER 1: Develop Purposes, Processes, and Strategies for College Reading

I. College reading: what is involved?
   A. Textbooks and other material.
   B. Learn strategies to improve.
II. What happens when you read? Ten ideas.
   A. Think and understand.
   B. Interact with the text.
   C. Use prior knowledge.
   D. Predict.
   E. Ask questions.
   F. Use the conventions of writing to understand.
   G. Relate reading to contexts that make sense.
   H. Collaborate to understand.
   I. Test your understanding.
   J. Have a purpose for reading.
III. Two main purposes for college reading.
   A. Study reading.
   B. Critical reading and thinking.
IV. Integrate study reading and critical reading and thinking.
V. Current process for reading right now.
   A. What do you do before, during, and after you read?
   B. What do you do to understand difficult material?
VI. Five prereading strategies to add to your process.
   A. Get organized to read. Decide when and where to read.
   B. Assign a purpose for reading.
   C. Identify the topic, call up prior knowledge, make predictions.
   D. Ask a question you think will be answered.
   E. Write at all stages of the reading process.

FIGURE 2-4 *An Outline of Chapter 1*

Option 3: Take Cornell reading notes.

Here are four steps for taking Cornell notes.

Step 1. Use notebook paper with a generous left-hand margin to take Cornell reading notes.

Write a title, and take enough notes so that you can easily understand them later.

Step 2. In the left-hand margin write notes on the notes.

Include labels, key words, and brief questions.

Step 3. At the end of the notes write a summary in complete sentences.

Refer to the marginal notes to help you write the summary.

Step 4. Later, when you study these notes, cover up the main notes on the right, refer to the key words and questions in the margin, and try to recite the contents of the notes.

If you cannot, look back and reread the notes. Then cover them again and try to recite them. Continue until you know the material. Then read the summary to check your understanding and fix the material in your mind.

Figure 2-5 provides an example of Cornell notes taken after a survey of Chapter 1. Notice that a modified outline form is used that places the main ideas by the margin, indents the sub-ideas, and sets them off with dashes. You may use the numbers and letters of a conventional outline in making these notes or follow the example below. Both show the relationship of the ideas, which is your objective.

CHAPTER 1: Develop Purposes, Processes, and Strategies for College Reading	
What are 4 goals?	*1. Four goals of the chapter:* 　—*to explain what happens when we read* 　—*to describe study reading and critical reading, the two main purposes for college reading* 　—*to help us understand our reading process and get ideas for improving it* 　—*to develop 5 new prereading strategies*
Describe college reading	*2. What is involved in college reading?* 　—*lots of textbooks, library books, journals, etc.* 　—*need to improve by developing new reading strategies*

FIGURE 2-5 *Cornell Notes on Chapter 1*

▶

10 ideas about readers?	3. *People use what is on the page and in their mind to develop meaning. Ten ideas to help understand ourselves as readers:* —*we think while we read* —*we interact with material on the page by using what we already know* —*we depend on our prior knowledge to help us understand* —*we make predictions* —*we ask questions to help us predict* —*we use what we know about writing conventions to help us make meaning* —*we put what we have read in a meaningful context to understand better* —*we collaborate with other readers to check our understanding* —*we test our understanding with tests made on the spot* —*we have a purpose for reading everything*
What are 2 purposes of college reading? Separate or not?	4. *Two main purposes for college reading: study reading and critical reading and thinking* —*study reading focuses on comprehending and learning* —*critical reading and thinking focuses on analysis and evaluation and developing our own ideas* —*These two purposes are not separate—we learn to integrate them.*
Describe present reading process	5. *How do we read right now? What is our process?* —*What do we do before we begin to read?* —*What do we do while we read?* —*What do we do when the material is difficult?* —*What do we do after we read?*
What are 5 strategies to improve prereading?	6. *We need to improve our process in all of those areas. Five prereading strategies will help:* —*Gather and organize reading materials and decide when and where to read* —*Assign a purpose for reading in each class* —*Identify the subject of a reading, call up what we know, make predictions* —*Ask a question that might be answered while reading* —*Write at all stages of the reading process to aid understanding and stay focused*
Summary	*Summary: College reading is complicated and involves thinking, interacting, drawing on prior knowledge, making predictions, asking questions, understanding writing conventions, putting new ideas in a meaningful context, collaborating, testing understanding, and always having a clear purpose. The two main purposes are study reading, or reading to learn, and critical reading and thinking, or reading to analyze, evaluate, and get new ideas. These purposes are integrated in most courses. We need to understand our present reading process by analyzing what we do before, during, and after reading, and also what we do when the material is hard to understand. We can improve our present process by adding five new prereading strategies: get organized and decide when and where to read, assign a purpose for reading, understand the subject and then call up prior knowledge and make some predictions, ask one question, and write at all stages of the process.*

FIGURE 2-5 Continued

▶

Survey and take some notes on this chapter (chapter 2). You may make a survey map, an outline, or Cornell notes. If you decide to make a survey map, the following map of this chapter has been started for you (Figure 2-6). Either complete it or use it as a guide to get you started making either an outline or Cornell notes instead.

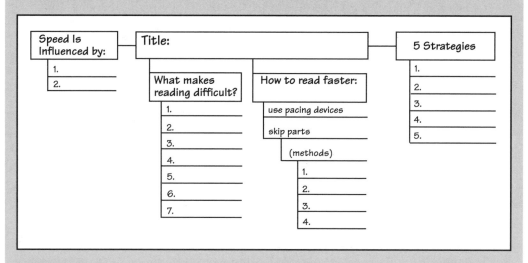

FIGURE 2-6

Strategy 5: Skim, scan, and read selected passages for research. Take research notes.

Skim the passage.

Get the subject of the passage well in mind by reading the title and the first paragraph. Read the last paragraph also to get a sense of how the author will complete the passage. Then move through the passage about twice as fast as you normally would. Read only the key words that carry most of the meaning and skip over the rest. Let your mind make connections and bridge the gaps. This will only work if you already know something about the subject. Try it on the passage that follows. Fifty percent of the words are omitted in Passage 1. They are restored in Passage 2.

WHY MEN FEAR WOMEN'S TEAMS

> Picture this.   flipping   channels   and
> land on   ABC.   on the screen   bas-
> ketball game.   players   sinking   pointers, slam-dunking,
>   usual things basketball players do.   high-fiving
>   patting   butt, and   sauntering to   locker
> room
>   imagine   players aren't men.   women, big sweaty
> ones,   uniforms   their version of
> bonding   scene   fantasy   remain so until women's
>   sports get   sponsors, television   are-
> nas, fan   and   well-trained players.

Passage 1

▶

WHY MEN FEAR WOMEN'S TEAMS

Picture this. You're flipping through the channels one night, and you land on a local network, let's say ABC. And there on the screen is a basketball game. The players are sinking three-pointers, slam-dunking, and doing the usual things basketball players do. They're high-fiving each other, patting one another on the butt, and then sauntering to the locker room to talk about long-term contracts.

Now imagine that the players aren't men. They're women, big sweaty ones, wearing uniforms and doing their version of what guys thrive on—bonding. So far, this scene is a fantasy and will remain so until women's professional team sports get corporate sponsors, television exposure, arenas, fan support, and a critical mass of well-trained players.[1]

Scan the passage.

To scan successfully, you need to look through material without slowing down to read. Get in mind exactly what you want to find and then move your eyes down the page in a zigzag, sweeping motion. If you cannot find the information, try looking at every third or fourth line. Move your eyes rapidly. You are looking, not reading. Try it. Take a second to scan the following passage to locate answers to these two questions:

1. What percentage of high school students drop out before graduating?

2. What is the dropout rate for blacks, Hispanics, and Native Americans?

Look for numbers and the two or three words on either side that describe what the numbers are about.

STUDENTS AT RISK

Daunting as the challenge of reform appears, its cost is insignificant when compared with the consequences of inaction. Over 25 percent of all high school students drop out before graduating; although half of these students do eventually receive an equivalency diploma, their detour is costly for them and for society. Among Blacks, Hispanics, and Native Americans, the dropout rate often exceeds 50 percent.

The majority of those who drop out are functionally illiterate and hardly any of them possess enough mathematical skills to make productive contributions to the American economy.[2]

[1] Kate Rounds, "Why Men Fear Women's Teams," *Ms.* January/February 1991.
[2] *Everybody Counts, A Report to the Nation on the Future of Mathematics Education* (National Academy Press, 1989) 12.

Read selected passages for research.

Four steps are involved in reading selected passages and using them for research:

1. Form a question that identifies your topic. Example: What is college reading?

2. Locate the topic in the index and find the page numbers on which it is discussed in the book. Example: College reading, 3–4.

3. Look up the topic on the page indicated in the text, scan to find the passage you need, and slow down and read to answer your question. Remember to survey the book before you draw on selected passages for research. You need to know a book's main subject, some of its contents, and the author's position on the subject to put your research in an accurate context.

4. Take research notes. You will take three kinds of notes on the material you read: direct quotes, paraphrases, and summaries. You may also write idea notes on original insights that occur to you as you read. Here are examples of these four types of notes. All notes are taken on the section "College Reading: What Is Involved?" on pages 3–4 of this book.

1. QUOTED MATERIAL. Quote material that is best stated in the author's words. Use it sparingly in a paper. Copy quoted material exactly as it is written and place it in quotation marks immediately. Introduce it with the author's name to show who made this statement. At the end of the quote, write the author's name, a brief title, and a page number so you will be able to find it and cite it when you use it in a paper. (Citation form is not demonstrated here. Your instructor will let you know which form to use.)

EXAMPLE OF A QUOTE:
According to Wood, "College textbooks are better than ever. They are big, beautiful, and reader friendly." (Wood, *College Reading*, p. 3)

2. PARAPHRASED MATERIAL. Paraphrasing is rewriting an author's ideas in your own words to make them fit more smoothly into your paper. You may introduce them with the author's name to make clear whose idea this was in the first place. You do not need quotation marks since you have rephrased the author's words.

EXAMPLE OF A PARAPHRASE:
Wood reminds us that college reading includes a great variety of different types of reading materials such as textbooks, library books, magazines and journals, lab manuals, test questions, and material on the Internet. (Wood, *College Reading*, p. 3)

▶

3. SUMMARIZED MATERIAL. At times you will want to summarize a section of a chapter, the entire chapter, or the book itself and include this information in a paper. A summary captures the ideas in a longer section of material than does a paraphrase. Again, it is best to indicate in the text who wrote the original material and where it can be found.

EXAMPLE OF A SUMMARY:
Wood cautions that students will be expected to read a great variety of reading materials while they are at college, but that, with practice and new strategies, they can soon become expert college readers. (Wood, *College Reading*, pp. 3–4).

4. IDEA NOTES. You will often get insights and ideas that are inspired by your reading. Write them down and label them as yours to use later in your paper.

EXAMPLE OF AN IDEA NOTE:
I think I read online material differently than printed textbooks. I can't turn pages to look ahead or to look back. It is harder to survey. I wonder if I need special strategies for reading online. (mine)

EXERCISES AND READINGS

THREE COLLABORATIVE CLASS EXERCISES

Exercise 1

Assess the level of difficulty. *Groups of students.*

This exercise will give you practice in determining how difficult different types of reading passages are for you. Form groups of three or four students. Each student should turn first to the three readings that are listed under "Three Reading Exercises" on page 58 and skim each of them for 5 minutes to assess their level of difficulty. Then rank them according to the level of difficulty. Which is easiest? Which is next easiest? Which is hardest? Discuss what makes these selections seem either easy or difficult for you to read. Report the results to the class.

Exercise 2

Survey this book and Chapter 3. *Groups of students.*

This exercise will teach you to use the surveying strategies taught in this chapter.

    a. **Survey the book.** Working in groups of three or four students, survey this entire book and complete the Survey Sheet for a Book, which follows.

    b. One person should **write the answers to the questions** on the lines below as they are discovered by the group.

    c. **Report the results to the class** and compare answers with other groups.

SURVEY SHEET FOR A BOOK

Step 1: Read the title of the book.

1. Focus on the title, and write the subject of the book in your own words.

   _____

2. Name three things that come to mind when you think of the subject.

   _____

3. Predict two topics that you think may be discussed in the book.

   _____

4. Ask one big question you think the book will answer.

   _____

Step 2: Read the title page and preface or introduction to the book.

1. When was the book written? Find the copyright date. _____

2. Who is the author? _____

3. Why did the author write this book? _____

4. Who does the author hope will read this book? _____

5. How well do you match the author's idea of who should read the book?

   _____

6. What type of book is it? Fiction or nonfiction? Technical or nontechnical? Informative or argumentative? Textbook or other? Modern or old?

   _____

Step 3: Read the table of contents of the book.

1. Consult the table of contents and list five important topics that are discussed in the book. _____

   _____

Step 4: Examine the special features of the book.

1. What are the special features of the book? Look in the front, in the back, and in one chapter. Make a list of some of the features that will help you read the book.

   _____

Step 5: Examine the first and last chapters of the book.

1. What is the first chapter about? _____

2. What is the last chapter about? _____

3. Why do you think the author begins and ends with these topics? _____

   _____

▶

Step 6: Read the title and first paragraph of the other chapters in the book.

1. Identify three major ideas that are developed in these chapters. _____

_____

2. What are five key words or terms that are used in this book? _____

_____

Step 7: Reflect on what you have learned about the book.

Complete this statement: "This book is about _____ , and it

covers the topics _____

_____."

To motivate yourself to read more of the book, write a sentence or two about what seems valuable or interesting in the book at this point.

_____

       d. Survey a chapter. Working in the same groups, survey Chapter 3, which is the next chapter you will read in this book. Have a scribe record the answers to the questions on the Survey Sheet for a Chapter, which follows, and report the results to the class.

SURVEY SHEET FOR A CHAPTER (OR AN ARTICLE)

Step 1: Read the title of the chapter.

1. What is the subject of the chapter? _____

2. Name three things that the subject makes you think of. _____

_____

3. Predict two topics that you think may be discussed in the chapter. _____

_____

4. Ask one big question that you think the chapter will answer. _____

_____

Step 2: Read the introduction to the chapter.

1. List three important ideas that are emphasized in the goals and first paragraph.

_____

▶

Step 3: Read the summary of the chapter.

1. What are the strategies that are summarized in the review section at the end of the chapter?

   _____

Step 4: Read the headings in the chapter.

1. What additional ideas do you find in the headings? _____

Step 5: Look at the visuals in the chapter.

1. List two ideas that are illustrated or explained by charts, diagrams, graphs, or

   pictures. _____

Step 6: Circle the key words in the chapter.

1. List three important words or terms in the chapter. _____

Step 7: Reflect on what you have learned about the chapter.

Complete this statement, "This chapter is about _____, and it

covers the topics _____

_____

_____."

To motivate yourself to read more, write a sentence or two about what seems valuable or interesting in the chapter at this point.

_____

_____

Exercise 3

Make a survey map, an outline, or Cornell notes for Chapter 3. *Groups of students.* First decide which note taking method your group will use. Then, draw on the information about Chapter 3 that you wrote on the survey sheet above. Follow one of the notetaking models that appears in Figures 2-2–2-6 on pages 47–51. One member of your group who serves as scribe should write what other members of the group contribute to the notes. Tape your group's notes to the wall and look at them. How are they different from notes taken by other groups? How are they the same? Are they all effective? How?

THREE READING EXERCISES:
ABOUT PEOPLE WHO MADE IT IN SPITE OF THE ODDS

The following three readings are drawn from a college history textbook and from two magazines *The Atlantic Monthly* and *Time.* You have already read an article, "My Father, the Graduate" (page 19), about the importance of persistence in meeting one's goals. These readings are also about people who persisted and made it in spite of the odds.

Reading 1

The Overland Trails[3]

JOHN MACK FARAGHER, MARI JO BUHLE, DANIEL CZITROM, AND SUSAN H. ARMITAGE

Explanatory Notes: *The following selection is taken from Chapter 14, "The Territorial Expansion of the United States, 1830s–1850s," which appears in the college textbook* Out of Many: A History of the American People. *The authors are college history professors.* **What do you know about westward expansion? What do you predict this will be about? Before you read "The Overland Trails," survey it by reading the title, the first and last paragraphs, and the first sentence in each of the other paragraphs (underlining and marginal notes are added to help you survey). Then turn to the directions and questions on page 60 entitled "Scan to Answer These Study Reading Questions." Form two teams and practice scanning to find the answers to the questions. When you have finished the scanning exercise, read the entire selection and answer the critical reading and thinking questions.**

description

The 2,000-mile trip on the Overland Trails from the banks of the Missouri River to Oregon and California usually took seven months, sometimes more. Travel was slow, dangerous, tedious, and exhausting. Pioneers often arrived at their destination with little food and few belongings, having been forced to lighten their loads as animals died and winter weather threatened. Uprooted from family and familiar surroundings, pioneers faced the prospect of being, in the poignant nineteenth-century phrase, "strangers in a strange land." Yet despite these risks, settlers streamed west: 5,000 to Oregon by 1845 and about 3,000 to California by 1848 (before the discovery of gold). Some arrived by ship, but this was more expensive than the overland journey, which itself was not cheap: a wagon, a team of oxen, food, clothing, and essential tools cost between $500 and $1,000.

motives

Pioneers had a number of motives for making the trip. Glowing reports from Oregon's Willamette Valley, for example, seemed to promise economic opportunity and healthy surroundings, an alluring combination to farmers in the malaria-prone Midwest who had been hard hit by the Panic of 1837. But rational motives

---

[3] John Mack Faragher, Mari Jo Buhle, Daniel Czitrom, and Susan H. Armitrage, *Out of Many: A History of the American People*, 2nd ed. (Upper Saddle River: Prentice Hall, 1997) 413–415.

do not tell the whole story. Many men were motivated by a ③sense of adventure, by a desire to experience the unknown, or, as they put it, to "see the elephant." Women were more likely to think of the trip as ④*A Pioneer's Search for an Ideal Home*, the title that Phoebe Judson chose for her account of her family's 1852 trip to Oregon.

Few pioneers traveled alone, partly because they feared Indian attack (which was rare) but largely because they needed help fording rivers or crossing mountains with heavy wagons. Most Oregon pioneers traveled with their families but usually also joined a larger group, forming a "train." In the earliest years, when the route was still uncertain, trains hired a "pilot," generally a former fur trapper. Often the men of the wagon train drew up semimilitary constitutions, electing a leader. Democratic as this process appeared, not everyone was willing to obey the leader, and many trains experienced dissension and breakups along the trail. But in essence all pioneers—men, women, and children—were part of a new, westward-moving community in which they had to accept both the advantages and disadvantages of community membership.

3

Traveled in groups

Wagon trains started westward as soon as the prairies were green (thus ensuring feed for the livestock). The daily routine was soon established. ①Men took care of the moving equipment and the animals, ②while the women cooked and kept track of the children. Slowly, at a rate of about fifteen miles a day, the wagon trains moved west along the Platte River, crossing the Continental Divide at South Pass in present-day Wyoming. West of the Rockies the climate was much drier. The long, dusty stretch along the Snake River in present-day southern Idaho finally gave way to Oregon's steep and difficult Blue Mountains and to the ①dangerous rafting down the Columbia River, in which many drowned and all were drenched by the cold winter rains of the Pacific Northwest. California-bound migrants faced even worse hazards: the complete ②lack of water in the Humbolt Sink region of northern Nevada and the looming Sierra Nevadas, which had to be crossed before the winter snows came. (Members of the ill-fated ③Donner party, snow-bound on the Nevada side of that range in 1846–47, resorted to cannibalism before they were rescued.)

4

daily routine

Hazards

In addition to the predominant experiences of tedium and exhaustion, there were other trail hazards such as ①illness and ②accidents. Danger from ③Indian attack, which all pioneers feared, was actually very small. Before the 1849 California Gold Rush, only thirty-four white people were killed (twenty-four in one wagon train) and twenty-five Indians. In subsequent years, as thousands of gold rushers flocked west, the deaths increased, but, significantly, more Indians than white people died. It appears that unprovoked white attacks on Indians were more common than the reverse.

5

Other hazards

In contrast, ④cholera killed at least a thousand people a year in 1849 and the early 1850s when it stalked sections of the trail along the Platte River. Spread by contaminated water, cholera caused vomiting and diarrhea, which in turn led to extreme dehydration and death, often in one night. In the afflicted regions, trailside graves were a frequent and grim sight. ⑤Drownings were not uncommon, nor were ⑥accidental ax wounds or shootings, and ⑦children sometimes fell out of wagons and were run over. The members of the wagon train community did what they could to arrange decent burials, and they provided support for survivors: men helped widows drive their wagons onward, women nursed and tended babies whose mothers were dead, and at least one parentless family, the seven Sager children, were brought to Oregon in safety.

6

By 1860 almost 300,000 people had traveled the Overland Trails to Oregon or California. Ruts from the wagon wheels can be seen in a number of places along the route even today. In 1869 the completion of the transcontinental railroad

Result   marked the end of the wagon train era (although many people made shorter trips to other western locations by wagon). In retrospect, the pioneers remembered their journey as more dangerous and less tedious than it actually was. The stories that came down to their grandchildren told of a heroic adventure. These "pioneers' tales" were not the truth as it had really happened but an effort to find the true heroism in an important episode by making a good story out of it.

7

920 words

Strategy Questions

1. What did you know about the subject before you began to read? What did you predict it would be about?
2. What did you learn from surveying? In one sentence describe what the chapter is about, and name some of the topics that were covered.

Scan to Answer These Study Reading Questions

Form two teams. The instructor will read the following questions, and team members will skim or scan "The Overland Trails," which begins on page 58, to find the answers. Remember to look for the answers, but do not slow down and read. The first person to find the answer to each question should call it out and win a point for that team. The team with the most points at the end wins.

1. How far is it from the Missouri River to Oregon and California?
2. How long did it take the pioneers to make this journey in the 1800s?
3. How many people were in Oregon and California by 1845?
4. How much money did a family need to make the trip?
5. What was one reason men made the trip?
6. What was one reason women made the trip?
7. How dangerous were the Indians?
8. What happened to the Donner party?
9. Name two hazards of traveling on the Overland Trails.
10. How many people had traveled to California and Oregon by 1860?

Critical Reading and Thinking Questions

1. What were some of the major differences between the men and women who crossed the country in covered wagons? Compare their reasons for making the trip and how they divided the work on the trip. If modern men and women made this same trip, do you think the motives for going and the division of labor now would be similar to or different from those of men and women in the 1850s?

2. At the end of this selection the authors suggest that the stories the pioneers told their grandchildren about their trips across the country exaggerated their hardships and did not represent the truth as it really happened. They were just making a good story. Judging from the evidence in the rest of the selection, do you think this is a fair conclusion? Why or why not?

3. What is some of the evidence in the selection for the statement that all pioneers became part of a community? What are some examples of cooperation in a community? Why was this important?

Exodus[4]

MARC COOPER

Explanatory Notes: *The author is a contributing editor of* The Nation *and is a senior fellow at the Institute for Justice and Journalism at the USC Annenberg School for Communication. This article is about the journey illegal Mexican immigrants make when they cross the border from Mexico into the United States. Draw on your prior knowledge: Do you know any illegal immigrants who have crossed the border and are working in this country? How are they treated? How should they be treated? The author of this article has accompanied immigrants on their trip across the border and describes their persistence along with the difficulties and dangers they encounter. What position do you think he will take on the problem of illegal immigration? Make a prediction.*

On January 6, celebrated as Three Kings Day in Mexico, the flow of border crossers heading north restarts its annual cycle. So when I arrive on the following Wednesday in the dusty, gritty Sonoran Desert town of Altar, two hours south of the border via a liver-jostling dirt road, the local merchants couldn't be more delighted. I have been to Altar before. And on this trip, I can readily agree with the local street entrepreneurs and hustlers that this year's crossing season, barely in its third day, looks to be as bountiful and profitable as ever—in spite of an also cyclical uproar, north of the border, over illegal immigration. Once an anonymous bus stop on Mexico's Route 2, Altar—a diesel-marinated ten-block grid of around 10,000 people—has become the primary staging area for Mexican migrants before they make their desperate bounce across the border. And the town's entire commercial life rests on this singular enterprise. 1

All around the central plaza that skirts the butternut-colored colonial-era church, small groups—mostly men, mostly young, mostly dressed in dark clothing 2

---

[4] Marc Cooper, "Exodus," *The Atlantic Monthly* May 2006: 123–127, 132.

and running shoes, though there are also some women with babies in their arms—await contact with the *coyote* or *pollero* who has promised to push them through a treacherous but in many ways invisible membrane from which they will emerge, almost magically, on the other side as our carpenters, gardeners, waiters, pickers, pluckers, and nannies. The going rate, door-to-door, from the fields of Veracruz or Oaxaca to the orange orchards of Florida or to a Brentwood kitchen: about $1,500. No need, even, to pay it all in advance: installments, with interest, will be drawn from future income.

On the streets adjoining the plaza, tiny, airless shops selling phone cards and converting currency are doing brisk business, as are the occasional youth gangs, who find few other places in Mexico where so many people are walking around with so much folding money in their pockets. Other Mexican migrants fleeing the impoverished south operate a warren of kiosks and stands, offering up for sale everything needed to ease the perilous crossing ahead: plastic gallon jugs of water; plastic baggies of combs, toothbrushes, aspirin tablets, and lip balm; dark jeans; black windbreakers; hooded sweatshirts; athletic shoes; baseball caps; bandanas; backpacks; and the black woolen ski masks favored by the salaried guides who lead the walkers across the desert. Also for sale are black plastic trash bags—$3 each—to be wrapped around the body; they're said to foil the heat-seeking sensors that the U.S. Border Patrol and the Department of Homeland Security have stitched into the other side of *la linea*. One Oaxacan vendor shows off a black cap with an embroidered green cannabis leaf. "They buy this one a lot," he says. "I tell them I don't think it's the best one to wear."

A few yards away, the Red Cross has just opened its first-aid trailer for this year's season, and its advice is also readily spurned. "I tell them that they run a great risk," says uniformed paramedic Amado Arellano. He even shows them a colorful but macabre wall map—provided by the Tucson-based Humane Borders group—that marks every spot where a migrant has died in the desert. Hundreds of fatal red dots cluster just above the border. "We try to tell them not to go," he says. "But no one listens. The necessity is too great." Right beside the medical trailer snakes a line—sometimes twenty to thirty vehicles long—of battered windowless ten-seater vans, their seats torn out and replaced with benches that allow twenty-seven, even thirty, passengers to be crammed in. These shuttle operations—charging an average of $10 a head—are some of the more lucrative businesses in Altar, and their overloaded vans rumble up the same rocky road I've just come down. The destination of "Sasabe" is written with washable white marker on the sides of the vans. They might be more honestly labeled "California" or "North California" or "Texas," as no sane person would voluntarily travel to the grim, un-paved Mexican border hamlet of Sasabe—except to use it as a location for a Robert Rodriguez movie or, more likely, as the final stepping stone over the line. By mid-day, the vans are departing with the perpetual rhythm of Disneyland people-carriers zipping into the Haunted House. Approximately 40,000 migrants per month make this trip through and out of Altar.

Accompanied by Jorge Solchaga, a thirty-eight-year-old diplomat who works with Mexican consulate in Phoenix, I walk through a nameless tortilla shop on a side street off the plaza, out its back door, and into a brick-and-cement court yard teeming with people getting ready to cross. This is one of Altar's countless unregulated and ill-named "guest house"—tenement flops that offer nothing except a body-sized patch of floor for $5 or $6 a night. On one side of the cramped courtyard, workmen plaster together an add-on to the tenement; its owners clearly realize that they are part of a growth industry. A rickety iron staircase leads us to some second-floor lodgings, a bare twenty-by-twenty-foot room in which about fifty people have put down their sleeping mats and backpacks.

In the courtyard once more, Solchaga spots a dark-skinned girl with a nursing-age infant in her lap. She stares at the ground as Solchaga gently warns her that she is about to put her life and that of her child at risk. When he presses her on the dangers, she barely nods. Almost inaudibly she says that she's twenty, but she looks five years younger and somewhat terrified. However, the die is cast. She's given up everything back home and will be heading out into a new world within a few minutes. "Make sure your husband carries three extra gallons of water for you, you hear?" Solchaga says, nodding to the man sitting behind her. As we exit the flop, Solchaga tells me that the blank look in that girl's eyes will surely haunt him. One of his jobs at the consulate is to process the deaths of Mexicans in the United States. Three years ago in Altar, he tells me, he warned another nursing mother not to make the crossing, and less than a week later, when a call came in to his Arizona office requesting him to help identify a "fatality" that had been found in the desert, he recognized the same young woman. "This is my job, and I am used to it," he says. Last year he processed the deaths of 219 Mexicans in the Phoenix area; some were migrants who had wandered in the desert for eight or nine days before their souls and bodies burned out. "It's the young women I never forget," he says, shrugging his shoulders.

The night before my trip to Altar, I had dinner with the Tucson-based journalist Charles Bowden, author of more than fifteen books, most of them set along the border. In perhaps his most acclaimed work, *Down by the River,* certainly a must-read for anyone researching the border, Bowden describes the poverty that swamps even the more prosperous Mexican border cities and that relentlessly churns the human flow northward. "Over there," he writes of Ciudad Juárez, just across from El Paso, Texas,

> most of the streets are unpaved, two thirds of the houses lack any sewage connection. At least 200,000 people in the city live as squatters . . . At least 350,000 more poor people descend on Juárez each year. Or sixty thousand, no one is sure. They take jobs at $3 to $5 a day that cannot sustain them.

When they realize that it's only the width of a river—or a twelve-foot wall, or three strands of cattle wire, or a three-day walk, for that matter—that separates them from a First World economy and some reasonable chance at a future, they push north. "The Mexican border is the only place," Bowden writes, "where the cyberspace world of a major economy rubs up against a world of raw sewage and mud huts. The world of mud is failing to sustain its people."

. . . .

With an estimated 11-to-1 manufacturing wage differential between the two countries (some experts put the agricultural wage gap at twice that), why is anyone shocked by what's happening? "You're looking at the biggest story of our lives," Bowden told me over dinner, "This is the largest cross-border human migration in history." Though rarely, if ever, posed in those terms, the staggering numbers tend to bolster Bowden's sweeping vision. Something like 15 million to 20 million migrants have crossed into the United States over the last two decades. An equal number are expected to do so in the next twenty-years. "People aren't coming here as much as they are leaving a cratered economy," Bowden said. "The only way you'll stop Mexicans coming to the U.S. is if you lower American wages to the same level as Vietnam. Someone worth maybe $100 a month in Mexico who comes to the U.S. becomes a human ATM machine. McCain-Kennedy, Kyl-Cornyn?" he said, referring to the hodge-podge of current immigration-reform proposals. "It's all bullshit. What we're seeing is something right out of the Bible. This is an exodus."

That's certainly the deep emotional impression I come away with as Solchaga and   10
I depart Altar. An hour up the road back toward the border, all vehicles are stopped at a checkpoint run by Mexico's orange-and-blue-uniformed Grupo Beta. Created last decade under U.S. pressure and with some American assistance, the Beta teams were intended to be elite Mexican immigration police that would work in tandem with the U.S. Border Patrol on the other side, to stanch the human flow. Then reality intervened. The Beta teams instead went into business, running their own lucrative shakedown schemes on the migrants. A few years ago, the Mexican government simply disarmed the Grupo Beta and reorganized it into a sort of community-assistance force for the migrants—seemingly a mix between the Automobile Club and the Eagle Scouts.

On our way up from Altar to the Beta checkpoint called El Tortuga, Solchaga   11
and I count thirty-one vans coming the other way. Something like 900 crossers have been delivered to the border in the previous hour. Now, at the Grupo Beta roadblocks, the vans coming behind us are arriving every three or four minutes. As each one arrives, two Beta officers unload the passengers and gather them by the side of the road for a short lecture—sometimes two or three vans' worth at a time. "However long the *pollero* told you it will take, it will take longer," says officer Julio Cesar Cancino. "If they told you it will be a two- or three-day walk, they lied. It will take longer." He advises them, in the event they get scattered, to look for the blue flags that demark water stations set up by American religious activists. Or to look for the red lights on the radio towers on the Mexican side of the border. "Whatever you do, don't run. The *migra*," he says, referring to the Border Patrol in Mexican slang, "isn't there only to arrest you, but also to help you. If you're in trouble, if you're lost and out of water, or if your *pollero* abandons you, go to them for help. But don't run. And don't reach for your pockets."

Like the girl that Solchaga had warned earlier in the day, these groups of   12
crossers don't quite know what to make of this advice. They don't know whether to trust fellow Mexicans in uniform. Isn't endemic corruption one of the reasons they're leaving Mexico, after all? They shuffle their feet and stare down at the ground, or off into the middle distance, and don't look the Grupo Beta officers in the eye. When asked, they quietly tick off their home states: Oaxaca, Veracruz,

Puebla, Chiapas, Michoacán. And they aren't shy about their destinations: Los Angeles, Phoenix, Houston, San Bernardino, Portland, New Jersey. Bowden is right. An exodus, indeed.

. . . .

All the migrants know is that the young man sitting with them in the van has   13
vowed to get them to the promised land, and that's where they're going. They're aware that the next three or four or more days will be tough—though few know just how tough. But the choice is, maybe, between working a cornfield for $4 a day in the south or picking grapes in the north for $60 or $70. By nightfall, all of the travelers will be moving across the border. The Grupo Beta officers, however, will be withdrawing. As has always been the case, the migrants will be on their own after dusk. "We leave at dark," Officer Cancino tells me. He points to the myriad bullet holes in the twisted road sign reading EL TORTUGO. "After that, it's way too dangerous."

Making the crossing ever more dangerous seems to be about the only tangible result   14
of U.S. border policy in the past decade. In 1994, the Clinton administration—fearing the political repercussions after the anti-immigrant Proposition 187 passed in California—implemented a "prevention through deterrence" border program. One after another, the traditional urban crossing points, near San Diego, Nogales, and El Paso, were simply blockaded and more or less shut down. Military-sounding campaigns like Operation Gatekeeper, Operation Hold-the-Line, Operation Safeguard, and Operation Rio Grande didn't do much to keep the migrants out of the United States. But driving them away from border cities got them—for a while, at least—out of the news. Historic and decades-old human streams were rerouted from California and Texas and funneled into the relatively unpopulated, inhospitable terrain along the Arizona border. Out of sight. Out of mind. Again, for a time.

No one was actually deterred, but more people died. Since the early 1990s, what-   15
ever the official policy, the Border Patrol has made about a million "apprehensions" per year (the number of detainees this past year was almost identical to that of 1993). And every year about half as many people—500,000 or so—elude arrest and make it across. But in 1994, the year of the Clinton clampdown, a total of twenty-three migrants died attempting passage. That number climbed to average 300 a year in the late 1990s and has topped 400 annually since 2000. Last year's toll set a new record: nearly 500, more than half of them in south-central Arizona.

. . . .

One thing is for certain: those battered vans in Altar will continue to load up every   16
afternoon, and every evening, their human cargo will find a way across the border. If the migrants run into some new [. . .] wall, they will simply go around it. Or over it. Or under it. Mexicans will show as much ingenuity in getting into the United States as Americans would in breaking into British Columbia if the Canadian minimum wage were $70 an hour. "Nothing really changes here," Charles Bowden said to me, as a chill night descended on the Tucson desert. "When people ask me what the solution will eventually be here, I say, 'This is it.' "

2523 words

Strategy Questions

1. When you predicted what position the author of this article might hold on illegal immigration, what did you predict? Were you correct? Were there any surprises that you could not have predicted? What were they?

Study Reading Questions

1. Where is the town of Altar, and why is it important to people from Mexico who are crossing into the United States illegally?
2. What is a coyote or pollero? What do these individuals typically charge each immigrant?
3. What is the Grupo Beta, and what is the migra? What are their roles?
4. Describe the preparations an immigrant makes before starting the journey across the border. Give three examples of objects they take with them.
5. What motivates immigrants to make this dangerous journey from Mexico to the United States? Give two reasons they might have for making the journey.

Critical Reading and Thinking Questions

1. Why is the flow of immigrants from Mexico called an exodus? What is this exodus compared to? How does this comparison affect your attitude towards illegal immigration from Mexico?
2. The three readings in this section are entitled "People Who Made It in Spite of the Odds." What qualities do illegal immigrants have that enable them to persevere in spite of hardships?
3. Make two columns on a piece of paper or on the board. In the first column write all of the problems associated with illegal immigration from the perspective of United States citizens. In the second column write some possible solutions to the problems. If you are doing this as a class, take a vote to determine what your class thinks might be the best solution on the list.
4. Agree or disagree with the following statement made at the end of the article and give reasons for your position: " 'Nothing really changes here,' Charles Bowden said to me, as a chill night descended on the Tucson desert. 'When people ask me what the solution will eventually be here, I say, This is it.' "

Reading 3

We've Overlooked One of Our Greatest Assets[5]

WILLIAM D. GREEN

Explanatory Notes: *The author is the CEO of his company Accenture. Like the two articles you have just read, this one is about an individual who persevered and accomplished more in life than he thought he would when he was younger. Take*

[5] William D. Green, "We've Overlooked One of Our Greatest Assets," *Newsweek* 1 May 2006: 22.

two minutes to survey the article. Read the title, the first and last paragraphs, and the first sentence of each of the other paragraphs. Then answer the "Strategy Questions." Now read the entire article and answer the other questions.

If you had told me back in 1971—the year I graduated high school—that I'd be going off to college soon, I would have assured you that you were sorely mistaken. I was the son of a plumber living in western Massachusetts, and we had all assumed that in the end I'd be a plumber, too. 1

I spent the year after high school working in construction. Then one day I went to visit some friends who were students at Dean College, a two-year residential college 45 minutes outside of Boston, and my mind-set began to change. As I walked around campus and listened to my friends talk about their experiences, I realized this was an opportunity to change my path that might not come again—an opportunity to take another shot at learning. So I enrolled at Dean, and I can honestly say it was a life-altering experience. 2

The school's philosophy is to educate, energize and inspire. In fact, it was a Dean professor, Charlie Kramer, who ignited my passion for economics and taught me how to think analytically. After all these years, I still have my notes from his economics classes, and I've referred back to them from time to time—even as I went on to Babson College, where I earned my bachelor of science degree in economics and then an M.B.A. I'm proud to say that today I'm a member of Dean College's board of trustees. 3

Would I be running a global consulting company with $17 billion in revenue and 130,000 employees today if I'd followed a different path? Who knows? But there is no doubt that my two years at Dean College not only prepared me for advancing my education and gearing up for a career, but also transformed me as a person. And that's not a bad start no matter where life takes you. 4

But while Americans are waking up to the idea that we need to sharpen our competitive edge in the world—[the] President [. . .] threw down the gauntlet in his State of the Union address earlier this year—many still overlook our system of community and junior colleges. The truth is, these schools can be the solution for what our K–12 programs might not be getting done. 5

Whenever I get the chance to talk to young people, I urge them to consider options other than four-year schools. Junior and community colleges can help them become better equipped to continue their education and to face real-world challenges. These colleges can smooth their transition from high school to work life, provide them with core decision-making skills and teach them how to think and learn. 6

In the United States there are more than 1,100 community colleges, most of them publicly funded, which serve nearly 12 million students. Almost two thirds of these students attend school part time, and many of them are holding down a full-time job. What's especially striking is the diversity of these schools: 47 percent of all African-American undergrads in this country attend community college, as do 56 percent of Hispanic undergraduates. 7

But what is it about these schools that make them so important to our competitive future? For starters, I can't think of any other institutions so tuned into the needs of our communities. The American Association of Community Colleges 8 estimates that more than half of new health-care workers get their training at community colleges. In 2003, 62 percent of the applicants who took the national exam to become licensed registered nurses were graduates of such programs.

Community colleges excel at working with local businesses to identify specific 9 needs, whether helping displaced autoworkers gain new job skills or helping local companies ensure they will have a steady supply of skilled workers. Chances are, if there's a large manufacturing plant in your town, your community college offers technical training in conjunction with the plant. Better skills and better pay lead to happier, more productive employees. That boosts the economy, which gives us all a better standard of living.

I believe that since businesses benefit from these institutions, we also have an 10 obligation to help them. This is especially true as state support, which constitutes an estimated 44 percent of community colleges' financial resources, continues to decline. We can show our support by donating funds, recruiting students, offering career counseling and encouraging our employees to teach classes.

An investment in your local junior or community college is a sound investment 11 in the competitiveness of our country and the potential of our citizens.

I should know. 12

760 words

Strategy Questions

1. Complete this sentence: "This article is about . . . , and it covers the topics. . . ."
2. Make a survey map, an outline, or a set of Cornell reading notes of this article. Include the title and the topics you identified for question 1 above. Add at least one detail about each part.

Study Reading Questions

1. What did Green think he would probably do for a living when he was young?
2. What changed his mind, and what did he do as a result?
3. What does he believe attributed to his success?
4. What are three benefits mentioned by Green that students experience when they attend community colleges?
5. What are two benefits that community colleges contribute to the community mentioned by Green?

Critical Reading and Thinking Questions

1. Green perseveres by modern standards. What does he have in common, if anything, with American pioneers (reading 1) and Mexican immigrants (reading 2)? How is he similar and how is he different from these two other groups, and how do those differences contribute to his achievements and success? Consider his personality, his opportunities, and his successes.

2. What is your idea of a modern-day hero? Write for three minutes, and then start a class list of heroic qualities on the board.
3. Green gives several examples of how community colleges directly serve the community in which they are located. Can you add examples from your experience? What are they?

TWO APPLICATION EXERCISES

Exercise 1

Survey one of your other textbooks or another book you are likely to read.

Follow the steps for surveying a book that appear on pages 44–45. Write a brief description of what the book is about and list some of the topics it covers. Write, also, what you find interesting about this book and how you think it may be valuable to you. Finally, how easy or difficult will it be for you to read?

Exercise 2

Survey the next chapter that you are assigned to read in one of your other courses or a magazine article you intend to read.

Follow the steps for surveying a chapter or article that appear on pages 45–46. Write a brief description of the chapter or article that states what it is about and that lists some of the topics it covers. Write what interests you in the chapter or article and what value it may have for you. Will it be easy or difficult to read?

REVIEW AND EVALUATE THE STRATEGIES

The following is a review of the five strategies you learned in this chapter:

1. Develop a range of reading speeds.
2. Survey books.
3. Survey chapters and articles.
4. Write a survey map, outline, or Cornell notes on the ideas in the book, chapter, or article.
5. Skim, scan, and read selected passages for research. Take research notes.

Make a personal evaluation of these strategies:

1. Underline your favorite strategies in the preceding list.
2. Make a check mark by those you want to continue to use.
3. Cross out any you probably will not continue to use. What are your reasons for rejecting them?

_____

_____

Increase Your Reading Vocabulary

CHAPTER GOALS:

1. **To show how increasing your vocabulary helps you read.**

2. **To motivate you to increase your vocabulary.**

3. **To explain the basics of vocabulary improvement.**

4. **To present five strategies for increasing your reading vocabulary.**

An Increased Vocabulary Improves Reading

The methods for increasing reading efficiency taught in Chapter 2, including surveying, skimming, scanning, and reading selected parts, only work when you know the meanings of most of the words. Increasing your vocabulary will improve both your rapid reading and your slower, more thorough reading. Reread Malcolm X's account at the end of Chapter 1 (see page 21), where he describes how he copied the dictionary while he was in prison in order to improve his vocabulary. Most people would agree that copying the dictionary showed a strong desire to improve. Malcolm X recognized the need for a better vocabulary when he tried to write intelligent letters and realized he did not know enough words to write them well. An improved vocabulary not only helped Malcolm write better, it also had a positive effect on his reading ability. Although he does not put it this way, by learning the meanings of many new words he also increased his prior knowledge, and he found that he could then use that new knowledge to understand reading material that had been too difficult for him to understand earlier. He could more easily make sense of things because he could understand the words.

What Will Motivate You to Increase Your Vocabulary?

Like Malcolm X, most students, especially at the college level, need to develop their own motivation to continue to improve their vocabularies. Vocabulary improvement is not usually assigned by instructors. Yet your instructors will expect you to improve on your own as part of your study and learning process. What will motivate you? Would you like to read and understand more easily? Would you enjoy writing more if you did not have to struggle for words? Can you imagine yourself speaking and saying exactly what you mean every time? Would you like the assurance that you could listen to lectures and understand them, or read an examination question and know exactly what it asks? Or will the desire to avoid embarrassment provide your motivation? Have you ever been in a discussion in which unfamiliar words were used, and you found yourself faking understanding because you were too shy or embarrassed to ask what a word meant? Many students have had that experience. When considering what is likely to motivate you to increase your vocabulary, realize that not all people are motivated by the same things or in the same ways.

Figure out what will motivate you to increase your vocabulary.

How can a better vocabulary help you? Jot down some personal reasons for improving your vocabulary.

_____

_____

_____

The end result of vocabulary improvement could turn out to be as valuable for you as it was for Malcolm X.

What Have You Done to Improve Your Vocabulary in the Past?

Vocabulary improvement is a lifelong task. It begins early and accelerates during school years. Some researchers say that during the first 12 years of school students learn as many as 8 to 11 new words per day. Others set the rate higher and say students learn closer to 20 new words a day. You already know the meanings of several thousand words.

Stop and think back about your vocabulary development.

How did you learn the words you know? Jot down some answers to these questions:

What did you do on your own? _____

What did your teachers assign you to do? _____

What is your favorite method for vocabulary improvement? _____

_____

It is a good idea to start with what you already do just as you did with the reading process in Chapter 1. Actually, research suggests that almost any method for improving vocabulary is better than no method at all. So start with what you do and use the most appealing suggestions from this chapter to make your present methods better.

Some students like to make vocabulary cards, either with one word or several words per card, like those shown in Figure 3-1. Other students like more systematic approaches and prefer to work through exercises in vocabulary workbooks; still others rely on lots of reading to help them learn new words. Many students like to make new word lists in their notebooks for each subject they are taking; some like to write definitions of new words right in the margins of their books. The four-column vocabulary sheet also works well for some students. Details for using several of these methods appear in the strategies section of this chapter.

Whichever method you decide to use will only work well if you keep in mind the three "basics" for improving vocabulary. First, you need to decide which words to learn; second, you need to figure out what these words mean; and third, you need to memorize the words and begin to use them.

Example 1

jocund–adj.	merry
jubilation–n.	rejoicing
judicious–adj.	wise; determined by sound judgment
junket–n.	a merry feast or banquet
junto–n.	group of persons joined in political intrigue; cabal
ken–n.	range of knowledge
kiosk–n.	summerhouse; open pavilion
kismet–n.	fate
kith–n.	familiar friends
kleptomaniac–n.	person who has a compulsive desire to steal
knavery–n.	rascality
knell–n.	tolling of a bell at a funeral; sound of the funeral bell
knoll–n.	little round hill
labyrinth–n.	maze
lacerate–v.	mangle; tear
lackadaisical–adj.	lacking spirit; languid
lackey–n.	footman
laconic–adj.	brief and to the point
laggard–adj.	slow; sluggish
lagniappe–n.	trifling present given to a customer
lagoon–n.	shallow body of water near a sea; lake
laity–n.	laymen; persons not connected with the clergy
lambent–adj.	flickering; softly radiant
laminated–adj.	made of thin plates or scales

Example 2

long-term memory "That much vaster system that holds everything else: Our long-term memory"	memory system that processes and keeps information for long time. Has large capacity Examples: how to drive a car, speak, read, recognize people and places, people's names.
Front	*Back*

FIGURE 3-1 *Vocabulary Cards*
Example 1 on page 72 is from a set of vocabulary cards made by a student who was preparing for a standardized exam. Example 2 shows a single term and its context on the front of a vocabulary card, with its meaning and examples on the other side. Long-term memory is a major concept for a psychology class.

Find Words and Decide to Learn Them

A conscious intent to locate and learn new words is a critical first step. Without it most readers read only the words they know, skip over the others, and wonder why they did not understand very well. You will not be able to learn all unfamiliar words at once. Instead, single out the words you have to know to understand the passage, along with specific words that particularly interest you.

As a top priority, you will need to identify and learn the **specialized vocabulary** that is associated with each of the courses you are taking. Every field of study has its own vocabulary, and the fastest way to become an "insider" and achieve success in a new field is to learn its vocabulary. Textbook authors often, but not always, make the specialized vocabulary easy to recognize by introducing it in chapter headings, by placing it in italics or boldface in the text itself, by defining it in the margins, or by summarizing it in a "Key Terms" or "Key Concepts" section at the end of a chapter.

Here are some examples of specialized vocabulary from some current textbooks. Some of these words will seem familiar to you, and you will wonder why they are identified as key terms. Familiar words are sometimes used in new and specialized ways in the context of a particular course, and you will need to learn these new meanings to make complete sense of the subject. Other words on the list will be both new and unfamiliar to you. You will probably need to know all of these words if you decide to take courses in these subject areas. They are also good "college-level" words since they are often used outside of their course context. Furthermore, since they represent major concepts, they can serve as brief introductions to each of these subjects. The exercise section at the end of this chapter will provide you with an opportunity to learn more about these words.

Specialized Vocabulary from Selected College Courses

- **Political Science:** *liberalism, conservatism, socialism*
- **Earth Science:** *hydrosphere, atmosphere, biosphere, geosphere*
- **History:** *market revolution, manifest destiny, expansionism*
- **Sociology:** *culture, nation, society, multiculturalism*
- **Biology:** *biodiversity, homeostasis, ecosystem*
- **Psychology:** *behaviorism, Gestalt psychology, cognitive psychology*
- **Business:** *entrepreneurs, capitalism, private enterprise*
- **Philosophy:** *free will, determinism, predestination, fatalism*

Find Out What the Word Means

There are three methods that you can use to help you understand the meanings of words: (1) study the word in context; (2) study the word's "parts"; and (3) look up the word in a glossary or dictionary. The words in the list you have just read represent fairly complicated concepts, and to understand them well, you might find it useful to use all three methods. For example, suppose you read in your philosophy book, "In the eighteenth century many people in the United States began to question the religious doctrine of *predestination.*" The context, or the words in the rest of the sentence, tells you that predestination is a religious doctrine. You look at the parts that make up this word: *pre* means before or ahead of time, and *destiny* is a familiar word to you. Destiny refers to what will irresistibly take place in the future, what is fated to happen. These two word parts, *pre* and *destiny*, suggest that predestination may mean to know one's fate ahead of time. Finally, you check the dictionary and learn that predestination is the idea that God has already decided from the beginning of time those individuals who will finally be saved and those who will not be saved. All three methods for learning a new word can thus be used together to help you gain a complete meaning for a word. Here is some additional information about each of these methods to help you use them with greater expertise.

Study the word in context. The context is the passage in which the word appears. Context either provides a complete definition or explanation of a word right in the passage itself, so that there is no mistaking the word's meaning, or it provides clues to the meaning of a word, in which case you use the context to help you guess the meaning of the word. The context for a word can be brief—a sentence or a picture—but it can also extend to a paragraph, a series of paragraphs, or even an entire essay accompanied by examples and illustrations that explain the meaning of the word. Lengthy explanations usually indicate that the word is a major concept or idea in the material you are reading, and you had better understand the word or your comprehension of much of the material will suffer.

Practice using context to determine a word's meaning.

Read the following paragraph and write the meaning of the boldfaced word in your own words, as much as possible, in the space below.

> **Behavior therapies** are based on the belief that all behavior, both normal and abnormal, is learned. Hypochondriacs *learn* that they get attention when they are sick; paranoid personalities *learn* to be suspicious of others. At the same time, behavior therapists assert, in opposition to insight therapists, that the therapist does not need to know exactly how or why people learned to behave abnormally in the first place. The job of the therapist is simply to teach people new, more satisfying ways of behaving.[1]

_____

_____

Can you also guess at the meanings of these words by using the context?

Hypochondriacs _____

Paranoid personalities _____

Insight therapists _____

Study the word's parts.   You can, as shown in the example of predestination, guess at a word's meaning by defining its prefix, root, or suffix. These are the elements that make up many words. They are often derived from other languages, and they contribute, often substantially, to a word's meaning. In fact, over 100,000 words in the English language are partly or wholly made up of bits and pieces of other languages, mostly Latin and Greek. Knowing the meanings of some of the most frequently used Latin and Greek elements can provide clues to the meanings of thousands of English words. For example, the word *benefactor* is made up of two Latin elements, *bene* and *fact*, which mean "good" and "do." Putting these two meanings together provides a strong clue to the meaning of this word: "someone who provides help or money in a charitable way, or someone who does good."

Practice guessing the meanings of words from their prefixes, roots, and suffixes.

Words and the word parts that form them, including prefixes, roots, and suffixes, are supplied here along with the meanings of the different word parts. Guess at the meaning of the word and jot it down in the space provided. Then, if you still are not sure of the meanings of the words, check them in the dictionary.

[1] Charles G. Morris, *Psychology: An Introduction*, 9th ed. (Upper Saddle River: Prentice Hall, 1996) 569.

Word	Prefix	Root	Possible Meaning
admonish	*ad-* (to, toward)	*mon* (warn)	_____
autograph	*auto-* (self)	*graph* (write)	_____
circumscribe	*circum-* (around)	*scribe* (draw)	_____
postpone	*post-* (after)	*pon* (place)	_____
predict	*pre-* (before)	*dict* (say)	_____
transport	*trans-* (across)	*port* (carry)	_____

Add Suffixes

Now add suffixes to these words and notice how the meanings change. Write what you think these words mean now.

Word	Suffix	Possible Meaning
admonisher	*-er* (one who does)	_____
autographer	*-er* (one who does)	_____
circumscriber	*-er* (one who does)	_____
postponement	*-ment* (state of)	_____
predictable	*-able* (to be)	_____
transportation	*-tion* (act of)	_____

Look up the word in the dictionary. Context and word parts often provide only partial meanings for a word. To gain a complete meaning, you will need to look up the word either in a dictionary or in the glossary of the book. A glossary is a short, specialized dictionary that appears in the back of a book and defines the book's most important terms and concepts. Not all books have glossaries, but textbooks that use a lot of specialized vocabulary often do. When there is no glossary, you can consult the dictionary. Some good ones include *Webster's New Collegiate Dictionary*, *The American Heritage Dictionary*, and *The Random House College Dictionary*. Buy one and learn to use it. Survey it first, as you would any other book, to find out what is in it. Look particularly at the sections that come before and after the A-to-Z listings. Much useful information is provided there. Then learn to read an entry for a word. The following entry for the word *comply* comes from *The Random House College Dictionary*. Below the entry is an explanation that details some of the possible information you will find for a word in that dictionary. Not all of this information is supplied for every word in the dictionary, however.

com·ply (kəm plī'), *v.i.*, **-plied,
-ply·ing. 1.** to act in accordance
with wishes, requests, demands,

How to Read a Dictionary Entry for a Word

1. The preferred spelling is listed first.
2. Syllables are separated with dots.
3. Hyphens indicate the word is hyphenated.

requirements, conditions, etc. (sometimes fol. by *with*): *to comply with regulations; They asked him to leave and he complied.* **2.** Obs. to be courteous or conciliatory. [< It *compli(re)* < Sp. *cumplir* (see COMPLIMENT) to fulfill, accomplish < L *complēre* = com-COM- + *plē* fill + -*re* inf. suffix—**com·pli'er**, *n.* —**Syn. 1.** acquiesce, yield, conform, obey. —**Ant. 1.** refuse, resist.[2]

4. The pronunciation is set off with lines or parentheses following the word.
5. The part or parts of speech are listed.
6. The language that was the origin for the word is listed.
7. The meanings are numbered. Usually, the most common or the oldest meaning is listed first.
8. Synonyms, or words that are similar in meaning, are listed at the end.
9. Antonyms, or words that are opposite in meaning, are also listed at the end when they are available. Not all words have antonyms.

Here are two more examples of dictionary entries, this time from *Merriam Webster's Collegiate Dictionary.* Notice that Webster's, in addition to presenting the word, the pronunciation, the part of speech, and the definition, also includes a date in parentheses. This is the date of the first recorded use of the word in English. You may be surprised how recently the two words below have become a part of the language.

In·ter·net \'in-tər-ˌnet\ *n* (1986): an electronic communications network that connects computer networks and organizational computer facilities around the world

World Wide Web *n* (1992): a part of the Internet designed to allow easier navigation of the network through the use of graphical user interfaces and hypertext links between different addresses—called also *Web*[3]

Keep your dictionary handy at all times, and consult it frequently. You may also find a thesaurus useful. A thesaurus is a dictionary of synonyms. It lists many similar or related words that can help you gain a fuller understanding of the word you seek to understand.

Memorize the word and use it.   There are various ways to commit a word to memory. Strategy 5 will provide you with some suggestions that will work. According to his account, Malcolm X wrote a new word, read it aloud several times, and then reviewed it the next day. That is a good method. It will work for you also.

INCREASING READING VOCABULARY: FIVE STRATEGIES

The strategies that follow suggest specific ways to apply the basics of vocabulary development explained in this chapter. That is, these points advise you on how to find the words you want to learn; they employ context, word parts, and dictionary definitions to help you understand them; and, above all, they demonstrate some ways to help you start learning and using these words.

▶

[2] *The Random House College Dictionary*, rev. ed. (New York: Random House, 1984).
[3] *Merriam Webster's Collegiate Dictionary*, 10th ed. (Springfield: Merriam Webster, 2001).

Strategy 1: Circle words and write their meanings in the margins.

Circle specialized vocabulary and other words you want to learn in your lecture notes and in your textbooks so that they will stand out from the rest of the text. Some of the words may be printed in boldface or italics or even be defined in the margins. Look at the context as a clue to the word's meaning. Then, in your own words, jot the meaning of the word in the margin. Practice by reading the following passage, circling the word **anomie**, and writing its meaning in the margin.

MODERNITY AND ANOMIE

Compared to traditional societies, modern societies impose fewer restrictions on everyone. Durkheim [an early sociologist] acknowledges the advantages of modern freedom, but he warned of a rise in **anomie**, *a condition in which society provides little moral guidance to individuals*. What so many celebrities describe as "almost being destroyed by their fame" is one extreme example of the corrosive effects of anomie. Sudden fame tears people away from their families and familiar routines, disrupting society's support and regulation of an individual, sometimes with fatal results. Durkheim instructs us, therefore, that the desires of the individual must be balanced by the claims and guidance of society—a balance that has become precarious in the modern world.[4]

Strategy 2: Make vocabulary sheets.

There are two types of vocabulary sheets.

Two-column vocabulary sheet.

Make these throughout the semester and keep them in your notebook. Or, make these just before an exam to help you learn key vocabulary quickly. The process of writing the word with its meaning will help you learn it. Practice using this type of sheet by writing the word **anomie** along with its meaning in the blanks below.

Word	Meaning

Four-column vocabulary sheet.

Figure 3-2 provides an example of a vocabulary sheet that incorporates all of the "basics" described in the chapter for learning new words: studying the context,

▶

---

[4] John J. Macionis, *Sociology*, 6th ed. (Upper Saddle River: Prentice Hall, 1997) 116.

Vocabulary Sheet			
(1) Word	(2) Context	(3) Meaning	(4) Association
rationalism	Rationalism says knowledge comes from our minds.	Relying on reasons rather than senses to find truth	math $e = mc^2$
euphoric	The good grade made her feel positively euphoric.	Extremely happy	eu–"good"
quantitative	Physics and chemistry are quantitative sciences.	Having to do with numbers	quantity lab beaker amount of force in physics
verdant	The verdant forest	Green and lush	verde—Spanish, "green"
dyad	Working in dyads can improve learning.	Group of two	dos—Spanish, "two"

FIGURE 3-2 *An Example of a Vocabulary Sheet That Contains Words of General Interest Gathered from Reading in Several Areas*
You may keep such a sheet in the front of your notebook and add interesting words when you encounter them.

looking up the definition, and analyzing word parts or making other associations to help you remember the meaning. Make a four-column vocabulary sheet by folding a piece of paper lengthwise twice in order to create four columns. Write the word in the first column, the context in which you found it in the second column, the meaning, in words that make sense to you, in the third column, and an association to help you remember it in the fourth column. Look at the example in Figure 3-2. Note that the association in the fourth column can be a picture, a bit of prior knowledge, a word from another language, a prefix or a root, an example, a comparison, a model or diagram, or an extended explanation. If you do not always write out all this information on a vocabulary sheet, at least go through these four steps mentally to fix the meanings of new words and concepts in your mind.

Practice using a four-column vocabulary sheet by writing the word **anomie** in the first column and then filling in the other three columns in the blanks on the top of page 80. Use the information provided in the paragraph about anomie. To help you make an association, you might think of rock stars or other people who have separated themselves from the guidance of society.

▶

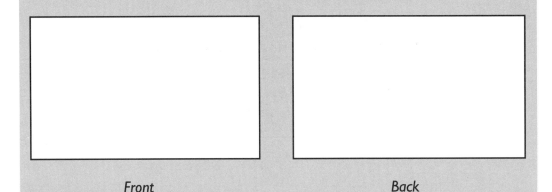

Word	Context	Meaning	Association

Strategy 3: Make vocabulary cards.

You may prefer to write a word that you want to learn on a 3" × 5" index card. Write the word and the context in which you found it on the front of the card. Write a brief definition on the back, using language that is easy to understand and remember. Use these as flash cards to help you memorize the meanings.

Look back at the vocabulary card in Example 2 of Figure 3-1 on pages 72–73. Then practice using a card by writing the term **behavior therapies**, along with the context in which it occurs, on the front of the blank card below (refer to the passage on this subject on p. 75). Next, write the meaning on the back.

Front   *Back*

Strategy 4: Organize related words on lists or maps.

It is often easier to learn words when you can see how some of them might be related to each other. Then you can learn them as a group. For example, you might organize words by categories. Thus you might write one list of words related to *ecology* and another related to *political philosophies*. Placing a title at the top of the list will show what the words have in common and this will help you remember them. Words can also be related to one another because they share a common root or prefix. The words in Exercises 2 and 3 on pages 90 and 95–97 have been organized in lists to show this relationship. Also, words can be mapped because they represent parts of a process. Figure 3-3 provides an example of six words that represent the six phases of the process of mitosis. By organizing these words on a map it is easier to see the process, which in turn will help you remember these words. Mapping is an especially useful technique for learning related scientific or technical terms.

▶

Strategy 5: Memorize the words and use them.

This is probably the most important of the five strategies, because without it your new words will only be half-learned, and you may forget them in a few days.

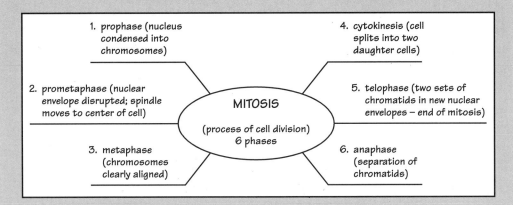

1. prophase (nucleus condensed into chromosomes)
2. prometaphase (nuclear envelope disrupted; spindle moves to center of cell)
3. metaphase (chromosomes clearly aligned)

MITOSIS
(process of cell division)
6 phases

4. cytokinesis (cell splits into two daughter cells)
5. telophase (two sets of chromatids in new nuclear envelopes – end of mitosis)
6. anaphase (separation of chromatids)

FIGURE 3-3 *A Map of the Process of Cell Division*

When you have written a new word, look away and see if you can repeat its meaning to yourself. Come back a few days later to see if you still remember what it means. Continue to do this until the word is a permanent part of your vocabulary. Then use the new words yourself in both your speaking and your writing.

EXERCISES AND READINGS

THREE COLLABORATIVE CLASS EXERCISES

Exercise 1

Understand words in context and write vocabulary sheets. *Small groups of students.*

This exercise will give you practice in locating specialized vocabulary in college textbooks and in writing the terms on four-column vocabulary sheets to help you learn them. Form groups of four or five students to read, discuss, and write about the words and concepts that appear in the textbook passages that follow. Each group selects one of the eight sets. Everyone reads the word in context, discusses its meaning, and then dictates information to a member of the group who has volunteered to be the scribe. This individual will record information about the word on a four-column vocabulary sheet like that in Figure 3-2 on page 79. Everyone should collaborate and contribute information to this sheet. Finally, one member of the group reports on the group's work by describing the entries on the vocabulary sheet to the rest of the class.

Set 1: Political Science. From the textbook, *Government by the People.*[5]
Words: *liberalism, conservatism, socialism.*

In its modern American usage, **liberalism** refers to a belief in the positive uses   1
of government to bring about justice and equality of opportunity. Modern-day
liberals wish to preserve the rights of the individual and the right to own private
property, yet they are also willing to have the government intervene in the economy to remedy the defects of capitalism. Contemporary American liberalism has
its roots in Franklin Roosevelt's New Deal programs, designed to aid the poor and
to protect people against unemployment and bank failures. Today, liberals also
seek protection against inadequate or deficient medical assistance and inadequate
or deficient housing and education. They generally believe in affirmative action
programs, regulations that protect workers' health and safety, tax rates that rise
with income, and the right of unions to organize as well as to strike.

. . . .

American **conservatism** has its roots in the political thinking of John Adams,   2
Alexander Hamilton, and many of their contemporaries. They believed in limited government and encouraged individual excellence and personal achievement.
Private property rights and belief in free enterprise are cardinal attributes of
contemporary conservatism. In contrast to liberals, conservatives want to keep
government small, except in the area of national defense. However, because conservatives take a more pessimistic view of human nature than liberals do, they
maintain that most people need strong leadership institutions, firm laws, and
strict moral codes to keep their appetites under control. Government, they think,
needs to ensure order. Conservatives are also inclined to believe that those who
fail in life are in some way the architects of their own misfortune and thus must
bear the main responsibility for solving their own problems. Conservatives have
a preference for the status quo and desire change only in moderation. A sample of conservative thinking can be found in *The National Review*, a weekly
magazine.

. . . .

Socialism is an economic and governmental system based on public ownership   3
of the means of production and exchange. Karl Marx once described socialism as a
transitional stage of society between capitalism and communism. In a capitalist
system, the means of production and most of the property are privately owned,
whereas in a communist or socialist system, property is "owned" by the state in
common for all the people. In the ultimate socialist country, justice is achieved by
having participants determine their own needs and take what is appropriate from
the common product of society. Marx's dictum was, "From each according to his
ability, to each according to his needs."[6]

[5] James M. Burns, J. W. Peltason, Thomas E. Cronin, and David B. Magleby, *Government by the People*, 2nd ed. (Upper Saddle River: Prentice Hall, 1997) 143–144, 146, 151.
[6] Karl Marx, "Critique of the Gotha Program," *Marx Selections*, ed. Allen W. Wood (New York: Macmillan, 1988) 190.

Set 2: Earth Science. From the textbook, *Earth Science.*[7] Words:
hydrosphere, atmosphere, biosphere, geosphere.

Hydrosphere

Earth is sometimes called the *blue* planet. Water more than anything else makes Earth unique. The **hydrosphere** is a dynamic mass of liquid that is continually on the move, evaporating from the oceans to the atmosphere, precipitating to the land, and running back to the ocean again. The global ocean is certainly the most prominent feature of the hydrosphere, blanketing nearly 71 percent of Earth's surface to an average depth of about 3800 meters (12,500 feet). It accounts for about 97 percent of Earth's water. However, the hydrosphere also includes the fresh water found in streams, lakes, and glaciers, as well as that found underground.

. . . .

Atmosphere

Earth is surrounded by a life-giving gaseous envelope called the **atmosphere.** When we view the atmosphere from the ground, it seems to be very deep. However, when compared to the thickness (radius) of the solid Earth (about 6400 kilometers, or 4000 miles), the atmosphere is a very shallow layer. One half lies below an altitude of 5.6 kilometers (3.5 miles), and 90 percent occurs within just 16 kilometers (10 miles) of Earth's surface. This thin blanket of air is nevertheless an integral part of the planet. It not only provides the air that we breathe but also acts to protect us from the dangerous radiation emitted by the Sun. The energy exchanges that continually occur between the atmosphere and Earth's surface and between the atmosphere and space produce the effects we call *weather* and *climate.*

. . . .

Biosphere

The **biosphere** includes all life on Earth. Ocean life is concentrated in the sunlit surface waters of the sea. Most life on land is also concentrated near the surface, with tree roots and burrowing animals reaching a few meters underground and flying insects and birds reaching a kilometer or so above Earth. A surprising variety of life forms are also adapted to extreme environments. For example, on the ocean floor, where pressures are extreme and no light penetrates, there are places where vents spew hot, mineral-rich fluids that support communities of exotic life forms. On land, some bacteria thrive in rocks as deep as 4 kilometers (2.5 miles) and in boiling hot springs. Moreover, air currents can carry microorganisms many kilometers into the atmosphere. But even when we consider these extremes, life still must be thought of as being confined to a narrow band very near Earth's surface.

. . . .

Geosphere

Lying beneath the atmosphere and the ocean is the solid Earth or **geosphere.** The geosphere extends from the surface to the center of the planet, a depth of 6400 kilometers,

[7] Tarbuck and Lutgens, *Earth Science*, 11th ed. (Upper Saddle River: Prentice Hall, 2006) 12–14.

making it by far the largest of Earth's four spheres. Much of our study of the solid Earth focuses on the more accessible surface features. Fortunately, many of these features represent the outward expressions of the dynamic behavior of Earth's interior. By examining the most prominent surface features and their global extent, we can obtain clues to the dynamic processes that have shaped our planet.

Set 3: History. **From the textbook,** *Out of Many: A History of the American People.*[8] **Words:** *Market revolution, expansionism, manifest destiny.*

The Market Revolution

The market revolution was the most fundamental change American communities ever experienced. It encompassed three broad, interrelated economic changes: exceptionally rapid improvements in transportation [. . .] which allowed both people and goods to move with new ease and speed; commercialization, the production of goods for a cash market rather than home use or local barter; and industrialization, in which power-driven machinery produced goods previously made by hand. These three aspects of the market revolution, taken together, rapidly knit the nation into a commercial market that supplied most ordinary Americans with abundant quantities of inexpensive manufactured goods.

. . . .

Manifest Destiny, an Expansionist Ideology

How did Americans justify their restless expansionism? After all, the United States was already a very large country with much undeveloped land. To push beyond existing boundaries was to risk war with Great Britain, which claimed the Pacific Northwest, and with Mexico, which held what is now Texas, New Mexico, Arizona, Utah, Nevada, California, and part of Colorado. Even if successful, such wars would reduce 75,000 Spanish-speaking people born on the continent and 150,000 Indian people to the status of conquered peoples. The United States needed a rationale for conquest.

In 1845 newspaperman John O'Sullivan provided it, coining the phrase by which expansionism became famous. It was, O'Sullivan said, "our *manifest destiny* to overspread the continent allotted by Providence for the free development of our yearly multiplying millions." O'Sullivan argued that Americans had a God-given right to bring the benefits of American democracy to other, more backward people—meaning Mexicans and Indian nations—by force, if necessary. The notion of manifest destiny summed up the thinking of many expansionists. Pride in what America had achieved combined with missionary zeal and racist attitudes toward other peoples made for a powerful combination. Americans were proud of their rapid development: the surge in population, the remarkable canals and railroads, the grand scale of the American enterprise. Why shouldn't it be even bigger? Almost swaggering, Americans dared other countries—Great Britain in particular—to stop them.

[8] John M. Faragher, Mari Jo Buhle, Daniel Czitrom, and Susan H. Armitage, *Out of Many: A History of the American People*, 2nd ed. (Upper Saddle River: Prentice Hall, 1997) 346, 411–412.

Set 4: Sociology. From the textbook, *Sociology*.[9] Words: *culture, nation, society, multicultural.*

Culture, Nation, and Society

At this point, we might well pause to clarify several similar terms—"culture," "nation," and "society." *Culture* refers to a shared way of life. A *nation* is a political entity, that is, a territory within designated borders such as the United States, Canada, Argentina, or Zimbabwe. *Society*, the topic of the next chapter, is the organized interaction of people in a nation or within some other boundary.

We correctly describe the United States, then, as both a nation and as a society. But many societies—including the United States—are *multicultural*, meaning that they encompass various ways of life that blend (and sometimes clash) in our everyday lives.

Set 5: Biology. From the textbook, *Life on Earth*.[10] Words: *biodiversity, homeostasis, ecosystem.*

The diversity of species and the complex interrelationships that sustain them are encompassed by the term **biodiversity**. In recent decades, the rate of environmental change has been drastically accelerated by a single species, *Homo sapiens* (modern human). Few species are able to adapt to this change, and in habitats most affected by people, many species are being driven to extinction. This concept is explored further in the box "Earth Watch: Biodiversity Is Threatened by Human Activities."

. . . .

To stay alive and function effectively, organisms must keep the conditions within their bodies fairly constant, a process called **homeostasis** (derived from Greek words meaning "to stay the same"). One of the many conditions regulated is body temperature. Among warm-blooded animals, for example, vital organs such as the brain and heart are kept at a warm, constant temperature despite wide fluctuations in environmental temperature.

. . . .

Beyond the individual organisms are broader levels of organization. A group of very similar, potentially interbreeding organisms constitutes a **species**. Members of the same species that live in a given area are considered a **population**. Populations of several species living and interacting in the same area form a **community**. A community plus its nonliving environment, including land, water, and atmosphere, constitute an **ecosystem**. Finally, the entire surface region of Earth inhabited by living things is called the **biosphere**.

[9] John J. Macionis, *Sociology*, 6th ed. (Upper Saddle River: Prentice Hall, 1997) 65–66.
[10] Teresa Audesirk and Gerald Audesirk, *Life on Earth* (Upper Saddle River: Prentice Hall, 1997) 4, 5, 14.

Set 6: Psychology. From the textbook, *Psychology.*[11] Words: *Gestalt psychology, behaviorism, cognitive psychology.*

Gestalt Psychology

Meanwhile in Germany a group of psychologists was attacking structuralism from another angle. Max Wertheimer, Wolfgang Köhler, and Kurt Koffka were all interested in perception, but particularly in certain tricks that the mind plays on itself. Why, they asked, when we are shown a series of still pictures flashed at a constant rate (for example, movies or "moving" neon signs), do the pictures seem to move? The eye *sees* only a series of still pictures. What makes us *perceive* motion?

Phenomena like these were the force behind a new school of thought, **Gestalt psychology**. Roughly translated from the German, *Gestalt* means "whole" or "form." When applied to perception, it refers to our tendency to see patterns, to distinguish an object from its background, to complete a picture from a few cues. Like James, the Gestalt psychologists thought that the attempt to break down perception and thought into their elements was misguided. When we look at a tree, we see just that, a tree, not a series of branches.

. . . .

John B. Watson: Behaviorism

John B. Watson was the first student to receive a doctorate in psychology from the University of Chicago. His dissertation was on learning in rats. One of the department's requirements was that he speculate on the kind of consciousness that produced the behavior he observed in his rats. Watson found this demand absurd; he doubted the rats had any consciousness at all. Nevertheless, he complied with the requirement, received his degree, and returned to his laboratory to think about consciousness.

Ten years and many experiments later, Watson was ready to confront both the structuralist and functionalist schools with his own ideas about consciousness and behavior. In "Psychology as the Behaviorist Views It" (1913), he argued that the whole idea of consciousness, of mental life, was superstition, a relic from the Middle Ages. You cannot define consciousness any more than you can define a soul, Watson argued. You cannot locate it or measure it, and therefore it cannot be the object of scientific study. For Watson, psychology was the study of observable, measurable behavior—and nothing more. Thus was the school of psychology known as **behaviorism** born. [. . .]

B. F. Skinner: Behaviorism Revisited

[. . .] Like Watson, Skinner fervently believed that psychology should study only observable and measurable behavior. He, too, was primarily interested in changing behavior through conditioning—and in discovering natural laws of behavior in the process.

. . . .

[11] Charles G. Morris, *Psychology*, 9th ed. (Upper Saddle River: Prentice Hall, 1996) 24, 25, 26.

Cognitive Psychology

In the past decade or two, a new perspective has emerged to reshape the field 6 of psychology. **Cognitive psychology** is the study of our mental processes in the broadest sense: thinking, feeling, learning, remembering, making decisions and judgments, and so on. Thus, cognitive psychologists are especially interested in the ways in which people perceive, interpret, store, and retrieve information.

In contrast to the behaviorists, cognitive psychologists believe that mental 7 processes can and should be studied scientifically. Although we cannot observe cognitive processes directly, we can observe behavior and make inferences about the kinds of cognitive processes that underlie that behavior. For example, we can read a lengthy story to people and then observe the kinds of things that they remember from that story, the ways in which their recollections change over time, and the sorts of memory errors that occur. Through systematic research of this kind, it is possible to gain insight into the cognitive processes that underlie human memory.

Set 7: Business. **From the textbook** *Business.*[12] **Words:** *entrepreneurs, capitalism, private enterprise.*

Entrepreneurs   An **entrepreneur** is an individual who accepts the risks and op- 1 portunities entailed in creating and operating a new business. AOL was started by James Kimsey, who had the technical skills to understand how the Internet works, the conceptual skills to see its huge future potential, and the risk-taking acumen to bet his own career and capital on the idea of AOL. Both Time Inc. and Warner Brothers Studios, two older companies that later merged into Time Warner, were also started (both in 1922) by entrepreneurs who risked personal fortunes on the success of their new ventures.

In 2001, the entrepreneurial and visionary leaders at both AOL and Time 2 Warner saw the potential benefits of merging the two firms. Most economic systems encourage entrepreneurs, both to start new businesses and to make the decisions that turn small businesses into larger ones big enough to move into new markets.

. . . .

Capitalism   Individuals, meanwhile, are free to work for Ford or anyone else, and 3 they are free to invest in Ford stock or to put their money elsewhere, whether saving it or spending it on products they need or want. Likewise, Ford can create the vehicles it chooses and sell them at the prices it chooses. Consumers, of course, are free to buy their next car from Ford or Toyota or BMW. This process contrasts markedly with that of a planned economy, in which individuals may be told where they can and cannot work, companies may be told what they can and cannot make, and consumers may have little or no choice in what they purchase or how much

[12] Ricky W. Griffin and Ronald J. Ebert, *Business*, 8th ed. (Upper Saddle River: Prentice Hall, 2006) 9–19.

they pay. The political basis of market processes is called **capitalism,** which sanctions the private ownership of the factors of production and encourages entrepreneurship by offering profits as an incentive. The economic basis of market processes is the operation of demand and supply.

. . . .

Private Enterprise and Competition in a Market Economy

Market economies rely on a **private enterprise** system—one that allows individuals to pursue their own interests with minimal government restriction. In turn, private enterprise requires the presence of four elements: private property rights, freedom of choice, profits, and competition.

- *Private property.* Ownership of the resources used to create wealth is in the hands of individuals.

- *Freedom of choice.* You can sell your labor to any employer you choose. You can also choose which products to buy, and producers can usually choose whom to hire and what to produce.

- *Profits.* The lure of profits (and freedom) leads some people to abandon the security of working for someone else and to assume the risks of entrepreneurship. Anticipated profits also influence individuals' choices of which goods or services to produce.

- *Competition.* If profits motivate individuals to start businesses, competition motivates them to operate those businesses efficiently. **Competition** occurs when two or more businesses vie for the same resources or customers. To gain an advantage over competitors, a business must produce its goods or services efficiently and be able to sell at a reasonable profit. To achieve these goals, it must convince customers that its products are either better or less expensive than those of its competitors. Competition, therefore, forces all businesses to make products better or cheaper. A company that produces inferior, expensive products is likely to fail.

Set 8: Philosophy. From the textbook, *Discovering Philosophy.*[13] Words: *free will, determinism, predestination, fatalism.*

The theory of **free will** expresses our everyday experience of feeling free. Those who argue for free will maintain that we have the capacity to size up a situation, think about our options, and choose how we will act. What we do, then, is the result of our own, deliberate free choice. **Determinism** maintains exactly the opposite. Determinists claim that everything in nature happens as a result of *cause and effect*, and this includes human behavior. If every effect already has a cause, then, our actions and our choices are simply the result of some preexisting causes that produce them, and they cannot be freely arrived at.

. . . .

[13] Thomas I. White, *Discovering Philosophy* (Upper Saddle River: Prentice Hall, 1991) 104, 109.

Determinism, Predestination, and Fate

Be sure to realize, however, that *determinism* is not the same thing as predestination or fatalism. 2

Predestination is a not-especially-comforting religious belief which maintains that God has decided from the beginning of time who will be "saved." This is already set. No matter what we do, no matter how hard we try, the outcome will not be changed. Our final destination—heaven or hell—is already logged into the heavenly computer. The argument for this is not philosophical but theological, and this idea raises the question of how a good God could predestine apparently decent people to eternal punishment. Christians who believe in predestination generally cite the argument of Saint Augustine (354–430) that the "original sin" of Adam and Eve, that is, their disobedience to God, was so terrible that God could justly condemn them and their descendants to hell. The central question then becomes why God chooses to save anyone, but that is another problem. 3

Fatalism is similar, in a way. If you believe that certain things are fated to happen, or that whatever happens to you is simply your destiny, or karma, you think these things take place no matter what you do—they're just "meant to be." Some people believe that there is someone out there that they're meant to meet, fall in love with, and marry. Somehow destiny will bring them together. Some people believe that they're fated to die on a certain day. Whether they're on a plane, in a car, or washing dishes in the kitchen, something fatal will happen. 4

Exercise 2

Analyze word parts: prefixes, roots, and suffixes. *Small groups.*

This exercise will teach the analysis of prefixes and roots as clues to the meanings of words. You will learn the most common prefixes and roots and use them to analyze the meanings of words and also to form words. Start with the warm-up exercise below to understand the basic method of Exercises 2 and 3, which is to analyze word parts. You will need dictionaries to complete these exercises.

Class warm-up.

Class members should guess at the meanings of the following words after examining the elements that compose them. Then someone in the class should check the dictionary to see how close the guesses were to the dictionary meanings of the words.

Word	Prefix and Meaning	Root and Meaning	Your Best Guess at the Meaning	Check the Dictionary. Were You Close? Yes or No
1. abduct	ab- (away from)	duct (lead)	_____	_____
2. advent	ad- (to)	vent (come)	_____	_____
3. avert	a- (away)	vert (turn)	_____	_____
4. biped	bi- (two)	ped (foot)	_____	_____
5. controversy	contro- (against)	vers (turn)	_____	_____
6. euphonious	eu- (good)	phon (sound)	_____	_____
7. impugn	im- (against)	pugn (fight)	_____	_____
8. inscribe	in- (on)	scrib (write)	_____	_____
9. interurban	inter- (between)	urb (city)	_____	_____
10. semiannual	semi- (half)	annus (year)	_____	_____

Add suffixes to half of these words and then guess the meaning.

Word	Suffix and Meaning	Your Best Guess at the Meaning	Check the Dictionary. Were You Close? Yes or No
1. abductor	-or (one who does)	_____	_____
2. bipedal	-al (relating to)	_____	_____
3. controversial	-ial (relating to)	_____	_____
4. euphoniously	-ly (like, characteristic of)	_____	_____
5. suburbanite	-ite (nature of, quality of)	_____	_____

a. Learn frequently used prefixes. *Small groups.*

Now work with some of the most common Latin and Greek prefixes, which have been organized by meaning on the lists that follow to help you learn them. Notice that the first list is different from the other six lists since it provides examples of words that contain the negative prefixes in this set. Study these examples to get you started, and then provide one additional example of a word along with a brief definition for each prefix in Set 1. In turn, do the same for each of the additional six sets. Write the words you discover along with their meanings in the spaces provided. Work in pairs or small groups of three or four and be prepared to report on your work to the class. You may use dictionaries, if necessary, to locate examples.

Set 1: Negative Prefixes

Prefix	Example	Meaning	Your Word	Meaning
1. *a-, an-*	anarchy	no government or law	_____	_____
2. *de-*	deforestation	no forests, destroyed	_____	_____
3. *dis-*	disrespect	no respect	_____	_____
4. *in-, il-, im-, ir-*	illiterate	not able to read or write	_____	_____
5. *non-*	nonentity	not significant	_____	_____
6. *un-*	undeveloped	not developed	_____	_____

Set 2: Size Prefixes

Prefix	Meaning	Your Word	Meaning
1. *hyper-*	excessive	_____	_____
2. *macro-*	large	_____	_____
3. *magni-*	large	_____	_____
4. *maxi-*	most, greatest	_____	_____
5. *media-*	half, middle, between	_____	_____
6. *micro-*	small	_____	_____
7. *mini-*	least, small	_____	_____
8. *multi-, poly-*	many	_____	_____
9. *omni-, pan-*	all	_____	_____
10. *over-*	excessive, too much	_____	_____
11. *semi-*	half, part	_____	_____
12. *semi-, hemi-*	half	_____	_____
13. *under-*	not enough	_____	_____

Set 3: Direction Prefixes

Prefix	Example	Your Word	Meaning
1. *ad-*	away	_____	_____
2. *ad-*	to, toward	_____	_____
3. *circum-*	around	_____	_____
4. *de-*	down, away, from	_____	_____
5. *dia-*	across	_____	_____
6. *dis-*	away	_____	_____
7. *ex-*	away from	_____	_____
8. *in-*	in, into	_____	_____
9. *per-*	through	_____	_____
10. *peri-*	around	_____	_____
11. *out-*	in a direction away	_____	_____
12. *re-*	back	_____	_____
13. *se-*	apart	_____	_____
14. *trans-*	across	_____	_____

Set 4: Place Prefixes

Prefix	Example	Your Word	Meaning
1. *con-*	with	_____	_____
2. *en-, em-*	in	_____	_____
3. *epi-*	on, upon	_____	_____
4. *extra-*	outside	_____	_____
5. *inter-*	between	_____	_____
6. *intra-*	within	_____	_____
7. *mid-*	middle	_____	_____
8. *para-*	beside	_____	_____
9. *sub-*	under	_____	_____
10. *sur-*	over	_____	_____
11. *syn-*	with	_____	_____

Set 5: Opposition Prefixes

Prefix	Example	Your Word	Meaning
1. *anti-*	against	_____	_____
2. *counter-*	against	_____	_____
3. *mis-*	wrong	_____	_____
4. *ob-*	against	_____	_____

Set 6: Time Prefixes

Prefix	Example	Your Word	Meaning
1. *after-*	after	_____	_____
2. *ante-*	before	_____	_____
3. *fore-*	before	_____	_____
4. *post-*	after	_____	_____
5. *pre-*	before	_____	_____

Set 7: Number Prefixes

Prefix	Example	Your Word	Meaning
1. *bi-, di-*	two	_____	_____
2. *centi-*	100	_____	_____
3. *dicu-, deci-*	ten	_____	_____
4. *hept-, sept-*	seven	_____	_____
5. *hex-, sex-*	six	_____	_____
6. *mil-, kilo-*	1000	_____	_____
7. *mono-, uni-*	one	_____	_____
8. *nona-*	nine	_____	_____
9. *oct-*	eight	_____	_____
10. *pent-, quint-*	five	_____	_____
11. *prim-, pro-*	first	_____	_____
12. *quad-, tetr-*	four	_____	_____
13. *tri-*	three	_____	_____

b. Review. The Most Common Prefixes

Approximately seventy percent of the words in the English language that begin with prefixes are formed with the prefixes in the list below. Continue to work with a partner or group and add your own example of words that begin with these prefixes.

Prefix	Meaning	Example	Your Example
1. *anti-*	against	antiwar, antifreeze	_____
2. *de-*	not, undo, opposite	decriminalize	_____
3. *dis-*	not, away	disrespect	_____
4. *en-, em-*	in, cause to	enfold, encode	_____
5. *fore-*	before	foretell	_____
6. *in-, im-*	in, on	impose	_____
7. *in-, im-, il-, ir–*	not	incomplete, impossible, illegal, irresponsible	_____
8. *inter-*	between	interpose, international	_____
9. *mid-*	middle	mid-Atlantic, mid-century	_____
10. *mis-*	not, bad, wrongly	misunderstand, misshapen	_____
11. *non-*	not	nontraditional	_____
12. *over-*	above, too much	overreact, oversee	_____
13. *pre-*	before	prepare, predict	_____
14. *re-*	again	review, reread	_____
15. *semi-*	half, part	semisoft, semicircle	_____
16. *sub-*	under, near	sub-basement, suburban	_____
17. *super-*	above	supervisor, supersonic	_____
18. *trans-*	across	transcontinental	_____
19. *un-*	not	uncover	_____
20. *under-*	under, not enough	understaffed	_____

Learn frequently used roots and suffixes. *Small groups.*

a. The following are twelve sets of some of the Latin and Greek roots that are frequently found in English words. Form small groups of three to four students. Each group will work with one set of roots. Group members may read the root word and its meaning and then write an example of an English word that contains that root along with a brief definition on a separate piece of paper. Notice that not all words begin with prefixes. Many words begin with root words. Assign a member of your group to report the results of your work to the class. Use a dictionary.

Example:	Root	Meaning	English Word	Definition
	alter	other, change	alternate	another person; substitute

Set 1		Set 2	
aero	air	*aqua*	water
ag, agi, ig, act	do, move, go	*arch*	chief, first, rule
ali, allo, alter	other	*aster, astr*	star
alt(us)	high, deep	*atmo*	air, vapor
am, amic	love, friend	*aud, aus*	hear, listen
Anni, annu, enni	year	*auto, aut*	self
anthrop	man, human	*biblio*	book
appell	name	*bio*	life

Set 3		Set 4	
ced, ceed, cede	move, yield, go	*cur, curs*	run
chrom	color	*cycl, cyclo*	wheel, circular
chron	time	*dem*	people
cide, cise	cut, kill	*dent, dont*	tooth
cogn	know	*dict*	say, speak
corp	body	*duc, duct*	lead
cosmo	universe, world	*eco*	habitat or environment
cred	believe	*ego*	I, self

Set 5

erg, ergon	work
fac, fact	do, make
fin	end
geo	earth
graph, gram	write
hetero	different
homo	same
hydr, hydra, hydro	water

Set 6

ject	throw
join, junct	join
juris, jus	law
kin	movement
liber	free
lith	stone
loc, loco, loq	place
log, logo, ology	word, study, speech

Set 7

luc, lum, lus, lun	light
man	hand
mar, mari, mer	sea, pool
meter	measure
migra	wander
mit, miss	send
mob, mot, mov	move
mon	warn, remind

Set 8

mor, mort	mortal, death
nat, nasc	to be from, to spring forth
nomen, nomin	name
path, pathy	feeling, suffering
ped, pod	foot
phil	love
phobia, phobos	fear
phon	sound

Set 9

photo	light
plu, plur, plus	more
pop	people
port	carry
pseudo	false
psych	mind, soul
reg, recti	straighten
rupt	break

Set 10

sanguin	blood
sci, scientia	know
scope, spec	see, watch
scrib, script	write
sent, sens	feel
sign, signi	sign, mark, seal
solus	alone
spec, spect, spic	look

Set 11		Set 12	
stat	stand	*urb*	city
tact, tang	touch	*ven, vent*	come
tempor	time	*ver, veri*	true
ten, tin, tain,	hold	*verb*	wordy
termin	end, boundary	*vid, vis*	see
terra	earth	*viv, vita, vivi*	alive, life
therm	heat	*volvo*	turn about, roll
tract, tra	draw, pull		

b. **Review.** Complete your group work by matching the definitions with the words in the lists that follow. Do not use the dictionary. Consult, instead, the lists of prefixes and roots that you have been learning.

	Definition	Word
_____	1. holding fast	a. bibliography
_____	2. not open to question	b. biography
_____	3. a written list of books	c. incontrovertible
_____	4. a warning before something happens	d. synergetic
_____	5. talkative, wordy	e. tenacious
_____	6. a written record of a life	f. loquacious
_____	7. working together	g. premonition
_____	8. wordiness	h. pseudonym
_____	9. a false name	i. misanthrope
_____	10. someone who hates humankind	j. verbose

c. **Make word families and put them on maps.** Practice grouping words that are related because of a common word part. Putting groups of related words on maps will help you learn them. Here is an example of a family of words that contains the root *chron* (time). Work in your same groups and map a similar family using one of the following elements listed after the example:

Example:

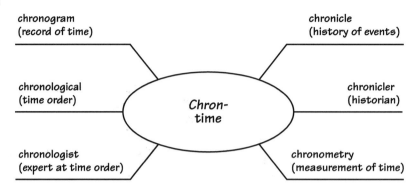

Map similar families using the elements:

dict- (say), *duct-* (lead), *cogn-* (know), *jus-, juris-* (law), *mit-, miss-* (send), *circum-* (around), and *pre-* (before).

d. **Add Suffixes.** Here is a list of common suffixes along with their meanings and examples of words that end with them. Write a second example in the column provided. Notice how a suffix changes the meaning of a word.

Common Suffixes

	Suffix	Meaning	Example	Your Example
1.	-able, -ible	able to be	understandable	_____
2.	-al, -ial	relating to	marginal	_____
3.	-an, -ian	native of	Canadian	_____
4.	-ance, -ancy	action, state	defiance	_____
5.	-ant	performing, agent	supplicant	_____
6.	-ary, -ery, -ory	relating to	dictionary	_____
7.	-cian	having a special skill	musician	_____
8.	-cule, ling	very small	molecule	_____
9.	-ee	one who receives the action	nominee	_____
10.	-en	made of	leaden	_____
11.	-er, -or	one who does	reader	_____
12.	-ful	full of	helpful	_____
13.	-fy	make	simplify	_____
14.	–ic	having characteristics of	poetic	_____

15.	-ion, -tion	act, process	connection	_____
16.	-ish	origin, nature	manish	_____
17.	-ism	act of, state of	pessimism	_____
18.	-ist	one who does	typist	_____
19.	-ite	nature of, quality of	socialite	_____
20.	-ity, -ty	state of	anonimity	_____
21.	-less	without	hopeless	_____
22.	-ly	like, characteristic of	hopefully	_____
23.	-ment	state of	excitement	_____
24.	-ness	state of	happiness	_____
25.	-(o)logy	study of	biology	_____

THREE READING EXERCISES:
ABOUT COMPUTERS

Computers have contributed a significant number of new words to the English language. "Computers" was selected as the subject of the readings for this chapter because these readings rely on a computer vocabulary that is useful across all college disciplines. When you read about computers, you will discover that some computer vocabulary is not in dictionaries yet. You will have to rely on context and meaning of word parts and then guess at the meanings of some of these computer-related words. The first two reading selections are drawn from college textbooks, and the third comes from *Time* magazine.

Reading 1

Data Communication Networks[14]

RICKY W. GRIFFIN AND RONALD J. EBERT

Explanatory Notes: *The following selection is drawn from a chapter titled "Managing Information Systems and Communications Technology" that appears in the business textbook,* Business. *As you read, underline the words that are either new to you or that you have not fully understood until now.*

Data Communication Networks

Data communication networks carry streams of digital data (electronic documents and other forms of video and sound) back and forth over telecommunication systems. The most prominent network, the Internet, and its companion 1

[14] Ricky W. Griffin and Ronald J. Ebert, *Business,* 8th ed. (Upper Saddle River: Prentice Hall, 2006) 443–447.

system, the World Wide Web, have emerged as powerful communication technologies. Let's look a little more closely at each of these networks.

The Internet The largest public data communications network, the **Internet** ("the Net"), is a gigantic system of networks that both serves millions of computers with information on business, science, and government and provides communication flows among more than 170,000 separate networks around the world. Originally commissioned by the Pentagon (**www.defenselink.mil**) as a wartime communications tool, the Internet allows personal computers in virtually any location to be linked. Because it can transmit information fast and at lower cost than long-distance phone service and postal delivery, the Net is also the most important e-mail system in the world. For thousands of businesses, it has joined—and is even replacing—the telephone, fax machine, and express mail as a communications tool.

Individuals can't connect directly to the Internet, but for small monthly usage fees, they can subscribe to the Net via an **Internet service provider (ISP),** such as EarthLink, AOL, or Verizon. An ISP is a commercial firm that maintains a permanent connection to the Net and sells temporary connections to subscribers.

Nearly 950 million Net users are active in more than 180 countries. The most intensive Net usage is in Malaysia, where 30 percent of the country's population is online, followed by the United States, China, and Japan. In early 2004, 151 million at-home and at-work Internet users were active in the United States alone. The Net's power to change the way business is conducted has been amply demonstrated in both large and small firms. Consider how it's changing just one industry—banking. Online banking by U.S. households nearly doubled from 2000 to 2003, growing to some 35 million households.[15]

The World Wide Web Thanks to the subsystem of computers known as the **World Wide Web** (WWW or "the Web"), the Internet allows users around the world to communicate electronically with little effort. The Web is a system with universally accepted standards for storing, retrieving, formatting, and displaying information. It provides the common language that allows us to surf the Net and makes it available to a general audience, not merely to technical users such as computer programmers. To access a Web site, the user specifies the *Uniform Resource Locator (URL)* that points to the unique Web address of the resource. Thus, the American Airlines URL is www.aa.com—a designation that specifies the storage location of American's Web pages.

Servers and Browsers Each Web site opens with a *home page*—a screen display that introduces the site to the visitor and may include graphics, sound, and visual enhancements. Additional pages present the sponsor's products and explain how

2

3

4

5

6

[15]Zoraini Wati Abas, "Internet Statistics and Online Growth," *New Straits Times–Management Times,* February 5, 2004 (EMEDIA-ACC-NO: 200402056940); "Internet Population Increased Nearly 20 Percent in 2001; Over 700 Million Users Projected by 2004," *Cableoptics Newsletter,* February 2002, 15; Kuldeep Kumar and Jos van Hillegersberg, "New Architecture for Financial Services: Introduction," *Communications of the ACM* 47:5 (2004): 26–30; Danny Sullivan, "Neilsen Ratings/Search Engine Ratings," *SearchEngineWatch* (February 23, 2004), searchenginewatch.com.

to get help in using the site. They often furnish URLs for related Web sites that the user can link into by simply pointing and clicking. The person who is responsible for maintaining an organization's Web site is usually called a *Webmaster.* Large sites use dedicated workstations—large computers—known as **Web servers,** which are customized for managing and supporting such sites.

With hundreds of thousands of new Web pages appearing each day, cyberspace now posts billions of pages of information. Sorting through this maze would be impossible without a Web **browser**—the software that permits users to access information on the Web. A browser runs on the user's PC and supports the graphics and linking capabilities needed to navigate the Web. Microsoft's Internet Explorer (**www.microsoft.com**) is the world's most widely used browser, even though Netscape Navigator (**www.netscape.com**) and some versions of Mozilla (**www.mozilla.org**) are free.[16]

Directories and Search Engines   Browsers offer additional tools—Web site directories and search engines—for navigating on the Web. Among the most successful cyberspace enterprises are companies such as Yahoo! (**www.yahoo.com**) that maintain free-to-use *directories* of Web content. When Yahoo! is notified about new Web sites, it classifies them in its directory. Users enter one or two keywords (for example, "compact disk"), and the directory retrieves a list of Web sites with Web pages containing those words.

In contrast, a **search engine** scans millions of Web pages without preclassifying them into a directory. It merely searches for pages containing the same words as the user's search terms, then displays addresses for those pages that come closest to matching, then the next closest, and so on. Some search engines, such as AltaVista (**www.altavista.com**) or Lycos (**www.lycos.com**), respond to more than 10 million inquiries a day. Not surprisingly, both directories and search engines are packed with paid ads.[17]

Intranets   Many companies have extended Net technology internally by maintaining internal Web sites linked throughout the firm. These private networks, or **intranets,** are accessible only to employees behind electronic **firewalls**—hardware and software security systems inaccessible to outsiders.[18] The Ford Motor Co. (**www.ford.com**) intranet connects 120,000 workstations in Asia, Europe, and the United States to thousands of Ford Web sites containing private information on Ford activities in production, engineering, distribution, and marketing. Sharing information has reduced the lead time for getting models into production from 36 to 24 months, and it has shortened customer delivery times. Ford's intranet has saved billions in inventory and fixed costs.[19]

7

8

9

10

[16]David Hewson, "Browsing for Alternatives," *Sunday Times* (London) (June 29, 2003), web.lexis-nexis.com.

[17]Sullivan, "Neilsen Ratings/Search Engine Ratings."

[18]Matt Villano, "Nokia Raises Security Bar for High-End Firewalls," *CRN,* May 24, 2004, 12.

[19]See Nancy Dixon, "Replicating Best Practice," *Strategic Direction,* July/August 2000, 15; Rick Gurin, "Online System to Streamline Ford's Delivery Process," *Frontline Solutions,* April 2000, 1, 8.

Extranets **Extranets** allow outsiders limited access to a firm's internal informa- tion system. The most common application allows buyers to enter a system to see which products are available for sale and delivery, thus providing convenient product-availability information. Industrial suppliers are often linked into customers' intranets so that they can see planned production schedules and prepare supplies for customers' upcoming operations.

950 words

Strategy Questions

1. Select five of the words from this textbook selection that you did not know. Fold a piece of paper twice to make four columns. Write the title "Computers" at the top of the paper. At the top of each of the four columns write the subtitles "word," "context," "definition," and "association." Enter the five words you have selected, and information about them, on the sheet.
2. Define Internet, intranet, and extranet. Refer back to "Set 4: Place Prefixes" on page 92 to review the meanings of prefixes.

Study Reading Questions

1. Define "data communication networks" and give an example of one.
2. Explain three reasons for the popularity of the Internet. What can it do that nothing else before it could do?
3. What is a Web browser? How does it differ from a search engine?
4. Why would a company install an intranet? How do firewalls help make intranets effective?
5. Why would a company set up extranets? Name two types of information outsiders might be able to access through a company's extranet.

Critical Reading and Thinking Questions

1. Drawing on your own experience, name and describe two companies that you are familiar with that use computers to manage information and communication both inside and outside of their daily operations. For what purposes do these companies use computers? Are the results more positive or more negative? Why do you think so?
2. In your opinion, how is the Internet changing business practices, especially when compared to business conducted before it was invented? Describe both positive and negative effects of the Internet on modern business practices.
3. The authors mention that Web directories and search engines are "packed with paid ads." Who do you think the advertisers pay to use this space? How effective do you think it is to advertise on Web directories and search engines? Why?

New Information Technology and Work[20]

JOHN J. MACIONIS

Explanatory Notes: *The following comes from a chapter titled "The Economy and Work" in the textbook* Sociology. ***What do you already know about how computers are affecting the work place? Underline all of the words in the essay, related to computers, that are new to you.***

July 2, Ticonderoga, New York. The manager of the local hardware store scans the bar codes of a bagful of items: "The computer doesn't just total the costs," she explains. "It also keeps track of inventory, placing orders from the warehouse and deciding which products to continue to sell and which to drop." "Sounds like what you used to do, Maureen," I respond with a smile. "Yep," she nods, with no smile at all.

Another workplace issue is the increasing role of computers and other new information technology. The Information Revolution is changing what people do in a number of ways. (Rule & Brantley, 1992; Vallas & Beck, 1996).[21]

1. **Computers are deskilling labor.** Just as industrial machinery replaced the master craftsworkers of an earlier era, computers now threaten the skills of managers. More business operations are based not on executive decisions but on computer modeling. In other words, a machine decides whether to place an order, stock a dress in a certain size and color, or approve a loan application.

2. **Computers are making work more abstract.** Most industrial workers have a hands-on relationship with their product. Postindustrial workers use symbols to perform abstract tasks, such as making a company more profitable or making software more user-friendly.

3. **Computers limit workplace interaction.** As workers spend more time at computer terminals, they become increasingly isolated from other workers.

4. **Computers increase employers' control of workers.** Computers allow supervisors to monitor employees' output continuously, whether they work at computer terminals or on assembly lines.

5. **Computers allow companies to relocate work.** Because computer technology allows information to flow almost anywhere instantly, the symbolic work in

---

[20] John J. Macionis, *Sociology*, 11th ed. (Upper Saddle River: Prentice Hall, 2007) 432–433.

[21] James Rule and Peter Brantley. "Computerized Surveillance in the Workplace: Forms and Delusions." *Sociological Forum.* Vol. 7, No. 3 (September 1992):405–23. See also Stephen P. Vallas and John P. Beck. "The Transformation of Work Revisited: The Limits of Flexibility in American Manufacturing." *Social Problems.* Vol. 43, No. 3 (August 1996):339–61.

today's economy may not take place where we might think. We have all had the experience of calling a business (say, a hotel or a toy store) located in our own town only to find that we are talking to a person at a computer workstation thousands of miles away. [. . .] McDonald's is [now] using new information technology to outsource the job of taking orders at the local drive-through to call centers hundreds or thousands of miles away.

Such changes remind us that technology is not socially neutral. Rather, it changes the relationships between people in the workplace, shapes the way we work, and often alters the balance of power between employers and employees. Understandably, then, people welcome some aspects of the Information Revolution and oppose others.

3

403 words

Strategy Questions

1. Select two more words or concepts from this textbook selection and add them to your "Computers" vocabulary sheet.
2. Review the meaning of these prefixes: de- (away); post- (after); inter- (between, among); out- (in a direction away). Using that information, guess at the meaning of the following words: deskilling, postindustrial, interaction, output, and outsource. Now go back to the reading selection, find these words, and read the context that surrounds them. How would you define these words now?

Study Reading Questions

1. What are five ways in which computers are changing the workplace?
2. Why are these changes referred to as "issues"?
3. What is the effect of these changes on employees and the way they work?

Critical Reading and Thinking Questions

1. React to the following generalization: "In other words, a machine decides whether to place an order, stock a dress in a certain size and color, or approve a loan application." Think about the advantages and disadvantages of changing the responsibility for decision making from humans to computers. What are the implications? How might they effect you?
2. Computers are often criticized for separating people and decreasing human interaction. What do you think of this criticism? Is it a problem or not? If yes, what could be done about it?
3. Have you personally had an experience of calling a business in your town or on the Internet and discovering that you are speaking with an individual from another country? Why is this becoming a common practice? Describe your experience: was it positive or negative? Why?

The Multitasking Generation[22]

CLAUDIA WALLIS

Explanatory Notes: *The author has coined a new name for the generation of students and others who "multitask": Gen M. Does this description fit you? Underline all of the vocabulary related to computers that is new to you as you read.*

1   It's 9:30 P.M., and Stephen and Georgina Cox know exactly where their children are. Well, their bodies, at least. Piers, 14, is holed up in his bedroom—eyes fixed on his computer screen—where he has been logged onto a MySpace chat room and AOL Instant Messenger (IM) for the past three hours. His twin sister Brontë is planted in the living room, having commandeered her dad's iMac—as usual. She, too, is busily IMing, while chatting on her cell phone and chipping away at homework.

2   By all standard space-time calculations, the four members of the family occupy the same three-bedroom home in Van Nuys, Calif., but psychologically each exists in his or her own little universe. Georgina, 51, who works for a display-cabinet maker, is tidying up the living room as Brontë works, not that her daughter notices. Stephen, 49, who juggles jobs as a squash coach, fitness trainer, event planner and head of a cancer charity he founded, has wolfed down his dinner alone in the kitchen, having missed supper with the kids. He, too, typically spends the evening on his cell phone and returning e-mails—when he can nudge Brontë off the computer. "One gets obsessed with one's gadgets," he concedes.

3   Zooming in on Piers' screen gives a pretty good indication of what's on his hyperkinetic mind. O.K., there's a Google Images window open, where he's chasing down pictures of Keira Knightley. Good ones get added to a snazzy Windows Media Player slide show that serves as his personal e-shrine to the actress. Several IM windows are also open, revealing such penetrating conversations as this one with a MySpace pal:

MySpacer: suuuuuup!!! (Translation: What's up?)
Piers: wat up dude
MySpacer: nmu (Not much. You?)
Piers: same

4   Naturally, iTunes is open, and Piers is blasting a mix of Queen, AC/DC, classic rock and hip-hop. Somewhere on the screen there's a Word file, in which Piers is writing an essay for English class. "I usually finish my homework at school," he explains to a visitor, "but if not, I pop a book open on my lap in my room, and while the computer is loading, I'll do a problem or write a sentence. Then, while mail is loading, I do more. I get it done a little bit at a time."

[22]*Time*, 27 March 2006, 48–55.

Brontë has the same strategy. "You just multitask," she explains. "My parents always tell me I can't do homework while listening to music, but they don't understand that it helps me concentrate." The twins also multitask when hanging with friends, which has its own etiquette. "When I talk to my best friend Eloy," says Piers, "he'll have one earpiece [of his iPod] in and one out." Says Brontë: "If a friend thinks she's not getting my full attention, I just make it very clear that she is, even though I'm also listening to music."

. . . .

Today 82% of kids are online by the seventh grade, according to the Pew Internet and American Life Project. And what they love about the computer, of course, is that it offers the radio/CD thing and so much more—games, movies, e-mail, IM, Google, MySpace. The big finding of a 2005 survey of Americans ages 8 to 18 by the Kaiser Family Foundation, co-authored by Roberts, is not that kids were spending a larger chunk of time using electronic media—that was holding steady at 6.5 hours a day (could it possibly get any bigger?)—but that they were packing more media exposure into that time: 8.5 hours' worth, thanks to "media multitasking"—listening to iTunes, watching a DVD *and* IMing friends all at the same time. Increasingly, the media-hungry members of Generation M, as Kaiser dubbed them, don't just sit down to watch a TV show with their friends or family. From a quarter to a third of them, according to the survey, say they simultaneously absorb some other medium "most of the time" while watching TV, listening to music, using the computer or even while reading.

. . . .

Is This Any Way to Learn?

Longtime professors at universities around the U.S. have noticed that Gen M kids arrive on campus with a different set of cognitive skills and habits than past generations. In lecture halls with wireless Internet access—now more than 40% of college classrooms, according to the Campus Computing Project—the compulsion to multitask can get out of hand. "People are going to lectures by some of the greatest minds, and they are doing their mail," says Sherry Turkle, professor of the social studies of science and technology at M.I.T. In her class, says Turkle, "I tell them this is not a place for e-mail, it's not a place to do online searches and not a place to set up IRC [Internet relay chat] channels in which to comment on the class. It's not going to help if there are parallel discussions about how boring it is. You've got to get people to participate in the world as it is."

Such concerns have, in fact, led a number of schools, including the M.B.A. programs at UCLA and the University of Virginia, to look into blocking Internet access during lectures. "I tell my students not to treat me like TV," says University of Wisconsin professor Aaron Brower, who has been teaching social work for 20 years. "They have to think of me like a real person talking. I want to have them thinking about things we're talking about."

On the positive side, Gen M students tend to be extraordinarily good at finding and manipulating information. And presumably because modern childhood tilts toward visual rather than print media, they are especially skilled at analyzing visual data and images, observes Claudia Koonz, professor of history at Duke University. A growing number of college professors are using film, audio clips and

PowerPoint presentations to play to their students' strengths and capture their evanescent attention. It's a powerful way to teach history, says Koonz. "I love bringing media into the classroom, to be able to go to the website for Edward R. Murrow and hear his voice as he walked with the liberators of Buchenwald." Another adjustment to teaching Generation M: professors are assigning fewer full-length books and more excerpts and articles. (Koonz, however, was stunned when a student matter-of-factly informed her, "We don't read whole books anymore," after Koonz had assigned a 350-page volume. "And this is Duke!" she says.)

Many students make brilliant use of media in their work, embedding audio files and video clips in their presentations, but the habit of grazing among many data streams leaves telltale signs in their writing, according to some educators. "The breadth of their knowledge and their ability to find answers has just burgeoned," says Roberts of his students at Stanford, "but my impression is that their ability to write clear, focused and extended narratives has eroded somewhat." Says Koonz: "What I find is paragraphs that make sense internally, but don't necessarily follow a line of argument." 10

Koonz and Turkle believe that today's students are less tolerant of ambiguity than the students they taught in the past. "They demand clarity," says Koonz. They want identifiable good guys and bad guys, which she finds problematic in teaching complex topics like Hutu-Tutsi history in Rwanda. She also thinks there are political implications: "Their belief in the simple answer, put together in a visual way, is, I think, dangerous." Koonz thinks this aversion to complexity is directly related to multitasking: "It's as if they have too many windows open on their hard drive. In order to have a taste for sifting through different layers of truth, you have to stay with a topic and pursue it deeply, rather than go across the surface with your toolbar." She tries to encourage her students to find a quiet spot on campus to just think, cell phone off, laptop packed away. 11

Got 2 Go. Txt Me L8er

But turning down the noise isn't easy. By the time many kids get to college, their devices have become extensions of themselves, indispensable social accessories. "The minute the bell rings at most big public high schools, the first thing most kids do is reach into their bag and pick up their cell phone," observes Denise Clark Pope, lecturer at the Stanford School of Education, "never mind that the person [they're contacting] could be right down the hall." 12

Parents are mystified by this obsession with e-communication—particularly among younger adolescents who often can't wait to share the most mundane details of life. Dominique Jones, 12, of Los Angeles, likes to IM her friends before school to find out what they plan to wear. "You'll get IMs back that say things like 'Oh, my God, I'm wearing the same shoes!' After school we talk about what happened that day, what outfits we want to wear the next day." 13

Turkle, author of the recently reissued *The Second Self: Computers and the Human Spirit*, has an explanation for this breathless exchange of inanities. "There's an extraordinary fit between the medium and the moment, a heady, giddy fit in terms of social needs." The online environment, she points out, "is less risky if you are lonely and afraid of intimacy, which is almost a definition of adolescence. Things get too hot, you log off, while in real time and space, you have consequences." Teen 14 venues like MySpace, Xanga and Facebook—and the ways kids can personalize their IM personas—meet another teen need: the desire to experiment with identity. By changing their picture, their "away" message, their icon or list of favorite bands, kids can cycle through different personalities. "Online life is like an identity workshop," says Turkle, "and that's the job of adolescents—to experiment with identity."

All that is probably healthy, provided that parents set limits on where their kids can venture online, teach them to exercise caution and regulate how much time they can spend with electronics in general. The problem is that most parents don't. According to the Kaiser survey, only 23% of seventh- to 12th-graders say their family has rules about computer activity; just 17% say they have restrictions on video-game time.

In the absence of rules, it's all too easy for kids to wander into unwholesome neighborhoods on the Net and get caught up in the compulsive behavior that psychiatrist Edward Hallowell dubs "screen-sucking" in his new book, *CrazyBusy.* Patricia Wallace, a techno-psychologist who directs the Johns Hopkins Center for Talented Youth program, believes part of the allure of e-mail—for adults as well as teens—is similar to that of a slot machine. "You have intermittent, variable reinforcement," she explains. "You are not sure you are going to get a reward every time or how often you will, so you keep pulling that handle. Why else do people get up in the middle of the night to check their e-mail?"

Getting Them to Log Off

Many educators and psychologists say parents need to actively ensure that their teenagers break free of compulsive engagement with screens and spend time in the physical company of human beings—a growing challenge not just because technology offers such a handy alternative but because so many kids lead highly scheduled lives that leave little time for old-fashioned socializing and family meals. Indeed, many teenagers and college students say overcommitted schedules drive much of their multitasking.

Just as important is for parents and educators to teach kids, preferably by example, that it's valuable, even essential, to occasionally slow down, unplug and take time to think about something for a while. David Levy, a professor at the University of Washington Information School, has found, to his surprise, that his most technophilic undergraduates—those majoring in "informatics"—are genuinely concerned about getting lost in the multitasking blur. In an informal poll of 60 students last semester, he says, the majority expressed concerns about how plugged-in they were and "the way it takes them away from other activities, including exercise, meals and sleep." Levy's students talked about difficulties concentrating and their efforts to break away, get into the outdoors and inside their head. "Although it wasn't a scientific survey," he says, "it was the first evidence I had that people in this age group are reflecting on these questions."

For all the handwringing about Generation M, technology is not really the problem. "The problem," says Hallowell, "is what you are *not* doing if the electronic moment grows too large"—too large for the teenager and too large for those parents who are equally tethered to their gadgets. In that case, says Hallowell, "you are not having family dinner, you are not having conversations, you are not debating whether to go out with a boy who wants to have sex on the first date, you are not going on a family ski trip or taking time just to veg. It's not so much that the video game is going to rot your brain, it's what you are not doing that's going to rot your life."

Generation M has a lot to teach parents and teachers about what new technol-   20
ogy can do. But it's up to grownups to show them what it can't do, and that there's life beyond the screen.—*With reporting by Wendy Cole/Chicago, Sonja Steptoe/Los Angeles and Sarah Sturmon Dale/Minneapolis*

2215 words

Strategy Questions

1. Add one more word or concept from this article to your "Computers" vocabulary sheet.
2. Review the word parts below and then guess at the meaning of the words that follow them that contain these parts:
   Prefixes: multi- (many); techno- (technical or technological); over- (exceeding, excessive); hyper- (excessively); inter- (between); e- (electronic).
   Roots: kine (movement, motion); phil (love); psycho (mind).
   Suffixes: -ic (having the characteristics of); -ity (state of); -ist (one who does); -less (without).
   Words drawn from the article: multiprocessing, multitasking, techno-psychologist, overcommitted; hyperkinetic, technophilic; informatics; interpersonal connectivity; media multitasking; wireless Internet access; problematic; e-communication; e-mail. Now find these words in the article and read about them in context. How would you define these words now?
3. Write a sentence in which you use the word "multitasking."

Study Reading Questions

1. What percent of children are online by the seventh grade?
2. About how much time do they spend online each day according to a recent survey of Americans from the age of 8–18?
3. Give an example of media multitasking. What might be involved?
4. According to college professors, how are college students who are in the habit of multitasking different from students who did not have a comparable access to technology?
5. What does the author say is the biggest problem for members of Generation M who spend hours every day multitasking?

Critical Reading and Thinking Questions

1. What types of electronic media do you use? Are you satisfied with the way you use them? Why, or why not? If you could make changes, what would they be?
2. Do any of your professors use media to teach in the classroom? Which media, and how do they use them? How do they help or hinder your learning?

3. Is there any media that should not be used in the classroom, or that should be used in specifically controlled ways? Which? What restrictions would you place on them?
4. React to the statement: "it's valuable, even essential, to occasionally slow down, unplug and take time to think about something for awhile." Do you agree or disagree, or would you modify this statement to read another way? Why?

THREE APPLICATION EXERCISES

Exercise 1

Locate specialized vocabulary in your other classes.

Bring at least one specialized vocabulary word from one of your other classes to your reading class. Be prepared to write the word on the chalkboard and to define it.

Exercise 2

Identify a major concept in another class.

What is one major concept that has been explained at length either in a textbook or in a lecture in one of your other classes? Report on it in your reading class by identifying the word and summarizing its meaning.

Exercise 3

Vocabulary in your textbooks.

Examine the way in which vocabulary is or is not emphasized and explained in your other textbooks. Do the authors of your textbooks tend to identify and define the words in context? In the margins? In special lists? Or do they usually merely provide hints to the meanings of key words?

REVIEW AND EVALUATE THE STRATEGIES

The following is a review of the five strategies you learned in this chapter:

1. Circle words and write their meanings in the margins.
2. Make vocabulary sheets (two-column and four-column).
3. Make vocabulary cards.
4. Organize related words on lists or maps.
5. Memorize the words and use them.

Make a personal evaluation of these strategies:

1. Underline your favorite strategies in the preceding list.
2. Make a check mark by those you want to continue to use.
3. Cross out any you probably will not continue to use. What are your reasons for rejecting them?

PART II

Study Reading:
Reading to Learn

Recognize the Organization of Ideas

CHAPTER 4

CHAPTER GOALS:

1. **To show that recognizing organization helps you predict.**

2. **To identify some common organizational formats and patterns.**

3. **To show how maps and outlines can make organization visual and help you learn.**

4. **To provide you with five strategies for recognizing and using organization to help you learn.**

What to Expect in the Next Chapters

The first three chapters of this book have provided you with an understanding of the reading process, a variety of ways to improve your reading efficiency, and a number of methods for increasing your vocabulary. All of the strategies presented in these first chapters provide a foundation for further improvement of study reading, critical reading, and critical thinking. The next four chapters focus on ways to improve study reading. You will learn to read closely, to study and learn the material, and to answer test questions that show you have learned.

This chapter teaches you to recognize and follow the format and organization of whole books and chapters. Chapters 5 and 6 focus on reading smaller parts of the whole: sections, paragraphs, and sentences, as well as visual material such as graphs and charts. Chapter 7 will help you organize a study reading system that will pave the way for preparing for exams and then taking them successfully.

Chapters 8 through 11 provide you with explanations and strategies to help you read critically, think critically, and answer test questions that require critical thinking. When you have finished working through the next eight chapters, you will be able to integrate study reading, critical reading, and critical thinking. That is the final goal of this book. You will also be equipped to take college exams that require all three abilities, as many exams do.

Recognizing Organization Helps You Predict

When you enter a music store and you are looking for a certain kind of CD, you can usually predict the area in which you will find it. The CDs are organized in categories, such as classical, country, rock, or easy listening. When you enter a grocery store you can predict that the different types of food will be organized in categories and kept in different locations. Likewise, when you enter a library, you can again expect to find different types of reading materials in different locations. Organizational plans are in place that enable you to predict where you will find what you are looking for in all of these places.

The same is true of reading material. It is organized. In fact, authors have a long tradition to draw on when they organize and write their ideas. For centuries, authors have organized material according to familiar **formats** and **patterns of organization.** Familiarizing yourself with these formats and patterns can help you recognize and use them to predict what is coming next. This makes following along and understanding the ideas much easier for the reader.

Organized material is also much easier to learn and commit to memory. There is a reason for this. Your memory is organized. It automatically sorts, selects, and files related items together. When you take the trouble to understand an author's organization and then to organize information from several sources into meaningful patterns of your own, your memory accepts and stores this information much more quickly and easily than it does disorganized material. Organized material in all aspects of life is easier to understand, locate, use, and remember.

Some Common Formats

Formatting is one way to organize material. You can think of formats as containers with separate parts waiting to be filled. Some examples are the personal letter, the job résumé, and the office memorandum. You can recognize at a glance the formats for these types of writing. You are also familiar with their usual parts. The personal letter format, for example, customarily includes the salutation, message, and closing signature. The format helps you predict these parts, which in turn helps you to comprehend. Here are some additional examples and descriptions of common formats that you will encounter in your college reading.

1. **The introduction, body, and conclusion format.** Articles in magazines and journals and the chapters in many types of nonfiction books are written according to the introduction, body, and conclusion (or summary) format. Knowing ahead of time what you can expect to find in each of these parts will help you read material that has been formatted in this way.
    a. The *introduction* includes any or all of the following:
        (1) A sentence explaining what the article or chapter is about.
        (2) A list of major ideas to be developed.
        (3) Background information to help the reader understand the subject.
        (4) An attention-grabbing story or anecdote.
        (5) Clue words or phrases that identify the material as introductory. Examples: *To begin with . . . ; my purpose is . . . ; this book (or chapter) will focus on . . . ;* or, *the three ideas that will be developed in this chapter are. . . .*
    b. The *body* includes:
        (1) A development of the major ideas, in logical order, with details, elaborations, explanations, and examples.

      (2) Clue words used to emphasize and separate the major ideas often include numbering (*first, second, third*) or such other words as *then* or *next*.
  c. The *conclusion* (or *summary*) may contain:
      (1) An important, final idea that the author wants to feature by putting it at the end.
      (2) A restatement or summary of all of the main points made in the body.
      (3) Clue words like *to conclude, in conclusion, finally* or, in the case of a summary, clue words like *to sum up, in summary,* or *to restate.*

2. The story format. Short stories usually conform to a conventional story format, or at least to a variation of it. Stories often begin with a setting that describes a time and place and, perhaps, the characters. This is followed by a series of episodes or events that cause the characters to interact. Often, the events introduce problems that need to be worked out and solved by the story's end. The conclusion usually resolves the problems. **Novels** also often follow this format on a longer scale.

3. The newspaper article format. The first paragraph of a typical news article often provides the most essential information and answers the questions: *who, what, where, when,* and *why.* The remainder of the article provides additional details that become less and less significant toward the end. The purpose of this format is to allow readers who are in a hurry to get the main parts of the news by reading the first paragraph of each story.

4. The feature article format. Articles in magazines and newspapers are often written according to the feature article format. These articles typically begin with one or more paragraphs that get your attention. These opening paragraphs may include stories about individuals, descriptions of vivid events, or any other information that is of high interest to "hook" you as a reader so that you will continue reading. The next section of the article provides the essential information that explains why the author is writing the article, including the central point of the article. The paragraphs that follow include additional ideas, details, and examples that provide more information about the central point. The final paragraph or paragraphs focus on a vivid idea or image that the reader can carry away. Sometimes the ending has an emotional impact as well to make it stronger and more memorable.

5. The textbook format. Textbooks are often divided into several parts, with each part further divided into several chapters that explain and develop these parts. The format of **textbook chapters** varies somewhat from one book to another. Usually, you can expect some information at the beginning of a textbook chapter to help you get started reading, like chapter goals or a list of the main ideas. Then, at the end, you can expect additional material to help you learn the chapter, such as summaries, questions, bibliographies, or lists of key words. You can usually expect the chapter itself to be divided into sections that are set off with headings and subheadings that appear in boldface type. These headings emphasize the main ideas and make them easier to recognize. Discover how each of your textbooks as a whole has been formatted. Then analyze the format of a typical chapter to help you predict what is coming next as you read subsequent chapters.

6. **The scientific or technical article format.** You will read and may even be asked to write articles about scientific experiments. The usual format includes:
   a. An abstract of the article that describes in brief what it is about.
   b. Previous research that leads to the experiment about to be described.
   c. An introduction that states the hypothesis or idea that is being tested.
   d. An explanation of the experimental design or procedure that has been followed.
   e. An analysis of the data, presented in tables and explained in the text.
   f. A summary of the results and final conclusions including, sometimes, recommendations for future research.

Notice that these formats have little, if any, influence on the ideas that they contain. They are empty forms until they are filled with ideas. Authors think about formats when they think about the type of material they are writing: a textbook, an article, a memorandum, or a story. Formats help them set up the parts. Authors turn to **organizational patterns,** however, when they begin to work with the ideas that will fill the parts.

Eight Common Organizational Patterns

1. **The whole into parts pattern.** Many broad subjects can be divided into subtopics or subcategories. Then each subtopic can be discussed and explained individually. Examples of this pattern include: dividing the types of rocks in a geology textbook into the subcategories of igneous, sedimentary, and metamorphic; dividing the government in a political science textbook into its three branches of legislative, executive, and judicial; or dividing psychological disorders in a psychology text into subtypes like schizophrenia or bipolar disorder.

Clues for the reader that a whole has been divided into parts include the following possibilities: (1) a brief list of the parts in the introduction; (2) headings and subheadings that identify parts; or (3) a restatement of the parts in a summary. Numbering, accompanied by a key phrase, may be used to make the parts easier to recognize, as in, *"The first branch of the government is the executive."* To read material that is organized according to the whole divided into parts, first identify the broad subject, then identify the parts, and finally read to understand the details that explain each part.

Look at an example.

An example of the whole into parts pattern of organization appears in the description of the World Wide Web on pages 99–102. Notice how the various components, or parts of this network, are described individually to show how they help make the Web function. Locate four parts of the World Wide Web and write them below.

Components of the World Wide Web

(1) _____   (3) _____

(2) _____   (4) _____

2. **The listing pattern.** Some material lends itself to organization that requires a title and a list. The title of the list is identified first, and a list of related items follows. The items in the list may all be of equal importance, and the sequence or order in which they appear may be arbitrary. You are reading a list right now of eight types of organizational patterns. These items are not parts of a whole; they are simply a list of examples, and they are all equally important. The order in which they are listed is not significant. Other examples of the listing pattern of organization might include: in a psychology textbook, a list of the criteria for choosing a psychotherapist; or, in a geology textbook, a list of the main sources of pollution.

Reader clues to lists are usually obvious. The items are numbered and listed. If they are written out in paragraphs, words such as *then*, *next*, or *finally* may separate the items so that the reader can more easily identify the items on the list. Numbering with a key phrase might also be used to emphasize the items on the list: "*The first source of pollution is . . .*" Whole to part and listing patterns of organization are used extensively in college textbooks. When you encounter the listing pattern, first identify the title of the list and then find the separate items on the list so that you can read about each of them in turn.

Look at an example.

An example of the listing pattern of organization appears on pages 103–104. The five workplace issues that have evolved with the increasing use of computers are listed and identified with numbers and boldface type to make them stand out. Locate these five issues and write them on the following list.

How Computers Are Changing Work

(1) _____   (4) _____

(2) _____   (5) _____

(3) _____

---

3. **The chronological pattern.** Some material can best be discussed as it occurs during a period of time. The time covered may be brief, a few hours or a day, or it can be extensive, several centuries or "ages" of the earth. There may be breaks in time, with large chunks of time skipped over. Also, flashbacks in time may interrupt a straight-forward chronological presentation. History books are usually organized chronologically; so is much narrative fiction.

Reader clues that chronological order is being followed are words or phrases that signal changes in time, like *first, next, soon, after, after that, the next day, an hour later, meanwhile, previously, earlier, at the same time, before that, at last, later, much later, then,* or *finally.* When you encounter material that has been arranged chronologically, notice how much time is covered, where the breaks in time occur, and whether flashbacks in time are included.

An example of the chronological pattern of organization appears on pages 61–65. "Exodus" describes the journey illegal immigrants from Mexico take to get into the United States. The author travels with a group of them. Look particularly at paragraphs 1 and 7–12. Describe where and when this journey starts _____

_____. Where does the description of the journey leave off?

_____ Roughly how much time is involved in the part

of the journey described here? _____

4. The process pattern. The emphasis here is on how to do something. The process pattern describes the steps needed to complete a project. Recipes are organized this way. Furthermore, the steps and the order of the steps are often (but not always) important if the final result is to be successful. You will find the process pattern used in lab manuals that describe how to set up and execute lab experiments, or you may find a process for writing a college paper described in your English textbook. Chapter 1 of this text encouraged you to describe your own reading process (see pages 10–11) and then to add additional strategies to your process to make it more powerful.

Look at two examples.

Two examples of the process pattern of organization are on pages 81 and 21–25.

1. The illustration that describes mitosis, or the process of cell division (see p. 81) is organized according to the process pattern. Write the stages of the process in the correct order:

Mitosis

(1) _____   (3) _____   (5) _____

(2) _____   (4) _____   (6) _____

2. Malcolm X describes the process he followed for improving his vocabulary (pp. 21–25). Identify the steps and the sequence in which he followed them.

Malcolm X's Process for Vocabulary Improvement

(1) _____

(2) _____

(3) _____

The same reader clues that are used to identify the chronological pattern are used to identify the process pattern. Numbers are often used to identify the steps and their order. When you are reading material that has been organized according to the process pattern, first understand what process is being described, then identify the steps, and finally take note of their order. Decide whether or not the order of the steps is important or not.

5. **The spatial pattern.** Sometimes authors describe material as it is located and arranged within a space or area. Examples of the spatial pattern might include a description in an art textbook of the arrangement of an art exhibit, or descriptions in a psychology textbook of the geography of the brain or the components of the eye.

Reader clues to spatial organization include place words or phrases like *over there, inside, outside, to the right, to the left, in the corner, behind,* or *in front of.* In biology, technical place words such as *anterior* (at the front), *dorsal* (on the back), or *ventral* (on the lower surface) may be used. The spatial pattern invites the reader to mentally visualize what is being described. Use the clue words to help you create a mental picture of each of the parts and where they are located in the total picture. This will help you understand and remember spatially organized material.

Look at an example.

An example of the spatial pattern of organization appears on pages 61–63. Read paragraphs 2 through 6 which describe the town of Altar where illegal Mexican immigrants congregate to prepare to cross into the United States. Notice the descriptions of the various enterprises and activities in this town and where they are located in relation to one another. Imagine a motion picture version of this town. Describe what you visualize.

_____

_____

_____

6. **The cause–effect pattern.** Sometimes an author develops a topic by explaining its causes and its effects. For example, a sociology textbook might include an explanation of the causes and effects of poverty, or a history textbook might present the causes and effects of the civil rights movement.

Reader clues that this pattern is being used include the words and phrases *cause, effect, so, then, consequently, because of this, therefore, for this reason, as a result, in consequence,* or *it follows.* The title of material arranged in this pattern might also provide a clue, as in "The Causes of the Civil War." Sometimes a statement such as "The effects of all this are . . ." signals the division between the cause and effect segments of the text. When you are reading material that describes causes and effects, identify the causes and identify the effects. Note also the order in which they appear. Sometimes, the effects are described first and at other times the causes are described first.

7. **The comparison–contrast pattern.** An author may develop a topic by showing what it is *like*, which is *comparison*, or what it is *unlike*, which is *contrast*. Some comparisons, however, include both a discussion of similarities and differences, and the term contrast is never used. Examples might include the comparison of computers and the human mind in a computer science textbook, or the contrast of modern and postmodern philosophy in a philosophy textbook.

A reader clue may be provided by a title, such as "A Comparison of the Plays of Shakespeare and Jonson" in a literature textbook. Or two key words, like Republican and Democrat, may be set up to identify the two subjects being compared and contrasted. These words will then be repeated to introduce each new point of comparison. Also, such words and phrases as *in comparison, in contrast, on the contrary, on the other hand, instead, likewise, similarly, like, unlike, however, similar to, dissimilar to, some, others, one another, the difference,* or *the same* are also clues. When reading material that compares and contrasts, notice what is being compared and identify the specific points of comparison or contrast.

8. **The problem–solution pattern.** Authors write about many topics that represent problems. In developing such topics, authors often propose solutions to the problems. Examples of topics that might be organized according to the problem–

solution pattern include: a discussion in a film history textbook of the problems faced by filmmakers of Eastern Europe after the collapse of communism in 1991, along with their efforts to solve them, or a discussion in a political science textbook of the problems the media can create during political campaigns, along with some ideas for solutions.

Topics that are traditionally presented as problems can be one clue that the problem–solution pattern will probably be followed. Thus when you encounter topics like the legalization of marijuana, what to do about poverty, or how to punish young criminals, you can often accurately predict a problem–solution pattern of organization. Other reader clues might include words like *problem, solution, solve, question,* or *answer.* Or sentences may signal a problem–solution pattern, as in "*A solution to the problem . . .*" or "*Some ways of dealing with this might include . . .*" Read material that has been organized with the problem–solution pattern by first finding and understanding the problem and then by finding and understanding the solution or solutions. Notice, also, which is described first—the problem or the solutions.

Look at an example.

An example of the problem–solution pattern of organization appears in "Join the Incredible Reading Rally" on pages 29–32. What problem is described in this essay? _____

What solutions are described? (1) _____ (2) _____

(3) _____

Mixed Patterns of Organization

As you read and analyze an author's use of patterns of organization, do not expect to find one single pattern throughout a chapter or essay. Instead, you can usually expect to find one dominant pattern, such as the chronological pattern for a history book, along with other subpatterns used within the overall pattern. A historian, writing mainly chronologically about the Civil War, might also at times describe the causes and effects of the war or the spatial relationships of the armies, discuss the problems President Lincoln faced and how he solved them, make a comparison of northern and southern attitudes toward slavery, or list the social classes in the pre–Civil War South. In effect, all the common patterns would be represented at various points in the book, even though the predominant pattern would be chronological. Notice that in the essay "Join the Incredible Reading Rally" (pages 29–32) the author explains what caused Tara Holland to become interested in people who could not read before he describes how she attempted to solve this problem. The cause–effect and problem–solution patterns are often combined because an explanation of a problem's cause often helps determine solutions. Examples of mixed patterns of organization appear in the readings at the end of this chapter.

Make the Organization Visible on Maps or Outlines

Organized facts and ideas are easier to learn if you can see them written out on maps or outlines. The parts are then more easily evident, as are the ways they are related to each other. Writing material on maps and outlines also helps you learn. Figures 4-1 through 4-8 provide examples of maps that show the organization of ideas. An example of an outline is also provided at the end of the section. Which would you find easier to study and learn from, a map or an outline? A third alternative is Cornell reading notes (see example on pages 49–50.)

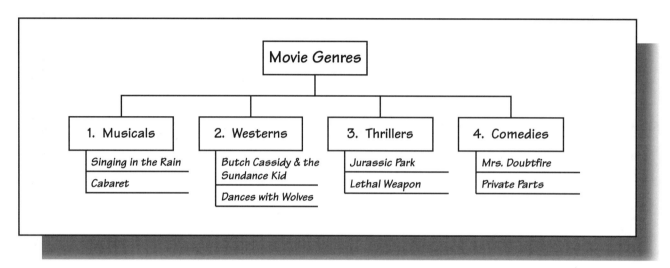

FIGURE 4-1 *Whole into Parts Map*[1]

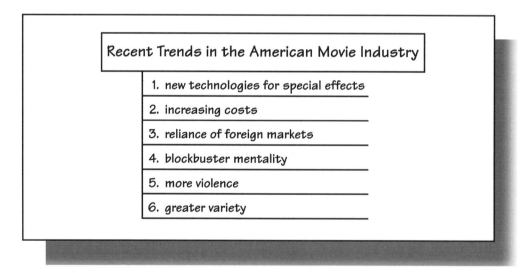

FIGURE 4-2 *Listing Map*

[1] Information for the maps and outlines in this section is drawn from Louis Giannetti and Scott Eyman, *Flashback: A Brief History of Film.* 3rd ed. (Englewood Cliffs: Prentice Hall, 1996) 14, 47–81, 140–143, 256, 259, 264–287, 463–487, 521–545.

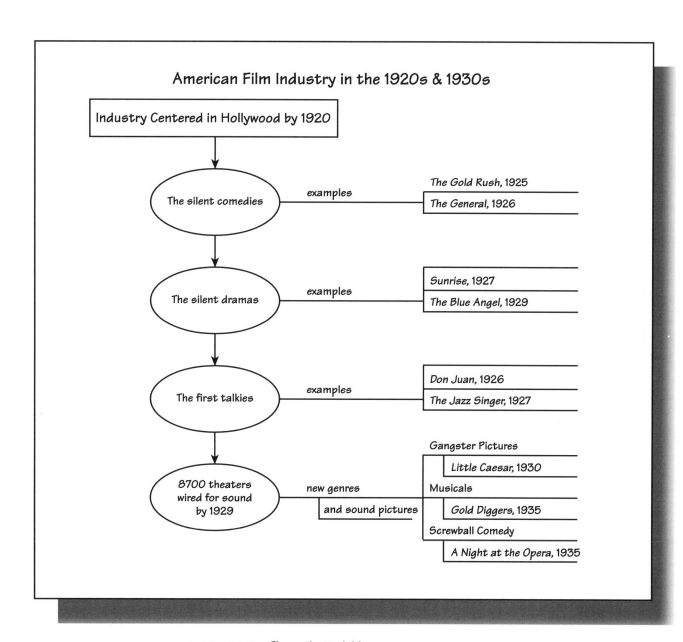

FIGURE 4-3 *Chronological Map*

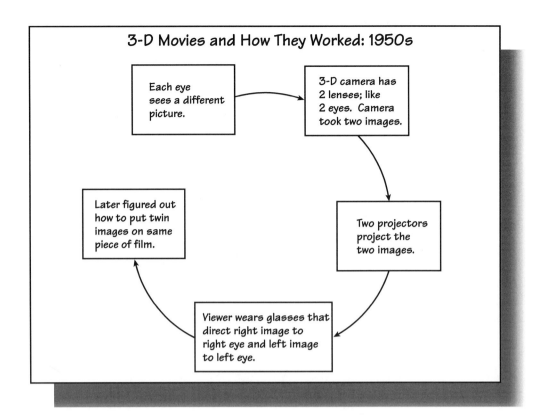

FIGURE 4-4 *Process Map*

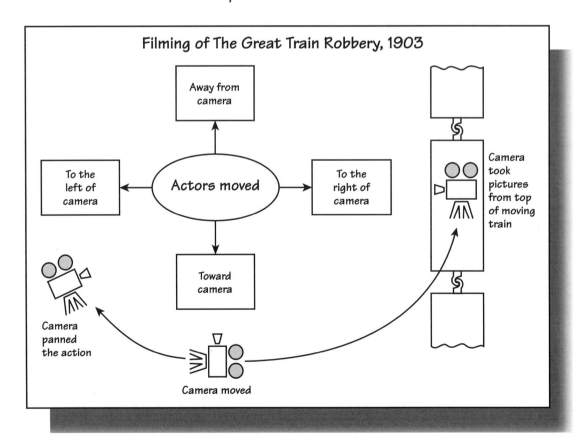

FIGURE 4-5 *Spatial Map*

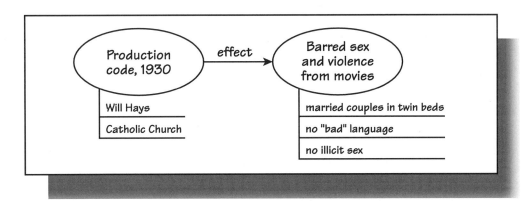

FIGURE 4-6 *Cause–Effect Map*

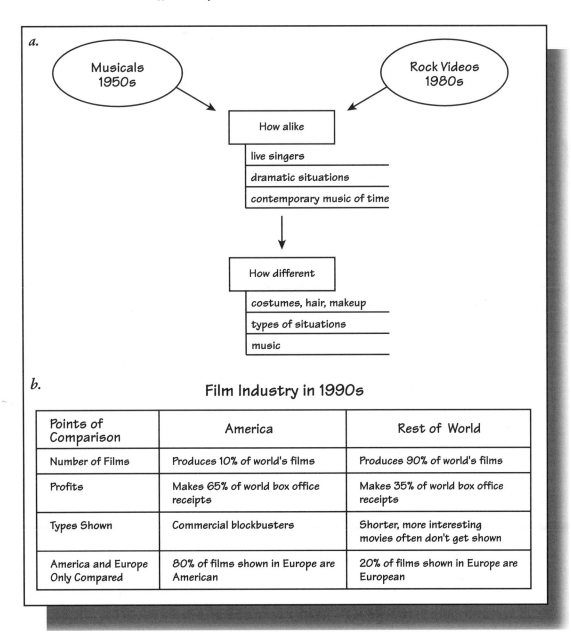

FIGURE 4-7 *Two Types of Comparison–Contrast Maps*

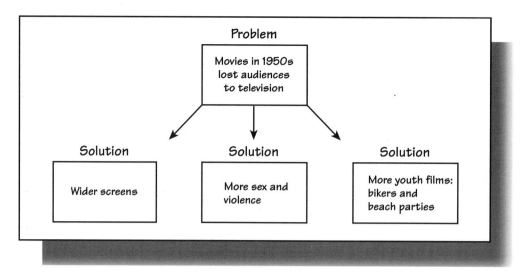

FIGURE 4-8 *Problem–Solution Map*

An alternative to mapping is the outline. An outline is like a map because it also is a visual representation of ideas and how they relate to one another. Some of your instructors—your writing instructors, for example—may require you to make formal outlines. Study outlines do not have to be so elaborate. The only requirement for a study outline is that the main ideas, or the ideas that you want to stand out the most, should be placed by the left-hand margin. Then all of the information about those ideas should be indented under them. You also need to write a title at the top of every outline. Here is an example of a simple study outline. Note that it goes into more detail than the survey outline and Cornell notes on pages 49–50. This outline shows the types of detail a reader would add to a survey outline after completing the survey and then reading for details.

Directors and Movies of the 1980s and Early 1990s

1. David Lynch—first film, *Eraserhead* in 1978. Eerie, surrealistic.
   a. *The Elephant Man*, 1980, story of nineteenth-century victim of horribly disfiguring disease.
   b. *Blue Velvet*, 1986, his masterpiece, about perversity, death, and the subconscious; movie is irrational, seductive, and terrifying.
   c. *Wild at Heart*, 1990. More mannered and not so good as the others.
2. Oliver Stone—won Academy Award for script for *Midnight Express* in early 1970s.
   a. *Platoon*, 1986, first film that achieved popular success. Vietnam war movie. Good and evil in two competing sergeants.
   b. *Born on the Fourth of July*, 1989, second in Vietnam war trilogy.
   c. The third, *Heaven and Earth* in 1993, least successful of the three.
3. Spike Lee—black artist, makes movies about blacks in Brooklyn.
   a. *She's Gotta Have It*, 1986, comedy about woman who doesn't want to commit to one man.
   b. *Do the Right Thing*, 1987, a day and a night in a black ghetto neighborhood, explodes into race riot. Black and white bigotry.

4. Tim Burton—studied animation and worked for Disney to get started. Comic book effect in his movies.
   a. *Pee-Wee's Big Adventure*, 1985, his feature directing debut, children's movie with Pee-Wee Herman.
   b. *Beetlejuice*, 1988, ghost story with special effects. Comic book characteristics.
   c. *Batman*, 1989, based on comic book, a big hit. Michael Keaton.
   d. *Edward Scissorhands*, 1990, fairy tale about a youth who has cutting shears instead of hands.

As you can see from these examples of maps and outlines, an outline format allows for more detail than a map. A map is good for showing the basic framework of ideas; an outline is good for condensing not only the major ideas but also a number of the details. Add marginal notes and a summary to your outline to help you learn it, and you will have a set of Cornell reading notes (see pages 49–50).

RECOGNIZE FORMAT AND ORGANIZATION: FIVE STRATEGIES

The next five strategies will explain exactly how to discover the format and organization of the material you read, how to make it visible on maps and outlines, and, finally, how to learn this material.

Strategy 1: Examine the table of contents and a sample chapter to discover formats.

When you survey, determine the type of material you are about to read and identify how it has been formatted. If you are looking at a book or an article, see if a familiar format has been followed, such as introduction/body/conclusion, and then look for the information that you can expect to find in each part. As part of your survey of a book, study the table of contents to see if it suggests how the book has been formatted, and then try to identify what that format is: Look for its parts and try to figure out what each part is likely to contribute to the whole. Also, examine a sample chapter in a book and analyze its format. Then look to see if all of the other chapters in the book are formatted in exactly the same way. Use your understanding of the formats and what they contain to help you predict and locate information.

Strategy 2: Recognize organizational patterns.

Get an idea of the organizational pattern of an entire book by reading the chapter titles in the table of contents. You will easily recognize a chronological pattern, for example. If the organization is not obvious, think about why chapters are presented in a particular order and make some predictions about the relationships among the chapters. When you read, use clue words and phrases, headings, and titles to help you recognize organizational patterns. Understand the relationships among the ideas, and use what you know about the pattern to help you predict and locate the ideas you can reasonably expect to find, such as the solution section of a problem–solution pattern. Also, use the patterns to organize the ideas in your mind so that they will be easier to remember.

▶

Strategy 3: Write organizational maps to help you visualize the ideas.

Write organizational maps that help you see how ideas have been organized and how they are related to each other. Create distinctive maps so that you can easily see what pattern of organization has been followed. You may map according to the examples in this chapter, or you may prefer to map with flowcharts or other configurations. Write quickly. The only requirement is that you be able to read your maps. Write a title for the map either at the top or in a box or circle in the middle of the map. Add important ideas to the title by writing them on attached lines. Add details and examples on other lines. Use clue words and phrases or arrows to show relationships. Be imaginative when you make maps.

Strategy 4: Write informal outlines to help you visualize the organization.

Not everyone likes to make maps. You may prefer to organize ideas in informal outline form instead, or you may want to switch from maps to outlines when you want to include more details than you could put on a map. Write the title of the outline at the top of the page so you will know what the outline is about. Write the main points by the left margin, and indent information about those ideas under them. You can number the ideas, or you may use bullets. You may also use bullets to separate the indented items. Don't make informal study outlines complicated, and don't spend much time writing them. The goal is to reduce material to a brief form so that you can see it and learn it more easily. Convert the outline to the Cornell note format by adding marginal notes and a summary.

Strategy 5: Learn the material on maps and outlines by reviewing, writing, and reciting.

You will need to review the material you have already read to determine the ideas to write on a map or outline. When you have finished writing a map or an outline, immediately look away and see if you can recite, or say to yourself, what you have written. *Do this without looking.* If you cannot remember what you have just read, read the map or the outline again, then look away and try again. Continue reading, looking away, and reciting until you can reproduce the material from memory. This activity transfers information to your long-term memory, where it will stay, especially if it is followed by additional review. Every week or two, read through your outlines and maps and refresh your recall of them. This will fix the information even more securely in your memory. Recitation and review as you write study materials takes only a little time and saves you much study time in the future. For example, these simple techniques can make studying much faster and easier when the time comes to prepare for a major exam. They can also help you in class discussion because you will know the material so thoroughly. Research shows that immediate recitation and periodic review can help you remember 70 to 80 percent, and sometimes even more, of the material that you learn. When exam time comes along, you may only have to learn 20 to 30 percent of the material. If you do not use these or any other measures to help transfer information to your permanent long-term memory, you will forget half of what you have learned within 24 hours

▶

and most of the rest of it within a week. Everyone forgets at this rate. The big difference between "just reading" and *study reading* is the amount of time you spend reviewing, writing to learn, reciting, and periodically reviewing.

———————————

Do reviewing, writing, and reciting work?

You have just **reviewed** several of the readings in this book in order to **write** answers to the questions in the "Look at an example" exercises in this chapter. Now look back at your answers, reread them, look away, and **recite** them to yourself. Repeat this until you can recite what you have written for all eight exercises from memory.

Now, without looking back, take the following quiz on this material. It calls for 20 answers. See how many of them you can answer correctly.

1. What are four component parts that make the World Wide Web function?

   (1) _____ (2) _____ (3) _____ (4) _____

2. The World Wide Web makes it possible for people all over the world to

   communicate on what worldwide network? (5) _____

3. What are the five workplace issues that have evolved with the increased use of

   computers in many businesses? (6) _____ (7) _____

   (8) _____ (9) _____ (10) _____

4. "Exodus" describes a journey that begins where? (11) _____
   Where does the journey described in this article leave off, even though it is not

   the final destination? (12) _____

5. What were two key features in Malcolm X's process for vocabulary

   improvement? (13) _____ (14) _____

6. Visualize the town of Altar as immigrants gather to prepare their journey. What

   two details come to your mind? (15) _____ (16) _____

7. What does the author of "We've Overlooked One of Our Greatest Assets" say

   was a major cause of his success in life? (17) _____

8. Name one way in which technology has changed GenM students as compared
   with earlier students who did not have the same access to technology.

   (18) _____

9. Name the problem and one solution in the article "Join the Incredible Reading
   Rally." (19) _____ (20) _____

Check your answers against the answers you wrote earlier in the chapter exercises. Subtract 5 points for each incorrect answer. What is your score? _____ Did you pass the test with a score of 70% or better? _____ What can you conclude about the effectiveness of reviewing, writing, and reciting? _____

EXERCISES AND READINGS

THREE COLLABORATIVE CLASS EXERCISES

Exercise 1

Recognize organizational patterns and clue words. *Pairs of students.*

This first exercise serves as a review of the organizational patterns you have learned to identify in this chapter. Work with a partner to match the titles with the patterns and write the answers in the blanks.

    a. What patterns of organization would you predict from reading the following titles? Match each title in the first column with an organizational pattern in the second column that could appropriately be used to develop it.

TITLES	ORGANIZATIONAL PATTERNS
1. _____ "Three Types of Movies: Horror, Western, and Romantic"	a. spatial
2. _____ "A History of Motion Pictures"	b. listing
3. _____ "Violent Movies and Children's Behavior"	c. problem–solution
4. _____ "The Layout of a Movie Set"	d. process
5. _____ "The Original Musicals and Modern Rock Videos"	e. chronological
6. _____ "Censoring Sex and Violence in the Movies"	f. whole into parts
7. _____ "How to Edit a Movie"	g. cause–effect
8. _____ "Some Criteria for Evaluating the Movies"	h. comparison–contrast

    b. Match the clue words and phrases with the pattern that you would expect to be associated with it.

CLUE WORDS AND PHRASES	ORGANIZATIONAL PATTERNS
1 _____ Rock videos are *different from* the musical comedies of the 1940s and 1950s.	a. spatial
2. _____ *In the center* is the stage. The director sits *directly in front.*	b. listing
3. _____ In this chapter, *three* major *types* of movies will be discussed.	c. problem–solution

CLUE WORDS AND PHRASES	ORGANIZATIONAL PATTERNS
4. _____ The *earliest* movies were silent. Sound wasn't used until *later.*	d. process
5. _____ There are no easy *solutions* to the *problem* of movie censorship.	e. chronological
6. _____ The *effect* of movies on children's behavior is difficult to prove.	f. whole into parts
7. _____ The *first criterion* to use for evaluating a movie is originality.	g. cause–effect
8. _____ The *next step* is to cut and splice the film	h. comparison–contrast

Exercise 2

Invent and map ideas to gain insight into organizational patterns. *Small groups of students.*

The purpose of this exercise is to help you get further insight into organizational patterns. First, working as a class, match the organizational patterns in the second column with the titles in the first column. Now form eight groups; each group will take one of the eight titles from the list that follows. The next step is to invent some ideas that might be used to develop each of the eight titles. Elect a scribe to write your group's title on a separate sheet of paper. Next to the title, write the organizational pattern that the class thought matched the title. For example, the title "Steps to Follow in Getting a Job" suggests a process. Now list four or five ideas under the title that could be used to develop the title using the organizational pattern the class has identified. For example, under the title "Steps to Follow in Getting a Job," you might list: 1) Decide what kind of job you want 2) Look in the classified ads, and so on. Use your imagination to develop the titles according to the organizational patterns they suggest. Display your results by taping up your lists of ideas and take a look at them. Are these brief outlines good examples of a few ideas that might be organized according to the eight organizational patterns described in this chapter?

EIGHT TITLES	EIGHT ORGANIZATIONAL PATTERNS
1. _____ "Steps to Follow in Getting a Job"	a. spatial
2. _____ "Types of Jobs"	b. problem–solution
3. _____ "An Efficient Work Area"	c. listing
4. _____ "What Will Happen If I Get a Job"	d. process
5. _____ "Dealing with the Difficulties of Finding a Job"	e. chronological
6. _____ "My Best Job and My Worst Job"	f. whole into parts

EIGHT TITLES	**EIGHT ORGANIZATIONAL PATTERNS**
7. _____ "My Requirements for a Job"	g. cause–effect
8. _____ "A History of the Jobs I Have Held"	h. comparison–contrast

Exercise 3

Map the ideas in essays. *Small groups of students.*

This exercise will provide you with practice in mapping the ideas you have reviewed in some of the essays from earlier chapters in this book. Form eight groups; appoint scribes to write the maps. The organizational pattern in each case has been identified for you. Your answers to the questions in the "Look at an example" exercises on pages 116–121 in this chapter will provide you with ideas to map. The page numbers of the articles themselves are also provided if you want to review them again. Draw your maps in any way you like. Be creative. Look again at the maps on pages 122–126 to get you started. Be sure to write a title and the type of organizational pattern at the top of each map. Also, make them large enough to display at the end of the class period.

a. Make a **whole into parts map** of the description of the World Wide Web that appears on pages 100–101.

b. Make a **listing map** of the five workplace issues that have emerged with the increased use of computers in business on pages 103–104.

c. Make a **chronological map** of the journey described in "Exodus" on pages 61–65. Where does it begin, where does it end, and approximately how long does it take?

d. Make a process map of Malcolm X's process for learning vocabulary, on pages 21–24.

e. Make a spatial map of paragraphs 2-6 of "Exodus" that describes the town of Altar, pages 61–63.

f. Make a cause-effect map of "We've Overlooked One of Our Greatest Assets," on pages 66–68.

g. Make a comparison-contrast map of "The MultiTasking Generation" on pages 105–109. Follow format b on page 125 that uses three columns. First list three or four points of comparison in the first column (for example, types of media). Then show how non-GenM students met these points of comparison in the second column (for example typewriter and books) and how GenM students meet them in the third column (for example, Instant Messaging, Word files, Websites, iPods, videogames, email).

h. Make a **problem–solution map** of "Join the Incredible Reading Rally," on pages 29–32.

THREE READING EXERCISES:
ABOUT THE PUNISHMENT OF CRIMINALS

The following readings will invite you to compare ideas about criminals and how they should be punished. The selections are drawn from a sociology textbook, a psychology textbook, and an essay in *The New Yorker* magazine, written by a judge who had to sentence a criminal to death.

The Criminal Justice System[2]

JOHN J. MACIONIS

Explanatory notes: *The following selection is taken from Chapter 9, "Deviance," which appears in the college textbook* Sociology. *The author is a college professor who teaches and writes about sociology.* **What do you know about the criminal justice system in the United States? What do you predict this will be about? Two organizational patterns are used in this selection. See if you can recognize them.**

The U.S. Criminal Justice System

The criminal justice system is a society's formal system of social control. We shall briefly introduce the key elements of the U.S. criminal justice system: police, the courts, and the system of punishment and corrections. First, however, we must understand an important principle that underlies the entire system, the idea of due process.

Due Process

Due process is a simple but very important idea: The criminal justice system must operate within the bounds of law. This principle is grounded in the first ten amendments to the U.S. Constitution—known as the Bill of Rights—adopted by Congress in 1791. The Constitution offers various protections to any person charged with a crime, including the right to counsel, the right to refuse to testify against yourself, the right to confront all accusers, freedom from being tried twice for the same crime, and freedom from being "deprived of life, liberty, or property without due process of law." Furthermore, the Constitution gives all people the right to a speedy and public trial, with a jury if desired, and freedom from excessive bail as well as "cruel and unusual" punishments.

In general terms, the concept of due process means that anyone charged with a crime must receive (1) fair notice of the proceedings, (2) a hearing on the charges conducted according to law and with the ability to present a defense, and (3) a judge or jury that weighs evidence impartially.[3]

[2] John J. Macionis, "Deviance," *Sociology*, 11th ed. (Upper Saddle River: Prentice Hall, 2007) 242–247.
[3] James A. Inciardi. *Elements of Criminal Justice.* 2nd ed. New York: Oxford University Press, 2000.

Due process limits the power of government, with an eye toward this nation's 4
cultural support of individual rights and freedoms. Of course, deciding exactly
how far government can go is an ongoing process that makes up much of the work
of the judicial system, especially the U.S. Supreme Court.

Police

The police serve as the primary point of contact between the criminal justice 5
system and a society's population. In principle, the police maintain public order by
enforcing the law. Of course, there is only so much that the 663,796 full-time police officers in the United States can do to monitor the activities of 300 million people. As a result, the police exercise considerable discretion about which situations
warrant their attention and how to handle them.

How do police carry out their duties? In a study of police behavior in five 6
cities, Douglas Smith and Christy Visher concluded that because they must act
swiftly, police officers quickly size up situations in terms of six factors. First, the
more serious they think the situation is, the more likely they are to make an arrest.
Second, officers take account of the victim's wishes in deciding whether or not to
make an arrest. Third, the odds of arrest go up the more uncooperative a suspect
is. Fourth, officers are more likely to take into custody someone they have arrested
before, presumably because this suggests guilt. Fifth, the presence of observers increases the chances of arrest. According to Smith and Visher, the presence of observers prompts police to take stronger control of a situation, if only to move the
encounter from the street (the suspect's turf) to the police department (where law
officers have the edge). Sixth, all else being equal, police officers are more likely to
arrest people of color than whites, perceiving suspects of African or Latino descent
as either more dangerous or more likely to be guilty.[4]

Courts

After arrest, a court determines a suspect's guilt or innocence. In principle, U.S. 7
courts rely on an adversarial process involving attorneys—one representing the defendant and another the state—in the presence of a judge, who monitors legal procedures.

In practice, however, about 90 percent of criminal cases are resolved prior to 8
court appearance through **plea bargaining,** *a legal negotiation in which a prosecutor reduces a charge in exchange for a defendant's guilty plea.* For example, the
state may offer a defendant charged with burglary a lesser charge, perhaps possession of burglary tools, in exchange for a guilty plea.

Plea bargaining is widespread because it spares the system the time and expense 9
of trials. A trial is usually unnecessary if there is little disagreement over the facts
of the case. In addition, because the number of cases entering the system annually
has doubled over the past decade, prosecutors could not bring every case to trial
even if they wanted to. By quickly resolving most of their work, the courts channel their resources into the most important cases.

[4] Douglas A. Smith, and Christy A. Visher. "Street-Level Justice: Situational Determinants of Police
Arrest Decisions." *Social Problems.* Vol. 29, No. 2 (December 1981): 167–77. See also Douglas A.
Smith. "Police Response to Interpersonal Violence: Defining the Parameters of Legal Control."
Social Forces. Vol. 65, No. 3 (March 1987):767–82.

But plea bargaining pressures defendants (who are presumed innocent) to 10 plead guilty. A person can exercise the right to a trial, but only at the risk of receiving a more severe sentence if found guilty. Furthermore, low-income defendants enter the process with the guidance of a public defender—typically an overworked and underpaid attorney who may devote little time to even the most serious cases.[5] Plea bargaining may be efficient, but it undercuts both the adversarial process and the rights of defendants.

Punishment

When a young man is shot dead on the street after leaving a restaurant, some 11 people may wonder why it happened, but almost everyone believes that someone should have to "pay" for the crime. Sometimes the desire to punish is so great that in the end, justice may not be done.

Why should a society punish wrongdoers? Scholars answer with four basic 12 reasons: retribution, deterrence, rehabilitation, and societal protection.

Retribution

The oldest justification for punishment is to satisfy people's need for **retribu-** 13 **tion,** *an act of moral vengeance by which society makes the offender suffer as much as the suffering caused by the crime.* Retribution rests on a view of society as a moral balance. When criminality upsets this balance, punishment in equal measure restores the moral order, as suggested in the ancient saying, "an eye for an eye, a tooth for a tooth."

In the Middle Ages, most people viewed crime as sin—an offense against God 14 as well as society—that required a harsh response. Today, although critics point out that retribution does little to reform the offender, many people consider vengeance reason enough for punishment.

Deterrence

A second justification for punishment is **deterrence,** *the attempt to discourage* 15 *criminality through the use of punishment.* Deterrence is based on the eighteenth-century Enlightenment idea that humans, as calculating and rational creatures, will not break the law if they think that the pain of punishment will outweigh the pleasure of the crime.

Deterrence emerged as a reform measure in response to the harsh punishments 16 based on retribution. Why put someone to death for stealing if theft can be discouraged with a prison sentence? As the concept of deterrence gained acceptance in industrial societies, the execution and physical mutilation of criminals in most high-income societies were replaced by milder forms of punishment such as imprisonment.

Punishment can deter crime in two ways. *Specific deterrence* is used to con- 17 vince an individual offender that crime does not pay. Through *general deterrence,* the punishment of one person serves as an example to others.

[5] Viveca Novak. "The Cost of Poor Advice." *Time* (July 5, 1999):38.

Rehabilitation

The third justification for punishment is **rehabilitation,** *a program for reforming the offender to prevent later offenses.* Rehabilitation arose along with the social sciences in the nineteenth century. Since then, sociologists have claimed that crime and other deviance spring from a social environment marked by poverty or a lack of parental supervision. Logically, then, if offenders learn to be deviant, they can also learn to obey the rules; the key is controlling their environment. *Reformatories* or *houses of correction* provided controlled settings where people could learn proper behavior.   18

Like deterrence, rehabilitation motivates the offender to conform. In contrast to deterrence and retribution, which simply make the offender suffer, rehabilitation encourages constructive improvement. Unlike retribution, which demands that the punishment fit the crime, rehabilitation tailors treatment to each offender. Thus identical crimes would prompt similar acts of retribution but different rehabilitation programs.   19

Societal Protection

A final justification for punishment is **societal protection,** *rendering an offender incapable of further offenses temporarily through imprisonment or permanently by execution.* Like deterrence, societal protection is a rational approach to punishment intended to protect society from crime.   20

Currently, about 2.2 million people are jailed in the United States. The crime rate has gone down in recent years, but the number of offenders locked up across the country has gone up, tripling since 1980. This rise in the prison population reflects both tougher public attitudes toward crime and punishing offenders and an increasing number of drug-related arrests. As a result, the United States now incarcerates a larger share of its population than any other country in the world.[6]   21

Critical review   The Summing Up table reviews the four justifications for punishment. However, an accurate assessment of the consequences of punishment is no simple task.   22

The value of retribution lies in Durkheim's claim that punishing the deviant person increases society's moral awareness. For this reason, punishment was traditionally a public event. Although the last public execution in the United States took place in Kentucky nearly seventy years ago, today's mass media ensure public awareness of executions carried out inside prison walls.[7]   23

Does punishment deter crime? Despite our extensive use of punishment, our society has a high rate of **criminal recidivism,** *later offenses committed by people*   24

---

[6] U.S. Bureau of Justice Statistics. *Capital Punishment, 2003.* Washington, D.C.: U.S. Government Printing Office, 2004. [Online] Available June 5, 2005, at http://www.ojp.usdoj.gov/bjs/pub/pdf/cp03.pdf and *Prison and Jail Inmates at Midyear 2004.* April 2005. [Online] Available October 14, 2005, at http://www.ojp.usdoj.gov/bjs/pub/pdf/pjim04.pdf

[7] Nicholas N. Kittrie. *The Right to Be Different: Deviance and Enforced Therapy.* Baltimore: Johns Hopkins University Press, 1971.

Four Justifications for Punishment

Retribution	The oldest justification of punishment. Punishment is society's revenge for a moral wrong. In principle, punishment should be equal in severity to the deviance itself.
Deterrence	An early modern approach. Deviance is considered social disruption which society acts to control. People are viewed as rational and self-interested; deterrence works because the pain of punishment outweighs the pleasures of deviance.
Rehabilitation	A modern strategy linked to the development of social sciences. Deviance is viewed as the result of social problems (such as poverty) or personal problems (such as mental illness). Social conditions are improved; treatment is tailored to the offender's condition.
Societal Protection	A modern approach easier to carry out than rehabilitation. If society is unable or unwilling to rehabilitate offenders or reform social conditions, people are protected by the imprisonment or execution of the offender.

previously convicted of crimes. About three-fourths of prisoners in state penitentiaries have been jailed before, and about half will be back in prison within a few years after release.[8] So does punishment really deter crime? Only about one-third of all crimes are known to police, and of these, only about one in five results in an arrest. The old saying "Crime doesn't pay" rings hollow when we realize that most offenses go unpunished.

General deterrence is even more difficult to investigate scientifically, since we have no way of knowing how people might act if they were unaware of the punishments handed down to others. Opponents of capital punishment point to

25

---

[8] Joan Petersilia. "Probation in the United States: Practices and Challenges." *National Institute of Justice Journal.* No. 233 (September 1997):4. See also Robert H. DeFina and Thomas M. Arvanites. "The Weak Effect of Imprisonment on Crime, 1971–1998." *Social Science Quarterly.* Vol. 83, No. 3 (September 2002):635–53.

research suggesting that the death penalty has limited value as a general deterrent and note that the United States is the only Western high-income nation that routinely executes serious offenders. Half of the 3,374 prisoners currently on death row are in just five states: California, Texas, Florida, Pennsylvania, and Ohio.

It is also true that some death sentences have been pronounced against innocent people. Between 1973 and 2003, almost 100 people were released from death row after new evidence established their innocence. How many did not get that chance? Before leaving office in January 2003, Illinois Governor George Ryan claimed that his state's judicial system was seriously flawed and commuted the sentences for all 167 of the state's death row inmates to life in prison.[9] In 2005, the U.S. Supreme Court struck a blow against capital punishment, ruling that offenders who were younger than eighteen when they committed their crimes cannot be put to death.

Despite growing controversy over the death penalty, a majority of U.S. adults (63 percent) say they support capital punishment for people convicted of murder.[10] Among first-year college students, support for the death penalty rose between 1970 and 1990 but has declined since then.[11]

Prisons provide short-term societal protection by keeping offenders off the streets, but they do little to reshape attitudes or behavior in the long term.[12] Perhaps we should not expect prisons to rehabilitate inmates because, according to Sutherland's theory of differential association, locking up criminals together for years probably strengthens criminal attitudes and skills. Incarceration also stigmatizes prisoners, making jobs hard to find later on.[13] In addition, prison breaks the social ties inmates may have in the outside world, which, following Hirschi's control theory, leaves these individuals more likely to commit new crimes upon release.

2060 words

Strategy Questions

1. What is the predominant pattern of organization in this selection? What clues helped you decide? What is the selection's title? What are its parts? What are two or three details that describe each part?

[9] Samantha Levine. "Playing God in Illinois." *U.S. News & World Report* (January 13, 2003):13.

[10] NORC. *General Social Surveys, 1972–2002: Cumulative Codebook.* Chicago: National Opinion Research Center, 2003.

[11] Alexander W. Astin, Leticia Oseguera, Linda J. Sax, and William S. Korn. *The American Freshman: Thirty-Five Year Trends.* Los Angeles: UCLA Higher Education Research Institute, 2002. See also Linda J. Sax et al. *The American Freshman: National Norms for Fall 2004.* Los Angeles: UCLA Higher Education Research Institute, 2004.

[12] Norman A. Carlson. "Corrections in the United States Today: A Balance Has Been Struck." *American Criminal Law Review.* Vol. 13, No. 4 (Spring 1976):615–47. See also Richard A. Wright. *In Defense of Prisons.* Westport, Conn.: Greenwood Press, 1994.

[13] Devah Pager. "The Mark of a Criminal Record," *American Journal of Sociology.* Vol. 108, No. 5 (March 2003):937–75.

2. What are the secondary patterns of organization in this selection? What clues helped you decide? What are the titles? What are the parts? What are two or three details that describe each part?
3. Make a map of the major ideas in this reading selection.

Study Reading Questions

1. What are the three key elements in the criminal justice system?
2. What is due process?
3. How many full-time police officers are employed in the United States? How many people live in the United States?
4. What are the four justifications for punishment? Describe each of them.
5. What is criminal recidivism? What is the rate of criminal recidivism in the United States?

Critical Reading and Thinking Questions

1. Rank the four justifications of punishment. Which would you put at the top of the list as the most important? Which would you rank as least important? Which would you put in second and third places? Justify your rankings.
2. What do you think this author's attitude is toward the general effectiveness of the criminal justice system in America? If this author were asked to give it a letter grade, what grade do you think he would give it? Why do you think so?
3. What do you think the consequences of the punishment of criminals are at present? Do you think they are adequate to fit the crimes that you read about or see on the television news each day? Justify your answer.
4. Did any of your opinions about the criminal justice system change as a result of reading this article? If yes, what changed? Why?
5. Compare the punishment of crime in the United States with the punishment of a thief in Iraq described in this selection. Which do you think is better? Why?

Reading 2

Punishment: The Opposite of Reinforcement[14]

STEPHEN F. DAVIS AND JOSEPH J. PALLADINO

Explanatory Notes: *The following is a selection from Chapter 5, "Basic Principles of Learning," from the college textbook* Psychology. *The authors are professors who teach and write about psychology. The material that precedes this in the chapter is about the concept of reinforcement. The authors provide a "Study Chart" that compares the ideas of reinforcement and punishment. Read it now to help you develop a context for reading the following material about punishment.* **As you read, determine what organizational patterns are used in this selection.**

---

[14] Stephen F. Davis and Joseph J. Palladino, "Basic Principles of Learning," *Psychology* (Englewood Cliffs: Prentice Hall, 1995) 224–227.

STUDY CHART
Positive and Negative Reinforcement Compared with Positive and Negative Punishment

Reinforcement—results in an increase in responding	Punishment—results in a decrease in responding
Positive—A stimulus is presented following a target response; an increase in responding occurs. For example, receiving good grades increases the amount of time one studies.	*Positive*—A stimulus is presented following a target response; a decrease in responding occurs. For example, washing a child's mouth out with soap for cursing reduces the number of curse words the child says.
Negative—A stimulus is removed following a target response; an increase in responding occurs. For example, if taking aspirin removes a painful headache, the frequency of taking aspirin increases.	*Negative*—A stimulus is removed following a target response; a decrease in responding occurs. For example, Saturday morning cartoon privileges are taken away because the child's chores have not been completed.

Joan, a 28-year-old parent, took her 2-year-old daughter, Jennifer, to the supermarket. Going to the supermarket is one of Jennifer's favorite activities. She likes to be pushed up and down the aisles in the shopping cart. Although she is typically quite well behaved, this trip proved to be different. While they were in the checkout line Jennifer decided to try out some of the "new" words she had heard Dad say last night when he closed the car door on his hand. Shocked, Joan told the child that she deserved to be punished for using such "bad" words.

Will punishment help correct Jennifer's choice of words?

You already know that the effect of a reinforcer (either positive or negative) is to increase the likelihood of a target response. So you should not be surprised to learn that the effect of a **punisher** is to *decrease* the likelihood or rate of responding of a target response.

Everyone seems to have an opinion about the usefulness of punishment. The typical view is that punishment does not work very well. This philosophy seems to have originated with the educator E. L. Thorndike. In the early 1900s, Thorndike developed a very influential theory of learning. One of the main components of that theory was the *law of effect*,[15] which stated that presenting a "satisfier" (a reinforcer) leads to the learning of new responses, whereas presenting an "annoyer" (a punisher) leads to the weakening or unlearning of responses. However, in his later writing Thorndike complicated matters: He concluded that punishment does not really lead to the unlearning of responses. If it does anything, it causes subjects to make some other response.

[15] E. L. Thorndike, *Animal Intelligence* (New York: Macmillan, 1911).

If punishment does not work, why use it? It appears that Thorndike may have been a bit premature in his dismissal of punishment. This technique for controlling behavior is more effective than he thought. We need to know how to use punishment effectively *and* to be willing to accept the consequences of its use. But before we discuss the effective use of punishment we need to know more about punishers.

Just as there are positive and negative reinforcers, there are positive and negative punishers. As you can see in [the figure below], positive punishers are aversive stimuli or events that are presented; negative punishers are pleasant stimuli or events that are removed. This sounds just like the description of reinforcement; what is the difference? The difference is that reinforcement (positive or negative) *increases* the rate of responding, whereas punishment (positive or negative) *decreases* the rate of responding. For example, if a rat in an operant conditioning chamber receives a mild electric shock for pressing a lever, its rate of responding decreases. Similarly, if a child is scolded for playing in the street, that behavior occurs less often. These are examples of positive punishers. Examples of negative

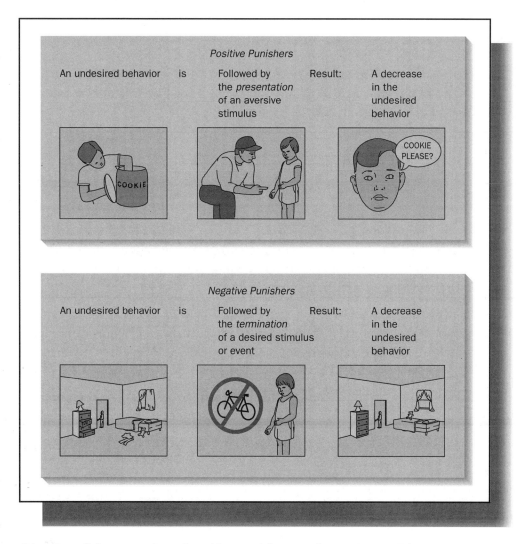

Diagram of the operation of positive punishers and negative punishers.

punishers include taking away a child's allowance, grounding a teenager, or suspending a basketball player for violating training rules.

Azrin and Holz[16] and Axelrod and Apsche[17] have suggested several procedures that should be followed if punishment is to be used effectively:

1. The punisher should be delivered (positive) or taken away (negative) *immediately after the response that is to be eliminated.* Spanking your cat for digging up your African violets while you were out will have no effect except perhaps to make you feel better.

2. The punisher should be *strong enough to make a real difference.* Being grounded for 2 days may not matter very much, but being grounded for 2 months is a different story. Similarly, there are spankings and then there are beatings. However, most people consider the use of extremely strong punishers unacceptable, if not ethically wrong. We do not want to inflict so much punishment that real damage results. This concern is reflected in society's negative view of child abuse.

3. The punishment should be administered *after each and every undesired target response.* Punishment is not as effective when you do not punish all of the undesired responses; it must be administered consistently.

4. There should be no *unauthorized escape from the punisher.* If the punishment is not applied uniformly, its effects will be weakened. Rats are very clever; frequently they learn how to hang upside down from the top of a cage to avoid an electric shock to their feet.

5. If you use punishment, you should be prepared for the possibility of *aggressive responding.* Rats do not like to be shocked, children do not like to have their television privileges taken away, and spankings can elicit other behaviors besides crying. Children who are spanked may retaliate by kicking and biting. Note that aggressive responding may be directed toward a person, animal, or object that cannot retaliate, such as a pet dog or cat; such behavior is called *displaced aggression.* Nor does aggressive behavior always end when the punishment ends. As a child, did you ever try to "get even" with your parents after being punished?

6. Provide the subject with an *alternative, desired behavior* that can be achieved and reinforced. This replaces the punished behavior with an acceptable behavior. Simply giving a child a spanking for playing in the street may not be especially effective if there is nowhere else to play.

You should now be able to answer the question we asked at the beginning of this section. Will punishment help correct Jennifer's choice of words? Assume that

---

[16] N. H. Azrin and W. C. Holz, "Punishment," in W. K. Honig, ed., *Operant Behavior: Areas of Application* (New York: Appleton-Century-Crofts, 1966) 380–447.

[17] S. Axelrod and J. Apsche, *The Effects of Punishment on Human Behavior* (New York: Academic, 1983).

you are Jennifer's parent; you are in a crowded supermarket and she has just yelled out a string of four-letter words. What would you do? Hitting a child is never an appropriate response. Besides, even with a strong punishment, the undesired response may disappear for a while, but it will return again. In sum, it is very difficult to use punishment effectively. Perhaps the best solution would be to reinforce an alternate, desired behavior such as politeness.

1130 words

Strategy Questions

1. What organizational pattern is used in the first four paragraphs under the heading, "Will punishment help correct Jennifer's choice of words?" What title might also be appropriate for this section of the material? What are the major ideas expressed here?
2. What organizational pattern is used in the next part of the article, which begins with paragraph 5, "Azrin and Holz . . ." and continues to the end? What title might also be appropriate for this section of material? How would you briefly write the ideas on a simple outline?

Study Reading Questions

1. What is a "punisher" in the context of this article? Provide an example of one.
2. What are two types of punishers? Provide an example of each.
3. What is an "aversive stimulus." Use the word parts *a* (away) and *vert* (turn) from Chapter 3, along with context, to help you understand the meaning of *aversive*.
4. What are the six procedures that should be followed if punishment is to be used effectively?
5. What is an alternate, desired behavior?

Critical Reading and Thinking Questions

1. How do the six procedures for effective punishment apply to capital punishment? Consider each of them separately and use them to critique the present system.
2. Does capital punishment meet the requirements of the six procedures? Are any of the procedures *not* applicable to capital punishment? Are any particularly applicable?
3. According to the procedures, is capital punishment an effective or an ineffective type of punishment?
4. Which do you consider more effective, positive punishers or negative punishers? For example, would you punish a child? How? Would you spank a child? Why or why not?
5. Agree or disagree with the following statement and provide reasons for your position: "In sum, it is very difficult to use punishment effectively."

Reading 3

Tinkering with Death[18]

ALEX KOZINSKI

Explanatory Notes: *This essay was first published in* The New Yorker *magazine in February 1997. The author is a death-penalty judge who reflects on the question, How does it feel to send another man to die?* **What is your present opinion about the death penalty? Are you in favor of this method of punishment or not? If you were a judge and you were responsible for sentencing people to death, how would you feel? What is the organizational pattern in this essay?**

1.

I woke with a start and sat upright in the darkness. 1

He must be dead by now. 2

The thought filled my head and gave me a weird sense of relief. But no, it 3
couldn't be. The execution was set for Sunday morning at seven—long after daybreak. The display on the digital clock showed 1:23. I fell back on my pillow and
tried to chase Thomas Baal from my mind.

I had first heard his name just three days earlier. My friend and mentor 4
Supreme Court Justice Anthony M. Kennedy had mentioned during a telephone
conversation that an execution was scheduled that night somewhere in my jurisdiction. As a judge on the United States Court of Appeals for the Ninth Circuit, I
hear cases from nine states and two territories spread over the Western United
States and Oceania.

"Must not be mine," I told him, "or I'd have heard about it by now." And left 5
for lunch. When I returned, the fax was chattering away.

"The clerk's office called," my secretary said. "Guess who's been drawn for 6
that execution?"

"How can it be? A man is scheduled to die tonight and this is the first I hear 7
of it?"

"He doesn't want a stay," my law clerk interjected. "I've been reading the doc- 8
uments and it looks like he's ready to swallow the bitter pill. It's his mom and dad
who are trying to stop the execution. They say he's not competent to waive his
right to appeal. The district court is holding a hearing even as we speak."

"Oh, good," I muttered. "Maybe the district judge will enter a stay." 9

"Fat chance," my secretary and my law clerk said in unison. "Better read those 10
papers."

2.

As I drifted back to sleep, I thought that Thomas Baal was not such a bad fel- 11
low compared with some of his neighbors on death row. On February 26, 1988,
Baal had robbed thirty-four-year-old Frances Maves at knifepoint. Maves gave

---

[18] Alex Kozinski, "Tinkering with Death," *The New Yorker* 10 February 1997: 48–53.

him twenty dollars, but Baal demanded more. She struggled. "You shouldn't have done that," Baal told her. "Now you pay. I sentence you to death." He stabbed Maves eight times.

I had seen my first death cases shortly after law school, when I clerked at the United States Supreme Court for former Chief Justice Warren E. Burger. That was almost two decades ago now, but I've never quite gotten over the experience. Whatever qualms I had about the efficacy or the morality of the death penalty were drowned out by the pitiful cries of the victims screaming from between the lines of dry legal prose: [12]

> On the afternoon of May 14, 1973, defendant and three others . . . drove to the residence of Jerry Alday. . . . The defendant and one of his companions entered the mobile home for the purpose of burglary. Shortly thereafter two members of the Alday family, Jerry and his father, Ned Alday, arrived in a jeep, were escorted at gunpoint into the trailer, and were shot to death at close range with handguns. . . .
>
> Shortly thereafter a tractor driven by Jerry's brother, Jimmy Alday, arrived at the trailer. After being forced to empty his pockets, he was placed on the living room sofa and killed with a handgun fired at close range.
>
> While one of the four was moving the tractor out of the driveway, Jerry's wife, Mary, arrived at her home by car. . . . Two other members of the Alday family, Aubrey and Chester, Jerry's uncle and brother, arrived in a pickup truck. Mary was forced into the bathroom while Aubrey and Chester were taken at gunpoint into the bedrooms and shot in a manner similar to the first two victims. . . .
>
> Mary Alday was then raped by two or more of the men. . . . She was then taken, bound and blindfolded, in her car about six miles to a wooded area where she was raped by two of the men, was beaten when she refused to commit oral sodomy, and her breasts mutilated. She was then killed with two shots. Her watch was then removed from her nude body.

Sometimes the victims had tiny voices, barely audible as they endured fates so horrible that they defy human comprehension: [13]

Over the . . . latter portion of Kelly Ann's short, torturous life the defendant [her father] did these things to her on one or many occasions:

1. Beat her in the head until it was swollen.

2. Burned her hands.

3. Poked his fingers in her eyes.

4. Beat her in the abdomen until "it was swollen like she was pregnant."

5. Held her under water in both the bath tub and toilet.

6. Kicked her against a table which cut her head then . . . sewed up her wound with needle and thread.

7. On one occasion beat her continuously for 45 minutes.

8. Choked her on the night she died and when she stopped breathing . . . placed her body in a plastic garbage bag and buried her in an unmarked and unknown grave.

Brutal facts have immense power; they etched deep marks in my psyche. Those 14
who commit such atrocities, I concluded, forfeit their own right to live. We tarnish
the memory of the dead and heap needless misery on their surviving families by
letting the perpetrators live.

Still, it's one thing to feel and another to do. It's one thing to give advice to a 15
judge and quite another to *be* the judge signing the order that will lead to the death
of another human being—even a very bad one. Baal was my first.

3.

Another start. The clock showed 3 A.M. Would this night never end? I knew I 16
had done the right thing; I had no doubts. Still, I wished it were over.

The district court had made its decision around 6 P.M. Thursday. Yes, Baal 17
was competent; he could—and did—waive his right to all appeals, state and federal.
This finding was based on the affidavits of the psychiatrists who had examined
Baal, and on Baal's courtroom responses:

> THE COURT: Do you want us to stop [the execution], sir, to give you
> an opportunity to appeal . . . ?
> THE DEFENDANT: No, I feel that I've gone through a lot of problems
> in there and I'm just—I feel that the death penalty is needed. And I don't
> feel that I have to stick around ten years and try to fight this thing out be-
> cause it's just not in me.
> THE COURT: You know that your act here in the Courtroom of saying,
> "Don't stop the execution," will result in your death. You're aware of that,
> are you not?
> THE DEFENDANT: Yes . . .
> THE COURT: Now, you know that the choice that you're making here
> is either life or death. Do you understand that?
> THE DEFENDANT: I understand. I choose death. . . .
> THE COURT: Is there anything else?
> THE DEFENDANT: Just bring me a hooker.
> THE COURT: Obviously the court can't grant requests such as that.
> Any other requests?
> THE DEFENDANT: Just my last meal and let's get the ball rolling.

In desperation, Baal's parents had submitted an affidavit from a psychiatrist 18
who, without examining Baal, could say only that he *might* not be competent. The
district judge didn't buy it. Stay denied.

The case officially landed in my lap just as I was leaving the office for dinner 19
at a friend's house. I arranged with the two other judges who had been selected to
hear the case for a telephone conference with the lawyers later that evening. Nothing stops the conversation at a dinner party quite like the half-whispered explanation "I have to take this call. It's a stay in a death case. Don't hold dessert."

Last-minute stay petitions in death cases are not unusual; they're a reflex. 20
Except in rare cases where the prisoner decides to give up his appeal rights, death
cases are meticulously litigated, first in state court and then in federal court—often
bouncing between the two systems several times—literally until the prisoner's
dying breath. Once the execution date is set, the process takes on a frantic pace.

The death warrant is usually valid only for a limited time—in some states only for a single day—and the two sides battle furiously over that piece of legal territory.

If the condemned man (only one woman has been executed in the last thirty-five years) can delay the execution long enough for the death warrant to expire, he will have bought himself a substantial reprieve—at least a few weeks, sometimes months or years. But, if the state can carry out the execution, the game ends in sudden death and the prisoner's arguments die with him. 21

The first time I had seen this battle was in 1977, when a platoon of American Civil Liberties Union lawyers descended on the United States Supreme Court in a vain effort to save Gary Gilmore's life. Gilmore's case was pivotal to death-penalty opponents, because he would be the first to be executed since the Supreme Court had emptied the nation's death rows in 1972 by declaring all existing death-penalty statutes unconstitutional. A number of states had quickly retooled their death statutes, but opponents hoped to use procedural delays to stave off all executions for many years. Gilmore upset this calculation by waiving his appeals after he was found guilty. 22

Gilmore was scheduled to face the firing squad on the morning of January 17, 1977. Efforts to obtain a stay from the lower federal courts during the night had proved unsuccessful, and the lawyers brought a stack of papers to the Supreme Court Clerk's office. The Court was due to hear cases at ten, which was also when the execution was scheduled. In the hour before the Justices took the bench, Michael Rodak, the Clerk of the Supreme Court, carried the petition to them in their chambers—first to one, then to another. The Justices entered the courtroom at the stroke of ten, and Rodak hurried back to his office. A few minutes after ten, he placed a call to the state prison in Draper, Utah, where Gilmore was being held. He first identified himself with a password: "This is Mickey from Wheeling, West Virginia." He continued, "I've presented the stay petition to the Justices, and it was denied. You may proceed with the execution." 23

Rodak then fell silent for a few seconds as he listened to the response from the other end of the line. 24

"Oh. . . . You mean he's already dead?" 25

4.

So as not to wake my wife with my tossing, I went to the kitchen and made myself a cup of tea. As I sipped the hot liquid, I thumbed through the small mountain of papers that had accumulated over the past seventy-two hours. 26

With the stakes in death cases so high, it's hard to escape the feeling of being manipulated, the suspicion that everything the lawyers say or do is designed to entice or intimidate you into giving them what they want. Professional distance—the detachment that is the lawyers' stock-in-trade in ordinary cases—is absent in death cases. It's the battle of the zealots. 27

And it's not just the lawyers. Death cases—particularly as the execution draws near—distort the deliberative process and turn judges into advocates. There are those of my colleagues who have never voted to uphold a death sentence and doubtless never will. The view that judges are morally justified in undermining the death penalty, even though it has been approved by the Supreme Court, was legitimized by the former Supreme Court Justices William J. Brennan, Jr., and 28

Thurgood Marshall, who voted to vacate as cruel and unusual every single death sentence that came before the Court. Just before retiring, in 1994, Justice Harry A. Blackmun adopted a similar view, by pronouncing, "From this day forward, I shall no longer tinker with the machinery of death."

Refusing to enforce a valid law is a violation of the judges' oath—something that most judges consider a shameful breach of duty. But death is different, or so the thinking goes, and to slow down the pace of executions by finding fault with every death sentence is considered by some to be highly honorable. In the words of Justice Brennan, this practice "embod[ies] a community striving for human dignity for all, although perhaps not yet arrived." 29

Judges like me, who support the death penalty, are swept right along. Observing manipulation by the lawyers and complicity from liberal colleagues, conservative judges often see it as their duty to prevent death-row inmates from diminishing the severity of their sentence by endlessly postponing the day of reckoning. [. . .] 30

Families of murder victims are among the most fervent supporters of the death penalty. They often use the press and political channels to agitate for the hasty demise of the monster who shattered their lives. Yet no one seems to have given serious thought to whether families are helped or harmed by the process, especially when it is long delayed. Does watching the perpetrator die help the families reach closure, or does the frustrated hope of execution in the face of endless appeals keep the psychological wounds open, sometimes for decades? 31

5.

Another hour passed, but sleep eluded me. Events of the last three days kept knocking around in my head. 32

Over my friend's kitchen telephone, the lawyers spoke with great urgency and took predictable positions. Afterward, my colleagues and I conferred. One of them—who has never seen a death sentence he liked—quickly voted to issue a stay. Almost instinctively, I took the opposite view. After some discussion, the third judge voted for a stay, and the execution was halted. 33

We spent all day Friday and most of that night preparing the stay order and my dissent. My colleagues argued that Baal's parents made a strong showing that he was not competent to surrender his life: he had a long history of "behavioral and mental problems," had attempted suicide on several occasions, and had been found to suffer from a variety of psychiatric disorders. Twice in the past, he had waived his legal remedies but had later changed his mind. 34

My dissent emphasized the diagnosis of the psychiatrists who had examined him; the state court's finding—just a week earlier—that he was competent; and Baal's lucid and appropriate answers to questions posed from the bench. I ended by arguing that Baal's decision to forgo the protracted trauma of numerous death-row appeals was rational, and that my colleagues were denying his humanity by refusing to accept his decision: 35

> It has been said that capital punishment is cruel and unusual because it is degrading to human dignity. . . . But the dignity of human life comes not from mere existence, but from that ability which separates us from the beasts—the ability to choose; freedom of will. *See* Immanuel Kant, "Cri-

tique of Pure Reason." When we say that a man—even a man who has committed a horrible crime—is not free to choose, we take away his dignity just as surely as we do when we kill him. Thomas Baal has made a decision to accept society's punishment and be done with it. By refusing to respect his decision we denigrate his status as a human being.

The idea that a long sojourn on death row is itself an excruciating punishment—and violates basic human rights—has gained some notable adherents. [. . .]   36

6.

Dawn broke as I drifted off into fitful sleep, but a part of me kept reaching out   37
to the man I knew was living the last hour of his life. Awareness of death is intrinsic to the human condition, but what is it like to know precisely—to the minute—when your life is going to end? Does time stand still? Does it race? How can you swallow, much less digest, that last meal? Or even think of hookers?

Though I've now had a hand in a dozen or more executions, I have never witnessed one. The closest I came was a conversation with Bill Allen, a lawyer from   38
my former law firm. I ran into him at a reception and his face was gray, his eyes—usually sharp and clear—seemed out of focus.

"Not well," Bill answered when I asked how he was doing. "I lost a client. His   39
name was Linwood Briley. I saw him die in the electric chair a couple of days ago."

"Was it rough?"   40

"What do you think? It was awful."   41

"What was it like when they turned on the juice?"   42

"Oh, by the time they got done strapping him down, putting the goop on his   43
head and the mask on his face, the thing sitting in that chair hardly looked human. But the really strange part was before: looking at him, talking to him, even joking with him, fully aware he'd be dead in half an hour."

"Why did you go?"   44

"I thought he should have a friend there with him in his final minutes."   45

The look on Bill's face stayed with me a long time. It was enough to persuade   46
me that I'd never want to witness an execution. Yet I sometimes wonder whether those of us who make life-and-death decisions on a regular basis should not be required to watch as the machinery of death grinds up a human being. I ponder what it says about me that I can, with cool precision, cast votes and write opinions that seal another human being's fate but lack the courage to witness the consequences of my actions.

After filing my dissent, at 2:59 A.M. Saturday, I put Baal out of my mind, figuring that it would be quite some time before I'd have to think about him again.   47
Much to my surprise, however, the Supreme Court issued an order that evening, lifting our stay. The execution was on. The Court had more or less adopted my reasoning—even cited me by name. I felt triumphant.

But, as Saturday turned to night, it began to sink in that Baal really *was* going   48
to die, and that I would have played a part in ending his life. The thought took hold of my mind and would not let go. It filled me with a nagging sense of unease, something like motion sickness.

7.

I finally plunged into a deep sleep from which I awoke long after the execution 49
was over. I was grateful not to have been awake to imagine in real time how Baal
was strapped onto a gurney, how his vein was opened, how the deadly fluids were
pumped into his body.

Lethal injection, which has overtaken the electric chair as the execution 50
method of choice, is favored because it is sure, painless, and nonviolent. But I find
it creepy that we pervert the instruments of healing—the needle, the pump, the
catheter, F.D.A.-approved drugs—by putting them to such an antithetical use. It
also bothers me that we mask the most violent act that society can inflict on one of
its members with such an antiseptic veneer. Isn't death by firing squad, with mutilation and bloodshed, more honest?

8.

Some three hundred and sixty people have been executed since Gary Gilmore. 51
The most we have dispatched in any one year was fifty-six, in 1995. There are
thirty-one hundred or so awaiting their date with the executioner, and the number
is growing. Impatient with the delays, Congress last year passed the Effective
Death Penalty Act, which will probably hasten the pace of executions. Even then,
it's doubtful we have the resources or the will even to keep up with the three hundred or so convicted murderers we add to our death rows every year.

With the pace of executions quickening and the total number of executions ris- 52
ing, I fear it's only a matter of time before we learn that we've executed the wrong
man. There have already been cases where prisoners on death row were freed after
evidence turned up proving them innocent. I dread the day we are confronted with
a case in which the conclusive proof of innocence turns up too late.

And I sometimes wonder whether the death penalty is not an expensive and 53
distracting sideshow to our battle against violent crime. Has our national fascina-
tion with capital punishment diverted talent and resources from mundane methods
of preventing violent crime? Take William Bonin, the notorious Freeway Killer,
who raped, tortured, and murdered fourteen teen-age boys, then dumped their
bodies along Southern California's freeways. If anyone deserved execution, surely
it was Bonin. And on February 23, 1996, after fourteen years on death row, he
went to his death, even then mocking the families of his victims. Asked if he had
any regrets, the confessed killer admitted that, indeed, he did: "Well, probably I
went in the [military] service too soon, because I was peaking in my bowling career. I was carrying, like, a 186 to a 190 average. . . . I've always loved bowling."

Yet, looking at the record in his case, one can't help noting that Bonin had 54
given us ample warning of his proclivities. While serving in Vietnam, he had sexually assaulted at gunpoint two soldiers under his command. After returning to
civilian life, he had been convicted of molesting four boys between the ages of
twelve and eighteen. He had served three years for those crimes and, upon his release, molested another boy. Again, he had served only three years and had then
been set free to commence his killing spree.

Bonin is not unique. My concurring opinion in his case lists a number of other 55
killers who gave us fair warning that they were dangerous but were nevertheless

set free to prey on an unsuspecting and vulnerable population. Surely putting to death ten convicted killers isn't nearly as useful as stopping a single Bonin before he tastes blood.

9.

It's late Saturday night. Another execution is scheduled for next week, and the 56 machinery of death is humming through my fax. And, despite the qualms, despite the queasiness I still feel every time an execution is carried out in my jurisdiction, I tinker away. I do it because I have taken an oath. But there's more. I do it because I believe that society is entitled to take the life of those who have shown utter contempt for the lives of others. And because I hear the tortured voices of the victims crying out to me for vindication.

3950 words

Strategy Questions

1. What is the predominant pattern of organization in this essay?
2. Make a map or a time line of the incidents in this essay. Indicate breaks in time and flashbacks so that you create a picture of how time flows in the essay.
3. How much real time passes in the main story of the essay, excluding the flashbacks and sections 8 and 9 at the end?

Study Reading Questions

1. What is the author's official position in the criminal justice system?
2. What is the name of the first person Judge Kozinski had to sentence to death, and what was his crime?
3. How does Judge Kozinski intellectually justify sentencing other people to death? How does he feel about it emotionally?
4. What year did the Supreme Court declare capital punishment unconstitutional? In what year was it reinstated? Who was the first person to die under the newly reinstated law?
5. Describe the attitude toward the death penalty that is usually held by the families of murder victims.

Critical Reading and Thinking Questions

1. What is your opinion about the death penalty now that you have read this essay? Did your opinion change as a result of reading? That is, (a) did reading make your original convictions stronger; (b) did reading change your beginning opinion; or (c) did reading awaken a new interest in the subject? Describe how reading this essay affected you.
2. Do you think that families of crime victims should be allowed to witness the execution of a person who victimized their family? Why or why not?

3. Review the four justifications of punishment on pages 135–137. Which of them applies to the death penalty, as it is described in this essay? What do you conclude from this application? Is the death penalty an effective punishment or not?
4. Review the six procedures that must be followed if punishment is to be carried out effectively, which appear on page 142. Which of these procedures are met in the case of capital punishment and which are not? Judging by these procedures, is capital punishment an effective mode of punishment?
5. Do you believe that death by lethal injection is a fit punishment for some of the crimes that are described in this essay? Provide reasons for your answer.

FOUR APPLICATION EXERCISES

Exercise 1

Describe the format of the chapters in this book.

Select one of the chapters and list its parts. Examine two other chapters to see if they are formatted in the same way. Use what you know about how the chapters are put together to help you make predictions and find information in future chapters.

Exercise 2

Describe the formats used in your other textbooks.

Examine the table of contents of one of your other textbooks and describe how the material seems to be organized. Identify the main parts and the order in which these parts occur. Examine the format of one chapter in your textbook and list its parts to show how it is formatted. Check a couple of other chapters. Do they all follow a common format?

Exercise 3

Identify an organizational pattern used in one of your other textbooks.

When you read your next assignment in another textbook, look for an example of an organizational pattern and identify it. How does recognizing it help you understand and remember the material? Be prepared to describe the pattern in class.

Exercise 4

Make a map or an outline of the information in another textbook.

Map or outline the information you identified in Exercise 3 and bring it to class.

REVIEW AND EVALUATE THE STRATEGIES

The following is a review of the five strategies you learned in this chapter:

1. Examine the table of contents and a sample chapter to discover formats.

2. Recognize organizational patterns.

3. Write organizational maps to help you see the ideas.

4. Write informal outlines to help you see the organization.

5. Learn the material on maps and outlines by reviewing, writing, and reciting.

Make a personal evaluation of these strategies:

1. Underline your favorite strategies in the previous list.

2. Make a check mark by those you want to continue to use.

3. Cross out any you probably will not continue to use. What are your reasons for rejecting them?

Understand Main Ideas and Details

CHAPTER GOALS:

1. **To help you recognize main ideas, supporting details, and transitions.**

2. **To teach you to read and understand difficult sentences, paragraphs, and longer sections.**

3. **To teach you to follow the UAS process for marking textbooks: Underline, Annotate, and Summarize.**

4. **To provide you with five strategies for learning and remembering the important ideas in everything you read.**

Reading for Ideas in Sentences, Paragraphs, and Longer Sections

Recognizing organizational patterns, as taught in the last chapter, helps you find and understand the important ideas in the material you read. This chapter also focuses on understanding the important or **main ideas.** You will often, however, run into trouble spots that make understanding difficult, especially in reading complex or demanding material. You will need special reading strategies to help you improve your understanding of such material.

You will know when you hit trouble spots if you are monitoring your comprehension as you read. Look away from time to time and mentally summarize what you have just read. Complete the sentences suggested in Chapter 2, "Most of this is about . . ." and "Some of the things said about it are . . ." If you try this and nothing comes to mind, you need to identify the problem areas where your comprehension is breaking down.

Begin by recognizing the meaningful units in the material you read: the sentences, the paragraphs, and the sections of several paragraphs that develop an idea. Where could you focus your attention to make the material immediately clearer in your mind?

In Chapter 1 you learned that writers follow certain conventions when they write (see p. 6), and that readers who know some of these conventions can follow along much better than readers who do not have this information. This chapter describes how authors typically write sentences, paragraphs, and longer sections of material. It also describes methods authors use to make the most important ideas in their material clearer and easier to understand. Finally, this chapter teaches a process for writing reading notes right in the book itself. This process involves **underlining** the main ideas in the text, writing **annotations** that capture the main ideas in the margins, and writing a paragraph **summary** based on your marginal notes that you can easily review when you need to. Think of this as the UAS process for taking notes in your textbook. The acronym will help you remember these steps.

Reading and Understanding Sentences

Your comprehension may break down at the sentence level, particularly if you are reading a long, difficult sentence. There are many different types of sentences, and authors try to vary the way they write them to make their material more interesting. All sentences express a complete thought. This means they have a **subject** and they have a **predicate that gives information about the subject**. To help you find the subject of a sentence, ask "What is this sentence about?"; to find its predicate, ask "What did the author say about it?" Then restate these parts of the sentence briefly in your own words to help you understand the main idea of the sentence better.

Everyone has trouble understanding difficult sentences at times. Richard Feynman, the Nobel Prize–winning physicist, tells of the difficulty he had reading about sociology at a meeting he attended:

> There was a sociologist who had written a paper for us all to read—something he had written ahead of time. I started to read the damn thing, and my eyes were coming out: I couldn't make head nor tail of it! I figured it was because I hadn't read any of the books on that list. I had this uneasy feeling of "I'm not adequate," until finally I said to myself, "I'm gonna stop, and read *one sentence* slowly, so I can figure out what the hell it means."
>
> So I stopped—at random—and read the next sentence very carefully. I can't remember it precisely but it was very close to this: "The individual member of the social community often receives his information via visual, symbolic channels." I went back and forth over it, and translated. You know what it means? "People read."[1]

Feynman has simplified the subject, "the individual member of the social community," to the word *people* and the predicate, "often receives his information via visual, symbolic channels" to the word *read*.

Try using Feynman's method on the following sentence from an essay about moviemaking.

Find the subject and discover what the author says about it. Restate the subject and predicate as simply and briefly as possible.

> Whether we say we're "creating a film" or merely "making a movie," the enterprise itself is sufficiently expensive and risky that it cannot be, and it will not be, undertaken without the hope of reward.[2]

[1] Richard P. Feynman, *"Surely You're Joking, Mr. Feynman!" Adventures of a Curious Character* (New York: W. W. Norton & Company, 1985) 281.

[2] Sydney Pollack, "The Way We Are," in Michael F. Petracca and Madeleine Sorapure, eds., *Common Culture* (Englewood Cliffs: Prentice Hall, 1995) 500.

How did you translate that sentence? _____

Basically, in simpler language, it says, *movies* (the subject) *must make money* (the predicate).

Most of the time you will understand sentences without having to stop and translate them. As you monitor your comprehension, however, and notice it occasionally slipping, you will need to locate the sentence that confused you. You may have to look up some of the words before you attempt to simplify and restate it. When you have simplified a difficult sentence, you will find it much easier to read the next sentences.

As you read a group of sentences, you will notice that they do not stand alone. They are related to one another, and they build on one another to create meaning. Authors make connections among their sentences that you can learn to recognize and follow.

How Authors Connect Sentences and Relate Ideas

Every sentence that you read carries the promise of more to come, of more information that is related to the idea just expressed. In fact, with the exception of the first sentence in a book or article, almost every sentence that you read will contain at least one word that connects it with the previous sentence. These connecting words tie sentences together, establish relationships between them, and make them easier to read. Unskilled writers who do not link sentences well create material that is comparatively difficult to read.

The prerequisites for writing linked sentences are that they all be on the same subject and that they follow a logical sequence. The links from sentence to sentence then help the reader concentrate on the subject and follow its development. Sentence links can even help the reader anticipate what is coming next. There are four main ways that sentences are most often linked together:

1. *Pronouns and antecedents.* Sentences can be linked with pronouns that refer back to words in previous sentences. These are called **antecedents.** Pronouns include such words as *I, you, we, he, she, it, they, one, mine, yours, his, theirs, them, who, what, whose,* and *which* among others. **Examples:**

    The *students* completed the course. Then *they* took the final. (*Students* is the antecedent for *they.*)

    I saw a *cat. It* was black. (*Cat* is the antecedent for *it.*)

2. *Related words.* Sentences can be linked with words other than pronouns that refer back to a related word in the previous sentence. **Examples:**

    The *cat* stalked the bird. Then the *beast* pounced.

    I saw a *cat.* The dumb *animal* was black.

    I saw a *bunch* of cats. The *smallest* was black.

3. *Repetition of key words.* Sentences are often linked with key words that are repeated throughout the paragraph. The repetition of a word that names the subject of the paragraph helps you keep your mind on it as you read. **Example:**

> At first, it may seem difficult to *speak* in public. Still, *speaking* is important in so many professions that most people need to develop this skill. One can improve public *speaking* skills by taking a course in *speaking* or by joining a toastmaster's club.

4. *Transitional words and phrases.* Sentences can be linked with **transitions,** words, and phrases that join ideas and also often express the relationship between them. In the last chapter you were taught to be aware of some of the transitional words and phrases that are associated with particular organizational patterns, such as *next* or *then* for the chronological pattern, *over there* or *here* for the spatial pattern, *first, second,* or *finally* for the topical pattern, and so on. You can review these on pages 116–121. Other examples of brief transitions that link ideas are *several, most, some, others, instead, the former, the latter, this, that, those, these, if . . . then, furthermore, likewise, in addition, in fact, and, yet, so, then,* and *however.* These are not the only possibilities, but they give you the idea. **Examples:**

> *Those* are a few. You may be able to think of *others.*
>
> *Most* families do not spend their entire incomes on necessities, but *instead* they buy a few luxuries.

Sentences make up paragraphs, and the next section provides you with insight and information that will help you read paragraphs when you have trouble understanding them.

Reading and Understanding Paragraphs

You can expect most of the paragraphs that you read to have certain predictable features. To begin with, most paragraphs have only one main idea, which the **topic sentence** in the paragraph introduces. Most of the time, the topic sentence is found at or near the beginning of the paragraph, but it can also appear in the middle or at the end. The rest of the paragraph provides detailed information about the main idea. This information can be of two types. Some of the material may qualify or add information about the topic sentence. Other information may provide very specific examples or other types of details. Here is an example of a paragraph from a biology textbook that has been written according to this usual paragraph format.

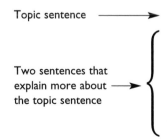

LIVING THINGS RESPOND TO STIMULI

Topic sentence ⟶ Living organisms perceive and respond to stimuli in their internal and external environments. Animals have evolved elaborate sensory organs and muscular systems that allow them to detect and respond to light, sound, chemicals, and many other stimuli from their surroundings. Internal stimuli are perceived by receptors for stretch, pain, and various chemicals. For

Two sentences that explain more about the topic sentence ⟶

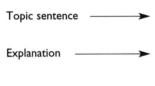

Examples ⟶ example, when you feel hungry, you are perceiving contractions of your empty stomach and low levels of sugars and fats in your blood. You then respond to external stimuli by choosing appropriate objects to eat, such as a piece of pie rather than the plate and fork. Animals, with their elaborate nervous systems and motile bodies, are not the only organisms to perceive and respond to stimuli. The plants on your windowsill grow toward the light, and even the bacteria in your intestine manufacture a different set of digestive enzymes depending on whether you drink milk, eat candy, or both.[3]

To help you establish the main idea of a paragraph, ask: What was most of this paragraph about? To get a sense of the details and development of the idea, ask: What did the author say about the main idea? Try this for the paragraph you have just read. What is the main idea? What details did the author add to explain it? Your answers may not be in these words exactly, but did you come up with something like this? Main idea: All living things respond to inside and outside stimuli. Details: hunger (inside); choosing pie (outside).

Here is a second example from a marketing textbook. The first sentence in this paragraph is the topic sentence. The other sentences provide additional explanation of the topic sentence. See if you can identify the main idea and briefly restate the explanation.

Topic sentence ⟶ Each company and marketing manager must work out a philosophy of socially responsible and

Explanation ⟶ ethical behavior. Under the societal marketing concept, each manager must look beyond what is legal and allowed and develop standards based on personal integrity, corporate conscience, and long-run consumer welfare. A clear and responsible philosophy will help the marketing manager deal with the many knotty questions posed by marketing and other human activities.[4]

Did you come up with something like this? Main idea: Companies must be responsible. Details: They need ethical standards and a responsible philosophy.

Notice that the explanation in this paragraph answers the questions *why* and *how*.

---

[3] Teresa Audesirk and Gerald Audesirk, *Life on Earth* (Upper Saddle River: Prentice Hall, 1997) 5.

[4] Philip Kotler and Gary Armstrong, *Marketing: An Introduction*, 4th ed. (Upper Saddle River: Prentice Hall, 1997) 580.

Restate the main idea and details in the following paragraph.

Read the paragraph, paying particular attention to the main idea and the details.

> The American dream, in other words, has two faces: the one communally egalitarian and the other competitively elitist. This contradiction is no accident; it is fundamental to the structure of American society. Even as America's great myth of equality celebrates the virtues of mom, apple pie, and the girl or boy next door, it also lures us to achieve social distinction, to rise above the crowd and bask alone in the glory. This land is your land and this land is my land, Woody Guthrie's populist anthem tells us, but we keep trying to increase the "my" at the expense of the "your." Rather than fostering contentment, the American dream breeds desire, a longing for a greater share of the pie. It is as if our society were a vast high-school football game, with the bulk of the participants noisily rooting in the stands while, deep down, each of them is wishing he or she could be the star quarterback or head cheerleader.[5]

Briefly state the main idea: _____

_____

Briefly state the details: _____

_____

When you examine the details that support and develop a main idea in a paragraph, you can expect to find various types. Here is a list of some of the types of details. You have just read examples of the first two on the list. You can easily find examples of the others in your textbooks. Learn this list so that you won't get the details in a paragraph confused with the main idea. Details are often more vivid and interesting than the main idea, and a common reading error is to remember the example or some other detail and forget the main idea it illustrates.

Types of Supporting Details

1. *Examples* give specific instances of the main idea.
2. *Explanations* answer *why, how, who, what, where,* and *when* questions about the main idea.

---

[5] Jack Solomon, "Masters of Desire," in Michael F. Petracca and Madeleine Sorapure, eds., *Common Culture* (Englewood Cliffs: Prentice Hall, 1995) 45.

3. *Comparisons* and *contrasts* show what the main idea is similar to or different than.
4. *Statistics* and *facts* that are true suggest the main idea is also true.
5. *Quotations* from people who are experts in the field are presented to support the main idea.
6. *Description* that you can visualize in your "mind's eye" creates a mental image of the main idea.
7. *Narration* provides an anecdote or story to illustrate the main idea.

Supporting details help the reader in a number of ways. They make main ideas clearer and easier to understand. They are usually interesting. Some supporting details, such as facts and quotes, are used at times to prove the truth of a main idea.

Analyze the details in this paragraph.

The following paragraph provides details about George Gerbner's research about crime on television, which was conducted at the University of Pennsylvania's Annenberg School of Communication. Underline the details in the paragraph and list the types of details in the margin. Refer back to the list you just read to help you.

On the small screen, crime rages about 10 times more often than in real life. But while other researchers concentrate on the propensity of TV mayhem to incite aggression, the Annenberg team has studied the hidden side of its imprint: fear of victimization. On television, 55 percent of prime-time characters are involved in violent confrontations once a week; in reality, the figure is less than 1 percent. In all demographic groups in every class of neighborhood, heavy viewers overestimated the statistical chance of violence in their own lives and harbored an exaggerated mistrust of strangers—creating what Gerbner calls a "mean-world syndrome." Forty-six percent of heavy viewers who live in cities rated their fear of crime "very serious" as opposed to 26 percent for light viewers. Such paranoia is especially acute among TV entertainment's most common victims: women, the elderly, nonwhites, foreigners and lower-class citizens.[6]

In addition to the main idea and details in a paragraph, you can also expect to find transitional words and phrases that will help you make the necessary mental connections between the main idea and the details. Some common transitional words and phrases that are often used to clarify the relationships among the various parts of a paragraph are *for example, on the other hand, in comparison, in con-*

[6] Harry Waters, "Life According to TV," in Petracca and Sorapure, eds., *Common Culture* 174.

trast, first, second, third, one, another, or *finally.* The paragraph that follows illustrates the parts you can expect to find in typical paragraphs that explain main ideas: The topic sentence is in boldface type; the sentences that provide additional information to explain the topic sentence are underlined; the details are in italics; and the transitions are boxed.

DECISION MAKING

<table>
<tr>
<td>Topic sentence in boldface</td>
<td>Decision making is a special kind of problem solving in which we already know all the possible solutions (choices). Therefore, the task is not to come up with new solutions, but rather to identify the best available solution or choice using a predetermined set of criteria. This might sound like a fairly simple process, but sometimes we have to juggle a large and complex set of criteria as well as a large number of possible choices. As the number of criteria and choices grows, so does the difficulty of making a good decision. For example, suppose that we are looking for an apartment. There are hundreds of apartments to choose from. And while the amount of rent is important, so are the neighbors, location, level of noise, and cleanliness. If we find a noisy apartment with undesirable neighbors but a bargain-basement rent, should we take it? Is it a better choice than the apartment in a more desirable location with less noise but with a higher rent? How can we weigh the various characteristics to ensure that we make the best possible choice among the hundreds of available apartments?[7]</td>
</tr>
</table>

The five examples of paragraphs from textbooks used as examples in this section about reading and understanding paragraphs all begin with topic sentences. Some researchers estimate that as many as 85 percent of the paragraphs in your textbooks begin this way. Other, less common variations of the main idea paragraph include those with the topic sentence at the end or in the middle. Sometimes there is no topic sentence, and you have to figure out the main idea by reading the paragraph and deciding what it is about. As you read your textbooks and other material, however, you will discover that most of the time the paragraphs begin with topic sentences and that the purpose of these paragraphs is to explain and develop main ideas.

Reading Other Types of Paragraphs

Besides main idea paragraphs, you will encounter four other types of paragraphs in your reading.

1. The **introductory paragraph** states the main subject of the entire book or chapter. Sometimes it also sets out the major topics to be discussed in the order in which the reader will encounter them.

---

[7] Charles G. Morris, *Psychology,* 9th ed. (Upper Saddle River: Prentice Hall, 1996) 287.

Analyze an introductory paragraph.

The following is an example of an introductory paragraph from an article about punk music. Underline the sentence that states the subject of the essay. Notice how the author lists the topics he will cover and basically creates a road map for the reader to follow in reading the article. This listing of ideas is called a **pre-outline** because it outlines the ideas readers will read about before they read them.

> Punk surfaced in Los Angeles in the late seventies as a curious blend of anarchy and anomie—as one last desperate attempt for white, urban, lower middle class youths to dramatically express their distaste for a society that had long since expressed its disinterest in them. What follows is a selective description of the movement; an analysis of its ideology and its symbiotic relationship to mainstream rock and roll and an attempt to contextualize punk as a unique moment in the history of American youth culture.[8]

What is the subject of the essay? _____

What are the three topics that the author will discuss? Rewrite them in simpler language. (1) _____ (2) _____

(3) _____

---

2. The **supporting paragraph** adds additional information or examples about a main idea introduced in the paragraph that precedes it.

Analyze a supporting paragraph.

The following is an example of a supporting paragraph from a philosophy textbook. The main idea in the paragraph that precedes this one is that <u>students cannot just memorize the theories of philosophers like Plato and Aristotle; they must also understand the ideas, think about them, and come up with their own personal reactions</u>. How does this next paragraph support that idea?

> For example, do you agree or disagree with Plato's description of the ideal society? Totally? Partially? What are the strengths and weaknesses of his ideas? What would you change? Why? How would you convince Plato to change his mind? Suppose the person sitting next to you disagrees with you. How would you try to change her mind?[9]

Your answer: _____

---

[8] Jon Lewis, "Punks in LA: It's Kiss or Kill," in Petracca and Sorapure, eds., *Common Culture* 328.
[9] Thomas I. White, *Discovering Philosophy* (Upper Saddle River: Prentice Hall, 1991) 6.

3. The **transitional** paragraph changes the subject. It signals to the reader that the author is finished discussing one topic and is about to start another.

Analyze a transitional paragraph.

Here is an example of a transitional paragraph from a philosophy textbook that changes the subject by summarizing one aspect of the topic that is being discussed, <u>the introspective, "inward" questions people ask</u>, and by announcing a new aspect of the topic. What is the new aspect of the topic? Underline it.

> So far our questions have focused mainly inward, on what it means to be a living person from the inside. When we turn our attention outward, however, we encounter different kinds of philosophical questions.[10]

4. The **summary** or **concluding paragraph** restates main ideas or emphasizes the most striking idea. Summary paragraphs may appear at the end of a chapter or article, or they may appear at one or more places in the middle of a chapter or article. Often an author will summarize the ideas in a section of material in the middle of a chapter before continuing with a brand-new idea.

Analyze a summary paragraph.

Here is an example of a summary paragraph (one of several in a section marked "Summary of Key Concepts") at the end of the first chapter of a biology textbook. This paragraph restates the ideas that were developed over several pages in the chapter.

BIOLOGY: THE SCIENCE OF LIFE

Biology is based on the scientific principles of natural causality, uniformity in space and time, and common perception. These principles are assumptions that cannot be directly proved but that are validated by experience. Knowledge in biology is acquired through the application of the scientific method. First, an observation is made. Then a hypothesis is formulated that suggests a natural cause for the observation. The hypothesis is used to predict the outcome of further observations or experiments. A conclusion is then drawn about the validity of the hypothesis. A hypothesis becomes a scientific theory when repeated tests have confirmed it and none have refuted it.[11]

[10] White, *Discovering Philosophy* 9.
[11] Audesirk and Audesirk, *Life on Earth* 5.

Check your understanding of the scientific method as described in this summary.

What are the four steps?

(1) _____ (3) _____

(2) _____ (4) _____

The main point about paragraphs is that each one of them **says** something—that is, it presents information. But every paragraph also **does** something—that is, it introduces, presents a main idea, supports an idea, changes the subject, or sums up or restates the idea. When you read paragraphs, be aware of both of these levels so that you will be able to answer these questions: *What does the paragraph say?* and *What does the paragraph do?*

Reading Sections of Material

A **section of material** develops one of a few major ideas in a chapter or essay. The reader learns more about the major idea by reading the sequence of paragraphs that make up the section. Each of these paragraphs may have a main idea of its own that explains more about the major idea. For example, in the summary paragraph from the biology text, which you just read, a major idea is the scientific method. It was described in several paragraphs, that is, in a section of material, one part of the chapter. Each part of the scientific method was explained in main idea paragraphs that were a part of the longer section.

Within a short essay you may only need to locate and understand two or three major ideas. Several paragraphs are used to develop each of them. In a chapter you may need to locate and understand only seven or eight major ideas that are the subjects of the sections within the chapter.

You can identify sections of material by paying attention to the clues that authors use to make their major ideas stand out. For example, the title of the chapter or article may suggest or even name some of the major ideas; the introduction may list them, the headings and subheadings in boldface type announce them; and transitional phrases or sentences may separate and identify them. Vocabulary also changes with the introduction of a new idea. Being sensitive to such changes will help you locate the major sections and the major ideas. Finally, a restatement of the major ideas in the summary gives you the opportunity to check again to see how successful you have been in locating the major ideas. A typical pattern of paragraphs in a chapter or essay might be as follows:

Introductory paragraph
Paragraph that introduces a major idea
   Paragraph that explains the major idea further
   Paragraph that gives examples of the major idea   } Section
   Transitional paragraph or sentence to change the subject

Paragraph that introduces another major idea
    Paragraph that analyzes the parts of the idea   } Section
    Paragraph that compares the idea to something else   }
Conclusion or summary paragraph that restates both
    ideas and/or draws a conclusion

Practice locating the sections of material in the following essay.

This essay has been printed as a list of sentences. (1) Read the title. What does it suggest about the major ideas in this essay? _____
(2) Locate the introduction, label it in the margin, and draw a line across the page at the end of it. (3) Locate the body of the essay and draw a line at the end of each of its sections. Number these sections in the margin. (4) Label the conclusion.

WHO WROTE THE WORKS OF SHAKESPEARE?

Shakespeare was an actor and some people think he lacked the ability and education to write the plays and poems.

Only 100 years after Shakespeare's death, some people were suggesting that Bacon wrote Shakespeare.

Delia Bacon wrote a book in 1856 that suggests Bacon and others were the real authors.

The Bacon Society was founded in England to further this view.

An American court of law handed down the decision "Francis Bacon is the author."

A more recent idea is that Christopher Marlowe wrote the works of Shakespeare.

Hoffman's book in 1955 was the first to suggest that Marlowe wrote his own plays as well as Shakespeare's.

Pro-Shakespeare scholars point out that Marlowe was murdered before some of the plays were written.

Hoffman thinks someone else was murdered and Marlowe escaped and continued to write.

Ann Whateley has also been suggested as the person who wrote Shakespeare's works.

Whoever wrote the works understood women so well that some people think only a woman could have written them.

A man could not understand the female mind as well as this author could.

Another popular theory is that the Earl of Oxford wrote Shakespeare's works.

Many books and articles have been written to show that only Oxford has the genius to write these works.

Shakespeare scholars point out that many of the major plays were written after Oxford's death.

In spite of the questions about who wrote Shakespeare, most modern scholars believe that Shakespeare wrote the works himself.[12]

Did you identify four sections with four major ideas? The four sections are about the four people who have been suggested as the possible authors of Shakespeare's works: Bacon, Marlowe, Anne Whateley, and the Earl of Oxford. Two types of clues are provided in this text to help you identify these four ideas: (1) transitional words and phrases that were used to change the subject, and (2) changes in vocabulary which, in this case, are the changes of the names of the people.

Go back and reread the list of sentences. Circle the names of the various contenders for Shakespearean authorship. Notice how a pattern begins to develop: four sentences about Bacon, four about Marlowe, three about Whateley, and three about Oxford. Underline the major transitional phrases as well. Did you spot "A more recent idea . . . ," "has also been suggested . . . ," and "Another popular theory . . ."? The transitional clues together with the changes in vocabulary make it possible to divide this essay into its four major sections even without the help of boldface headings.

Write Reading Notes in Your Textbooks

As college students your textbooks now belong to you, which means you may write in them as much as you want. This practice will increase their value for you. A well-marked textbook provides a record of what you have learned and thought about while in college. You can use these textbooks as reference tools and memory aids for many years to come if you keep them instead of selling them when your class is over. Make your well-read and well-marked textbooks a part of your personal library.

There are other reasons for taking notes in your textbooks. This practice helps you focus and concentrate while you are reading, helps you learn the material as you write about it in the margins, and helps you think and make mental connections with what you already know. Writing in your textbooks also saves you time, helps you find important material quickly when you have to look for it, and helps you review for class discussions or exams. Strategy 5 on page 169 describes and provides an example of the UAS process for marking your textbooks that involves underlining, writing annotations, and writing summaries.

[12] Adapted from George McMichael and Edgar M. Glenn, *Shakespeare and His Rivals: A Casebook on the Authorship Controversy* (New York: The Odyssey Press, 1962).

UNDERSTAND THE MAIN IDEAS: FIVE STRATEGIES

All five of the strategies that follow are designed to help you concentrate on the most important ideas as you read and to help you reduce them to a brief form that is easy to recite, review, and remember.

Strategy 1: Monitor your comprehension of sentences, paragraphs, and sections.

This is such an important strategy that it is repeated here in the strategies section. Make frequent comprehension checks mentally or in writing by jotting down some notes. See if you can say to yourself what you have learned and what you now understand from your reading. Ask the questions, What is the subject? and What did the author say about it? Practice this regularly. When you monitor your comprehension and find you have been staring at words instead of reading, try one of the following four strategies to get you back on track.

Strategy 2: Use the author's clues to help you find the main ideas.

A few of the clues to main ideas that authors use to emphasize what is important are mentioned in this chapter. Here is a complete list. All of these possibilities will not be present in everything you read, but when they are, they can help you identify the most important ideas in what you are reading.

Twelve Clues to Main Ideas

1. *Titles, heads, and subheads.* These announce major subjects and ideas in bold-face type.

2. *Purpose sentence.* Look for a sentence in the first paragraphs of a book, chapter, or article that states what the rest of the text will be about.

3. *Pre-outline.* Look for sentences listing the ideas that will be developed in the coming paragraphs.

4. *Topic sentences.* Recognize the sentences in paragraphs and sections of material that state the subject and focus of the rest of the discussion.

5. *Italics.* Sometimes main ideas appear in italics as well as in boldface type to make them stand out from the rest of the text.

6. *Repetition.* Repetition of a key word or idea throughout a text is a signal that it is a major topic in the discussion.

7. *Questions.* Questions invite readers to look for answers, and the answer is often one of the major ideas being developed.

8. *Numbering.* Ideas that are numbered are important to notice. Either write them or make them into a mental list and put a label or title at the top.

▶

9. *Visuals.* Pictures, graphs, diagrams, figures, and other visual materials are often used to highlight and emphasize main ideas. Study them carefully.

10. *Details.* The use of examples, statistics, and other details always signals a main idea is being clarified, proved, or developed. Look back or ahead and discover the idea.

11. *Organizational patterns.* The major parts of the pattern, such as the topics, the divisions in time, the two objects being compared, the cause and the effect, or the problem and the solution, are the main ideas. Recognize the pattern and look for the ideas.

12. *Summary.* Summaries restate the main ideas in brief form.[13]

Strategy 3: Reduce and simplify difficult sentences.

When you have difficulty understanding a sentence, first find the subject (what the sentence is about) and then the predicate (what the author says about the subject). Next, look up the words that you don't know. Finally, resay or rewrite the complicated sentence in your own words to understand it better. Try this one more time. Read the following sentence and then reduce it to two or three words.

There is probably no group among the animal kingdom that has foresworn aggression altogether; fighting has been observed in virtually all species.[14]

Your rewrite: _____

Did you write *animals fight?* That is an acceptable translation of the sentence. Did you look up any words that you did not know first?

Strategy 4: Read paragraphs to discover what they say, and also what they do.

To discover what each paragraph SAYS, read it for meaning. Look for a topic sentence at or near the beginning to help you focus on the main idea. Look for sentences that qualify or further explain the topic sentence, and look for examples and other forms of supporting detail. Notice how the author has linked the sentences to one another. Be aware of pronouns and their antecedents, related words, the repetition of key words, and transitions. This will help you keep your mind on the subject and follow the author's line of thought. When you finish reading, be able to describe what most of the paragraph was about. Remember, however, that not all paragraphs are main idea paragraphs, so you also have to be aware of what a paragraph does, or how it functions in its context.

To discover what a paragraph DOES, read it for function. Does the paragraph introduce a chapter or a section of material in a chapter, present a main idea, sup-

▶

[13] Nancy V. Wood, *College Reading and Study Skills*, 5th ed. (Fort Worth: Harcourt Brace, 1996) 204.
[14] Virginia Walbot and Nigel Holder, *Developmental Biology* (New York: Random House, 1977) 5.

port an idea in a previous paragraph, use a transition to change the subject, or sum up or restate one or more of the main ideas? Be aware of both of these levels when you read paragraphs so that you can answer the questions: What does this paragraph say? and What does this paragraph do?

Strategy 5: Follow the UAS process for marking a book.

Step 1: Underline.

Read first and then underline selectively. Underline just enough so that you can look back at the paragraph, read what you have underlined, and get a quick review of what that paragraph was about. Circle words you want to emphasize, because they capture the main points, and number ideas when that is appropriate. For example, number ideas in a list, the parts of a whole, cause and effect, problem and solution, etc. It may also help to box transitions like *for example, next,* and *finally.*

You can add other symbols of your own:

1. Circle a word that you don't understand and put a V for Vocabulary next to it in the margin so that you can look it up or ask about it in class.
2. Write a Q for Question in the margin, and write your question to bring up in class or check on later.
3. Write a P for Paper Idea and write the idea in the margin, especially if you are assigned a paper in the class, and you are responsible for coming up with a topic.
4. Write your original ideas in the margin and use square brackets [ ] to set them off. This practice will make your reading more meaningful to you.

Step 2: Annotate.

Using your own words and as few words as possible, write the main idea, or what most of each paragraph is about, in the margin. This is called an annotation. Annotations should be brief, clear, and easy to understand so that you can read them later. If the material is difficult and condensed, and you must read it closely and thoroughly, make a note on every paragraph. If you do not need such complete and detailed notes, make annotations on some of the paragraphs or only at the end of each section. Do not write too much. Your purpose is to reduce the text to a manageable size that is easy to study later.

Step 3: Summarize.

Using your marginal annotations as a guide, write a summary, in your own words, of the main points made in the section of material you have just read. Write in complete thoughts and complete sentences so that your summary will be easy to understand later when you refer back to it. You may write summaries at the end of sections of material, at the end of chapters, and even at the end of books.

▶

A summary written on the white pages at the end of a book will help you remember that book forever.

How to Write a Summary:

1. Reread all of your underlinings and annotations.
2. Include the author's name, the title of the selection, and the main idea of the summary in the first sentence to focus the summary, thus: In "Title," Author explains / describes / argues that / shows that . . .
   Example: In "Learning to Read," Malcolm X describes how he got a homemade education in prison.
3. Write one-sentence summaries for each paragraph or major section of material. If one idea is developed in several paragraphs, write one sentence summarizing them as a group. Use your annotations in the margins and some of the ideas you underlined in the text to help you write these sentences. Don't copy. Put the author's ideas in your own words. You will understand and remember your own words better than someone else's words.
4. Reread the underlinings, annotations, and the draft of your summary. Cut material that doesn't contribute new information or that seems repetitive. Add material if you have left something out. Say what you have to say in as short a space as possible. Your summary should only be 10% to 20% as long as the original material you are summarizing.

Example of the UAS Process for Marking a Book

The following section of material comes from a psychology textbook. It has been underlined and annotated. The summary appears at the end.

WAYS OF REDUCING PREJUDICE[15]

Stephen F. Davis and Joseph Palladino

Reduce prejudice and break stereotypes

Need: ① equal status

Prejudice and its outward manifestation, discrimination, are common occurrences that everyone has experienced in one form or another. How can prejudice be reduced? Four decades ago Gordon Allport proposed that "equal status contact between majority and minority groups in the pursuit of common goals"[16] would reduce prejudice. His hypothesis predicts that close and extensive contact between group members will result in greater understanding because such contact shows that stereotypes are inaccurate.

Before this hypothesis becomes workable, however, several additional qualifications are needed. First, for contact to be effective in reducing prejudice, the parties in both groups must be of equal status. The importance of this factor is shown in the problems encountered in attempting to integrate public schools and urban neighborhoods. When one group is perceived as having lower status than another, it is difficult to overcome prejudice. ▶

---

[15] Stephen F. Davis and Joseph Palladino, *Psychology* (Englewood Cliffs: Prentice Hall, 1995) 743–744.
[16] Gordon Allport, *The Nature of Prejudice* (Reading: Addison Wesley, 1954) 281.

Second, contact is more effective in breaking down stereotypes and reducing prejudices when both groups are united in the pursuit of a common goal. For example, Muzafer Sherif and his colleagues demonstrated that competition between groups at a summer boys' camp resulted in strong prejudice and discrimination. But when the groups were forced to cooperate to achieve a common goal (starting the water-tank truck on which the camp's water supply depended), prejudice and discrimination decreased.[17] In sum, cooperation that is successful in achieving a goal generally leads to reduced prejudice and discrimination.

The Summary.

In "Ways of Reducing Prejudice" Davis and Palladino report on Gordon Allport's ideas for reducing prejudice and breaking stereotypes. Allport suggests that groups need to be placed in a situation where they have equal status and where they work together to reach a common goal that is important to them. Competition increases prejudice. Cooperation reduces it.

Handwritten margin note:
② Common goal
Cooperation works
Competition doesn't

EXERCISES AND READINGS

FOUR COLLABORATIVE CLASS EXERCISES

Exercise 1

Reduce and simplify sentences. *Whole class.*

Read the following five sentences and look up the words you do not know. Then, on a separate piece of paper, write in the briefest form the subject of the sentence and what the author says about it. Finally, rewrite the sentence in your own words as simply as possible. Share your rewrites with the rest of the class.

a. From a chapter in a sociology textbook entitled "Race and Ethnicity":

A race is a category composed of people who share biologically transmitted traits that members of a society deem socially significant.[18]

b. From a chapter in a political science textbook entitled "Political Parties and Interest Groups":

The story of women's movements in the United States is the story of groups whose members originally lacked political power, developed a sense of group consciousness, entered politics despite countless frustrations and setbacks, and, after long struggles, achieved some of their major political goals.[19]

---

[17] Muzafer Sherif et al., *Intergroup Conflict and Cooperation: The Robber's Cave Experiment* (Norman: Institute of Group Relations, 1961).

[18] John J. Macionis, *Sociology*, 6th ed. (Upper Saddle River: Prentice Hall, 1997) 320.

[19] James MacGregor Burns et al., *Government by the People*, 2nd ed. (Upper Saddle River: Prentice Hall, 1997) 201.

c. From a chapter in a marketing textbook entitled "Understanding Marketing and the Marketing Management Process":

Customer satisfaction depends on a product's perceived performance in delivering value relative to a buyer's expectations.[20]

d. From a political science textbook chapter entitled "The American Political Landscape":

Because where we live and what we are in terms of our religion and occupation affect how we vote, many who study voting and make predictions about it do so in terms of these factors—what are called **demographics.**[21]

e. From an essay entitled "Popular Music and Individual Differences":

By virtue of their growing presence in the lives of young people, electronic media play an increasingly important role in socialization, which is the acquisition, maintenance, and modification of the social beliefs, attitudes, and values that form the core of an individual's understanding of social reality.[22]

Exercise 2

Underline and make annotations on paragraphs. *Groups of students.*

Form groups of four students. Practice the first two steps of the UAS process, underlining and annotating, on the paragraphs below.

Paragraph 1: From a history textbook. This paragraph has been underlined and annotated for you. It is an example. Read the paragraph and discuss the underlining and annotating in this example. What strikes you about it?

THE NEW IMMIGRANTS

The Census Bureau figures show largest increase in population ever in 1990s.

The 2000 census showed that the nation's population during the 1990s grew by 32.7 million, a number greater than that of any other decade in U.S. history. Even the 1950s, which witnessed the post–World War II baby boom, could not compete against a decade marked by a huge number of immigrants and a birthrate that surpassed the death rate. At the beginning of the new millennium, Americans numbered 281.4 million.[23]

[20] Philip Kotler and Gary Armstrong, *Marketing: An Introduction*, 4th ed. (Upper Saddle River: Prentice Hall, 1997) 8.

[21] Burns et al., *Government by the People* 191.

[22] Christine Hall Hansen and Ronald D. Hansen, "Popular Music and Individual Differences," in Michael F. Petracca and Madeleine Sorapure, eds., *Common Culture* (Englewood Cliffs: Prentice Hall, 1995) 315.

[23] John Mack Faragher et al., *Out of Many*, 5th ed. (Upper Saddle River: Prentice Hall, 2006) 968.

Paragraph 2: From a psychology textbook. This paragraph has been underlined. Read the paragraph and the underlining. Then write an annotation that sums up the main idea in the paragraph. Read these annotations to your group and create a group annotation that everyone in the group finds acceptable.

NONVERBAL COMMUNICATION

Teachers often say that the first class session in a course is the most important one. As a student, your <u>initial impression</u> of the teacher may greatly influence your enjoyment of that first class. The <u>instructor's nonverbal communication</u> plays an important role in determining this initial impression. Which course would you rather take, <u>one in which the instructor never looks the students in the eye</u> and has (unusual mannerisms) (such as blinking rapidly, a behavior associated with anxiety) or <u>one in which the instructor looks each student in the eye,</u> (smiles frequently) and has an (easygoing, relaxed manner?) People's mannerisms and other nonverbal communications influence our impressions of them.[24]

Paragraph 3: From a biology textbook. This paragraph has been annotated. Read the paragraph and underline the words and phrases that capture the idea expressed in the margin. Students should work alone and then get together to discuss and negotiate how they want to underline this paragraph.

BIOTECHNOLOGY MAY EVENTUALLY ALLOW ALTERATIONS IN HUMAN GENOMES

The greatest concern of many observers is that genetic engineering offers the potential to change the human genome. As we pointed out, it is not yet possible to eliminate, say, insulin-dependent diabetes by cutting the defective gene out of fertilized eggs and inserting a functional one. But suppose that it does become possible (few molecular geneticists would be willing to bet against it). Then what? Could humankind agree on what constitutes a "bad" gene? Even if we could, would we be right? Probably most people could agree on diabetes, cystic fibrosis, and muscular dystrophy. But what about more subtle changes? What about genes that might alter personality? Or length of life? Or predisposition to take risks? Are we wise enough to direct our own evolution—or, if we develop the capability, are we wise enough to refrain?[25]

The author questions whether or not people will make wise decisions about genetic engineering.

Exercise 3

Read and write a summary of a section of material. *Groups of students.*

Form groups of four students. Half of the groups will read and write a summary of the first section of material, "Diversity in the Movies," and the other half will read and write a summary of the second section, "Dolphin Emotions." Prepare a report for the class by following the instructions for writing a group summary.

[24] Stephen F. Davis and Joseph J. Palladino, *Psychology* (Englewood Cliffs: Prentice Hall, 1995) 703.
[25] Audesirk and Audesirk, *Life on Earth* 261.

How to Write a Group Summary

Each member of the group, working individually, should first read the passage and study the underlining and the annotations for one of the following passages on pages 174–176. Each of these passages is a section of material from a college textbook. Then select one of the members of the group to write the summary, while the others contribute ideas and wording. Work for consensus among group members about what to include in the summary. Use the example of a summary on page 171 as a guide.

Follow these directions for writing a group summary.

1. Begin the summary with a sentence that includes the author's name, the title of the selection, and the main idea of the summary. The authors' names are in footnotes at the bottom of each page.

2. Using the marginal notes as a guide write four or five sentences that explain the ideas that are developed in the paragraphs.

3. Briefly write a concluding idea, if there is one.

4. Reread the summary and add or delete material if necessary. Discuss the wording and rewrite until the group is satisfied that the summary is clear and accurate.

Read the summary that your group has written to the rest of the class.

Passage 1: From a history of film textbook.

DIVERSITY IN THE MOVIES

African Americans are having a big influence on movies today.

Now for the good news. There is probably more variety in the contemporary American cinema than in any previous period. Nowhere is this better illustrated than in the recent proliferation of African American filmmakers. The 1990s saw an explosion of black talent on the screen. Although blacks account for only 13 percent of the American population, over 25 percent of movie audiences in the United States are black, and they have supported a wide variety of movies about African American life.

We are seeing many different kinds of movies about African Americans.

These movies range from neo-blaxploitation films like *New Jack City*, *Juice*, and *Gunmen*, to traditional biography pictures of famous African Americans like Spike Lee's *Malcolm X* (1992) and *What's Love Got to Do With It?* (1993, about singer Tina Turner), to comedies like the *House Party* movies and the Whoopie Goldberg blockbuster hit *Sister Act* (1992), to police thrillers like Carl Franklin's superb *One False Move* (1991), to avant-garde experimental films like Charles Burnett's *To Sleep With Anger* (1990) and Julie Dash's *Daughters in the Dust* (1990). There were also many black-and-white buddy films like *White Men Can't Jump* and the *Lethal Weapon* movies, which featured prominent roles for African American actors. [. . .]

Gays and people from ethnic minorities are making more movies.

Other minorities have also found representation on the American screen, though to a lesser extent. Throughout the 1990s, the cherished ideal of the American melting pot could certainly be substantiated by such movies as *My Own Private Idaho* (1992), directed by the gay filmmaker Gus Van Sant; Robert Rodriguez's Mexican American *El Mariachi* (1992); *Mississippi Masala*

(1992), by Mira Nair from India; the Chinese American sleeper hit *The Joy Luck Club* (1993), directed by Wayne Wang, from a novel by Amy Tan; and literally dozens of movies directed by émigré filmmakers like Hong Kong's John Woo, Holland's Paul Verhoeven, Brazil's Hector Babenco, Sweden's Lasse Hallström, Germany's Wolfgang Petersen, and Brits and Aussies galore.

The status of women filmmakers has also vastly improved. Today there are about two dozen women directors working in the mainstream Hollywood cinema, more than in any previous period. As with any other grouping, women filmmakers have made all sorts of movies, at different levels of accomplishment. In the real world, as opposed to theoretical wishful thinking, talent and sensitivity are more important determinants of success than gender. [. . .]

At their best, women directors have brought something entirely new and valuable to the table. Some of them have made their mark with small, personal movies that probably could not have been made as effectively by male directors simply because the materials required a sympathetic insider's point of view. Allison Anders's *Gas Food Lodging* (1992) as well as Martha Coolidge's bittersweet *Rambling Rose* (1991) and *Angie* (1994) clearly reveal a feminine sensibility at work.[26]

More women are making movies than ever before.

They bring a unique perspective to their film-making.

440 words

Passage 2: From a philosophy textbook.

DOLPHIN EMOTIONS

Many people say that we cannot claim that animals have personalities or emotions like our own. Because we can't get a first-hand report from animals about their subjective states, we do not know what's going on inside them. The best we can do, then, is to infer internal states and motivations from outward behavior, and we certainly have to be careful doing that. Nonetheless, many scientists believe that a number of animals do experience emotions of one sort or another, and dolphins may be among them.

animals experience emotion

No one disputes that dolphins feel isolation from other dolphins keenly. Some individuals who have been cut off from their families and schools behave in ways that suggest grief. Some have stopped eating and died. Mothers whose calves have died have become listless, apparently mourning their loss.

dolphins feel isolated

Some trainers claim that individual dolphins have distinct personalities, differing in terms of curiosity, timidity, playfulness, aggression, speed of learning, and patience. ① Some enjoy swimming with humans more than others. ② Some like learning new behaviors more than others. ③ Even mothers differ; some refuse to cut the apron strings, while others encourage their young to become independent. Dolphins also seem to have what we call moods. They can be eager to work some days, lackadaisical on others, and stubbornly uncooperative on still others.

personalities

moods

[26] Louis Giannetti and Scott Eyman, *Flashback*, 3rd ed. (Englewood Cliffs: Prentice Hall, 1996) 540–543.

Perhaps most impressive, however, is that dolphins can act in ways that suggest that they're <u>sensitive to the moods of humans</u> they've come to know. Laura Urian, of Florida's Dolphin Research Center, tells the following story. She was particularly fond of a dolphin named Halley. One day she arrived at the Center to find that the dolphin had died. Upset by Halley's death, Laura approached her work with the other dolphins visibly saddened. While Laura was doing the morning feeding, however, a dolphin named Theresa did something very unusual. Theresa *never* does flips, but while Laura was feeding her, she executed a series of six of them. Had Theresa taken note of Laura's mood? While it is impossible to know precisely what Theresa's sense of things was, certainly one interpretation is that she could understand Laura's emotional state because she is capable of similar feelings herself and was trying to cheer Laura up in her own way.[27]

sensitive to others

example

390 words

Exercise 4

Practice the UAS process for marking books. *Individuals, then Groups of Students.*

Form groups of four students. Turn to Reading 2, "The Mechanisms of Learning and Memory Are Poorly Understood" by Teresa Audesirk and Gerald Audesirk on page 182. Working individually, read, underline, and write annotations on this textbook passage. With your group, compare and discuss what you have underlined and what you have written in the margins. Then write a group summary. Follow the steps in Exercise 3 above.

Read the summary your group has written to the rest of the class.

THREE READING EXERCISES: ABOUT LEARNING AND MEMORY

The following three readings are drawn from a book and from college textbooks for biology and psychology. All three provide different perspectives on learning and memory, including what recent research tells us about learning and memory and some ideas about how to improve them.

[27] Thomas I. White, *Discovering Philosophy* 84.

"We're Born to Learn"[28]

RITA SMILKSTEIN

Explanatory Notes: *The following passages come from a book that explains how the brain works when it is learning. It also suggests how students can work with the brain's natural learning process to help them become better learners. Have you ever tried to improve your ability to learn? As you read this essay, underline selected passages and write some annotations in the margins.*

How the Brain Learns

One challenge for educators is to learn about the brain's innate and natural learning, thinking, and remembering processes if they are to teach the way the brain naturally functions.   1

Dendrites and Learning

Figure 5-1 is a picture of dendrites growing. This is a picture of learning because, as we are learning, specific neurons are growing specific new dendrites for that specific new object of learning. Then other neurons' axons connect with these dendrites, as well as with other neurons' bodies, at connection points called synapses. [. . .]   2

The growing and connecting of dendrites *are* learning. [. . .] In fact, as we feel ourselves learning, instead of saying, "I feel I'm getting it; I'm learning it," we could more accurately say, "I feel my dendrites growing and my synapses connecting."   3

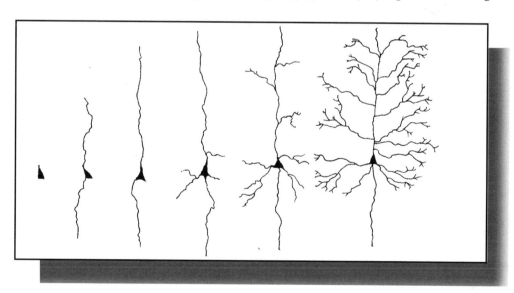

FIGURE 5-1 *Growing Dendrites = Learning*

[28] Rita Smilkstein, *We're Born to Learn* (Thousand Oaks: Corwin Press, 2003) 52, 56, 71–73, 86, 90–91, 102–103.

The Brain's Innate Resources and Rules

The brain's innate abilities and processes constitute the brain's innate resources for learning. 4

The Brain's Innate Resources

- The brain has a natural learning process.

- The brain has an innate sense of logic.

- The brain is an innate pattern seeker.

- The brain is an innate problem solver.

- The brain is innately imaginative and creative (can see in new ways).

- The brain is innately motivated to learn.

. . . .

Five Rules of How the Brain Learns

1. *Dendrites, synapses, and neural networks grow only from what is already there.* We learn by connecting new learning to something we already know and then constructing new levels of neural/knowledge structures, level by level, twig by twig, from that prerequisite foundation. Thus, to teach or learn something new, we must always start with something familiar as the foundation from which to construct the next level of knowledge or skill. [. . .] 5

2. *Dendrites, synapses, and neural networks grow for what is actively, personally, and specifically experienced and practiced.* As people actively practice an object of learning, they get better at what they are practicing because their brains are growing more dendrites, synapses, and neural networks for that specific object of learning. The larger the networks get, the more naturally and automatically they can think about, remember, and use that object of learning. Unfortunately, in the same way, if an experience is negative or abusive and it is repeated—practiced—often enough, that network will get stronger; and learners will become better at (become more and more accustomed to) being abused.[. . .] 6

3. *Dendrites, synapses, and neural networks grow from stimulating experiences.* Because learning, thinking, and remembering are active physiological, chemical, electrical phenomena, stimulation is needed to arouse the brain to grow new neural structures and fire synapses. For example, a stimulating experience would be processing with others, as when getting and giving feedback about an object of learning. Stimulating experiences also arouse the brain to use its innate resources, that is its impulsion to seek patterns, solve problems, and understand how the world works and how to make it work. These are activities that cause neural structures to grow and connect. And, again, even negative and abusive experiences are stimulating because they impel us to see how that abusive world works and how to act and survive in it. 7

4. *Use it or lose it.* If people stop doing something that they had previously learned, even if it is enjoyable or useful, after a while they might, because of neural pruning, forget some or all of it:

   a. A boy takes skiing lessons for 3 months when he is 8 and then does not ski again for 10 years. He might have to start over again from the beginning because he will probably have lost the small amount of dendrites, synapses, and neural networks he had grown in those earlier few months. As noted above, the brain prunes structures that are not being used.

   b. A girl rides her bike every day from the age of 8 until she goes to college 10 years later and then does not ride a bike for the next 10 years. She might have trouble starting again after that hiatus, but it will not take long before she recovers her skill because she will not have totally lost the vast volume of dendrites, synapses, and neural networks she had previously grown. Although the brain prunes unused structures, when those structures are vast and deeply embedded from years of constant use, pruning will have less of an effect.

   c. A student takes a first-level math course during the spring term and does not think about math all summer. The following fall, in the second-level math course, she cannot remember everything she knew from the previous spring term.

   d. A young man who had been emotionally abused as a child is always repeating, as negative self-talk, what his alcoholic father had told him, that he is stupid, a loser, worthless. But the young man, seeking help, joins a therapy group. In this group, he comes to understand where his negative self-image and self-talk came from and that, by understanding and using the "use it or lose it" rule, he can lose that negative network by not repeating its negative words, by rejecting them. He also starts to practice positive self-talk in order to grow a new, positive neural network. The more he practices the positive self-talk and ignores and rejects the negative talk, the stronger the positive network will grow and the weaker the negative one will become, perhaps atrophying altogether over time. [. . .]

5. *Emotions affect learning.* Emotions produce chemicals that enter the brain and physiologically affect the synapses and, consequently, the brain's ability to think, learn, and remember. Thus, emotions and thinking, learning, and remembering are inextricably bound together.

. . . .

Learning from Experience

Dendrites, Synapses, and Neural Networks Are Our Eyes

Our dendrites, synapses, and neural networks, which grow as a result of our personal experiences, are our knowledge; they are the eyes with which we see. A student brought this home to me. He was in his 50s and, having suffered a debilitating physical injury that had ended his career as a mechanic, was at the community college to retrain for a new career. He was in my basic grammar course because he needed to improve his reading and writing skills. He was an excellent student, mature, motivated, a fast learner, and one of the highest achievers in the class.

About halfway through the term, he had to go to the hospital for surgery and missed a week of school. When he returned, I invited him to my office for tutoring so he could catch up. As he sat next to my desk and I stood by my office chalkboard about to go through the lessons he had missed, I thought to myself, "He's very smart and catches on quickly. I can go through these lessons faster with him by himself than I was able to do with the whole class." So I began writing one of the new grammatical constructions on the board, explaining as I went, not giving him the time he would have had in class to try it on his own, talk about it, practice it, get feedback, assess his work, and try it again. [. . .] 15

After I had finished, I asked him to write a sentence using the new construction. He sat silently staring at the board. He was not able to do it. He had not understood. I asked why not, had I talked too fast? Then he said something that taught me a lesson I have never forgotten: 16

"No. But if you don't have eyes to see it, you can't see it." 17

I had not given him the opportunity to grow his new eyes. He had not had the opportunity to grow his new dendrites and synapses that would have made it possible for him to see, to understand, to use this new grammar concept. It was not that he was not fully capable of learning this concept; it was that he had not had the time and practice every learner needs in order to grow the specific new dendrites, synapses, and neural networks for seeing, understanding, and having skill for a specific new object of learning. 18

. . . .

A Handout for Students

Students appreciate receiving a handout of "The Major Points About Learning," in the box below, along with the following advice: 19

"Put this in your notebook, tape it to your bathroom mirror, and read it at least three times a day." 20

Major Points About Learning

1. Your brain was born to learn, loves to learn, and knows how to learn.

2. You learn what you practice.
   - Practice is making mistakes, correcting mistakes, learning from them, and trying over, again and again.
   - Making and learning from mistakes is a natural and necessary part of learning.

3. You learn what you practice because when you are practicing your brain is growing new fibers (dendrites) and connecting them (at synapses). This is what learning is.

(continued)

> **Major Points About Learning** (continued)
>
> 4. Learning takes time because you need time to grow and connect dendrites.
>
> 5. If you don't use it, you can lose it. Dendrites and synapses can begin to disappear if you don't use them (if you don't practice or use what you have learned).
>
> 6. Your emotions affect your brain's ability to learn, think, and remember.
>   - Self-doubt, fear, etc., prevent your brain from learning, thinking, and remembering.
>   - Confidence, interest, etc., help your brain learn, think, and remember.
>
> 7. Remember, you are a natural-born learner.

1581 words

Strategy Questions

1. Read the following paragraph from the book excerpts you just read and circle every word that the author has used to link the sentences to one another. Circle pronouns and their antecedents, related words, the repetition of key words, and transitions. This exercise has been started for you.

   3. Dendrites, synapses, and neural networks (grow) from (stimulating experiences.) Because learning, thinking, and remembering are active physiological, chemical, electrical phenomena, (stimulation) is needed to arouse the brain to (grow new) neural structures and fire synapses. For example, a stimulating experience would be processing with others, as when getting and giving feedback about an object of learning. Stimulating experiences also arouse the brain to use its innate resources, that is its impulsion to seek patterns, solve problems, and understand how the world works and how to make it work. These are activities that cause neural structures to grow and connect. And, again, even negative and abusive experiences are stimulating because they impel us to see how that abusive world works and how to act and survive in it.

2. What types of supporting details are found in this reading selection? Refer to the list on pages 159–160.

3. Write a summary of the selection. Use the instructions and the model on page 171 to help you.

Study Reading Questions

1. What are dentrites, synapses, and neural networks? How are they related to learning?

2. What are the innate resources in the brain that facilitate learning?

3. What are the five rules of how the brain learns? Put these in your own words.

4. When the student who had missed classes told the author that he did not "have eyes to see it," what did she take that to mean?

5. What are the 7 major points about learning? Put these in your own words.

Critical Reading and Thinking Questions

1. Reflect on the brain's "innate resources" listed on page 178. Think about yourself as a learner and provide examples of your own personal experiences with these innate resources. Are they all true of you? Are some more true than others? Which? Why?

2. How do positive emotions (e.g., excited about the topic, motivated to learn, feel you can learn, etc.) influence your learning? How do negative emotions (e.g., fear of failure, lack of confidence) influence your learning? How can you adjust your emotional state to help you learn?

3. Reread the "Major Points About Learning" on pages 180–181. Select one of those points and write a paragraph in which you elaborate on it to show how you could use it to help you learn.

Reading 2

The Mechanisms of Learning and Memory Are Poorly Understood[29]

TERESA AUDESIRK AND GERALD AUDESIRK

Explanatory Notes: *The following is taken from a college biology textbook. The authors are married and teach at the University of Colorado at Denver.* **What do you think biologists can teach us about memory?** *As you read this selection, underline selected words and phrases, use your own words to write annotations in the margins, and then write a summary of the selection. Use the example on page 171 as a guide.*

Although theories abound as to the cellular mechanisms of learning and memory, we are a long way from understanding these phenomena. In mammals, and particularly in humans, however, we do know a fair amount about two other aspects of learning and memory: the time course of learning and some of the brain sites involved in learning, memory storage, and recall.

Memory May Be Brief or Long Lasting

Experiments show that learning occurs in two phases: an initial **working memory** followed by **long-term memory**. For example, if you look up a number in the phone book, you will probably remember the number long enough to dial but for-

[29] Audesirk and Audesirk, *Life on Earth* 503–504.

get it promptly thereafter. This is working memory. But if you call the number frequently, eventually you will remember the number more or less permanently. This is long-term memory.

Some working memory seems to be electrical in nature, involving the repeated activity of a particular neural circuit in the brain. As long as the circuit is active, the memory stays. If the brain is distracted by other thoughts, or if electrical activity is interrupted, such as by electroconvulsive shock or by a concussion, the memory disappears and cannot be retrieved no matter how hard you try. In other cases, working memory involves temporary biochemical changes within neurons of a circuit, with the result that synaptic connections between them are strengthened.

Long-term memory, on the other hand, seems to be structural—the result, perhaps, of persistent changes in the expression of certain genes. It may require the formation of new, permanent synaptic connections between specific neurons or the permanent strengthening of existing but weak synaptic connections, for example, by increasing the area of synaptic contacts. These new or strengthened synapses last indefinitely, and the long-term memory persists unless certain brain structures are destroyed. Working memory can be converted into long-term memory, apparently by the hippocampus, which processes new memories then transfers them to the cerebral cortex for permanent storage.

Learning, Memory, and Retrieval May Be Controlled by Separate Regions of the Brain

Learning, memory, and the retrieval of memory seem to be separate phenomena, controlled by separate areas of the brain. Ample evidence shows that the hippocampus (part of the limbic system) is involved in learning. For example, intense electrical activity occurs in the hippocampus during learning. Even more striking are the results of hippocampal damage. A person whose hippocampus is destroyed retains most of his or her memories but is unable to learn anything that occurs after the loss. One victim was still unable to recall his address or find his way home after 6 years at the same residence. He could be entertained indefinitely by reading the same magazine over and over, and people whom he saw regularly required reintroduction at each encounter. People with extensive hippocampal damage can recall events momentarily, but the memory rapidly fades, as does the memory of a dream upon awakening. This phenomenon has led to the hypothesis that the hippocampus is responsible for transferring information from working into long-term memory.

Retrieval, or recall, of established long-term memories is localized in another area of the brain, the outer **temporal lobes** of the cerebral hemispheres. In a famous series of experiments in the 1940s, neurosurgeon Wilder Penfield electrically stimulated the temporal lobes of conscious patients undergoing brain surgery. The patients did not merely recall memories but felt that they were experiencing the past events right there in the operating room!

The site of storage of complex long-term memories is much less clear. The psychologist Karl Lashley spent many years training rats and subsequently damaging parts of their brains in an effort to locate the site of the memory, but failed. None of the injuries could erase a memory completely. In 1950, a frustrated Lashley wrote: "I sometimes feel, in reviewing the evidence on the localization of the memory trace, that the necessary conclusion is that learning is not possible."

Some researchers suggest that each memory is stored in numerous distinct places in the brain. Or perhaps memories are stored like a hologram image, both everywhere and nowhere at the same time: The memory is more precise if the whole brain is intact, but each "bit" (probably several thousands of neurons) of cerebral hemisphere can store an essentially complete memory. Further research might provide definitive answers, but for now, the storage site of memories remains an unsolved mystery.

8

800 words

Strategy Questions

1. Monitor your comprehension of the essay that you have just read. Jot down on paper all that you can remember from reading it. Answer these questions: What was the subject? and What did the author say about it? Now check what you have written against your underlining and marginal notes. Have you left anything out?
2. Were any of the clues to main ideas present in this essay? Recheck the list on pages 167–168 to see if any of these were used to make the main ideas stand out. Which were used? What main ideas did they emphasize and clarify?
3. Write a summary of the essay. Use the instructions and the model on page 171 to help you.

Study Reading Questions

1. What are the two types of memory discussed here? Describe them.
2. Working memory seems to be electrical. What is the nature of long-term memory?
3. Where is the retrieval of long-term memory located?
4. Where do researchers believe memory is stored?

Critical Reading and Thinking Questions

1. What do you think about the methods of testing memory used by Penfield and Lashley? Do you think it is ethical to test animals and human beings in such a manner? Why or why not? Can you think of any alternative ways to test memory?
2. What information and explanations in the first article ("We're Born to Learn") helped you read and understand this second selection from a biology textbook? How were these two selections similar, and how were they different?
3. Speculate on why memory storage is still such a mystery to scientists. Why is it more difficult to test memory than something like vision or hearing?

8. **Use retrieval cues.** The more retrieval cues you have, the more likely it is that 11
you will remember something. One way to establish automatic retrieval cues
is to create routines and structure. For example, when you come in the door,
put your house and car keys in the same place every time. Then when you ask
yourself, "Where did I put my keys?" the fact that you have a special place for
the keys serves as a retrieval cue. Sometimes something that is clearly not routine or structured can serve as a retrieval cue. For example, if you want to remember to do something before you go to bed, leave an unusual item on your
bed (perhaps a shoe or a sock); when it's time to go to bed, you'll see the unusual object, and that should help remind you of what you wanted to do.

Similarly, if you are having difficulty remembering something, you might 12
find it useful to return to the setting where you last used that information.
That way the cues present when you used that information will be available
and may help you remember. If you can't do that, try to recreate the setting
vividly in your mind in as much detail as possible, including the thoughts and
feelings you were having at the time. This may provide enough contextual cues
to pry the information from you.

9. **Rely on more than memory alone.** Human memory is less than perfect, so 13
it's wise to make use of other tools. Write down the things you need to remember, and then post a note or list of those things somewhere obvious, such
as on your bulletin board or refrigerator door. Put all the dates you want to
remember on a calendar, and then put the calendar in a conspicuous place. If
you witness an accident, immediately write down everything you saw and
heard in as much detail as you can; then use your written account to refresh
your memory periodically.

10. **Be aware that your own personal schemata may distort your recall of** 14
events. As noted earlier, people sometimes unknowingly "rewrite" past events
to fit their current image or their desired image of themselves and their past decisions. Being on guard against such distortions may help you avoid them.

Finally, while you're working to improve your memory, keep in mind that 15
forgetting is not always a bad thing. Most of us have many experiences we would
like very much to forget, and forgetting them might be a blessing. A study of children whose home life had been so troubled that they had been placed for a time in
a child guidance clinic found that changing or "rewriting" their memories of early
childhood made a difficult, disadvantaged life less of a liability. For example, when
these children were interviewed 30 years later, those who incorrectly recalled their
childhood as fairly normal were also the ones who had been able to develop a basically stable, conventional life of their own.[32] Forgetting is sometimes a blessing,
rather than a curse.

. . . .

---

[32] L. N. Robins, S. P. Schoenberg, S. J. Holmes, K. S. Ratcliff, A. Benham, & J. Works. (1985). Early
home environment and retrospective recall: A test for concordance between siblings with and without psychiatric disorders. *American Journal of Orthopsychiatry, 55,* 27–41.

Improving Your Memory for Textbook Material

You can use all the principles discussed in this chapter to help you remember material from textbooks in most of your courses. The key to storing new material in long-term memory is making associations between that material and information that is already in LTM. If you simply passively reread the chapter over and over, you are not likely to store, retain, or retrieve information effectively.[33] Highlighting or underlining passages makes for a slight improvement, if only because you are at least thinking about which material is most important.

A more effective technique is to prepare an outline of the chapter before reading it so that you have associations and links ready to be made when you actually read the material. Some textbooks (including this one) provide you with a ready-made outline at the beginning of the chapter, but creating one yourself forces you to start thinking about the content of the chapter and how one section relates to another. Then, as you read, write comments under the headings of your outline. Your personal summary will not only help you remember material as you are reading the chapter, but will be useful when you are reviewing the material for a test.

Another memory-enhancing technique is to rehearse the material as you read the chapter. You might write in the margin of the text as you go along, recording your reactions, questions, ideas about how the new material may relate to other material, thoughts about how you might apply what you are learning in your own life, and so on. Try to relate the new material to all sorts of things you already know, expressing this relationship in your own words. You can also work with a friend, taking turns challenging each other with questions that draw on material from different sections or paragraphs. However you go about it, integrating and elaborating on the textual material forces you to process it and to form new associations among the pieces of information that you are storing.

Elaborative rehearsal offers two distinct benefits: It ties the new material to information already in memory, and it generates a multitude of retrieval cues to help you recall the material when you need it. Even after you feel well prepared, continued rehearsal may improve your retention. In fact, studies have shown that if you *overlearn* a subject in school, such as a foreign language or a part in a school play, you may be able to remember much of it for the rest of your life.[34]

A more ambitious, and even more effective, system for studying is known by the letters of its five stages: SQRRR (or SQ3R, for short):

1. **Survey.** Before you even start to read, look quickly at the chapter outline, the headings of the various sections in the chapter, and the chapter summary. This

16

17

18

19

20

21

[33] M. A. McDaniel, P. J. Waddill, P. S. Shakesby. (1996). Study strategies, interest, and learning from text: The application of material appropriate processing. In D. Herrmann, C. McEvoy, C. Hertzog, P. Hertel, & M. K. Johnson (Eds.), *Basic and applied memory research: Theory in context* (pp. 385–397). Mahwah, NJ: Erlbaum. See also R. R. Wilke. (2001). The effect of active learning on college students' achievement, motivation, and self-efficacy in a human physiology course for non-majors. *Dissertation Abstracts International Section A: Humanities and Social Sciences, 61,* 4329.

[34] H. P. Bahrick. (1984). Semantic memory in permastore: Fifty years of memory for Spanish learned in school. *Journal of Experimental Psychology: General, 113,* 1–31, and H. P. Bahrick & L. K. Hall. (1991). Lifetime maintenance of high school mathematics content. *Journal of Experimental Psychology: General, 120,* 20–33, and T. Noice & H. Noice. (2002). The expertise of professional actors: A review of recent research. *High Ability Studies, 13,* 7–20.

gives you an overview of what you will be reading, and helps you organize and integrate the material as you go along.

2. **Question.** Before you start to read, translate each heading in the chapter into 22 questions about the text to follow. Before reading a chapter, for example, that includes the heading "Short-Term Memory", you might form questions such as "Why is it called 'short-term'?" "Is there another type of memory that lasts longer?" "What good is memory if it's only short-term?" "Why do memories fade?"

3. **Read.** Now read the first section in the chapter, looking for answers to the ques- 23 tions you have posed. If you discover major points not directly related to your questions, either revise your old questions to encompass the new material or make up new questions.

4. **Recite.** Once you finish reading a section, close the book, and recite from mem- 24 ory the answers to your questions and any other major points that you can remember. You can also jot down your answers in outline form or recite them to someone else. Then open the book and check to make sure that you have covered all the key points raised in the section. Repeat steps 3 and 4 for each section of the chapter.

5. **Review.** After reading through the whole chapter, review your notes, and then 25 recite or say mentally your questions and answers from memory. Relate the material to other ideas, to experiences in your own life, or to familiar things. Try to think of particularly good examples or illustrations of key points or concepts in the chapter. Get involved.

The SQ3R method forces you to react—to enter into a dialogue with the text. This 26 interaction makes the material more interesting and meaningful and improves your chances of recalling it. It also organizes the material and relates it to what you already know. This method certainly takes longer than simply reading a chapter does, but you will save time later on when studying for exams.

2180 words

Strategy Questions

1. Were any of the clues to main ideas present in this essay? Recheck the list on pages 167–168 to see if any of these were used to make the main ideas stand out. Which were used? What main ideas did they emphasize and clarify?
2. What did you underline, and what did you jot in the margin for the last section titled "Improving Your Memory for Textbook Material?" Compare the way you marked these paragraphs with the rest of the class.
3. Write a summary of the essay. Use the instructions and the model on page 171 to help you.

Study Reading Questions

1. What are mnemonics? Give an example.
2. What are three factors that interfere with memory?
3. What are three ways you can use to improve your memory?
4. What are three ways to improve your memory when reading textbook material?

Critical Reading and Thinking Questions

1. List three methods from this selection you might use to improve your own memory. Why do they appeal to you?
2. What are the authors' purposes for writing about memory? Identify at least two purposes and explain how the authors meet them.
3. Why is the subject of memory an important and interesting issue for biologists, psychologists, and students? Think about how an understanding of memory affects each of these groups and the work they do. Refer to the three readings in the chapter to support your answers.
4. Compare the subject matter of all three articles on memory. How are they the same? How are they different? Account for these similarities and differences.

THREE APPLICATION EXERCISES

Exercise 1

Locate and copy a difficult sentence in one of your other textbooks.

Reduce and simplify the sentence by rewriting it briefly in your own words. Bring it to class to use as an example of this strategy.

Exercise 2

Underline and take marginal notes in one of your other textbooks.

Bring your book to class. Open the book to a representative page, and compare your underlining and notes with those of other students in your class.

Exercise 3

Write a summary of one chapter in one of your other textbooks and bring it to class.

Discuss what you included in your summary and why. Discuss any problems you had and how you solved them.

Review and Evaluate the Strategies

The following is a review of the five strategies you learned in this chapter:

1. Monitor your comprehension of sentences, paragraphs, and sections.
2. Use the author's clues to help you find the main ideas.
3. Reduce and simplify difficult sentences.
4. Read paragraphs to discover what they say, and also what they do.
5. Follow the UAS process for marking a book.

Make a personal evaluation of these strategies:

1. Underline your favorite strategies in the preceding list.
2. Make a check mark by those you want to continue to use.
3. Cross out any you probably will not continue to use. What are your reasons for rejecting them?

_____

_____

CHAPTER

6

Understand Visual Materials

CHAPTER GOALS:

1. **To increase your awareness of visual material.**

2. **To identify types of visual materials along with their special characteristics.**

3. **To suggest some ways to interact with visual material.**

4. **To provide you with five strategies for reading visual materials and relating them to the rest of the text.**

Why Is It Important to Study the Visuals?

You may be wondering why this book includes an entire chapter on reading and understanding visual material. In Chapter 1 the observation was made that modern college textbooks are big, beautiful, and reader friendly. One reason for this is the amount of **visual materials** they contain: You can expect your college textbooks to include photographs that represent events from modern times and times past, illustrations and drawings of various types, reproductions of paintings and other fine art, summary charts of information, all types of graphs and analytical charts, as well as cartoons, diagrams, and geographical maps. Many of these visuals have been generated by computer programs that create imaginative, original, and effective displays and features designed to help you understand the rest of the chapter. Visuals make written explanations clearer, more interesting, and more memorable.

This chapter focuses on visuals that organize and present information. These include charts, graphs, tables of figures, geographical maps, and diagrams. Such visual materials appeal mostly to your logic and reason, and they are widely used in textbooks. The emphasis in this chapter, like all the chapters in this first half of the book, is on study reading, which, in this case, means understanding these types of visuals and how they relate to the text that surrounds them. Chapter 11 will focus on a different type of visual material. There you will be taught to recognize visual argument that appeals to emotions as well as to reason, and you will be taught to analyze, interpret, and evaluate these types of visuals as they appear in all types of media, including the World Wide Web. The emphasis in Chapter 11, like the other chapters in the second half of the book, is on critical reading and thinking.

Every visual you encounter is there for a specific purpose. For example, visuals can show general trends, point out similarities and differences, summarize and organize information, illustrate causes and effects, describe step-by-step processes, or illustrate the relationship between parts and the whole. Visuals sometimes teach facts, and at other times they serve as examples that clarify or prove major concepts. They are an integral part of the text, and learning to read them is a major part of reading comprehension.

Textbooks are not the only place that you will encounter quantities of visual material while you are in college. Your professors may illustrate their lectures with slides, films, maps, and various types of computer-generated models, charts, and graphs. Furthermore, some of your assignments may be on the Internet, the largest and most visual "textbook" in the world. Learning to read and interpret visual material is now an essential college skill.

Even though visual material can be of great benefit to comprehension, research shows that readers have a strong tendency to ignore it as they read. Or, they notice it only briefly, without stopping to understand and relate it to the rest of the text. Some professors have observed that their students seem to be afraid to try to figure out complicated visuals. If you are a typical beginning college reader who may often ignore the visual material in your books, this chapter and Chapter 11 will help you reverse that trend.

An Example of an Information-Packed Visual

Look at the chart in Figure 6-1 on page 194, which is taken from a biology textbook.[1] It teaches units of measurement for biology. Notice how much information has been included in this chart. The units of measurement are listed on the left, ranging from the largest unit at the top to the smallest unit at the bottom. Additional information about the units is listed across the bottom of the chart. Examples of objects that illustrate the comparative size of the units of measurement appear at the right to give you a better idea of sizes. Finally, in the shaded boxes to the left you are told what would be required to make each of the objects visible. The explanation of the figure in the caption below it provides more information about units of measurement in biology.

This visual presentation is clear and easy to understand because it follows a familiar numerical order and because it provides specific examples. It would be harder to grasp and remember this material if it were explained as a written text. The chart encourages you to learn by making associations: The picture of the tree is associated with the measurement of 100 meters, and a meter is associated with a yard. You learn from the chart that a yard is a bit shorter than a meter, so you imagine a tree that is somewhat taller than 100 yards. You can then make a quick

---

[1] Teresa Audesirk and Gerald Audesirk, *Life on Earth* (Upper Saddle River: Prentice Hall, 1997) 75.

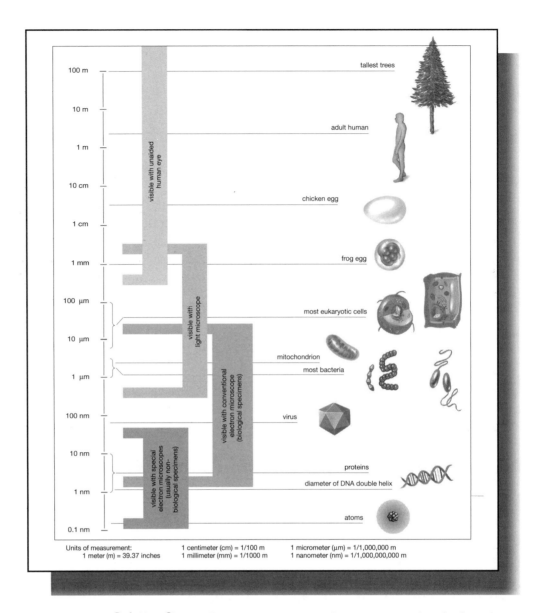

FIGURE 6-1 *Relative Sizes* Dimensions commonly encountered in biology range from about 100 meters (the height of the tallest redwoods) through a few micrometers (the diameter of most cells) to a few nanometers (the diameter of many large molecules). Note that, in the metric system (used almost exclusively in science), separate names are given to dimensions that differ by factors of 10, 100, and 1000.

association with something more familiar, like a football field, which is 100 yards long. The mental picture you create of the tree and its size will now stay in your memory longer than a verbal explanation of the same concept. One hundred meters will have instant meaning for you whenever you see this unit of measurement.

The chart you have just examined is an example of one type of visual presentation or tool. There are a number of other types. The next section will identify those types, along with some of their special characteristics.

Eight Types of Visuals That Present Information

Here is a list of eight common types of visual material you will encounter often in your reading, along with a description of their special characteristics and purposes.

1. **Pie Charts.** A pie chart looks like a pie that has been cut into pieces. These charts emphasize the various parts of a whole and what each part of the whole represents. If the parts of a pie chart are reported as percentages, the whole pie will represent 100%.

Examine a pie chart.

The pie charts in Figure 6-2 are taken from a government textbook, and they show the political party affiliations of people who report that they regularly watch the Fox news channel or the CNN news channel. Both charts show the parts that make up the whole of the regular viewers of these channels. The unidentified portion of the pie would presumably represent people who do not regularly view these news channels or who do not identify themselves as Republicans or Democrats. To the right of the charts is a brief explanation from the text itself that adds additional information about them.

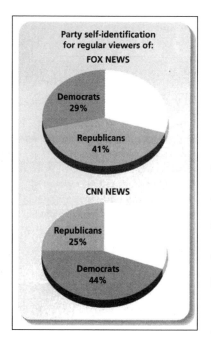

A conservative Republican from Arizona might watch the "liberal eastern networks" and complain about their biased news coverage while sticking to her own opinions. A liberal from New York will often complain about right-wing talk radio, even if he listens to it some nights on the way home from work (see Figure 6-2).[2]

(1) Which channel is watched by more Republicans than Democrats?

_____

(2) Which channel is watch more by Democrats than Republicans?

_____

(3) What conclusions would you draw from the preferences identified by these groups?

_____

FIGURE 6-2 *Partisanship and Preferred News Source*

Source: *The New York Times*, July 18, 2004.

---

[2] David B. Magleby, et al. *Government by the People*, 21st ed. (Upper Saddle River: Prentice Hall, 2006) 260.

2. **Flowcharts.** Flowcharts show the sequential steps of a process. The steps are usually boxed or circled and connected by lines to make it easier to see how the process flows from the beginning, through the steps, to the end.

Examine a Flowchart.

The flowchart in Figure 6-3 is from a chapter on producing services. It appears in a business textbook. The process described here is the time and steps involved in getting a roll of film developed in a store. Notice the steps, the arrows, and the explanations. What do the arrows contribute to this flow of activity?

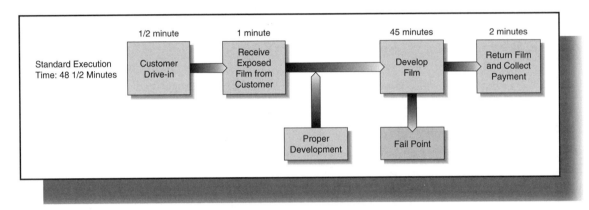

FIGURE 6-3 *Service-Flow Analysis*[3]

(1) What is the total amount of time used in this process?_____ Which step takes the most time? _____

(2) What do the two boxes below the main line of activity identify?_____ Why do the arrows attached to them point in different directions?

_____

(3) How does the flowchart help you understand the film development process? What can you conclude about the process?

_____

[3] Ricky W. Griffin and Ronald J. Ebert, *Business,* 4th ed. (Englewood Cliffs: Prentice Hall, 1996) 395.

3. Organization Charts. Organization charts describe the hierarchy and relationships among the employees or members of an organization.

Examine an organization chart.

The organizational chart in Figure 6-4 shows the over all organization of a large national union. The heads of the different departments on this chart might also have separate organizational charts that show how each department is organized. This chart comes from a business textbook.

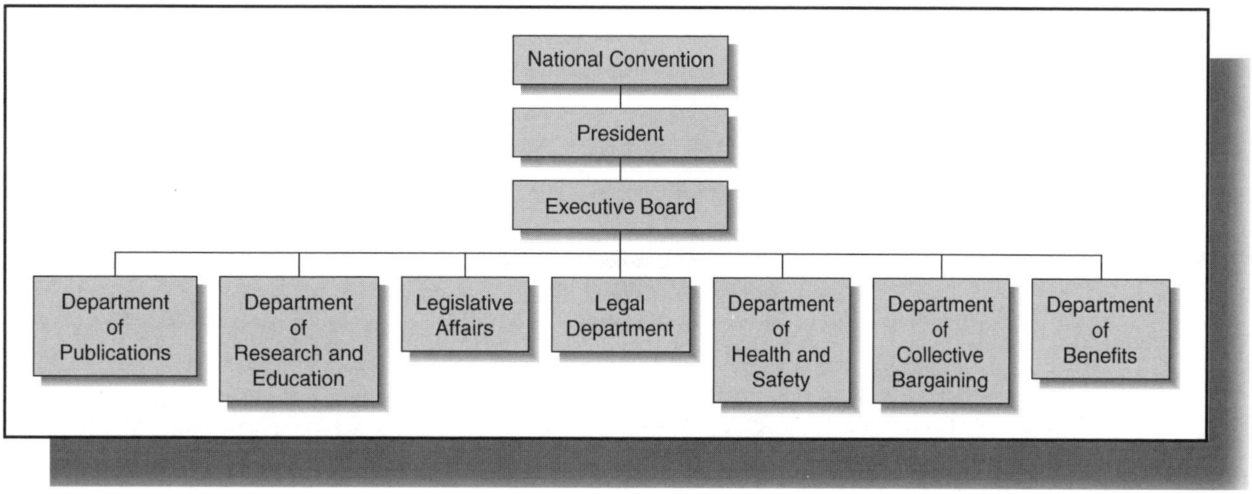

FIGURE 6-4 *Organization of a Large National Union*[4]

(1) Which entity has the most responsibility for this national union?_____

(2) What other two entities provide the rest of the leadership of this organization?

_____ How many departments carry on the

daily activities of the organization? _____

(3) What have you learned from examining this organization chart? What can you conclude?

_____

[4] Griffin and Ebert, *Business*, 4/e 328.

4. Line Graphs. A line graph has a vertical axis, which goes up and down; a horizontal axis, which goes across the page; and a line or lines plotted on the graph that show trends. To read a line graph you need first to understand what the graph is about in general. Read the caption and any verbal explanations that appear under the graph or in the text in which it is embedded. Then figure out what is plotted on the horizontal axis and what is plotted on the vertical axis.

Examine a line graph.

Figure 6-5 shows the curve of forgetting, or how rapidly people forget what they learn if they do not take any steps to help them remember it. The paragraphs of text that accompany this graph provide additional information. Notice what is plotted on the vertical and horizontal axes and what the lines represent.

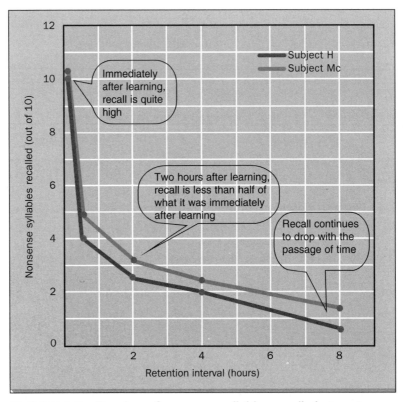

FIGURE 6-5 *Number of nonsense syllables recalled at various intervals following learning for two participants.* Recall dropped dramatically with time, but it was higher if they slept after learning. In agreement with Ebbinghaus's research, the greatest decrease in recall occurred very shortly after learning had taken place.
Source: *Jenkins and Dallenback (1924).*

The Curve of Forgetting

One of the most important findings of Ebbinghaus's research is the curve of forgetting. Ebbinghaus found that memory for learned material is best right after the learning session. As time passes, we forget more and more. This basic finding has been replicated (reproduced) numerous times since Ebbinghaus discovered it. As you can see from Figure 6-5, Jenkins and Dallenbach found that participants recalled the most when they were tested immediately after learning. The participants learned a list of 10 nonsense syllables and then were asked to recall the list 1/2 hour and 2, 4, and 8 hours later. One-half hour after the initial training session, the participants were able to recall only half of the list; their performance continued to deteriorate with the passage of time.[5] The importance of these results is clear: You can expect your best recall shortly after a learning session. Another important finding from the Ebbinghaus laboratory involves what is called *distributed practice.* Simply put, it is better to distribute learning trials across a period of time than to mass them in a single block of learning. "When it comes to learning, a little every day is the optimal way."[6] Of course, distributed practice is exactly the opposite of what students do when they cram for exams. Students who cram are relying on the high rate of recall immediately after learning trials. They often ignore the high rate of *forgetting* that occurs even immediately after learning. Most students cram because they don't properly plan their study time.[7]

Hermann Ebbinghaus (1850–1909) was a pioneer in the study of human memory.

(1) What is plotted on the vertical axis?_____

(2) What is plotted on the horizontal axis?_____

(3) What do the lines on this graph demonstrate?_____

_____ What conclusions can you draw about what people

have to do to remember what they learn? _____

[5] J. G. Jenkins & K. M. Dallenbach (1924). Oblivescence during sleeping and waking. *American Journal of Psychology, 35,* 605–612.

[6] A. Baddeley (2004). *Your memory: A user's guide.* Buffalo, NY: Firefly Books.

[7] Stephen F. Davis and Joseph Palladino, *Psychology,* 5th ed. (Upper Saddle River: Prentice Hall, 2007) 284–286.

5. **Bar Graphs.** On a bar graph information is plotted on bars that usually go up and down on the page, as in Figure 6-6, although they also sometimes go across the page, sideways, as on page 216. Read these graphs much as you would a line graph. Bar graphs usually plot numbers or percentages on the vertical axis. The bars represent items that are labeled either below or next to the bar. Bar graphs invite you to consider amounts and to make comparisons.

Examine a bar graph.

Figure 6-6 provides information about the careers beginning college students say they think they want to pursue. A paragraph of text that provides additional information appears to the right of the graph. Examine the vertical and horizontal axes and understand what each represents.

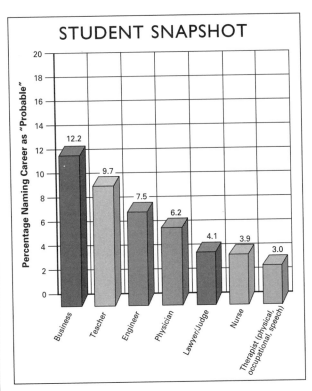

In almost all cases, professional work requires not just a college degree but also a graduate degree. Not surprisingly, therefore, professions are well represented among the occupations beginning college students say they hope to get after graduation, as shown in Figure 6-6.

FIGURE 6-6 *The Careers Most Commonly Named as Probable by First-Year College Students, 2004* Today's college students expect to enter careers that pay well and carry high prestige.

Source: *Sax et al. (2004).*[8]

[8] John J. Macionis, *Sociology.* 11th ed. (Upper Saddle River: Prentice Hall) 429.

(1) Notice the numbers on the vertical axis represent percentages, but the percentages only extend from 0% to 20%. Why? _____ _____ Calculate the total percent of students represented by the seven bars. Notice that slightly less than half of all beginning students are represented on this graph. What would you guess the remaining half of beginning students might report?

_____

(2) Notice that the bars on the horizontal axis are plotted from most to least. What is the effect of this placement?_____

(3) What do you conclude about the aspirations of entering college students?

_____

_____

6. Tables of Figures. Tables of figures present summaries of numerical data that are usually explained more fully in the text. It is important to read and understand all captions and labels that accompany tables of figures. Such tables often show trends, similarities, and differences, or they simply summarize data by presenting it in a format that is easy for the reader to examine.

Examine a table of figures.

Figure 6-7 appears in the Appendix of an American history textbook where demographics of the United States are reported. Note the subject of the table, the way in which the numbers are reported, and identify the information that appears in each of the four columns.

Immigration, by Origin (in thousands)			
Period	Europe	Americas	Asia
1820–30	106	12	—
1831–40	496	33	—
1841–50	1,597	62	—
1851–60	2,453	75	42
1861–70	2,065	167	65
1871–80	2,272	404	70

(continued)

FIGURE 6-7

Immigration, by Origin (in thousands) (continued)			
Period	Europe	Americas	Asia
1881–90	4,735	427	70
1891–1900	3,555	39	75
1901–10	8,065	362	324
1911–20	4,322	1,144	247
1921–30	2,463	1,517	112
1931–40	348	160	16
1941–50	621	355	32
1951–60	1,326	997	150
1961–70	1,123	1,716	590
1971–80	800	1,983	1,588
1981–90	762	3,616	2,738
1991–2000	1,100	3,800	2,200

Source: *Historical Statistics of the United States* (1975), *Statistical Abstract of the United States* (1991), Population Estimates Program, Population Division, U.S. Census Bureau, April 2001.

FIGURE 6-7[9] *(continued)*

(1) How are the numbers reported in this table? What do 12 and 3,800 represent in actual numbers?

_____

(2) What parts of the world would you guess are included in the column the "Americas?"

_____

(3) Which ten year period saw the greatest number of immigrants entering the United States?_____ Which saw the next greatest?

_____ What do you conclude about immigration in the

United States?_____

7. Geographical maps with legends. Geographical maps are used to show local, national, or worldwide trends, to invite comparison among various geographical locations, or to emphasize the special characteristics of particular locations. The legend on a map explains what the differently colored regions represent.

[9] John Mack Faragher, et al. "Appendix," *Out of Many: A History of the American People.* 5th ed. (Upper Saddle River: Prentice Hall) A–18.

Examine a geographical map with a legend.

The map in Figure 6-8 comes from a chapter about crime in a sociology textbook. Look at the legend to help you read this map. Read all of the text that accompanies the map to help you interpret it.

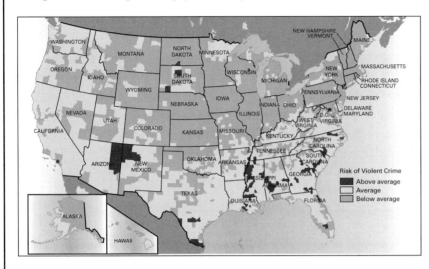

FIGURE 6-8 *Seeing Ourselves— National Map: The Risk of Violent Crime across the United States* This map shows the risk of becoming a victim of violent crime. In general, the risk is highest in low-income, rural counties that have a large population of men between the ages of fifteen and twenty-four. After reading through this section of the text, see whether you can explain this pattern.
Source: American Demographics magazine, December 2000 issue. Copyright © 2004 by Crain Communications, Inc.

Crimes against the person, also called *violent crimes,* are *crimes that direct violence or the threat of violence against others.* Violent crimes include murder and manslaughter (legally defined as "the willful killing of one human being by another"), aggravated assault ("an unlawful attack by one person upon another for the purpose of inflicting severe or aggravated bodily injury"), forcible rape ("the carnal knowledge of a female forcibly and against her will"), and robbery ("taking or attempting to take anything of value from the care, custody, or control of a person or persons by force or threat of force or violence and/or putting the victim in fear"). National Map 6-8 shows the risk of violent crime in counties all across the United States.[10]

(1) Identify four locations in the United States where the risk of violent crime is

above average: _____

(2) Identify four areas where the risk of violent crime is below average:_____

_____

(3) What have you learned from this map and the explanations about violent

crime in the United States? What do you conclude? _____

_____

[10] Macionis, *Sociology* 237.

8. **Diagrams.** Diagrams are used to show specific types of relationships among ideas. They may display cause-effect or comparison-contrast relationships, or they may lay out the steps in a chronological process. The maps you learned to make in Chapter 4 (pp. 122–126) to clarify organization are good examples of diagrams that show relationships. Another example is the diagram of the process of growing dendrites to illustrate how the brain learns on page 177. Notice the chronological organization in the dendrite diagram.

Examine a diagram.

The diagram in Figure 6-9 comes from a marketing textbook and compares two concepts described in the book. Read both the diagram and the accompanying text to help you understand the diagram.

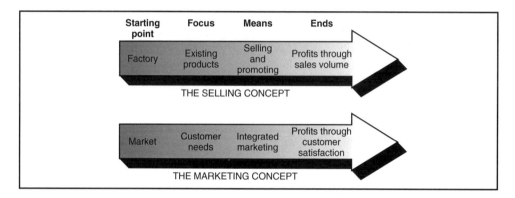

FIGURE 6-9 *The Selling and Marketing Concepts Contrasted*

Figure 6-9 contrasts the selling concept and the marketing concept. The selling concept takes an *inside-out* perspective. It starts with the factory, focuses on the company's existing products, and calls for heavy selling and promotion to obtain profitable sales. It focuses primarily on customer conquest—getting short-term sales with little concern about who buys or why.

In contrast, the marketing concept takes an *outside-in* perspective. As Herb Kelleher, Southwest Airlines' colorful CEO, puts it, "We don't have a marketing department; we have a customer department." And in the words of one Ford executive, "If we're not customer driven, our cars won't be either."[11] The marketing concept starts with a well-defined market, focuses on customer needs, and integrates all the marketing activities that affect customers. In turn, it yields profits by creating lasting relationships with the right customers based on customer value and satisfaction.[12]

[11] See David Lewis, "Southwest Staff Go Nuts (for Customers!)," *Sales & Marketing Institute*, May 2005, accessed at www.salesmarketing.org.nz/article623.html. For more on market orientation and firm performance, see Ahmet H. Kirca, Satish Jayachandran, and William O. Bearden, "Marketing Orientation: A Meta-Analytic Review and Assessment of Its Antecedents and Impact on Performance," *Journal of Marketing*, April 2005, pp. 24–41.

[12] Gary Armstrong and Philip Kotler, *Marketing: An Introduction*, 8th ed. (Upper Saddle River: Prentice Hall) 11.

(1) What is the first concept? _____ Where does it begin?

_____ Where does it end? _____

(2) What is the second concept? _____ Where does it begin?

_____ Where does it end? _____

(3) What have you learned about selling and marketing? _____

What do you conclude about these concepts as they affect your life as a consumer? _____

Create Visuals of Your Own When They Are Not Supplied by the Author

Making an effort to create mental pictures of descriptive passages wherever you encounter them, including those in poems, stories, and novels, can increase your understanding and memory of this material. Description also occurs in non-fiction writing. Look back at "Dolphin Emotions" on pages 175–176, for example. No pictures are supplied, but you can create a picture in your mind of the dolphin doing flips to raise the spirits of the person who feeds her. Even better, you can create a moving picture of what you see as you read. Many readers create mental pictures quite easily. Other readers who have never created mental pictures find they can do so quite easily once they become familiar with the concept. You can also learn to create other types of visuals when these are not supplied by the author. They might include summary tables of information, graphs, drawings, or flowcharts to help you summarize, visualize, and learn new information.

READING VISUALS: FIVE STRATEGIES

Here are five strategies that will help you focus on visual material in the first place and then read and interact with it critically to help you understand and remember the major concepts it represents.

Strategy 1: Make reading visuals a part of your reading process.

Look for visual material when you survey. As part of the survey, slow down and look at all of the visuals and read their captions. This is a quick way to become acquainted with many of the major ideas in a chapter before you read it. When you

▶

read, notice all cross references to visuals in the text (for example, Figure 3-2, Table 2-1, etc.) and then find those visuals and read them in the context that describes them. Relate the visuals to the explanations that tell more about them. Finally, take another look at the visual materials when you review. Visuals help you remember new material.

Strategy 2: Ask five questions to help you read visuals.

These questions will help you with *study reading* of visual material.

1. What is the *subject?* Read the title and the caption to discover what the visual is about.

2. What are the *details* or *parts?* What additional information does the author provide about the subject?

3. What is the *organizational pattern?* The most common patterns that you will find in visual materials are *chronological, comparison–contrast, cause–effect,* and *topical.* You may, however, also find *spatial* and *problem–solution* patterns at times. Identifying the organization pattern of a visual will help you think about it in the same way that the author has.

4. What is the *purpose?* Does the visual clarify, attempt to prove, and add interest, or does it condense and summarize? Does it show trends and special relationships, emphasize parts, or present data?

5. How does the visual *relate to the rest of the text?* Is there additional information in the body of the text that further explains it? Read the text and study the visual together for complete understanding.

How to apply the five study reading questions: An example.

Figure 6-10 presents an example of how these five questions can be applied when reading a line graph, along with the paragraph from a sociology textbook that explains more about it.

THE DECLINE OF AGRICULTURAL WORK[13]

The paragraph: In 1900, about 40 percent of U.S. workers were farmers. In 2004, just 1.6 percent were employed in agriculture. The family farm of yesterday has been replaced by *corporate agribusinesses.* Land is now more productive, but this change has caused painful adjustments across the country as a way of life is lost.[14] Figure 6-10 shows the shrinking role of the primary sector in the U.S. economy.

▶

[13] John J. Macionis, *Sociology.* 11th ed. (Upper Saddle River: Prentice Hall) 428.
[14] Kathryn Marie Dudley, *Debt and Dispossession: Farm Loss in America's Heartland.* Chicago: University of Chicago Press, 2000.

The line graph:

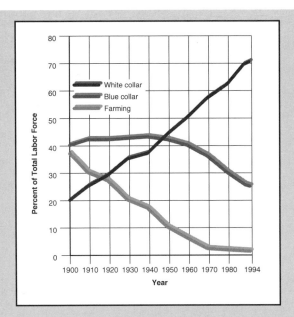

FIGURE 6-10 *The Changing Pattern of Work in the United States, 1900–2004* Compared to a century ago, work in the United States now involves mostly white-collar service jobs.

Source: *Estimates based on U.S. Department of Labor (2005).*

FROM FACTORY WORK TO SERVICE WORK

A century ago, industrialization swelled the ranks of blue-collar workers. By 1950, however, a white-collar revolution had moved a majority of workers into service occupations. By 2004, 77 percent of the labor force worked in the service sector, and 92 percent of new jobs were being created in this sector (U.S. Department of Labor, 2005).[15]

Answers to the five reading questions.

1. *What is the subject?* <u>The change in work patterns in the U. S. since 1900.</u>

2. *What are the parts?* <u>The changes in white collar, blue collar, and farming work.</u>

3. *What is the organizational pattern?* <u>Chronological, traces trends over time.</u>

4. *What is the purpose?* <u>Presents summary data to show that blue collar and farming have declined and white collar has increased.</u>

5. *How does the graph relate to the text?* <u>The graph represents visually the percentages and key dates identified in the text.</u>

▶

[15] U.S. Department of Labor. Bureau of Labor Statistics, *Employment and Earnings.* Vol. 52, No. 1 (January 2005). [Online] Available October 17, 2005, at http://www.bls.gov/cps

Strategy 3: Summarize the information in the visual.

Make reading notes on visuals just as you would on other parts of the text. Underline important words and ideas, jot the main idea of the visual in the margin, and add a note or two about what you think. Write in the margins of your book, on self-stick notes, or on cards inserted in your book. For example, the line graph in Figure 6-10 on page 207 could be summarized in this way:

Summary: The jobs people hold in the United States have changed between 1900 and 2004. Changes include major drops in farming jobs (from 40% to 1.6%) and in blue collar jobs (from 41% to 22%). An increase has taken place in white collar jobs (from 20% to 77%). A majority of these are service occupations, like sales, clerical, hospital, and restaurant jobs. The organizational pattern is chronological, but comparisons are also made.

Strategy 4: Draw a conclusion: What have you learned?

Go a step further and answer the question, so what? Explain the significance of what you have learned from examining a visual. Here is an example of a conclusion you might have drawn for yourself after you had examined and summarized the line graph in Figure 6-10.

Conclusion: When I graduate my best chances for employment may lie in the white collar area. White collar jobs include both service and professional jobs. I want to major in business, so I will probably look for a white collar professional job in that general area.

Strategy 5: Trace or redraw complicated visuals or create your own.

A good way to understand and remember a complicated visual is to trace or redraw it, paying particular attention to the parts and how they make up the whole. This is an especially effective technique to use with the complicated diagrams or charts in your math and science books. Try redrawing the line graph in Figure 6-10. Notice how much more easily you can understand this graph now.

When you encounter a descriptive passage and no visual is provided, mentally visualize what is being described and make a sketch or drawing of your own to help you understand and remember the passage.

EXERCISES AND READINGS

THREE COLLABORATIVE CLASS EXERCISES

Exercise 1

Read visual materials. *Pairs of students.*

The emphasis in this exercise is on study reading of visual materials. Work with another student and practice reading the figures that follow on pages 210–220. They represent the 8 different types of visuals that are described in this chapter, and they are numbered for easy reference. For each of these figures, answer the five questions for reading visuals (see Strategy 2, pp. 206–207, and the list below). Then write a brief summary of the visual and draw a conclusion (see Strategies 3 and 4, p. 208). Prepare to report to the class. Write your summary and conclusion in the space provided below each visual or on a separate piece of paper.

Five Questions to Help You Read Visuals

1. What is the *subject?* Read the title and the caption to discover what the visual is about.

2. What are the *details* or *parts?* What additional information does the author provide about the subject?

3. What is the *organizational pattern?* The most common patterns that you will find in visual materials are *chronological, comparison-contrast, cause-effect,* and *topical.* You may, however, also find *spatial* and *problem-solution* at times. Identifying the organizational pattern of a visual will help you think about it in the same way that the author has.

4. What is the *purpose?* Does the visual clarify, prove, and add interest, or does it condense and summarize? Does it show trends and special relationships, emphasize parts, or present data?

5. How does the visual *relate to the rest of the text?* Is there additional information in the caption or accompanying text that further explains it? Read the caption and parts of the text and study them together for complete understanding.

1. A pie chart from a chapter on small businesses in a business textbook.

Popular Areas of Small-Business Enterprise

Not surprisingly, small businesses are more common in some industries than in others. The major small-business industry groups are *services, construction, finance and insurance, wholesaling,* and *transportation and manufacturing.* Each industry differs in its needs for employees, money, materials, and machines, but as a general rule, the more resources required, the harder it is to start a business and the less likely an industry is dominated by small firms. Remember, too, that *small* is a relative term. The criteria (number of employees and total annual sales) differ from industry to industry and are often meaningful only when compared with truly large businesses. Figure 6-11 shows the distribution of all U.S. businesses employing fewer than 20 people across industry groups.

Services

Small-business services range from marriage counseling to computer software, from management consulting to professional dog walking. Partly because they require few resources, service providers are the fastest-growing segment of small business. A retailer, for example, sells products made by other firms directly to consumers. Usually, people who start small retail businesses favor specialty shops—say, big men's clothing or gourmet coffees—that let them focus limited resources on narrow market segments.

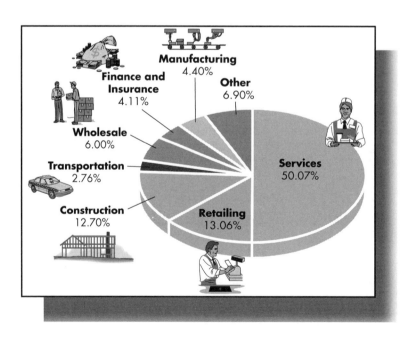

FIGURE 6-11 *Small Business by Industry*

Construction

About 13 percent of businesses with fewer than 20 employees are involved in construction. Because many construction jobs are small local projects, local firms are often ideal contractors.

Finance and Insurance

Financial and insurance firms account for about 4 percent of all firms with fewer than 20 employees. Most of these businesses are affiliates of or agents for larger national firms.

Wholesaling

Small-business owners often do well in wholesaling; about 6 percent of businesses with fewer than 20 employees are wholesalers. Wholesalers buy products from manufacturers or other producers and sell them to retailers. They usually purchase goods in bulk and store them in quantities at locations convenient for retailers. For a given volume of business, therefore, they need fewer employees than manufacturers, retailers, or service providers.

Transportation and Manufacturing

Some small firms—about 3 percent of all companies with fewer than 20 employees—do well in transportation and related businesses. These include taxi and limousine companies, charter airplane services, and tour operators. More than any other industry, manufacturing lends itself to big business, but this doesn't mean that no small businesses do well in manufacturing; rather, about 5 percent of firms with fewer than 20 employees are involved in manufacturing. Indeed, small manufacturers sometimes outperform big ones in such innovation-driven industries as electronics, toys, and computer software.[16]

Summary:

_____

_____

Conclusion:

_____

_____

[16] Ricky W. Griffin & Ronald J. Ebert, *Business,* 8th ed. (Upper Saddle River: Prentice Hall, 2006) 92–93.

2. **A flowchart from a business textbook that shows the process for deciding whether or not a company should go international.**

Going International

As the world economy becomes globalized, more firms are conducting international operations. Wal-Mart, for example, was once the quintessential U.S. growth company. But as managers saw both fewer expansion opportunities inside the United States and stronger competition from domestic competitors, they decided that foreign expansion was the key to future growth.

By aggressively opening new stores and buying existing retail chains in other countries, Wal-Mart more than quintupled foreign sales, to $40 billion, between 1997 and 2003. Because this total still represents only 15 percent of total revenues, Wal-Mart has made international sales growth its primary goal for the future. Today, the firm has more than 1,000 stores in the United Kingdom, Mexico, Canada, Germany, Brazil, Argentina, China, and South Korea, and it has ambitious plans for continued international expansion. When asked to explain why his firm set up shop in Germany, one Wal-Mart executive simply noted that "Germany, being the third-largest economy in the world, is very important to us and one obviously that we can't ignore."

This route, however, isn't appropriate for every company. If you buy and sell fresh fish, you'll find it more profitable to confine your activities to limited geographic areas because storage and transport costs may be too high to make international operations worthwhile. As Figure 6-12 shows, several factors affect the

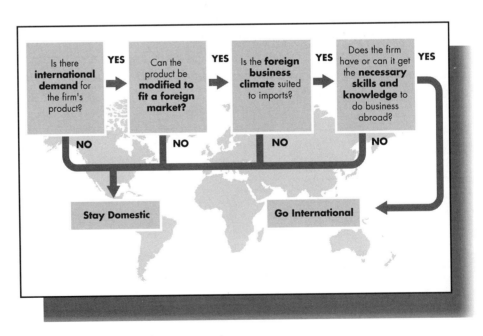

FIGURE 6-12 *Going International*

decision to go international. One key factor is the business climate in other nations. Even experienced firms have met cultural, legal, and economic roadblocks (problems that we discuss in more detail later in this chapter).

Gauging International Demand In considering international expansion, a company should also consider at least two other questions:

1. Is there a demand for my products abroad?
2. If so, must I adapt those products for international consumption?

Summary:

_____

_____

Conclusion:

_____

_____

3. **An organization chart for a landscaping service company from a business textbook.**

Chain of Command

Most businesses prepare **organization charts** to clarify structure and to show employees where they fit into a firm's operations. Figure 6-13 is an organization chart for Contemporary Landscape Services Inc., a small but thriving business in Bryan, Texas. Each box in the chart represents a job. The solid lines define the **chain of command,** or *reporting relationships,* within the company. For example, the retail shop, nursery, and landscape operations managers all report to the owner and president, Mark Ferguson. Within the landscape operation is one manager for residential accounts and another for commercial accounts. Similarly, there are other managers in the retail shop and the nursery.

The organization charts of large firms are far more complex and include individuals at many more levels than those shown in Figure 6-13. Size prevents many large firms from even having charts that include all their managers. Typically, they create one organization chart showing overall corporate structure, separate charts for each division, and even more charts for individual departments or units.[17]

---

[17] Griffin & Ebert, B*usiness* 8/e 133–134.

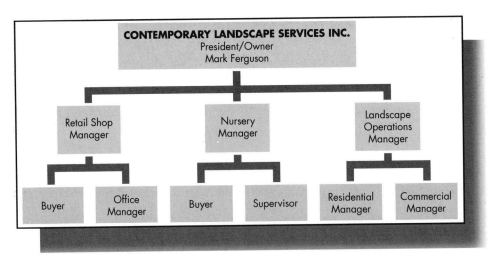

FIGURE 6-13 *The Organization Chart*[18]

Summary:

_____

_____

Conclusion:

_____

_____

4. **A line graph that shows the percentage of bachelor's degrees awarded to men from a political science textbook.**

Some women still complain of a "glass ceiling" in large corporations, preventing their advancement. But there is no denying that major progress has been made, with more and more women going to college and professional schools and into media and business. Indeed, during the past three decades, the percentage of women graduating from colleges and universities has outpaced that of men (see Figure 6-14)

Summary:

_____

_____

Conclusion:

_____

_____

[18] Griffin and Ebert, *Business* 183.

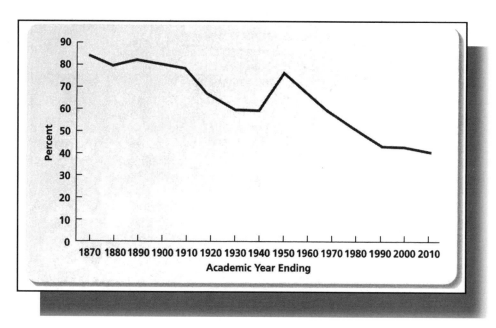

FIGURE 6-14 *Percentage of Bachelor's Degrees Awarded to Men*
*Percentage for 2010 is projected by the Pell Institute for the Study of Opportunity in Higher Education, National Center for Education Statistics.[19]
Source: *Michael A. Fletcher, "Degrees of Separation," The Washington Post, June 25, 2002, p. A1.*

5. A bar graph that shows the numbers of Americans killed in wars from the Revolutionary War to the present from a sociology textbook.

War and Peace

Perhaps the most critical political issue is war, *organized, armed conflict among the people of two or more nations, directed by their governments.* War is as old as humanity, but understanding it is crucial today because humanity now has weapons that can destroy the entire planet.

At almost any moment during the twentieth century, nations somewhere in the world were engaged in violent conflict. In its short history, the United States has participated in eleven large-scale wars. From the Revolutionary War to the Iraq War, more than 1.3 million U.S. men and women have been killed in armed conflicts, as shown in Figure 6-15 and many times that number have been injured. Thousands more died in "undeclared wars" and limited military actions in the Dominican Republic, Nicaragua, Lebanon, Grenada, Panama, Haiti, Bosnia, and elsewhere.

[19] Magelby, *Government by the People* 437.

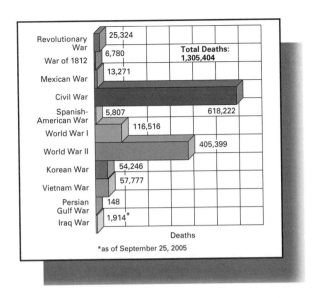

FIGURE 6-15 *Deaths of Americans in Eleven U.S. Wars* Almost half of all U.S. deaths in war occurred during the Civil War (1861–1865).[20]
Source: *Compiled from various sources by Maris A. Vinovskis (1989) and the author.*

Summary:

_____

_____

Conclusion:

_____

_____

6. A table of figures that shows men's and women's median salaries according to their educational level from a sociology textbook.

Completing college brings many rewards, including intellectual and personal growth, as well as higher income. In the last forty years, as our economy has shifted to work that requires processing information, the gap in average income between people who complete only high school and those who earn a four-year college degree has more than doubled. Today, a college degree adds as much as $1 million to a person's lifetime income. Figure 6-16 gives details. In 2004, men with an eight-grade education typically earned $21,659, high school graduates averaged $35,725, and college graduates averaged $57,220. The ratios in parentheses show that a man with a bachelor's degree earns more than two-and-one-half times as much as a man with eight or fewer years of schooling. Across the board, women

[20] Macionis, *Sociology* 458–459.

Education	Men	Women
Professional degree	$100,000 (4.6)	$75,036 (4.4)
Doctorate	82,401 (3.8)	68,875 (4.0)
Master's	71,530 (3.3)	51,316 (3.0)
Bachelor's	57,220 (2.6)	41.681 (2.4)
1–3 years of college	41,895 (1.9)	30,816 (1.8)
4 years of high school	35,725 (1.6)	26,029 (1.5)
9–11 years of school	26,277 (1.2)	19,162 (1.1)
0–8 years of school	21,659 (1.0)	17,023 (1.0)

*Persons aged twenty-five years and over working full time, 2004. The earnings ratio, in parentheses, indicates how many times the lowest income level a person with additional schooling earns.

FIGURE 6-16 *Median Income by Sex and Educational Attainment**
Source: *U.S. Census Bureau (2005).*

earn less than men; added years of schooling boosts women's income, but more slowly. Keep in mind that for both men and women, some of the increased earnings have to do with social background, because those with the most schooling are likely to come from relatively well-off families to begin with.[21]

Summary:

_____

_____

Conclusion:

_____

_____

7. **A map with a legend that shows the areas in Africa where the greatest numbers of individuals infected with AIDS live, from a sociology textbook.**

The Impact of AIDS on Africa

Now in its third decade, HIV/AIDS may become one of the deadliest epidemics in modern human history. As of 2003, two-thirds of the 40 million HIV/AIDS cases in the world were found in Sub-Saharan Africa, and it was estimated that the epidemic may have already claimed 17 million lives in the region. The virus is thought to have originated in the forests of the Congo, possibly crossing over from chimpanzees to humans sometime in the 1950s. Yet it was not until the 1980s that the impact of the disease was widely felt. On average, 8 percent of all adults in

[21] Macionis, *Sociology* 535–537.

Sub-Saharan Africa (ages 15–49) are infected with the virus. Yet in some countries the infection rate is three times this level. Women account for 58 percent of the reported HIV/AIDS cases in the region, which is the opposite of the pattern in Europe and North America, where men make up the majority of the cases. In this region, as in much of the developing world, the disease is transmitted by unprotected heterosexual encounters. Until the late 1990s, many African governments were unwilling to acknowledge publicly the severity of the situation or to discuss frankly the measures necessary for prevention. The consequences of this inaction have been deadly.

Southern Africa is ground zero for the AIDS epidemic that is ravaging the region (Figure 6-17). In South Africa, the most populous state in southern Africa,

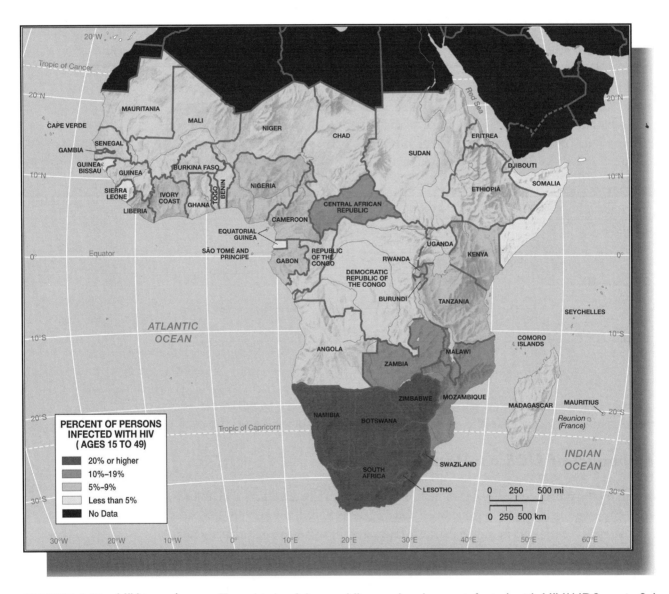

FIGURE 6-17 *HIV prevalence* Two-thirds of the world's people who are infected with HIV/AIDS are in Sub-Saharan Africa. It is estimated that more than 17 million lives have been lost in the region due to AIDS. Infection rates in 2004 were highest in southern Africa, especially Botswana (37.3 percent) and Swaziland (39 percent).

Source: *Data from Population Reference Bureau,* World Population Data Sheet, 2004.

TWO READING EXERCISES WITH VISUALS:
ABOUT CHANGE

The common theme in the next two readings is change. Visuals appear in each reading to make some of the possibilities for change more vivid. The essays come from a sociology textbook and a biology textbook. Read the essays and think about the visuals that illustrate them.

Reading 1

Cultural Change[27]

JOHN J. MACIONIS

Explanatory Notes: *John Macionis is a professor of sociology at Kenyon College in Gambier, Ohio. The following essay about cultural change among college students comes from his sociology textbook. The visual that accompanies the essay documents change in college students' attitudes.* **Interact with this visual and decide whether or not it accurately reflects your current values and aspirations.**

Cultural Change

Perhaps the most basic human truth of this world is that "all things shall pass." Even the dinosaurs, which thrived on this planet for 160 million years (see the timeline), remain today only as fossils. Will humanity survive for millions of years to come? All we can say with certainty is that given our reliance on culture, for as long as we survive, the human record will show continuous change. 1

Figure 6-19 shows changes in attitudes among first-year college students between 1969 (the height of the 1960s counterculture) and 2004. Some attitudes have changed only slightly: Today, as a generation ago, most men and women look forward to raising a family. But today's students are less concerned with developing a philosophy of life and much more interested in making money. 2

Change in one part of a culture usually sparks changes in others. For example, today's college women are much more interested in making money because women are now far more likely to be in the labor force than their mothers or grandmothers were. Working for income may not change their interest in raising a family, but it does increase both the age at first marriage and the divorce rate. Such connections illustrate the principle of **cultural integration,** *the close relationships among various elements of a cultural system.* 3

[27] Macionis, *Sociology* 79–80.

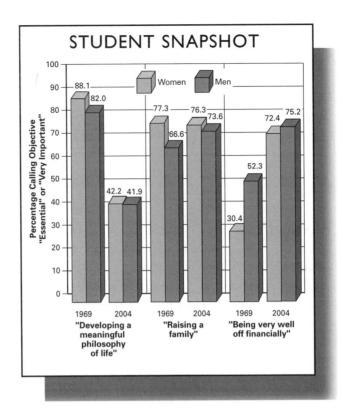

FIGURE 6-19 *Life Objectives of First-Year College Students, 1969–2004* Today's students are less interested in developing a philosophy of life and more interested in making money.

Source: *Astin et al. (2002) and Sax et al. (2004).*

Cultural Lag[28]

Some elements of culture change faster than others. William Ogburn observed that technology moves quickly, generating new elements of material culture (things) faster than nonmaterial culture (ideas) can keep up with them. Ogburn called this inconsistency **cultural lag,** *the fact that some cultural elements change more quickly than others, disrupting a cultural system.* For example, in a world in which a woman can give birth to a child by using another woman's egg, which has been fertilized in a laboratory with the sperm of a total stranger, how are we to apply traditional ideas about motherhood and fatherhood?

Causes of Cultural Change

Cultural changes are set in motion in three ways. The first is *invention,* the process of creating new cultural elements. Invention has given us the telephone (1876), the airplane (1903), and the computer (1947), each of which has had a tremendous impact on our way of life. The process of invention goes on con-

[28] William F. Ogburn, *On Culture and Social Change* (Chicago: University of Chicago Press, 1964).

stantly, as indicated by the thousands of applications submitted annually to the U.S. Patent Office. The timeline on the inside cover of this text shows other inventions that have helped change our way of life.

Discovery, a second cause of cultural change, involves recognizing and better understanding something already in existence—perhaps a distant star or the foods of another culture or women's athletic ability. Many discoveries result from painstaking scientific research, and others from a stroke of luck, as in 1898, when Marie Curie left a rock on a piece of photographic paper, noticed that emissions from the rock had exposed the paper, and thus discovered radium.

The third cause of cultural change is *diffusion*, the spread of cultural traits from one society to another. Because new information technology sends information around the globe in seconds, cultural diffusion has never been greater than it is today.

Certainly our own society has contributed many significant cultural elements to the world, ranging from computers to jazz music. Of course, diffusion works the other way, too, so that much of what we assume to be "American" actually comes from elsewhere. Most of the clothing we wear and the furniture we use, as well as the watch we carry and the money we spend, all had their origin in other cultures.[29]

594 words

Strategy Questions

1. What is the subject of the bar graph for this reading?
2. What information does the bar graph add to the text about cultural change?
3. Several organizational patterns are combined in this bar graph. Identify as many as you can.

Study Reading Questions

1. Who are the people interviewed for the survey that is summarized in the bar graph?
2. According to the graph, which two life objectives among this group of people changed the most from 1969 to 2004? Which changed the least?
3. Reread the second paragraph, which provides information about the chart. Why was 1969 chosen as the beginning date for the study?
4. Were more or fewer men interested in raising a family in 2004 compared with 1969? What about women?
5. What are the three causes of cultural change described in the essay?

[29] Ralph Linton, "One Hundred Percent American," *The American Mercury* 40: 160 (April 1937): 427–429.

Critical Reading and Thinking Questions

1. Which of the three life objectives in the bar graph seem centered on concern for the community and which seem centered on concern for the individual? Give reasons for your answer.
2. Think of two life objectives and probable responses to them that you might add to the graph. What additional information do you think they might suggest to researchers about modern college students?
3. Look at the first and last objectives. Why do you think there has been a large decrease in developing a philosophy of life and a large increase in trying to be well off financially? Do you think there is any connection between the two changes? Do you think that these results are reflective of our whole society? Explain your answers by giving examples to support your thoughts.
4. Imagine that you have been asked to complete the survey. Would you mark any of these life objectives as essential or very important to you? How accurately do the 2004 results for each life objective reflect your values and attitudes? Are you in the majority or the minority? Explain why your attitudes might be the same as or different than these first-year college students.

Reading 2

Habitat Change and Destruction Are the Leading Causes of Extinction[30]

TERESA AUDESIRK AND GERALD AUDESIRK

Explanatory Notes: *The authors are professors of biology at the University of Colorado at Denver. The following essay comes from their biology textbook,* Life on Earth. *This essay is illustrated with three different types of visuals: maps, a line graph, and a photograph. What do each of these visuals contribute to the essay? Which do you think is the most striking and memorable? Why?*

Habitat change, both contemporary and prehistoric, is the single greatest cause of extinctions. Presently, habitat destruction due to human activities is proceeding at a frightening pace. Perhaps the most rapid extinction in the history of life will occur over the next 50 years, as tropical forests are cut for timber and to clear land for cattle and crops. As many as half the species presently on Earth may be lost because of tropical deforestation.

Prehistoric habitat alteration usually occurred over a longer time span but nevertheless had serious consequences. Climate changes, in particular, caused many extinctions. Several times, moist, warm climates gave way to drier, colder climates with more variable temperatures. Many plants and animals failed to adapt to the harsh new conditions and became extinct. One cause of climate change is continental drift (Figure 6-20). As the continents move about over the surface of Earth,

---

[30] Audesirk and Audesirk, *Life on Earth* 324–326.

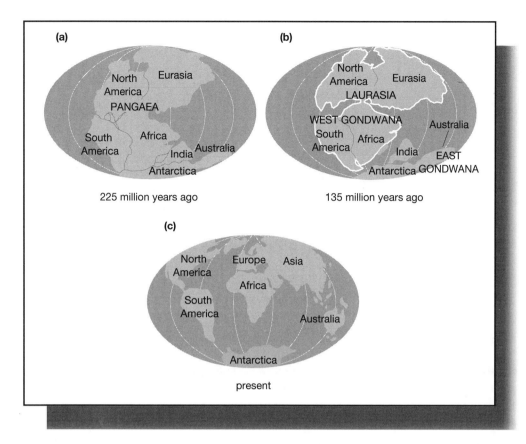

(a)

North America
Eurasia
PANGAEA
South America
Africa
India
Australia
Antarctica

225 million years ago

(b)

North America
Eurasia
LAURASIA
WEST GONDWANA
South America
Africa
Australia
India
EAST GONDWANA
Antarctica

135 million years ago

(c)

North America
Europe
Asia
Africa
South America
Australia
Antarctica

present

FIGURE 6-20 *Continental Drift Has Caused Climate Change* Although slow, continental drift can cause tremendous environmental changes, as land masses are moved about on the surface of Earth. The solid surfaces of the continents slide about over a viscous, but fluid, lower layer. (a) About 225 million years ago, all the continents were fused together into one gigantic land mass, which geologists call Pangaea. (b) Gradually, Pangaea broke up into Laurasia and West and East Gondwana. (c) Further drift eventually resulted in the modern positions of the continents. Continental drift continues today: The Atlantic Ocean, for example, widens by a few centimeters each year.

they change latitudes. Much of North America was located around the equator many millions of years ago, an area characterized by consistently warm and wet tropical weather. But drift carried the continent up into temperate and arctic regions. As a result, the tropical weather was replaced by cooler temperatures, less rainfall, and seasonal changes.

An extreme, and very sudden, type of habitat destruction might be caused by catastrophic geological events, such as massive volcanic eruptions. Several prehistoric eruptions, which would make the Mount St. Helens explosion look like a firecracker by comparison, wiped out every living thing for dozens of miles around and probably caused global climatic changes as well. 3

The fossil record reveals episodes of extensive worldwide extinctions, especially among marine life (Figure 6-21). Enormous meteorites, several kilometers in 4

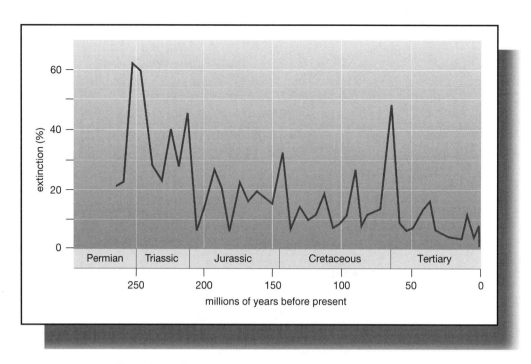

FIGURE 6-21 *Episodes of Mass Extinction* This graph plots the percentage of genera of marine animals that have become extinct during geologic time. The higher the peak, the greater the extent of extinctions. Marine animals were chosen for this study because their fossils are abundant in sedimentary rocks and are easily dated. The large peak of extinctions near the boundary between the Cretaceous and Tertiary periods also approximately coincides with the end of the dinosaurs. Many paleontologists are convinced that the dinosaurs were going downhill for millions of years before this time, so there is hot debate over whether the Cretaceous-Tertiary extinction event (such as a meteorite impact) provided the final blow to the dinosaurs or whether the dinosaurs would have died out at that time anyway.

diameter may have hit Earth at these times. If a huge meteorite struck land, it would kick up enormous amounts of dust. The dust might be thick enough, and spread widely enough, to block out most of the sun's rays. Fires started by the impact might be widespread, adding soot to the atmosphere. Many plants would die because they couldn't photosynthesize. Many animals, all of which ultimately depend on plants for food, would also die. Smaller amounts of dust might still block out enough sunlight to cause global cooling, perhaps even triggering an ice age. Widespread extinctions would result.

Did such massive meteorite strikes really occur, and if so, would they cause 5
extinctions? No one knows for sure, but considerable evidence points to meteorites as the causes of at least some major extinctions (Figure 6-22). Recently, two groups of researchers have suggested that the Chicxulub crater near the Yucatan Peninsula of Mexico was the impact site of the meteorite that might have killed the dinosaurs.

730 words

FIGURE 6-22 *Meteorites May Have Triggered Some Mass Extinctions*
The Manicouagan crater in Quebec is about 45 miles in diameter. Giant impact craters such as this one often contain a central dome of rock that splashes up after the meteorite has buried itself in the ground, leaving a ring-shaped depression between the outer crater wall and the inner dome. In this satellite photo, water backed up behind a dam fills the crater ring. The Manicouagan meteorite struck a little over 200 million years ago; geologist Paul Olsen suggests that its impact triggered the mass extinction near the Triassic-Jurassic boundary (see Figure 6-21). *NASA Headquarters*

Strategy Questions

1. What is the subject matter of Figure 6-20?
2. What is the organizational pattern of Figure 6-21?
3. What is the purpose of Figure 6-22? What additional information about this figure is in the text?

Study Reading Questions

1. What phenomena does Figure 6-20 illustrate?
2. The extinction of what type of animals is documented in Figure 6-21? Why were these chosen for the study?
3. Look at Figure 6-21. Approximately how many years ago did the Jurassic period begin? When did it end? How long did it last? What period are we in now?
4. What substance fills the crater ring shown in Figure 6-22?

Critical Reading and Thinking Questions

1. Refer to the entire article and list the ways in which changes in the earth affect various forms of life. What are at least three changes that environmentalists are

concerned about today? What brought about these changes? What dangers do these changes pose to life? Do you share environmentalists' concerns? Explain your answer.

2. Recent movies and television programs have presented scenarios of what would happen if the earth were hit by a meteor or asteroid. Compare the results shown in movies and TV with the results described in this textbook selection. Are the results similar or different? Why? In your opinion, why are so many people interested in natural disaster movies?

3. Do you think it is important that scientists study the changes that have occurred on the earth over the past 300 million years? What information might these studies provide that could be helpful today and in the future? Do you think that these studies provide interesting information about the past, but do not tell us anything about the present and future? Defend your answer.

TWO APPLICATION EXERCISES

Exercise 1

Analyze the visual materials in your textbooks.

Turn the pages of your textbooks and look at the visuals in them. What types seem to be most typical of each of the subjects you are studying? Why do you think some types of visuals are more often associated with certain subjects than with others?

Exercise 2

Select one visual that interests you in one of your textbooks.

Answer the five study reading questions about the visual (see pp. 206 and 209). Add a summary and a conclusion. Write your answers on a separate piece of paper. Bring your answers to class and give a brief report on the visual you selected. Include in your report why you were attracted to the visual you selected in the first place. What types of visuals seem to have caught the attention of the members of your class? Does one type predominate, or is there a variety of types? Speculate about what makes successful visuals and how they contribute to your understanding of your textbooks.

REVIEW AND EVALUATE THE STRATEGIES

The following is a review of the five strategies you learned in this chapter:

1. Make reading visuals a part of your reading process.
2. Ask five questions to help you read visuals.
3. Summarize the information in the visual.
4. Add a conclusion: What did you learn?
5. Trace or redraw complicated visuals or create your own.

Make a personal evaluation of these strategies:

1. Underline your favorite strategies in the list above.
2. Make a check mark by those you want to continue to use.
3. Cross out any you probably will not continue to use. What are your reasons for rejecting them?

_____

_____

CHAPTER

7

Organize a Study Reading Process, Study for and Take Exams

CHAPTER GOALS:

1. **To suggest how to organize study materials to help you prepare for exams.**

2. **To teach ways to condense and review material for exams.**

3. **To acquaint you with the requirements of different types of exams.**

4. **To provide you with five strategies to help you take exams successfully.**

Study Reading Focuses on Learning

Study reading was defined as a major purpose for college reading in Chapter 1 (page 8). Study reading has also been the main topic of the second part of this book. Figure 7-1 provides a set of questions that serves as a reminder of some of the mental activities involved when your main purpose is to study and learn reading material. This last chapter in Part II will help you review the study reading strategies you have learned in earlier chapters and will suggest ways to organize some of them for efficient exam study. You will also practice some new strategies that will help you learn and remember material for exams. In addition, you will learn about different types of college exams and what they will require of you. The strategies in this chapter are all practical ones. They present some powerful ways to help you first learn information and then demonstrate to your professors how much you have learned when you take their exams.

What Will You Study for Exams?

Information in your college courses comes from two main sources: (1) your textbooks and other reading assignments and (2) the notes you take on lectures and

QUESTIONS THAT GUIDE STUDY READING

1. What does the professor expect me to learn?
2. How does this relate to what I already know?
3. What is this about? What is the main point?
4. What are the parts? Subpoints? Details? What is the organization?
5. Do I understand? If not, what words do I need to look up? What background do I need to develop? Who can I talk to? What else can I read?
6. How can I summarize, outline, or retell this to make it easier to learn?
7. Do I know this material well enough to take an exam? What do I have to do to learn it?
8. Can I explain this material by answering questions or writing about it?
9. What questions can I ask and practice answering?

FIGURE 7-1 These questions will help you focus your reading purpose on study reading, or reading and learning the material.

discussion. You will need to review, organize, and learn information from both sources when you prepare for an exam.

1. Your reading assignments. You will need to review and study your reading assignments as part of your exam preparation. Figure 7-2 (on pp. 234–235) provides a self-assessment of your current study reading strategies. Evaluate your use of these strategies by completing the checklist. Are you now able to check "yes" for at least some of the strategies for each phase of the study reading process? A well-developed study reading process is the first step for effective exam preparation.

2. Your lecture notes. You will also need to read your lecture notes and study them just as you would any other reading assignment. Of course, in order to do that, you must take good notes in the first place. Students who have trouble taking lecture notes usually write disorganized or illegible notes that are difficult to read, or they write skimpy, incomplete notes that don't make much sense. Avoid both of these problems by focusing on the subject of the lecture, concentrating and listening, and writing rapidly and legibly throughout the lecture. You should plan to take five to seven pages of notes during a 50-minute lecture. Begin by writing a title for the notes; then write the major ideas out by the left-hand margin and indent the material that supports them. Include diagrams and other visuals in your notes. Abbreviate some of the words. The aim is to record ideas rather than to try to write every word you hear.

When you finish taking a set of notes, go back, reread, and revise them before they are "cold" and you have forgotten what the professor was talking about. This

SELF-EVALUATION: USING STUDY READING STRATEGIES

	Yes	No

Before reading.

1. I focus on the title, concentrate on the subject, and set a purpose.

2. I call up my prior knowledge on the subject.

3. I make some predictions.

4. I ask a big question about the subject.

5. I survey a book before I read it.

6. I survey a chapter before I read it, and make a survey map or survey outline.

7. I identify some of the key vocabulary words I don't know.

While reading.

8. I pay attention to the author's clues to locate the major ideas.

9. I recognize formats and organizational patterns.

10. I notice how supporting details are used to develop ideas.

11. I notice how transitions separate and emphasize ideas.

12. I reduce and simplify difficult sentences to understand them better.

13. I look up words I don't know.

14. I read the visual material and relate it to the rest of the text.

15. I underline important ideas and jot some notes in the margin.

16. I monitor my comprehension from time to time.

After reading.

17. I write summaries and add details to survey outlines or maps to capture the most important ideas.

18. I recite the main points until I can reproduce them from memory.

19. I review my notes, maps, or summaries every two or three weeks.

20. I quiz other students and have them quiz me on practice exam questions.

▶

Give yourself a score on the self-evaluation for study reading. Count all of the check marks in the Yes column, multiply that number by 5, and write your score in the blank: _____. A score of 70 or better on this self-evaluation is excellent, and 50–65 is also very good since it shows you are using half or more of the strategies. If your score is 45 or lower, you should probably look through the strategies again and add a few to what you are doing now to make your study reading process more powerful.

FIGURE 7-2 Evaluate your study reading strategies.

means you need to rework them within 24 hours. Fill in words where you need them. Make certain everything makes sense. Then underline the main ideas, jot some additional notes in the margin, and write brief summaries of each set of lecture notes, just as you would any other reading assignment. Figure 7-3 is a self-assessment of lecture note taking strategies that will help you evaluate your current practices. A well-developed lecture note taking system is the second step in effective exam preparation.

SELF-EVALUATION: TAKING LECTURE NOTES

	Yes	No
1. I read the assignment before the lecture and bring plenty of paper and pens to class.	___	___
2. I write the subject of the lecture as a title for my notes and focus on it to help me concentrate.	___	___
3. I relate the lecture to the reading assignment and make some cross-references.	___	___
4. I think and understand as I write; I monitor my comprehension as I listen and write.	___	___
5. I take notes in outline form.	___	___
6. I take several pages of notes on each lecture and write in complete thoughts, not just phrases, so I can understand them later.	___	___
7. I abbreviate some words and reduce and simplify some of the ideas.	___	___

▶

FIGURE 7-3 Evaluate your lecture note taking strategies.

	Yes	No

8. I include the professor's diagrams and drawings in my notes.

9. I write in ink on one side only of full-size notebook paper so my notes are easier to read.

10. I write legibly and leave space so that I can revise and add words later.

11. I take notes throughout a lecture, even when it is boring or difficult.

12. I keep my mind on note taking and ignore distractions in class.

13. I sit as close as I can to the front of the room to make it easier to concentrate.

14. I write my own ideas and reactions into my notes and put them in brackets to identify them as mine.

15. I spell unfamiliar words the best I can and check the correct spelling later.

16. I read and revise my notes within 24 hours.

17. I underline my notes and jot the main ideas in the margins.

18. I write brief summaries of each set of notes.

19. I review my notes every two or three weeks.

20. I file my notes in consecutive order in a notebook or file folder so that they eventually form a "book" that I can study like any other book.

Count all of the check marks in the Yes column, multiply that number by 5, and write your score in the blank: _____. A score of 70 or better on this self-evaluation is excellent, as long as you have checked at least two of the last five items. A score of 50–65 is also very good since it shows you are using half or more of these strategies. If your score is 45 or lower, you can improve your lecture note taking by adding some strategies. Be sure to include one or more of the last five items on the checklist. These require you to do something with your notes after you have taken them to help you learn and remember them.

FIGURE 7-3 Continued.

When you begin exam study, gather all of your lecture notes and all of the memory aids you have made for your reading assignments (underlining, marginal notes, summaries, maps, outlines, Cornell notes). Begin your review with the source of information that has been the backbone of the course. Are the *readings* the central part of the course, with lectures and discussions used to clarify and elaborate on the readings? Or are the *lectures* the main source of information, with the readings used to amplify and clarify them? Begin with the main source of information in the course and add material from other sources later. You will have a lot of information to study. To learn it all, you need to use the "3 R's" for exam study: Reduce, Recite, and Review.

How Will You Study for Exams?

1. Use the 3 R's. In Chapter 5 you learned to **reduce** and simplify difficult sentences and paragraphs and to write them in simpler language to help you understand them better. You also learned to **reduce** material by underlining, annotating, and writing summaries. In Chapter 4 you learned to **review** the material you have just read, to **reduce** the volume of this material by condensing and writing it on maps and outlines, and then to **recite** the ideas aloud or in writing to help you learn them. These three R's—Reduce, Recite, and Review—should now be a part of your regular study reading process.

2. Make study sheets. You can use the 3 R's again when it is time to begin to study for an exam. First, **reduce** the main topics that have organized the course to a simple list. Write them in the order they were presented in class on one side of a single sheet of paper. Use the titles of your lecture notes or the table of contents of your textbook to help you make this list. Its purpose is to identify topics you will need to study later in more detail. Next, make detailed study sheets for each of the items on your list. Write the topic at the top and add all of the details, in brief form, that you think you will need to know for the exam. You will need to **review** both your reading notes and your lecture notes to make study sheets. Strategy 2 at the end of this chapter teaches you exactly how to make study sheets and also provides examples.

Writing study sheets is active and helps you learn as you write. Learn the rest by **reciting** the information on your study sheets until you know it without looking back. You may do this by yourself, or you may work with another student. Both of you should repeat what you want to learn to the other person until you both know the material. This is the surest way to learn it.

Review your study sheets by reading through all of them the night before the exam and just before you go to sleep. Then review them again just before you go into the exam. Your mind will be full of information, and you will be able to concentrate on the requirements of the exam. Figure 7-4 on page 238 provides a chart of the types of exams that you can expect to encounter in college, along with their requirements.

Types of College Exams			
Type	Description	Strategy for Taking	Preparation
Objective	Multiple-choice, true–false, fill-in-the-blank, and matching items	Look at the questions from professor's point of view. Decide what is correct and incorrect. Complete or rearrange the parts of the answer.	Learn all of the ideas and facts you can. Use study sheets.
Essay	Broad questions that ask you to organize and explain what you have learned in the class in well-organized essays written in paragraphs	Read carefully, number the parts, write a brief outline, get right to the point, write complete answers for each part. Proofread.	Organize information and your own ideas on study sheets.
Quantitative	Problem solving in math and science classes	Read the questions. Answer all parts. Proof and check your answers for logic.	Write math facts, theorems, and strategies on cards or study sheets. Include examples of problems.

FIGURE 7-4 The major types of exams you will encounter in college.

GETTING ORGANIZED AND TAKING EXAMS: FIVE STRATEGIES

The strategies that follow will help you organize your study time, make study sheets, and learn the information on them. These strategies also teach you how to take exams and learn from your mistakes so you will avoid making them again on future exams.

▶

Strategy I: Organize study processes for reading textbooks and taking lecture notes.

Follow a study reading process each time you read an assignment throughout the semester to use your time efficiently and to learn the material as you go along. You will then have less to learn just before an exam. Here is a two-hour study reading process that you can adjust to meet the length and difficulty of individual reading assignments.

A Study Reading Process

1. Review your last assignment and predict ideas for the new assignment. (10 minutes)

2. Survey the new assignment. (10 minutes)

3. Read, underline, annotate, and write section summaries. (45 minutes)

4. Survey again to get the main ideas straight. (5 minutes)

5. Make memory aids: outlines, maps, chapter summaries, vocabulary sheets, study sheets—whichever you prefer. (25 minutes)

6. Reread your memory aids and recite the information on them until you know it. (25 minutes)

Notice that you allow slightly more time for surveying, making memory aids, reciting, and reviewing than you allow for reading. This is what it takes to read *and* learn new material. You will discover significant benefits from following this format. You *will* learn, and the more you learn the more you will find you *can* learn because of the increase in your prior knowledge.

Follow a similar organized study process for learning your lecture notes. You may follow this process throughout the semester so that you will have less to learn just before an exam. As with reading, you will spend at least as much time rereading, revising, marking, summarizing, and reviewing your lecture notes as you spend actually taking them.

A Study Process for Lecture Notes

1. Read the notes from the day before while you are waiting for class to begin. (5 minutes)

2. Get set to take notes: Start a new sheet of paper, write the class and date in the corner, and write the subject of the lecture as a title. (2 minutes)

3. Take well-organized and legible lecture notes. (45–50 minutes)

4. Read and revise your notes within 24 hours so that they make sense to you. Underline the important points and take notes on your notes in the margin. (20 minutes)

▶

5. Write a brief summary of your notes at the end. Pull the main ideas together. (5 minutes)

6. Recite the material in these notes until you know them. (15 minutes)

If you follow these study processes for reading and taking lecture notes, exam study will be much easier for you. When you begin to prepare for an exam, you will already know a great deal of the material, and your main task will be to reduce and organize it on study sheets so that you can learn the rest and recall it easily in the exam.

Strategy 2: Make study sheets.

1. Write a list of the topics you will need to study.

This will take 5 to 10 minutes and will organize the rest of your study. Draw these topics from the chapter titles, chapter outlines and goals, and chapter headings in your textbook or from the titles of your lecture notes. Figure 7-5 provides an example of a list of topics to study for a history exam.

2. Write a study sheet for each item on the list.

Make a separate study sheet for each item on the list. Write each topic at the top of a new sheet. Write brief lists or outlines of the material you want to learn. Concentrate on writing only the material you need to know but have not yet learned.

> **New Middle Class**
> **1790s–1840s**
>
> 1. Wealth and class
>
> 2. Religion and personal life
>
> 3. Middle class family
>
> 4. Motherhood
>
> 5. Sentimentalism
>
> 6. Transcendentalism and self-reliance

FIGURE 7-5 This list of subjects from a history course provides the topics for individual study sheets. The list shows you what you need to study.[1]

▶

---

[1] Topics drawn from a chapter outline in John M. Faragher et al., *Out of Many*, 2nd ed. (Upper Saddle River: Prentice Hall, 1997) 341.

Include key words that identify major concepts. Reduce all material to only a few words. Write just enough to help you remember additional details about each item. Abbreviate words. Include diagrams. Study sheets should trigger your memory. Figure 7-6 provides an example of a study sheet that develops one of the topics on the list in Figure 7-5. It is about "Religion and Personal Life" in general and focuses specifically on the "Second Great Awakening," a religious movement of the time.

Making study sheets is an active study process because you have to write the information. When you have completed several, read them over and mentally rehearse the information they contain. This is an active process also. Review the study sheets just before you go in to take an exam. You will find it reassuring to look at them and realize how much you know.

Religion and Personal Life
Second Great Awakening: 1790s–1820s

Change from Puritan religion
    -Original sin replaced with optimism
    -Salvation through personal faith
        -Democratic and optimistic

Religion of new middle class
    -Evangelical
    -Camp meetings, revival meetings, sinners saved, conversions, repentance
    -Women especially involved

Beginning of organized Protestant religion
    -Widespread
    -Dramatic in frontier towns
    -African Americans converted, both slaves and free, and blended
    Christianity with African religions
        -Hypocrisy in white religions—lack of equality

Effects:
    -Emphasis on individual achievement, self-discipline, individual responsibility
    -Saved people supposed to act moral, upright, disciplined, hardworking
    -Good for business—kept everyone on straight and narrow road

FIGURE 7-6 Example of a study sheet for history.[2]

---

[2] Information from Faragher et al., *Out of Many* 261, 323, 360–361.

Strategy 3: Use test taking strategies.

When you enter a college exam, you will need to know exactly what to do. Here are some suggestions to help you.

1. Get control of the situation.

Get enough sleep, eat a nutritious meal, arrive on time, ignore other students' nervous talk, get a comfortable seat, and look at your study sheets until you receive the exam. Then *focus* on the exam.

2. Analyze the test.

Look through the exam quickly. Read the directions. Determine the exam type, what you will be expected to do, the time allowed for each part, which parts will be easy and which will be difficult. Start with the easy parts. Focus, concentrate, and watch the time. You may want to jot down the amount of time you want to spend on each part or each question. Proceed, and stay within your time limits. You will be graded on what you complete. You want to complete the entire exam.

3. Use different strategies for different types of tests.

a. **Objective.** Read with concentration and focus. Visualize the answers on your study sheets. Eliminate and cross out incorrect multiple-choice answers. Change true–false statements to read the opposite way to help you make a judgment. Cross out matching items as you use them.

b. **Essay.** Read, underline, and number the parts of the question. Make a brief outline of only a few words. Come right to the point in the first sentence. Use plenty of details and examples, but don't pad your answer. Make the answer easy to read: Write legibly, use clear topic sentences and transitions, and, at the end, summarize or conclude. Check to see if you have answered all parts of the question. Proofread and insert corrections.

c. **Quantitative.** Read and mark the important parts of the question, use all the data, and check to see if the answer is logical. If you are unsure of an answer, work the problem again to check your answer. Proofread for careless errors. Careless errors are one of the biggest problems in quantitative exams.

4. Make special preparations for take-home or open-book exams.

If you are allowed to take an exam at home, create the necessary time and choose the right place to work. Then proceed as you would for any other exam, focusing and concentrating without interruption. If you are told you may use your text during an exam, turn the book into a reference book before the exam. Use labeled self-stick notes to mark key passages so that they will be easy to find. Write other material on fact cards and summary cards for fast reference.

▶

5. Proofread and check answers.

Change your answers on objective questions only when they are obviously wrong.

Strategy 4: Manage test anxiety.

1. What is test anxiety?

That nervous feeling you sometimes get in an exam is known as test anxiety. Think of test anxiety as extra energy that will help you perform well on the test. You will be able to keep it at a manageable level by studying and learning the material and by getting enough sleep before the exam. Then use this extra energy to help you concentrate and recall the answers to the questions. If your energy level is so intense that it makes you uncomfortable, seek further advice in your college counseling office. Counselors are trained to help you manage excessive or debilitating test anxiety.

2. Use positive self-talk while you are taking the test.

Keep telling yourself that you are well prepared, that you can do it, that you may miss a few but so will everyone, and that you are as smart as anyone else.

3. Plan for the worst before you are given the test.

Think through a worst-case scenario. Make acceptable plans in case you do not make the score you want to make. This will help you avoid negative talk (I have to pass; I won't be able to pass, etc.). Negative talk interferes with your efficiency and can lower your score.

4. Say "focus" to yourself every time your mind wanders.

Repeating this word will help you concentrate.

Strategy 5: Learn from your mistakes.

Analyze returned exams and learn from your mistakes. Most errors on exams fall into one of the following categories:

1. Not reading the question well and writing on something else.

2. Not knowing enough and answering with the wrong material.

3. Not writing enough; failing to give examples or leaving out whole parts of the question.

4. Not knowing the key vocabulary words and being unable to interpret the question.

Most of these problems can be avoided by organizing material on study sheets, learning it, reading and answering all parts of each question, and checking your answers.

EXERCISES AND READINGS

THREE COLLABORATIVE CLASS EXERCISES

These exercises will teach you to study a selection from a chapter in a history text-book about the 1960s and the Vietnam War and to take an exam on it. Prepare for the collaborative class exercises that follow by reading the major excerpt from the chapter, which begins on page 247. It is the only reading included in this chapter. Before class, survey the chapter. Then read, underline the main ideas, and make some marginal notes. Finally, make a study sheet on the information in the selection. Follow the example of study sheets in Strategy 2 and bring your study sheet to class. The actual studying for the exam will be done with your classmates in class. Follow the steps in Exercises 1, 2, and 3.

Exercise 1

Practice the 3 R's: Reduce, Recite, and Review. *Small groups.*

Form groups of three or four students and prepare for the exam on the history selection that appears at the end of this chapter.

  a. **Reduce.**   You reduced the history chapter yourself when you wrote your study sheet. Now compare the study sheets made by members of your group. Select the one that is most complete and add useful or omitted information to it from the other study sheets made by your group members. Create a complete composite study sheet that will be easy for all of you to study.

  b. **Recite.**   Take turns asking other members of your group questions about the information on the composite study sheet. Each member should answer the questions without looking at the sheet. Check it only when you absolutely must. Continue in this way until all of you know the information on the study sheet.

  c. **Review.**   Each student should now, from memory as much as possible, write their own summary of the information memorized from the study sheet. Look back if you need to. Include as many details as possible. Read these summaries to your group and continue to learn from each other.

Exercise 2

Read, analyze, and take the exam on the history selection.

Work alone on this exercise and proceed as follows:

  a. Turn to page 254 and read all the general directions for the exam. Then glance through the exam to see what you will be required to do. Read, underline, and number the main parts of the two essay questions. Write a brief outline for answers to each of them.

  b. Before you actually begin to take the exam, change the following examples of negative self-talk to positive self-talk. The first two are started for you.

NEGATIVE SELF-TALK	POSITIVE SELF-TALK
1. I'm too tired.	I got enough sleep last night.
2. I feel sick.	I feel great.
3. I'm hungry.	_____
4. I can't think.	_____
5. I'm dumb.	_____
6. I can't do this.	_____
7. There isn't enough time.	_____
8. I didn't study.	_____
9. This test is too hard.	_____
10. The professor is out to get us.	_____
11. This question isn't fair.	_____
12. The teaching assistant must have written this test.	_____
13. I'm always unlucky.	_____
14. I can't concentrate.	_____
15. The person next to me knows more.	_____

c. Now that you are in a positive frame of mind, write the answers for the exam on a separate piece of paper. Answer the objective questions first, and then write the two essays. In writing each essay, begin with a clear introductory sentence that comes right to the point, develop your answer in paragraphs, and end with a concluding sentence. Proofread and insert corrections. Try to complete the exam within the time frame allowed. Most exams are timed and, with practice, you can learn to meet the time requirements. If meeting them is very difficult or even impossible for you, discuss the possibility of special accommodations for extending the time with your instructor.

Exercise 3

Evaluate your answers.

Trade your exam with another member of your group. Check your answers for the objective questions against the answer key on page 505 at the back of the book. Read the scoring guide for the two essay answers (also on p. 505), notice what each of the essay answers should contain, and note how the points should be distributed for each part of each answer. Now read the essays, check to see that they contain the parts identified in the scoring guide, and assign points for each part. Add the points on the objective test and the points for each of the essay answers, write the total score on the test paper, and return the test to the person who took it.

A perfect score is 100. If you did not receive 100, try to figure out why. Use the self-assessment in Figure 7-7 to help you evaluate your exam. When you have completed this evaluation, take a look at the "No" answers. What can you do to improve your exam taking in the future? Discuss your observations in your group and report out to the class about what your group did well and in what ways you can also improve.

SELF-EVALUATION: TAKING EXAMS

	Yes	No
1. Were your study sheets complete enough?	___	___
2. Did you know enough to take this exam?	___	___
3. Did you read, understand, and answer each of the objective questions?	___	___
4. Did you understand all of the vocabulary in the questions?	___	___

For the essay answers.

	Yes	No
5. Did you underline and number the parts of each of the essay questions?	___	___
6. Did you make brief outlines?	___	___
7. Did you write in paragraphs with an introduction and a conclusion?	___	___
8. Did you organize each answer and use transitions?	___	___
9. Did you give examples and details?	___	___
10. Did you answer all parts of both essay questions?	___	___
11. Did you respond to the questions, or did you get off the subject and write on something else?	___	___
12. Did you come right to the point in the first sentence?	___	___
13. Did you avoid padding your answers with irrelevant material?	___	___
14. Did you write answers that are legible and easy to read?	___	___

FIGURE 7-7 Evaluate your test taking strategies.

READING EXERCISE:
FROM A HISTORY TEXTBOOK

The following is a major section from a long chapter entitled "War Abroad, War at Home, 1965–1974," which appears in a history textbook. This is the only reading at the end of this chapter. Finish underlining and annotating; this work has been started for you.

Reading

A Generation in Conflict[3]

JOHN MACK FARAGHER, MARI JO BUHLE, DANIEL CZITROM, SUSAN H. ARMITAGE

Explanatory Notes: *The authors are history professors at Yale University, Brown University, Mount Holyoke College, and Washington State University. They explain in their text that both President John Kennedy and President Lyndon Johnson believed there was a danger that communism would spread in Southeast Asia and perhaps throughout the world. These presidents believed that North Vietnam, which was communist and had the support of the major communist powers, was intent on conquering South Vietnam, and that if they got a foothold there, other parts of the world would come under attack as well, including the United States. The Vietnam War, which was supposed to prevent the spread of communism, began in 1965 when Johnson was president and became more and more unpopular as time went on. More than 50,000 Americans died, the war seemed unwinnable, and American citizens became deeply divided about continued participation. The war finally ended with the Paris Peace Agreement in 1973 when Richard Nixon was president.* **Do you know anyone who participated in this war? Have you ever seen a movie about the Vietnam War? What do you know about the counterculture (the hippies) in the 1960s? Survey this selection, read it, underline it, make some marginal notes, and then make a study sheet to summarize the information in it. Learn the information on your study sheet and take the practice examination that follows on pages 254–255.**

Presidents thought other countries would adopt communism

1965–1973

As the war in Vietnam escalated, Americans from all walks of life demanded an end to U.S. involvement. Debates raged everywhere, from families to informal community meetings to the halls of Congress. Eventually the antiwar movement won over a majority. But between 1965 and 1971, its years of peak activity, it had a distinctly generational character. At the forefront were the baby boomers who were just coming of age.

This so-called sixties generation, the largest generation in American history, was also the best educated so far. By the late 1960s, nearly half of all young adults between the ages of 18 and 21 were enrolled in college. In 1965 there were 5 million college students; in 1973 the number had doubled to 10 million. Public universities made the largest gains; by 1970 eight had more than 30,000 students apiece. These

Baby boomer generation protested war

[3] Faragher et al., *Out of Many* 933, 936–940.

young people combined a massive protest against the war in Vietnam with a broader, penetrating critique of American society. Through music, dress, and even hairstyle, a large number expressed a deep estrangement from the values and aspirations of their parents' generation. As early as 1967, when opposition to the war had begun to swell, "flower children" were putting daisies in the rifle barrels of troops stationed to quash campus protests, providing a seemingly innocent counterpoint to the grim news of mass slaughter abroad.

These young adults believed they heralded a "culture of life" against the "culture of death" symbolized by the war. Campus organizations such as SDS [Students for a Democratic Society], which had begun in the early 1960s as an attempt to build community, now turned against a government that lied to its citizens and sent its young men to kill and be killed. SDS encouraged many college students to take a militant stand against the war, calling for an immediate and unconditional withdrawal of U.S. troops from Vietnam.

" 'The Times They Are A-Changin' "

The first sign of a new kind of protest was the free speech movement at the University of California at Berkeley in 1964. That fall, civil rights activists returned to the campus from Freedom Summer in Mississippi. They soon began to picket Bay Area stores that practiced discrimination in hiring and to recruit other students to join them. When the university administration moved to prevent them from setting up information booths on campus, eighteen groups protested, including the arch-conservative Students for Goldwater, claiming that their right to free speech had been abridged. The administration responded by sending police to break up the protest rally and arrest participants. University president Clark Kerr met with students, agreed to not press charges, and seemed to grant them a small space on campus for political activity. Then, under pressure from conservative regents, Kerr backed down and in November announced that the university planned to press new charges against the free speech movement's leaders. On December 2 a crowd of 7,000 gathered to protest this decision. Joining folk singer Joan Baez in singing "We Shall Overcome," a group of students marched toward the university's administration building where they planned to stage a sit-in until Kerr rescinded his order. The police arrested nearly 800 students in the largest mass arrest in California history.

Mario Savio, a Freedom Summer volunteer and philosophy student, explained that the free speech movement wanted more than just the right to conduct political activity on campus. He spoke for many students when he complained that the university had become a faceless bureaucratic machine rather than a community of learning. Regulating the activities of students while preparing them for colorless lives as corporation clerks, the university made them "so sick at heart" that they had decided to put their "bodies upon the gears" to make it stop.

The critique of the free speech movement reverberated. Across the country college students began to demand the right to participate more fully in structuring their own education. Brown University students, for example, demanded a revamp of the curriculum that would eliminate all required courses and make grades optional. Students also protested campus rules that treated students as children instead of as adults. After a string of campus protests, most large universities, including the University of California, relinquished *in loco parentis* (in the place of parents) policies and allowed students to live off-campus and to set their own hours.

Across the bay in San Francisco, other young adults staked out a new form of community—a counterculture. In 1967, "the Summer of Love," the population of the Haight-Ashbury district swelled by 75,000, as youthful adventurers gathered for the most celebrated "be-in" of the era. Although the *San Francisco Chronicle* featured a headline reading "Mayor Warns Hippies to Stay Out of Town," masses of long-haired young men and women dressed in bell-bottoms and tie-dyed T-shirts were undeterred. They congregated in "the Haight" for no other purpose but to listen to music, take drugs, and "be" with each other. "If you're going to San Francisco," a popular rock group sang, "be sure to wear some flowers in your hair . . . you're going to meet some gentle people there." In the fall, the majority returned to their own communities, often bringing with them a new lifestyle. *Time* magazine announced the appearance of new "hippie enclaves . . . in every major U.S. city from Boston to Seattle, from Detroit to New Orleans."

This generational rebellion took many forms, including a revolution in sexual behavior that triggered countless quarrels between parents and their maturing sons and daughters. During the 1960s more teenagers experienced premarital sex— by the decade's end three-quarters of all college seniors had engaged in sexual intercourse—and far more talked about it openly than in previous eras. With birth control methods widely available, including the newly developed "pill," many young women refused to remain virgins. "We've discarded the idea that the loss of virginity is related to degeneracy," one college student explained. "Premarital sex doesn't mean the downfall of society, at least not the kind of society that we're going to build." Many heterosexual couples chose to live together outside marriage, a practice few parents condoned. A much smaller but significant number formed communes—approximately 4,000 by 1970—where members could share housekeeping and child care as well as sexual partners.

Psychedelic and other hallucinogenic drugs played a large part in this counterculture. Harvard professor Timothy Leary urged young people to "turn on, tune in, drop out" and also advocated the mass production and distribution of LSD (lysergic acid diethylamide), which was not criminalized until 1968. Marijuana, illegal yet readily available, often paired with rock music in a collective ritual of love and laughter. Singer Bob Dylan taunted adults with the lyrics of his hit song, "Everybody must get stoned."

Music played a large part in defining the counterculture. Beginning in 1964, with the arrival of the British rock group the Beatles, popular music began to express a deliberate generational identity. Folk music, which had gained popularity on campuses in the early 1960s with the successful recordings of Peter, Paul and Mary, Phil Ochs, Judy Collins, as well as Joan Baez, continued to serve the voice of protest. Shortly after Freedom Summer, folk singer Bob Dylan issued a warning to parents:

Your sons and your daughters are beyond your command
Your old road is rapidly aging.
Please get out of the new one
If you can't lend a hand
For the times they are a-changin'[4]

---

[4] "'The Times They Are A-Changin'" Copyright © 1963 by Warner Bros., Inc., renewed by Special Rider Music. All rights reserved and administered by Special Rider Music, New York.

By 1965 Dylan himself had electrified his guitar and turned to rock, which triumphed as the musical emblem of a generation.

At a farm near Woodstock, New York, more than 400,000 people gathered in August 1969 for a three-day rock concert and to give witness to the ideals of the counterculture. Thousands took drugs while security officials and local police stood by, some stripped off their clothes to dance or swim, and a few even made love in the grass. "We were exhilarated," one reveler recalled. "We felt as though we were in liberated territory."

The Woodstock Nation, as the counterculture was renamed by the media, did not actually represent the sentiments of most young Americans. But its attitudes and styles, especially its efforts to create a new community, did speak for the large minority seeking a peaceful alternative to the intensifying climate of war. "We used to think of ourselves as little clumps of weirdos," rock star Janis Joplin explained. "But now we're a whole new minority group." Another interpreter, Charles Reich, whose *The Greening of America* (1970) became a best-seller, defined the counterculture as a generation's attempt to create "a form of community in which love, respect, and a mutual search for wisdom replace the competition and separation of the past." The slogan "Make Love, Not War" linked generational rebellion and opposition to the U.S. invasion of Vietnam.

From Campus Protest to Mass Mobilization

Three weeks after the announcement of Operation Rolling Thunder [a campaign of gradually intensifying air attacks ordered by President Johnson in March 1965], peace activists called for a day-long boycott of classes so that students and faculty might meet to discuss the war. At the University of Michigan in Ann Arbor, more than 3,000 students turned out for sessions held through the night because administrators bowed to pressure of state legislators and refused to cancel classes. During the following weeks, "teach-ins" spread across the United States and as far away as Europe and Japan.

Students also began to protest against war-related research on their campuses. The expansion of higher education in the 1960s had depended largely on federally funded programs, including military research on counterinsurgency tactics and new chemical weapons. Student protesters demanded an end to these programs and, receiving no response from university administrators, turned to civil disobedience. In October 1967, the Dow Chemical Company, manufacturers of napalm, a form of jellied gasoline often used against civilians, sent job recruiters to the University of Wisconsin at Madison despite warnings that a group of students would try to prevent them from conducting interviews. A few hundred students staged a sit-in at the building where the recruitment interviews were scheduled, and 2,000 onlookers gathered outside. Ordered by university administrators to disperse the crowd, the city's police broke glass doors, dragged students through the debris, and clubbed those who refused to move. Suddenly the campus erupted. Students chanted "Sieg Heil" at the police, who attempted to disperse them with tear gas and Mace. Undergraduate students and their teaching assistants boycotted classes for a week. During the next three years, hundreds of similar strikes took place on campuses in every region of the country.

Courtesy of Bernie Boston
An antiwar demonstrator places a flower, a symbol of peace, in the rifle barrel of troops during the March on the Pentagon in October 1967. Nearly 100,000 opponents of the Vietnam War gathered in Washington, D.C., and hundreds were arrested as they attempted to storm the entrance to the Pentagon.

Many student strikes merged opposition to the war with other campus and community issues. At Columbia University, students struck in 1968 against the administration's plans to evict Harlem residents in order to erect new campus buildings. In the Southwest, Mexican American students demonstrated against the use of funds for military projects that might otherwise be allocated to antipoverty and educational programs. 16

By the late 1960s the peace movement had spread well beyond the campus and commanded a diverse following. While some protesters marched, others held prayer vigils, staged art fairs, distributed leaflets door to door, or simply engaged friends and neighbors in conversation about the war in Vietnam. In April 1967 the largest demonstration in American history to this time, at Sheep's Meadow in Manhattan's Central Park, drew more than 300,000 people to a day-long rally. Meanwhile, 60,000 protesters turned out in San Francisco. By summer, Vietnam Veterans Against the War began to organize returning soldiers and sailors, encouraging them to cast off the medals and ribbons they had won in battle. 17

The steadily increasing size of antiwar demonstrations provoked conservatives and prowar Democrats to take a stronger stand in support of the war. On the weekend following the huge turn-out in Central Park, the Veterans of Foreign Wars staged a "Loyalty Day" parade in New York City under the banner "One Country, One Flag, Love It or Leave It." Although only 7,500 people participated, the event signaled the hardening of opposition to the peace movement. Several newspaper and magazine editorialists called for the arrest of antiwar leaders on charges of treason. Secretary of State Dean Rusk, appearing on NBC's *Meet the* 18

Press, expressed his concern that "authorities in Hanoi" might conclude, incorrectly, that the majority of Americans did not back their president and that "the net effect of these demonstrations will be to prolong the war, not to shorten it."

Many demonstrators themselves concluded that mass mobilizations alone made little impact on U.S. policy. Some sought to serve as moral witness. Despite a congressional act of 1965 providing for a five-year jail term and a $10,000 fine for destroying a draft card, nearly 200 young men destroyed their draft cards at the April Sheep's Meadow demonstration and encouraged approximately a half-million more to resist the draft or refuse induction. Two Jesuit priests, Daniel and Philip Berrigan, raided the offices of the draft board in Catonsville, Maryland, in May 1968 and poured homemade napalm over records. A few protesters even doused their clothes with gasoline and set fire to themselves, as Buddhist monks protesting the war had done in Vietnam. Other activists determined to "bring the war home." An esti-

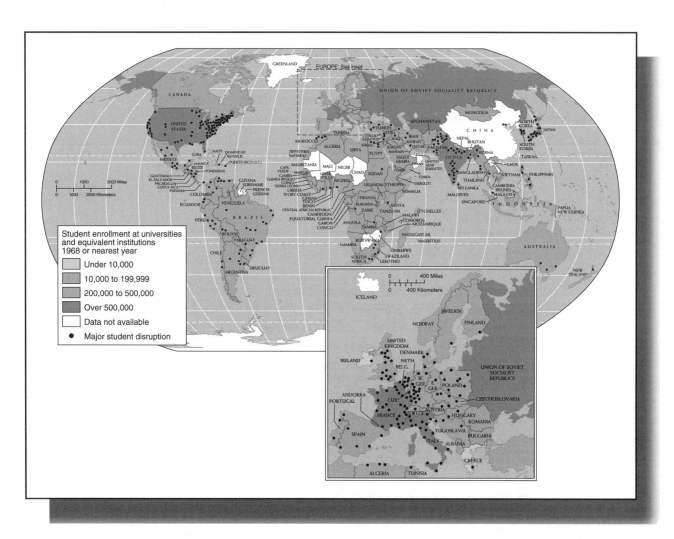

Antiwar Protests on College and University Campuses, 1967–1969 Campus-based protests against the war in Vietnam, at first centered on the east coast and in California, spread to nearly every region of the country and around the world by the decade's end.

mated 40,000 bombing incidents or bomb threats took place from January 1969 to April 1970; more than $21 million of property was damaged, and forty-three persons were killed. The majority of the perpetrators never became known.

Observers at the time noted a similarity between the violence in Vietnam and the violence in the United States. Parallel wars were now being fought, one between two systems of government in Vietnam, another between the American government and masses of its citizens. Those Americans sent to Vietnam were caught in between.

Teenage Soldiers

The Vietnam War era witnessed not only a generation gap but a fissure within the generation of young adults. Whereas the average age of the World War II soldier was twenty-six, the age of those who fought in Vietnam hovered around nineteen. Until late 1969 the Selective Service Act—the draft—allowed male students to request educational deferments, and, overall, college graduates constituted only 12 percent of all soldiers and 9 percent of those in combat. Meanwhile, the army recruited hard in poor communities, advertising the armed forces as means of vocational training and social mobility. Working-class young men, disproportionately African American and Latino, were registered in large numbers under this program. They also bore the brunt of the combat. High school dropouts were the most likely to be sent to Vietnam, and by far the most likely to die there. This disparity forced a rupture that would last well past the actual war.

Yet the soldiers were not entirely apart from the changes affecting their generation. GIs in significant numbers smoked marijuana, listened to rock music, and considered themselves part of the sexual revolution. In 1968 more than 200 soldiers from Fort Hood, Texas, attended a be-in. But most resented the protests at home as the voice of privileged peers who did not have to fight. Only a small number spoke out against the war. As the war dragged on, however, soldiers began to show their frustration and their desperation to escape psychologically. Flagrantly using heroin as well as the more "countercultural" marijuana and LSD both off and on duty, they frequently entered decades of personal addiction. Meanwhile, thousands of soldiers simply refused to enter battle, and hundreds took their revenge with murderous results, "fragging" their commanding officers with grenades meant for the enemy. Some African American soldiers complained about being asked to fight "a white man's war" and sported helmets emblazoned with slogans like "No Gook Ever Called Me Nigger." By 1971 hundreds of GIs were joining marches against the war or staging antiwar marches to celebrate what they called "Armed Farces Day."

The nature of the war fed these feelings. U.S. troops entering South Vietnam expected a welcome from the people whose homeland they had been sent to defend. Instead, Americans viewed anti-American demonstrations and placards with messages like "End Foreign Dominance of Our Country." Vietnamese civilians risked their lives to help drive the invaders out. Worse, armed guerillas refused to face American forces with vastly superior arms and air support. Instead, American soldiers had to chase their elusive enemies through deep swamps, crawled through dense jungles, found themselves covered with leeches and fire ants, and stumbled into deadly booby-traps. Through all this, they remained uncertain about who

20

21

22

23

they should consider friend or foe. Patently false U.S. government press releases heralding glorious victories and grateful civilians not only fooled no one but deepened bitterness on the front lines.

Vietnam veterans returned to civilian life quietly and without fanfare, denied the glory earned by the soldiers of previous wars. They reentered a society badly divided over the cause for which they had risked their lives. Tens of thousands suffered debilitating physical injuries. Many more came home with drug dependencies or posttraumatic stress disorder, haunted and depressed by troubling visions and memories of atrocities. Many had trouble getting and keeping jobs; they lacked skills to cope with a shrinking industrial economy. Perhaps a majority felt betrayed either by their own generation or by their government.

2980 words

EXAM ON HISTORY TEXTBOOK SELECTION

Objective Portion 40%   15 minutes

Matching

Choose the appropriate answer from the list below and write the corresponding letter in the blank.

1. _____ Three-day concert held in New York in 1969   A. Mississippi

2. _____ Location of Freedom Summer   B. Charles Reich

3. _____ Author of *The Greening of America*   C. Timothy Leary

4. _____ Location of the Summer of Love   D. Woodstock

5. _____ Professor who urged students to "Turn on, tune in, drop out"   E. San Francisco

True/False

Determine if the following statements are true or false and put a T or an F in the blank.

6. _____ Television played a large part in defining the counterculture.

7. _____ In the late 1960s, nearly one half of all adults between the ages of 18 and 21 were enrolled in college.

8. _____ The average age of Vietnam soldiers was 21.

▶

Fill in the blank

Fill in the missing word or words.

9. Communities where members could share housekeeping and child care as well as sexual partners are called _____.

10. The manufacturer of napalm that students at the University of Wisconsin at Madison prevented from conducting on-campus interviews was _____

_____.

Multiple choice

Read the following statements and determine which answer is correct. Write the letter in the blank.

11. _____ The Summer of Love occurred during the summer of:

A. 1960. B. 1970. C. 1967. D. 1965.

12. _____ Students at various universities did which of the following?

A. boycotted classes B. demanded the elimination of required courses and grades C. staged sit-ins D. all of the above

13. _____ Who staged a pro-war parade under the slogan, "One Country, One Flag, Love It or Leave It"?

A. President Johnson B. Veterans of Foreign Wars
C. Secretary of State Dean Rush D. NBC

14. _____ Who was heavily recruited for the war?

A. college students B. high school dropouts
C. professional businessmen D. none of the above

15. _____ Who is the folk singer who sang "We Shall Overcome" at a University of California at Berkeley student protest?

A. Bob Dylan B. Judy Collins C. Joan Baez D. Janis Joplin

Essay Portion 60%   30 minutes

1. List four ways in which some U.S. soldiers expressed their frustration with the Vietnam War. Name three of the problems the soldiers faced when they returned home. What were the causes of each of these problems?
2. List and describe four ways in which the Sixties generation showed they were the counterculture to previous generations. Describe one change in attitude in the Sixties generation that particularly affected the way many young people thought about the Vietnam War.

Four Application Exercises

1. **Try the study reading process explained in Strategy 1 in this chapter in another course.**

Be prepared to discuss your experience with this process in class.

2. **Take a set of lecture notes in another class, as explained in Strategy 1 in this chapter.**

Revise your notes, underline them, take further notes in the margin, and write a brief summary. Be prepared to discuss your experience with this process in class.

3. **Make study sheets for your next exam in another class.**

Bring one of your study sheets to class and be prepared to discuss your experience in making it.

4. **Analyze the errors in your next graded exam in another class.**

Use the self-evaluation for taking exams on page 246 to help you. Write a brief explanation of what you need to improve for your next exam.

Review and Evaluate the Strategies

The following is a review of the five strategies you learned in this chapter:

1. Organize study processes for reading textbooks and taking lecture notes.
2. Make study sheets
3. Use test taking strategies
4. Manage test anxiety
5. Learn from your mistakes

Make a personal evaluation of these strategies:

1. Underline your favorite strategies in the list above.
2. Make a check mark by those you want to continue to use.
3. Cross out any you probably will not continue to use. What are your reasons for rejecting them?

PART III

Critical Reading and Thinking: Reading to Analyze, Evaluate, Think

Understand the Context, Purpose, Point of View

CHAPTER 8

CHAPTER GOALS:

1. **To shift the focus from study reading to critical reading.**

2. **To teach you to recognize and understand some major features of argument.**

3. **To teach you to recognize the author's argumentative purpose and point of view.**

4. **To provide five strategies for reading and reacting to argument.**

A Shift of Focus

Shift from study reading to critical reading.   The focus in this chapter now shifts from study reading to critical reading. Study reading emphasizes what you know as a result of reading. Critical reading and thinking focus on what you think as a result of reading. Critical reading is the subject of Chapters 8 through 11, and critical thinking is the subject of Chapter 12. Critical reading centers on the text itself and teaches strategies for **analysis** and **evaluation** of what you have read. Critical thinking is expansive and invites you to go beyond the text and think about the new ideas you have as a result of reading. Here are some other mental shifts that you will need to make to help you read the next chapters.

Shift from exposition to argument.   The two most common types of reading material you will encounter in college are exposition and argument. The purpose of **exposition** is to inform, to describe, to explain, or to report facts and ideas that everyone would accept without controversy or disagreement. Examples include the facts and tables in almanacs and reference books; weather reports; government, business, and scientific technical reports; some news stories; and much of the information in your college textbooks. In the first chapters of this book you were provided with comprehension strategies to help you understand such material.

   Argument deals with controversial subjects that have not yet been settled and that are still open to inquiry or debate. The purpose of argument is to convince you to think about a controversial subject in a particular way. Examples include newspaper editorials, articles that defend distinctive views on controversial subjects, and scholarly arguments that make a case for particular views or interpretations of some of the subjects you are studying in your college courses. In these last chapters you will be provided with critical reading and thinking strategies to help you think about and analyze controversial material.

Exposition, because it presents facts and information, is usually associated with study reading in college. Argument, because it invites people to take sides and to come up with ideas and judgments of their own, is usually associated with critical reading.

It is not always easy to distinguish between exposition and argument, and they are often mixed within a single piece of writing. Most works you read, however, can be classified as predominantly one or the other. Classifying reading material as mainly expository or mainly argumentative can help you know what to look for as you read. Knowing the difference can help you predict.

Shift from your reading purpose to the author's writing purpose.   Your purpose for reading, the subject of earlier chapters, is still important. You have to have a purpose, know what it is, and use it to guide your reading. These next chapters, however, will now focus more on the author's purpose for writing. Is it to inform, to convince, to entertain, to describe, or to express personal feelings and experiences? Those are the broad categories that usually identify the author's purpose in such common types of written material as exposition, argument, imaginative literature, descriptive writing, and personal journals. Knowing the author's broad purpose helps you know what to look for as you read, and it also helps you predict.

Shift from the language of exposition to the language of argument.   You were taught in earlier chapters to determine the subject of what you are reading by asking, *What is the subject?* You were also advised to ask the question, *What does the author say about it?* This question helps you discover the main ideas and details. When you read and discuss argumentative writing, the language used to describe the subject, main idea, and details often shifts. The subject of argument is usually called the **issue**. Issues, by definition, are controversial. The sentence that states the author's position on the issue is usually called the **claim**. The claim is the thesis or purpose sentence in an argument. The main ideas and details in argument are usually called *reasons* and *evidence*. Argument, in fact, is often described as a *claim supported by reasons and evidence*. It may help you to think of the overall structure of an argument as a completed version of the following statement: "I think (make the claim) . . . , because (give the reasons) . . .

Shift from a single point of view to multiple points of view.   Your textbook authors write from their own points of view, even though they often also summarize those of many other researchers and scholars within their own writing. The focus of the first seven chapters in this book has been to help you comprehend a single author's point of view. The readings at the ends of the first six chapters, however, have presented selections on a single subject written from different points of view. This has prepared you for reading about argumentative issues that typically invite many perspectives and points of view. You can predict multiple perspectives and points of view on issues when you read argument.

Shift from writing to learn to writing to think.   You were told in Chapter 1 that at least one strategy in each chapter would be a writing strategy. Writing helps you learn the material you have read, and it also helps you think about it. Note that the writing strategies in previous chapters have helped you learn by teaching you to clarify and condense material in the form of reading notes, summaries, lists, maps, vocabulary sheets, and outlines. The writing strategies taught in the remaining chapters will help you analyze, think, react, work out, and express positions and original ideas in summary response papers, reaction papers, and free-writing exercises.

Shift your reading process.   As you make the shift from study reading to critical reading, you will continue to use the comprehension strategies you have practiced in the first seven chapters. To read critically, however, you will add to your present strategies or apply them in new ways. For example, you will still survey to find the subject, introduction, body, and conclusion, but you will add discovering the issue and the author's position on it. You will still read to identify the subject, the main ideas, the explanations, and the details, but you will now think of these as the issue, the claim, the reasons, and the evidence. You will still recognize organizational patterns and transitions, but you will also be interested in analyzing how particular patterns have been used to make an argument more convincing. You will still continue to look up words you do not know, and you will study visual materials; but now you may also become aware of the argumentative appeal of some words over others, and you will examine visuals to see how they contribute to the overall argument or make an argument of their own. As a result of these additions, you will modify your reading process to make it more effective for reading argument.

What Is Argument? Where Is It Found?

We can begin a definition of argument by stating what it is not. It is not "an argument" that is angry and contentious and not aimed at settling anything. Argument focuses instead on mental reasoning that may change perceptions, introduce new ways of thinking, and encourage new conclusions. Look at the front page of the daily newspaper to find examples of argumentative topics. Here are some: How much of the national budget should be set aside for defense? Should U.S. industry stop trading goods with countries that are regarded as potential enemies of the United States? Should the military draft be reinstated? Or, Should industry, the government, or both be responsible for reducing global warming? Here are some other examples you may find closer to your own experience: How will you meet both family and school responsibilities while you are in college? Should you change your major or stick with what you have chosen? Should you try to work and go to school at the same time? Should you try to study in a group or by yourself? Should you live at home or in an apartment? Final decisions on these topics may result in action, but the argument itself focuses on the issues and the reasons for thinking about them in particular ways.

Definitions of argument range from identifying opposing views, taking sides, providing reasons, and declaring winners to emphasizing common values and ideas and reaching consensus or agreement on controversial topics. Both definitions of argument are useful, depending on the argumentative context and purpose. Court-room argument and contest debate focus on polarizing issues as pro and con, taking sides, arguing both sides, and declaring winners. Scholarly argument is more likely to focus on understanding and clarifying issues along with the different perspectives people hold on them, and finally even negotiating agreement. Most people would agree that constructive argument in which the arguing parties look for points of agreement and ways to solve a problem is finally better than verbal fighting and standoffs that benefit no one. Most of the argument you will read as a college student will focus on differences in perspective but will also urge reasoned resolutions when that is possible.

Unresolved issues surround us, and once you become aware of them, you will find them in every class you take and in every book you read in college. Here are some examples of paragraphs from modern textbooks, like the ones you will read as a college student, that will demonstrate this idea. These examples identify a variety of issues and some of the perspectives people take on them. Read the paragraphs and answer the questions that follow them. These questions will call your attention to the issues in these passages.

Examples of Issues in Textbooks

I. The starting date for Renaissance art is the controversial subject in this passage from an art history textbook. Notice that this is a complicated date to establish and that there are various views on how to resolve this issue.

'LATE GOTHIC' PAINTING, SCULPTURE, AND GRAPHIC ARTS

As we narrow our focus from the Renaissance as a whole to the Renaissance in the fine arts, we are faced with many questions. When did Renaissance art start? Did it, like Gothic art, originate in a specific center, or did it arise in several places at the same time? Should we think of it as one coherent style or as a new "Renaissance-conscious" attitude that might be embodied in more than one style? "Renaissance consciousness" was an Italian idea, and there can be no doubt that Italy played the leading role in the development of Renaissance art, at least until the early sixteenth century. This fact does not necessarily mean, however, that the Renaissance was confined to the South. So far as architecture and sculpture are concerned, modern scholarship agrees with the traditional view, first expressed more than 500 years ago, that the Renaissance began soon after 1400. For painting, however, an even older tradition argues that the new era began with Giotto. Scholars hesitate to accept such a claim at face value, for they must then assume that the Renaissance in painting dawned about 1300, a full generation before Petrarch. Similarly, as we have seen, Giotto himself did not reject the past.[1]

[1] H. W. Janson and Anthony F. Janson, *A Basic History of Art,* 5th ed. (Upper Saddle River, NJ: Prentice Hall, 1997) 240.

Answer these questions.

1. What is the traditional date for the beginning of the Renaissance?_____
2. What is another date some scholars cite as the beginning of Renaissance painting? _____

---

2. Whether the 1963 film *Cleopatra,* with Elizabeth Taylor and directed by Joseph L. Mankiewicz, was a good film or a bad film is the controversial issue in this passage from a film studies textbook. Notice that the authors take a position on this issue and provide reasons and evidence for their evaluation.

CLEOPATRA

Corbis

Cleopatra (U.S.A., 1963), *with Elizabeth Taylor, directed by Joseph L. Mankiewicz.*

Cleopatra was described as the most costly fiasco in the history of movies—a project that was originally budgeted at $1.2 million and eventually ran away at nearly $40 million. A four-hour exercise in overkill, it groans under the weight of its mindless extravagance. The project was stalled for years because of production foul-ups, illness of its star Elizabeth Taylor, various personnel changes (including new leading men), new rewrites for the script, and a new director. (Mankiewicz was more suited to sophisticated drawing-room comedy than to epic spectacles, but he did his best with a bad situation.)

Taylor was one of the top stars of the 1960s, commanding a salary of $1 million per picture plus a percentage of the profits. During the production of the film, she was engaged in a much-publicized love affair with leading man Richard Burton, who later became her husband—twice. Among the many extravagances of the picture was Taylor's insistence that Twentieth Century-Fox hire hairdresser Sidney Guilaroff at $1700 per week to style her hair. She was so burdened by gaudy headdresses and costumes that her beauty was actually undermined—she looks like a plump gilded pigeon about to topple over from the sheer weight of it all. The same thing happened to the movie. Twentieth Century-Fox almost toppled with it. (*Twentieth Century-Fox*)[2]

[2] Louis Giannetti and Scott Eyman, *Flashback: A Brief History of Film*, 3rd ed. (Englewood Cliffs: Prentice Hall, 1996) 32.

Answer these questions.

1. Would these authors give *Cleopatra* a "thumbs up" to recommend it or a "thumbs down" to discourage viewers?_____

2. What are two of their reasons?

   (a) _____

   (b) _____

   _____

   _____

3. Whether there is a difference in the way men and women behave toward other people, and what causes this difference, is the subject of the next paragraphs. Notice that the position about men's and women's behavior presented here is that of researcher Carol Gilligan. Other people, including you, may not agree with her. Gilligan believes that men and women develop fundamentally different self-concepts when they are children. Men learn to be independent and women learn to care for others and to become more intimately connected to other people than do men. This passage explains the results of this possible difference. It is from a philosophy textbook.

MALE AND FEMALE SELF-CONCEPTS AND ETHICAL VALUES

To make matters more complicated, Gilligan proposes another theory. . . . In essence, she suggests that the different thought processes and values of mature men and women result from the self-concept we form when we are very young.[3] We end up with one of two different self-concepts, she says, one individual, autonomous, and essentially separate from others, the other intimately connected to other people. Gilligan claims that most men develop the former self, most women, the latter.

In essence, Gilligan argues that our ethical outlook stems largely from the psychological makeup associated with our gender. Take the "masculine" view of the self. Men are separate, autonomous individuals, out in the world doing what they want. Inevitably they come into conflict with each other. Many men may want the same thing, but only one of them can have it, or they find their individual interests in total opposition. How do they protect their "separateness" and yet live in the same society? The most logical way is to adopt an ethic of fairness, equality, and impartiality, the rules of which specify the rights of all and apply the same way to all. Thus Kohlberg's ethic of "justice" is appropriate in a society of "separate" masculine selves.

On the other hand, if we see ourselves as essentially connected to other people, we will develop a different ethic. In a reality based on relationships,

---

[3] See Chapter 3, "Concepts of Self and Morality," from Carol Gilligan, *In a Different Voice: Psychological Theory and Women's Development* (Cambridge: Harvard University Press, 1982) for the details of this process.

the chief threat is a lack of care for other people. Because we must inevitably accept different responsibilities to different people, the ethical dilemmas that people with this orientation face stem mainly from the fact that they have competing or conflicting responsibilities. Which responsibility gets priority? One must look at the specifics of each situation very carefully and then decide who gets special treatment. Thus, a view of the self as "connected" implies the primacy of Gilligan's ethic of care.[4]

Answer these questions.

1. Do you agree that men's early training causes them to compete and to come into conflict with others more than women do? Yes or no? _____ Why do you think so? _____

_____

2. Do you agree that women's early training causes them to compete less than men and to be more likely to care for others than men? Yes or no? _____ Why do you think so?_____

_____

---

4. The issue in the following paragraphs concerns water pollution. How serious is this problem? What should be done about it? Most people recognize this as a serious issue, and the author of this geologic environment textbook makes his position on these questions clear.

CONTAMINATION OF OUR NATION'S WATER RESOURCES

The increasing contamination of our nation's water resources is one of the three most important environmental problems in this country. The other two are soil pollution and air pollution. Immense societal effort and vast amounts of money are needed to correct existing contamination/pollution, which has built up over two centuries in the United States. Unless we begin now, the problems may become unsolvable. The old adage "out of sight, out of mind" is true, but is disastrous when applied to polluted groundwater, which cannot be ignored. Once surface or groundwater becomes polluted, it is very difficult—often impossible—to purify it. An ounce of prevention is worth a ton of cure.

The largest non-governmental polluters are the chemical industries. They unavoidably produce large amounts of synthetic and nonsynthetic compounds that become effluent from their plants. State governments have controlled these effluents inadequately as they strive to offer a "friendly" environment for industrial growth. The result of this policy is clearly evident in the lower Mississippi River area, particularly the delta region of southern

---

[4] Thomas I. White, *Discovering Philosophy* (Upper Saddle River: Prentice Hall, 1991) 421.

Louisiana, where the river is a soup of toxic chemicals, pesticides, fertilizers, and misplaced nutrients.

Pesticides, poorly designed sanitary landfills, and inadequate sewage treatment are other major sources of water pollution. The use of pesticides should be decreased and eventually abandoned. Communities should closely regulate landfill construction and sewage treatment. Protection of a community's drinking water must receive high priority.[5]

Answer these questions.

1. What is this author's position on the problem of water pollution? _____
   _____

2. What does the author say should be done about water pollution? Identify three solutions. (a) _____ (b) _____

   (c) _____

---

5. You may not expect some subjects to be controversial at all, but they are. At issue in this paragraph from a sociology textbook is the definition of death. Notice that the definition has recently changed. You can assume that there may have been considerable discussion and argument before this new definition was negotiated and agreed upon.

WHEN DOES DEATH OCCUR?

Common sense suggests that life ceases when breathing and heartbeat stop. But the ability to revive or replace a heart and to artificially sustain respiration have rendered such notions of death obsolete. Medical and legal experts in the United States now define death as an *irreversible* state involving no response to stimulation, no movement or breathing, no reflexes, and no indication of brain activity.[6, 7]

Answer these questions.

1. What was the old definition of death? _____

2. What is the new definition of death? _____

3. Why was the definition changed? _____

These examples are included here to help you begin to recognize controversial topics in your textbooks. Additional information to help you recognize argument is provided in the next section.

[5] Harvey Blatt, *Our Geologic Environment* (Upper Saddle River: Prentice Hall, 1997) 225.

[6] John Ladd, "The Definition of Death and the Right to Die," in *Ethical Issues Relating to Life and Death,* John Ladd, ed. (New York: Oxford University Press, 1979) 118–45; and Thomas F. Wall, *Medical Ethics: Basic Moral Issues* (Washington: University Press of America, 1980).

[7] John J. Macionis, *Sociology*, 6th ed. (Upper Saddle River: Prentice Hall, 1997) 544.

How to Recognize Argument

Obvious argument.   Argument appears in different forms. The most obvious and the easiest to recognize is when the author states an issue, takes a position on it, and argues in favor of that position. It is clear that the author wants to convince you either to strengthen or change your current position or beliefs. Articles that openly argue for the abolishment of capital punishment or for providing more scholarships and loans for college students are examples. The paragraphs you just read from the textbook on the environment is another good example.

Hidden argument.   Sometimes when reading apparently informative material, such as a textbook, a newspaper, or a newsmagazine, you will discover that the author actually has an argumentative intent. For example, in a history textbook you may find an author arguing that the Constitution was written to further the business interests of its authors. You had always thought that these individuals had more idealistic motives. Furthermore, you can find other sources that agree with you. You decide that the author is biased on this issue and that the material about the Constitution represents just one view on this issue. You also notice that the only evidence provided in the article supports the author's point of view. In addition, you notice that the author uses some fairly emotional examples to prove this point. These stacked details that represent only one side of the issue and the emotional examples alert you to the fact that this author probably holds biased opinions on this issue and is presenting an argument to change your mind about the authors of the Constitution. Much material that is written primarily to inform also contains argumentative passages, and the intention, even though concealed, is at least partly to convince.

Unconscious argument.   Sometimes authors are aware when they switch from writing information to writing argument, and other times they are not. Imagine the author who is opposed to legalizing marijuana for medical purposes and who is assigned to write an article that explains the advantages of this practice. In spite of this author's best efforts to remain neutral on this issue, bias will often creep in. The result may be an unconscious effort to change people's minds about the medical benefits of the drug. You are alerted to the author's unconscious argumentative purpose when you notice that the evidence in the article is more likely to demonstrate the dangers than the benefits of marijuana, that the authorities quoted in the article confirm the danger, that the pictures give a negative impression, and that the examples seem to show more harms than benefits. At the same time, the author affirms that the drug can and should be used for medical purposes. It is up to you as a reader to try to figure out what is really going on in such an article and what the author really thinks.

Exploratory argument.   Sometimes the author's purpose is to explain several different views on an issue without taking a particular position or siding with any one of them. Newspaper and magazine authors often write about issues in this way. So do your textbook authors. As a reader you will want to determine whether or not each position receives equal treatment, or whether one view seems to be favored over another, thus revealing the author's bias. When there is no apparent bias and each position is simply explained rather than advocated, writing that explores an issue is informative rather than argumentative. The purpose is to help the reader understand the different views and perhaps to think about them and discuss them but not necessarily to accept one of them. The four justifications for punishment in the "Criminal Justice System" on pages 133–138 is an example of exploratory argument.

Some Ways to Predict Controversy and Argument

Besides the types of argument that have just been explained, there are other clues that can alert you to an argumentative purpose and help you predict that you will be reading argument. Gathering information about the subject, the author, the point of view, the context for the argument, and the source will help you discover possible signs of controversy and author bias.

The subject.   The length of a 12-inch ruler, especially if you measure it yourself to make sure that it is 12 inches long, is not controversial. You would not argue about its length. People do, however, argue about issues. They argue, for example, about whether women should serve side by side with men in military combat, about how to cure AIDS, about how to treat young criminals, and about a host of other public issues that can affect people's lives in significant ways. Scholars and scientists have their own issues to argue about: Do we really have free will? What is the nature of black holes? Is chemical use threatening the ozone layer and causing a greenhouse effect? Will computers ever duplicate human thought processes? Some subjects, by their very nature, are controversial. When you pick up a book or an article, take a look at the title, skim the table of contents, and read the preface and the first paragraph to get an idea of the subject. Call up what you already know to help you determine whether the subject is controversial. Knowing that a subject is controversial before you begin to read will help you predict argument.

The author.   Figure out if the author is taking a stand on a controversial issue and predict what that stand will be. Sometimes authors reveal their positions in the preface or introduction. Or, an editorial note about the author may provide just enough information to signal a possible argumentative purpose. Look particularly for an author's affiliations with groups, organizations, governments, companies, or societies that might result in a particular position or point of view. Vietnam veterans, black ministers, wealthy industrialists, small businesspeople, students, property owners, medical doctors, and women's rights activists are all likely to think about particular issues in ways that reflect their values, experiences, affiliations, or backgrounds. Use what you already know about the values and beliefs of these groups of people to anticipate an author's possible position on an issue.

The point of view.   To say an author takes a stand, expresses a position, or has a "take" on an issue is the same as saying that the author has a particular point of view. Modern issues are complex, and they often invite many different points of view, and certainly more than two. Television debates, often shown on the nightly news in the form of two talking heads, encourage people to polarize issues and to think of them as having only two points of view, for or against. In reality, there are a variety of points of view that can be taken on virtually every issue. For example, the issue of what to do with young criminals may invite a tough point of view (put them in with hardened criminals) or a soft point of view (send them to juvenile facilities). There are, however, other ways of thinking about these problems that might involve education, parents, the church, or organized support groups. Or, the focus may be on unique forms of punishment like community service that may be particularly appropriate for the young. Identify the author's point of view and approach to an issue as soon as you can. Knowing the point of view will help you predict the ideas that the author will make, and this, in turn, will enable you to read and follow along more easily. Understanding the author's point of view can also help you discover your own point of view on an issue, an important by-product of critical reading.

The context for argument. Argument does not suddenly appear out of nowhere. Something usually happens to cause issues to surface and get people's attention. For example, unusually hot summer temperatures cause people to speculate about the present status of global warming, an oil spill raises environmental protection issues, new legislation on gay marriage raises the issues associated with what constitutes a family in America, crowded schools trigger discussion of immigration issues, and an increase in the number of homeless people invites discussion of who should take responsibility for them. On campus, crowded parking lots may cause discussion about parking issues, or too many closed classes may cause students to question class scheduling policies. Pay attention to what is going on both inside and outside of your school. If a dramatic, real-life situation occurs that captures people's attention, you can usually predict that many people will begin to discuss and write about the associated issues. When you read controversial material, see if you can figure out what happened that motivated the author to write on that issue at that particular time.

The source. Sometimes the title of a book, magazine, or journal will alert you to the possibility that you might be reading argument. A title might also convey a possible point of view and even a possible context for the argument. *Ms.*, a magazine associated with the feminist movement, or *Modern Maturity*, a magazine for retired people, are examples. You might also pay attention to the date of publication. Issues can surface and get a lot of attention for a while and then lie dormant until something happens to bring them back up again. Look at the date of the publication to help you figure out if the issue is a current one. Also, try to discover if the issue has been argued repeatedly, off and on, over a long period of time and thus is an enduring issue. Under what conditions to declare war, how to describe women's roles and responsibilities, and how to respond to the poor and homeless are examples of enduring issues that have engaged human beings for centuries.

When it is not possible to gather enough information about the subject, author, point of view, context, and source before you begin to read argument, you will need to look for this information while you read. To help you read, make sure you understand the general issue in the argument. Then locate the claim, which states the main point of the argument and answers the question, What is the author trying to prove? It is the main point of the argument, and locating it right away will help you understand and follow the rest of the argument.

Types of Claims and Argumentative Purpose

There are five types of claims in argument, and each of them represents a different argumentative purpose. Knowing the types of claims and being able to recognize them as you read will help you figure out each author's purpose. Virtually every argument can be placed into one of the following five categories of claims. Notice also that each claim attempts to answer the question or questions that are associated with it. These questions all invite different points of view. They all lead to argument.

The Types of Claims

1. **Claims of Fact:** Did it happen? Is it true?
2. **Claims of Definition:** What is it? How should we define it?
3. **Claims of Cause:** What caused it? What are the effects?
4. **Claims of Value:** Is it good or bad? How do we know?
5. **Claims of Policy:** What should we do about it?

The five brief examples of argument that were used to introduce you to argument earlier in this chapter (see pp. 262–266) exemplify the five types of claims and the five associated purposes for argument. Here is a brief analysis of each of them.

Claims of Fact

Example: From an art history textbook, " 'Late Gothic' Painting, Sculpture, and Graphic Arts" (review pp. 262–263).

Issue: When did Renaissance art begin?

Claim: "So far as architecture and sculpture are concerned, modern scholarship agrees with the traditional view . . . that the Renaissance began soon after 1400."

Purpose: To establish a date for the beginning of the Renaissance. To establish what happened and when. To refute the view that the Renaissance in painting began earlier.

Claims of fact are often central to the argument in courtroom debate. Lawyers argue about what happened in order to prove innocence or guilt. Historians also argue about what happened as they sort through historical evidence to try to establish historical fact. Other examples of claims of fact: Women are as effective as men in combat; modern students care more about making money than establishing a philosophy of life; women are better than men at building consensus. Notice that all of these are apparent statements of fact, but not everyone would agree with them. They are all arguable.

Claims of Definition

Example: From works on ethics and a sociology textbook, "When Does Death Occur?" (review p. 266).

Issue: How should we define death?

Claim: "Medical and legal experts in the United States now define death as an *irreversible* state involving no response to stimulation, no movement or breathing, no reflexes, and no indication of brain activity."

Purpose: To establish that former definitions of death are now obsolete and to argue for a new definition.

Entire arguments can center around the definition of a term. Here are some examples of claims of definition: The fetus must be defined as a human being, not just a bunch of cells; wars conducted by the United States in this century can all be defined as just rather than unjust wars; sexual harassment must be defined in terms of behavior and not sexual desire. Notice that the arguments will focus on the definitions of fetus, just and unjust war, and sexual harassment in these claims. If you agree with the definition, you agree with the claim. If you do not, you may want to argue.

Claims of Cause

Example: From a philosophy textbook, "Male and Female Self-Concepts and Ethical Values" (review pp. 264–265).

Issue: How is the ethical behavior of men and women different?

Claim: "In essence, Gilligan argues that our ethical outlook stems largely from the psychological makeup associated with our gender."

Purpose: To suggest that the cause of people's ethical outlook, or how they relate to other people as described in the rest of the passage, is caused by gender rather than something else. Thus men behave one way because they are men, and women behave another way because they are women.

People often disagree about what causes something to happen, and they also disagree about the effects. Here are some other examples of claims of cause: Overeating causes disease and early death; a healthy economy causes people to have faith in their political leaders; sending infants to day care can result in psychological problems later on. The cause–effect relationship is at issue in these statements.

Claims of Value

Example: From the film history textbook, "*Cleopatra*" (review pp. 263–264).

Issue: Was the film *Cleopatra* a success or a failure?

Claim: "*Cleopatra* was described as the most costly fiasco in the history of movies. . . ."

Purpose: To argue that the film *Cleopatra*, in spite of its famous stars and enormous cost, was a failure. It did not make money, and it nearly ruined Twentieth Century-Fox.

Claims of value, as their name implies, aim at establishing whether the item being discussed is either good or bad, valuable or not valuable, desirable or not desirable. It is often necessary to establish criteria for goodness or badness in these arguments and then to apply them to the subject to show why something should be regarded as either good or bad. Here are some additional examples of claims of value: Public schools are better than private schools; science fiction novels are more interesting to read than romance novels; dogs are the best pet; mercy killing is immoral.

Claims of Policy

Example: From a geologic environment textbook, "Contamination of Our Nation's Water Resources" (review pp. 265–266).

Issue: What should we do about contaminated water?

Claim: "Immense societal effort and vast amounts of money are needed to correct existing contamination/pollution, which has built up over two centuries in the United States."

Purpose: To argue that it is time to put a lot of money and effort into purifying the water in the United States.

A claim of policy often describes a problem and then suggests ways to solve it. Here are some additional examples of policy claims: We should stop spending so much on prisons and start spending more on rehabilitation; children in low income families should receive medical insurance from the government; social security should be abolished in favor of private savings accounts. Deciding what to do in the face of problems has always been one of the major purposes of argument.

How to Read Argument

You have been introduced to a number of important features of argumentative writing in this chapter. Understanding and recognizing these features will help you predict and read more critically and analytically. One characteristic of an educated person is to be able to recognize the difference between undisputed fact and issues that are still open to question and that invite opinion. Your professors spend much of their time reading argument. As a college student, you will read a great deal of argument also.

There are a number of possible effects that reading argument can have on you: You may decide to stay with your original position; you may change your position completely; you may change your position somewhat; or you may take a neutral position, at least until you read and think more about it. Try to decide what you think for now, and recognize that you could change your mind in the future. Finally, regard argument as a continuing conversation with many voices, one of which can be yours.

UNDERSTANDING CONTEXT, PURPOSE, POINT OF VIEW: FIVE STRATEGIES

The five strategies that follow will help you recognize the issues and claims in written argument and understand the author's motivation and point of view. They will also suggest ways that you can maintain an active interest as you read, develop your own point of view, and respond to what you have read.

▶

Strategy 1: Identify the issue and form an issue question.

Identify the broad general issue area when you read controversial material. Examples of broad issue areas are crime, health care, or computers. Then identify the specific related issue that focuses on an aspect of the broad general issue area. Formulate the specific issue as an issue question: What should we do about overcrowded prisons? How are we to define dangerous levels of secondhand smoke? How are computers changing the people who use them? Either locating the author's issue question or formulating such a question yourself will help you identify exactly what is at issue in an article or chapter. This will help you answer the question, What is at issue in this argument?

Strategy 2: Identify the claim. Determine the type of claim.

The claim states the author's position on the issue. The claim is usually located at or near the beginning of an argument, but it can also appear at the end or even in the middle. Sometimes there is no one sentence that functions as a claim, and you will need to put parts of sentences together to describe what the argument is about. These parts then become the claim. When you cannot find the claim at the beginning of an argument, look at the end to see if it is there. Authors may lead up to the claim and place it at the end for special emphasis. The claim organizes everything in the argument and provides you with a focus for reading. All of the rest of the argument supports the claim.

The claim is always a statement rather than a question. The author answers the issue question with the claim. To help you find the claim, ask, What does this author think about the issue? Or, How does this author answer the issue question? For example, in response to the issue question, What should we do about overcrowded prisons? the claim might be, Old and feeble prisoners should be released to society to make room in prison for younger and more dangerous criminals. In response to the issue question, How are we to define dangerous levels of secondhand smoke? the claim might be, The smoke from a single smoker's cigarette can be defined as producing dangerous levels of toxic smoke for nonsmokers. In answer to the issue question, How are computers changing the people who use them? the claim might be, Computers isolate, dehumanize, and depress the people who spend most of their time working on them.

Identify the type of claim. In the three examples used here, the claim about what to do with prisoners is a policy claim. The claim about secondhand smoke is a definition claim. The claim about computers is a value claim. Sometimes more than one type of claim appears in a single argument. One type of claim will predominate, however, and the others will appear as subclaims that further develop the main argument expressed by the predominant claim.

Identifying the claim helps you understand the author's position and purpose in the argument. The claim also helps you predict the organizational pattern, which will help you follow the argument. Fact argument is often arranged chronologically,

▶

particularly when the objective is to establish what happened in the past. Definition argument often involves comparison, since one way to define is to show how something is either like or different from something else. Cause argument usually follows a cause–effect or effect–cause organizational pattern. Value argument often includes a list of criteria to apply to the object being evaluated in order to establish whether it is good or bad. Policy argument usually has a problem–solution pattern of organization.

Strategy 3: Speculate about the context for the argument.

Make some guesses about what happened to motivate a writer to write about an issue. If the context is not explained in the text, draw on your own background to guess what caused the author to write. Guessing about an author's motivation will help you generate interest in the material. For example, a policy claim that English should become the common language in Europe may be motivated by the special interests of people in business. It is easier to sell American goods in Europe if the advertising that goes with it does not have to be translated into a number of other languages. Or, the decision to find a new definition for death may be motivated by a physician's ability to keep peoples' hearts beating with machines even when there are no other signs of life. Look at the front page of your daily newspaper for some recent examples of newsworthy incidents that may be generating argument.

Strategy 4: Write out your point of view before you read and compare it with the author's as you read.

As soon as you have figured out the issue, jot down your ideas about it before you begin to read and even before you find the claim and determine the author's point of view. Writing your ideas will help you maintain active interest in your reading, which will also help you interact with the ideas in the text.

Strategy 5: Look for common ground, decide what you think, and write your reactions.

As you read, identify the author's point of view and argumentative purpose and try to understand the reasons that support that point of view. Analyze the common ground that you have with the author. Do you share any common experiences or opinions? If you do, then you will be more likely to agree with at least some of the author's ideas. When you finish reading, decide what you think now. Look back at your preliminary notes to see if you have changed any of your original ideas as a result of reading. The purpose of argument is to cause readers to change their views. Was the author successful with you? Reflect on what you have read and think about the effect the material has had on your thinking. Write out some of your thoughts and reactions to help you remember them for discussion and exams.

EXERCISES AND READINGS

THREE COLLABORATIVE CLASS EXERCISES

Exercise 1

Read and react to an argumentative essay. *Whole class.*

This exercise will give you practice in comparing your point of view with those of two different authors, in analyzing any changes in your opinions that result from reading, and in reacting to the essays in writing. The following essays express two different points of view on the issue of sexual harassment.

a. First, write out all of your present opinions, experiences, and thoughts on the issue of sexual harassment. Write your present point of view.

b. Second, before you read the essays, read the five questions and complete Test 1, which begins below and continues on the next page, by indicating in column 1 whether you agree or disagree.

c. Now read Essay 1 and answer the five questions on Test 2 as you think the author would answer them. Next, read Essay #2 and answer the questions on Test 3 as you think the author of Essay 2 would answer them. Finally, take Test 4 and answer the questions yourself. Have any of your answers changed since your original answers for Test 1?

d. Underline the sentence in each essay that, in your opinion, best states the author's claim and write answers to the following questions: What type of claim is it? Are other types of claims made in this essay? What other types of claims? (*Note:* There may be disagreement on the claims and types of claims in your class. Just be able to defend your answer and see if the class can reach some agreement on these questions.)

e. Write answers to these questions: How does Rush Limbaugh define sexual harassment? How does Macionis define it? How do you define it?

f. Write a reaction statement in which you express either agreement or disagreement with either one or both of the two authors, and state why. Give your present point of view on sexual harassment. Also, indicate how your point of view changed, if it did, as a result of reading. Read and discuss with the class both your answers to the questions in items *d* and *e* and your reaction statement on sexual harassment.

Check "agree" or "disagree" after each statement	Before You Read	After You Read		
	Test 1 How would you answer?	Test 2 How would the author of essay 1 answer?	Test 3 How would the author of essay 2 answer?	Test 4 How would you answer now?
1. Feminists think normal male behavior is sexual harassment.	agree _____ disagree _____	agree _____ disagree _____	agree _____ disagree _____	agree _____ disagree _____
2. Sexual harassment laws will inhibit men and make them shy.	agree _____ disagree _____	agree _____ disagree _____	agree _____ disagree _____	agree _____ disagree _____

▶

Check "agree" or "disagree" after each statement	Before You Read	After You Read		
	Test 1 How would you answer?	Test 2 How would the author of essay 1 answer?	Test 3 How would the author of essay 2 answer?	Test 4 How would you answer now?
3. Real sexual harassment should be defined as real rape.	agree ____ disagree ____	agree ____ disagree ____	agree ____ disagree ____	agree ____ disagree ____
4. Women can avoid sexual harassment by just saying no.	agree ____ disagree ____	agree ____ disagree ____	agree ____ disagree ____	agree ____ disagree ____
5. Men need women to civilize them.	agree ____ disagree ____	agree ____ disagree ____	agree ____ disagree ____	agree ____ disagree ____

Essay 1: Sexual Harassment and the Feminist "Front"

RUSH LIMBAUGH

Explanatory Note: *Rush Limbaugh is well known as a conservative radio talk-show host. He is a provocative political commentator, and in this excerpt from his book* See, I Told You So, *Limbaugh describes his views on the issue of sexual harassment.*

Do you think looking at someone is sexual harassment? Do you think all men are rapists? Do you think all sex is rape? If your answer to any or all of these questions is no, you are simply not, by definition, a feminist. Don't forget, you mainstream women out there who may think I am exaggerating: It is not you who defines feminism or sets the movement's agenda. You may prefer to think of the feminist movement as an innocuous, well-meaning organization committed to equality between the sexes. Wishing it so doesn't make it so. And I'm here to tell you, as painful or unpleasant as it may be to your ears, there is nothing innocuous about the feminist leadership in this country. And make no mistake, these women are the ones who set the agenda for the feminist movement. 1

The people who define modern feminism are saying that normal male deportment is harassment, near rape, abuse, and disrespect. These extremists, who make up the intellectual leadership of the modern feminist movement, are attempting to make the case that any expression of interest by a man in a woman is harassment. Inevitably, this is going to lead to several serious problems. 2

First among those is that men will become fearful about making any advances. This attitude will confuse men about what is right and what kind of behavior is acceptable. If no approach is welcome, then women will, by necessity, have to become the aggressors. Men will be afraid of crossing the line. 3

The second major problem with this trend is that it trivializes real sexual harassment, real rape. When people are labeling everyday, normal, male–female con- 4 duct as sexual harassment, we not only obliterate relations between the sexes, but we greatly trivialize true sexual harassment. Harassment is now being so broadly defined by some that it entails any behavior that offends or annoys or interrupts your life.

The fact of the matter is that women have far more power than most of them realize. It's a biological fact that males are the aggressors. We all know this is true. That means that the ultimate power—the power to say yes or no—lies with women. [. . .]

Some militant feminists apparently harbor such animosity for the opposite sex that they want to criminalize the process of courtship—the old-fashioned "chase." I have news for these people: It's normal for boys to pursue girls. It's natural for men to pursue women. This normal and natural process, once called the fine art of seduction, is being confused with harassment. What was once considered an important part of the process of finding a mate is being mischaracterized as rape.

How should you channel normal masculinity and the aggressive nature of the male? Would these women prefer men as husbands, or leaders of marauding gangs? That is basically the choice. Because women can be—and need to be—a great civilizing influence over men.

Do you realize that in some cities today men can be arrested for making a wolf whistle at a comely woman? Now, I'm not suggesting that this is the kind of behavior we should encourage, but should it be criminalized? And what are the consequences of this sort of overreaction? The consequences are manifold. It's no wonder so many men and women have problems interacting. Rules and regulations like these are presumably meant to foster improved relations between men and women, but their effect is just the opposite. What is being fostered is an adversarial relationship between the sexes.

Take, for instance, the young star of "The Wonder Years," Fred Savage. The then sixteen-year-old was hit with a sexual-harassment suit by a former staffer of the show, Monique Long, who claimed that Savage repeatedly asked her to have an affair with him and—egads!—touched her by holding her hand. The lawsuit also charged that Jason Hervey, another actor on the show, harassed Long during her two years on the show as a costume designer, at one point touching her "in a sexual way." Long, thirty-two, claimed she was asked not to return to the show because of her complaints about the actors.

Have things gotten to the point where a man, or boy, can't ask a woman out? Can't flirt? Is it a crime to hold somebody's hand? Wouldn't a more appropriate response to questionable behavior have been for this thirty-two-year-old woman to call the teenager's parents? Or even slap him in the face? Is our society so confused now about relations between men and women that a mature adult doesn't know how to deal with a flirtatious sixteen-year-old?[8]

870 words

[8] From Rush Limbaugh, *See, I Told You So* (New York: Pocket Star Books, 1993) 224–227.

Essay #2: Sexual Harassment[9]

JOHN J. MACIONIS

Explanatory Note: *This next selection about sexual harassment comes from a sociology textbook. The author defines the subject of sexual harassment as the current laws define it, and presents examples. Two laws are currently in place that protect individuals from sexual harassment: Title VII of the Civil Rights Act of 1964 prohibits sexual harassment in the workplace. Complaints are filed with the U.S. Equal Employment Opportunity Commission, and the employer is responsible for stopping the objectionable behavior. Title IX of the Education Amendments of 1972 prohibits sexual harassment of students and employees in educational institutions that receive federal funding. Any institution that does not respond to complaints of sexual harassment could lose federal funding.*

Sexual harassment refers to *comments, gestures, or physical contact of a sexual nature that are deliberate, repeated, and unwelcome.* During the 1990s, sexual harassment became an issue of national importance that rewrote the rules for workplace interaction between women and men. [1]

Most (but not all) victims of sexual harassment are women. The reason is that, first, our culture encourages men to be sexually assertive and to see women in sexual terms. As a result, social interaction in the workplace, on campus, and elsewhere can easily take on sexual overtones. Second, most people in positions of power—including business executives, doctors, bureau chiefs, assembly-line supervisors, professors, and military officers—are men who oversee the work of women. Surveys carried out in widely different work settings show that half of the women respondents receive unwanted sexual attention.[10] [2]

Sexual harassment is sometimes obvious and direct: A supervisor may ask for sexual favors from an employee and make threats if the advances are refused. Courts have declared such *quid pro quo* sexual harassment (the Latin phrase means "one thing in return for another") to be a violation of civil rights. [3]

More often, however, sexual harassment is a matter of subtle behavior—sexual teasing, off-color jokes, the display of pinups—that may not even be *intended* to harass anyone. But by the *effect* standard favored by many feminists, such actions add up to creating a *hostile environment*. Incidents of this kind are far more complex because they involve different perceptions of the same behavior. For example, a man may think that by repeatedly complimenting a co-worker on her appearance he is simply being friendly. The co-worker may believe that the man is thinking of her in sexual terms and is not taking her work seriously, an attitude that could harm her job performance and prospects for advancement. [4]

302 words

[9] John J. Macionis, *Sociology*, 11th ed. (Upper Saddle River: Prentice-Hall, 2007) 348, 350.
[10] NORC. *General Social Surveys, 1972–2002: Cumulative Codebook.* (Chicago: National Opinion Research Center, 2003).

Predict the issue, the author's point of view, and the context. *Small groups.*

Form small groups of three or four students and work with the following lists. Be prepared to report your conclusions to the class.

a. **Book Titles.** The following list of actual book titles and authors probably signal that they will contain at least some controversy and argument.

- *Down the Tube: An Inside Account of the Failure of American Television* by William F. Baker, president of New York's public television station, and George Dessart, professor of radio and television at the City University of New York.

- *$40 Million Slaves: The Rise, Fall, and Redemption of the Black Athlete.* By William C. Rhoden, sports columnist for the *New York Times.*

- *Hostile Takeover: How Big Money and Corruption Conquered Our Government—and How to Take It Back.* By David Sirota, former Democratic staff member on Capitol Hill and now a Montana-based blogger.

- *Exporting America: Why Corporate Greed Is Shipping American Jobs Overseas.* By Lou Dobbs, business journalist and CNN anchor.

- *The End of Iraq: How American Incompetence Created a War Without End.* By Peter W. Galbraith, an authority on the Kurdish people in Iraq.

- *Godless: The Church of Liberalism.* By Ann Coulter, a conservative columnist who argues that liberalism is a religion.

  (1) What **issue** or issues would you predict each of these authors will discuss?
  (2) What possible **points of view** might you find in these books?
  (3) Speculate as well about the possible **contexts** for these books. (They were all published in 2006, except for *Down the Tube,* which was published in 1998.) Answer the question, What may have happened to cause these authors to write about these issues? Use your imagination.

b. **Magazine Titles.** Now make the same predictions about the titles of some actual magazines. Identify at least one issue that you would expect to find discussed in each of these magazines.

- *AFL-CIO News*
  Issue: _____

- *American Rifleman*
  Issue: _____

- *The American School Board Journal*
  Issue: _____

- *Business Today*
  Issue: _____

- *Black Issues in Higher Education*
  Issue: _____

- *Hispanic*
  Issue: _____

Author's Affiliation and Context. Read the following list of made-up authors, affiliations, contexts for their argument, and titles of their essays. What point of view would you anticipate in each essay?

Author	Affiliation	Occasion	Essay Topic
1. Henry Jones	Trustee of the Council to Protect the Environment	Recent national meeting on the "greenhouse effect" and global warming	"The Natural Environment and Industry"

Anticipated point of view: _____

2. Nancy Cromwell	Caseworker, Planned Parenthood	Recent report that abortion pills will soon be available	"The Abortion Pill"

Anticipated point of view: _____

3. Bill Williams	President, pro-life group	Recent report that abortion pills will soon be available	"The Abortion Pill"

Anticipated point of view: _____

4. Mary Maxwell	Single, working mother	Pending legislation on whether federal government should or should not provide day-care funds	"The Day-Care Issue: Who Is Responsible?"

Anticipated point of view: _____

5. Richard Jones	President, school board; executive, IBM	Student attacks teacher on school grounds	"Discipline in the Schools"

Anticipated point of view: _____

THREE READING EXERCISES:
ABOUT ETHICS

The following three readings are drawn from a college marketing textbook and from two modern newspapers, the *New York Times* and the *Washington Post.* These articles present different points of view on various ethical subjects. The first reading addresses invasion-of-privacy issues in direct marketing. Direct marketing is Internet marketing. It can also be conducted by mail or telephone, and it is often associated with the compilation of huge databases of information about its customers. The second reading examines student-teacher e-mailing and asks whether rules or standards should be set to create more appropriate e-mail communication. The third alerts readers to some of the problems with physician-assisted suicide, a practice widely debated that is still against the law in America.

Reading 1

Public Policy and Ethical Issues in Direct Marketing[11]

GARY ARMSTRONG AND PHILIP KOTLER

Explanatory Notes: *The following selection is taken from Chapter 13, "Communicating Customer Value: Personal Selling and Direct Marketing," in the textbook* Marketing, An Introduction. *Both authors are university professors. They address the invasion of privacy issue in direct marketing. This is an example of a controversial subject being treated as a serious issue in a textbook.* **Do you ever worry about privacy when you provide credit card and other personal information by phone or on the Internet when you are making a purchase? Do you ever wonder whether or not your purchase will be delivered to you after you have given your credit card information?**

Direct marketers and their customers usually enjoy mutually rewarding relationships. Occasionally, however, a darker side emerges. The aggressive and sometimes shady tactics of a few direct marketers can bother or harm consumers, giving the entire industry a black eye. Abuses range from simple excesses that irritate consumers to instances of unfair practices or even outright deception and fraud. The direct marketing industry has also faced growing concerns about invasion-of-privacy issues. [. . .]

Invasion of Privacy

Invasion of privacy is perhaps the toughest public policy issue now confronting the direct marketing industry. These days, it seems that almost every time consumers enter a sweepstakes, apply for a credit card, take out a magazine subscription, or order products by mail, telephone, or the Internet, their names are entered into some company's already bulging database. Using sophisticated computer technologies, direct marketers can use these databases to "microtarget" their selling efforts.

Consumers often benefit from such database marketing—they receive more offers that are closely matched to their interests. However, many critics worry that marketers may know *too* much about consumers' lives and that they may use this knowledge to take unfair advantage of consumers. At some point, they claim, the extensive use of databases intrudes on consumer privacy.

[11] Gary Armstrong and Philip Kotler, *Marketing: An Introduction,* 8th ed. (Upper Saddle River: Prentice Hall) 428–430.

For example, they ask, should AT&T be allowed to sell marketers the names 4
of customers who frequently call the 800 numbers of catalog companies? Should a
company such as American Express be allowed to make data on its millions of
cardholders worldwide available to merchants who accept AmEx cards? Is it right
for credit bureaus to compile and sell lists of people who have recently applied for
credit cards—people who are considered prime direct marketing targets because of
their spending behavior? Or is it right for states to sell the names and addresses of
driver's license holders, along with height, weight, and gender information, allowing apparel retailers to target tall or overweight people with special clothing offers?

In their drives to build databases, companies sometimes get carried away. For 5
example, when first introduced, Intel's Pentium III chip contained an embedded
serial number that allowed the company to trace users' equipment. When privacy
advocates screamed, Intel disabled the feature. Similarly, Microsoft caused substantial privacy concerns when one version of its Windows software used a "Reg-
istration Wizard" that snooped into users' computers. When users went online to
register, without their knowledge, Microsoft "read" the configurations of their
PCs to learn about the major software products they were running. Users
protested loudly and Microsoft abandoned the practice.

These days, it's not only the large companies that can access such private in- 6
formation. The explosion of information technology has put these capabilities into
the hands of almost any business. For example, one bar owner discovered the
power of information technology after he acquired a simple, inexpensive device to
check IDs.

> About 10,000 people a week go to The Rack, a bar in Boston. . . . One by
> one, they hand over their driver's licenses to a doorman, who swipes them
> through a sleek black machine. If a license is valid and its holder is over 21,
> a red light blinks and the patron is waved through. But most of the cus-
> tomers are not aware that it also pulls up the name, address, birth date, and
> other personal details from a data strip on the back of the license. Even
> height, eye color, and sometimes Social Security number are registered.
> "You swipe the license, and all of a sudden someone's whole life as we
> know it pops up in front of you," said Paul Barclay, the bar's owner. "It's
> almost voyeuristic." Mr. Barclay soon found that he could build a database
> of personal information, providing an intimate perspective on his clientele
> that can be useful in marketing. Now, for any given night or hour, he can
> break down his clientele by sex, age, zip code, or other characteristics. If he
> wanted to, he could find out how many blond women named Karen over
> 5 feet 2 inches came in over a weekend, or how many of his customers have
> the middle initial M. More practically, he can build mailing lists based on
> all that data—and keep track of who comes back.[12]

Such access to and use of information has caused much concern and debate 7
among companies, consumers, and public policy makers. Consumer privacy has
become a major regulatory issue.

The direct marketing industry is addressing issues of ethics and public policy. 8
For example, in an effort to build consumer confidence in shopping direct, the
Direct Marketing Association (DMA)—the largest association for businesses prac-

[12] Jennifer Lee, "Welcome to the Database Lounge," *New York Times,* March 21, 2002, p. G1.

ticing direct, database, and interactive marketing, with more than 4,700 member companies—launched a "Privacy Promise to American Consumers." The Privacy Promise requires that all DMA members adhere to a carefully developed set of consumer-privacy rules. Members must agree to notify customers when any personal information is rented, sold, or exchanged with others. They must also honor consumer requests to "opt out" of receiving further solicitations or having their contact information transferred to other marketers. Finally, they must abide by the DMA's Preference Service by removing the names of consumers who wish not to receive mail, telephone, or e-mail offers.[13]

9

Direct marketers know that, left untended, such problems will lead to increasingly negative consumer attitudes, lower response rates, and calls for more restrictive state and federal legislation. "Privacy and customer permission have become the cornerstones of customer trust, [and] trust has become the cornerstone to a continuing relationship," says one expert. Companies must "become the custodians of customer trust and protect the privacy of their customers."[14]

10

Most direct marketers want the same things that consumers want: honest and well-designed marketing offers targeted only toward consumers who will appreciate and respond to them. Direct marketing is just too expensive to waste on consumers who don't want it.

11

972 words

Strategy Questions

1. Identify the broad issue of this reading selection. Then identify the specific issue and formulate it as a question.
2. What is the author's claim? Where is it located? What type of claim is it?
3. What is the context for this issue? Look at some of the examples the authors provide to help you answer.
4. Do you share any common ground with these authors? On what points? What effect does common ground, or a lack of it, have on your acceptance or rejection of the authors' position on the issue?

Study Reading Questions

1. Why is the invasion of privacy the "toughest public policy issue now confronting the direct marketing industry?"
2. What is the DMA? How many member companies belong to it?
3. Describe the DMA's "Privacy Promise to American Consumers." What are its rules?
4. How does direct marketing benefit the company? How does it benefit the consumer?

[13] Information on the DMA Privacy Promise obtained at www.the-dma.org/privacy/privacypromise.shtml, November 2005.
[14] Debbie A. Connon, "The Ethics of Database Marketing," *Information Management Journal*, May–June 2002, pp. 42–44.

Critical Reading and Thinking Questions

1. Why might you not want to have personal information, such as that collected by the bar in Boston, available to strangers? How could that harm you?
2. Do you think direct marketing companies will abide by the DMA's Privacy Promise? Do you personally see evidence that this promise is influencing the way companies conduct marketing now?
3. What might be some of the benefits of companies being able to access personal information about you? Do you think the benefits might outweigh the liabilities, or not? Give reasons for your answer.

Reading 2

To: Professor@University.edu. From: Your Student. Subject: Why It's All About Me[15]

JONATHAN D. GLATER

Explanatory Notes: *This article first appeared in the* New York Times *and considers professors' points of view on the e-mail they receive from students. Student opinion on this subject is also briefly included.* **Have you ever e-mailed a professor? Did you receive a response that satisfied you? Why, or why not?**

1 One student skipped class and then sent the professor an e-mail message asking for copies of her teaching notes. Another did not like her grade, and wrote a petulant message to the professor. Another explained that she was late for a Monday call because she was recovering from drinking too much at a wild weekend party.

2 Jennifer Schultens, an associate professor of mathematics at the University of California, Davis, received this e-mail message last September from a student in her calculus course: "Should I buy a binder or a subject notebook? Since I'm a freshman, I'm not sure how to shop for school supplies. Would you let me know your recommendations? Thank you!"

3 At colleges and universities nationwide, e-mail has made professors much more approachable. But many say it has made them too accessible, erasing boundaries that traditionally kept students at a healthy distance.

4 These days, they say, students seem to view them as available around the clock, sending a steady stream of e-mail messages—from 10 a week to 10 after every class—that are too informal or downright inappropriate.

5 "The tone that they would take in e-mail was pretty astounding," said Michael J. Kessler, an assistant dean and a lecturer in theology at Georgetown University. " 'I need to know this and you need to tell me right now,' with a familiarity that can sometimes border on imperative."

[15] Jonathan D. Glater, "To: Professor@University.edu. From: Your Student. Subject: Why It's All About Me," *New York Times* 21 February 2006: A1, A14.

He added: "It's a real fine balance to accommodate what they need and at the same time maintain a level of legitimacy as an instructor and someone who is institutionally authorized to make demands on them, and not the other way round." 6

While once professors may have expected deference, their expertise seems to have become just another service that students, as consumers, are buying. So students may have no fear of giving offense, imposing on the professor's time or even of asking a question that may reflect badly on their own judgment. 7

For junior faculty members, the barrage of e-mail has brought new tension into their work lives, some say, as they struggle with how to respond. Their tenure prospects, they realize, may rest in part on student evaluations of their accessibility. 8

The stakes are different for professors today than they were even a decade ago, said Patricia Ewick, chairwoman of the sociology department at Clark University in Massachusetts, explaining that "students are constantly asked to fill out evaluations of individual faculty." Students also frequently post their own evaluations on Web sites like *rateyourprofessor.com* and describe their impressions of their professors on blogs. 9

Last fall, undergraduate students at Syracuse University set up a group in Facebook.com, an online network for students, and dedicated it to maligning one particular instructor. The students were reprimanded. 10

Professor Ewick said 10 students in one class e-mailed her drafts of their papers days before they were due, seeking comments. "It's all different levels of presumption," she said. "One is that I'll be able to drop everything and read 250 pages two days before I'm going to get 50 of these." 11

Kathleen E. Jenkins, a sociology professor at the College of William and Mary in Virginia, said she had even received e-mail requests from students who missed class and wanted copies of her teaching notes. 12

Alexandra Lahav, an associate professor of law at the University of Connecticut, said she felt pressured by the e-mail messages. "I feel sort of responsible, as if I ought to be on call all the time," she said. 13

Many professors said they were often uncertain how to react. Professor Schultens, who was asked about buying the notebook, said she debated whether to tell the student that this was not a query that should be directed to her, but worried that "such a message could be pretty scary." 14

"I decided not to respond at all," she said. 15

Christopher J. Dede, a professor at the Harvard Graduate School of Education who has studied technology in education, said these e-mail messages showed how students no longer deferred to their professors, perhaps because they realized that professors' expertise could rapidly become outdated. 16

"The deference was probably driven more by the notion that professors were infallible sources of deep knowledge," Professor Dede said, and that notion has weakened. 17

Meanwhile, students seem unaware that what they write in e-mail could adversely affect them, Professor Lahav said. She recalled an e-mail message from a student saying that he planned to miss class so he could play with his son. Professor Lahav did not respond. 18

"It's graduate school, he's an adult human being, he's obviously a parent, and it's not my place to tell him how to run his life," she said. 19

But such e-mail messages can have consequences, she added. "Students don't 20 understand that what they say in e-mail can make them seem very unprofessional, and could result in a bad recommendation."

Still, every professor interviewed emphasized that instant feedback could be 21 invaluable. A question about a lecture or discussion "is for me an indication of a blind spot, that the student didn't get it," said Austin D. Sarat, a professor of political science at Amherst College.

College students say that e-mail makes it easier to ask questions and helps them 22 to learn. "If the only way I could communicate with my professors was by going to their office or calling them, there would be some sort of ranking or prioritization taking place," said Cory Merrill, 19, a sophomore at Amherst. "Is this question worth going over to the office?"

But student e-mail can go too far, said Robert B. Ahdieh, an associate professor 23 at Emory Law School in Atlanta. He paraphrased some of the comments he had received: "I think you're covering the material too fast, or I don't think we're using the reading as much as we could in class, or I think it would be helpful if you would summarize what we've covered at the end of class in case we missed anything."

Students also use e-mail to criticize one another, Professor Ahdieh said. He 24 paraphrased this comment: "You're spending too much time with my moron classmates and you ought to be focusing on those of us who are getting the material."

Michael Greenstone, an economics professor at the Massachusetts Institute of 25 Technology, said he once received an e-mail message late one evening from a student who had recently come to the realization that he was gay and was struggling to cope.

Professor Greenstone said he eventually helped the student get an appointment 26 with a counselor. "I don't think we would have had the opportunity to discuss his realization and accompanying feelings without e-mail as an icebreaker," he said.

A few professors said they had rules for e-mail and told their students how 27 quickly they would respond, how messages should be drafted and what types of messages they would answer.

Meg Worley, an assistant professor of English at Pomona College in California, said she told students that they must say thank you after receiving a professor's response to an e-mail message.

"One of the rules that I teach my students is, the less powerful person always 29 has to write back," Professor Worley said.

1132 words

Strategy Questions

1. What is the author's claim? Where is it located? What type of claim is it?
2. What sides of the argument are presented in this article? Who holds them?
3. Speculate on the context of this argument. What event or events took place that created an interest in this issue?
4. Write a short reaction paper to this article. What is your opinion about student e-mail? Do you share common ground with any of the professors quoted here? Do you think regulations are needed for this type of communication? What would you recommend?

Study Reading Questions

1. What are the subjects of the three examples of student e-mail messages sent to professors that are cited in paragraph 1?
2. The author states that professors are troubled by some of their students' e-mail for several reasons. Name two of them.
3. Why, according to the author, do students like to send e-mail messages to their professors?
4. How could student e-mail adversely affect them?
5. How could it benefit them?

Critical Reading and Thinking Questions

1. Have you or one of your friends ever sent an e-mail message to a professor? What was it about? What was the result?
2. Consider the examples of the subjects students e-mail their professors about in this article. Which, in your opinion, are legitimate subjects, and which are not? Give reasons for your opinions.
3. If you were a college professor, would you encourage your students to send you e-mail? Would you set any limits on the subjects or style of these e-mails? Why, or why not?
4. Do you believe that faculty should create rules for more appropriate student e-mailing? Or, do you believe faculty should deal with student e-mail on a case-by-case basis? Explain your answer.

Reading 3

Could You Please Die Now?[16]

EVAN J. KEMP, JR.

Explanatory Notes: *This selection is taken from the* Washington Post National Weekly. *Kemp is a former chairman of the Equal Employment Opportunity Commission and is senior partner of Evan Kemp Associates, Inc., a health and mobility company owned and operated by disabled people.* **Before you read this article, speculate on why some disabled people might either favor or oppose assisted suicide. Then compare your speculations with Kemp's argument.**

On Jan. 8, the Supreme Court heard oral arguments in *Washington v. Glucksberg* and *Vacco v. Quill*. At issue was the question of whether or not "terminally ill" individuals have an inherent "right to die." And, if so, should a licensed physician be granted the legal right to assist in the "suicide" of a patient?   1

As the case was argued inside the court, thousands kept vigil outside the court. I was among them.   2

---

[16] Evan J. Kemp, Jr., "Could You Please Die Now?" *Washington Post National Weekly Edition* 13 January 1997: 23.

You might ask, "Why would a conservative Republican who served as the chair of the U.S. Equal Employment Opportunity Commission in the Bush administration join Clinton Democrats, representatives of the Catholic Church, Orthodox Jews, civil rights advocates, and a large congregation of disabled and elderly people in a noisy street demonstration?" 3

The answer is simple: I do not believe that doctors should kill their patients. 4

At the outset, I must acknowledge that the right to die proponents have a certain undeniable logic to their argument. I agree with the proposition that every individual has a right to control his or her life. Unfortunately, this logic does not take into account the institutional ramifications of physician-assisted suicide and thus misses a much more basic point. In this age of soaring health care costs, I believe the right-to-die option inevitably will be transformed into a means of rationing health care. 5

As a matter of fact, we've already taken our first few steps down this exceedingly steep and slippery slope. At present, a patient checking into a hospital is routinely given the option of signing a "do not resuscitate" order (DNR), requesting that "heroic measures," such as cardiopulmonary resuscitation, not be taken should such measures be required to keep the person alive. 6

DNR consent is supposed to be voluntary. In practice, however, that has not always been the case. Some disabled people report instances in which hospitals have pressured patients—most notably, people with disabilities, the uninsured, and the severely ill—to sign DNR orders. 7

In some cases, the DNR is not explained clearly. The patient, or the patient's family or other representative, is not adequately informed of the nature of the order—especially the fact that it is supposed to be voluntary. The DNR is often included with other routine administrative papers to be signed. This cannot be construed as "informed consent." 8

Joe Ehman, a news reporter in Rochester, N.Y., who uses a wheelchair, told me he was "literally hounded by social workers" to sign a DNR when he was hospitalized in 1995 for back surgery. "A few hours after surgery, still delirious from the anesthesia and from postsurgical morphine and demerol, I had to hear from yet another social worker who wanted to force-feed me a DNR. I mustered my strength and screamed, 'I'm 30 years old. I don't want to die!'" 9

Maria Matzik, a woman in her thirties who lives and works in Dayton, Ohio, says she had a frightening battle with nurses during a 1993 hospital stay. "They kept asking me to sign a DNR order," she told me. "When I wouldn't sign it, they said it didn't matter anyway. Because I use a ventilator, they told me nothing would be done if I had a cardiac arrest." Matzik escaped that fate, but others have not. 10

Marjorie Nighbert, a 76-year-old Florida woman, was hospitalized in 1996 after a stroke. Before her hospital admission, she signed an advance directive that no "heroic measures" should be employed to save her life. On the basis of that directive and at the request of her family, the hospital denied Nighbert's requests for food and water, according to reports in the *Northwest Florida Daily News*. A hurriedly convened hospital ethics committee ruled that she was "not medically competent to ask for such a treatment." Until her death more than 10 days later, Nighbert was restrained in her bed to prevent her from raiding other patients' food trays. 11

The larger point is that, in evaluating the right-to-die movement, one should not overlook the fundamental importance of money. In the *Washington v. Glucksberg* decision, federal Judge Stephen Reinhardt tried to put the best possible face on the economic pressures involved in life and death decisions: ". . . in a society in which the costs of protracted health care can be so exorbitant, we are reluctant to say that it is improper for competent, terminally ill adults to take the economic welfare of their families and loved ones into consideration." 12

When it comes to spending money on health care, however, "families and loved ones" often are not in a position to call the shots. Insurance companies, hospitals, nursing homes and HMOs are—and they would prefer that the dirty little secret of money be kept out of the public debate about assisted suicide. After all, it's much easier for them to justify their actions on the basis of humanitarian principle than financial self-interest. Once physician-assisted suicide is given the sanction of law, our health care institutions are likely to devise contractual mechanisms that make sure members of targeted groups die as efficiently as possible. 13

All of this will be justified by the holy grail of the right-to-die movement: "choice." But the laws of economics virtually guarantee that, in practice, those who "choose" assisted suicide will disproportionately come from the lower end of the socioeconomic ladder: people without health insurance, as well as from people who are said to possess a low "quality of life"—i.e., people with disabilities. 14

As former Surgeon General C. Everett Koop declared at a Washington, D.C., press conference in November, "Toleration of doctor-assisted suicide can lead to acceptance of involuntary euthanasia." 15

As a disabled person, I am especially sensitive to the "quality of life" rationale that is frequently introduced in the debate. For the past 47 years, I have lived with a progressive neuromuscular disease that first began to manifest itself when I was 12. My disease, Kugelburg Weylander Syndrome, has no known cure, and I have no hope for "recovery." 16

Upon diagnosis, my parents were informed by the physicians treating me that I would die within two years. Later, another group of physicians was certain that I would live only to the age of 18. Yet here I am at age 59, continuing to have an extraordinarily high quality of life. 17

And my case is by no means unique. The majority of families I have encountered in my lifetime, and who have been close enough to share details of their extended family life, have had at least one member who defied the medical establishment by living a far longer and more productive life than expected. Should we permit the medical establishment to assist these individuals with disabilities to die before their time at the hands of their physicians? I don't think so. 18

If physician-assisted suicide is decriminalized, the next question to arise will be how to pay for the service. If the suicide services, dubbed "obitiatry" by Dr. Jack Kevorkian, become billable, those services could dovetail all too well with our nation's current drive to cut health care costs. Health maintenance organizations may view the cost of obitiatry as especially cost-effective in that the practice will require neither referrals to specialists nor repeat visits to physicians' offices. 19

In managed-care parlance, the portion of the premium dollar spent on medical 20
care is called the "medical-loss ratio." Insurance companies and health maintenance organizations could cut that ratio by providing assisted suicide rather than
bypass surgeries and the like. After all, many people are cheaper dead than alive.

The American Medical Association has twice affirmed its opposition to 21
physician-assisted suicide and recently filed an amicus brief with the Supreme
Court. The AMA wishes for physicians to maintain their role as healers, and not
to become potential killers, even for reasons of mercy.

The experience of Nazi Germany is relevant here, not because the advocates of 22
assisted suicide are incipient fascists (they're not) but because of the historical fact
that the Holocaust had its beginnings in the systematic elimination of Germans
with disabilities. As Hugh Gregory Gallagher noted in his 1990 book, *By Trust
Betrayed: Physicians, Patients and the License to Kill in the Third Reich*, Adolf
Hitler's order of September 1939 called for physicians to assist in the killings of citizens with illnesses and disabilities. Nazi propagandists, led by a small number of
physicians, said that such citizens were "useless eaters" and "life unworthy of life."
Today American health planners, while driven by a very different ideology, also
speak a dehumanizing language about "health care consumers" and the dubious
"quality of life" of our citizens with illnesses and disabilities.

From where I sit, it is undeniably clear that giving physician-assisted suicide 23
the sanction of law will have unintended consequences which vastly outweigh any
benefits that might accrue. As Koop puts it, "Society must not allow doctors to be
killers as well as healers."

1140 words

Strategy Questions

1. Identify the broad issue of this reading. Then identify the specific issue and formulate this as a question.
2. What is the author's claim? What type of claim is it? Where is it located?
3. Speculate about the context for the author's argument. What event or events
   may have caused him to write this article?
4. Write a short reaction paper to this reading. Do you think disabled persons
   should feel threatened by the legalization of physician-assisted suicide? Do you
   believe that money is a deciding factor in whether or not to resuscitate a
   disabled person? Why or why not?

Study Reading Questions

1. What is a DNR?
2. Using context clues, determine the meaning of "obitiatry" in paragraph 19.
3. If given the chance, the author fears that insurance companies and HMOs
   would support physician-assisted suicide. Why might these groups support this
   practice?
4. What disease does the author have? Describe its characteristics. When did he
   know he had the disease, and how long was he told he would live? How old was
   he when he wrote this article?

Critical Reading and Thinking Questions

1. Why does Kemp compare assisted suicide to Nazi Germany and the Holocaust? Do you think this is a fair comparison? Why or why not?
2. How does the issue of physician-assisted suicide relate to discussions about whether or not deformed fetuses should be aborted? What do those who *oppose* both actions have in common? What do those who *support* both actions have in common?
3. Kemp's main concern is that if assisted suicide is legalized, targeted groups such as people without insurance and people with disabilities will be forced to "choose" it over resuscitation. What are some ramifications of forcing such individuals to sign a DNR?

THREE APPLICATION EXERCISES

Exercise 1

Search for issues in your other classes.

Every subject you study in college will have some issues associated with it. These are subjects that have not yet been settled and that scholars are still debating. Review your lecture notes and look through your textbooks. Find at least one controversial issue from each of your other classes and be prepared to contribute it to a class discussion on "Argument in the Academic Disciplines." Do you have opinions on any of these issues? What more will you need to learn to be able to contribute an educated opinion?

Exercise 2

Look for critical reading and critical thinking assignments in your textbooks.

Survey your textbooks and look for questions or special readings that are labeled "critical reading" or "critical thinking." It is very common for textbook authors to include such material in their books. Critical reading and critical thinking are widely regarded as an important part of a college education, and textbook authors frequently teach these abilities with special assignments, readings, and sets of questions. Be prepared to describe what you have found.

Exercise 3

Contribute assignments from your other classes that require critical reading or critical thinking.

Review your assignments from your other classes this semester. Which of them required study reading? Which of them required critical reading and critical thinking? Be able to describe assignments from your other classes that require at least some critical reading and critical thinking. Discuss what you are expected to do to complete them successfully.

REVIEW AND EVALUATE THE STRATEGIES

The following is a review of the five strategies you learned in this chapter:

1. Identify the issue and form an issue question.
2. Identify the claim. Determine the type of claim and its purpose.
3. Speculate about the context for the argument.
4. Write out your point of view before you read and compare it with the author's as you read.
5. Look for common ground, decide what you think, and write your reactions.

Make a personal evaluation of these strategies:

1. Underline your favorite strategies in the list above.
2. Make a check mark by those you want to continue to use.
3. Cross out any you probably will not continue to use. What are your reasons for rejecting them?

_____

_____

Evaluate the Support, Reasoning, and Conclusions

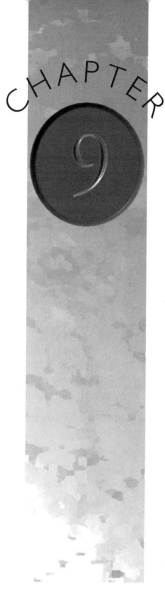

CHAPTER

9

CHAPTER GOALS:

1. **To teach you to recognize the support in argument.**

2. **To teach you to recognize refutation and conclusions in argument.**

3. **To alert you to signs of bias when an argumentative purpose is not obvious.**

4. **To provide you with five strategies for evaluating support and conclusions.**

The Importance of Support in Argument

In Chapter 5 you learned about the importance of supporting details. Main ideas don't mean much of anything until they are explained and clarified with supporting details. In argument, support includes good reasons and evidence, which clarify and explain the claim and also often prove it. Supporting evidence used in argument has traditionally been described as having certain types of audience appeal. It can, for instance, appeal to your reason and common sense. This type of support is called **logical support.** It can also appeal to what you admire most in other people, including their authority, good character, credibility, admirable accomplishments, and general trustworthiness. This type of support establishes the **personal credibility** of the individuals being described. Finally, some of the support in argument appeals mainly to your emotions, including your values and your motivation to achieve personal happiness and success in your life. This type of support is called **emotional support.** When the support in an argument is effective and convincing, you are much more likely to accept the author's conclusions. When it does not work effectively, you may feel manipulated by the author, and you will reject the conclusions.

Here is an example of the first few paragraphs of an argumentative essay about breaking racial stereotypes. Notice that the claim is expressed in the first two sentences. The remaining paragraphs support the claim. Look at the variety of types of support that are used in this essay. Each type is labeled in the margin. The intent of all of this support is to make the claim memorable, interesting, and, above all, convincing. Read and decide whether you think the support is effective or not. Figure out also what you are expected to conclude. Do you believe this conclusion as a result of reading this support? If you are convinced by this argument, what did you find most convincing about it?

Practice Essay
THE BLACK GEN X NOBODY KNOWS[1]

Ellis Cose

Claim	African-American kids don't all fit one hip-hop mold. Many quietly defy the stereotypes of their generation. Imagine a sixteen-year old Harlem boy whose parents are both dead, and odds are high you won't conjure up
Example	
Admirable traits & accomplishments used to convince	Antwan Allen. Yet Antwan—number one in his class, president of the drama club, president of the student council, editor of his school's paper and head of its honor society—insists, with passion and conviction, that he is not an aberration, that he is just as representative of his race and generation as the hip-hop boys of the 'hood.
Literal comparison comparing two types of students	

Slender, bespectacled, shy and yet calmly self-assured, Antwan concedes that many black youngsters prefer the streets to school: "But I think that group overshadows all the exceptional African-American students who are out there. I mean, not every African-American person is a basketball player or a thug.... Not all black people speak in slang, wear jeans hanging off them [and are] getting high. That's what's portrayed on TV."

Description

Emotionally loaded language
Refutation of stereotype

Historical comparison

Nonetheless, those who consider the street corner their turf have a disproportionate influence on the rest. A couple of decades ago things were different. Nerds were teased but also supported, recalls Thierry Fortune, of Motivational Educational Entertainment, a Philadelphia market-research firm specializing in "at risk urban youth." There was "a constant reinforcement in terms of doing well in school," observes Fortune. That is largely missing today, he believes, because the generation is raising itself to a substantial degree. Although many of its members hunger for greater adult presence, they find refuge in a culture of alienation.

Quote from authority

Generalization from a single example

Even among archetypal good kids, the pressure to be "down" (hard, street-smart) is strong. Antwan points to a friend at La Salle Academy, the Catholic high school they both attend, as an example. His buddy is extremely bright but is "so caught up in the whole thing of being 'down,' 'keeping it real,' he's completely lost all sense of who he is," observes Antwan. "He slacks off in his work . . . because he doesn't want to be perceived as being 'white' or being a nerd or being a geek."

Sign: slacking off is a sign of being "real"

Antwan understands his friend's dilemma, since his own respectful deportment has led some acquaintances to suggest he was "not being black." But the charge strikes him as nonsensical. "What is being black?" he asks rhetorically. It's a great deal more, he believes, than embodying a stereotype.

Opinion

[1] Ellis Cose, "The Black Gen X Nobody Knows," *Newsweek* 17 March 1997: 62.

"I can 'keep it real' on the street corner with my homies," he says, "but where Cause–effect
is that going to get me in life? Is it going to get me a good job? Is it going to
get me a good family? No! I think that the only way you can honestly, truly Conclusion
get ahead in life is by staying true to who you are."

465 words

Are you convinced by this argument? Did you agree with the conclusion that one must stay true to one's ideals? Or, did you supply other evidence and examples from your own experience that led you to a different conclusion?

The rest of this chapter will help you understand why you found the support in the above argument convincing or not. You will learn to identify the different types of support in argument. The strategies at the end of the chapter will teach you to evaluate support. You will also learn to evaluate the conclusion of an argument. When you finish reading the chapter, you will be prepared to answer these important bottom-line questions: Do you believe the author? Do you agree or disagree? Are you convinced? Is the argument effective or not? Why or why not?

The next three sections of this chapter provide information about the most commonly used methods for supporting and developing a claim in argument: logical support, opinions and personal credibility used as support, and emotional support.

Logical Reasons and Logical Support

Logical reasons.   Find the author's reasons by stating the claim, adding the word "because," and making a list of the main reasons the author provides that cause you to believe and accept the claim. You will usually believe and accept the reasons if they make sense and seem logical to you. For example, in the essay you just read about the black Generation X, the claim is, *All African-American kids do not fit a common stereotype.* Follow this claim with the word "because" to help you find the reasons. Here are two reasons given by the author. (1) *because some African-American kids are different from the television stereotypes*, and (2) *because some of them want to prepare for college, family, and a good job.* To find the claim, ask What does the author want me to believe? To find the reasons, ask What reasons are provided to make me believe the claim? You will need to regard the reasons as good reasons to find them convincing.

Types of logical support.   Once you have identified the claim and the reasons, you need to notice the specific support that is offered to make you believe the reasons. Logical support appeals to your common sense, experience, and your ideas about what is verifiable or logical. Here are five types of logical support that are commonly used in argument.

- *Facts*. **Facts** include real examples of people or places, data, and statistics. To be convinced, the reader must believe the facts are true. Facts may be selected to support only one side of an issue, however. Notice whether the facts presented support mainly one point of view or several points of view on the issue.

- *Definitions.* Important terms are usually defined in argument, and the reader must accept the definitions for the argument to be convincing. In the last chapter you read two articles that argued for different definitions of sexual harassment (pages 276–278). The author of the first essay defined it as normal male behavior. The author of the second essay defined it as any comments, gestures, or physical contact of a sexual nature that are unwelcome to either sex. If you disagreed with either of these authors on the definition of this term, you probably also rejected their argument.

- *Cause–effect.* **Cause–effect reasoning** in argument usually suggests that certain actions produce certain results. The cause-effect reasoning in the Gen X article on page 294 suggests that being a member of the hip-hop culture produces less desirable results than do studying and finding a job. The author of "We've Overlooked One of Our Greatest Assets" on pages 66–68 argues that his community college education is the main cause of his success in life.

- *Signs.* **Signs** are frequently used in argument to prove that the existence of one thing indicates that something else is true. For example, the presents under a Christmas tree are a sign that Santa Claus has been there, or red spots are a sign of measles. You can see immediately that some signs are true indicators of what is alleged and some are not.

- *Comparison.* There are two types of comparison that appeal to your sense of logic and reason: (1) **historical comparison** and (2) **literal comparison.**

  (1) *Historical comparison* suggests that what happened in the past may also happen again, that is, that history repeats itself. For example, some people argued that the United States should not withdraw from the war in Iraq in 2006 because the same thing that happened in Afghanistan when the Russians withdrew from that country could happen in Iraq as well. In Afghanistan the Taliban took over; therefore, in Iraq terrorists would take over. Historical comparisons may also be used to suggest that times have changed. Someone who disagrees with the comparison of Afghanistan and Iraq might point out that these two countries are so dissimilar that the same results would not necessarily occur in both countries.

  (2) *Literal comparison* shows how items in the same general category are either the same or different. Two car insurance plans might be compared in an advertisement, for example, with one of them recommended as better than the other. Or, someone might make the argument that installing a dress code in one high school reduced discipline problems, so other schools should also install dress codes.

Analyze the logical support.

Practice analyzing types of logical support by reading the **first five paragraphs** of an article from *Newsweek* magazine by Anna Quindlen: "Undocumented, Indispensable." This is an article about the issues associated with illegal immigration in the United States. The title of the article provides a clue to the author's position on this issue. The **last five paragraphs** of this article, which are also included here, are used in subsequent exercises in this chapter to show examples of a statement of personal credibility, emotional support, refutation, and a conclusion. You may read them now or later. As you read the first five paragraphs, look for some of the types of logical support that have just been identified in this chapter and label them in the margin. Then answer the questions.

Practice Essay
UNDOCUMENTED, INDISPENSABLE[2]

Anna Quindlen

On May Day a persistent rumble came from Market Street in San Francisco, but it was not the oft-predicted earthquake, or at least not in the geologic sense. Thousands of people were marching down the thoroughfare, from the Embarcadero to city hall, holding signs. NO HUMAN BEING IS ILLEGAL. I AM A WORKER, NOT A CRIMINAL. TODAY I MARCH, TOMORROW I VOTE. I PAY TAXES.

1

The polyglot city by the bay is so familiar with the protest march that longtime citizens say it handles the inconveniences better than anyplace else. Some of them remember the Vietnam War marches, the feminist rallies. The May Day demonstration bore some resemblance to both, which was not surprising. Immigration is the leading edge of a deep and wide sea change in the United States today, just as those issues were in their own time.

2

Of course, this is not a new issue. The Founding Fathers started out with a glut of land and a deficit of warm bodies. But over its history America's more-established residents have always found ways to demonize the newcomers to the nation needed to fill it and till it. It was only human, the contempt for the different, the shock of the new.

3

Today, because so many immigrants have entered the country illegally or are living here on visas that expired long ago, the demagoguery has been amped up full throttle. Although the conventional wisdom is that immigrants are civic freeloaders, the woman with a sign that said I PAY TAXES was reflecting the truth. Millions of undocumented immigrants pay income taxes using a special identification number the IRS provides. They pay into the Social Security system, too, even though they're not eligible to collect benefits. In fact, they may be helping to keep the system afloat, with $7 billion currently in a designated suspense file, much of which is believed to have come from undocumented workers.

4

[2] Anna Quindlen, "Undocumented, Indispensable," *Newsweek*, 15 May 2006: 78.

A man carrying a sign saying I AM A WORKER, NOT A CRIMINAL said he pays taxes, too, through his construction job. All three of his children were born in the United States. Although he said he had a hard time deciphering government forms—and don't we all?—he had applied for a green card and had been waiting for four years. In 2004 there was a backlog of more than 6 million unprocessed immigration petitions, a record high. So much for suggestions that immigrants are lax about regularizing their status. Clearly the laxity is at least partly federal.

It's true that immigrants use government services: schools, public hospitals. It's also true that many pay their way through income and sales taxes. Despite the rhetoric, no one really knows whether they wind up being a loss or a gain for the economy. Certainly lots of them work. A state like Arizona, for instance, could not keep pace with the demand for new homes at reasonable cost without immigrant workers, many of them undocumented.

The counterargument is that that drives down the wages of American citizens. It's galling to hear that argument from members of Congress, who have not raised the federal minimum wage for almost a decade. Most of those politicians blame the workers for their willingness to accept low wages. Don't hold your breath waiting for significant sanctions against those companies that shut their eyes to the immigration status of their employees—and that also make large political contributions.

Americans who are really incensed by millions of undocumented immigrants can take action, just as those marching in the streets did. They can refuse to eat fruits and vegetables picked by those immigrants. They can refuse to buy homes on which they worked. After all, if a migrant worker like Cesar Chavez could organize a national boycott of grapes, then opponents of immigration could surely organize something similar. But they won't. We like our cheap houses and our fresh fruit. And our government likes the bait-and-switch, taking taxes from workers whose existence it will not recognize. The borders are most porous in Washington, D.C.

Full disclosure: I'm the granddaughter of immigrants, and I know how much of the melting pot is a myth. My grandparents always referred to my father as "an American boy," which meant he was not from Italy. It was not a compliment. They didn't melt; their daughter did, although one of the only times I ever saw her bitter was when she explained what the word "dago" meant.

There are big decisions to be made about the vast wave of undocumented workers in this country, issues that go beyond slogans and placards. But there's no premium in discussing those issues in xenophobic half-truths, in talking about what undocumented immigrants cost the country without talking about what they contribute, in talking about them as illegals when they are nannies, waiters, roofers and the parents of American citizens. One fact is indisputable: the essence of America is free enterprise and human rights. It's why people come here in the first place. WE ARE ALL IMMIGRANTS, read signs on Market Street. Some of us just got here sooner.

846 words

1. **Examine a sign:** In *paragraph 1,* the rumbling in the streets of San Francisco might be a sign of an earthquake, but it isn't. What is it a sign of instead?

   _____

   Describe the scene._____ What are the possible

   effects of this description on readers?_____

2. **Examine a historical comparison:** In *paragraph 2,* the march described in this

   article is compared with what in the past? _____

   What is the significance of this comparison? What does Quindlen claim the

   present march shares with those in the past?_____

3. **Examine cause-effect reasoning:** In *paragraph 3,* Quindlen describes the effect that newcomers sometimes have on the permanent residents of a country.

   What, according to her, causes this effect? _____

   How does she characterize the result and how serious does she seem to consider it?

   _____

4. **Examine definitions:** In *paragraph 4,* immigrants are defined in two different ways. What is the definition she attributes to "conventional wisdom"?

   _____

   What is the definition she claims is more true?_____

   _____

5. **Examine the facts:** Identify some of the facts that are used in *paragraph 5.*

   _____

   Look back through the other four paragraphs, and identify additional facts.

   _____

Opinions and Personal Credibility Used as Support

Opinions.   **Opinions** are commonly used to support arguments. You will need to decide for yourself whether the opinions are the informed opinions of experts or whether they are the uninformed opinions of nonexperts. You can believe experts because they possess information and experience that makes them believable. You are less likely to believe nonexperts whose information and experience with the subject is limited, if it exists at all.

You will need to try to establish the degree of expertise of both the people who are quoted by authors and also of the authors themselves. Authors sometimes establish the expertise of the individuals they quote by citing some of these individuals' credentials in the text. The author of the Gen X article on page 294 establishes the authority of Thierry Fortune, whom he quotes in his essay. He says Fortune is a member of "Motivational Educational Entertainment, a Philadelphia market-research firm specializing in 'at risk urban youth.'" This individual's opinion about urban youth is now more believable than it would have been without this explanation about his background. Authors also give their own opinions in their work, so it is important to try to find out something about them.

Personal credibility. Sometimes authors reveal who they are and establish their credibility with statements that begin, "As president of the university . . ." or "Having held the position of city tax collector for twenty years . . ." or "Having studied this matter extensively . . ." Such credentials are meant to strengthen the author's position and make it more believable.

Use information about an author from the preface, notes, or the reading material itself to help you assess the author's expertise and credibility. The Explanatory Notes for each of the readings in this book, for example, provide information about the authors of the readings that will help you decide whether or not they have sufficient expertise for you to believe them.

Analyze the credibility of the author.

If you were to go to Anna Quindlen's Home Page on the Internet, you would find that she is a bestselling author of novels, nonfiction books, and children's books. For many years she wrote a regular column called "Public and Private" for the *New York Times* newspaper. This column won a Pulitzer Prize in 1992. She now writes a regular column called "The Last Word" that appears every other week in *Newsweek* magazine. Those are her credentials in general.

In this next paragraph taken from her article "Undocumented, Indispensable," Quindlen pauses in paragraph 9 to establish some of her unique credentials for writing on this particular topic:

> Full disclosure: I'm the granddaughter of immigrants, and I know 9 how much of the melting pot is a myth. My grandparents always referred to my father as "an American boy," which meant he was not from Italy. It was not a compliment. They didn't melt; their daughter did, although one of the only times I ever saw her bitter was when she explained what the word "dago" meant.

1. How does this paragraph help to establish Quindlen's authority to write on this particular subject?_____

2. What effect does this paragraph have on the common ground Quindlen may or may not share with her readers?_____

3. How are you personally affected by her "disclosure?"_____

_____

Emotional Support

Many controversial issues provoke emotion, and authors often use emotional support of various types to convince their readers to think like they do. Emotional support is effective in an argument when the subject itself is emotional and when it does not distract the reader from drawing a logical conclusion. Here are five types of emotional support that are commonly used in argument.

1. **Emotionally loaded language.** Many words have two types of meaning: their **denotative meaning** and their **connotative meaning.** Denotative meaning is the literal meaning that can be found in the dictionary. Connotative meaning encompasses all the additional negative or positive associations that most people have with a word.

    Read through the two lists that follow. Do not think about these words' denotative meaning or what they would mean if you looked them up in the dictionary. Instead, think only about their connotative meaning, or how they make you feel. Words that appeal to your feelings are called "emotionally loaded" words.

List 1		List 2	
I am usually	*uneasy*	I am usually	*capable*
	anxious		*caring*
	despairing		*cheerful*
	bored		*bright*
	frightened		*relaxed*
	desperate		*proud*
	stupid		*contented*
	a failure		*confident*

One list, especially if you apply it to yourself, will make you feel good, and one will make you feel bad because of the positive and negative connotations of the words. Other examples of words with strong connotative meanings include *home, dreams, family values, neighborhood, friends,* or *sneak thief, murderer, junkie, derelict,* and *drunkard.* Authors expect you to experience feelings and to call up special associations when you read such words. They also expect these feelings to affect your understanding of the material you read. Look back at the Gen X article (page 294) and locate the emotionally loaded words in the second paragraph.

2. **Emotional examples.** An emotional example can be extremely convincing. Specific examples of a hungry baby in Africa or a young girl in Afghanistan who is not permitted to go to school appeal to the emotions far more than statistics on hunger or education.

3. **Emotional comparisons.** Some comparisons carry emotional weight. Even though the items being compared may be very different, they may share qualities or outcomes that appeal to the emotions and can be shown to be desirable and

convincing. For example, notice how Quindlen associates past earthquakes in San Francisco with the immigration marches she describes. They both shake up the status quo and bring about change. Readers who are sympathetic to her position would regard this as a positive comparison with good connotations.

4. **Vivid description of an emotional scene.** A vivid, detailed description of an emotional scene is convincing. For instance, a description of a fatal accident caused by a drunken driver could be used to convince people to vote for stronger penalties for drunken driving. Or a vivid description of members of a gang hanging out on streets, taking drugs, and getting killed could make readers fear and reject the gang culture. Quindlen allows us to see the marchers and their signs in the opening paragraph of her article. She describes them in positive terms to help her strengthen her argument.

5. **Appeals to needs and values.** Authors often appeal to our motivation to acquire the things we think we need, such as food, warmth, shelter, sex, security, self-esteem, excitement, creativity, or self-expression. They also sometimes appeal to the opposites of these needs and values, including hunger, cold, fear, self-doubt, boredom, or other types of dissatisfaction to motivate people to change their behavior and restore themselves to a more positive state of being. Advertisements aimed at convincing young people that they should avoid taking illegal drugs often show the negative effects of drugs to appeal to people's sense of fear.

We also have emotional associations with our values. Consider, for example, how you feel about honesty, loyalty, freedom, creativity, equality, faithfulness, integrity, and so on. Authors engage our emotions by reminding us that by accepting their positions, we will satisfy our sense of values. In general, you will share much more common ground with an author and find it much easier to accept the conclusion if you also happen to share the author's values in regard to the issue.

Analyze emotional support.

Emotional support appears throughout "Undocumented, Indispensable" by Anna Quindlen because her subject is strongly emotional. Read the short selection below, which comes from *paragraph 10* in the essay. Underline all of the emotionally loaded words.

> There are big decisions to be made about the vast wave of undocu- 10
> mented workers in this country, issues that go beyond slogans and plac-
> ards. But there's no premium in discussing those issues in xenophobic half-
> truths, in talking about what undocumented immigrants cost the country
> without talking about what they contribute, in talking about them as ille-
> gals when they are nannies, waiters, roofers and the parents of American
> citizens.

1. Which words did you identify as emotionally loaded?_____

2. Do they carry positive or negative connotations?_____

3. What are xenophobic half-truths? (Xeno means foreign, and phobic means fear.) Does this term carry positive or negative connotations? Whom is it used to describe?

_____

Refutation

Besides using support to make their claims more convincing, authors also sometimes identify positions that are different from their own and use support to demonstrate what is wrong with these other positions. This practice is called refutation, and it can be used to strengthen the author's position. Sometimes counterarguments, or arguments that challenge the author's position, are identified and spelled out so that the author can go into detail about what is wrong with them.

Analyze refutation.

Take a look at how Anna Quindlen handles **refutation** in her article, "Undocumented, Indispensable." The following are paragraphs 6-8 of her article. Read them to identify the positions taken by her opposition and then notice how she answers them.

    It's true that immigrants use government services: schools, public hospitals. It's also true that many pay their way through income and sales taxes. Despite the rhetoric, no one really knows whether they wind up being a loss or a gain for the economy. Certainly lots of them work. A state like Arizona, for instance, could not keep pace with the demand for new homes at reasonable cost without immigrant workers, many of them undocumented.   6

    The counterargument is that that drives down the wages of American citizens. It's galling to hear that argument from members of Congress, who have not raised the federal minimum wage for almost a decade. Most of those politicians blame the workers for their willingness to accept low wages. Don't hold your breath waiting for significant sanctions against those companies that shut their eyes to the immigration status of their employees—and that also make large political contributions.   7

    Americans who are really incensed by millions of undocumented immigrants can take action, just as those marching in the streets did. They can refuse to eat fruits and vegetables picked by those immigrants. They can   8 refuse to buy homes on which they worked. After all, if a migrant worker like Cesar Chavez could organize a national boycott of grapes, then opponents of immigration could surely organize something similar. But they won't. We like our cheap houses and our fresh fruit. And our government likes the bait-and-switch, taking taxes from workers whose existence it will not recognize. The borders are most porous in Washington, D.C.

1. Examine the first counterargument and Quindlen's refutation in paragraph 6. What does Quindlen identify as one argument people use against illegal immigrants working in the United States?_____

_____

What is her answer to this argument?_____

_____

2. Examine the second counterargument and Quindlen's refutation in paragraph 7. What effect do some people think illegal immigrants have on the pay scale of legal workers?_____

What is her answer to this argument?_____

3. In paragraph 8, what does Quindlen suggest her opposition do to express their objections to illegal immigration?_____

How does she expect her opposition to respond to her suggestion?_____

_____ Why?_____

The Conclusion

Authors draw conclusions on the basis of the support and refutation they provide. The support is either convincing, and the reader accepts the conclusion, or it is not convincing, and the reader rejects it. Locate the conclusion of an argument by asking the question, What does the author finally want me to believe about the claim?

The conclusion can appear at various places in an essay. Sometimes the conclusion is identical with the claim and appears at the beginning of the essay. The rest of the essay supports the claim, which becomes the main point and the conclusion of the essay. Other times, the author leads up to the conclusion and presents it at the end. A variation is stating the claim itself as the conclusion at the end of an essay. When you read the first paragraphs of an essay and are not quite sure what the author wants you to think, look at the last two or three sentences. You will often find the claim/conclusion stated there. Sometimes the author does not state the claim or the conclusion at all, but expects the reader to infer it. The next chapter will help you learn to make inferences.

Analyze a conclusion.

Anna Quindlen's conclusion to her article "Undocumented, Indispensable" appears in paragraph 10 at the end of her article. Consider this paragraph along with the title of the article and state her conclusion in your own words.

> There are big decisions to be made about the vast wave of undocumented workers in this country, issues that go beyond slogans and placards. But there's no premium in discussing those issues in xenophobic half-truths, in talking about what undocumented immigrants cost the country without talking about what they contribute, in talking about them as illegals when they are nannies, waiters, roofers and the parents of American citizens. One fact is indisputable: the essence of America is free enterprise and human rights. It's why people come here in the first place. WE ARE ALL IMMIGRANTS, read signs on Market Street. Some of us just got here sooner. 10

1. What is Quindlen's concluding idea?_____

2. Do you find it convincing or not?_____ Why? _____

Go back and reread the entire Quindlen essay that appears on pages 297–298. Then answer these questions:

1. What is Quindlen's claim in "Undocumented, Indispensable?" Complete the statement, The author wants me to think. . . .

2. What are Quindlen's reasons for her claim? Complete the phrase, because. . . . Add as many reasons as you can that are developed in the article.

3. What human needs does Quindlen appeal to in this article?

4. What values does she appeal to? Do you share them?

5. Evaluate the support in this article. Describe her use of logic, emotion, and personal credentials as support. How effective is her support? Why do you think so?

_____

Now practice what you have learned in this chapter by analyzing another essay.

Practice analyzing the support, the refutation, and the conclusion.

Read the essay that follows and locate the types of support used by the author. All of the types of support on the list below are present in the essay. When you locate each of type of support, underline the support in the essay, label the type of support in the margin, as in the example on pages 294–295, and cross the item off the list. Then answer the questions that appear at the end of the essay. Look for:

vivid description

emotionally loaded language

emotional examples

appeals to needs and values

literal comparison (two similar items)

establishment of the personal credibility of the smoker (Jan Binder)

historical comparison (present with past)

emotional comparisons (two unlike items)

cause–effect

opinions of authorities

statistics

Practice Essay
A SLAVE OF SMOKE IN AN ANTI-SMOKE LAND[3]

Dirk Johnson

SYCAMORE, Ill., Nov. 18—It was not quite 8 A.M. as Jan Binder stood on the sidewalk in a cold Midwestern drizzle. Her fellow workers hustled past her toward the office, some of them shaking their heads in dismay.   1

"They're thinking," Ms. Binder said, "she doesn't have the sense to come in from the rain."   2

Despite the shivers, Ms. Binder, a tall woman with auburn hair, stood in the drizzle, her fingers clutching the last precious inch of a burning cigarette.   3

To be a smoker in America today, in most circles, is to be an outcast. It means being viewed as weak, offensive and, perhaps most of all, dimwitted. These are people, after all, who do not seem to have the sense to come in from a toxic thunderstorm.   4

Most people who have never smoked cannot fathom why anyone would put a cigarette in her mouth, one after the next, and draw the noxious fumes. It should be simple to stop. But almost anyone who has smoked heavily knows otherwise.   5

There are few riddles in life more enigmatic than the spell that smoking can cast, even to smokers like Jan Binder, a smart 38-year-old who has walked the horror chamber of nicotine.   6

It was two years ago, sitting in a hospital room, that a doctor looked into the eyes of her husband, James, and told him, "Mr. Binder, you have lung cancer."   7

That evening her husband walked through the door at home, switched on a lamp, turned to her and sized up his life.   8

[3] Dirk Johnson, "A Slave of Smoke in an Anti-Smoke Land," *The New York Times* 19 November 1998: A1, A20.

"I don't regret anything," he told her, "except a few million cigarettes." 9

Seven months later, he was dead. He was 37. Their daughter Mary 10
was 7 years old. Kate was 5.

"When they told Jim he was going to die," Ms. Binder said, "and I 11
saw the look on his face, I knew I would never smoke again."

She was certain sheer willpower could do it. But it was like willing 12
herself to stop drawing breath.

She has tried going cold turkey. She has tried the nicotine patch. She 13
has tried the drug Zyban.

Nothing has worked for more than a week. 14

"People look at me and think, 'How can you still smoke?'" said Ms. 15
Binder, who goes through a pack a day. "And God knows, I don't want
to smoke. But I am like a slave to it. It rules your life."

This is a woman who scarcely lacks fortitude. Besides her full-time 16
job for a state consortium that oversees programs for disabled students,
she fills her late husband's partnership in his pizza business, doing the
books and overseeing the payroll.

She digs deep into her pockets to pay for her daughters to attend pri- 17
vate school, to take piano lessons, to play soccer and softball. She rises
before daybreak to clean the house and wash school uniforms. She carries 50-pound bags of water softener down the stairs to her basement.

But when it comes to those feather-light sticks of tobacco, she feels 18
helpless. [. . .]

It is the rare smoker who does not wish to quit. A recent survey found 19
that two-thirds of smokers had seriously tried to stop, most of them at
least three times. Medical experts say nicotine has a powerful effect on
the chemistry of the brain, improving mood and in some cases masking
depression, an illness that can be treated with an anti-depressant like
Zyban.

What is not as commonly understood is how smoking can make peo- 20
ple feel guilty and ashamed. [. . .]

After Jim Binder was diagnosed with cancer, he tried valiantly to live 21
a pristine life. Facing death, he bore a crushing guilt, a husband and father leaving his family behind.

"He wanted so desperately to undo what he had done," his widow 22
said.

To extend his days, he ate organic foods and drank herbal tea. He 23
meditated. He prayed.

And he tried his very damnedest to give up cigarettes. 24

But there were moments, early in the morning before the children 25
would rise, that he would sit out on the back porch, gazing into the distance, drawing hard on a cigarette, shrouded in a smoky cloud that, for
the moment at least, served as a kind of veil.

It is now his wife who carries the guilt, a mother who cries in the 26
shower about her fatherless children and about their terrible, completely
logical fears when they see her light up, a woman who threw out every
ashtray when her husband died.

27

She has vowed so many times to her children that she will quit, often setting a date. And when that time comes, she tries. The minutes crawl like years, and she feels as if she is coming out of her skin, a jangle of nerves and emotion. And suddenly her hand is reaching for a pack. Or she is standing in a convenience store, with the $3 that will feed an insatiable craving.

"I am going to quit—I have to," she vowed one recent day, as a cigarette burned on a plate, a makeshift ashtray, in the kitchen of a house that falls quiet, too quiet, in the nighttime. "I just don't know how."

780 words

1. What is the claim of this essay? _____

2. What are one or two reasons that support the claim? _____

   _____

3. Write out one example of refutation in the essay. _____

4. What conclusion are you expected to draw about smokers? _____

   _____

5. Is the support in this essay sufficiently convincing to cause you to accept the conclusion? Why or why not? _____

How to Recognize a Biased Point of View: The Signs of Bias

You learned in Chapter 8 that you will need to read closely at times to recognize an author's real purpose for writing. Some of the material you read may appear at first to be informative and totally unbiased, but you will find, on closer reading, that it actually contains many argumentative elements that are aimed at convincing rather than informing you. It was also suggested in Chapter 8 that you analyze some of the influences outside of the text that might cause the author to be biased. These included gathering information about the possible controversial nature of the subject itself, searching for elements in the author's own background that might cause opinionated thinking about the subject, understanding the context or occasion that motivated the author to write in the first place, and understanding the possible biases that might be associated with the source of publication. Some magazines and newspapers, for example, are associated with causes or political parties and are openly biased in favor of a particular point of view.

Bias is not bad. It would be a very boring world if everyone held the same views on every topic. As a reader, however, you need to be able to recognize both a biased point of view and the position the author is taking on the issue. You cannot achieve total comprehension without an understanding of the author's basic purpose for writing.

Besides the influences identified above that exist outside of the text and that might cause bias, signs of bias can also occur within the text itself. Recognizing them can alert you to an author's biased point of view. All of these signs of bias, by the way, can be very effective and convincing within the context of an argument. They are effective ways for supporting an argument.

The Signs of Bias in the Text

1.   **The author's attitude.** Authors may indirectly exhibit positive or negative attitudes toward their subject, even if they do not directly express these attitudes. These attitudes come from the values, opinions, and assumptions that authors hold as true and that often influence the way they present their ideas. When you read, ask if a particular attitude toward the subject seems to be influencing the way the author expresses the ideas. Ask, What basic ideas, values, or beliefs are causing the author to write in this way? In the case of the article by Ellis Cose at the beginning of this chapter, the author's attitudes are favorable to enterprising students who are willing to work hard to get ahead and less favorable to young people who hang out in the streets and have no apparent ambition. He does not say this directly, but these attitudes are apparent from the examples he uses and from the reasons he gives.

2.   **The use of emotional support.** A preponderance of emotional support and strong feeling is almost always a sign of bias in favor of a particular point of view. Emotionally loaded language, emotional examples and descriptions, emotional comparisons that compare two unlike items in emotional ways, pictures and other visual materials that engage one's emotions, and emotional opinions all signal a strong possibility of bias and an argumentative purpose for writing.

3.   **Alluding to credentials that identify a point of view.** When an author refers to personal credentials, background experiences, or particular expertise in the text itself that one would associate with a particular point of view on an issue, you can anticipate bias and an argumentative purpose. Thus, if the author lets you know in the text that she is a Jew who is writing about the Holocaust, a Roman Catholic who is writing about birth control, or a member of Mothers Against Drunk Drivers who is writing about teenage drinking, you can usually anticipate quite accurately what positions they will take on these issues.

4.   **Stacking evidence in favor of a particular point of view.** All arguments do not present both sides of an issue. Often, authors present their sides, and not others, and then carefully select the evidence to support what they think. Statistics are often selected to support a particular position as well. When evidence seems to be one-sided and stacked to favor one point of view, this is usually a sign of an author's bias on the subject. For example, imagine someone arguing that cloning is a dangerous and unethical practice. The evidence is all about cloning people and the chaos and confusion that might result from that. The possible benefits of cloning microorganisms for medicine or animals for food are not mentioned.

Analyze the signs of bias.

Practice analyzing the signs of bias in the article you just read on pages 306–308, "A Slave of Smoke in an Anti-Smoke Land."

1. Review the section in Chapter 8 on how to recognize argument (see pp. 267–268). Do you think this essay is an argument? _____ Why? _____ If you answered yes, would you say this essay is an example of obvious argument, hidden argument, unconscious argument, or exploratory argument? _____ Explain your answer. _____

   _____

2. Do signs of bias signal an argumentative purpose in this article? _____ If yes, identify some of the signs of bias. (Refer to the list on page 309.) _____

   _____

   _____

   _____

EVALUATE THE SUPPORT, REASONING, AND CONCLUSIONS: FIVE STRATEGIES

The purpose of the following five strategies is to help you recognize productive argument. They will teach you to distinguish good reasons and sound evidence from misleading and inaccurate evidence that could manipulate you to accept a false and irrational conclusion. They will also help you recognize and evaluate refutation and the author's conclusion. Then you will be able to decide whether you want to accept the author's conclusion for now, at least until you receive other information that might cause you to change your mind later.

Strategy I: Evaluate the logical support.

Ask if the reasons are "good" reasons that you can accept. Ask if the facts, data, and statistics are verifiable, whether there are enough of them to be convincing, whether they represent all sides of the issue, or whether they have been selected and "stacked" to represent only one side. Check definitions to see if they are accurate and acceptable, test cause–effect reasoning to see if you think a particular cause will really result in the effect described, decide whether signs are true representations of what is happening or are not true signs at all. Test comparisons by

▶

asking whether the two items being compared are similar as claimed, and prove the point their comparison is meant to illustrate, or whether they are in fact so different that they do not prove anything.

Strategy 2: Evaluate opinions and personal credibility used as support.

Ask who is being quoted and if that individual knows enough to contribute a valuable and convincing opinion. To evaluate personal credibility statements, ask whether the individual's experience, background, and reputation are sufficiently impressive to make you accept the argument.

Strategy 3: Evaluate emotional support.

Ask how the emotional materials contribute to the argument. Do they actually prove anything, or do they simply engage my emotions? Emotionally loaded language, figurative analogies, and made-up emotional examples and descriptions cannot logically prove anything because these kinds of appeals are not factual. You will find them convincing only if you share the author's feelings about the claim and the support for the claim.

You can also ask if the emotional materials are appropriate to the subject. Emotional materials are appropriate when the subject and the context for the argument are themselves emotional. Finally, ask if the emotional appeal is used to further a good cause or a bad cause. Use your own judgment to decide the moral worth of an emotional argument. Emotion itself is not bad. But you may conclude that emotional support that contributes to an unworthy or immoral cause is bad, while emotion that contributes to a good cause is more acceptable. Compare, for example, the emotional arguments of Hitler condemning people to death and the emotional arguments of a conservationist who is trying to save an endangered animal species.

Strategy 4: Evaluate the effectiveness of the refutation.

Ask if the position being refuted is represented accurately, along with convincing reasons and support that make you want to reject it. Ask also if other positions should have been identified and refuted to make the author's conclusion even stronger. To do this, you will need to think about the different possible points of view that could be taken in response to the issue.

Strategy 5: Evaluate the conclusion and write a reaction.

Use both what you already know about the subject before you begin to read and what the author says about the subject in the text to help you make a judgment about the validity, accuracy, and moral worth of the conclusion. Try to identify the author's values and attitudes. Do you share them or not? Write a reaction in which you answer the following questions: Do I believe and accept this conclusion? Why or why not? Is it, according to my standard of values, a moral or immoral, good or bad conclusion? What conclusion might I prefer to draw instead? What are my reasons for wanting to adopt a different conclusion?

EXERCISES AND READINGS

Three Collaborative Class Exercises

Exercise 1

Identify bias in three short reading selections. *Small groups.*

The following three passages about fast food come from a newspaper, a magazine, and a Website. Review the section in this chapter on the signs of bias (see pp. 308-309). Form small groups of four students each. First, discuss briefly among yourselves any positive or negative biases you might have about fast food. Next, each student should read the three passages and then discuss whether or not bias exists in each of them. Each reader should be prepared to provide evidence of bias. Study the language to get a sense of each author's attitude towards this subject, look for emotional support either in favor of or against the subject, consider the author's credentials and how they might contribute to bias, and look for evidence that has been stacked in favor of a particular point of view. Report to the class when you have finished. Identify the amount of bias and the nature of the bias in each selection. Give evidence for your conclusions.

Practice Essay
SELECTION 1: SURGERY WITH A SIDE OF FRIES[4]

Andrew Weil

Explanatory Notes: *This first selection is an excerpt from an editorial in a daily newspaper. The author is the director of the integrative medicine program at the University of Arizona College of Medicine. He is a wellness expert who writes frequently about how people can be more healthy.*

FOUR years ago, a group of researchers at the University of Michigan conducted a survey of hospitals and found that 4 out of 10 had fast food restaurants on their premises. Today, I'm afraid, that number can only have gone up—judging by how often I and my colleagues cringe at the sight of new burger and pizza places in medical centers. 1

. . .

Expelling fast food from hospitals is an obvious step to better health, but suggest it and you run into the same tangle of inertia and apathy that has kept hospitals from serving patients appetizing and wholesome food—and has instead allowed large food service corporations to put profit ahead of quality. I hold my profession responsible for much of the apathy. Nutrition is slighted in medical education. It is considered a "soft" subject akin to home economics, not worthy of the time and attention commanded by important fields like biochemistry and pharmacology. 2

[4] Andrew Weil, "Surgery with a Side of Fries," *The New York Times* 6 July 2006: A23.

We must have nutritionally literate doctors, but getting fast food out of hospitals will also require the kind of grassroots activism that has removed sugary sodas and candy from vending machines in many schools. Doctors should model healthy life-styles for their patients, and hospitals should be places of inspiration and education as well as centers for the treatment of disease. Fast food has no place in them. 3

224 words

Practice Essay

SELECTION 2: FAST FOOD NATION:
THE TRUE COST OF AMERICA'S DIET[5]

Eric Schlosser

Explanatory Notes: *This is an excerpt from an article that appeared in the* Rolling Stone *magazine in 1998. Later the author expanded on this article to write the book* Fast Food Nation: The Dark Side of the All-American Meal, *published in 2001. Five years later he published another book about fast food,* Chew on This: Everything You Don't Want to Know About Fast Food, *published in 2006. He is an award-winning journalist who also writes for a number of magazines.*

During the last four decades, fast food has infiltrated every nook and cranny of 1 American society.[. . .] Fast food is now served not only at restaurants and drive-thrus but also at stadiums, airports, college campuses and elementary schools, on cruise ships, trains and airplanes, at Kmarts, Wal-Marts, gas stations and even hospital cafeterias. In 1970, Americans spent about $6 billion on fast food. Last year they spent more than $100 billion on fast food.

The McDonald's Corp. has become a powerful symbol of America's service 2 economy, the sector now responsible for ninety percent of the country's new jobs. In 1968, McDonald's operated about 1,000 restaurants. Today it has about 23,000 restaurants worldwide and opens roughly 2,000 new ones each year. An estimated one of every eight Americans has worked at McDonald's. The company annually trains more new workers than the U.S. Army. McDonald's is the nation's largest purchaser of beef and potatoes. It is the second-largest purchaser of poultry. A whole new breed of chicken was developed to facilitate the production of McNuggets. The McDonald's Corp. is the largest owner of retail property in the world. Indeed, the company earns the majority of its profits not from selling food but from collecting rent. McDonald's spends more money on advertising and marketing than does any other brand, much of it targeted at children. A survey of American schoolchildren found that ninety-six percent could identify Ronald McDonald. The only fictional character with a higher degree of recognition was Santa Claus. The impact of McDonald's on the nation's culture, economy and diet is hard to overstate. Its corporate symbol— the Golden Arches—is now more widely recognized than the Christian cross.

279 words

---

[5] Eric Schlosser, "Fast Food Nation: The True Cost of America's Diet," *Rolling Stone,* Issue 794, 3 September 1998. Available at <u>http://www.mcspotlight.org/media/ press/rollingstone l.html</u>

Practice Essay

SELECTION 3: WENDY'S TO SWITCH TO HEALTHIER COOKING OIL[6]

Mark Williams

Explanatory Notes: *This is an excerpt from an article that appears on the* Fast Food Source *Website. The author is an Associated Press Business Writer.*

Wendy's International Inc. said Thursday it will begin frying french fries and breaded chicken items with non-hydrogenated oil, continuing a shift to offer healthier menu choices. 1

The country's third-largest burger chain said the blend of corn and soy oil has zero grams of artery-clogging trans fat per serving and will cut trans fat in those menu items by 95 percent. Wendy's will begin using the oil in its 6,300 restaurants in the U.S. and Canada in August. 2

"The trend is for a bit healthier," said Lori Estrada, Wendy's senior vice president for research and development. "We wanted to look at our products and improve our nutritional profile." 3

Trans fat raises bad cholesterol and lowers good cholesterol. Eating just 5 grams a day raises the risk of heart disease by 25 percent, research shows. 4

The new oil will reduce trans fat to zero grams for Wendy's chicken sandwiches, chicken nuggets and chicken strips. A large order of french fries will go from 7 grams to 0.5 grams while an order of fries from the kids' menu will have zero grams. 5

. . .

Earlier this year, Wendy's cut all trans fat from salad dressings and last year the chain started offering margarine with zero grams of fat per serving for baked potatoes. 6

In 2004, it began offering combo meal choices that allowed customers to pick chili, a baked potato or a side salad instead of fries, and offering milk and fruit for substitution in kids' meals. 7

245 words

[6] Mark Williams, "Wendy's to Switch to Healthier Cooking Oil." Available at http://www.fastfoodsource.com/forum/portal.php?article=0

Evaluate the advertisements. *Small groups.*

Form small groups of four students each. Then, drawing on the information in the chapter, analyze the following advertisements. Prepare answers to these questions:

    a. What is the author's claim? Complete the statement, This author wants me to think . . .

    b. What are the reasons? Use the statement form, because . . .

    c. What is the evidence? What is offered as proof? Look particularly for different types of proof. Describe how they function in the advertisement.

    d. Are you convinced by the advertisement? Why or why not?

Advertisement 1.

Ad for the iMac Apple computer. *Chic* is a French word that means "stylish and fashionable." Pronounce it "sheek" to rhyme with "geek." [7]

Courtesy of Apple Computer, Inc.

[7] *Newsweek* 17 August 1998: 12.

Advertisement 2.

Ad for Energizer batteries.[8]

NOTE For dependable performance use Energizer AA batteries. After all, they last longer than ordinary Duracell in cellular phones. But go ahead, tempt fate, live on the edge. Just don't come crying to us when your phone decides to clam up while you're booking the order that would have paid for your house in the Hamptons, the boat of your dreams and the 50 million retainers your kids managed to misplace.

Energizer. Designed to keep your high-tech stuff going and going and...

Analyze the evidence and conclusion; write a reaction. *Small groups.*

This exercise provides you with additional practice in recognizing all the types of support and in evaluating the author's conclusion. The essay you will read is titled "Alcohol" by Mike Barnicle. The author is a newspaper columnist in Boston, Massachusetts.[9]

---

[8] *Newsweek* 27 July 1998: 7.

[9] In 1998 Barnicle was a subject of controversy himself about his own use of sources and evidence, though the validity of this article was never at issue.

- Before you begin to read, jot down three or four ideas that come to your mind when you think about people drinking alcohol while they are at college.
- Read the following essay. Then form small groups of four students each and answer the following questions. One member of the group should jot down the answers. When you finish, discuss your answers with the rest of the class.

   a. What is the conclusion? Complete the statement, The author wants me to think . . .

   b. What are the reasons? Complete the phrase, Because . . .

   c. Find some examples of logical proof: facts, definitions, cause–effect, signs, comparisons.

   d. Find some examples of author credibility and also descriptions of the credibility of people described in the article.

   e. Find some examples of emotional proof: emotionally loaded language, emotional examples, emotional comparisons, vivid descriptions, appeals to needs and values, and emotional visuals.

   f. What is the author's attitude toward this subject? Do you share this attitude, or are you and the author "worlds apart"? How much common ground would you say you have with this author?

- When you have finished reading and discussing the essay, write a one-page reaction in response to the following questions: Do I believe and accept the author's conclusion? Why or why not? Is it, according to my standard of values, a moral or immoral, a good or bad conclusion? What conclusion might I prefer to draw instead? What are my reasons for wanting to adopt a different conclusion?

Alcohol[10]

MIKE BARNICLE

Here they were, the dead boy's family, parked in pretty much the same spot, 1 doing some of the same things they did less than a month ago, only in reverse order. An enormous sadness overwhelmed them, as they carried the contents of his room down the steps and out the door of the fraternity house. A rite of June was being conducted on the last day of September.

All the clothes, books and pictures belonged to Scott Krueger. He arrived a few 2 weeks ago to begin his freshman year at the Massachusetts Institute of Technology. He arrived as bright and attractive as they come, ready and quite able to take his initial step away from home and right into a life that offered spectacular opportunity.

---

[10] Mike Barnicle, "Alcohol," *Boston Globe* 6 October 1997: op-ed. This essay was also printed in *The Dallas Morning News* 6 October 1997: op-ed.

Now, with the academic year still in its infancy, Scott is gone, and his college is flunking common sense. With alcohol identified as the weapon that killed one of its students, MIT's response is to assemble a team of professors and administrators to study campus drinking and issue university guidelines as if what occurred the other day was a laboratory accident. 3

God knows, it is impossible to legislate human behavior. And, certainly, a school can't be held legally responsible for whatever it is individual students choose to do with themselves—or to themselves—once they walk out a classroom door. 4

But it is too bad that MIT and other institutions don't view a six-pack or a pint of vodka as posing the same potentially lethal threat to life as a cigarette. The college is littered with no-smoking signs, but nowhere is there a sign that says, "Get caught drinking, and there will be no diploma." 5

On the surface, America currently faces few threats. The Soviet Union has crumbled and disappeared. The Cold War is a relic and something for history books. The economy is booming, and crime supposedly has been reduced. 6

So our great modern enemy, the largest evil we confront, has become smoking. The Marlboro Man has replaced Nikita Khrushchev and Josef Stalin. Instead of bomb shelters and air raid drills, we stigmatize anybody with a pack of Salems. 7

Yet in the course of a normal day, alcohol absolutely ruins more families and destroys more individual lives than a whole warehouse of filter tips. However, because Jim Beam and Coors Lite employ better marketing experts and ad agencies, we read more editorials about lung cancer than about cirrhosis. 8

Courtesy of Eleanor Mill.

Now, on a pleasant fall weekend, we have an elite set of students, truly gifted people, using binge drinking as a badge of admission to some fraternity. Is there a parent on this earth tossing and turning because his son or daughter might smoke a cigarette on a Saturday night? But how many suffer from sleep deprivation, hoping against hope that their child isn't behind the wheel, drunk, racing home to beat a curfew? 9

There aren't enough fingers to point at who caused the tragic events leading toward Scott Krueger's death: Who sold the booze? Who purchased it? Who, if anyone, forced him to drink and drink and then drink some more? 10

Go to almost any city neighborhood, pause by nearly any corner or park in the smallest of towns, and you will witness a 11 huge national problem: Teenagers thinking they can act beyond their years by sneaking a couple of beers.

Of course, part of the reason this story is so awful, so penetrating, is the picture of Scott Krueger's face, high school graduation picture, handsome, smiling, confident, self-assured, eyes focused on a future open only to a favored few. He was a freshman at one of the world's most famous schools. He was a student at a university whose very name—MIT—is an unmatched calling card for potential employers. What ever could happen to such a young man?

12

In the lineup of dark nightmares any parent thinks possible to befall a child— automobile crashes, robbery victim—death by drinking isn't even on the list. But as his family packed his things for the long trip back to New York, they drove off with the agonizing knowledge that their son was killed by alcohol and died within a culture that glibly assumes smoking is the only lethal social evil around.

13

625 words

Three Reading Exercises:
About Medical Marijuana

The following three readings are drawn from the weekly magazines, *Newsweek* and *U.S. News and World Report*. All three are arguments that provide different points of view about whether or not marijuana should be legalized for medicinal purposes. These articles were occasioned by referendums in California and Arizona that asked citizens of those states to vote either for or against the legalization of marijuana for medicinal purposes in those states. Both states voted in favor of these propositions, but after the votes, as you will see, many continued to argue the pros and cons of this issue. ***As you read these essays, identify the positions the authors take, evaluate their evidence, and, when you have completed your reading, come to a conclusion of your own on this issue.***

Reading 1

We're on a Perilous Path[11]

BARRY R. McCAFFREY

Explanatory Notes: *This essay comes from* Newsweek *magazine. McCaffrey is a retired army general and, writing as the director of the Office of National Drug Control Policy, represents the point of view of that office.* Newsweek *refers to him as "the drug czar."* **Find the conclusion in this essay and decide whether the evidence used is effective enough for you to accept it.**

[11] Barry R. McCaffrey, "We're on a Perilous Path," *Newsweek* 3 February 1997: 27.

Why is it dangerous for Americans to use marijuana as medicine? The answer is: it may not be. It may surprise you to hear the national drug-policy director say this, but I don't think we should automatically reject the possibility that marijuana may have some medicinal benefits. In fact, a synthetic version of THC, the main active ingredient in marijuana, is already approved by the FDA and available with a doctor's prescription. Called Marinol, it's used to ease nausea in cancer patients and help people with AIDS keep up their appetites.

Does that mean the new California law legalizing marijuana as medicine is a good idea? Absolutely not. The truth is, despite the insistence of legalization activists, there is no proof that smoked marijuana is the most effective available treatment for anything. Don't take my word for it. The National Institutes of Health recently examined all of the existing clinical evidence about smoked marijuana. Its conclusion: "There is no scientifically sound evidence that smoked marijuana is medically superior to currently available therapies." This isn't an argument between advocates for legalizing marijuana and the federal government. It's an argument between the legalizers and the American Medical Association, and the American Cancer Society, and the American Ophthalmological Society—all of which oppose the California marijuana initiative.

It seems to me entirely sensible that before we go rushing to embrace the medicinal use of marijuana—or LSD, heroin or any other illicit drug—we ought to find out if it is safe and effective. Every other drug on the market was required to undergo exhaustive testing by the FDA before it was made available to the public. As far as I'm concerned, the door is wide open to marijuana or any other substance—but first it has to pass scientific scrutiny and be subject to peer-group review. (It surprises many people to learn that methamphetamines and even cocaine have been approved for specific medical purposes.)

We have made $1 million available to the Institute of Medicine at the National Academy of Sciences to ask physicians and scientists for all that is known about smoked pot, and what questions need to be asked about it. And I have asked Dr. Harold Varmus, the Nobel laureate and head of the National Institutes of Health, to examine the potential benefits of marijuana. If researchers find there are compounds in marijuana that may have medicinal benefits (cannabis is made up of more than 400 different substances), we must immediately make them available to the American medical community. If they can demonstrate that they are safe and effective, then let's approve them.

Until then, though, it is inconceivable to allow anyone of any age to have uncontrolled use of marijuana for any alleged illness—without a doctor's examination or even prescription. But that is precisely what the California law lets people do. Can you think of any other untested, homemade, mind-altering medicine that you self-dose, and that uses a burning carcinogen as a delivery vehicle?

I think it's clear that a lot of the people arguing for the California proposition and others like it are pushing the legalization of drugs, plain and simple. It sends a very mixed and confusing message to the young. We've got 68 million kids age 18 and below. They're using drugs in enormously increasing numbers. Drug use among eighth graders alone has more than tripled in the last five years. Pretending pot is just another choice makes their decision to stay off drugs that much harder.

575 words

Strategy Questions

1. Identify the author's values and attitudes toward medicine, research, and drugs.
2. Is McCaffrey a credible author? What is his title? Why do you think that makes him reliable or not?
3. Is the evidence in this article stacked? In other words, does the author fairly represent all sides of the issue or just enough to support his own claim? Explain your answer.
4. Evaluate the author's conclusion. Write a short reaction piece to this conclusion. What is your opinion about the legalization of medical marijuana? Do you agree with the author? Why or why not?

Study Reading Questions

1. What is the main active ingredient in marijuana? What is the name of the synthetic version?
2. What are two reasons that individuals who are ill might use marijuana?
3. What is the government agency that tests drugs before they are made available to the public?
4. What controversial drugs have been approved for specific medical purposes?
5. How many different substances does marijuana have in it?

Critical Reading and Thinking Questions

1. Why do you think marijuana is an illegal substance? Do you believe it should be made available to patients, if it is proven to be effective? Why or why not?
2. McCaffrey states that under the California law anyone of any age is allowed uncontrolled use of marijuana for any alleged illness without a doctor's examination or prescription. Do you believe this is an effective way to legalize marijuana for medical purposes? What alternatives might you suggest? In other words, what should someone have to do to acquire medical marijuana?
3. Reread the last paragraph. Do you agree that the push for legalization sends a mixed message to the young? Why or why not?

Reading 2

This Is Smart Medicine[12]

MARCUS CONANT

Explanatory Notes: *This article also appeared in* Newsweek *magazine, as a companion piece to the article by McCaffrey that you have just read. It is written by a*

[12] Marcus Conant, "This Is Smart Medicine," *Newsweek* 3 February 1997: 26.

Anyone who has ever smoked marijuana will tell you he gets hungry afterward. That kind of anecdotal evidence led doctors and patients to experiment with marijuana as a treatment for extreme nausea, or wasting syndrome. I have seen hundreds of AIDS and cancer patients who are losing weight derive almost immediate relief from smoking marijuana, even after other weight-gain treatments—such as hormone treatments or feeding tubes—have failed. But it's not just individuals who have recognized the medicinal benefits of marijuana. No less an authority than the FDA has approved the use of Marinol, a drug that contains the active ingredient in marijuana. 1

The problem with Marinol is that it doesn't always work as well as smoking marijuana. Either you take too little, or 45 minutes later you fall asleep. Even though insurance will pay for Marinol—which costs about $200 a month—some patients spend their own money, and risk breaking the law, for the more effective marijuana. That's fairly good evidence that smoking the drug is superior to taking it orally. How would we keep patients from giving their prescribed marijuana to friends? The same way we keep people from abusing other prescription drugs: by making patients understand the dangers of giving medication to other people. A physician who prescribes marijuana without the proper diagnoses should be held up to peer review and punished. There are drugs available at the local pharmacy—Valium, Xanax, Percodan—that are far more mood-altering than marijuana. They aren't widely abused. It's not important that a few zealots advocate the wholesale legalization of marijuana. The federal government can't craft policy based on what a few irrational people say. This is a democracy, and what the people of California voted for was to make marijuana available for medical use for seriously ill people. 2

For skeptics, a study devised at San Francisco General Hospital would test the benefits of smoking marijuana once and for all. It, too, was endorsed by the FDA—but the federal government won't provide the marijuana for the study. Washington recently offered to fund a $1 million review of literature on medical marijuana, but it refuses to allow a clinical trial, which is what's really needed. 3

When citizens even speak up in favor of legalizing marijuana for medicinal use, as happened this fall in California and Arizona, the government tries to stop them. Gen. Barry McCaffrey and the Justice Department have threatened to revoke the prescription-drug licenses of doctors who prescribe marijuana. This is a truly dangerous step. The government has no place in the examination room. Our society has long felt that certain relationships require privileged communication, such as those between a priest and a parishioner or a lawyer and a client. If a patient wants to discuss marijuana, I don't want to have the responsibility of reporting him, and I have to feel comfortable that the patient will not report me. This is a First Amendment issue of freedom of speech between doctor and patient. 4

Perhaps the most persuasive argument for medicinal marijuana I've encountered came two years ago, when the California Assembly was debating a medical-marijuana bill. One GOP assemblyman said he had had a great deal of trouble with 5 the issue. But when a relative was dying a few years before, the family had used marijuana to help her nausea. That story helped the bill pass. Wouldn't it be awful if people changed their minds only after someone close to them had died?

525 words

Strategy Questions

1. Reread the final paragraph. What does this emotional story contribute to the argument? Does it prove anything, or does it simply engage the reader's emotions? Explain.
2. Is the evidence in this article stacked? In other words, does the author fairly represent all sides of the issue or just enough to support his own claim? Explain your answer.
3. Can you identify any fallacies in this piece? If so, what are they and why are they fallacies? If not, why do you believe this argument is a sound one?
4. Conant discusses the argument that patients could pass marijuana on to friends or sell it on the street. How does he refute this argument? Is his refutation successful? Why or why not?
5. Evaluate the author's conclusion. Write a short reaction piece to this conclusion. What is your opinion about the legalization of medical marijuana? Do you agree with the author? Why or why not?

Study Reading Questions

1. What two other weight-gaining treatments have not been as successful as smoking marijuana?
2. What are two reasons that taking Marinol may not be as effective as smoking marijuana?
3. What three prescription drugs does the author find to be even more mind-altering, and therefore more dangerous, than marijuana?
4. Why couldn't San Francisco General Hospital test the effectiveness of smoking marijuana, even though the study was endorsed by the FDA?

Critical Reading and Thinking Questions

1. Conant draws on several examples of the government's practice of putting a stop to the testing of medical marijuana. Imagine Conant and McCaffrey, the author of the first article, discussing the testing of marijuana for medicinal purposes. Why would each of them think the government stops some of these studies? What is at stake, or at risk, for the government in these studies? What do you think about this issue? Explain.
2. The author argues that "a physician who prescribes marijuana without the proper diagnosis should be held up to peer review and punished." What kinds of punishment do you believe would be suitable for this crime?
3. The author argues that the use of medical marijuana is a First Amendment issue of freedom of speech between doctor and patient, a communication similar to the confidentiality between lawyer and client. Do you believe this is an accurate

analogy? In other words, should the discussion of the use of medical marijuana be protected information? Would McCaffrey agree with Conant on this matter? Justify your answer.

Lost in the Weed[13]

RICHARD BROOKHISER

Explanatory Notes: *This article appeared originally in* U.S. News and World Report. *The author, Richard Brookhiser, writes as a senior editor of* National Review, *a weekly magazine that is traditionally associated with a conservative political point of view.* **Brookhiser uses personal experience in this essay as proof, and he refutes three arguments on the opposing side that he claims are mistaken. See if you can recognize the problems with these three arguments. Summarize these arguments. How does Brookhiser discredit each of them?**

1   Last November, the voters of California and Arizona made it legal to use marijuana as a medicine. Last week, the Clinton administration said these actions were too rash. But for me, they came in the wrong states and four years too late. In 1992, my doctor in New York told me that I had metastasized testicular cancer, which required chemotherapy. To deal with the resulting nausea, I took legal antiemetic drugs, but after a while they didn't work. Then, I turned to pot.

2   I hadn't smoked marijuana since college—I had quit because I didn't like the smoke, the high or the jokes of potheads. But I went back to it because the craving to eat that pot induces in the healthy ("the munchies") fights nausea in the sick. None of my doctors or nurses discouraged me from smoking dope. They had all treated patients who successfully used marijuana to keep food down. It worked for me, too.

3   Cancer patients are not the only sick people who get relief from smoking pot. Marijuana has reportedly restored the appetite of AIDS patients, arrested the deterioration of the eyes of glaucoma sufferers and relieved the symptoms of chronic migraines, epilepsy and multiple sclerosis. But anyone with a disease who turns to pot must break the federal law that makes marijuana illegal in all circumstances.

4   Opponents of medical marijuana typically make three arguments, all of them mistaken.

5   The first is that THC, the main active ingredient in the drug, is legally available in a pill (marketed as Marinol). But the pill, besides being expensive, seems to cause higher levels of anxiety and depression. Since I was trying to combat vomiting, I didn't think a pill was the smart way to go. The second argument is that marijuana hasn't been thoroughly tested. But that's mainly because the government gives scientists the runaround. Dr. Donald Abrams, an AIDS researcher, has been trying to get marijuana from the National Institute on Drug Abuse. All he gets is the

[13] Richard Brookhiser, "Lost in the Weed," *U.S. News and World Report* 13 January 1997: 9.

brushoff. If it supplies Abrams, NIDA says, it might be overwhelmed by requests from other researchers. Can't have that—then there might be some research.

The third objection is that legalizing marijuana for the sick would set a bad example for children targeted by drug pushers. But how? A bald-headed cancer patient lounging by an IV pole is not an image of cool.

Attorney General Janet Reno is threatening to prosecute doctors who prescribe marijuana to patients. For an administration composed, in part, of former recreational drug users (including President "Didn't Inhale"), the decision to harass doctors who use these same drugs to treat the sick is unseemly. Supporting this policy is also unseemly for my fellow Republicans, whose aim is supposed to be reforming Big Government.

In a few months, I will finish my fifth year free from cancer. God forbid that any policy makers in Washington should go through what I did in 1992. But inevitably some will—and will turn to marijuana for relief. They should extend that same liberty to their fellow citizens.

510 words

Strategy Questions

1. Identify the three fallacies from the opposing side that Brookhiser refutes. Are his refutations successful? Why or why not?
2. Is the author a credible source to argue for the legalization of medical marijuana? Defend your answer.
3. Identify the author's values and attitudes toward illness, drugs, and the government.
4. Evaluate the author's conclusion. Write a short reaction piece to this conclusion. What is your opinion about the legalization of medical marijuana? Do you agree with the author? Why or why not?

Study Reading Questions

1. Why did Brookhiser stop smoking marijuana in college?
2. For what reasons might individuals who are ill use marijuana?
3. What are two drawbacks of Marinol?
4. Why didn't NIDA provide Dr. Abrams with marijuana for AIDS research?

Critical Reading and Thinking Questions

1. Brookhiser mentions that he had smoked marijuana in college, but had not smoked it again until the legal antiemetic drugs failed to cure his chemotherapy-induced nausea. Why do you think he mentions his previous experience with the drug? Does this help or hurt his argument? Explain your thoughts.
2. Brookhiser raises the argument that legalizing medical marijuana "would set a bad example for children targeted by drug pushers." Do you believe this is true? Why or why not?
3. What is the final argument in paragraph 8? Would either McCaffrey or Conant agree with Brookhiser's conclusion? Do you agree with his conclusion? Justify your answers.

THREE APPLICATION EXERCISES

Exercise 1

Analyze the claim and support in an advertisement.

Bring in an advertisement from a magazine or newspaper and prepare to state the claim and the reasons given in the ad. Describe the evidence, and state why you do or do not find the ad convincing.

Exercise 2

Look for signs of bias in your textbooks.

Read about a controversial subject in one of your other textbooks and decide whether the author has remained completely objective in writing about this subject or, indeed, has let biased opinion creep in and influence the way the ideas are presented. Bring the example you find to class to discuss.

Exercise 3

Discover evidence in your textbooks.

Find one section in one of your other textbooks that is on a controversial subject and make a list of all of the types of support and evidence that occur there. What does the author finally conclude? Is the conclusion adequately supported by the evidence?

REVIEW AND EVALUATE THE STRATEGIES

The following is a review of the five strategies you learned in this chapter:

1. Evaluate the logical support.
2. Evaluate opinions and personal credibility used as support
3. Evaluate emotional support.
4. Evaluate the effectiveness of the refutation.
5. Evaluate the conclusion and write a reaction.

Make a personal evaluation of these strategies:

1. Underline your favorite strategies in the list above.
2. Make a check mark by those you want to continue to use.
3. Cross out any you probably will not continue to use. What are your reasons for rejecting them?

Make Inferences and Analyze Values and Beliefs

CHAPTER
10

CHAPTER GOALS:

1. **To teach you to supply part of the meaning by making inferences.**

2. **To identify the types of inferences associated with critical reading.**

3. **To teach you to infer the author's values and beliefs and decide if you share them.**

4. **To provide five strategies for making inferences and analyzing values and beliefs.**

You Make Inferences All the Time, Whether You Know It or Not

Older reading books sometimes advised students to "read between the lines." The idea behind this was that authors themselves put all the meaning on the page, though some of it was concealed and invisible to the reader. Readers had to somehow read between the lines and guess what the author meant. Now we realize that readers themselves, interacting with the material they read, supply part of the meaning by drawing on their own store of knowledge and experience with the topic. Meaning in reading is created by the reader who uses prior knowledge to interpret and add to the author's ideas on the page. This chapter focuses on that interaction between mind and page and provides you with strategies to help you do it better.

You will need to know two key terms to read this chapter: **imply** and **infer.** *Authors imply meaning* when they leave part of it for the reader to figure out. *Readers infer meaning* when they supply part of it. Making inferences is the process of supplying part of the meaning as one reads. You make **inferences** often. Look at the cartoon on the next page.

I think you would agree that not all of the meaning in this cartoon has been spelled out. You know enough about situations of this type to recognize that this

"I don't have an answer, but you've given me a lot to think about." [1]

student perhaps has not done his homework and that he is trying to flatter his teacher and divert her attention so that he won't get in trouble. The boy is gambling that the teacher won't mind or notice that he hasn't learned anything, especially if she thinks she has inspired him to think. You may not have filled in the meaning for this cartoon in exactly this way, but if you "got" the point of this cartoon, you did fill in some meaning that is probably close to that explanation. One of the pleasures of listening to jokes or reading comics or cartoons is in supplying the part of the meaning that has been left out. This allows you to "get the point."

Authors Expect You to Supply Both Literal Meaning and Inferential Meaning

An unwritten agreement exists between authors and readers that authors do not have to spell everything out. Authors regularly omit explanations and information that they think their readers will be able to supply. When authors write for readers who know as much as or more than they do about their subjects, they omit more information than when they write for readers who know less. Reading would be boring if authors always assumed that their readers knew nothing about the subject.

[1] *The New Yorker* 10 February 1997: 57.

Supplying Literal Meaning

Here are the opening sentences of three college textbooks for psychology, biology, and history. Notice what you learn from reading these sentences, and notice also the meaning you add to these sentences to make them more meaningful to you. You can understand the literal meaning of these sentences without looking up words in the dictionary or asking someone what the sentences mean.

From psychology: "Almost every day we encounter events in our personal life or in the mass media that involve what we call "psychology.""[2]

From biology: "On your way across campus tomorrow morning, take a moment to look around you."[3]

From history: " 'Why do you call us Indians?' a Massachusetts native complained to Puritan missionary John Eliot in 1646."[4]

All of these authors expect you to be able to define the words in these sentences, to come up with some examples of your own, to place yourself imaginatively in situations, and to predict what will come next. They assume that you already have enough information stored in your memories so that you can do that. It would be boring if the authors of the first sentence, for example, thought they had to spell out the meaning of *personal life*, *mass media*, and *psychology*, or if the authors of the second sentence thought they had to describe everything you might possibly see as you walk on your campus.

Supplying Inferential Meaning

It would also be boring if the author spelled out the meaning of this next sentence: *The girl crossed the street so that the black cat would not cross in front of her.* In this sentence, the author expects the reader to supply the meanings of the words, the literal meaning, and also to supply information about superstition that is not directly explained in the sentence. That the girl is superstitious is, however, implied or hinted at by the situation and the girl's action. The implied, or unstated, meaning that the author expects the reader to "get" is that the girl is avoiding the cat so that she will avoid bad luck. *When readers use clues provided by the author and also add information from their own background to draw logical conclusions about meaning, they are making inferences.* Readers make inferences quite naturally whenever they realize that the literal meaning is not adequate for understanding and that additional meaning must, therefore, be inferred.

Try making some inferences. Drawing on your prior knowledge, what would you immediately call up or infer if someone started to tell you a joke about one of the following?

---

[2] Stephen F. Davis and Joseph J. Palladino, *Psychology* (Englewood Cliffs: Prentice Hall, 1995) 2.

[3] Teresa Audesirk and Gerald Audesirk, *Life on Earth* (Upper Saddle River: Prentice Hall, 1997) 1.

[4] John M. Faragher et al., *Out of Many*, 2nd ed. (Upper Saddle River: Prentice Hall, 1997) 5.

1. A joke about an "aggie." The "aggie" is usually _____.

2. A joke about a lawyer. The lawyer is usually_____.

Henry James, the American novelist, says in one of his essays that an author actually pays a compliment to the reader by leaving out information and then expecting the reader to supply it. The author thereby suggests that the reader is intelligent, educated, and able to supply added meaning.

What If You Do Not Have Enough Information to Make an Accurate Inference?

Sometimes you will not have enough prior knowledge about a subject to make an accurate inference. If you are an international student and have never heard an "aggie" joke, for instance, you will not infer anything when asked about this type of joke.

A great deal of detailed information is supplied in the passage below. Yet for most readers, the author has not supplied enough clues to help them figure out what process is being described here, and the subject itself remains puzzling. The literal meaning is simple enough to get, but you must infer the subject to understand what the whole passage is about. See if you are one of the rare readers who can guess the subject of this passage.

The procedure is actually quite simple. First, you arrange the items into different groups. Of course one pile may be sufficient depending on how much there is to do. If you have to go somewhere else due to lack of facilities that is the next step; otherwise, you are pretty well set. It is important not to overdo things. That is, it is better to do too few things at once than too many. In the short run this may not seem important but complications can easily arise. A mistake can be expensive as well. At first, the whole procedure will seem complicated. Soon, however, it will become just another facet of life. It is difficult to foresee any end to the necessity for this task in the immediate future, but then, one never can tell. After the procedure is completed one arranges the materials into different groups again. Then they can be put into their appropriate places. Eventually they will be used once more and the whole cycle will then have to be repeated. However, that is part of life.[5]

This is the subject printed backward: *Sehtolc Gnihsaw.* Now go back and reread the passage with the title in mind. It should be much easier to understand now that you have inferred the subject.

Here is a second example that presents some unusual problems with making inferences. The following letter from a student to the student's parents requires the reader to make inferences. Notice, however, that the clues in the body of the letter deliberately invite incorrect inferences so that they can be disclaimed later in the postscript. The inferences made about the postscript will, then, seem less severe than the inferences made about the letter itself, and this will get the student off the hook, so to speak.

[5] From D. J. Dooling and R. Lauchman, "Effects of Comprehension on Retention of Prose," *Journal of Experimental Psychology* 88 (1971): 216–222.

```
Dear Mom and Dad,

    I'm sorry for not writing, but hope you will understand.
First, sit down before you read further.
    I'm doing much better now after recovering from the
concussion and the broken leg I received when I jumped from
my dorm window after it caught fire last month. I can almost
see and walk normally thanks to the loving care of the
wonderful man who risked his life to save me. He more than
saved me; he has become my whole family. You see, I have
been living with him since the fire and we are planning to
get married. We haven't set a date yet but plan to have one
soon, before my pregnancy starts to show.

Love Always,


P.S.: There was no fire, I am perfectly healthy and not
pregnant. In fact, I do not even have a boyfriend. However,
I did get a D in German, a D- in physics, and I failed
college algebra. I wanted you to keep this all in
perspective.[6]
```

Here is a final example of inference making that poses another kind of a problem. This example comes from an essay that explains inference making as the process of inferring the unknown on the basis of the known. The first two sentences provide known, factual information that can be verified. The third sentence is an inference based on the first two sentences.

Manny Freebus is 5 feet 8 inches and weighs 235 pounds.

Manny Freebus is grossly fat.

Manny Freebus eats too much.

The author goes on to say, however, that the third sentence is an incorrect inference because Manny Freebus actually has a glandular condition that keeps him overweight. He eats a normal amount of food.[7]

[6] Davis and Palladino, *Psychology* 391.
[7] Neil Postman and Steve Powers, "The Bias of Language, The Bias of Pictures," in *Common Culture*, Michael F. Petracca and Madeleine Sorapure, eds. (Upper Saddle River: Prentice Hall, 1995) 469.

As you can see, inference making is not clearly predictable, and it is sometimes inaccurate. People do not all make the same inferences in response to the same texts. Different individuals bring different information and experiences to the page, and thus their inferences differ. Readers also sometimes make incorrect inferences because they misinterpret the clues in the text, or because they base their inferences on information that is unrelated to the topic. You should expect these misreadings to occur from time to time and view them with interest. When inferences about the same passage differ from reader to reader, discussion among the readers can often finally establish inferential meanings that are more or less agreeable to all. In the process, readers discover interesting information about one another as well as new approaches to reading that they may never have thought about on their own.

Inference making is an important part of the reading process. The next section identifies situations in which authors expect their readers not only to make inferences but to make inferences that will actually change the literal meaning of the text. Readers who do not make inferences in these situations miss the intended meaning altogether.

Make Inferences That Change the Literal Meaning

A clue that you may need to make inferences that change the literal meaning of the text occurs when the literal meaning does not make sense or seems odd or wrong in some way. Examples of material that, if taken literally, will not make sense include all types of **figurative language**, including **idioms, proverbs, metaphors, and similes. Irony** and **sarcasm** are other types of material that cannot be taken literally.

If you were from another country and did not know very much English, imagine what sort of images would go through your mind if you heard a conversation full of nonstandard English like this one: "Let's *shoot the breeze* for a while." "No thanks, I'm finally *off the hook,* and I'm going to *hit the hay.*" "Okay, be a *wet blanket* if you want to. But that's all right. I know what it's like to feel that you're *at the end of your rope.*" The phrases in italics are examples of idioms, one type of figurative language that can be confusing to people who have studied only the literal meanings of English words. People who understand these idioms would immediately translate them to mean that the person addressed does not want to talk anymore, has finished something hard, and wants to go to bed, not because she wants to be boring but because she is exhausted.

Like idioms, *proverbs* and other sayings also mean something different from their literal meanings. Consider the proverbs, "The early bird catches the worm," "A stitch in time saves nine," or "If the shoe fits, wear it." In every case, the reader or listener is expected to infer meaning that is quite different from that expressed literally.

Now imagine a student who has studied only the literal meaning of English words sitting down in an American classroom for the first time and overhearing the other students comment on their fellow students as they enter the room: "Those are a couple of cute *chicks* over there." "Here comes a *necktie.*" "I bet that other guy is a *brain.*" These are examples of *metaphors.* You "get" them if you are familiar with these types of comparisons and are thus able to infer what the students mean. These remarks may seem meaningless, odd, or strange, however, to an international student.

Similes, like metaphors, also make comparisons between items that are very different. Similes use the word *like* to make the comparison, while metaphors do not. "That car runs like a dream" and "That engine purrs like a cat" are examples of similes. As a reader, you infer the qualities that the two items being compared share, just as you do when you figure out the meaning of metaphors. These qualities are the unexpressed meaning that the author expects you to get when you read similes and metaphors.

Irony and *sarcasm* both present cases of the author saying one thing but really meaning something else. The real meaning, in fact, is usually the exact opposite of what the author actually says. To sneeringly remark "That's a *great* idea" to a friend who wants to drop out of school when you think she shouldn't is an example of sarcasm. You actually mean that dropping out is a terrible idea. Here is an example of irony—the first paragraphs of an essay entitled "A Liberating Curriculum" written by Roberta F. Borkat, a professor of English and comparative literature at San Diego State University. As you read these paragraphs, underline the words and phrases that make you think the author is saying one thing but actually meaning something else.

A blessed change has come over me. Events of recent months have revealed to me that I have been laboring as a university professor for more than 20 years under a misguided theory of teaching. I humbly regret that during all those years I have caused distress and inconvenience to thousands of students while providing some amusement to my more practical colleagues. Enlightenment came to me in a sublime moment of clarity while I was being verbally attacked by a student whose paper I had just proved to have been plagiarized from "The Norton Anthology of English Literature." Suddenly, I understood the true purpose of my profession, and I devised a plan to embody that revelation. Every moment since then has been filled with delight about the advantages to students, professors and universities from my Plan to Increase Student Happiness.

The plan is simplicity itself: at the end of the second week of the semester, all students enrolled in each course will receive a final grade of A. Then their minds will be relieved of anxiety, and they will be free to do whatever they want for the rest of the term.

The benefits are immediately evident. Students will be assured of high grade-point averages and an absence of obstacles in their march toward graduation. Professors will be relieved of useless burdens and will have time to pursue their real interests.[8]

Answer these questions.

1. What does the author literally say? _____

2. What do you infer the author actually means? _____

[8] *Newsweek* 23 April 1993: 11.

Your past experience as a student will make you question the real intentions of a college professor who says she will give all A's just because her students want them.

Make Accurate Inferences

You have already seen that one of the pitfalls of inference making is to "take things in the wrong way" and end up with inaccurate inferences that distort the meaning of the text. In the case of irony or figurative language, the author fully intends you to infer meaning that is not literally stated. In the cartoon at the beginning of this chapter, the artist also clearly expects you to supply background information about the boy and the teacher in order to infer the point of the cartoon. Such inferences are expected and intended by the author or the artist. If you do not "get" these inferences, you miss the point.

A range of accepted meanings and inferences exists for most things you read. When readers go outside of this range and contribute extreme and unusual meanings that do not seem warranted by the text, other readers will usually complain. Inferences made within an accepted range that can be supported with evidence from the text, however, can usually make a book or article much more interesting and memorable to all readers. Most of the time, you will know enough to find the evidence and make accurate inferences that fall within the accepted range.

What Inferences Are Important in Critical Reading?

In reading critically, you will need to infer several types of meaning when it is not explained directly in the text. To do this, you will need to use clues provided within the text and make the best guesses you can. Specifically, you need to try to make some inferences about:

1. The claim/conclusion, if it is not stated.
2. The author's purpose, if it is not obvious.
3. The author's background, if it is not explained.
4. The context or motivation that caused the author to write.
5. The presence of bias, especially if an argumentative purpose and point of view is not obvious.
6. The reading audience that the author seems to have had in mind.
7. The intended meaning in the case of sarcasm, irony, or figurative language.

Practice making inferences.

The following excerpts from an essay about a public defender supply enough information to help you make guesses about most of the items just listed. You will not receive direct information about all of the items, however. Read the essay and use the information in it, along with your own experience, to infer answers to the questions that are written in the margins next to the essay.

Practice Essay
EQUAL BEFORE THE LAW⁹

Tamara Rice Lave

How can you represent *those* people? How can you be a public defender?" Jane (not her real name), a former nurse, asked me both questions. The daughter of a California police officer, she is young, pretty and white. Jane was charged with, and pleaded guilty to, stealing from a disabled patient. Taken aback, I stared at her: "But I am representing you!"

This "us/them" philosophy lies at the heart of such questions. There are some defendants, white and middle class, who do not see themselves as criminals. They believe it is "them"—the poor and minorities—who violate the law.

I represent those individuals that the Janes of society presume to be guilty. When I graduated from Stanford Law School, I chose to work as a public defender rather than as a corporate lawyer or prosecutor. This was hard for my family and friends to understand. Intellectually, they agreed that everyone should have a lawyer; they just didn't want me to be that person. "How could you represent a murderer? How could you sleep at night knowing that you let a dangerous person loose on the streets?" demanded my Aunt Heather at a family gathering.

. . . .

Most trying is dealing with prosecutors who aren't sympathetic to the tribulations of lives unlike their own. In one memorable case, a city attorney argued that a homeless client should get 60 days behind bars for illegal possession of a shopping cart because he had prior convictions for the same offense and didn't seem to be "learning his lesson."

Despite the frustrations, I've never regretted becoming a public defender. If I had gone to a law firm or become a prosecutor, I would have been surrounded by people like me. This would have given me little opportunity—and indeed, in the case of a prosecutor, little reason—to challenge my own prejudices. As a public defender, I must bridge the divide between us and them, myself and my client, proving that everyone is equal before the law. Doing so requires empathy and patience, two characteristics that everyone, particularly the Janes of society, could use.

Lave is a deputy public defender in San Diego, Calif.

What criticism is implied by Jane's question? _____
_____
_____

What social context has motivated the author to write this essay? _____
_____
_____

What is the author's background?
_____
_____
_____

Who is the possible intended audience? _____

Check for signs of bias:
Author's attitude? _____
Emotional support? _____
Author's credentials? _____
Stacked evidence? _____

What is the author's purpose for writing? _____
_____

What is the claim/conclusion?
_____
_____

⁹ Tamara Rice Lave, "Equal Before the Law," *Newsweek* 13 July 1998.

When reading critically, it is also important to infer the author's unstated values and beliefs regarding an issue. As you learned in Chapter 9, an author's values and beliefs can cause him or her to exhibit a negative or positive attitude toward an issue and, as a result, to exhibit a biased point of view. You need to be able to answer the question What does this author value and believe about the issue? even if the values and beliefs are not explicitly stated. This is a key reading skill for critical reading. The next section explains why.

Infer the Author's Values and Beliefs

In conversation, you are always aware of the person you are talking to. You listen to what is being said, and you form ideas about "where that person is coming from." In other words, you make some inferences about the other person's values and key beliefs and about the basic assumptions that cause that person to express a point of view on an issue in a particular way. You can do the same thing while you read.

Authors often have strong attitudes and beliefs that cause them to present their ideas in a certain way. In "Equal Before the Law," the essay you just read, the author says she values equality, empathy, and patience. We can also infer that she is sympathetic to defendants who are "down and out" and cannot afford an expensive lawyer. She assumes that all people deserve to be defended and are thus equal before the law.

In reading argument, you will need to determine whether or not you share the author's values and beliefs on this issue. If you agree with the author on basic values and beliefs, you will also usually accept the author's claim/conclusion. If you do not agree and hold a whole different set of beliefs and values, you may reject the claim/conclusion. In the next-to-last paragraph, Lave describes a city attorney who wanted to send a homeless person to jail for persisting in the illegal possession of a shopping cart. This attorney is obviously not sympathetic to the people Lave defends and holds values and beliefs that are different from Lave's. The city attorney probably would not be impressed by Lave's arguments for the type of law she has chosen to practice. What about your values and beliefs? Are you more sympathetic with Lave's or with the city attorney's values on the issue of defending the poor and minorities who violate the law? If you were a lawyer, who would you choose to defend?

Practice inferring values and beliefs.

Read the following paragraphs, which come from an essay entitled "Making the Grade" by Kurt Wiesenfeld, a physics professor who teaches at Georgia Tech in Atlanta. As you read, identify this professor's values and beliefs about students' grades, and then identify the values and beliefs that some of his students hold on this issue. Finally, examine your own values and beliefs about grading and answer the questions that follow.

Practice Essay
MAKING THE GRADE[10]
Kurt Wiesenfeld

It was a rookie error. After 10 years I should have known better, but I went to my office the day after final grades were posted. There was a

[10] Kurt Wiesenfeld, "Making the Grade," *Newsweek* 17 June 1996: 16.

tentative knock on the door. "Professor Wiesenfeld? I took your Physics 2121 class? I flunked it? I wonder if there's anything I can do to improve my grade?" I thought: "Why are you asking me? Isn't it too late to worry about it? Do you dislike making declarative statements?"

After the student gave his tale of woe and left, the phone rang. "I got a D in your class. Is there any way you can change it to 'Incomplete'?" Then the e-mail assault began: "I'm shy about coming in to talk to you, but I'm not shy about asking for a better grade. Anyway, it's worth a try." The next day I had three phone messages from students asking me to call them. I didn't.

Time was, when you received a grade, that was it. You might groan and moan, but you accepted it as the outcome of your efforts or lack thereof (and, yes, sometimes a tough grader). In the last few years, however, some students have developed a disgruntled-consumer approach. If they don't like their grade, they go to the "return" counter to trade it in for something better.

What alarms me is their indifference toward grades as an indication of personal effort and performance. Many, when pressed about why they think they deserve a better grade, admit they don't deserve one but would like one anyway. Having been raised on gold stars for effort and smiley faces for self-esteem, they've learned that they can get by without hard work and real talent if they can talk the professor into giving them a break. This attitude is beyond cynicism. There's a weird innocence to the assumption that one expects (even deserves) a better grade simply by begging for it. With that outlook, I guess I shouldn't be as flabbergasted as I was that 12 students asked me to change their grades after final grades were posted.

1. Describe the author's values and beliefs about grading. _____
   _____

2. Describe some of his students' values and beliefs about the grades they receive.
   _____

3. Where do you stand on the issue of grades and what they should represent?
   _____

4. Do you accept the author's conclusions? _____ Explain _____
   _____

Notice that if you agree with the author's values and beliefs, you will accept his position on this issue. If you agree with the values and beliefs of the students described in the article, you will be more likely to accept their position. Inferring the unstated values and beliefs that are present in every argument can help you understand why you can accept the ideas of some but not all of the authors you read.

MAKING INFERENCES AND ANALYZING ASSUMPTIONS: FIVE STRATEGIES

The five strategies that follow suggest specific questioning strategies, along with practice examples to help you learn to make accurate inferences of all types. Making inferences is an important reading skill for all kinds of reading purposes, but it is particularly important for critical reading.

Strategy I: Understand both literal and inferential meaning.

Ask these questions to help you make inferences:

a. What is the literal meaning of this statement? What can I understand simply by understanding the meaning of the words?

b. What additional meaning can I infer?

When you have answered these questions and have made a tentative inference, test it against the evidence in the text and from your own background, and revise it if necessary.

Here are some examples of pairs of sentences that require the reader to make inferences to understand them fully. As you read these examples, practice answering the questions: What is the literal meaning? and What else can I infer? The first one is done for you.

Examples.

1. The cat jumped. The bird flew away.

Possible Inference: The cat was trying to catch the bird and missed.

2. I walked into the room. It was very bright even though it was midnight.

*Possible Inference:*_____

3. The student looked at the returned exam, tore it up, and threw it in the wastebasket.

*Possible Inference:*_____

4. The child took a toy off of the shelf in the store. Her mother spoke to her, and she began to cry.

*Possible Inference:*_____

5. The student took a book from the shelf in the library, looked at it, and put it back.

*Possible Inference:*_____

6. The man dialed the phone. Then he hung up without speaking.

*Possible Inference:*_____

Strategy 2: Make an inference that changes the literal meaning for figurative language, sarcasm, and irony.

Whenever you encounter literal meaning that seems exaggerated, odd, unlikely, or that simply does not make sense, you can usually assume that the intended meaning is different or even opposite from the literal meaning. To help you establish the intended meaning, ask the following questions:

a. What does the author say literally?

b. What does the author really mean?

These questions will help you infer the author's intended meaning for all types of figurative language, sarcasm, and irony. You will also need to look for clues in the text itself and add information of your own to figure out what the author really means.

Here is an example of two sentences that literally say the same thing, but notice how the inflection changes the meaning.

a. "I am really *glad* you finally showed up."

b. "I am really glad you *finally* showed up."

The first expresses genuine pleasure, and the second may be a sarcastic comment made to someone who is late. In speech, the tone of voice gives away the author's intention. In a written text, you will need to use context clues to help you infer the tone and intention of the person speaking. Notice that in the second example the implied meaning is the opposite of the literal meaning.

Strategy 3: Make accurate inferences that you can defend with evidence from the text.

Infer unstated meanings that the author expects you to "get." Add additional inferences when you have evidence from the text itself or from reliable outside sources to justify them.

When reading critically, make inferences about the following when they are not spelled out in the text: the claim/conclusion; the author's purpose; the author's background; the context or motivation that caused the author to write; the presence of bias, especially if an argumentative purpose is not obvious; the reading audience that the author seems to have had in mind; and the intended meaning when it is different from the stated meaning. To make accurate inferences ask:

- What does the author intend me to infer?

- What else can I infer?

- What evidence in the text and in my experience supports this inference?

▶

Strategy 4: Infer the author's values and beliefs, and decide if you share them.

The author's values and beliefs are not always stated, but they do influence the way in which the author argues for a particular position on an issue.

Here is an example: *I should take the easiest classes I can to keep my grades up.* The unstated values and beliefs that cause the author to say this: *Grades are more important than what I might learn in harder classes.* See if you can supply the unstated values and beliefs for the next three examples.

1. I should quit school and get a job so that I can get a better car.

   _____

2. Politicians should exhibit higher standards of behavior than ordinary citizens.

   _____

3. Women should not be allowed to participate in military combat.

   _____

Discuss in class the values and beliefs you inferred. You will not all agree on exactly the same values and beliefs, but all of your answers should at least be suggested by the statements themselves. To infer values and beliefs, ask:

- What is the issue?
- What is the author's position on the issue?
- What values or beliefs are causing the author to take this position?
- In other words, where is this author "coming from"?

Then compare your values and beliefs on the issue with those of the author by asking these questions:

- Where am I "coming from" on this issue?
- Do I agree or do I disagree with the author's position?
- If I disagree, what values or beliefs do I hold that are different from the author's?

Strategy 5: Decide if your values and beliefs allow you to accept the conclusion.

If you share the author's values and beliefs, you will usually also agree with the author's conclusion. If you disagree with the author's values and beliefs, you will usually reject the conclusion. If you partially agree with the author's values and beliefs, you will at least share some common ground with the author, and you may find yourself partially in agreement with the conclusion. Decide to what degree you can accept the author's conclusion.

EXERCISES AND READINGS

THREE COLLABORATIVE CLASS EXERCISES

Exercise 1

Make some inferences. *Whole class.*

This exercise will provide you with practice in making inferences. Read the following instructions to high school seniors about preparing for their senior trip. Make inferences about what students have done in the past and what the author thinks they may do again. Jot down some of your inferences.

> All seniors will be required to attend school Thursday morning! Seniors will be excused at lunch. Please eat lunch before you board the train on Thursday! Your passport will be distributed to you on the train with your name on it. Do not lose it! All luggage will be opened and checked before departure. Students are to limit luggage to one traveling bag. Girls are permitted to have an overnight or cosmetic bag, also. Do not leave anything on the train! Watch cameras carefully!! You may not walk barefooted (or stocking footed) from one car to another!! If a student becomes a discipline problem such as drinking, or any other behavioral problem, he/she will be placed on the first available transportation home, and parents notified of his/her arrival time. The return transportation will be at parents' expense.[11]

Questions for Group Discussion

1. What inferences can you make about some of the things that have gone wrong on past senior trips?
2. What evidence is there for the accuracy of your inferences?

Exercise 2

Evaluate the inferences. *Small groups.*

This exercise asks you to critically evaluate the inferences that someone else has made. You will look at the evidence provided in the essay below about a student and decide whether or not the inferences made by the student's teacher are probably accurate or inaccurate. Read the essay and form groups of four students. Have the scribe in your group jot down your answers to the questions that follow the essay. Then discuss your answers with the class.

---

[11] Excerpts from letter written to high school seniors at Coronado High School, El Paso, Texas.

Passing and Failing[12]

AMBER DAHLIN

Passing problems along is unethical, right? Passing students to ensure that you won't see them again is wrong, isn't it? But sometimes (at least I thought so then) it's better to send trouble on its way, not invite it in for dinner or a research paper. So when I had a suspected murderer/child molester in a research-writing course several years ago, I practiced every avoidance strategy at my command, and then I sent the man on his way with a D. His passing illuminates my failing.

I teach at Metropolitan State College in Denver, an urban undergraduate college with an eclectic student population of job-changers, recent high school graduates, and street-smart radicals. During the first week of class, which we spend getting to know one another, I am prepared to hear accounts of job worries, concerts, high school events, family troubles, an assortment of hobbies, and complaints about education in general. John went to another level entirely.

As we went through the circle of introductions, John stated, with an air of mystery, that he was in a "serious political situation." Other students, their curiosity piqued, of course asked what he meant. He was referring to the molestation and murder of a six-year-old boy on a bike path in Denver. John was under suspicion for the crime. He said that he and his roommate were being harassed by the police after having been questioned several times. While answering inquiries about what one student called "that astounding murder thing," John maintained an aura of nonchalance, seeming to enjoy the notoriety of being a murder suspect.

I should explain my own reactions at this point. Child abuse, domestic violence, sexual abuse—these topics literally make me cry. I was depressed to be reminded of the boy's murder, which had caused a tumult in the city. Why, I wondered, would a person bring this incident up during a round of casual introductions?

Furthermore, I was raised in Wyoming, where teachers were like ranchers and students were the cattle; where if you had problems you handled them yourself, in stoic silence; where dirty little secrets were supposed to stay put in prairie dog holes. When John finished his introduction my instinct was to say, We just don't talk about those things. And we moved on (sort of like, Oh, Sandy likes to snowboard and John is a murder suspect. Next?).

Internally, though, my thoughts stampeded. Did he really do it? Was he actually an eccentric victim himself, hassled by the police? If he had done it, why would he bring it up here? If he hadn't, why would he bring it up here? How was I supposed to react? Was I in danger? Was the rest of the class in danger? I decided to believe his version—that he was indeed being hassled by the police. I was relieved, though, when he didn't attend class much. His writing skills were adequate in the work he did turn in. At midterm he had a D.

[12] Amber Dahlin, "Passing and Failing," in *Oops: What We Learn When Our Teaching Fails*, ed. Brenda M. Power and Ruth S. Hubbard (York: Stenhouse, 1996) 18–20.

Right after that, I held conferences to discuss each student's major research   7
project for the rest of the semester. I dreaded John's conference. I didn't want to
be alone with him. Here is how it went:

> **ME:**   Hi, John. What topic are you thinking about?
> **JOHN:**   Computers.
> **ME:**   (*That seems safe enough*) I see. What exactly about computers are you interested in?
> **JOHN:**   I want to create a computer program that can hypnotize people.
> **ME:**   (*What?*) Hmm.
> **JOHN:**   Yeah, see, people would get into the program and you'd be able to hypnotize people and control their thoughts.
> **ME:**   (*This is sick*) Is such a thing actually possible?
> **JOHN:**   Yeah, I've found some stuff on it already.
> **ME:**   Oh.
> **JOHN:**   And I'd call it Computerized-Hypnosis-Inducing-Learning-Device. C.H.I.L.D.
> **ME:**   (*Oh, no! That acronym! He did do it. He is a child molester. I'm going to throw up*) Oh.

And then he left, with me having said nothing of substance. I didn't express the   8
revulsion I felt. I never said, John, this topic makes me think you're seriously disturbed. Or, John, I'm going to recommend that you see a counselor. Or, What is
the *matter* with you? I felt an overwhelming urge to flee, simply to be a hundred
miles away from this horrible person who even if he hadn't murdered a child was
definitely sick. After he left I sat in my office and thought, I hate this place, I hate
this place, I hate this place.

Looking back, I can analyze this gut-level reaction and play out the options. I   9
have always avoided conflict and confrontation, partially from upbringing and
partially from personal preference. Realistically, what can a writing teacher do
about a murderer? If everyone did as I did, though, let John pass through without
even acknowledging there was something wrong, then he would go blithely
through life doing whatever he wanted. Yet if I had confronted John, told him he
was sick, he might have flown at me in a rage, started sending me threatening letters, stalked me at school.

I know that I failed as a teacher because I did not teach John. I didn't want to   10
teach him—I wanted him to disappear. I avoided him as much as possible throughout the semester, I gave shallow responses to his writing, and I pretended that
everything was normal when clearly it was not. John, I am certain, learned nothing about research or writing in that class.

Part of my uncertainty in dealing with this student was a result of feeling iso-   11
lated myself, a new faculty member who had not yet established a support system.
That semester was my first at an urban institution, where, frankly, there is greater
likelihood of running into disturbed people. My naïveté and inexperience were
contributing factors, and I hope that if a similar situation occurred now I would
call upon more resources, both personal and institutional.

Yet I am haunted. I did not act as a responsible human being. I wonder if my   12
inability to confront John somehow contributed to his continued illness. John was
not convicted of the murder, but I wonder where he is. I'm afraid I'll see a computerized hypnosis program in a catalog someday or read his name in the newspaper in connection with another murder.

I wish I could say that a realization of my own culpability came in time to matter, but it didn't. John never came back to class. I got a phone call from him at the end of the semester. He wondered if there was any way he could make up his absences or take an incomplete. I thought, If I fail him he might register for my session again. He might find out that I have a seven-year-old daughter and come after her. Rationally I know that this was unlikely, but at the time it seemed possible.

I thought, If I pass him I'll never see him again.

But I was wrong. He is still here with me.

13
14
15

1025 words

Questions for Discussion

1. What is literally true about the student and his behavior? What factual evidence can by verified by others observing this situation?
2. What does the teacher infer is true about the student?
3. In your opinion, does the teacher have sufficient evidence to make these inferences? Would you have made the same inferences? Why or why not?
4. What conclusion does the teacher make about herself?
5. Do you share her assessment of herself and accept her conclusion? Why or why not?
6. On the basis of the factual evidence, if you were the teacher in this case, what inferences would you have made and what actions would you have taken in regard to this student?

Exercise 3

Compare the author's values and beliefs with your own. *Individuals and whole class.*

This exercise provides you with practice in locating the author's values and beliefs and in comparing them with your own, both before and after you read the essay. The issue in the following essay is: How should young criminals who have committed particularly horrible crimes be treated by the judicial system? Before you begin to read, write down your values and beliefs about young offenders and the types of punishment you think they should receive. Then read the article and answer the questions that follow. Discuss your answers with the class.

Juvenile Justice: Facts vs. Anger[13]

JEROME G. MILLER

With every new tragedy involving children accused of murder, there is a louder drumbeat of demands for harsher laws to deal with what some experts say is a new

1

---

[13] Jerome G. Miller, "Juvenile Justice: Facts vs. Anger," *The New York Times* 15 August 1998: A23.

breed of killer. So it was again this week when two Chicago boys, ages 7 and 8, were charged with the murder of an 11-year-old girl, and two Arkansas boys were sentenced for the shooting deaths of four classmates and a teacher.

Many politicians and others have called for allowing children under the age of 2
10 to be tried in adult courts and sentencing them to adult prisons. The Texas Legislature has even debated imposing the death penalty on children as young as 11 years old, although the actual execution would be postponed until he or she turned 17.

But as the former commissioner of youth corrections in Massachusetts and 3
Pennsylvania, I know from experience that punishing children with harsher sentences and conditions is not the solution.

First, there has not been a surge in child killers. Children under the age of 18 4
have been responsible for fewer than one-twentieth of the murders committed in this country for the last two decades at least. (Approximately 10 percent of these crimes involve young people who have killed their parents, often within the context of abusive relationships.)

After reviewing 975 homicides in Cuyahoga County, Ohio, over 42 months 5
in the early 1970's, for example, the Cleveland deputy coroner found five homicides committed by children 8 years of age and younger—some of them unusually brutal. According to the Justice Policy Institute, which analyzed F.B.I. statistics, nationally there were 25 recorded homicides committed by children under the age of 13 in 1965, versus 16 in 1996. And despite the rash of school shootings in recent months, fewer incidents occurred this year than in some past years. For example, school shootings caused 55 deaths in 1992–93, in contrast with 40 in 1997–98.

This is not to deny that juvenile violence is an important problem. But consider 6
what effects harsher penalties for young people had in the past. In Massachusetts and Pennsylvania, for example, children were brutally treated in both adult and juvenile correctional institutions a generation ago. Boys as young as 14 were often sentenced to three to five years for offenses as minor as vandalism and small burglaries. Beatings and long stretches in solitary confinement were common.

In the early and mid-1970's, I helped several states deinstitutionalize their 7
juvenile justice systems. In Massachusetts, Gov. Frank Sargent, a Republican, replaced all the reform schools with some 200 different nonprofit programs, including group homes and individual intensive treatment for the worst cases. In some instances, we had one worker supervising no more than one or two youngsters. Institutionalization is so expensive—it currently costs $50,000 to $70,000 a year per child in most states—that these options did not cost the state more money.

More important, making the juvenile justice system less strict had positive re- 8
sults. Independent studies found that a decade after Massachusetts closed its reform schools, the recidivism rate was much lower than in states that continued to rely on reform schools and prisons. In Massachusetts, 24 percent of juveniles who had been released for 36 months were reincarcerated or recommitted.

In contrast, Texas had a recidivism rate of 43 percent, and California's rate was 9
62 percent. And when Massachusetts juveniles committed new crimes, the violations were less serious than those by offenders in states with stricter laws.

Perhaps our reforms were successful because they spoke to civility and decency.   10
Many people would argue that today's young criminals deserve nothing of the kind.
But they should know that harsher penalties will do nothing to protect society.

630 words

Questions for Discussion

1. To help you read critically, either find or make inferences about the following information in the essay selection. Then answer the remaining questions about assumptions.
   a. What is the claim/conclusion?
   b. What is the author's purpose? What in the essay makes you think so?
   c. What is the author's background?
   d. What is the context that caused the author to write this essay?
   e. What type of reading audience does the author probably have in mind?
2. What were your values and beliefs about the treatment of young offenders before you began to read?
3. What are the author's values and beliefs about the treatment of young offenders that are stated in the text? What additional values are implied?
4. Compare what you believed before you began to read with what the author believes:
   a. Do you agree with the author? How do you agree?
   b. Did you disagree with the author initially, but now find you are at least partly in agreement with him? How have you changed?
   c. Do you continue to disagree with the author? How do you disagree?
   d. Do you accept the author's claim/conclusion? Why or why not?

FOUR READING EXERCISES:
ABOUT LANGUAGE AND CULTURE

The following four readings are drawn from a sociology textbook, *Newsweek* magazine, a book of essays, and *The New York Times*. The first selection, from the sociology textbook, provides background information on language and how it influences human communication and behavior. The second article, by Rachel Jones, is an argument that shows some of the problems with using Black English in some contexts. This essay was originally published in *Newsweek* in 1982. The third article, by Paule Marshall, is also about Black English, as spoken by immigrants from Barbados. She writes about the value of this form of English for creative writers. The final article is about Spanglish, the hybrid language that is a mixture of English and Spanish, spoken by some Latinos in parts of the country. **Before you read these four essays, think about the values and beliefs that you have about the language you speak and the language you write. As you read the essays, notice the influence that language has on people and their relationships with others and decide if any of your original values and beliefs about language change in any way as a result of your reading.**

Language[14]

JOHN J. MACIONIS

Explanatory Notes: *This selection on language and culture is taken from a sociology textbook written by John J. Macionis who teaches at Kenyon College. As you read, think about the roles that language plays in our lives. What would it be like if you were unable to communicate with others through any language? Do you think language affects the ways we experience the world? In what ways?*

Helen Keller (1880–1968) became a national celebrity because she overcame the daunting disability of being blind and deaf from infancy. The loss of two key senses cut off this young girl from the symbolic world, greatly limiting her social development. Only when her teacher, Anne Mansfield Sullivan, broke through Keller's isolation by teaching her sign language did Helen Keller begin to realize her human potential. This remarkable woman, who later became a renowned educator herself, recalls the moment she grasped the concept of language.

1

> We walked down the path to the well-house, attracted by the smell of honeysuckle with which it was covered. Someone was drawing water, and my teacher placed my hand under the spout. As the cool stream gushed over one hand, she spelled into the other the word *water*, first slowly, then rapidly. I stood still, my whole attention fixed upon the motions of her fingers. Suddenly I felt a misty consciousness as of something forgotten—a thrill of returning thought; and somehow the mystery of language was revealed to me. I knew then that "w-a-t-e-r" meant the wonderful cool something that was flowing over my hand. That living word awakened my soul; gave it light, hope, joy, set it free![15]

Language, the key to the world of culture, is *a system of symbols that allows members of society to communicate with one another.* These symbols take the form of spoken and written words, which are culturally variable and composed of the various alphabets used around the world. Even conventions for writing differ: In general, people in Western societies write from left to right, people in northern Africa and western Asia write from right to left, and people in eastern Asia write from top to bottom.

2

[A] global map shows where in the world one finds the three most widely spoken languages. Chinese is the official language of 20 percent of humanity (about 1.2 billion people). English is the mother tongue of about 10 percent (600 million) of the world's people, with Spanish the official language of 6 percent (350 million). Notice, too, that one can travel virtually anywhere in the world other than much of western Africa and "get by" speaking English. Due to the worldwide economic

3

[14] John J. Macionis, *Sociology*, 6th ed. (Upper Saddle River: Prentice Hall, 1997) 68–70.
[15] Helen Keller, *The Story of My Life* (New York: Doubleday 1903) 21–24.

and political clout of Great Britain and, more recently, the United States, English is now becoming a global tongue that is a favored second language in most of the world's nations.

For people everywhere, language is the major means of **cultural transmission,** *the process by which one generation passes culture to the next.* Just as our bodies contain the genes of our ancestors, so our symbols carry our cultural heritage. Language gives us the power to gain access to centuries of accumulated wisdom.   4

Throughout human history, people have transmitted culture through speech, a process sociologists call the *oral cultural tradition.* Only as recently as five thousand years ago did humans invent writing, and, even then, just a favored few ever learned to read and write. It was not until this century that nations (generally the industrial, high-income countries) have boasted of nearly universal literacy. Still, 10 to 15 percent of U.S. adults (20 to 25 million people) cannot read and write—an almost insurmountable barrier to opportunity in a society that increasingly demands symbolic skills. In low-income countries of the world, illiteracy rates range from 30 percent (People's Republic of China) to as high as 80 percent (Sierra Leone in Africa).   5

Language skills not only link us with others and with the past, they also set free the human imagination. Connecting symbols in new ways, we can conceive of an almost limitless range of future possibilities. Language—both spoken and written—distinguishes human beings as the only creatures who are self-conscious, mindful of our limitations and aware of our ultimate mortality. Yet our symbolic power also enables us to dream, to envision a better world, and to work to bring that world into being.   6

. . . .

Does Language Shape Reality?

Do the Chinese, who think using one set of symbols, actually experience the world differently from North Americans who think in English or Spanish? The answer is yes, since each language has its own, distinct symbols that serve as the building blocks of reality.   7

Edward Sapir[16] and Benjamin Whorf,[17] two anthropologists who specialized in linguistic studies, noted that each language has words or expressions with no precise counterparts in other tongues. In addition, all languages fuse symbols with distinctive emotions. Thus, as multilingual people can attest, a single idea often "feels" different if spoken in, say, Spanish rather than in English or Chinese.[18]   8

Formally, then, what we now call the **Sapir-Whorf hypothesis** states that *people perceive the world through the cultural lens of language.* Using different sym-   9

[16] Edward Sapir, "The Status of Linguistics as a Science," *Language* 5 (1929): 207-214. Also, David G. Mandelbaum, ed., *Selected Writings of Edward Sapir in Language, Culture, and Personality* (Berkeley: University of California Press, 1949).

[17] Benjamin Lee Whorf, "The Relation of Habitual Thought and Behavior to Language," in *Language, Thought, and Reality* (Cambridge: The Technology Press of MIT/New York: Wiley, 1956) 139–159.

[18] Gerhard Falk, personal communication, 1987.

bolic systems, a Filipino, a Turk, and a Brazilian actually experience "distinct worlds, not merely the same world with different labels attached."[19]

Of course, the capacity to create and manipulate language also gives humans 10 everywhere the power to alter how they experience the world. For example, many African Americans hailed it as a step toward social equality with white people when the word "Negro" was replaced by the term "black" and, more recently, by "African American" or "person of color." In short, a system of language guides how we understand the world but does not limit how we do so.

900 words

Strategy Questions

1. Consider the following statement from paragraph 4: "Just as our bodies contain the genes of our ancestors, so our symbols carry our cultural heritage." What is the literal meaning of this statement? What can you understand simply by understanding the meaning of the words? What additional meaning is implied? What prior knowledge can you draw on to help you understand the implications of this statement?
2. Consider the following statement in paragraph 6: "Language skills not only link us with others and with the past, they also set free the human imagination." What is the author literally saying? What does the author also imply?
3. What are Macionis's values and beliefs about language and culture?

Study Reading Questions

1. Who was Helen Keller?
2. What is the author's definition of language?
3. What is the most widely spoken language? How many people speak Spanish?
4. What is "the process by which one generation passes culture to the next"?
5. What percentage of American adults cannot read or write?

Critical Reading and Thinking Questions

1. Imagine what it would be like to be deaf and blind like Helen Keller. How would you acquire knowledge? How might you communicate with other people? How might you use your other three senses to aid you?
2. The Sapir-Whorf hypothesis finds that people who speak Spanish, German, or Swahili, for example, actually experience the world differently than people who speak English, Italian, or Chinese. Why is this an important discovery? How can we use this hypothesis when communicating with people who speak different languages from ours? Explain your answers.
3. According to the author, we can actually alter the way in which we experience the world by creating new language or by manipulating the language we already use. The example given was the replacement of "Negro" by "black" or "African

[19] Edward Sapir, *Selected Writings of Edward Sapir in Language, Culture, and Personality* 162.

American." Although the literal meaning of these three terms is the same, they imply somewhat different meanings. How does the implied meaning change for each of the three terms? Think of another example of two or more words used for the same thing and describe the differences in the implied meanings for each of the words.

What's Wrong with Black English?[20]

RACHEL JONES

Explanatory Notes: *This essay comes from* Newsweek *magazine and has been reprinted nearly 50 times since 1982. When Jones wrote this article she was a student at Southern Illinois University, and this column launched her professional writing career and changed the course of her life. In 1997 she published "Not White, Just Right" in* Newsweek *to reaffirm her earlier arguments. Jones is now a science reporter for National Public Radio and has served as president of the Journalism and Women Symposium.* **Before you read, think about what you already know concerning the debates about Black English, or Ebonics. Why has this been such a contested issue these past few years? What is your opinion on the issue? What do you expect the author to say about the issue?**

William Labov, a noted linguist, once said about the use of black English, "It is the goal of most black Americans to acquire full control of the standard language without giving up their own culture." He also suggested that there are certain advantages to having two ways to express one's feelings. I wonder if the good doctor might also consider the goals of those black Americans who have full control of standard English but who are every now and then troubled by that colorful, grammar-to-the-winds patois that is black English. Case in point—me.

I'm a 21-year-old black born to a family that would probably be considered lower-middle class—which in my mind is a polite way of describing a condition only slightly better than poverty. Let's just say we rarely if ever did the winter-vacation thing in the Caribbean. I've often had to defend my humble beginnings to a most unlikely group of people for an even less likely reason. Because of the way I talk, some of my black peers look at me sideways and ask, "Why do you talk like you're white?"

The first time it happened to me I was nine years old. Cornered in the school bathroom by the class bully and her sidekick, I was offered the opportunity to swallow a few of my teeth unless I satisfactorily explained why I always got good grades, why I talked "proper" or "white." I had no ready answer for her, save the fact that my mother had from the time I was old enough to talk stressed the importance of reading and learning, or that L. Frank Baum and Ray Bradbury were my closest companions. I read all my older brothers' and sisters' literature textbooks more faithfully than they did, and even lightweights like the Bobbsey Twins

1

2

3

---

[20] Rachel Jones, "What's Wrong with Black English?" ("My Turn" column) *Newsweek* 27 December 1982.

and Trixie Belden were allowed into my bookish inner circle. I don't remember exactly what I told those girls, but I somehow talked my way out of a beating.

'*White pipes.*'   I was reminded once again of my "white pipes" problem while apartment hunting in Evanston, Ill., last winter. I doggedly made out lists of available places and called all around. I would immediately be invited over—and immediately turned down. The thinly concealed looks of shock when the front door opened clued me in, along with the flustered instances of "just getting off the phone with the girl who was ahead of you and she wants the rooms." When I finally found a place to live, my roommate stirred up old memories when she remarked a few months later, "You know, I was surprised when I first saw you. You sounded white over the phone." Tell me another one, sister.

I should've asked her a question I've wanted an answer to for years: how does one "talk white"? The silly side of me pictures a rabid white foam spewing forth when I speak. I don't use Valley Girl jargon, so that's not what's meant in my case. Actually, I've pretty much deduced what people mean when they say that to me, and the implications are really frightening.

It means that I'm articulate and well-versed. It means that I can talk as freely about John Steinbeck as I can about Rick James. It means that "ain't" and "he be" are not staples of my vocabulary and are only used around family and friends. (It is almost Jekyll and Hyde-ish the way I can slip out of academic abstractions into a long, lean, double-negative-filled dialogue, but I've come to terms with that aspect of my personality.) As a child, I found it hard to believe that's what people meant by "talking proper"; that would've meant that good grades and standard English were equated with white skin, and that went against everything I'd ever been taught. Running into the same type of mentality as an adult has confirmed the depressing reality that for many blacks, standard English is not only unfamiliar, it is socially unacceptable.

James Baldwin once defended black English by saying it had added "vitality to the language," and even went so far as to label it a language in its own right, saying, "Language [i.e., black English] is a political instrument" and a "vivid and crucial key to identity." But did Malcolm X urge blacks to take power in this country "any way y'all can"? Did Martin Luther King Jr. say to blacks, "I has been to the mountaintop, and I done seed the Promised Land"? Toni Morrison, Alice Walker and James Baldwin did not achieve their eloquence, grace and stature by using only black English in their writing. Andrew Young, Tom Bradley and Barbara Jordan did not acquire political power by saying, "Y'all crazy if you ain't gon vote for me." They all have full command of standard English, and I don't think that knowledge takes away from their blackness or commitment to black people.

Soulful.   I know from experience that it's important for black people, stripped of culture and heritage, to have something they can point to and say, "This is ours, we can comprehend it, we alone can speak it with a soulful flourish." I'd be lying if I said that the rhythms of my people caught up in "some serious rap" don't sound natural and right to me sometimes. But how heartwarming is it for those same brothers when they hit the pavement searching for employment? Studies have proven that the use of ethnic dialects decreases power in the marketplace. "I be" is acceptable on the corner, but not with the boss.

Am I letting capitalistic, European-oriented thinking fog the issue? Am I selling out blacks to an ideal of assimilating, being as much like white as possible? I have not formed a personal political ideology, but I do know this: it hurts me to hear black children use black English, knowing that they will be at yet another disadvantage in an educational system already full of stumbling blocks. It hurts me to sit in lecture halls and hear fellow black students complain that the professor "be tripping dem out using big words dey can't understand." And what hurts most is to be stripped of my own blackness simply because I know my way around the English language.

I would have to disagree with Labov in one respect. My goal is not so much to acquire full control of both standard and black English, but to one day see more black people less dependent on a dialect that excludes them from full participation in the world we live in. I don't think I talk white, I think I talk right.

1100 words

Strategy Questions

1. Can you infer Jones's purpose for writing this essay? What might have motivated her to write about Black English?
2. Infer who the reading audience is. Did Jones have several audiences in mind? Who are they? How do you know this?
3. Infer some of the author's values and beliefs about language.
4. Decide if your values and beliefs allow you to accept Jones's conclusion that she "doesn't talk white," she "talks right." Explain your answer.

Study Reading Questions

1. How did Jones learn to speak standard English so well?
2. What did Jones's roommate conclude after first speaking with her on the telephone?
3. What does Jones believe it means to "talk white"?
4. Jones describes two unpleasant incidents that occurred because she spoke standard English. What were they?

Critical Reading and Thinking Questions

1. What values and beliefs do Jones, Ellis Cose, and Antwan Allen (review pp. 294–295) have in common? Do you share any of their values and beliefs?
2. How would Jones react to the notion that "language shapes reality" from the essay on language by Macionis (see pp. 347–349)?
3. What is your opinion about Black English? Do you agree with Jones or with those who argue against her? In other words, do you think that speaking standard English means selling out and talking "white"? Or, should African Americans speak only Black English to stay in touch with their "culture"? Justify your answer.

Reading 3

Poets in the Kitchen[21]

PAULE MARSHALL

Explanatory Notes: *This selection was written by Paule Marshall, who has been a professor of English at Columbia University and is the author of the novella "Merle." She is a daughter of immigrants from Barbados. As you read, think about the ways in which other people's use of language may have influenced you. Also consider the importance of identifying with people of your own race or religion. How might language play a role in this identification?*

Some years ago, when I was teaching a graduate seminar in fiction at Columbia University, a well known male novelist visited my class to speak on his development as a writer. In discussing his formative years, he didn't realize it but he seriously endangered his life by remarking that women writers are luckier than those of his sex because they usually spend so much time as children around their mothers and their mothers' friends in the kitchen. 1

What did he say that for? The women students immediately forgot about being in awe of him and began readying their attack for the question and answer period later on. Even I bristled. There again was that awful image of women locked away from the world in the kitchen with only each other to talk to, and their daughters locked in with them. 2

But my guest wasn't really being sexist or trying to be provocative or even spoiling for a fight. What he meant—when he got around to explaining himself more fully—was that, given the way children are (or were) raised in our society, with little girls kept closer to home and their mothers, the woman writer stands a better chance of being exposed, while growing up, to the kind of talk that goes on among women, more often than not in the kitchen; and that this experience gives her an edge over her male counterpart by instilling in her an appreciation for ordinary speech. 3

It was clear that my guest lecturer attached great importance to this, which is understandable. Common speech and the plain, workaday words that make it up are, after all, the stock in trade of some of the best fiction writers. They are the principal means by which characters in a novel or story reveal themselves and give voice sometimes to profound feelings and complex ideas about themselves and the world. Perhaps the proper measure of a writer's talent is skill in rendering everyday speech—when it is appropriate to the story—as well as the ability to tap, to exploit, the beauty, poetry and wisdom it often contains. 4

"If you say what's on your mind in the language that comes to you from your parents and your street and friends you'll probably say something beautiful." Grace Paley tells this, she says, to her students at the beginning of every writing course. 5

[21] Paule Marshall, "Poets in the Kitchen," in *Reena and Other Stories* (Old Westbury: Feminist Press, 1983) 3–12.

It's all a matter of exposure and a training of the ear for the would-be writer in those early years of apprenticeship. And, according to my guest lecturer, this training, the best of it, often takes place in as unglamorous a setting as the kitchen. 6

He didn't know it, but he was essentially describing my experience as a little girl. I grew up among poets. Now they didn't look like poets—whatever that breed is supposed to look like. Nothing about them suggested that poetry was their calling. They were just a group of ordinary housewives and mothers, my mother included, who dressed in a way (shapeless housedresses, dowdy felt hats and long, dark, solemn coats) that made it impossible for me to imagine they had ever been young. 7

Nor did they do what poets were supposed to do—spend their days in an attic room writing verses. They never put pen to paper except to write occasionally to their relatives in Barbados. "I take my pen in hand hoping these few lines will find you in health as they leave me fair for the time being," was the way their letters invariably began. Rather, their day was spent "scrubbing floor," as they described the work they did. 8

Several mornings a week these unknown bards would put an apron and a pair of old house shoes in a shopping bag and take the train or streetcar from our section of Brooklyn out to Flatbush. There, those who didn't have steady jobs would wait on certain designated corners for the white housewives in the neighborhood to come along and bargain with them over pay for a day's work cleaning their houses. This was the ritual even in the winter. 9

Later, armed with the few dollars they had earned, which in their vocabulary became "a few raw-mouth pennies," they made their way back to our neighborhood, where they would sometimes stop off to have a cup of tea or cocoa together before going home to cook dinner for their husbands and children. 10

The basement kitchen of the brownstone house where my family lived was the usual gathering place. Once inside the warm safety of its walls the women threw off the drab coats and hats, seated themselves at the large center table, drank their cups of tea or cocoa, and talked. While my sister and I sat at a smaller table over in a corner doing our homework, they talked—endlessly, passionately, poetically, and with impressive range. No subject was beyond them. True, they would indulge in the usual gossip: whose husband was running with whom, whose daughter looked slightly "in the way" (pregnant) under her bridal gown as she walked down the aisle. That sort of thing. But they also tackled the great issues of the time. They were always, for example, discussing the state of the economy. It was the mid and late 30's then, and the aftershock of the Depression, with its soup lines and suicides on Wall Street, was still being felt. 11

Some people, they declared, didn't know how to deal with adversity. They didn't know that you had to "tie up your belly" (hold in the pain, that is) when things got rough and go on with life. They took their image from the bellyband that is tied around the stomach of a newborn baby to keep the navel pressed in. 12

They talked politics. Roosevelt was their hero. He had come along and rescued the country with relief and jobs, and in gratitude they christened their sons Franklin and Delano and hoped they would live up to the names. [. . .] 13

And their talk was of war and rumors of wars. They raged against World War II when it broke out in Europe, blaming it on the politicians. "It's these politicians. 14

They're the ones always starting up all this lot of war. But what they care? It's the poor people got to suffer and mothers with their sons." If it was *their* sons, they swore they would keep them out of the Army by giving them soap to eat each day to make their hearts sound defective. Hitler? He was for them "the devil incarnate."

Then there was home. They reminisced often and at length about home. The old country. Barbados—or Bimshire, as they affectionately called it. The little Caribbean island in the sun they loved but had to leave. "Poor—poor but sweet" was the way they remembered it. 15

And naturally they discussed their adopted home. America came in for both good and bad marks. They lashed out at it for the racism they encountered. They took to task some of the people they worked for, especially those who gave them only a hard-boiled egg and a few spoonfuls of cottage cheese for lunch. "As if anybody can scrub floor on an egg and some cheese that don't have no taste to it!" 16

Yet although they caught H in "this man country," as they called America, it was nonetheless a place where "you could at least see your way to make a dollar." That much they acknowledged. They might even one day accumulate enough dollars, with both them and their husbands working, to buy the brownstone houses which, like my family, they were only leasing at that period. This was their consuming ambition: to "buy house" and to see the children through. 17

There was no way for me to understand it at the time, but the talk that filled the kitchen those afternoons was highly functional. It served as therapy, the cheapest kind available to my mother and her friends. Not only did it help them recover from the long wait on the corner that morning and the bargaining over their labor, it restored them to a sense of themselves and reaffirmed their self-worth. Through language they were able to overcome the humiliations of the work-day. 18

But more than therapy, that freewheeling, wide-ranging, exuberant talk functioned as an outlet for the tremendous creative energy they possessed. They were women in whom the need for self-expression was strong, and since language was the only vehicle readily available to them they made of it an art form that—in keeping with the African tradition in which art and life are one—was an integral part of their lives. 19

And their talk was a refuge. They never really ceased being baffled and overwhelmed by America—its vastness, complexity and power. Its strange customs and laws. At a level beyond words they remained fearful and in awe. Their uneasiness and fear were even reflected in their attitude toward the children they had given birth to in this country. They referred to those like myself, the little Brooklyn-born Bajans (Barbadians), as "these New York children" and complained that they couldn't discipline us properly because of the laws here. "You can't beat these children as you would like, you know, because the authorities in this place will dash you in jail for them. After all, these is New York children." Not only were we different, American, we had, as they saw it, escaped their ultimate authority. 20

Confronted therefore by a world they could not encompass, which even limited their rights as parents, and at the same time finding themselves permanently separated from the world they had known, they took refuge in language. "Language is the only homeland," Czeslaw Milosz, the emigré Polish writer and Nobel Laureate, has said. This is what it became for the women at the kitchen table. [. . .] 21

For me, sitting over in the corner, being seen but not heard, which was the rule   22
for children in those days, it wasn't only what the women talked about—the content—but the way they put things—their style. The insight, irony, wit and humor they brought to their stories and discussions and their poet's inventiveness and daring with language—which of course I could only sense but not define back then.

They had taken the standard English taught them in the primary schools of   23
Barbados and transformed it into an idiom, an instrument that more adequately described them—changing around the syntax and imposing their own rhythm and accent so that the sentences were more pleasing to their ears. They added the few African sounds and words that had survived, such as the derisive suck-teeth sound and the word "yam," meaning to eat. And to make it more vivid, more in keeping with their expressive quality, they brought to bear a raft of metaphors, parables, Biblical quotations, sayings and the like:

"The sea ain' got no back door," they would say, meaning that it wasn't like a   24
house where if there was a fire you could run out the back. Meaning that it was not to be trifled with. And meaning perhaps in a larger sense that man should treat all of nature with caution and respect.

"I has read hell by heart and called every generation blessed!" They sometimes   25
went in for hyperbole.

A woman expecting a baby was never said to be pregnant. They never used that   26
word. Rather, she was "in the way" or, better yet, "tumbling big." "Guess who I butt up on in the market the other day tumbling big again!"

And a woman with a reputation of being too free with her sexual favors was   27
known in their book as a "thoroughfare"—the sense of men like a steady stream of cars moving up and down the road of her life. Or she might be dubbed "a freebee," which was my favorite of the two. I liked the image it conjured up of a woman scandalous perhaps but independent, who flitted from one flower to another in a garden of male beauties, sampling their nectar, taking her pleasure at will, the roles reversed.

And nothing, no matter how beautiful, was ever described as simply beautiful.   28
It was always "beautiful-ugly": the beautiful-ugly dress, the beautiful-ugly house, the beautiful-ugly car. Why the word "ugly," I used to wonder, when the thing they were referring to was beautiful, and they knew it. Why the antonym, the contradiction, the linking of opposites? It used to puzzle me greatly as a child.

There is the theory in linguistics which states that the idiom of a people, the   29
way they use language, reflects not only the most fundamental views they hold of themselves and the world but their very conception of reality. Perhaps in using the term "beautiful-ugly" to describe nearly everything, my mother and her friends were expressing what they believed to be a fundamental dualism in life: the idea that a thing is at the same time its opposite, and that these opposites, these contradictions make up the whole. [. . .]

By the time I was 8 or 9, I graduated from the corner of the kitchen to the   30
neighborhood library, and thus from the spoken to the written word. The Macon Street Branch of the Brooklyn Public Library was an imposing half block long edifice of heavy gray masonry, with glass-paneled doors at the front and two tall metal torches symbolizing the light that comes of learning flanking the wide steps outside. [. . .]

I sheltered from the storm of adolescence in the Macon Street library, reading 31 voraciously, indiscriminately, everything from Jane Austen to Zane Grey, but with a special passion for the long, full-blown, richly detailed 18th- and 19th-century picaresque tales: "Tom Jones," "Great Expectations," "Vanity Fair."

But although I loved nearly everything I read and would enter fully into the lives 32 of the characters—indeed, would cease being myself and become them—I sensed a lack after a time. Something I couldn't quite define was missing. And then one day, browsing in the poetry section, I came across a book by someone called Paul Laurence Dunbar, and opening it I found the photograph of a wistful, sad-eyed poet who to my surprise was black. I turned to a poem at random. "Little brown-baby wif spa'klin' / eyes / Come to yo' pappy an' set on his knee." Although I had a little difficulty at first with the words in dialect, the poem spoke to me as nothing I had read before of the closeness, the special relationship I had had with my father, who by then had become an ardent believer in Father Divine and gone to live in Father's "kingdom" in Harlem. Reading it helped to ease somewhat the tight knot of sorrow and longing I carried around in my chest that refused to go away. I read another poem. " 'Lias! 'Lias! Bless de Lawd! / Don' you know de day's / erbroad? / Ef you don' get up, you scamp / Dey'll be trouble in dis camp." I laughed. It reminded me of the way my mother sometimes yelled at my sister and me to get out of bed in the mornings.

And another: "Seen my lady home las' night / Jump back, honey, jump 33 back. / Hel' huh han' an' sque'z it tight . . ." About love between a black man and a black woman. I had never seen that written about before and it roused in me all kinds of delicious feelings and hopes.

And I began to search then for books and stories and poems about "The Race" 34 (as it was put back then), about my people. While not abandoning Thackeray, Fielding, Dickens and the others, I started asking the reference librarian, who was white, for books by Negro writers, although I must admit I did so at first with a feeling of shame—the shame I and many others used to experience in those days whenever the word "Negro" or "colored" came up.

No grade school literature teacher of mine had ever mentioned Dunbar or James 35 Weldon Johnson or Langston Hughes. I didn't know that Zora Neale Hurston existed and was busy writing and being published during those years. Nor was I made aware of people like Frederick Douglass and Harriet Tubman—their spirit and example—or the great 19th-century abolitionist and feminist Sojourner Truth. There wasn't even Negro History Week when I attended P.S. 35 on Decatur Street!

What I needed, what all the kids—West Indian and native black American 36 alike—with whom I grew up needed, was an equivalent of the Jewish shul, someplace where we could go after school—the schools that were shortchanging us—and read works by those like ourselves and learn about our history.

It was around that time also that I began harboring the dangerous thought of 37 someday trying to write myself. Perhaps a poem about an apple tree, although I had never seen one. Or the story of a girl who could magically transplant herself to wherever she wanted to be in the world—such as Father Divine's kingdom in Harlem. Dunbar—his dark, eloquent face, his large volume of poems—permitted me to dream that I might someday write, and with something of the power with words my mother and her friends possessed.

When people at readings and writers' conferences ask me who my major influences were, they are sometimes a little disappointed when I don't immediately name the usual literary giants. True, I am indebted to those writers, white and black, whom I read during my formative years and still read for instruction and pleasure. But they were preceded in my life by another set of giants whom I always acknowledge before all others: the group of women around the table long ago. They taught me my first lessons in the narrative art. They trained my ear. They set a standard of excellence. This is why the best of my work must be attributed to them; it stands as testimony to the rich legacy of language and culture they so freely passed on to me in the wordshop of the kitchen.

2700 words

Strategy Questions

1. Although Marshall does not directly tell her readers what her economic background was as a child, she provides several clues. What clues can you find? Infer what her background was.
2. Consider this sentence in paragraph 8: "Nor did they do what poets were supposed to do—spend their days in attic rooms writing verses." What is the literal meaning of this statement? What does the author imply about such poets?
3. Consider these statements from paragraphs 20 and 21: ". . . Their talk was a refuge." ". . . They took refuge in language." "Language is the only homeland." What is the literal meaning of each statement? Infer what the author also means.

Study Reading Questions

1. What country is Marshall's mother from?
2. What does Marshall's mother do to make a living?
3. What is the name the women had for their American-born children?
4. What are the two phrases used for a woman who is pregnant?
5. Who is the first black poet that Marshall read?

Critical Reading and Thinking Questions

1. Both Rachel Jones and Paule Marshall describe their early love for reading. How do you think reading has affected their lives and their experiences as writers? How might their reading affect the language they use to speak and write?
2. Even though reading had a huge influence on Marshall's language development, she also credits her mother and her mother's friends as her first and greatest influence. How did these women influence Marshall? Can you think of anyone who has influenced your language development in a significant way? Who influenced you? How?
3. Look at the quote from Grace Paley that says, "If you say what's on your mind in the language that comes to you from your parents and your street and friends you'll probably say something beautiful" (page 353). What do you think she means? How would such language make what you had to say beautiful? Do

you agree? Why or why not? Marshall mentions some of her mother's phrases, such as "the sea ain't got no backdoor." Think of an example from your background and state it in "your language."

4. Imagine a conversation between Rachel Jones and Paule Marshall about the value of reading black authors. What positions do you think each of them would take? Where might they agree and where might they disagree?

It's the Talk of Nueva York: The Hybrid Called Spanglish[22]

LIZETTE ALVAREZ

Explanatory Notes: *This selection on Spanglish was published in* The New York Times. *Spanglish is the mixing of Spanish and English words or the contortion of English words into something more like Spanish. As you read, think about the advantages and disadvantages of Spanglish. Why do you think Spanish-speaking people might like or dislike Spanglish? How might you compare Spanglish and Black English?*

Nely Galan, guest host for a day, and the television actress Liz Torres plop down onto the plump, oversized chairs that dominate the late-night talk show set, and without missing a beat, slip into the language that comes most naturally to both of them.   1

"Oye, oye, check out those red lips, girlfriend," Ms. Galan says.   2

"Madonna Red," Ms. Torres replies, pouting her full lips.   3

"Madonna Red, una belleza," Ms. Galan says. "You look beautiful."   4

"Sí, gracias," Ms. Torres remarks, returning the compliment. "Y tú te ves tan linda."   5

Ms. Galan tells her late-night audience: "It's a Latina girlfest. We love makeup."   6

Never mind that the talk show, "Later," appears on NBC and is geared to an English-speaking audience. Ms. Galan, born in Cuba and reared in New Jersey, and Ms. Torres, Puerto Rican and raised in Hell's Kitchen in Manhattan, were speaking the hybrid lingo known as Spanglish—the language of choice for a growing number of Hispanic-Americans who view the hyphen in their heritage as a metaphor for two coexisting worlds.   7

"I think Spanglish is the future," said Ms. Galan, 32, the president of Galan Entertainment, a Los Angeles television and film production company that focuses on the Latino market. "It's a phenomenon of being from two cultures. It's perfectly wonderful. I speak English perfectly. I speak Spanish perfectly, and I choose to speak both simultaneously. How cool is that?"   8

Immigrants struggling to learn a new tongue have long relied on a verbal patchwork to communicate in their adopted land. But Spanglish today is far from the   9

---

[22] Lizette Alvarez, "It's the Talk of New York: The Hybrid Called Spanglish," *The New York Times* 25 March 1997: A1–A14.

awkward pidgin of a newcomer. As millions of Hispanic-Americans, first, second and third generation, take on more prominent roles in business, media and the arts, Spanglish is traveling right along with them.

The headlines of a glossy new magazine aimed at young Hispanic women spout a hip, irreverent Spanglish. Young Hispanic rappers use the dialect in recordings, and poets and novelists are adapting it to serious literacy endeavors. Spanglish has few rules and many variations, but at its most vivid and exuberant, it is an effortless dance between English and Spanish, with the two languages clutched so closely together that at times they actually converge. Phrases and sentences veer back and forth almost unconsciously, as the speaker's intuition grabs the best expressions from either language to sum up a thought. Sometimes entirely new words are coined. 10

Some Spanish-language purists still denounce Spanglish as a debasement of their native tongue. And many Latinos, wary of the Ebonics controversy that flared over the suggestion that black English should be considered a separate language, are unsure just how far they want to push their own hybrid. Many see it as a purely colloquial form of communication best suited to popular culture, and there is little talk of introducing a Spanglish curriculum in schools or demanding that Spanglish be accepted in the workplace. 11

Most speakers fall into Spanglish only among other bilingual Latinos, and when they do, it is often with a sense of humor. 12

"If in addition to, quote, 'taking all those good fruit-picking jobs' we then begin bastardizing the language, we are really going to catch it," said Christy Haubegger, publisher of *Latina* magazine. "We don't need another strike against us." 13

But those reservations have not limited Spanglish's popularity. Ms. Haubegger, a Mexican-American lawyer, began Spanglish's most successful foray into the magazine world last June when she started *Latina* magazine, a bilingual glossy in New York for young Hispanic women. The magazine peppers its stories and headlines with Spanglish. "When He Says Me Voy . . . What Does He Really Mean?" one headline reads. ("Me voy" is "I'm leaving.") "Mi padre's infidelity. Are cuernos genetic?" another reads. ("Cuernos" are horns.) The magazine, published six times a year, has been so successful that this summer it will go monthly. 14

In Miami, *Generation ñ*, another bilingual magazine, found an audience in part because of a regular humor column by Bill Cruz called Cubanamericanisms. Nothing more than a list of Webster-style definitions of Spanglish words, now dubbed Cubonics in Miami, it had Miami's Cuban community guffawing over their own expressions. In January, the magazine printed 4,000 novelty books featuring excerpts from the column, and they sold faster than a maicrogüey (microwave) can cook up a Weigüache (Weight Watchers) meal. 15

The much-praised Hispanic writers Sandra Cisneros, Julia Alvarez and Roberto G. Fernandez routinely drop Spanglish into their novels and poetry, believing it to be a legitimate, creative form of communication. 16

"Language is not a little, airtight, clean, finished container of something," said Ms. Alvarez, a Dominican-American author (who is not related to this writer). "It's permeable, alive. It moves." 17

Ms. Haubegger, 28, the publisher of *Latina* magazine, also believes that Spanglish is good business. 18

"If we were an English magazine, we would just be general market," she said. 19 "If we were a Spanish-language magazine, we would be Latin American. We are the intersection of the two, and we reflect a life between two languages and two cultures that our readers live in."

There are two basic approaches to Spanglish, with countless variations: switch- 20 ing and borrowing. Borrowing words from English and Spanishizing them has typically been the creation of immigrants, who contort English words for everyday survival. This method makes new words by pronouncing an English word "Spanish style" (dropping final consonants, softening others, replacing M's with N's and V's with B's), and spelled by transliterating the result using Spanish spelling conventions.

Thus, a grandfather suffering from a chest cold in Miami will walk into a drug- 21 store and ask for "Bibaporrú," ordinarily called Vick's VapoRub. A teen-ager will buy a pair of "chores"—"shorts"—for the gym. A housekeeper will plug in the "bacuncliner" to vacuum the rug. And, since regional differences exist in Spanglish, Latinos in New York might complain about "el estín" during winter if the steam shuts off.

Sometimes, an English word is borrowed for reasons of efficiency, since Span- 22 ish is famously multisyllabic. Instead of saying, "estacionamiento" for "parking," Spanglish speakers opt for "parquin." Instead of "escribir a máquina" for "to type," they say "taipear." Swiftly advancing technology has also added the verbs "bipiar" (from the noun "beeper") and "i-meiliar" ("to E-mail") to the vocabulary.

"Dame un bipeo later," said Mike Robles, a stand-up comic from the Bronx 23 who does a whole riff on Spanglish. Give me a beep. "There are whole generations out there that speak exactly that," he said.

The children of immigrants, who grow up speaking or hearing Spanish at 24 home, and English everywhere else, use these borrowed words, but they take Spanglish one step further. Ask them what they speak among themselves or at home and the answer is inevitably the same: Hablo un mix de los dos languages, a mix of the two.

Traditionalists have sometimes deplored this "code-switching" between lan- 25 guages, often calling it a product of laziness and ignorance. And it is true that as Spanish gets fuzzier to American-born Hispanics, they come to rely on English words to fill the gap. But a new school of thought has recently emerged that says that Spanglish illustrates a high degree of fluency in both languages.

"It's a sign of linguistic dexterity," said Ana Celia Zentella, a linguist at Hunter 26 College and at the CUNY Graduate Center who has written a book on bilingualism in New York. "It's like a complex juggling act or a train car able to run on two tracks at the same time, shifting from one to the other at the appropriate time. It's a skill that is often misunderstood."

Luz de Armas, chief creative officer and managing partner of Conill Advertis- 27 ers in New York, who said she and her co-workers speak mostly Spanglish among themselves, agreed. She often switches into Spanish, she said, to convey anger, joy, love or embarrassment, because Spanish is a more descriptive, emotional language than English—not because she doesn't know the word.

That is also true for Ms. Alvarez, the novelist. "For me, Spanish is my child- 28 hood language," she said. "I came to this country when I was 10. It's the language of sensations and emotions, of the day to day."

As with other foreign languages, some Spanish words simply cannot be translated. 29

"English is very concise and efficient," said Gustavo Perez Firmat, a Duke University professor and poet who has written a collection of poems called "Bilingual Blues." "Spanish has sabrosura, flavor." 30

It is also a statement of identity. "The reality is, because you do have a constant influx, we don't assimilate, we acculturate," said Ms. de Armas, whose parents are from Spain. "I'm not turning my back on what I came from. You pick and choose and accommodate, and that's what Spanglish is." 31

Glossary

Talking the Talk

Of the two basic forms of Spanglish, borrowing—saying English words "Spanish style" and spelling them accordingly—is more common among first-generation speakers; later generations tend to switch back and forth. Here are examples of the hybrid language—often spoken with a sense of humor—that has vaulted from streets to talk shows to the pages of magazines like Latina and *Generation ñ*.

bacuncliner vacuum cleaner

biper beeper, pager

boyla boiler

chileando chilling out

choping shopping

espresgüey expressway

fafu fast food

jangear hang out

joldoperos muggers, holdup artists

liqueo leak

malcrogüey microwave oven

pulóver T-shirt

roofo roof

sangüiche sandwich

tensén 10-cent store, like Kmart or Woolworth's

SPANGLISH

EL Oye, me estoy frisando y el estín esta broken—close the door. ¿Vamos a lonchar, or what? I need to eat before I go to my new job as a chiroquero.

ELLA ¿Quieres que te cocine some rice en la jitachi, or should I just get you some confley con leche? By the way, you embarkated me el otro dia. ¿What did you do, pick up some fafu en vez de ir al restaurante where I was waiting? Eres tan chipero.

TRANSLATION

HE Hey, I'm freezing and the steam [or heat] is broken—close the door. Are we going to have lunch or what? I need to eat before I go to my new job as a sheetrocker.

SHE Do you want me to cook you some rice in the Hitachi [catchall term for all steam cookers], or should I just get you some cornflakes [ditto for any kind of cereal] with milk? By the way, you stood me up the other day. What did you do, pick up some fast food instead of going to the restaurant where I was waiting? You're so cheap.

1700 words

Strategy Questions

1. Consider the statement, Spanglish is "like a complex juggling act or a train car able to run on two tracks at the same time, shifting from one to the other at the appropriate time." What is the literal meaning of this statement? Infer what the author is really saying.
2. Consider Christy Haubegger's statement, "If in addition to, quote, 'taking all those good fruit-picking jobs' we then begin bastardizing the language, we are really going to catch it." What is she literally saying? What does she really mean? What additional meaning is implied about the history of the Hispanic culture?
3. The author does not directly tell how she feels about Spanglish. Can you infer from the article what her feelings are about it? What values and beliefs might she hold about language?

Study Reading Questions

1. What are two reasons that some Hispanic people do not favor Spanglish?
2. What is the name of the bilingual magazine from Miami?
3. What are some characteristics of pronouncing English words "Spanish style"? Give an example.
4. What is the term for going back and forth between two languages?
5. What are two reasons some people have given for using Spanglish instead of just English?

Critical Reading and Thinking Questions

1. Aside from the reasons listed in the article, think of two advantages and two disadvantages of Spanglish. How do you feel about Spanglish? Defend your opinion.
2. How does Spanglish relate to issues concerning Black English? In what ways is it similar? In what ways is it different?
3. Imagine Jones, Marshall, and Alvarez discussing the different versions of English they describe in their essays. How and under what circumstances might each value standard English? What value might each of them express for the variations in English spoken by members of their individual cultures?
4. Macionis, in the essay "Language," defines language as follows: "Language, the key to the world of culture, is a system of symbols that allows members of a society to communicate with one another." How do you think Jones, Marshall, and Alvarez would each react to that definition? Explain what each might say about how members of their cultures either communicate or fail to communicate with one another.

THREE APPLICATION EXERCISES

Exercise 1

Infer the author's assumptions in one of your textbooks.

Read the introduction to one of your textbooks. Find a general statement about the subject of the book. What does the author believe about the subject and expect you to believe also?

Here is an example that can serve as a model. This comes from a book of readings about popular culture. The author makes this generalization about popular culture: "Analyzing popular culture with a critical eye allows you to begin to free yourself from the manipulation of the media; it is an important step toward living an examined life."[23] The author's beliefs might be expressed as follows: You are manipulated by the media, and it is best to live an examined life.

Exercise 2

Infer the point of a cartoon.

Find a cartoon or comic strip and bring it to class. What information are you expected to add to get the point?

Exercise 3

Infer the assumptions in an editorial or letter.

Clip and bring to class a newspaper editorial or letter to the editor. What is the issue? What are the author's values and beliefs? Do you agree with them? Can you accept the conclusion?

REVIEW AND EVALUATE THE STRATEGIES

The following is a review of the five strategies you learned in this chapter:

1. Understand both literal and inferential meaning.
2. Make an inference that changes the literal meaning for figurative language, sarcasm, and irony.
3. Make accurate inferences that you can defend with evidence from the text.
4. Infer the author's values and beliefs and decide if you share them.
5. Decide if your values and beliefs allow you to accept the conclusions.

Make a personal evaluation of these strategies:

1. Underline your favorite strategies in the list above.
2. Make a check mark by those you want to continue to use.
3. Cross out any you probably will not continue to use. What are your reasons for rejecting them?

_____

_____

[23] Michael F. Petracca and Madeleine Sorapure, eds., *Common Culture: Reading and Writing about American Popular Culture* (Englewood Cliffs: Prentice Hall, 1995) 2.

Develop Media Literacy*

CHAPTER 11

CHAPTER GOALS:

1. **To help you understand media literacy and apply key media literacy concepts to analyze and evaluate media, including Web sites and Web-based materials.**

2. **To teach you to recognize, analyze, and evaluate visuals that present arguments.**

3. **To teach you to recognize misleading evidence, faulty reasoning, and fallacies in both visual and written materials.**

4. **To provide you with five strategies for developing media literacy.**

The Modern Media and Media Literacy

You already interact on a daily basis with what is now referred to as the modern media. It includes radio, television, newspapers and magazines, billboards, signs, packaging and marketing materials, the Internet, movies, music recordings, email messages, Web sites, video games, cell phones, and books. A recent study by the Kaiser Family Foundation found that young people ages 8–18 now spend up to six and a half hours a day listening, watching, reading, or interacting with materials that they access through the modern media. Reflect on the amount of time you spend each day taking in or sending information via the media, and you may be surprised how much your life is impacted. Much of the material you access is available through the mass media, which means that it is distributed world wide and that people all over the world are contributing to and accessing the same information you are. For example, when Hurricane Katrina hit New Orleans people in every part of the world were able to watch the devastation on their television sets. During the Israeli-Lebanon bombings in 2006, Larry King interviewed both Palestinians and Israelis on his evening show and asked the interviewees to imagine they were talking with people from the opposing side since the chances were very good that both friends and foes were watching and listening to the participants on this television broadcast from the United States.

*Larry Johnson and Andrew Tibble contributed much of the material about Web sites and media literacy to this chapter.

The modern mass media has changed the way people all over the world live and interact with each other. Consider how much you rely on the media for news, entertainment, information, and daily communication with friends and family, and you will understand why the media is now identified as a significant part of every culture that has access to it. The media is so pervasive, in fact, that many people refer to the culture in which we now live as the media culture.

The media culture has also contributed to what has been identified as the consumer culture. The constant advertising that appears in the media encourages many people to spend more money and acquire more goods than did their grandparents, who were not exposed to the same amount of advertising.

As a college student you will be expected to draw on many different types of media in the reading, research, and writing that you do for your college courses. In order to use media well, you will need to develop media literacy, which involves learning to understand, analyze, and evaluate different types of media. This chapter defines media literacy and presents five core media literacy concepts that will help you develop your media literacy. You will also become aware of the ways in which the media influence your ideas and personal values. We will next focus on the visual images that you encounter in the media, including on the Internet, on television, and in textbooks. Many images are subtly and deliberately persuasive, and you will learn to recognize, analyze, and evaluate them as arguments, just as you have done with print materials in earlier chapters in this book. You will then learn to locate and evaluate Web sites and various other types of materials that appear on the World Wide Web. Since you will be using web materials for some of your assignments in college, you will need to recognize that not all of it is of equal quality, and that some of it presents arguments. Finally, you will be taught to recognize misleading evidence, faulty reasoning, and fallacies as they appear in various types of media. Some media, for example, is manipulative and may influence you in ways you will want to resist. At the end of the chapter you will learn five strategies to help you develop media literacy.

Media Literacy: What Is It?

According to the Web site of the Center for Media Literacy, "media literacy is a twenty-first century approach to education. It provides a framework to access, analyze, evaluate, and create messages in a variety of forms—from print to video to the Internet. Media literacy builds an understanding of the role of the media in society as well as essential skills of inquiry and self-expression necessary for citizens of a democracy."[1]

Sometimes we don't realize how much media messages affect our culture as well as our individual choices. The following questions help us recognize some of these influences.

- Why do many of us pay more for clothes that have the logos of recognizable companies on them?

---

[1] Center for Media Literacy *http://www.medialit.org/reading_room/rr2def.php*

- Why do millions of Americans buy tobacco products that will probably shorten their lives?
- Why are so many alcohol ads associated with sporting events?
- How do magazine ads and other media messages encourage young women to view themselves as overweight or unattractive?

Developing media literacy skills provides a framework to help us address these and other media issues and answer the questions raised by them. A study of media issues involves the use of critical thinking strategies that allow us to become "wise consumers of media."[2] The Media Awareness Network presents five core media literacy concepts that we can use to help us analyze media messages:

Five Core Media Literacy Concepts

1. **All media messages are constructed.** Media messages are **created** with a purpose. The purpose may be to sell a product, entertain, or convince us to support a political position. Sometimes we see a commercial that catches our attention or makes us laugh, but we don't think about the preparation that goes into an advertisement. A national advertisement may require millions of dollars and often requires months to complete. A marketing strategy is developed by an ad agency, scripts are written, and actors are cast. A video production team uses specialized lighting and composes dozens of video shots over several weeks. This footage is integrated with computer graphics, music, and a professional voice-over. Post video editing retouches or recreates images that do precisely represent what the production team has in mind.

2. **Media messages are constructed using a creative language with its own rules.** Media messages attempt to create an artificial world and draw the viewer into it. Entertaining ads or programs often use humor to connect to the viewer. Products are sometimes marketed by convincing potential customers that the product will make them more attractive to the opposite sex. If someone drives the right car, uses the right cell phone, and applies the right deodorant, they are "cool." Failure to purchase the correct products could lead to the label of "loser."

3. **Different people experience the same messages differently.** A beer commercial with actresses wearing bikinis and participating in a wild party is targeted for males of a certain age. It is clear that this ad is not aimed for women or married men. The humor in an ad for a minivan might appeal to parents with several children, but young adults, under age 25, may not find the ad to be humorous or interesting.

4. **Media have embedded values and points of view.** Media messages communicate the values of the dominant culture, including youth, sex appeal, humor, power, success, and fitting-in with groups that demonstrate these qualities. The majority of television shows have main characters who are white, middle class, attractive and successful people. Many movies are written for teenage audiences. In these movies teens are the people who understand problems and solve them. Adults are often confused and ineffective.

---

[2] From the New Mexico Media Literacy Project, *http://www.nmmlp.org/media_literacy/index.html*

5. Media messages are constructed to gain profit and/or power. Advertisements, movies, television shows, and music are created to make money. If they are entertaining and informative, but are not profitable, they are removed from distribution. News programs may offer important information, but networks are aware that their programs must contain entertaining elements to maintain high ratings.[3]

Become Aware of Media Issues

As you might imagine, since the media is such a large part of life, many issues are associated with it. Here are some titles of issues for media literacy study. As you read through this list, other titles for the study of media issues may occur to you.

- Obesity, media messages, and their possible connections
- Advertising techniques, their truth and accuracy, and what makes them effective
- Stereotyping (by sex, race or ethnicity) and how that affects perceptions
- The consumer culture and its effect on buyers
- Bias in the news and how to recognize and react to it
- Violent and sexual content in the media and its effect on people, young and old
- Excessive television viewing, health problems, low achievement in school, and their possible connections.
- Violent video games and their possible effects
- Children and the media, including setting time limits and restrictions
- Unsupervised Internet use by children and its dangers.

A media literacy organization promotes "Turnoff TV Week." This group asks families to refrain from watching television for a week and record the changes that occur in family activities relationships. Many families have reported that they find alternate activities that are more interesting and involve more family interaction. Family members often discover time for reading and other hobbies.

Even if parents don't choose to eliminate television viewing, they may restrict television access for their children. Instead of allowing young children unsupervised access to television programs with adult content, some parents enable the lock-out capabilities that are available on new television sets. Another option to control television content would be for parents to record programs, preview them, and only allow their children to view screened programs. When children are old enough to ask questions about adult issues, it may be helpful for them to view adult-oriented shows with their parents. This provides a valuable opportunity for discussion of sensitive issues in a supportive environment.

Not all media issues are negative. Issues are also associated with positive uses of the media, including public service messages, entertainment, educational programs, positive role models in all types of programs, and news programs. Issues associated with these types of media often center on evaluation, which includes identifying the best programs and also figuring out how to improve and make some of them more useful.

---

[3] These five core media literacy concepts and the discussions that accompany them are available at the Media Awareness Network Web site, *http://www.media-awareness.ca/english/teachers/media_literacy/key_concept.cfm*

What Is Visual Argument? Why Is It Convincing?

A major part of the media is the visual argument that appears there. It comes in a variety of forms and includes photographs, both moving and still, drawings, illustrations, paintings, sculptures, and cartoons. It also sometimes includes the types of visuals you worked with in Chapter 6: diagrams, flowcharts, various types of graphs, visual demonstrations, tables of numbers, and even maps, especially when they have been developed to advance a position on a controversial issue.

All of these types of visual argument are used by a variety of people to persuade you to see things their way: advertisers use images to persuade you to buy their goods, politicians use images to get you to vote for them, journalists use images to get your attention and influence your interpretation of the news, people on Myspace, an Internet chat site, use images so you will become interested in them and become their Internet friends or associates. Visual argument can also take other forms. Recently a school in California outlawed both the Mexican and United States flags at school and further forbade students to wear politically provocative clothing or to paint their faces. The students had been responding to the immigration issue. In that context, flags, clothing, and painted faces also become potent and potentially disruptive forms of visual argument.

You can learn to recognize visual argument by asking two questions: *Is this visual about an issue that has not been resolved or settled? Does this issue potentially inspire two or more different views?* If the answer to both questions is yes, the next step is to describe the issue and the position it appears to take on the issue. You will often have to infer this information because it will not always be directly stated in words either on or near the visual itself.

Recognize and analyze a visual argument.

Figure 11-1 provides an example of a visual argument. This is the same photograph that appears in the history textbook chapter on page 251 of this book. Here this photograph has been enlarged so that you can study it carefully. Use what you have learned in Chapters 8 and 9 to make your initial analysis. You will also need to make inferences, taught in Chapter 10, to answer the questions about visual argument that follow it.

Courtesy of Bernie Boston

FIGURE 11-1 *A Vietnam War Protester Placing Flowers in the Rifle Barrels of Troops Guarding the Pentagon during an Antiwar Demonstration, 1967.*

Source: John Mack Faragher et al., *Out of Many: A History of the American People,* 2nd ed. (Upper Saddle River, NJ: Prentice Hall, 1997), 938.

1. Determine the subject, occasion, audience, and purpose:

   What is this about? _____

   What was going on at the time, and when did it occur? _____

   Who might the audience have been? _____

   Why do you think the photographer took this picture? _____

2. Does this photograph qualify as a visual argument? _____

   Is it about an issue that had not been resolved or settled? _____

   What issue does it raise? _____

   Does this issue potentially inspire two or more views? _____

3. How would you state the claim or the main point that is being made?

   _____

4. Describe the support for the claim. Does it appeal primarily to logic, to emotions, to developing the photographer's credentials, or to a mix of these?

   _____

5. What values are implicit in the argument? Do you share them? (If you do, you will find this an interesting and convincing argument. If you don't, you may reject it.) _____

The Special Features of Visual Argument

Visual argument has a number of unique features that make it particularly convincing and effective for advancing argument. Not all visual argument demonstrates all of these features, and sometimes these features combine or overlap with one another.

Before you read about these special features, look at the image in Chapter 1 on page 16. It is a photograph of one of the small towns on the Mexico-United States border that has the "Lots for Sale" sign in the foreground and that has been classified as one of the poorest communities in the United States. This photograph will be used as an example as we examine the eight special features of visual argument.

1. Visual argument is immediate and tangible and pulls you into the picture. It works on a different level of perception than written argument. Communication is fast, and it evokes a rich, dense, and immediate response. The picture of the town shows the dry earth, lack of vegetation, and small, crowded community. The Lots for Sale sign shows that people can still join this community and makes the viewer consider whether or not this would be a good place to buy land. You see these details quickly and react.

2. Visual argument inspires personal identification with the characters, the action, and the scene, and it does so more quickly than print. When you have read the article about the town and have examined the picture, you may feel sympathy for people who live here and identify with the difficult conditions, like a lack of running water, that often exist in these communities.

3. Visual argument often evokes an emotional response. It operates more directly on the emotions than written argument because images communicate more directly than words do. We may not be as critical and suspicious of a visual argument as we would be of a written argument. We see it, respond to it emotionally, and accept or reject it. Most viewers would respond emotionally to the

picture of the town. It confirms the problems described in the article about it. The picture evokes a negative emotional response.

4. Visual argument often relies on the juxtaposition of materials by putting unlike objects next to each other in a new combination. The purpose is to invite the viewer to make new links and associations. A Lots for Sale sign is usually associated with more attractive lots than those depicted here. This Lots for Sale sign is juxtaposed with the desolate and dry desert landscape, including the lack of running water and the poverty of those who live here. Juxtaposition of sign and landscape invites a comparison with more attractive property and strengthens the argument that this is a substandard place for people to live.

5. Visual argument often employs icons to prompt an immediate response from a viewer. Icons are images that people have seen so often that they respond to them immediately and in predictable ways. National flags are iconic for individuals in the countries they represent. The Lots for Sale sign is iconic in this visual because it is familiar, and the viewer responds to it immediately and in a predictable way: one could buy a lot and live here.

6. Visual arguments also employ symbols. Icons are symbolic, and they are so common that they evoke a common reaction. Not all symbols used in argument are so familiar that they can be considered iconic. Symbols and icons both have a lot of visual power because they both call up associations with past experiences and feelings and apply them to a new object. For some viewers the town itself will symbolize a way of life that they would want to avoid for themselves and for other people as well.

7. Visual argument is selective. When you look at a visual, think about what is included and what you are intended to see. Everything else has been left out. In the picture of the town and the sign, the sign is in the foreground and receives the most emphasis in the picture. It reminds the viewer that people are still buying here and that they will continue to live in this type of poverty unless something happens to improve the situation.

8. Visual argument invites unique interpretations from viewers. Usually no two people looking at a visual argument will interpret it in exactly the same way since individuals bring information and associations from their own past experience and use it to fill in some of the meaning in the visual. Much of the meaning of a visual argument has to be inferred. Sometimes the artist helps the viewer by adding a few words, but only a few, and they are short, fragments usually. The only words in the picture we have been using as an example are on the sign. All who view it will not interpret the sign and the rest of the photograph in the same way. It depends on whether the viewer might want to consider living here or not. How would you interpret this visual argument?[4]

    When you have finished reading about this image as an argument, answer these questions for yourself:

    Would I want to live there?

    Should anyone have to live there, with those conditions?

    What can be done about poverty in this country?

    This picture raises those issues.

[4] Nancy V. Wood, *Perspectives on Argument,* 5th ed. (Upper Saddle River: Prentice Hall, 2007) 409–415.

Now apply each of these features to the photograph of the antiwar demonstrator in Figure 11-1, and draw some conclusions about the effectiveness of this photograph as a visual argument.

Apply the special features of visual argument to the photograph of the antiwar demonstrator in Figure 11-1.

1. **Is the photo immediate and tangible? Does it pull you in?** What do you notice first? What can you say about the composition of this picture that draws you in?

2. **Does the photo establish common ground?** Is there anything or anyone in this picture you can identify with?

3. **Does the photo arouse your emotions?** What is your emotional reaction to this picture?

4. **Does the photo rely on juxtaposition?** What is placed in juxtaposition here, and what is the effect?

5. **Does the photo use icons?** Are there icons in this visual? If yes, what are they?

6. **Does the photo use symbols?** What objects in this visual would you say are symbolic, and what do they symbolize?

7. **Is the photo selective?** What is included in this visual? What is left out? What is the effect?

8. **How would you interpret this photo?**

   What do you think the photographer's purpose was?

   What is the final effect?

   What do you conclude about this photo?

Everything we have said here about still visual argument also applies to moving visuals. Motion picture directors and editors can create powerfully persuasive effects through the selection and juxtaposition of shots that lead the audience to see links and make associations that otherwise would not occur to them. Motion pictures also draw in the audience, engage their emotions, establish common ground, invite multiple interpretations, and rely on icons and symbols to create some of their meaning.

Visuals that stand by themselves or that accompany written text are found everywhere on the World Wide Web. The next section will help you become an effective Web reader as you learn to browse and find the information that interests you. You will also learn to evaluate its quality and effectiveness as you search for the best materials for your purpose.

How to Locate and Evaluate Internet Information

When you need to find an address or telephone number, you will usually use a telephone book to locate that information. Or, to find a book or article in the library, you will consult the card or the online catalogue. Finding material on the Internet requires its own special procedures.

Locating Information on the Internet

To find a Web site that provides information on a topic, most Internet users use an Internet search engine. There are dozens of Internet search engines, but students frequently use Google (google.com) or Yahoo (yahoo.com) to locate information on the Internet.

After entering the Web address of the search engine, a text window appears on the search engine's opening screen. This text window is the starting point for an Internet information search. A user may begin a search by typing a name, topic, place, or phrase into the text window. Some search engines, like Google, allow the user to search specifically for images, recent news stories, or scholarly information.

Internet search engines are powerful tools, and like any powerful tool, they must be used properly to produce useful results. Two common problems that students experience when performing Internet searches are incorrect spelling or punctuation and a lack of understanding of how to narrow search results. For example, if a user begins a search for information on Vietnam, the name of the country must be spelled correctly when entering it into the search engine text window. Typing **Vietnam** into the text window causes another problem, though. It will result in a listing of hundreds of millions of Web sites. To narrow the search, the user could enter more specific terms enclosed in quotes, such as, **"Hanoi 1970."** In this case, the search engine looks through the Internet for the specific phrase, "Hanoi 1970." Typing **Hanoi and 1970**, without quotes, produces a list of Web sites that uses both terms, but not necessarily together in a phrase.

Evaluating Web sites and Web-based Materials

Locating information on the Internet is only the first step toward actually using the information in an academic setting. It is easy to locate Internet information, but that information must be carefully evaluated. You need to understand that only a very small fraction of information from the Internet can be used in college classes. It is important to develop strategies to help you determine which Internet-based information is acceptable and which should be discarded. Various criteria exist for evaluating materials you find on the World Wide Web. Here are five that are drawn from the Lesley Libraries Web site. Ask these five questions to help you determine the usefulness of material you locate on the Web.

1. What is the purpose of the Web site?
2. Does the author of the information have sufficient background or demonstrated expertise to be considered an authority on the subject?
3. How objective is the information on the site?
4. Is the information current?
5. Is the information presented in a format that is clear, understandable, and professional?

Let's look at these five criteria for evaluation in more detail.

1. **What Is the Purpose of the Internet Web site?** A Web site could have a variety of purposes. It may have been created to sell a product, persuade the reader to vote for a political candidate, provide entertainment, or offer educational information. Sometimes the purpose of a Web site is easily determined, but it can be hidden, and the reader must make some inferences to determine its purpose.

Understanding how to read a Web site address can provide valuable clues to help you determine the purpose of a site. The following examples demonstrate common Web site extensions that provide important information about a Web site's purpose:

- The .gov extension means the Web site was created by a government agency. An example is irs.gov.
- The .com extension means the Web site has a commercial purpose. An example is Honda.com.
- The .edu extension means a higher education institution produced the Web site. An example is Stanford.edu.
- The .org extension means the Web site was produced by a nonprofit organization. An example is NPR.org.

Sometimes a Web site can provide entertaining and educational information, but if it has a .com extension, its main purpose is to sell a product. A Web site written in a scholarly format that provides information on Franklin Roosevelt and has an .edu extension could be a history paper written by a college student or professor.

2. **What Authority Does the Web site Author Have to Write on the Subject?** Since anyone can create a Web site and post opinions on a topic, you should try to verify that the author of Web-based materials is an authority on the subject. Ask the following questions:
- Can the author be identified? Sometimes the name of the author or publishing organization is not available on a Web site.
- Does the author have credentials that clearly identify him or her as an expert on the subject? To find out if the author is an authority on a subject, enter the author's name into an Internet search engine like Google or Yahoo, and you will probably find information on the author's occupation and published works. This will help establish his or her credentials to write on the subject.

- Is there a way to contact the author? Look for an email address. When an author includes that address, it usually indicates a willingness to answer questions or provide more information.
- Does the Web site have an organizational or corporate sponsor? Some organizations publish reliable research conducted by expert researchers while others publish information that is based on the personal experience of only one or a few individuals, which may be less valuable.

3.   How Objective Is the Web site? Though biased information presents a particular way of looking at the world, this information may still be useful. Students shouldn't always reject biased information, but should instead try to identify the nature of the biases in the material that they read. All of us have biases. One person might prefer to buy a foreign car while another person would only buy an American car. If we understand these people's preferences, we can more easily understand the reasons each person might give for preferring one type of car over another.

Objective, or unbiased information, is difficult to locate in the real world, but it is even more difficult to find on the Web. The Internet has an ample supply of material that promotes a particular political candidate, offers justifications for a corporation to act irresponsibly, or promotes hate for various ethnic or racial groups.

Students must think critically about the source of Web-based information and look for evidence that a Web site author may be motivated to present a specific point of view. Here are some examples. Tobacco and alcohol companies present information that they claim emphasizes their "corporate responsibility." News Web sites blend newsworthy events with celebrity news to increase the number of viewers. An employee who is paid to provide information that supports a specific political point of view may write a Government Web site. Ask yourself, how reliable is this information?

4.   How Current Is the Web site? Students should look for information on a Web site that indicates when it was published. Many topics are time sensitive. A Web site that discusses foreign policy in the Middle East, but is dated before 9/11/01, might have limited value unless you are examining the history of foreign policy in this area. Information on automobile safety or gas mileage for new cars must be current to be useful.

5.   How Clear and Professional Is the Web site? The Web site author should present information in a clear and understandable format. If a Web site has misspelled words and uses incorrect punctuation, its credibility should be questioned. Some Web sites create an unprofessional appearance by including flashing text or distracting graphics. Someone who is not an expert on the content of the site may author a Web site that has an amateur appearance.[5]

---

[5] For more information on these and other criteria for evaluating Web sites, go to *http://www.lesley.edu/library/guides/research/evaluating.web.html*

Practice locating information and evaluating Web sites by answering the following questions.

1. If you are looking for information on hybrid automobiles, what search words would you enter into the text window of an Internet search engine? _____
   _____

2. What is the main purpose of the Web sites at crayola.com and moveon.org?
   _____

3. Is a Web site on race relations credible if its author is a physics professor?
   _____

4. Why should a student rely or not rely on information from Apple Computer Inc. that compares its IPOD product with other MP3 players? _____
   _____

5. A Web site presents information on global warming. Describe why each of the following could indicate that the information is not reliable.

   a) The date the site was created is not listed. _____

   b) The Web site has a .com extension._____

   c) The Web site uses several different text colors on one page._____

   d) The Web site refers to global warming as globual warming. _____

   _____

Think Critically about Images and Statistical Figures

Here are some questions you can ask to help you critically evaluate the visual material you encounter in all kinds of media, including that on the Web. You can apply these questions to the graphs, tables of figures, and drawings you learned about in Chapter 6 as well as to the visual images and Web materials you have learned about in this chapter.

1. **For a picture that you have identified as a visual argument, ask if the image may have been selected or changed to represent a particular point of view.** In viewing photographs, for example, ask whether the photo represents a unique or

exaggerated way of looking at the subject or is an accurate picture of what really happened. For example, a photo of several people carrying off TV sets and other appliances during a riot is used to show that people were looting. You can ask whether this picture is typical of citizens' actions or is an extreme example of what only a few people did. The photos taken of disasters, like floods, usually depict the worst, most extreme results of the disaster. You can at least wonder how representative these pictures are of what actually has happened. Remember, too, that computers can be used to augment or change pictures. Tabloid newspapers sometimes create humorous composite images by placing one person's head on another person's body. See if there is any evidence that a visual has been changed, doctored, or recreated in any way so that you will see what the author wants you to see.

2. **For graphs and tables of figures, ask if statistical material has been manipulated so that it will make a stronger statement.** Take a close look at the numerical data in graphs and tables of figures. For example, on one graph you may read that the average income in America has increased to $38,000, and in another chart you read that it has increased to $23,000. This is puzzling until you realize that the $38,000 figure represents household income, or the amount made by all members of a household, and that the $23,000 figure represents individual income, or the amount made by only one person. This difference accounts for the disparity in the figures. Read all explanations and titles so that you will understand exactly what the data in the visuals are saying.

In reading graphs, notice the range of figures on the horizontal and vertical axes. Do they go from 0 to 100, or do they represent a smaller range, say, 80 to 100? A recent line graph in a newspaper that claims a popular stock is "plummeting" actually plots a change from $117 to $103 per share on the vertical axis and shows how this occurred over a period of several months on the horizontal axis. The graph visually suggests a greater decline than what actually exists.

3. **For samples of information, ask if the sample as shown in tables and charts is fair and accurate.** Many visuals that summarize trends, such as the information from opinion polls, a history of research results, or a report of common cultural practices, present only sample data because all possible data would be too massive to gather and interpret. In reading visuals that present a sample of material, try to determine what the sample is supposed to represent and whether or not the sample is fair. At the very least, try to determine the source of the data. Figure 11-2 on page 379 is a table of figures that claims to report how the United Nations is doing. It appears in a political science textbook. Omitted, however, is information on *who was queried for this poll* and *how many were queried*. One cannot ascertain whether or not the sample in this poll is a fair and accurate representation of the people who are affected by the United Nations. The value of this figure is diminished as a result. Such a visual provides, at best, only a rough estimate of a particular trend. Spend some time reading and pondering visual materials. Try to understand what is really going on in them, and make some judgments about their accuracy and value as well.

How Is the United Nations Doing?				

Question: In general, do you feel that the United Nations is doing a good job or a poor job in trying to resolve the problems it has to face?

	1975	1985	1993	1995
Good job	33%	38%	52%	35%
Poor job	51	44	44	56
Don't know or no answer	16	18	4	9

FIGURE 11-2

Source: *Gallup Organization, 1996.*[6]

How to Recognize Misleading Evidence, Faulty Reasoning, and Fallacies in Print and Visual Material

Authors sometimes resort to using misleading evidence, faulty reasoning, and fallacies when they try to be convincing. Advertisements and political campaign literature are two sources that often furnish examples of these unreliable types of support. These faulty types of support may at first seem convincing and may appear to strengthen an argument, but when they are evaluated by a knowledgeable reader, they usually actually weaken an argument. They signal that the author is using unreliable information and reasoning to manipulate a reader to accept a particular point of view. The use of one or more of these types of faulty evidence certainly weakens the conclusion. Here are some examples of misleading evidence, faulty reasoning, and fallacies.

1. **Distorting the evidence, using insufficient or unreliable evidence, and lying with statistics can weaken an argument.** Evidence should be verifiable, which means you should be able to look it up in another source and find the same information. There should also be enough evidence, and major information that could change the way one interprets the evidence should not be omitted. For example, the owner of a company argues that salaries in the company are good, since the average salary is $40,000. What is left out is that one individual makes $120,000 while four others make only $20,000 each. Presenting the average salary to suggest an equitable pay scale distorts the truth.

2. **Exaggerating or oversimplifying evidence also weakens an argument.** An argument that claims all nuclear power plants should be abolished because nuclear accidents are inevitable, and provides evidence of two such accidents, exaggerates to the

[6] James M. Burns et al., *Government by the People,* 2nd ed. (Upper Saddle River: Prentice Hall, 1997) 400.

point of distortion. An argument in favor of handgun ownership that suggests that guns be sold only to "good" people and not to criminals oversimplifies. You can see that it would be difficult to accept a conclusion based on evidence of this sort.

3. **Relying on one's own authority instead of on evidence weakens an argument.** Have you ever encountered people who claim something is true because they say it is true? If the individual is a recognized authority on the issue, then such a claim may be accurate and reliable. Imagine, however, a politician who claims that a work of art is immoral because he thinks it is. No criteria for judging the morality or immorality of art are provided. We are simply asked to accept the subjective opinion of someone who may know very little about art. Opinions that are supported with evidence from expert sources are much stronger than unsupported opinions from nonexperts.

4. **Misusing emotional materials weakens an argument.** Irrelevant and unrelated emotional materials or stories that are unrelated to the subject are sometimes used to try to prove a point. For example, providing horrible details about the suffering of the terminally ill to prove that assisted suicide should be legal can be irrelevant and unrelated to the claim. This is particularly true when the patient's suffering can be relieved with drugs. *Faulty analogies*, like comparing governments to hungry wolves; *distorted visuals*, like showing how happy people can become by doing abdominal exercises; *extreme slogans*, like those printed on placards in public demonstrations; and *hate language* aimed at particular groups of people represent misuse of emotional appeal and, on close scrutiny, they can be exposed as ineffective proof.

5. **Creating false needs can mislead a reader.** Advertisers who convince readers that they need a new car or a different type of blue jeans often create false needs. People who fall for this type of manipulation may have a need to show off, to display wealth or power, or to be distinctive. Creating false needs is often used by advertisers who know people will not buy their product without first being persuaded that they need it. "Do you have messy soap dishes?"an advertiser asks. The goal is to persuade you to switch to liquid soap and to give up soap dishes altogether. Until this moment, however, you may never have wondered whether your soap dishes are messy or not. They certainly are not *very* messy. The needs created often have nothing to do with reality. You can always ask if you really need what is being recommended.

6. **Relying on some of the common fallacies to prove a point weakens an argument.** The fallacies often seem attractive, but they are misleading. Notice how they represent incomplete or distorted ways of thinking. Here are some of the most common types of fallacies.

a. **Hasty generalization.** Readers are expected to accept a conclusion based on insufficient evidence. For example, people read an article that says Italians are healthy because they drink red wine. They jump to the conclusion that everyone should drink red wine. The same holds true of deciding to take vitamin supplements, to give up coffee, to go back to butter, or to eat more fiber, when the "facts" that support these conclusions may be very sparse and inconclusive.

b. **Red herring.** Evidence is used to support a claim that is actually unrelated to the claim. Arguing that a politician would be incompetent politically because of her personal life or family background is a red herring. Claiming that chat rooms on the Internet destroy marriages to prove that computers have a negative effect on society is also a red herring. These examples have nothing to do with the central arguments about political competence or the overall value of computers.

c. **Faulty cause.** A faulty cause–effect relationship is used to prove a claim when the cause, in fact, has nothing to do with the effect. For example, we read about laboratory tests that have been performed on animals that may also cause cures in humans. We assume that if a mouse is cured of cancer, people can be cured in the same way. This is an example of faulty cause–effect reasoning. Many experiments need to be performed to establish whether animals and humans will be affected in the same way or not.

d. **Faulty comparison.** A faulty comparison compares items from two radically different categories. Such comparisons invite the reader to transfer the emotional qualities of one of the items being compared to the other item. Here is an example: Higher education is sometimes compared to business, students are compared to customers, and education is compared to goods one might buy in a store. Central to these comparisons is the idea that higher education should try to become more like profit-making businesses because businesses are usually viewed as successful and, as a result, are valued in our society. If you agree that education can profit by becoming more like business, this comparison will be convincing to you. If, on the other hand, you decide that business and education are so different that they cannot be compared, or if you do not value business as much as you do education, this comparison will not be convincing to you.

   Another example of a faulty comparison is the comparison that is sometimes made between mercy killing and abortion to demonstrate that both take lives and, consequently, both should be against the law. This is an emotional comparison on two life-and-death issues, and you will find such a comparison convincing only if you agree that mercy killing and abortion kill in similar ways and that killing of any kind should always be against the law. If, on the other hand, you decide that an abortion kills someone who has never lived and mercy killing kills someone who has lived a long time, the comparison may break down for you, and you may not find this comparison convincing. Notice that these two examples of faulty comparisons—education and business and mercy killing and abortion—engage your emotions more than your logic and sense of reality.

e. **Straw man.** The straw man fallacy attributes an argument to an opponent that the opponent never made and then refutes it. Thus, it is sometimes easier to go after a "straw man" than a real issue. For example, a student who fails an exam argues that his teacher wants to flunk him out of school and ruin his life. This is easier than arguing with the real issue of whether or not the student has demonstrated sufficient learning to pass.

f. **Guilt by association.** This fallacy suggests that people's character can be judged by the character of their associates. Thus, if a group is considered suspect, any member of that group, even though innocent, may be suspected as well. For example, if a company conducts business in an illegal manner, individuals who work for the company may be suspected of illegal activity. Another way of putting this is that an individual may be judged unfairly by the company he (or she) keeps.

g. **Slippery slope.** The slippery slope is a scare tactic. The suggestion is made that if we allow one thing to happen, then many other things just like it will inevitably happen as well. For example, if one student is allowed to leave class early, then everyone in the class will want to leave early. Or, if we permit children to watch TV, they may want to watch it all the time and never do anything else. Thus they will slide down the slippery slope to disaster.

h. **Bandwagon appeal.** This fallacy claims that if everyone is doing something, then you should too, like drinking at fraternity parties or cheating on exams. It is obvious what is wrong with this reasoning.

i. **Either–or.** Some arguments are oversimplified with only two unsatisfactory possibilities or choices recommended and with no alternative or compromise positions suggested. Some examples are: Either this country continues the welfare program or children will starve to death; or, A woman can either have a career or stay home and raise a family; or, Terminally ill people can either suffer extreme pain or commit suicide.

Identify fallacies, misleading evidence, and faulty reasoning.

1. Take another look at the advertisement for computers that appears on page 315. Read the print that accompanies it. What is the fallacy in this statement?

   _____

   Name the fallacy._____

2. Look at the advertisement on page 316 for energizer batteries. Look at the image and read the small print. Do you detect any misleading evidence, faulty

   reasoning, or fallacies in this ad? Describe it._____

   _____

DEVELOP MEDIA LITERACY: FIVE STRATEGIES

Here are five strategies that will help you locate, analyze, and evaluate media, including Web sites and Web-based materials as well as the visual argument that so often appears in the media.

Strategy 1: Analyze media using the five core media concepts.

These five statements about the media and the questions that accompany them will help you analyze any media, whether you encounter it on the television set, the motion picture screen, the Internet, a billboard, or in a print source such as a magazine, newspaper, or book. As you read these questions, apply them to the advertisement for a Fujitsu ScanSnap in Figure 11-3.

1. All media messages are constructed for a purpose.
   - Who created it?
   - What is its purpose?
   - Describe as much of the production process as you can.

2. Media messages are constructed using a creative language with its own rules.
   - Describe the scene created for the media message.
   - What draws you into this scene?
   - What effect does the message have on you?

3. Different people experience the same messages differently.
   - Describe the target audience.
   - Are you a part of the target audience?
   - How do you experience the message?

4. Media have embedded values and points of view.
   - What values of the dominant culture are present in the message?
   - What type of audience might share these values?
   - How well do your values match those expressed in the message?

5. Media messages are constructed to gain profit and/or power.
   - Does this message aim for profit or power?
   - Is it interesting and engaging enough to gain your attention?
   - Is it convincing to you? Why, or why not?

▶

FIGURE 11-3 *Apply the five core media concepts and questions to this scanner advertisement.*[7]

---

[7] *Wired* November 2006: p. 055.

Strategy 2: Recognize visual argument.

Not every image presents an argument, so you will first need to determine whether or not an image takes a position on a controversial issue. Study the visual, read any accompanying text, and answer these questions:

1. What is the context in which it occurs?
   - What is the subject?
   - What is the occasion?
   - Who is the audience?
   - What is the purpose?

2. Is this an issue that has not been resolved or settled and that potentially inspires two or more views?

3. What is this issue, and what views on it do different people hold?

Practice Recognizing Visual Argument

Turn back to the drawing on page 317 that accompanies the essay "Alcohol" by Mike Barnicle, and answer the questions above as they apply to this drawing.

Strategy 3: Analyze the special features of a visual argument.

Here is the list of questions about the special features of visual argument that you read earlier in this chapter. Not all apply to every visual argument. Also, some are used more effectively than others in a particular case. As you read through the following questions, apply them to the 1951 advertisement for television sets that appears in Figure 11-4.

1. Is the image immediate and tangible? Does it pull you in? What do you notice first? What can you say about the composition?

2. Does the image establish common ground? Is there anything or anyone in this image you can identify with?

3. Does the image arouse your emotions? What is your emotional reaction?

4. Does the image rely on juxtaposition? What is placed in juxtaposition? What is the effect?

5. Does the image use icons? If yes, what are they?

6. Does the image use symbols? What is symbolic, and what does it symbolize?

7. Is the image selective? What is included? What is left out? What is the effect?

8. How would you interpret this image?
   What do you think the photographer's purpose was?
   What is the final effect?

▶

What do you conclude about this image?

Advertisement:

FIGURE 11-4 *Radio and Television Ownership* A Motorola television advertisement from *Woman's Home Companion*, 1951. Manufacturers designed TV sets as living room furniture and emphasized their role in fostering family togetherness.[8]
Gaslight Advertising Archives, Inc., N.Y.

Strategy 4: Evaluate Web sites and Web-based materials.

Answer the following questions to establish the quality and reliability of the material you locate on the World Wide Web.

1. What is the purpose of the site? Is it consistent with your purpose for consulting or using it?

2. Does the author or organization have the information and expertise to be a valuable source of information?

3. How objective is the information on the site? If you detect bias, what is the nature of the bias, and how will you explain it if you use the source?

4. How current is the information? Do you need to search further for more current information?

▶

[8] Faragher et al., *Out of Many* 879–880.

5. Is the format of the site clear and professional looking, or is it poorly presented and possibly created by unreliable parties?

Practice answering these questions:

Go to the following Web sites and practice answering the five questions. Use Google to help you find them.

MSNBC.com

Texasminutemen.org

theshadowlands.net

Strategy 5: Expose misleading evidence, faulty reasoning, and fallacies.

You may have trouble remembering all of the names of the fallacies. Concentrate instead on the illogical thinking they represent: introducing irrelevant material, providing inadequate or misleading support, drawing irrelevant conclusions, and oversimplifying or exaggerating the choices. Here are the fallacies organized in the same categories as the types of support, including logical support, opinions and personal credibility used as support, and emotional support.

1. Look for the fallacies associated with logical reasoning and discredit them as effective evidence. These include distorted or inaccurate evidence, faulty cause, faulty comparison, hasty generalization, red herring, and straw man.

2. Look for the fallacies associated with opinion and personal credibility and discredit them as effective evidence. They include guilt by association and relying on authority instead of evidence to prove a point.

3. Look for the fallacies associated with emotional support and discredit them as effective evidence. They include creating false needs, misuse of emotional material such as exaggerated visuals or hate language, the bandwagon appeal, the either–or fallacy, and the slippery slope.

Practice Looking for Fallacies

Look again at the advertisement for a scanner in Figure 11-3. What fallacies are present in this ad? Write a paragraph that explains the persuasive strategies used in this ad.

EXERCISES AND READINGS

FOUR COLLABORATIVE CLASS EXERCISES

Exercise 1

Use the core concepts to analyze advertisements. *Small groups.*

Two advertisements follow. The first is for a sleeping pill, and the second is for a body spray. Form small groups of four students each. Half of the groups may work with the sleeping pill advertisement and half with the body spray advertisement. For each of these advertisements, discuss and arrive at answers to the following questions that are based on the core media concepts explained in this chapter. When you complete your discussion, assign an individual from your group to report your findings to the class.

1. Who created each of these ads, and what was the purpose?

2. What techniques are used to attract my attention? Describe the fantasy worlds created in the ads.

3. How might different people understand this message differently from me? Who is the "target market" for each ad? Am I part of the target market?

4. What lifestyles, values, and points of view are represented in or omitted from these ads? Comment on the values that are implied in particular. Do you share these values?

5. Why were these ads created? Who benefits if each of these ads successfully achieves their goals?

6. What do you conclude about the effectiveness of the ad? Would you buy the product?

Advertisement 1:

FIGURE 11-5 *An ad for Lunesta sleeping pills.*[9]
Courtesy of Sepracor.

[9] *Time* 14 August 2006: 19.

Advertisement 2:

FIGURE 11-6 *An ad for Wild Card body spray by Tag.*[10]

Courtesy of the Gilette Co.

[10] *Rolling Stone* 10 August 2006: 110.

Exercise 2

Gain insight into how the creators of advertisements make their ads more attractive and persuasive for consumers. *Individuals.*

The purpose of this exercise is to provide you with an example of one way that ad makers create ads that are appealing to consumers.

1. Visit the Web site at http://demo.fb.se/e/girlpower/retouch/

2. Click on the link that says, "Retouch Web site". When the window opens, click on the icon that says, "Click Here to Reveal the Fraud." Select each of the 12 items that have been retouched. Study the before and after pictures, answer the following questions, and discuss them with the class.

   a) Why do magazines digitally manipulate images that are targeted for girls and women?

   b) Explain how the self-image of young girls might be affected by altered images in magazines.

   c) How can a magazine or advertiser benefit from digitally enhanced photos of women?

   d) In what ways might a magazine for men alter digital images?

Exercise 3

Form groups for the purpose of creating an anti-ad. *Pairs of students.*

Sometimes the truth of advertising can be challenged by an anti-ad or a spoof ad that intentionally creates feelings and perceptions that are the opposite of the original advertisement. A famous anti-smoking ad shows a poor, disheveled, homeless person who is smoking. Attached is the caption, "Smoking is Very Sophisticated." A second example is a spoof version of "Joe Camel," the cartoon character who promoted Camel cigarettes for many years. In an ad by Adbusters Magazine, "Joe Camel" was called "Joe Chemo" and was shown in a hospital gown dragging an IV cart.

1. With your partner, visit the Web site http://adbusters.org/spoofads/index.php to see examples of anti-ads. Click on each category of anti-ad to see additional examples.

2. With your partner, brainstorm and make a list of ads that you have seen on television or in print and select one of them. Or use one of the ads on pages 389 or 390.

3. Discuss how you could change one of these ads to make an anti-ad.

4. Describe your concept for the anti-ad to the class and draw a conclusion about it.

Analyze visual argument. *Small groups.*

Create small groups of four students each. Half of the groups may work with Visual #1, a photograph of the mushroom cloud created by an atomic bomb. This photograph comes from a history textbook that describes the first time these bombs were used during the Second World War. President Harry Truman decided to use the atomic bomb, and the war with Japan ended a week after the first bomb was dropped. The decision to use it, however, was controversial at the time, and still is because of the bomb's deadly power.

The other half of the groups may work with Visual #2, a cartoon titled "Revenge of the Environment." It is drawn from a textbook on the geologic environment. It appears in the front of the book so that it is the first thing readers see when they turn the first page.

Each group should answer the following questions about their visual and then report their conclusions to the class.

A. Establish whether or not the image is a visual argument.

1. What is the context in which it occurs?

   - What is the subject?

   - What is the occasion?

   - Who is the audience?

   - What is the purpose?

2. Is this an issue that has not been resolved or settled and that potentially inspires two or more views?

3. What is this issue, and what views about it do different people hold?

B. Establish which special features of visual argument are present in the image.

1. Is the image immediate and tangible? Does it pull you in? What do you notice first? What can you say about the composition of the image?

2. Does the image establish common ground? Is there anything or anyone in this image you can identify with?

3. Does the image arouse your emotions? What is your emotional reaction?

4. Does the image rely on juxtaposition? What is placed in juxtaposition? What is the effect?

5. Does the image use icons? If yes, what are they?

6. Does the image use symbols? What is symbolic, and what does it symbolize?

7. Is the image selective? What is included? What is left out? What is the effect?

8. How would you interpret this image?

What do you think the photographer's purpose was?

What is the final effect?

C. Draw a conclusion. What have you learned from examining this visual?

Visual # 1. A photograph from a chapter in a history book about World War II, 1941–1945.

FIGURE 11-7 *The Atomic Bomb*   On August 6, 1945, a U.S. B-29 fighter plane dropped "Little Boy," an atomic bomb, on Hiroshima, killing nearly 80,000 Japanese civilians and injuring another 70,000. Three days later, "Fat Man" destroyed Nagasaki, killing 40,000 and injuring 60,000 more. On August 14, the government of Japan surrendered, bringing an end to the war.[11]
Courtesy of AP/Wide World Photos.

[11] John Mack Faragher et al., *Out of Many* 2nd ed. (Upper Saddle River: Prentice Hall, 1997) 824.

Visual #2. A cartoon from a textbook on the geologic environment.

FIGURE 11-8 *An Environmental Cartoon*

Source: *Reprinted with special permission of King Features Syndicate.*[12]

© *King Features Syndicate.*

[12] Harvey Blatt, *Our Geologic Environment* (Upper Saddle River: Prentice Hall, 1997).

THREE READING EXERCISES:
ABOUT THE MEDIA AND ITS EFFECTS

The following three readings are drawn from the *San Francisco Chronicle,* a daily newspaper, the National Public Radio (NPR) Web site, and *Time,* a weekly news magazine. All three examine issues associated with the media. Before you begin to read, think a few minutes about your own ideas and values in regard to under-age drinking of alcoholic beverages, children and teenagers having uncontrolled access to the Internet, and the debate over a constitutional amendment to ban flag burning in the United States.

Reading 1

"Alcohol's Allure"[13]

EDITORIAL PAGE STAFF WRITER

Explanatory Notes: *The authors of editorials are not always identified, but editorials are usually written by capable staff writers who work for the newspaper, in this case, the* San Francisco Chronicle. *This article examines advertisements for alcoholic beverages that are targeted for under-age drinkers.* **Notice at the end of the article there are a list of facts and a list of recommendations for what you can do to change under-age drinking trends. How do you react to these facts and recommendations?**

Along with ads for milk in this month's issue of Rolling Stone magazine you'll find a half dozen seductive ads for Michelob, Skyy Blue and Absolut Vanilia.   1

Never mind that fully a third of the magazine's readers are between ages 12 and 20. Similar ads appear in Spin, Vibe and other youth-oriented publications.   2

Everywhere—in print, on the Internet, on television and radio—young people are bombarded by alcohol ads. Increasingly, the goal is to reach a legal-age audience, but the "spillover effect" to under 21-year-olds is undeniable. Coors, for example, has shifted its theme from Rocky Mountain outdoorsiness to beer as a way for rowdy young males to impress blond twins in skimpy tank tops.   3

Advertising for hard liquor hasn't made it to the major networks—yet. In 1996 the distilled spirits industry abandoned its voluntary code against TV advertising. Since then, hard-liquor advertising has appeared on hundreds of local television stations, radio stations and cable TV networks.   4

A new entrant on the youth landscape are malt-based sweetened drinks. Ads for Smirnoff Ice and Bacardi Silver, made by brewing companies which add distilled spirits "flavorings," have popped up on shows like "Friends," with large teen audiences.   5

[13] "Alcohol's Allure," *San Francisco Chronicle,* editorial page, 6 April 2003.

Not surprisingly, teens now consume at least 12 percent of all alcohol sold in the United States. In California alone, alcohol companies rake in nearly $1.5 billion annually from underage drinkers. Peer pressure, parents and price play a part. But advertising is clearly a factor, as a series of studies at UC Berkeley's Prevention Research Center has shown. "Kids who are exposed to alcohol advertising drink more, and more often, than those who aren't," says Joel Grube, the center's senior research scientist. 6

Talk to groups of young people, and they'll tell you that alcohol in various forms is smuggled onto high school campuses, disguised in soda cans or water bottles. During lunch or class they're passed around among students. Hard liquor such as Remy Martin, Courvoisier, and Bacardi—typically blended with soft drinks—are now common drinks for the teen crowd. At teenage parties, Smirnoff Ice competes with beer as a drink of choice. 7

Pity the parent who tries to resist the pressure to supply alcohol to their teenage children and their friends. "It is a foul parent who has a party without alcohol at his house," says Dr. James Hanson, director of the intensive care unit at Children's Hospital in Oakland, who has seen firsthand alcohol's potentially lethal effects. Each year, Hanson says, between 5 and 10 young patients arrive at Children's in alcohol-induced comas. Many more are admitted as a result of alcohol-related accidents, including bizarre stunts such as nighttime go-cart racing. 8

Representatives of the beer and distilled spirits industries insist that their advertising is not directed to underage drinkers. They point to a range of programs that they sponsor to discourage underage drinking. The industry's voluntary code recommends against advertising on any medium where more than 50 percent of readers, viewers or listeners are under the age of 21. 9

But the guidelines do little to shield children from alcohol advertising. A 1999 Federal Trade Commission report found that "the 50 percent standard permits placement of ads on programs where the underage population far exceeds its representation in the population." 10

Several sophisticated studies by the Center on Alcohol Marketing and Youth (*www.camy.org*) found that underage youth are far more likely to see alcohol ads than the adult audience for which they were ostensibly intended. 11

"Whether or not they are intending to target this market, they are capturing a substantial proportion of it," says David Jernigan, the center's research director. "Like the rest of society, they have to take responsibility for it." 12

As a start, the beer and distilled spirits industries must lower their 50 percent standard to further restrict advertising that currently reaches too many teens. For more responsible advertising, they need look no further than the wine industry which voluntarily advertises on outlets with far smaller teen audiences. Surveys show the wine industry is successful in reaching its intended target: adult drinkers. 13

Berating parents to do more will only have a limited impact. What is needed is a much broader approach that mirrors the successful anti-smoking campaigns of recent years. That includes restricting advertising, raising the price of offending products, limiting outlets, and creatively educating young people about alcohol's dangerous effects. 14

This issue goes far beyond racy ads. The lives of young people are at stake. 15

Teen drinking facts

—Underage drunk drivers accounted for 1,452 fatal car crashes in 2001.

—One-third of 11th-graders in California qualified as "excessive alcohol drinkers," according to last year's California Student Survey.

—4 out of 10 children who begin drinking at age 13 or younger become alcohol dependent.

—Underage drinking has been linked to unwanted pregnancies, date rape, other illegal drug use and gun violence.

What You Can Do

—Work to limit liquor outlets and alcohol billboard ads in your community, as well as alcohol sponsorship of rock concerts, sports events, and other events attended by teenagers.

—Join campaigns to encourage alcohol companies to reduce the amount of alcohol advertising seen by young people.

—Urge your representative to support legislation in the Legislature such as AB216 and SB5 that encourage the alcohol industry to be more responsible, and helps deal with the negative effects of underage drinking.

—Cooperate with your local police to help them enforce liquor laws.

—As a parent, reduce the availability of alcohol in your home.

—Work to make sure schools have clear and enforceable no-alcohol policies. Encourage **media literacy** programs to help students resist the impact of alcohol advertising.

—As a young person, join peer education programs to inform young people about the dangers of drinking. And join some of the campaigns mentioned above.

This editorial is part of a series on reclaiming childhood from consumerhood. We 16 would like to hear from you. Do you think alcohol advertising contributes to underage drinking? If you're a teenager, do you think underage drinking is a problem? If so, what can be done about it? Send your comments to *editorials@sfchronicle.com*

822 words

Strategy Questions

1. Who seems to be the target audience for many of the ads for alcohol discussed in this article? Why do you think so?
2. What values are implicit in the "What You Can Do" section? Whose values are they? Do you share them?
3. Would the ads for Coors beer (paragraph 3) be effective with the young audience described in this article? Why?

Study Reading Questions

1. Name two of the "youth-oriented" publications mentioned in this article that carry liquor ads.
2. What percent of all alcohol sold in the United States is now consumed by teens?
3. How much money per year do liquor companies make in California on alcohol sold to teenage drinkers?

Critical Reading and Thinking Questions

1. How does each of the following groups contribute to the problem of under-age drinking: parents? alcohol marketers? teens? What realistic changes could each of these groups make to change the trend described in the article?
2. What effect does the list of "Teen drinking facts" at the end of the article have on the reader? How effective do you think it is to list facts in this way? Why?
3. Pick one item on the list titled "What You Can Do" and describe how you think it might help solve the problems described in this article. Why do you think it might work?

Reading 2

Monitoring Teens' Media Intake Poses Challenges

NEDA ULABY AND MARC SILVER

Explanatory Notes: *The two essays that appear below are drawn from the NPR (National Public Broadcasting) Web site. The site is produced here exactly as you would find it on the Internet. Neda Ulaby , the author of the first segment, has worked as a reporter for NPR since 2000. You can go to the Web address for this site and listen to a longer version of this essay online. The Web address is listed at the bottom of each Web page below. Marc Silver, the author of the second segment, is an editor at* U.S. News and World Report *who writes for a variety of magazines and newspapers. Here he interviews author Debra W. Haffner for an NPR radio program.* **As you read this material, analyze the format of these Web pages. What are some of their special characteristics? Comment on content and layout.**

Young People and the Media
Monitoring Teens' Media Intake Poses Challenges
by Neda Ulaby
All Things Considered, August 2, 2006 • If you go to online spaces popular with teenagers, you'll find plenty of smart, funny, charming material. But you'll probably also find things that would make the most liberal parents cringe, such as one Internet-based animated game allowing players to sexually humiliate a popular singer.

It's easy for teens and pre-teens to access hardcore images of sex and violence that would have been hard for adults to find 20 years ago. Some Web advertisements blindside kids such as 15-year-old Angela Black.

http://www.npr.org/templates/story/story.php?storyID=5599056   8/31/2006

Many teens have a multitude of devices at their finger-tips today, making it harder for parents to know what they are being exposed to.
Corbis

Popular Teen Web Sites
MySpace
Xanga
Facebook

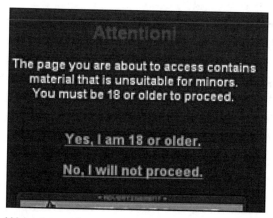

Web sites with mature content often have screens nominally meant to keep out underage users, but it's usually not difficult to circumvent them.
Common Grounds

"Pop-ups come up sometimes, and it's just like, 'Delete,' " Black says. "That's all I do, because that's disgusting, porn stuff."

Every day, Angela updates her social networking Web sites—all three, on Myspace, Xanga and Facebook. Most of the stuff isn't anything Angela's mother needs to worry about: Angela and her friends fill their pages with silly, supportive messages. They post pictures of bad hair days and muse about life, faith, and love.

But the pages of Angela's classmates aren't always as wholesome.

"I see people talk about their adventures with boys or girls—and sometimes it's freaky, but not shocking anymore, because you get used to it," Black says.

But the ability to disguise one's identity online can make it harder for parents to determine exactly what their children are doing. Ashley Hutchinson, a 21-year-old volunteer who helps educate teens on sexual-health issues, notes that parents have lost their historic advantage of being the first to know how to use communication tools. Teens use cell phones, gaming consoles and other portable media devices to exchange content in ways that don't always occur to their elders, such as text-messaging sex hotlines.

If experts agree on one thing, it's that most parents are clueless about the media lives of their children. It can be tricky for parents to define what is appropriate, especially when mainstream culture has become so casually risqué. Susannah Stern, who teaches communications at the University of San Diego, notes that kids have "learned very well from adults what we value and what gets people to pay attention."

Recently, the Kaiser Family Foundation did a study showing that over the past seven years, sexual content on network television has increased from more than half of all shows to seven out of every 10 shows. The number of sexual scenes in those shows has gone up, too.

Teenagers do not respond identically to media messages, says Susannah Stern, so there's no one way to help guide them. She says adults should make clear that their interest is not in removing teenagers' autonomy but in helping them develop their own internal controls.

"What's hard is that parents [want] a list of the 20 things you should do and the 20 things you shouldn't do," Stern says. "I just don't think in this day and age dealing with adolescents that you can give that kind of prescriptive list."

Volunteer counselor Hutchinson describes hers as a guinea-pig generation: the first to grow up immersed in a brave new world of technology and media culture, and the first to master it—more or less—on their own.

523 words

Parents: Don't Let the Media Be the Boss of You!
by Marc Silver

Debra W. Haffner is the author of *Beyond the Big Talk* and, more recently, From *Diapers to Dating: A Parent's Guide to Raising Sexually Healthy Children.*

The motto of today's media sometimes seems to be "defeat the parents." Let's see: raunchy sitcoms, vulgar movies, violent video games, explicit Web sites, not to mention provocative personal Web pages and instant messages. That's a lot of crudity and lewdity for mom and dad to keep tabs on.

Rev. Debra W. Haffner, director of the Religious Institute on Sexual Morality, Justice and Healing, *regularly blogs* on sexuality and related topics. She offers practical guidance for put-upon parents.

NPR: Should you ever spy on your kids to see what Web sites they visit?
I don't like the word "spy," but I think it's perfectly appropriate to say to a child under 16, "I plan to check the history of sites you've visited every day, and together we will set rules and limits on Internet use."

What rules would you suggest?
A Kaiser study found that about one-third of kids have access to the Internet in their bedroom. That's a really bad idea. If you care about what your kids are doing on the Internet, the computer should be in a family room where you can observe their use.

One of the most important things to say to kids today is you may NEVER go to meet someone you met online unless I go with you. I don't have too many absolute rules as a parenting expert, but that should be an absolute rule.

Another rule is that you can only instant message (IM) with people on your list, and I give approval for who's on the list. I tell my 13-year-old son, "If I don't know the person or the person is more than two years older than you, I will say no." And I check to make sure there aren't people on the IM list I don't know.

And I think it's OK to say to your child that periodically you want to look at their e-mails. Not to open their e-mails but to know they're from people they know.

Do parental controls—limits on the sites they can visit—work?
I don't happen to believe in parental controls for children over 12. For children under 12 it makes sense, but the controls limit too much access to health care information your child might want or need.

http://www.npr.org/templates/story/story.php?storyID=5599056

Should you let your child have a personal Web page?

If your child does, get an account as a parent so you can check your kid's site once a week to make sure the child isn't showing pictures in provocative clothing or giving out too much personal information. Kids might go, "I didn't give out my last name." But they'll give out where they go to school, what club they're in. That's a lot of information.

What if a parent sees a sexually provocative IM exchange that the child left on the computer screen?

The first question is, how did you happen to see it? Did you go look for it? I think it is important to respect your child's privacy (unless you suspect drug use and then all bets are off; privacy is a secondary concern when it comes to well-being).

In this case, you have a teachable moment, and ignoring that would be silly. Say, "Honey, guess what? You left up this piece and I started to read it. I really want to talk about it because it makes me feel uncomfortable knowing that you're having these sexualized conversations." Then talk about what's going on with them sexually.

Many parents might be a bit tongue-tied.

There's a three-part process you can use for kids from 3 through 30. You find out what they already know. You correct misinformation or incorrect information. And then you give your values.

So if the topic is oral sex . . .

"I read this and I'm concerned there's all of this talk about oral sex. I'm wondering what's going on with you—or your friends. I hope you know oral sex can cause any number of sexually transmitted diseases and you need to be protected when it does occur." And you state your family values: "In our family, we hope that you never do this, or that you wait until you are older before you think about doing this, or that you only do it in a committed monogamous relationship." The important thing is to clarify the values about sexuality you want to give your children.

What if your under-17 kid wants to see an R-rated movie, and says everybody is going?

My rule is it's illegal to go see an R movie unless you're 17 or older. But I'm happy to go with you if for every hour and a half of the movie we get 30 minutes to talk about what you've seen. I took my daughter to see *American Pie* and we talked a long time about how children make decisions, about whether you need to lose your virginity by the end of high school. The movie had lots of good opportunities in its grossness.

What if your child defies you and sees an R movie anyway?

There needs to be a discussion about the consequences of going to the multiplex and telling me you're seeing a PG movie, then going to an R movie. I always tell my children that I know the people who go to the movies around here. If you go to an R movie, there's a good chance I'm going to find out. And the consequence will be that you don't get to go to the movies alone for the next three months.

Do you believe in censoring a child's TV viewing?

It depends how old your kid is. I don't believe kids 12 and younger should watch TV without a grown-up to mediate sexual content. After the age of 15, you have to hope you've done a good enough job to have your child mediate messages. A Kaiser study says an enormous number of kids have a TV set in their own room. If you're concerned about what kids are watching, don't put a TV in their room.

What about violent video games? What's the point of banning them at home if your kids will play them at a friend's house?

You have the right to limit materials coming into your home. You may not be able to stop your kid from playing *Grand Theft Auto* at somebody else's house, but you have the right to say, "I don't want materials with people using violence and sex to hurt each other in my home."

http://www.npr.org/templates/story/story.php?storyID=5599056

Which won't make your kid a happy camper.

It is OK to make your child unhappy. Starting from when your kid says, "I'm not going in the booster seat," there are lots of opportunities to make your child unhappy. A child's being temporarily mad or even hateful to you does not override your need as a parent to make sure your child is safe and healthy.

1011 words

Strategy Questions

1. How does the material in the left-hand column of this Web site relate to the printed material on the right? Give examples.
2. Comment on the quality of this Web site. What grade would you give it on a scale of A–F? Why?
3. What is the purpose of this Web site?

Study Reading Questions

1. What are Myspace, Zanga, and Facebook?
2. Why do some children disguise their identity when they are online?
3. According to the Kaiser Family Foundation, what has increased over the past seven years on network television? By what percent has it increased?

Critical Reading and Thinking Questions

1. What, in your opinion, are the most serious problems described in the articles on this Web site? Why do you think they are serious?
2. What is Silver referring to in his opening statement, "The motto of today's media sometimes seems to be 'defeat the parents'." What does he mean by that? Can you provide some examples of this tendency yourself?
3. Haffner, in her interview with Silver, makes a number of suggestions for how parents can protect their children from objectionable material on the Internet. Which of her suggestions would you accept? Which would you reject? Why?

Reading 3

Forget Flag Burning[14]

MAJOR GENERAL ROBERT SCALES (RET.)

Explanatory Notes: *The author, a retired Major General, commanded two units in Vietnam and was awarded a Silver Star. He served 34 years in the Army. His essay appeared on the last page of* Time *magazine on July 3, 2006. It includes three visuals: the marines raising the flag on Iwo Jima in 1945, the flag being burned in the United States in 1967, and the flag being folded and presented to mourning fam-*

14 Robert Scales, "Forget Flag Burning," *Time* 3 July 2006: 100.

*ilies who have lost family members in Iraq in 2006. **What do each of these visuals contribute to the essay, how are they related to each other, and which of them is the most striking and memorable?***

Joe Rosenthal, "Marines raising the American flag at Iwo Jima" Courtesy of AP/Wide World Photos
Leonard Detrick, "Anti-Vietnam War Protestors" Courtesy of Leonard Detrick/The New York Daily News
Andrew Lichtenstein, "Memorial with people holding folded flags" Courtesy of Andrew Lichtenstein/Getty Images USA, Inc.

Some in congress appear to be taking a sabbatical from the long war on terrorism to introduce a constitutional amendment banning the burning of the flag. The debate over such an amendment may or may not be worth having, but one thing is clear: at a time when the country is at war, now is not the time for such tertiary considerations. 1

I understand reverence for the flag. It comes naturally to soldiers. We commit our lives to serving intangibles, swearing oaths to a piece of parchment or saluting an expanse of cloth decorated with stars and stripes. We understand symbolism because symbolism is what in large measure compels us to do a job that might result in our demise. 2

The American flag symbolizes freedom. The Constitution we soldiers are pledged to defend guarantees freedom of expression even when freedom of expression includes the right to deface the flag, however obnoxious that act may be. Of course, I'm old enough to remember flag burning when flag burning was "cool." I was in Hawaii, on R. and R., halfway through my tour in Vietnam. My wife and I were watching television when student war protesters in California—none of whom had the slightest chance of facing violent death in combat—illuminated their campus by torching Old Glory. I was appalled by the sight. A short time later, Walter Cronkite informed the world that my unit, the 101st Airborne, was beginning an offensive in the A Shau Valley. I left for Vietnam the next day to confront an enemy that undoubtedly would have punished those protesters had they burned the North Vietnamese flag in Hanoi. 3

But that was then. The image of the flag that soldiers see today is different. Instead of flags aflame, we see flags covering coffins of soldiers and Marines returning the hard way from Iraq and Afghanistan. Pushing forward a constitutional amendment is labor-intensive work. I'm concerned how such a diversion during wartime might appear to those who are still serving in harm's way. 4

Please don't get me wrong. I have many friends in Congress, patriots all. Each one of them has been to Iraq and Afghanistan many times. Although he refuses to advertise the fact, one was wounded there during an inspection tour last year. My 5 concern relates not to the sincerity of Congress but to the perceptions among our young men and women that their overseers are suddenly distracted at a time when attention to their needs has never been more necessary.

Our soldiers want to be assured that Congress is doing all it can to reduce losses in what Lincoln ruefully termed the "terrible arithmetic" of war. They want to know that Congress is doing all it can to give them the weapons they need to maintain the fighting advantage over the enemy. They are concerned that their equipment is wearing out under constant use. They and their families are worried that not enough soldiers are in the pipeline to replace them.

We know from letters and conversations that our young soldiers returning from combat are concerned about the future of their institutions. They want to know who is focused on reshaping our Army and Marine Corps so that both services will be better able to fight the long fight against radical Islam. How will Congress fund the future? Where will the new weapons and equipment come from? They are also worried about more personal issues like housing and health care for themselves and their families.

Dan Brown was my First Sergeant in Vietnam. I was new to war. He had served in two. He gave me a piece of advice then that Congressmen intent on changing the subject should heed: "In combat the main thing is to keep the main thing the main thing. Otherwise, you die." The main thing today for Congress and the nation should be the war in Iraq. Soldiers are sworn to defend the right to free speech with their lives even if "speech" is expressed in despicable ways. What they want in return is the assurance that our lawmakers will hold their interests dear.

So the message from most of us soldiers is clear: Debate a flag-burning amendment if you wish. But don't create the perception among our young men and women in combat that there are more important issues than their welfare at the moment. Wait a while. At least for their sake, wait until the last flag-draped coffin comes home.

743 words

Strategy Questions

1. What are the visual arguments made by each of the three photographs?
2. What is the claim of this essay? Which of the photographs illustrates that claim? How does it do that?
3. What do you think the flag symbolizes as it appears in each of the three photographs?
4. What is the effect created by placing these three photographs next to each other in this order?

Study Reading Questions

1. What was the subject of a constitutional amendment being recommended by some members of Congress when this article was written?

2. Where does the author think Congress should focus its interest instead? Why?
3. What does the author say the American flag symbolizes to military personnel?

Critical Reading and Thinking Questions

1. Why is this essay illustrated with three photographs of the American flag? What are the dates of the three photos? Describe the contexts of each of them. What do they all have in common? How is each different from the others?
2. Evaluate the personal credibility of the author? Is he authorized to write on this subject? Why, or why not?
3 Do you agree or disagree with this author about what he claims should be the main concern of Congress at this time? Give reasons for your answer.

FOUR APPLICATION EXERCISES

Exercise 1

Find a fallacy

Locate an advertisement that contains a fallacy, bring it to class, and explain the fallacy.

Exercise 2

Find a visual argument

Look at magazines, newspapers, or the Internet and find a visual argument. Cut it out or print it so that you can hand it around in class. Say why you think it is an argument, and describe how the eight features of visual argument are or are not present in it.

Exercise 3

Turn off the media

Turn off all televisions, DVDs, and computer games in your home for one week. Keep a journal to record your reactions and describe changes in your daily routine. Report on positive or negative outcomes from this activity.

Exercise 4

Turn off the cell phone

Turn off your cell phone for one week. Record the same information described in Exercise 3 above.

Review and Evaluate the Strategies

The following is a review of the five strategies you learned in this chapter:

1. Analyze media using the five core media concepts.
2. Recognize visual argument.
3. Analyze the special features of a visual argument.
4. Evaluate Web sites and Web-based materials.
5. Expose misleading evidence, faulty reasoning, and fallacies.

Make a personal evaluation of these strategies:

1. Underline your favorite strategies in the list above.
2. Make a check mark by those you want to continue to use.
3. Cross out any you probably will not continue to use. What are your reasons for rejecting them?

_____

_____

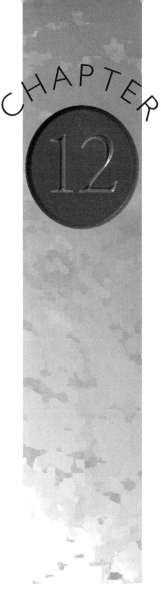

Use Reading to Help You Think

CHAPTER 12

CHAPTER GOALS:

1. **To show how reading can be used to generate ideas and insights.**

2. **To describe thinking in the major academic disciplines.**

3. **To teach you to synthesize and make mental connections as you read.**

4. **To provide five strategies that will encourage critical thinking, problem solving, and creative thinking while you read.**

Reading, Learning, and Thinking

You have now developed strategies for study reading that will help you learn and remember the material that you read in college. To those you have added strategies for critical reading that will help you **analyze** and evaluate argumentative writing. Figure 12-1 provides a reminder of the questions that guide critical reading. Figure 12-2 is a self-assessment of the critical reading strategies you learned in Chapters 8 through 11. Complete this assessment to help you review and evaluate your critical reading process. You should be able to check "yes" for at least a few of the strategies for each of the phases of the process.

QUESTIONS THAT GUIDE CRITICAL READING

1. Is the subject controversial? What are some possible points of view? What is the author's point of view? What is my point of view before reading? After reading?

2. Does this reading material contribute to a larger, ongoing conversation about an issue? What does it contribute? What big ideas have been expressed in the past about this issue?

3. What is the author's purpose for writing? Is an argumentative purpose clear, or, if not, are there any signs of bias that indicate a possible hidden or unconscious argumentative purpose?

▶

4. What is the social context for the argument? What motivated the author personally to write about this issue?

5. What is the claim? What type of claim is it? What are some of the reasons that support the claim?

6. What are the author's values and beliefs regarding the issue? How do they match my own values and beliefs regarding the issue? How much common ground do I share with the author on this issue?

7. What is the possible nature of the targeted reading audience?

8. What is the evidence? Consider both fact and opinion. How reliable is the evidence? Is the opinion well informed?

9. What types of comparison are used: Literal? Historical? False? Why are comparisons used? How effective are they?

10. Is cause–effect reasoning used? Is it valid? That is, do the causes lead to the effects?

11. How are the key concepts defined? Are any of the definitions controversial? Do I accept the definitions?

12. If a problem is posed, what are the solutions? Are they good solutions?

13. Does the author use emotional support? How effective is the emotional support?

14. Is there any refutation? Is the refutation effective?

15. What should I infer? Would the author expect me to make these inferences, as in the case of irony?

16. What is the conclusion? What am I supposed to believe as a result of reading? Can I accept the conclusion? Why or why not?

17. What is the value of the conclusion? Is the conclusion good or bad? Moral or immoral? Useful or useless?

18. Do any of the visuals contribute to the argument? How?

FIGURE 12-1 These questions will help you focus your reading purpose on critical reading, or reading, analyzing, and evaluating the material.

SELF-EVALUATION: USING CRITICAL READING STRATEGIES

(Add these strategies to those you have developed for study reading; see pp. 234–235)

	Yes	No

Before reading.

1. I survey and decide what is at issue.   ___ ___

2. I think about my present position on the issue.   ___ ___

3. I try to learn about the author's background and
   experience.   ___ ___

4. I try to discover the author's motivation for writing.   ___ ___

5. I speculate about the author's purpose and point of view.   ___ ___

6. I imagine the audience the author may have had in mind.   ___ ___

While reading.

7. I look for the claim and identify some of the reasons.   ___ ___

8. I look for signs of bias if an argumentative purpose is
   not clear.   ___ ___

9. I evaluate the logical support.   ___ ___

10. I evaluate the emotional support.   ___ ___

11. I evaluate the use of personal credentials to build trust.   ___ ___

12. I analyze and discredit misleading evidence, faulty
    reasoning, and fallacies.   ___ ___

13. I locate and evaluate refutation of other positions.   ___ ___

14. I analyze the author's values and beliefs.   ___ ___

15. I compare my values and beliefs with the author's
    and look for common ground between us.   ___ ___

16. I make inferences about the unknown on the basis of
    the known.   ___ ___

17. I recognize irony.   ___ ___

18. I locate and decide whether or not to believe the
    conclusion.   ___ ___

▶

After reading.

19. I compare the author's position on the issue with my own initial position and analyze any change in my position as a result of reading.   ____ ____

20. I think about the value of the author's conclusion, that is, if it is good or bad, moral or immoral, according to my standard of values.   ____ ____

Give yourself a score on the self-evaluation for critical reading. Count all of the check marks in the "yes" column, multiply that number by 5, and write your score in the blank: _____. A score of 70 or better on this self-evaluation is excellent, and 50–65 is also very good, since it shows you are using half or more of the strategies. If your score is 45 or lower, you should probably look through the strategies again and add a few to what you are doing now to make your critical reading process more powerful.

FIGURE 12-2 Evaluate your critical reading strategies.

This final chapter adds a few more strategies to those you have already developed to help you think critically and creatively about what you read. You will learn to think in two ways: You will think critically about the author's ideas as you read, and you will think creatively about your own original ideas as they are inspired by your reading. Thus you will learn to use your reading as a springboard to help you think. The purpose of this chapter is to teach you ways to use reading in conscious and deliberate ways to help you think. The final exercises, readings, and practice exam at the end of the chapter will give you the opportunity to integrate strategies for study reading, critical reading, and critical thinking. You will need to integrate and use all three types of strategies to be successful in most of your other college courses.

What Is Critical Thinking?

In his autobiography, the Nobel Prize-winning physicist Richard Feynman describes his experiences as a visiting professor of science with a group of students who had been taught only to memorize, not to think. Even though you may not understand the scientific concepts in this passage, you will still be able to understand these students' approach to learning and why it frustrated their professor.

These students had already had many courses, and this was to be their most advanced course in electricity and magnetism—Maxwell's equations, and so on.

The university was located in various office buildings throughout the city, and the course I taught met in a building which overlooked the bay.

I discovered a very strange phenomenon: I could ask a question, which the students would answer immediately. But the next time I would ask the question—the same subject, and the same question, as far as I could tell—they couldn't answer it at all! For instance, one time I was talking about polarized light, and I gave them all some strips of polaroid.

Polaroid passes only light whose electric vector is in a certain direction, so I explained how you could tell which way the light is polarized from whether the polaroid is dark or light.

We first took two strips of polaroid and rotated them until they let the most light through. From doing that we could tell that the two strips were now admitting light polarized in the same direction—what passed through one piece of polaroid could also pass through the other. But then I asked them how one could tell the absolute direction of polarization, from a single piece of polaroid.

They hadn't any idea.

I knew this took a certain amount of ingenuity, so I gave them a hint: "Look at the light reflected from the bay outside."

Nobody said anything.

Then I said, "Have you ever heard of Brewster's Angle?"

"Yes, sir! Brewster's Angle is the angle at which light reflected from a medium with an index of refraction is completely polarized."

"And which way is the light polarized when it's reflected?"

"The light is polarized perpendicular to the plane of reflection, sir." Even now, I have to think about it; they knew it cold! They even knew the tangent of the angle equals the index!

I said, "Well?"

Still nothing. They had just told me the light reflected from a medium with an index, such as the bay outside, was polarized: they had even told me which way it was polarized.

I said, "Look at the bay outside, through the polaroid. Now turn the polaroid."

"Ooh, it's polarized!" they said.

After a lot of investigation, I finally figured out that the students had memorized everything, but they didn't know what anything meant. When they heard "light that is reflected from a medium with an index," they didn't know that it meant a material such as water. They didn't know that the "direction of the light" is the direction in which you see something when you're looking at it, and so on. Everything was entirely memorized, yet nothing had been translated into meaningful words.[1]

Notice that these students were not expected to come up with new, original insights, but simply to think about and understand what they had learned. Thinking

---

[1] From Richard P. Feynman, *Surely You're Joking, Mr. Feynman! Adventures of a Curious Character* (New York: W. W. Norton and Company, 1985) 212–213.

and understanding, in this case, meant translating difficult concepts into more familiar language and applying these concepts to familiar objects. This professor finally led his students to engage in some critical thinking.

Critical thinking, as you can see by now, does not invite you to criticize or find fault. Instead, critical thinking, when used as a reading strategy, invites you to employ a variety of mental activities to acquire greater understanding and insight into the material you are reading. Here are some examples of critical thinking strategies that can engage you as you read.

Critical Thinking Strategies

1. Ask "why" at every opportunity.
2. Notice comparisons and contrasts described in the text and make some comparisons of your own.
3. Analyze the causes and effects described in the text and infer additional possible effects.
4. Notice the problems, locate the suggested solutions, and add possible solutions of your own.
5. Understand the current status of a topic that is in the process of change and anticipate or forecast future changes.
6. Think about the past status of the topic, and ask how the past may have influenced the present.
7. Apply new information to familiar situations to understand the implications of the ideas, as in the example of the science students that you just read.
8. Elaborate and add explanations and examples until you are able to understand a difficult concept more easily.
9. Associate something unfamiliar with something familiar to help you understand it better.
10. Agree and disagree with a controversial position to understand more than one perspective and to discover new perspectives.
11. Think about implications. Ask, What would happen if . . . , and think about future possibilities.
12. Make a final evaluation of the conclusion, decide whether you can or cannot accept it, and be able to say why.

Practice applying the critical thinking strategies.

The critical thinking strategies are only useful if you can apply them to a specific subject or idea that you want to think about.

Practice applying each one of these strategies to one of the subjects listed below. Make some notes on the ideas you generate:

1. Water shortages in the southwestern U. S.

2. Cutting back on fossil fuels.

3. The minimum wage.

4. Poverty in the U. S.

The critical thinking strategies you have just practiced could be applied to many subjects across the academic subject areas. You have already applied some of these strategies in answering the critical reading and thinking questions that accompany the readings in this book. You will probably never use all of the strategies while reading any one assignment. Some strategies will be more appropriate than others for thinking about particular topics. Make an effort to use some of them, however. When you do, your reading will become more meaningful because you will be thinking about the subject and relating new ideas to information you already possess.

What Is Problem Solving?

Problem solving, as the name implies, involves identifying problems and testing solutions to them until one solution is found that seems to work best. Problem solving encourages new insights and creative procedures. Here is one approach to problem solving that is similar to what you might encounter in some of your science classes.

A Problem Solving Process

1. Recognize and define the problem. Discover the problem by reading or by some other means.
2. Get additional information about the problem by reading some more, by discussing, and by observing.
3. Form a tentative solution to the problem.
4. Test the tentative solution to see if it works.
5. Decide what else you might need to do to make certain you have found a good solution.

Understand the problem solving process.

Here is an example of how this problem solving process works in real life. Each year *Discover* magazine, which publishes stories about contemporary science, presents awards to the individuals who have made especially striking scientific breakthroughs. The following describes a recent award for the discovery of an imaging system that detects the dangerous skin cancer, melanoma.

For the third year in a row, the Christopher Columbus Fellowship Foundation, an independent federal government agency established to encourage and support new discoveries, has given a $100,000 grant to one of the DISCOVER Awards entrants. The 1998 Columbus Scholar is Marek Elbaum, for his work in developing an imaging system for the early detection of melanoma.

As you read the following account of the scientists' work on this discovery, notice how the problem solving process guided them and helped them think:

Winner: Electro-Optical Sciences' Spectral Lesion Imaging System

SKIN DEEP

Innovator: Marek Elbaum

Melanoma killed more than 7,000 Americans last year, in part because the malignant lesions it causes look just like freckles or moles when they first appear. Almost all patients survive this form of skin cancer when it's diagnosed early, but dermatologists fail to catch it by visual inspection one time in three.

"We went to the oncologists and we asked, 'What is difficult for you?'" recalls Elbaum. "And they said, 'If you could help us discriminate early melanoma from benign pigmented lesions, this would be of great help.' And we said with great arrogance, 'Yes, we can do such things.'"

Elbaum and his colleagues at Electro-Optical Sciences in Irvington, New York, then wondered if malignant lesions might look different from benign ones when examined under different frequencies of light. And they found, in fact, that infrared light, which has a longer wavelength than visible light, can penetrate deeper into the skin, revealing the buried portion of a malignant lesion and making it stand out in computer images. So they built a probe that captured infrared and visible-light images. "Instead of providing one color image that the human eye acquires and then the brain analyzes, we are using ten images, each of which is obtained at a different wavelength," explains Elbaum. "What emerges is a completely different pattern from what physicians are accustomed to." A computer then analyzes the pattern to determine if it fits a preprogrammed set of parameters for melanoma.

Elbaum's device can diagnose a malignant growth in less than a minute. Since unveiling it in April 1997, he has tested several hundred patients. Preliminary results suggest that the device is more accurate than a doctor's visual inspection and produces fewer false positives. If so, it could eliminate hundreds of thousands of unnecessary biopsies and maybe even save a few lives. If all goes well, it will be on the market in two years.[2]

[2] "Skin Deep," *Discover* July 1998: 51.

What is the problem? _____

What led the scientists to identify the problem? _____

How did they get more information about the problem? _____

What did they discover that resulted in a possible solution to the problem?___

_____

How did the scientists test their solution to make certain it would work? ____

_____

Problem solving can be used in a variety of academic subject areas, but it is particularly associated with thinking and experimentation in science and engineering. The approach described here, however, can be useful in helping you think about solving any problem, whether it is scientific or not.

What Is Creative Thinking?

Critical thinking and problem solving can, on occasion, lead to **creative thinking,** the "Aha!" type of thinking that is associated with new discoveries, new insights, new combinations of ideas, and new conclusions. Two examples of twentieth-century creative thinkers may provide you with insight into creative thinking and help you define it for yourself.

Stephen Gary Wozniak, otherwise known as "Woz," is one of the most famous creative thinkers of the twentieth century. He is responsible for inventing the Apple II computer and for helping launch the personal computer industry. Here is how he describes the way he works: "The way I work requires so much concentration," Woz says. "Getting to know the problem well enough by thinking, thinking, thinking, thinking. And then you try every day to make it a little better, go through it again and again, cutting something off here or there."[3]

Here is a description of a creative thinker by another creative thinker. Marvin Minsky, who works with artificial intelligence, in discussing Richard Feynman, the physics professor you read about earlier in this chapter, describes Feynman as a thinker in this way:

When [Richard] Feynman faced a problem he was unusually good at going back to being like a child, ignoring what everyone else thinks, and saying, "Now, what have we got here?"

He was so "unstuck" and if something didn't work he would look at it in another way. He had so many different good ways. He would do something in ten minutes that might take the average physicist a year, so he

[3] Gary Wolf, "The World According to Woz," *Wired* September 1998: 184.

was . . . wonderfully productive. I attribute what they call "genius" to having a bunch of characteristics:

- Don't respond to peer pressure.
- Keep track of what the problem really is; less wishful thinking.
- Have a lot of ways of representing things. If one way doesn't work, switch quickly to another one.

The important thing is not to persist; I think the reason most people fail is that they are too determined to make something work only because they are attached to it. Talking to Feynman, whatever came up he would say, "Well, here's another way to look at it."
The least stuck person I have ever known.[4]

As you can see, Feynman had ways to get unstuck in his thinking when he had to. Everyone gets stuck from time to time. One of the best ways to get unstuck and be more creative is to do more reading and writing. Reading fills your mind with information that you can connect to material you already know. Reading helps you discover new relationships that no one else would ever see in quite the same way you do because others do not have the same prior knowledge you have. Recall that your prior knowledge helps you to learn and to think. Thus reading helps you understand and learn an author's ideas, but it also invites you to take off and create your own original ideas as a result of reading.

Writing helps you explain your ideas to yourself and to others so that you can understand them better. For instance, an original idea is suggested to you by something you have just read. The idea is half-formed in your mind at this point. You stop reading and write out the idea in some detail. This helps you figure out what you think. Now you can use this idea to help you think of other ideas, to write papers, to participate in class discussions, or to respond to exam questions that ask for your ideas. Reading and writing are a powerful combination for generating original and creative thinking.

Besides reading and writing, you also need to set aside some prime time to think in an environment that is free from distractions.

At what time of day do you do your best thinking? _____

Where do you do your best thinking? _____

You can learn to become a critical thinker, a problem solver, and a creative thinker while you are in college. These abilities are valued both by professors and employers. Thinking is also satisfying and fun. Thinking provides you with your own individual response to what you are learning. Thinking makes your education uniquely your own.

[4] Marvin Minsky, from *No Ordinary Genius: The Illustrated Richard Feynman*, ed. Christopher Sykes. Quoted in *Discover* October 1996: 102.

Thinking in the Academic Disciplines

Thinking varies somewhat from subject to subject, and it is useful to know some of the general questions professors in different courses ask in order to focus their thinking on their subjects. Also, textbook authors sometimes identify some of the big questions in their disciplines in the prefaces and introductions to their textbooks. Watch for the big questions and learn to ask them yourself to help you think about your college courses. Here are examples of questions you might expect to encounter in six college courses.[5]

1. **Historians ask *why* questions to understand the causes and effects of historical events.** For example, a historian might ask why the Vietnam War was so unpopular, or why the hippie counterculture appealed to so many young people in the 1960s. Historians also ask, "What evidence from the past provides the best answers about what really happened?" and "What do the answers from the past suggest about what may occur in the future?"

2. **Political scientists ask, "Who is benefited?" "Who is burdened?" and "Who governs?"** These questions provide insight into different types of governments. Political scientists, for example, might ask, "Who is benefited by capitalism, communism, socialism, or fascism?" They might also ask questions about who is burdened by these forms of government and who has the primary responsibility for governing for each of them.

3. **Psychologists ask, "What influenced this individual's behavior?"** Psychologists seek to understand why individual people behave as they do. A psychologist might ask, for example, "What is the most significant influence on human behavior: our genes, our parents, or our peers?"

4. **Sociologists ask, "What are social trends?"** As sociologists seek to understand different groups and cultures, they might ask, for example, about recent trends in education, work habits, or the use of leisure time, and compare them across several different societies.

5. **Scientists ask, "What am I observing?" and "What can I conclude from my observations?"** Scientists rely on inductive reasoning to reach conclusions. Inductive reasoning bases conclusions on a series of specific instances or examples. Thus the scientist who invented the new way to detect melanoma observed the results of his experiment with many individuals before he concluded that his new device would work.

6. **Mathematicians ask, "What is the whole, and what are its parts?"** This question is basic to most mathematical problems that involve slotting information (parts) into an equation (the whole) so that one can do the math and reach an answer. Mathematicians also need to ask how to work a problem to decide on the appropriate equation to use.

---

[5] These examples are drawn from conversations with professors and from the prefaces of college textbooks.

What are some of the big questions in your courses?

Think about the big questions your professors ask in your courses. Read the prefaces to your textbooks to gain further insights into the questions the experts ask in their disciplines. Then write the names of the courses you are taking at present, along with one or two big questions that are probably asked in each of them. The first one is started for you.

	Course	Big Questions
1.	Reading	How do we understand and describe reading?
		How can individuals improve their reading?
2.	_____	_____
		_____
3.	_____	_____
		_____
4.	_____	_____
		_____
5.	_____	_____
		_____

As you have read through the sample questions from the various disciplines, you may have noticed some similarities in the types of questions asked in different fields. Noting similarities and making connections between disciplines is an important type of thinking in college, and the next section will provide you with some ideas about how to make such connections.

Synthesize and Make Mental Connections

Synthesis involves drawing ideas and materials from a variety of sources and putting them together in ways that form new ideas. You synthesize when you draw information from several readings and then use these ideas, facts, and cases to write research papers. You also synthesize when you study for an exam. Besides drawing information from the textbook, you usually synthesize additional information from lectures, discussions, and other readings to prepare yourself to take an exam. You will practice synthesis when you do the collaborative exercises at the end of this chapter. You will synthesize information from several readings and write it on study sheets to prepare to take the practice exam that appears there.

Making **mental connections** is related to synthesis because it relates two or more sources and identifies what they have in common. Work to make mental connections among all of the sources of information in a particular class and also among all of the classes that you take. You can begin to try now. Notice how your history class can help you understand your literature class and how your math class can help you understand an engineering or computer class. Notice how the scientific method can help you think in your biology class and also how it can be useful in your sociology or psychology class. Synthesizing and making original mental connections are important ways you can personalize your education to make it uniquely your own.

Heighten Your Awareness of Reading, Learning, and Thinking with Metacognition

Most people would agree that we accomplish tasks more successfully if we are aware of how we accomplish them. A major purpose of this book has been to heighten your awareness of what goes on in your mind as you read, learn, and think so that you will be able to improve your abilities in these areas. Such heightened awareness is called metacognition. **Metacognition** is thinking about how we think. It involves becoming conscious of one's thought processes and then using these thought processes in systematic ways to think and learn. Well-developed metacognitive abilities lead to reading, learning, and thinking that is better directed, better controlled, and more productive.

In reading this book, you have learned to heighten your awareness of how you read, learn, and think in three critical areas. First, you have become more aware of your prior knowledge and how this knowledge helps you understand new material. Associating new material with previously learned material enables you to learn and think about the new material. Furthermore, when you lack prior knowledge for a reading assignment, the material will seem "hard" until you develop sufficient background to understand the assignment. The readings in this book are selected to help you develop your prior knowledge in a wide variety of academic subjects. They should provide you with background for many of the subjects you will read about in your other classes. Wide and varied reading will increase your prior knowledge in still other areas. The more you read, in fact, the better reader you will become.

A second area of awareness you have developed is an understanding of how authors use conventions in their writing. In other words, you have learned more about what you can expect on the printed page. You can now focus on important parts of a book or chapter, such as the title, the introduction, the conclusion, the headings and subheadings, the examples, transitions, topic sentences, organizational patterns, and visual materials, and use them to help you read. Noticing these special features helps you find and organize the important ideas so that you can understand, remember, and think further about them.

Finally, you are now aware of many special active reading and thinking strategies that will help you understand, analyze, synthesize, evaluate, and think about the material that you read. These strategies are designated "active" strategies because you have to *do* something to use them. They call on you to think; to read and think; to speak and think; and to read, think, and write. In other words, all require active thought. Use the metacognitive abilities you have developed in all three of these areas to direct your reading, learning, and thinking.

USING READING TO HELP YOU THINK: FIVE STRATEGIES

The five strategies that follow provide specific suggestions and questions to help you think. The questions are deliberately left "open" to invite you to explore your own ideas and come up with your own answers. The final strategy combines reading, thinking, and writing and can be used to develop ideas that are inspired by your reading.

Strategy 1: Set a thinking goal and brainstorm to access your prior knowledge.

This may seem obvious, but if you are to think effectively, you must know exactly what you are thinking about. You may want to think about an idea inspired by reading, by discussion, or by a topic or problem assigned by the professor. Write the topic down: My goal is to think about . . . Focus on the topic and make certain that you understand it. Rewrite the topic in simpler language, if necessary.

The readings that follow (see p. 425) are all on the subject of the environment. You are invited to apply the strategies detailed in this chapter to the general topic of environmental protection as you read and mentally try out the next few thinking strategies. Thinking about this topic will also serve as a good prereading activity for the environmental readings at the end of the chapter, when you get to them.

Use your prior knowledge to help you begin to think about a topic. One very good way to access your prior knowledge of a topic is to brainstorm. Try brainstorming this aspect of the environmental protection topic: *ways to protect the natural environment.*

The Rules for Brainstorming

1. Set a time limit, say, 5 to 10 minutes.

2. Write the topic, and then quickly write every related idea that comes to mind. Work for quantity not quality.

3. Some ideas may seem better than others as you write, but write them all down. Do not stop to evaluate or elaborate on the ideas. Just write a phrase or two to capture each idea and keep going.

4. When the time is up, go back and read what you have written to see what you can use. Circle the best ideas.

You now have a good start. Ask the questions in Strategies 2, 3, and 4 to add additional thoughts and ideas about your topic.

▶

Strategy 2: Ask critical thinking questions.

The following questions can be used to help you think about new ideas that particularly strike you as you read, or they can be used to help you think about a specific topic that you have already identified and brainstormed. Try asking these questions about the topic you just brainstormed: *ways to protect the natural environment.*

Critical Thinking Questions

1. How can I describe or define the topic? Why should I be interested in this topic?

2. What is this topic similar to? What is it different from? What can I associate with this topic to help me understand it better?

3. What causes and effects are associated with this topic?

4. Are problems and solutions associated with this topic? What are some possible solutions?

5. What might happen to this topic in the future?

6. How has the past contributed to current ideas about this topic?

7. Can I apply any information about this topic to other situations to help me understand the topic better?

8. How can I elaborate on this topic with my own explanations and examples to help me understand it better?

9. Can I associate this topic with something more familiar to help me understand it better?

10. What are the different perspectives on the topic? Which do I agree with and with which do I disagree?

11. What are the future possibilities and implications for this topic? What would happen if . . . ?

12. What is my conclusion about this topic? What are my reasons for reaching this conclusion?

Write out the answers to these questions, and you will be pleasantly surprised at the amount of thinking they generate. Use these questions to help you generate thoughts for any assignment that requires critical thinking.

▶

Strategy 3: Ask problem solving questions.

Strategy 2, question 4 asks that you decide whether the topic you have chosen to think about represents a problem. If your answer to that question is yes, use the following questions to help you think further about the problem and its solutions. Try asking these questions about this problem: *protecting the environment is not important to many people in the world.*

Problem Solving Questions

1. What is the problem?

2. What causes the problem?

3. What are the significant effects of the problem?

4. What do I need to do or read to find out more about the problem?

5. What is a tentative solution to the problem?

6. How can I test this solution to see if it will work?

7. What else do I need to do to make certain I have a workable solution?

8. What can I finally conclude about the problem and the solution?

Strategy 4: Ask creative thinking questions.

The following questions can be used to stimulate creative and original thought about a topic. Usually, you will use only a few of these questions each time you read. Look for the "hot spots" on the list, the questions that will generate the most creative thinking for you. Practice asking these questions about this topic: *How can more people be persuaded to protect the natural environment?*

Creative Thinking Questions

1. What is my starting point for thinking? What strikes me? What interests me? Why?

2. How can I think about this topic in a new and original way?

3. What new ideas and answers are occurring to me as I think (or read)?

4. What connections can I make with other ideas or other related topics that I know about?

5. What parts can I divide this topic into? How should I think about each part separately? What could I learn from that?

6. What is this topic a part of? Can I synthesize this topic with other related material to form a new and larger idea or set of ideas? What could I learn from that?

▶

7. What is my best insight?

8. What is the value, excellence, or potential use of my insight?

9. How do I feel about this topic?

10. Do I have closure on this topic, or should I continue to think about it? How?

Strategy 5: Read and freewrite to start your thinking.

Brainstorming can help you think before you begin to read. Freewriting after you have read can help you think when you have finished reading.

The Rules for Freewriting

1. As soon as you finish reading, start writing about whatever comes to your mind as a result of your reading.

2. Continue to write without stopping for 10 or 15 minutes. Write quickly to catch the flow of your thoughts. Do not worry about incomplete sentences, misspellings, or punctuation. Write in phrases at times. Leave blank spaces if you cannot think of a word. Just get down the ideas and keep going.

3. If you find you do not have very much to write, do some more reading and try again.

4. Read what you have written and circle or underline the best ideas. Use some of the questions in Strategies 2, 3, and 4 to help you think about and develop one or more of these ideas. Write out your answers.

EXERCISES AND READINGS

THREE COLLABORATIVE CLASS EXERCISES

Prepare for the collaborative class exercises that follow by reading the three short essays and the excerpt from a sociology textbook that begin on page 426 These are the only readings included in this chapter, and all of them are about the environment. Survey each reading first. As you begin to read, underline and make some marginal annotations. Notice that marginal annotations are already provided for the first essay that begins on page 426. Use these as an example to get you started underlining and annotating the others. Also write out original ideas that occur to you, either in the margins or on separate pieces of paper. Next, work through the following exercises that will help you prepare for and take the exam that appears at the end of this chapter.

Exercise 1

Make a group study sheet. *Small groups.*

This activity will prepare you for questions on the exam that will demonstrate that you have *learned* the material you have read.

Form groups of four students. Work as a group to synthesize factual information on a study sheet. You will draw this information from the four selections you have just read. Use the example of the study sheet on page 241 as a model. Select a scribe who will write for all members of the group. Start with the article by environmentalist Alan Thien Durning and write in brief form the information you think you will need to learn from this chapter. Use the headings and subheadings to guide you. Then add information to the study sheet from the historical essay about the forests by naturalist John Muir, from the brief statement about the land by Native-American N. Scott Momaday, and from the excerpt from a textbook chapter about the water and air by John Macionis. Include specialized vocabulary that is unfamiliar to you.

Exercise 2

Add ideas to your study sheet that are generated by critical thinking and creative thinking questions. *Small groups.*

These activities will prepare you for questions that require you to demonstrate that you have *thought* about the material you have read.

a.   Each member of your group should select a topic on the study sheet that is of particular interest to that individual. Write these four topics on separate sheets of paper. Then each group member answers in writing two or three of the critical thinking questions about the selected topic (see p. 421). Finally, members share their critical thinking answers with other members of the group and add the best ideas to the group study sheet.

b.   Next, each member of your group selects one of the four reading selections at the end of the chapter by authors Durning, Muir, Momaday, and Macionis, and then takes 5 minutes to survey and review it. Each member freewrites for five minutes on the ideas generated by the reading selection. Group members next read their freewrites to the group, select the best ideas from them, and add their ideas to the group study sheet.

Exercise 3

Prepare for and take the exam on pages 436–437. Evaluate your answers.

a.   Prepare for the exam by quizzing one another on the information on the study sheet your group has made. When each of you can repeat most of this information to other members of the group, turn to the exam.

b.   Read the general directions for the exam and glance through the rest of it to see what you will be required to do. Read, underline, and number the main parts of the essay questions. Write a brief outline for answers to each of them.

c. Write the answers for the exam on a separate piece of paper. Answer both the objective questions and the essay questions. Begin each essay answer with a clear introductory sentence that comes right to the point, develop your answer in paragraphs, include plenty of detail, include evidence of critical and creative thinking, and end with a concluding sentence. Proofread and insert corrections.

d. Evaluate your answers. Trade your exam with another member of your group. Check the objective answers against the answer key that appears at the back of the book on page 508. Check the essay answers against the scoring guide, just as you did at the end of Chapter 7. Assign points for the parts that are correct, compute the score, and return the exam to the student who wrote it. A perfect score is 100. If you did not receive 100, figure out why. Use the self-assessment instrument in Figure 7-7 on page 246 to help you evaluate your exam. Notice particularly whether or not each of you responded to the parts of questions that asked you to present your own ideas. Discuss your observations about how each of you did in your group and report out to the class about how well your group did and how it can improve.

FOUR READING EXERCISES:
ABOUT LOOKING AFTER THE ENVIRONMENT

The following four readings include a contemporary essay written by Alan Durning about some simple ways individuals can protect the environment, first published in the *Utne Reader* in 1994; a selection from an essay written by naturalist John Muir, first published in *The Atlantic Monthly* in 1901; a short essay entitled "The Land," written by Native American N. Scott Momaday and originally published in 1970; and a section about water and air by John Macionis from his sociology textbook published in 2007. All four selections present arguments for the importance of caring for and preserving the natural environment. Follow the instructions on pages 424–425 for reading these essays and preparing study sheets that reflect your study reading, critical reading, and critical thinking. Then take the exam, which begins on page 436, and follow the instructions for scoring it.

The Seven Sustainable Wonders of the World[6]

ALAN THEIN DURNING

Durning, a past senior researcher at Worldwatch Institute, is now the director of Sightline Institute (formerly Northwest Environment Watch) in Seattle. He writes about consumerism and the environment. He wrote this piece for the Utne Reader *magazine. As you read through this article, try to think of other environmentally friendly objects that we use every day.*

I've never seen any of the Seven Wonders of the World, and to tell you the truth I wouldn't really want to. To me, the real wonders are all the little things— little things that work, especially when they do it without hurting the earth. Here's my list of simple things that, though we take them for granted, are absolute wonders. These implements solve every-day problems so elegantly that everyone in the world today—and everyone who is likely to live in it in the next century—could make use of them without Mother Nature's being any the worse for wear.

The author believes that the real wonders of the world are simple inventions that solve problems in environmentally-friendly ways.

1. The Bicycle

The most thermodynamically efficient transportation device ever created and the most widely used private vehicle in the world, the bicycle lets you travel three times as far on a plateful of calories as you could walking. And they're 53 times more energy efficient—comparing food calories with gasoline calories—than the typical car. Not to mention the fact that they don't pollute the air, lead to oil spills (and oil wars), change the climate, send cities sprawling over the countryside, lock up half of urban space in roads and parking lots, or kill a quarter million people in traffic accidents each year.

Bicycles are an energy efficient, clean form of transportation.

The world doesn't yet have enough bikes for everybody to ride, but it's getting there quickly: Best estimates put the world's expanding fleet of two-wheelers at 850 million—double the number of autos. We Americans have no excuses on this count: We have more bikes per person than China, where they are the principal vehicle. We just don't ride them much.

There are plenty of bicycles— unfortunately we don't use them much in the U.S.

2. The Ceiling Fan

Appropriate technology's answer to air conditioning, ceiling fans cool tens of millions of people in Asia and Africa. A fan over your bed brings relief in sweltering climes, as I've had plenty of time to reflect on during episodes of digestive turmoil in cheap tropical hotels.

Ceiling fans provide relief from the heat and are an environmentally-friendly alternative to air conditioning.

Air conditioning, found in two-thirds of U.S. homes, is a juice hog and the bane of the stratospheric ozone layer because of its CFC coolants. Ceiling fans, on the other hand, are simple, durable, and repairable and take little energy to run.

3. The Clothesline

A few years ago, I read about an engineering laboratory that claimed it had all but perfected a microwave clothes dryer. The dryer, the story went, would get the

[6] Alan Thein Durning, "The Seven Sustainable Wonders of the World," *Utne Reader* (March/April 1994) 96–97.

moisture out of the wash with one-third the energy of a conventional unit and cause less wear and tear on the fabric.

I don't know if they ever got it on the market, but it struck me at the time that if simple wonders had a PR agent, there might have been a news story instead about the perfection of a solar clothes dryer. It takes few materials to manufacture, is safe for kids, requires absolutely no electricity or fuel, and even gets people outdoors where they can talk to their neighbors.

7 Drying clothes in the sun is simple, clean and gets you outside in the fresh air.

4. The Telephone

The greatest innovation in human communications since Gutenberg's printing press, telephone systems are the only entry on my wonders list invented in this century, and—hype of the information age not withstanding—I'll wager that they never lose ground to other communications technologies. Unlike fax machines, personal computers and computer networks, televisions, VCRs and camcorders, CD-ROM, and all the other flotsam and jetsam of the information age, telephones are a simple extension of the most time-tested means of human communication: speech.

8 The telephone is a simple technology that helps us talk to one another. It's likely to be with us a long time.

5. The Public Library

Public libraries are the most democratic institutions yet invented. Think of it! Equal access to information for any citizen who comes inside. A lifetime of learning, all free. Libraries foster community, too, by bringing people of different classes, races, and ages together in that endangered form of human habitat: noncommercial public space.

9 Libraries are free and accessible to everyone.

Although conceived without any ecological intention whatsoever, libraries are waste reduction at its best. Each library saves a forestful of trees by making thousands of personal copies of books and periodicals unnecessary. All that paper savings means huge reductions in energy use and water and air pollution, too. In principle, the library concept could be applied to other things—cameras and camcorders, tapes and CDs, cleaning equipment and extra dining chairs—further reducing the number of things our society needs without reducing people's access to them. The town of Takoma Park, Maryland, for example, has a tool library where people can check out a lawn mower, a ratchet set, or a sledgehammer.

10 Sharing books (and other items) through libraries conserves precious resources.

6. The Interdepartmental Envelope

I don't know what they're really called: those old-fashioned slotted manila envelopes bound with a string and covered with lines for routing papers to one person after another. Whatever they're called, they put modern recycling to shame.

11 A great example of recycling.

7. The Condom

It's a remarkable little device: highly effective, inexpensive, and portable. A few purist Greens might complain about disposability and excess packaging, but these objections are trivial considering the work the condom has to do—battling the scourge of AIDS and stabilizing the human population at a level the earth can comfortably support.

12 A simple device that can prevent disease and slow population growth.

830 words

The American Forests[7]

JOHN MUIR

In 1892 John Muir founded the Sierra Club, a group that devotes itself to the study and protection of the Earth's scenic and ecological resources. Muir also worked with President Theodore Roosevelt to establish several national parks in the late 19th and early 20th centuries. This is an excerpt from an article published by Muir in The Atlantic Monthly *in 1901.*

Notwithstanding all the waste and use which have been going on unchecked like a storm for more than two centuries, it is not yet too late—though it is high time—for the government to begin a rational administration of its forests. About seventy million acres it still owns—enough for all the country, if wisely used. These residual forests are generally on mountain slopes, just where they are doing the most good, and where their removal would be followed by the greatest number of evils; the lands they cover are too rocky and high for agriculture, and can never be made as valuable for any other crop as for the present crop of trees. It has been shown over and over again that if these mountains were to be stripped of their trees and underbrush, and kept bare and sodless by hordes of sheep and the innumerable fires the shepherds set, besides those of the millmen, prospectors, shakemakers, and all sorts of adventurers, both lowlands and mountains would speedily become little better than deserts, compared with their present beneficent fertility. During heavy rainfalls and while the winter accumulations of snow were melting, the larger streams would swell into destructive torrents, cutting deep, rugged-edged gullies, carrying away the fertile humus and soil as well as sand and rocks, filling up and overflowing their lower channels, and covering the lowland fields with raw detritus. Drought and barrenness would follow.

In their natural condition, or under wise management, keeping out destructive sheep, preventing fires, selecting the trees that should be cut for lumber, and preserving the young ones and the shrubs and sod of herbaceous vegetation, these forests would be a never failing fountain of wealth and beauty. The cool shades of the forest give rise to moist beds and currents of air, and the sod of grasses and the various flowering plants and shrubs thus fostered, together with the network and sponge of tree roots, absorb and hold back the rain and the waters from melting snow, compelling them to ooze and percolate and flow gently through the soil in streams that never dry. All the pine needles and rootlets and blades of grass, and the fallen, decaying trunks of trees, are dams, storing the bounty of the clouds and dispensing it in perennial life-giving streams, instead of allowing it to gather suddenly and rush headlong in short-lived devastating floods. Everybody on the dry side of the continent is beginning to find this out, and, in view of the waste going on, is growing more and more anxious for government protection. The outcries we hear against forest reservations come mostly from thieves who are wealthy and steal timber by wholesale. [. . .]

[7] John Muir, "The American Forests," *The Atlantic Monthly* (1901), rpt. in John Muir, *Our National Parks* (San Francisco: Sierra Club Books, 1991).

Emerson says that things refuse to be mismanaged long. An exception would seem to be found in the case of our forests, which have been mismanaged rather long, and now come desperately near being like smashed eggs and spilt milk. Still, in the long run the world does not move backward. The wonderful advance made in the last few years, in creating four national parks in the West, and thirty forest reservations, embracing nearly forty million acres; and in the planting of the borders of streets and highways and spacious parks in all the great cities, to satisfy the natural taste and hunger for landscape beauty and righteousness that God has put, in some measure, into every human being and animal, shows the trend of awakening public opinion. The making of the far-famed New York Central Park was opposed by even good men, with misguided pluck, perseverance, and ingenuity; but straight right won its way, and now that park is appreciated. So we confidently believe it will be with our great national parks and forest reservations. There will be a period of indifference on the part of the rich, sleepy with wealth, and of the toiling millions, sleepy with poverty, most of whom never saw a forest; a period of screaming protest and objection from the plunderers, who are as unconscionable and enterprising as Satan. But light is surely coming, and the friends of destruction will preach and bewail in vain.

The United States government has always been proud of the welcome it has extended to good men of every nation, seeking freedom and homes and bread. Let them be welcomed still as Nature welcomes them, to the woods as well as to the prairies and plains. No place is too good for good men, and still there is room. They are invited to heaven, and may well be allowed in America. Every place is made better by them. Let them be as free to pick gold and gems from the hills, to cut and hew, dig and plant, for homes and bread, as the birds are to pick berries from the wild bushes, and moss and leaves for nests. The ground will be glad to feed them, and the pines will come down from the mountains for their homes as willingly as the cedars came from Lebanon for Solomon's temple. Nor will the woods be the worse for this use, or their benign influences be diminished any more than the sun is diminished by shining. Mere destroyers, however, tree-killers, wool and mutton men, spreading death and confusion in the fairest groves and gardens ever planted—let the government hasten to cast them out and make an end of them. For it must be told again and again, and be burningly borne in mind, that just now, while protective measures are being deliberated languidly, destruction and use are speeding on faster and farther every day. The axe and saw are insanely busy, chips are flying thick as snowflakes, and every summer thousands of acres of priceless forests, with their underbrush, soil, springs, climate, scenery, and religion, are vanishing away in clouds of smoke, while, except in the national parks, not one forest guard is employed.

All sorts of local laws and regulations have been tried and found wanting, and the costly lessons of our own experience, as well as that of every civilized nation, show conclusively that the fate of the remnant of our forests is in the hands of the federal government, and that if the remnant is to be saved at all, it must be saved quickly.

Any fool can destroy trees. They cannot run away; and if they could, they would still be destroyed—chased and hunted down as long as fun or a dollar could be got out of their bark hides, branching horns, or magnificent bole backbones.

Few that fell trees plant them; nor would planting avail much towards getting back anything like the noble primeval forests. During a man's life only saplings can be grown, in the place of the old trees—tens of centuries old—that have been destroyed. It took more than three thousand years to make some of the trees in these Western woods—trees that are still standing in perfect strength and beauty, waving and singing in the mighty forests of the Sierra. Through all the wonderful, eventful centuries since Christ's time—and long before that—God has cared for these trees, saved them from drought, disease, avalanches, and a thousand straining, leveling tempests and floods; but he cannot save them from fools—only Uncle Sam can do that.

1300 words

The Land[8]

N. SCOTT MOMADAY

N. Scott Momaday is a Native-American author who is best known for his book The Way to Rainy Mountain. *He originally contributed the passage reproduced here to a handbook for environmental activists published by the Sierra Club.*

I am interested in the way that a man looks at a given landscape and takes possession of it in his blood and brain. For this happens, I am certain, in the ordinary motion of life. None of us lives apart from the land entirely; such an isolation is unimaginable. We have sooner or later to come to terms with the world around us—and I mean especially the physical world, not only as it is revealed to us immediately through our senses, but also as it is perceived more truly in the long turn of seasons and of years. And we must come to moral terms. There is no alternative, I believe, if we are to realize and maintain our humanity, for our humanity must consist in part in the ethical as well as the practical ideal of preservation. And particularly here and now is that true. We Americans need now more than ever before—and indeed more than we know—to imagine who and what we are with respect to the earth and sky. I am talking about an act of the imagination essentially, and the concept of an American land ethic.

It is no doubt more difficult to imagine in 1970 the landscape of America than it was in, say, 1900. Our whole experience as a nation in this century has been a repudiation of the pastoral ideal which informs so much of the art and literature of the nineteenth century. One effect of the Technological Revolution has been to uproot us from the soil. We have become disoriented, I believe; we have suffered a kind of psychic dislocation of ourselves in time and space. We may be perfectly sure of where we are in relation to the supermarket and the next coffee break, but

[8] N. Scott Momaday, "The Land," in *Ecostatics: The Sierra Club Handbook for Environmental Activists*, ed. John G. Mitchell with Constance L. Stallings (New York: Simon and Schuster, 1970) 102–104.

I doubt that any of us knows where he is in relation to the stars and to the solstices. Our sense of the natural order has become dull and unreliable. Like the wilderness itself, our sphere of instinct has diminished in proportion as we have failed to imagine truly what it is. And yet I believe that it is possible to formulate an ethical idea of the land—a notion of what it is and must be in our daily lives—and I believe moreover that it is absolutely necessary to do so.

It would seem on the surface of things that a land ethic is something that is 3 alien to, or at least dormant in, most Americans. Most of us in general have developed an attitude of indifference toward the land. In terms of my own experience, it is difficult to see how such an attitude could ever have come about.

420 words

Water and Air[9]

JOHN J. MACIONIS

The following selection is part of a chapter entitled "Population, Urbanization, and Environment" in a sociology textbook by John Macionis. It provides information about the world water supply and problems with water pollution as well as information about air pollution and its effect on global warming. The two visuals in this selection are good examples of visual argument.

Oceans, lakes, and streams are the lifeblood of the global ecosystem. Humans 1 depend on water for drinking, bathing, cooking, recreation, and a host of other activities.

According to what scientists call the *hydrologic cycle,* Earth naturally recy- 2 cles water and refreshes the land. The process begins as heat from the sun causes Earth's water, 97 percent of which is in the oceans, to evaporate and form clouds. Because water evaporates at lower temperatures than most pollutants, the water vapor that rises from the seas is relatively pure, leaving various contaminants behind. Water then falls to Earth as rain, which drains into streams and rivers and finally returns to the sea. Two major concerns about water, then, are supply and pollution.

Water Supply

Only about 1 percent of Earth's water is suitable for drinking. It is not sur- 3 prising, then, that for thousands of years, water rights have figured prominently in laws around the world. Today, some regions of the world, especially the tropics, enjoy plentiful fresh water, using a small share of the available supply. However, high demand, coupled with modest reserves, makes water supply a matter of concern in much of North America and Asia, where people look to rivers rather than rainfall for their water. In China, deep aquifers are dropping rapidly. In the Middle East, water supply is reaching a critical level. Iran is rationing water in its

[9] John J. Macionis, *Sociology,* 11th ed. (Upper Saddle River: Prentice Hall, 2007) 600–604.

capital city. In Egypt, the Nile River provides just one-sixth as much water per person as it did in 1900. Across northern Africa and the Middle East, as many as 1 billion people may lack the water they need for irrigation and drinking by 2025.[10]

Rising population and the development of more complex technology have greatly increased the world's appetite for water. The global consumption of water (now estimated at 4 billion cubic feet per year) has tripled since 1950 and is rising steadily. As a result, even in those parts of the world that receive plenty of rainfall, people are using groundwater faster than it can be replenished naturally. In the Tamil Nadu region of southern India, for example, so much groundwater is being used that the water table has fallen 100 feet over the last several decades. Mexico City—which has sprawled to some 1,400 square miles—has pumped so much water from its underground aquifer that the city has sunk 30 feet during the past century and continues to drop about 2 inches per year. Farther north in the United States, the Ogallala aquifer, which lies below seven states from South Dakota to Texas, is now dropping by about 18 inches a year, raising fears that it will run dry within several decades.

In light of such developments, we must face the reality that water is a valuable, finite resource. Greater conservation of water by individuals (the average person consumes 10 million gallons in a lifetime) is part of the answer. However, households around the world account for just 10 percent of water use. It is even more crucial that we curb water consumption by industry, which uses 20 percent of the global total, and farming, which consumes 70 percent of the total for irrigation.

Perhaps new irrigation technology will reduce the future demand for water. But here again, we see how population increase, as well as economic growth, strains our ecosystem.[11]

Water Pollution

In large cities from Mexico City to Cairo to Shanghai, many people have no choice but to drink contaminated water. Infectious diseases like typhoid, cholera, and dysentery, all caused by waterborne microorganisms, spread rapidly through these populations. Besides ensuring ample *supplies* of water, then, we must protect the *quality* of water.

Water quality in the United States is generally good by global standards. However, even here the problem of water pollution is steadily growing. According to the Sierra Club, an environmental activist organization, rivers and streams across the United States absorb some 500 million pounds of toxic waste each year. This pollution results not just from intentional dumping but also from the runoff of agricultural fertilizers and lawn chemicals.

A special problem is *acid rain*—rain made acidic by air pollution—which destroys plant and animal life. Acid rain (or snow) begins with power plants burning

[10] Sandra Postel. "Facing Water Scarcity." In Lester R. Brown et al., eds., *State of the World, 1993: A Worldwatch Institute Report on Progress toward a Sustainable Society,* New York: Norton, 1993:22–41, and "China Faces Water Shortage," *Popline* (December 2001):1–4.

[11] Sandra Postel, "Facing Water Scarcity" and Population Action International. *People in the Balance: Population and Resources at the Turn of the Millennium.* Washington, D.C.: Population Action International, 2000.

Water is vital to life, and it is also in short supply. The state of Gujarat, in western India, has experienced a decade-long drought. In the village of Natwarghad, people crowd together, lowering pots into the local well, taking what little water is left.

fossil fuels (oil and coal) to generate electricity; this burning releases sulfuric and nitrous oxides into the air. As the wind sweeps these gases into the atmosphere, they react with the air to form sulfuric and nitric acids, which turns atmospheric moisture acidic.

This is a clear case of one type of pollution causing another: Air pollution (from smokestacks) ends up contaminating water (in lakes and streams that collect acid rain). Acid rain is truly a global phenomenon because the regions that suffer the harmful effects may be thousands of miles from the original pollution. For instance, British power plants have caused acid rain that has devastated forests and fish in Norway and Sweden, up to 1,000 miles to the northeast. In the United States, we see a similar pattern as midwestern smokestacks have harmed the natural environment of upstate New York and New England.   10

Air Pollution

Because we are surrounded by air, most people in the United States are more aware of air pollution than contaminated water. One of the unexpected consequences of industrial technology, especially the factory and the motor vehicle, has been a decline in air quality. In London in the mid-twentieth century, factory smokestacks, automobiles, and coal fires used to heat homes all added to what was probably the worst urban air quality of the last century. What some British jokingly called "pea soup" was in reality a deadly mix of pollution: Over five days in 1952, an especially thick haze that hung over London killed 4,000 people.   11

Air quality improved in the final decades of the twentieth century. Rich nations passed laws that banned high-pollution heating, including the coal fires that   12 choked London fifty years ago. In addition, scientists devised ways to make factories as well as automobiles and trucks operate more cleanly.

If high-income countries can breathe a bit more easily than they once did, the problem of air pollution in poor societies is becoming more serious. One reason is that people in low-income countries still rely on wood, coal, peat, and other "dirty" fuels for cooking fires and to heat their homes. In addition, nations eager to encourage short-term industrial development may pay little attention to the longer-term dangers of air pollution. As a result, many cities in Latin America, Eastern Europe, and Asia are plagued by air pollution as bad as London's pea soup fifty years ago.

The Rain Forests

Rain forests are *regions of dense forestation, most of which circle the globe close to the equator.* The largest tropical rain forests are in South America (notably Brazil), west-central Africa, and Southeast Asia. In all, the world's rain forests cover some 2 billion acres, or 7 percent of Earth's total land surface.

Like other global resources, rain forests are falling victim to the needs and appetites of the surging world population. As noted earlier, to meet the demand for beef, ranchers in Latin America burn forested areas to increase their supply of grazing land. We are also losing rain forests to the hardwood trade. People in rich nations pay high prices for mahogany and other woods because, as the environmentalist Norman Myers puts it, they have "a penchant for parquet floors, fine furniture, fancy paneling, weekend yachts, and high-grade coffins."[12] Under such economic pressure, the world's rain forests are now just half their original size, and they continue to shrink by about 1 percent (65,000 square miles) annually, which amounts to about an acre every second. Unless we stop this loss, the rain forests will vanish before the end of this century, and with them will go protection for Earth's biodiversity and climate.

Global Warming

Why are rain forests so important? One reason is that they cleanse the atmosphere of carbon dioxide (CO_2). Since the beginning of the Industrial Revolution, the amount of carbon dioxide produced by humans, mostly from factories and automobiles, has risen sharply. Much of this carbon dioxide is absorbed by the oceans. But plants also take in carbon dioxide and expel oxygen. This is why rain forests are vital to maintaining the chemical balance of the atmosphere.

The problem is that production of carbon dioxide is rising while the amount of plant life on Earth is shrinking. To make matters worse, rain forests are being destroyed mostly by burning, which releases even more carbon dioxide into the atmosphere. Experts estimate that the atmospheric concentration of carbon dioxide is now 20 to 30 percent higher than it was 150 years ago.[13]

---

[12] Norman Myers. "The Mega-Extinction of Animals and Plants." In Sir Edmund Hillary, ed., *Ecology 2000: The Changing Face of the Earth.* New York: Beaufort Books, 1984b:88.

[13] Andrew C. Revkin. "Can Global Warming Be Studied Too Much?" *New York Times* (December 3, 2002):D1, D4.

Members of small, simple societies, such as the Tan't Batu in the Philippines, live in harmony with nature; they do not have the technological means to greatly affect the natural world. Although we in complex societies like to think of ourselves as superior to such people, the truth is that there is much we can—and must—learn from them.

High above Earth, carbon dioxide acts like the glass roof of a greenhouse, letting heat from the sun pass through to the surface while preventing much of it from radiating away from the planet. The result of this *greenhouse effect,* say ecologists, is **global warming,** *a rise in Earth's average temperature due to an increasing concentration of carbon dioxide in the atmosphere.* Over the past century, the global temperature has risen about 1 degree Fahrenheit (to an average of 58° F). Scientists warn that it could rise by 5° F to 10° F during this century, which would melt vast areas of the polar ice caps and raise the sea level to cover low-lying land around the world. Were this to happen, water would cover all of Bangladesh, for example, and much of the coastal United States, including Washington, D.C., right up to the steps of the White House. On the other hand, the U.S. Midwest, currently one of the most productive agricultural regions in the world, probably would become arid. 18

Not all scientists share this vision of future global warming. Some point out that global temperature changes have been taking place throughout history, apparently with little or nothing to do with rain forests. Higher concentrations of carbon dioxide in the atmosphere might speed up plant growth (since plants thrive on this gas), and this increase would correct the imbalance and push Earth's temperature downward once again. But a consensus is building that global warming is a problem that threatens the future of all of us.[14] 19

[14] Kim A. McDonald. "Debate over How to Gauge Global Warming Heats Up Meeting of Climatologists." *Chronicle of Higher Education.* Vol. 45, No. 2 (February 5, 1999):A17. and Richard A. Kerr. "Climate Models Heat Up." *Science Now* (January 26, 2005):1–3.

EXAM ON ENVIRONMENTAL SELECTIONS

Objective Portion 40%   15 minutes

Matching

Choose the appropriate answer from the following list and write the corresponding letter in the blank.

1. _____   How earth naturally recycles water through evaporation and rain   A. governmental administration

2. _____   John Muir's solution to deforestation.   B. hydrologic cycle

3. _____   A gas produced by industry and automobiles that causes the green house effect.   C. John Muir

4. _____   Who said, "Any fool can destroy trees."   D. N. Scott Momaday

5. _____   Who said, "None of us lives apart from the land entirely; such an isolation is unimaginable.   E. carbon dioxide

True/False

Determine if the following statements are true or false and put a T or an F in the blank.

6. _____   Ninety-seven percent of the water in the world is in the oceans.

7. _____   Households around the world account for 70% of water use.

8. _____   John Muir believed that if residual forests on mountain slopes were cut down, the lowlands and slopes would become little better than deserts in terms of fertility.

Fill in the blank

Fill in the missing word or words.

9. _____   are regions of dense forestation, most of which circle the globe close to the equator.

10. Alan Durning's example of waste reduction at its best, because it saves a forest full of trees, even though it was not designed with any ecological intention, is

_____.

▶

Multiple choice

Read the following statements and determine which answer is correct. Write the letter in the blank.

11. _____ Major environmental concerns about water include:

    A. acid rain   B. population growth   C. drought
    D. all of the above

12. _____ John Muir finds that the loss of forests is due to:

    A. bulldozing   B. flooding   C. fires set by shepherds
    D. Christmas tree business

13. _____ Durning's list of world wonders includes:

    A. insect repellent   B. the Internet   C. interoffice envelopes
    D. fireplaces

14. _____ Which of the following consumes 70 percent of the total water supply in the world?

    A. households   B. industry   C. agricultural irrigation
    D. water parks

15. _____ Which is commonly given as the most important reason for protecting the rain forests?

    A. they absorb carbon dioxide from the air
    B. They provide wood for fuel
    C. They provide wood for building
    D. They are beautiful

Essay Portion 60%   30 minutes

Question 1: 30 points

What is global warming? What causes it? What do some scientists believe will result if no efforts are made to slow or stop global warming? How might it affect you? Use your problem solving skills and discuss what can be done to stop or reverse the effects of global warming.

Question 2: 30 points

List Alan Durning's seven "little things that work . . . without hurting the earth." Add short descriptions that show how each of these work to protect the environment. Expand on this list by adding two additional items that you use on a regular basis that protect the environment. Explain their environmental benefits. Then identify two additional items you use regularly that are potentially or actually harmful to the environment. Explain why they are harmful.

THREE APPLICATION EXERCISES

Exercise 1

Identify one topic for critical thinking in one of your other classes and bring a critical thinking question about this topic.

Refer to the critical thinking questions on page 421 and identify those questions that would help you think about this topic.

Exercise 2

Clip an editorial or a letter to the editor in a newspaper or magazine, read it, and freewrite in response to it for five minutes.

Bring the clipping and your freewrite to class. Volunteers may want to read a few of these. Discuss the types of thinking generated by this activity.

Exercise 3

Write a critical thinking test question on one or more of the four articles about the environment.

Bring your question to class to trade with a classmate. Practice answering these questions and report on your experiences to the class.

REVIEW AND EVALUATE THE STRATEGIES

The following is a review of the five strategies you learned in this chapter:

1. Set a thinking goal and brainstorm to access your prior knowledge.
2. Ask critical thinking questions.
3. Ask problem solving questions.
4. Ask creative thinking questions.
5. Read and freewrite to start your thinking.

Make a personal evaluation of these strategies:

1. Underline your favorite strategies in the list.
2. Make a check mark by those you want to continue to use.
3. Cross out any you probably will not continue to use. What are your reasons for rejecting them?

_____

_____

APPENDIX

Practice Reading
Sample Chapters

Memory

CHAPTER OUTLINE

Reprinted from *Psychology*, Fifth Edition, by Stephen F. Davis & Joseph Palladino (2007), Prentice-Hall, Inc.

I n Chapter 5 we examined the basic learning processes, especially classical conditioning and operant (instrumental) conditioning, that are characteristic of a wide variety of organisms. In this chapter we highlight some uniquely human aspects of learning and memory. We begin with early studies of memory, giving special attention to the pioneering work of Hermann Ebbinghaus. We then examine the phenomenon of memory in detail and discuss several recent developments in the study of memory. After a look at some techniques for improving your memory, we explore the physiological basis of learning and memory.

In addition to helping us adapt more effectively to our environment, the processes covered in this chapter clear the way for improved communication and the storage of knowledge. As you might have sensed, we are beginning to focus on the processes that define what makes us human and the way we function as individuals and as members of groups.

Before we begin an in-depth examination of memory, let's define our topic. This task may be more difficult than you think; memory is one of those abilities we take for granted. Certainly memory is related to learning. If we did not learn or acquire new knowledge, we would have nothing to store in our memories. In many instances, memories last an incredibly long time. Putting these ideas together, we can tentatively define **memory** as a system or process by which the products or results of learning are stored for future use.

INITIAL STUDIES

When Sue graduated from high school, she enrolled in a college several hundred miles from her home. After completing college, she accepted a job as a YMCA program director in a large metropolitan area. Because her trips back home were infrequent, she lost contact with her high school classmates. She has not seen most of them in years. Her 25th high school reunion is approaching, and Sue wonders how good her memory is. How many of her former classmates will she recognize? *How good is our memory for faces after a long interval of time?*

The scientific study of human memory is almost as old as scientific psychology itself. The pioneer in this area was Hermann Ebbinghaus, a patient and thorough German psychologist who conducted his studies of memory in the late 1800s and early 1900s (Ebbinghaus, 1885). Ebbinghaus asked questions such as "What conditions are favorable (or unfavorable) for linking or associating the words, sounds, and visual stimuli that make up our store of learned knowledge?"

Because everyday words already have meanings and associations attached to them (that is, some learning has already taken place), Ebbinghaus used other stimuli in many of his experiments. A focus of his research was on **nonsense syllables**, which are usually composed of three letters arranged in a consonant-vowel-consonant sequence. For example, *gok*, *taf*, *keb*, and *tup* are nonsense syllables. Because nonsense syllables were supposed to have no meaning, Ebbinghaus believed he could study how associations between these stimuli are formed without any other factors, such as previous learning, complicating the results.

memory
System or process by which the products or results of learning are stored for future use

nonsense syllables
Stimuli used to study memory; typically composed of a consonant-vowel-consonant sequence

Armed with these new stimuli, Ebbinghaus began his studies with only one research participant: himself. In most instances the task consisted of memorizing lists of nonsense syllables. Before you start questioning the importance of studying how one learns a sequence of nonsense syllables, think about all the lists or sequences that we learn (Curran & Keele, 1993). As grade school children, we learn the alphabet, the names of the presidents, and the multiplication tables. As we grow up, we learn telephone numbers, ZIP codes, addresses, and lock combinations. Ebbinghaus's studies of lists were actually quite relevant.

Psychological Detective

Ebbinghaus's next step was to devise a way to measure memory. Now, if someone says that all you have to do to measure memory is to ask a participant what he or she has learned, you might be skeptical. Measuring memory is more complicated than that. Before you read further, write down some ideas about how you might measure memory when a participant is learning a list of nonsense syllables. Be sure to identify the specific response you are measuring.

Ebbinghaus's method for measuring memory of lists of nonsense syllables was called **serial learning** (also known as *ordered recall*). As a participant, you are given a set of items to remember and asked to reproduce the sequence in the exact order in which it was presented (Marshuetz, 2005). This technique reveals whether you have mastered the correct sequence of the syllables or other stimuli like numbers (Baddeley, Papagno, & Andrade, 1993). For example, if you dial or key in 343-7355 on the telephone instead of 343-3755 (the number that was supposed to be learned), serial learning is not perfect.

A second method, **paired-associate learning,** was developed by Mary Whiton Calkins (1863–1930), the first woman to serve as president of the American Psychological Association (see Chapter 1; Madigan & O'Hara, 1992). In this task you associate an unfamiliar word or nonsense syllable with a familiar word. This technique is often used to learn the vocabulary for a foreign language—remember the flash cards you used to learn Spanish or French? The test consists of presenting the familiar word and then producing the foreign word associated with it.

A third method of measuring memory is **free recall.** Here the task is to remember as many items as possible, regardless of the sequence (Baddeley, 2004). Naming the major parts of a neuron (see Chapter 2), the major sleep disorders (see Chapter 4), or the components of classical conditioning (see Chapter 5) are examples of free recall. Free recall is now the preferred method of measuring learning. You can experience this method right now. Cover each word in Table 7-1 with a card and then read one word at a time at a comfortable pace. When you get to the bottom of the list, you will find the instruction to "Recall" the words. Write down as many of the words as you can remember.

One of the most interesting findings from studies of free recall is that the position or order of the material to be recalled affects the chances that it will be remembered. For example, items near the beginning of the list are typically recalled well (the *primacy effect*); items near the end of the list are also recalled well (the *recency effect*). Items in the middle of the list tend to be recalled less well than items at the beginning or end of the list. This phenomenon, called the **serial position effect** (Baddeley, 2004), was discovered by Mary Whiton Calkins (Madigan & O'Hara, 1992; see Figure 7-1).

The Curve of Forgetting

One of the most important findings of Ebbinghaus's research is the curve of forgetting. Ebbinghaus found that memory for learned material is best right after

Hermann Ebbinghaus (1850–1909) was a pioneer in the study of human memory.

serial learning
Learning procedure in which material that has been learned must be repeated in the order in which it was presented; also known as *ordered recall*

paired-associate learning
Learning procedure in which items to be recalled are learned in pairs. During recall, one member of the pair is presented and the other is to be recalled

free recall
Learning procedure in which material that has been learned may be repeated in any order

serial position effect
Tendency for items at the beginning and end of a list to be learned better than items in the middle

TABLE 7-1

Free Recall

Instructions: Try to remember the words in this list. Place a card over the list and then reveal one word at a time. When you get to the bottom of the list, close the book and write down as many of the words as you can remember.

Hospital

Lawn

Doorbell

Laundry

Street

Mouse

Radio

Wood

Sofa

Garage

Recall

the learning session. As time passes, we forget more and more. This basic finding has been replicated (reproduced) numerous times since Ebbinghaus discovered it. As you can see from Figure 7-2, Jenkins and Dallenbach (1924) found that participants recalled the most when they were tested immediately after learning. The participants learned a list of 10 nonsense syllables and then were asked to recall the list 1/2 hour and 2, 4, and 8 hours later. One-half hour after the initial training session, the participants were able to recall only half of the list; their performance continued to deteriorate with the passage of time. The importance of these results is clear: You can expect your best recall shortly after a learning session. Another important finding from the Ebbinghaus laboratory involves what is called *distributed practice*. Simply put, it is better to distribute learning trials across a period of time than to mass them in a single block of learning. "When it comes to learning, a little every day is the optimal way" (Baddeley, 2004, p. 70). Of course,

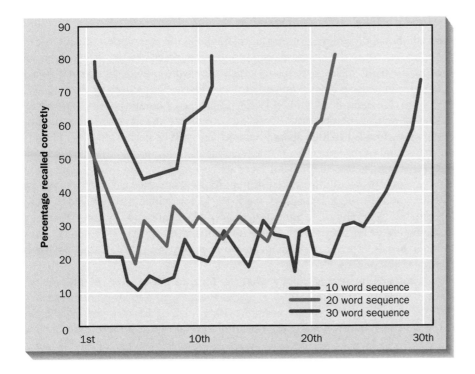

FIGURE 7-1 The tendency for items at the beginning of a list or at the end of a list to be recalled more easily than items in the middle of a list is called the *serial position effect*. As you can see, this phenomenon occurs with lists of various sizes.

Source: Baddeley (2004).

FIGURE 7-2 Number of nonsense syllables recalled at various intervals following learning for two participants. Recall dropped dramatically with time, but it was higher if they slept after learning. In agreement with Ebbinghaus's research, the greatest decrease in recall occurred very shortly after learning had taken place.

Source: Jenkins and Dallenbach (1924).

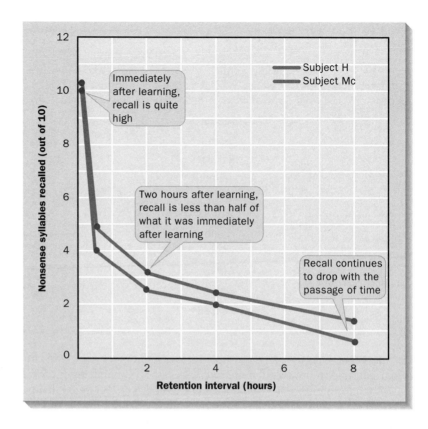

distributed practice is exactly the opposite of what students do when they cram for exams. Students who cram are relying on the high rate of recall immediately after learning trials. They often ignore the high rate of *forgetting* that occurs even immediately after learning. Most students cram because they don't properly plan their study time. There are effective techniques that you can use to improve the way you study. You will find several suggestions for improving your studying in the section on Techniques for Improving Memory later in this chapter.

7.1

Recognition and Relearning

Two additional procedures for measuring memory, the recognition test and the relearning test, supplement the three methods just described. In the **recognition test,** participants pick out items to which they were previously exposed from a longer list that also contains unfamiliar items (Haist, Shimamura, & Squire, 1992; Yonelinas, Hockley, & Murdock, 1992). This type of memory task is involved in taking a multiple-choice test. Recall Sue from this chapter's opening vignette. When she attends her high school reunion, Sue will be performing a similar task in attempting to recognize her former classmates.

How good is our memory for faces after a long interval of time? The results of a research project indicate that our ability to remember faces for a long time is quite good (Bruck, Cavanagh, & Ceci, 1991). Participants were asked to match current photographs of former high school classmates with photos taken approximately 25 years earlier. Those individuals did much better at matching photos than did a group of participants who had not gone to high school with the people in the photos.

A **relearning test** is exactly what the term implies. After the passage of a certain amount of time (called a *retention interval*), the original material is learned again. For example, you might study a list of 15 nonsense syllables on Monday afternoon. You study the list until you can repeat it three times without an error; this level of performance, your *performance criterion*, is established by

recognition test
Test in which retention is measured by the ability to pick out previously learned items from a list that also contains unfamiliar items

relearning test
Test of retention that compares the time or trials required to learn material a second time with the time or trials required to learn the material the first time

the researcher. One week later you study the same list. The researcher calculates the amount of time, or number of trials, it takes to relearn the material so that you can match your performance criterion, and the two scores are compared. If learning occurred more rapidly the second time you studied the list, this difference is reported as a **savings score** (or *relearning score*). A good example of relearning is studying for a comprehensive final exam. Chances are good that, with the right concentration, it will take you less time and effort to relearn the material.

Although the work of Ebbinghaus and other early psychologists provided a basic understanding of human memory, much more has been discovered since then. Today few psychologists study how people learn lists of nonsense syllables; they are more interested in examining the processes by which memories are formed, stored, retrieved, and used. This shift in interest occurred because most psychologists abandoned the mechanical association-based model of memory in which items were simply linked to other items. A new view of the mind began to emerge—one suggesting that the mind is an active agent with many other organizational properties. This developing view prompted different questions. How do we store items in memory? Once memories are stored, how do we retrieve them?

savings score
Difference between the time or trials originally required to learn material and the time or trials required to relearn the material; also known as *relearning score*

MODELS OF MEMORY

Ann is phenomenal! She knows every client by name and can recall the details of particular accounts with ease. She always makes the right decision, often under extreme pressure, and never seems ruffled or disturbed. Business appointments with her are a pleasure. Her friends have frequently commented that her memory is "like a computer." *In what ways might a computer and human memory be alike?*

7.2

Human Memory as an Information Processing System

Like the computer, researchers have characterized human memory as an information processing system that has three separate stages: an *input* or *encoding stage*, a *storage stage*, and a *retrieval stage* during which an already stored memory is called into consciousness (see Figure 7-3). Let's take a closer look at each of these stages.

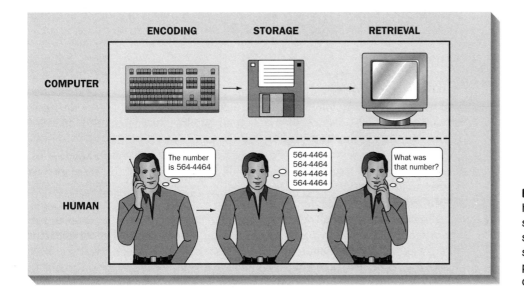

FIGURE 7-3 Because it has separate encoding, storage, and retrieval stages, human memory is similar to an information processing system like the computer.

What memories does this grade school science class help you retrieve?

Encoding. In the **encoding** stage, sensory information is received and coded, and then transformed into neural impulses that can be processed further or stored for later use. Just as the computer changes keyboard entries into usable electronic symbols that may be stored on a computer disk, sensory information is *transduced*, or converted, into neural impulses (see Chapter 3) that can be used and stored by the brain. In addition to transduction, a great deal of the encoding process appears to be devoted to rehearsing (practicing or repeating) the input, organizing it into groups, and relating the groups to already stored information. Encoding may even involve giving this information a special name or label.

Suppose that as you drive to school, you listen to a new song on the radio. The sounds are transduced into neural impulses, which are then recognized as making up a song. You remember hearing similar songs and classify the one you are listening to as belonging to that group—for example, "smooth jazz" or "oldie." This procedure is very much like installing a computer program; information is encoded in the central processing unit, and the user gives it a name and file path that helps relate it to similar programs.

Storage. The second stage of memory processing is **storage**. Like the computer program, the encoded information must be stored in the memory system if we plan to retain it for any length of time or use it more than once. Although some bits of information are stored briefly, used only once, and then discarded, others, like certain telephone numbers, are used frequently and are therefore stored on a more permanent basis.

Retrieval. Once a computer program has been named and stored, we can "call it up" by its name and use it again. Human memory works in much the same way. When we recall or bring a memory into consciousness, we have retrieved it. This recall process is known as memory **retrieval.**

We do not store information in memory randomly. The information is organized and related to already stored information in ways that allow us to use certain cues to retrieve it.

Psychological Detective

To see how the retrieval process works, write down the name of your fourth-grade teacher. After you have done so, describe the process that led you to that particular name.

The words *fourth-grade teacher* are the stimuli that activated your memories of the fourth grade. As you retrieve these memories while searching for the name of your teacher, you may recall your school building, your fourth-grade classroom, the ride to school on the bus, and the names of your classmates. In turn, each of these memories could serve as a stimulus to retrieve related memories. There are probably many stimuli that could help you retrieve the name of your fourth-grade teacher.

In some instances, the network of related memories is small and only a few specific cues will successfully retrieve a certain memory. For example, suppose you are in the supermarket trying to choose a brand of detergent when an apparent stranger begins a conversation with you. The "stranger" is talking as if you have known each other for some time, but you have no idea what this person's name is. Why do we find it so difficult to recall some names? Knowing about retrieval cues

encoding
First stage of the memory process; in it information is transformed or coded (a transduction process) into a form that can be processed further and stored

storage
Second stage of the memory process; in it information is placed in the memory system. This stage may involve either brief or long-term storage of memories

retrieval
Third stage of the memory process; in it stored memories are brought into consciousness

helps answer this question. When the stranger reminds you that you met last Saturday at a party, it is as though a light goes on. Suddenly you remember who this person is and where you met. Because you met under special circumstances, the party, only cues related to that situation will retrieve the memory of the meeting. When those specific cues are presented, the memory returns.

Myth or Science

How often have you heard that someone has a "photographic memory"? Although it is likely that this comment refers to people with very good memories, some people do appear to have photographic memory. People with **eidetic imagery** (the technical term for photographic memory) say that they can look at a written page, person, slide, or drawing and then later mentally see that image (Guenther, 1998; Haber, 1969). The visual image persists after stimulation (for example, a slide is turned off), can be scanned like a photograph, and offers relatively accurate detail. In fact, it appears as if these people take photographs and store them in their minds for future use. For example, when you need information from a page in a book, you retrieve that page from memory and read it. Leonardo da Vinci and Napoleon Bonaparte are two famous people who had photographic memory. Leonardo could draw detailed portraits of people after meeting them only once. Napoleon could glance at a map briefly and later recall the location of every stream, town, and hill. Eidetic imagery appears to be relatively rare, however. Estimates of the percentage of the population with eidetic imagery are often in single digits (Haber & Haber, 1964). Would this ability be great at test time? Perhaps. It seems, however, that once the image has faded (such images last for up to 4 minutes), the memory seems no better than the memories of those who do not possess eidetic imagery (Haber, 1969; Haber & Haber, 1964).

eidetic imagery
A form of memory, often called *photographic memory*, which consists of especially vivid visual recollections of material

STUDY TIP

Construct a visual diagram showing the human memory as an information processing system, including the stages from the stages-of-memory model. Include a short definition of each stage in your diagram.

The Stages-of-Memory Model

Our encoding-storage-retrieval model of memory would serve our purpose quite well if we had only one type of memory to store. We have, however, at least three well-defined types of memory: sensory memory, short-term memory, and long-term memory. So the information processing model must be modified to read as follows:

$$\text{Encoding} \rightarrow \text{"type" of storage} \rightarrow \text{retrieval}$$

The rest of this section describes the three types of memory and the ways they are used in our daily lives. The stages-of-memory model (also called the *traditional model*) that we discuss is shown in Figure 7-4, it was developed by Richard Atkinson and Richard Shiffrin (1968).

Sensory Memory. As the name implies, **sensory memory** is a memory or storage of sensory events such as sights, sounds, and tastes, with no further processing or interpretation. Because sensory memory provides us with a fleeting image of the stimuli present at a particular moment, it has the potential to be huge. Because many stimuli are received all the time, sensory memory appears to last only briefly, about 0.5 to 1.0 second, depending on which sensory system is involved.

Sensory information that is not selected for further processing by higher brain centers decays and is replaced by incoming stimuli. As you saw in Chapter 3, we cannot attend to and process all the stimuli we receive; some of them must be filtered out. Stimuli that we attend to are those that are selected from sensory memory for further processing; other stimuli are lost.

sensory memory
Very brief (0.5 to 1.0 second for visual stimuli and 2 to 3 seconds for auditory stimuli) but extensive memory for sensory events

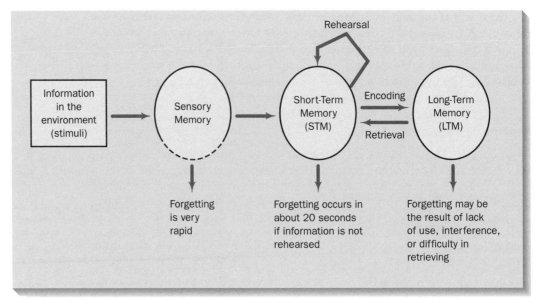

FIGURE 7-4 The stages-of-memory model.

After a moment's reflection, you might ask, "If sensory memories last such a short time, how can you demonstrate that they really exist?" In a compelling set of experiments, researchers presented a display of 12 letters to participants (Sperling, 1960). The pattern might look like this:

D	C	R	M	← High tone
Y	N	S	V	← Medium tone
I	E	G	Z	← Low tone

The entire pattern was flashed for only 1/20th of a second. The participants then recalled and wrote down as many letters as possible. Typically, they were able to identify only 4 or 5 of the 12 letters. That does not seem like good evidence for any kind of memory! Some changes made in later experiments, however, produced dramatic improvement. One modification involved assigning a different audible tone to each row of the stimulus pattern: a high tone to the top row, a medium tone to the middle row, and a low tone to the bottom row. As before, the entire pattern of 12 letters was flashed for 1/20th of a second. Immediately afterward, one of the three tones was sounded, and the participants were asked to write down the letters in the row designated by the tone. When tones accompanied the presentation of the letters, participants correctly identified three or four letters in a row, regardless of which row was signaled. Clearly, much more information was potentially available in memory than the original experiment had indicated. Because they did not know in advance which row would be signaled, the participants had to have a memory of all the letters when one of the tones was sounded. Timing is important, however; when the tone was sounded a second after the letters were presented, participants could remember only one or two letters in the designated row. Thus a significant amount of information is lost from sensory memory very quickly after the stimuli are presented.

The amount of information lost from sensory memory is not a fixed quantity. Rather, it depends on the amount of processing effort that is expended in the next stage of memory. We can either process a few items very thoroughly and lose a great deal from sensory memory or we can process a larger number of items less thoroughly and retain more from sensory memory.

Because it is important and easy to study, we have been talking exclusively about visual sensory memory. Do we have brief sensory memories for our other senses? Although less research has been done on this topic, the answer appears to be yes. Ulric Neisser (1967) proposed the existence of an *auditory* or *echoic sensory memory*. His proposal was supported by a study in which participants heard simultaneous lists of letters from three loudspeakers in different locations (Darwin, Turvey, & Crowder, 1972). If students tried to report the letters from all three loudspeakers, they did poorly; if they were asked to repeat the letters from a specific speaker immediately after the list was read, they did much better. If a delay was imposed, their performance decreased noticeably. These results are similar to those Sperling reported for visual stimuli with one major exception. Echoic sensory memory lasts a bit longer—closer to 2 to 3 seconds (Lu, Williamson, & Kaufman, 1992), although, some research suggests that it may last as long as 10 seconds (Sams, Hari, Rif, & Knuutila, 1993). You can also experience auditory sensory memory. Hit your hands against the top of your desk. Do you still hear the sound for a brief instant after you have stopped? This sound is an auditory sensory memory.

Psychological Detective

Consider the following situation. Jim is sitting in class but is not really paying attention to the lecture. His mind is on the movie he is planning to see that evening. Without realizing it, he is rubbing one hand along the edge of the desk. After rubbing his hand on the desk several times, Jim becomes aware of his behavior. Each time his hand leaves the desk, he is sure he is still feeling the sensation. What causes the sensation that Jim experiences after he rubs his hand along the edge of the desk? Write down some possibilities before reading further.

Sensory memory appears to be involved in the sensation Jim is experiencing. Try it yourself. Rub your hand quickly along the edge of your desk or a table—heel first, fingertips last. For a brief instant after your hand leaves the desk, you will have the sensation that you are still touching it. You have just experienced an example of *tactile (touch) sensory memory*.

According to the stages-of-memory model, what happens to the information that is selected from sensory memory and not lost? To answer this question, we need to continue our exploration of the various types of memory.

Short-Term Memory.   Once information has been attended to or selected from sensory memory, it is transferred to conscious awareness (Engle, Cantor, & Carullo, 1993; Laming, 1992). According to the stages-of-memory view, information must be processed in **short-term memory (STM)** before it can be transferred to more permanent storage in long-term memory. What is this STM? As the name implies, STM lasts for only a short period—perhaps several seconds. Although researchers have not determined exactly how long such memories endure, it appears that items are lost from STM in about 10 to 20 seconds.

For example, research in which participants recalled a three-letter stimulus found that recall fell from 90% correct immediately after presentation of the stimulus to 10% correct after 18 seconds (Brown, 1958; Peterson & Peterson, 1959). Why? Two processes appear to be at work: (a) Unless memories are practiced or rehearsed, they become weaker and fade away; and (b) to make room for new incoming information, some of the memories in STM are pushed out or displaced. In the Brown and Peterson and Peterson studies, the participants counted backward by threes to prevent practice after learning the three-letter stimulus. Their results indicated that much of this displaced information is simply lost, but some is transferred to long-term memory.

short-term memory (STM)
Memory stage in which information is held in consciousness for 10 to 20 seconds

Without rehearsal, STM does not last very long.

Psychological Detective

Study the following phone numbers for 15 seconds:

316-343-5800

401-246-4531

912-692-3423

Now write them on a piece of paper without looking at this page. You probably found this task difficult. You would be able to handle two phone numbers better. Why? Write down some possible answers before reading further.

George Miller, former president of the American Psychological Association, proposed that we can hold 7 +/− 2 items in STM at any one time.

Exercises like this one, coupled with extensive research, prompted psychologist George Miller (1956) to propose that we can hold approximately seven items (plus or minus two) in STM (often called the "magic number") at any one time. After a moment's reflection, you might be sure that this 7 +/− 2 proposal is incorrect. When we remember two telephone numbers, we are dealing with more than nine items (7 +/− 2). That would be true if we counted each digit separately. Most people remember telephone numbers (with area code) not as 10 separate digits but as three *chunks*. Think of a chunk as a meaningful unit of information (Gobet et al., 2001). Try this: Say the first telephone number aloud, and you can "hear" the chunks. When you said the telephone number aloud, you probably said 316 (pause), 343 (pause), 5800. A chunk is like a pail into which we pour several individual items that can then be recalled together from memory. With two phone numbers, each having an area code, you have only six chunks to remember.

What Miller demonstrated with the principle of grouping or chunking is that although STM may be limited to five to nine items (7 +/− 2), each item may consist of a chunk or group of items. In this way the capacity of STM can be increased significantly.

Psychological Detective

What would you do if you wanted to remember the following list? Study it for 15 seconds; then close your book and write down as many of the items as possible.

telephone	Ford	pine	Toyota
poplar	fax	Chevrolet	cherry
oak	compact disk	walnut	radio
Buick	Mazda	television	DVD
cedar	mail	audiocassette	Pontiac
Saturn	maple	elm	Honda

FIGURE 7-5 Chunking helps us create categories that increase the amount of information we can hold in STM.

There are 24 items in this list, considerably more than the magic number 7 +/− 2. Hence it will be difficult for you to remember each word by itself. If, however, you set up three categories (trees, automobiles, and communication devices) and put each item into the appropriate category, you should have no trouble remembering all 24 items (see Figure 7-5).

The original concept of STM posed a major problem: It was too short. Although 10 or 20 seconds was sufficient to input and store new information, it did not allow time for processing information (Ashcraft, 2006). The initial 10- to 20-second STM period often leads to a second phase, **working memory**, during which attention and conscious effort are brought to bear on the material at hand. Working memory is like a mental workbench or a place where mental effort is applied (Baddeley, 2004; Nairne, 2003). If you attempt to solve the following problem, you will probably find that you held the intermediate answer in memory while computing the next part, then held the updated intermediate value, and so forth:

$$2 \times \frac{5/6 + 4}{\frac{1}{2} \times (6 + 3)}$$

working memory
Second stage of short-term memory; in it attention and conscious effort are brought to bear on material

What's more, comprehension of sentences can sometimes tax our immediate memory processes. Try to understand the following:

I know that you are not unaware of my inability to speak German.

While you are trying to make sense of this sentence you learn it piece by piece, then put the pieces together (Ashcraft, 2006). When we retrieve words from long-term memory and put them together in a sentence, the process of putting words together occurs in working memory. For example, let's say that you are listening to a lecture in which your instructor makes an interesting but very complicated point. While you hold the sentence in STM, you retrieve word meanings from long-term memory. Then, in light of what you already know (retrieval from long-term memory), you use working memory to make sense of the new sentences you've just heard. Using brain-imaging techniques (see Chapter 2), researchers have begun to isolate brain regions that are active when we use working memory. For example, order and item memory are separable, and different brain regions seem to be involved (Marshuetz, 2005). Other research reveals that "human spatial working memory is partly mediated by regions in the parietal and prefrontal cortex" (Smith, 2000, p. 45). Future research using brain imaging techniques will define these and other brain regions involved in working memory more precisely.

Long-Term Memory. What would your interactions with your environment be like if STM was the only type of memory you had? Because you lacked any capacity for permanent memory storage, you would have to learn the same things *over* and *over* again. (We describe a person who has only STM later in this chapter.) It is critical to be able to transfer information from STM to more permanent storage in **long-term memory (LTM).** The stages-of-memory model stresses the importance of rehearsal or practice in this transfer. Items that are rehearsed seem more likely to be transferred than unrehearsed items. For example, you will remember your friend's new telephone number better if you repeat (rehearse) it several times rather than repeating it just once.

There are different types of rehearsal; some types aid in transferring information to LTM, and others do not. One researcher conducted a series of studies of a phenomenon known as *directed forgetting* (Björk, 1975). In these experiments two groups of participants were asked to learn several lists of items, such as nonsense syllables or telephone numbers. Both groups were given the same amount of time to rehearse each list after it was presented. A retention test was given before presentation of the next list. Before beginning the experiment, one group was told to forget all the items from a given list immediately after the retention test. The second group was told to remember all the lists. A typical directed-forgetting experiment (see Fleck, Berch, Shear, & Strakowski, 2001) is diagrammed in Figure 7-6.

Although no differences were found between the groups in retention of individual lists of nonsense syllables, large differences were apparent on a retention test given after all the lists had been presented. The participants who had been directed to forget did much worse than those who had been directed to remember. These differences appear to be caused by different types of rehearsal.

Two types of rehearsal—maintenance and elaborative—have been studied. We use **maintenance rehearsal** when we want to save or maintain a memory for a short period. Examples of maintenance rehearsal include the telephone number for the pizza restaurant you have just looked up or the material you tried to cram for a test. Maintenance rehearsal ensures that the memory remains until it has been used and is then discarded; research participants who are directed to forget a list as soon as they have learned and repeated it use this type of rehearsal. Participants who are instructed to remember a list use **elaborative rehearsal,** which adds meaning to

long-term memory (LTM)
Memory stage that has a very large capacity and the capability to store information relatively permanently

maintenance rehearsal
Rehearsal used when we want to save or maintain a memory for a specified period of time

elaborative rehearsal
Rehearsal in which meaning is added to the material to be remembered

FIGURE 7-6 Design of a directed-forgetting experiment.

> **Group 1:** Instructed to learn each list of nonsense syllables for a test and then forget the list before learning the next list
>
> **Group 2:** Instructed to learn and store all lists of nonsense syllables

Learn List 1	Test List 1	Learn List 2	Test List 2	Learn List 3	Test List 3	Test All Lists

| **RESULTS** | Both groups equal | | Both groups equal | | Both groups equal | | Group 2 superior to Group 1 (evidence of directed forgetting) |

material that we want to remember. For example, you increase your chances of remembering someone's name if meaningful elements are present when you are introduced. Where does the person work or live? What are his or her hobbies? An introduction such as "I would like you to meet my friend Jason Downey. Jason works as the chief parole officer for the state. He is an avid sky diver" provides several elements that are useful to memory. Earlier we saw that the more meaningful material is, the better it is learned. Elaborative rehearsal is an example of this process at work; it results in a more permanent memory and promotes the transfer of information to LTM (Bartlett, 1932; Best, 1999). Unlike STM, LTM has a very large, if not unlimited, capacity.

7.3

Forgetting. Once a memory has been transferred from STM to LTM, it is supposed to be there on a *permanent* basis. If that is true, why do we forget? Some memory loss may be due to the fading or *decay* of memories (Dosher & Ma, 1998), but much loss appears to be caused by *interference*. Old memories that are already stored may be recalled instead of the specific memory we are seeking. This effect is called **proactive interference.** Proactive interference occurs when old information hinders our memory of the new information. When you move to a new house or apartment, you have a new address and telephone number. How often do you find yourself using the old address or phone number? Sometimes this problem lasts for years. Another example of proactive interference can be seen every January, when millions of people continue to write the previous year on their bank checks.

Similarly, information that was learned *after* the material we want to remember may hinder the recall of the earlier learned material. This process is called **retroactive interference.** Sometimes it is important to remember old addresses and phone numbers, but try as we might, new addresses and phone numbers are the only ones that come to mind. The other information may be stored in LTM, but we simply cannot retrieve it. Proactive and retroactive interference are diagrammed in Figure 7-7.

What happens when we retrieve a memory from LTM? As we saw in Figure 7-3, the stages-of-memory model suggests that when a memory is recalled from LTM and enters consciousness, it is placed directly into STM. There it may be combined with new information that has been received, creating a new memory. If this new memory is properly rehearsed, it may be transferred to LTM for more permanent storage. The following Study Chart summarizes the main components of the stages-of-memory model.

proactive interference
Situation in which previously learned information hinders the recall of information learned more recently

retroactive interference
Situation in which information learned more recently hinders the recall of information learned previously

The stages-of-memory approach is not the only model of memory that has been developed. We explore a second influential model, the levels-of-processing model, in the next section.

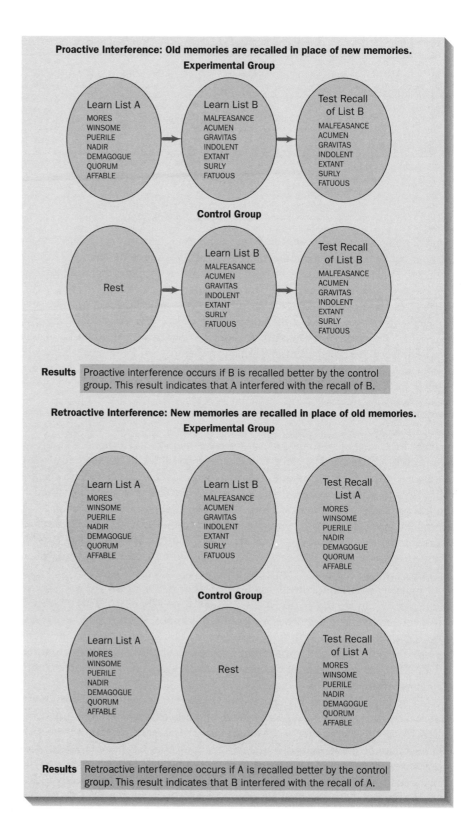

FIGURE 7-7 Research designed to test proactive and retroactive interference.

Study CHART

Types of Memory According to the Stages-of-Memory Model

Type	Description	Example
Sensory	Storage of a large number of sensory events for 0.5 to 1.0 second.	Rubbing your hand across a table top and feeling the sensation for a brief instant after you stop.
Short-term (STM)	Working memory is a second stage of STM. Lasts for a few seconds unless rehearsal takes place. Conscious awareness is involved.	Remembering the name of a person you just met.
Long-term (LTM)	More permanent form of memory storage. Rehearsal or practice is important for transferring memories from STM to LTM.	Your telephone number or home address.

REVIEW SUMMARY

1. Hermann Ebbinghaus conducted pioneering research on **memory** in the late 1800s. Ebbinghaus devised nonsense syllables, which he believed had no meaning attached to them, to study how associations between stimuli are formed. Through the use of **serial learning**, Ebbinghaus determined that much of what we learn is forgotten very shortly after a learning session. When we try to recall a list of items, we tend to recall items at the beginning (primacy effect) and the end (recency effect) better than items in the middle. This phenomenon is called the **serial position effect**. Other methods of studying memory include **paired-associate learning** and **free recall**.

2. These basic methods were developed and expanded by incorporating additional tasks, such as the **recognition test** and the **relearning test**. The **savings score** is produced by the relearning method.

3. Some investigators have drawn a parallel between the computer and human memory. Computers and human memory have (a) an input or **encoding** stage, (b) a **storage** stage, and (c) a **retrieval** stage.

4. The stages-of-memory (traditional) model proposes that there are three types of memory: sensory, short-term, and long-term. **Sensory memory** is a very brief (lasting 0.5 to 1 second) memory for a large array of (visual) stimuli. **Eidetic imagery** (photographic memory) occurs when after stimulation a visual image persists longer than normal. This ability appears to be relatively rare. **Short-term memory (STM)** is more limited in capacity than sensory memory but lasts longer (about 10 to 20 seconds). **Working memory** is the second stage of STM, during which attention and conscious effort are brought to bear on material. With practice or rehearsal, memories may persist even longer and ultimately may be transferred to more permanent storage in **long-term memory (LTM)**.

5. Memories may not be retrievable from LTM because they have faded or because of interference by other memories.

6. Proactive interference occurs when old material interferes with the retrieval of material learned more recently. **Retroactive interference** occurs when recently learned material interferes with the retrieval of material learned earlier.

✓ CHECK YOUR PROGRESS

1. Kevin and Sharin are participants in a memory experiment. Their task is to learn a list of items such as *bok* and *gex*. What are these items called? Why are they used in the study of memory?

2. Explain the statement "Human memory is like an information processing system."

3. Indicate whether each of the following statements describes sensory memory, STM, or LTM.
   a. very large capacity
   b. capacity of 7 +/− 2 items
   c. "permanent" storage
   d. lasts only .5 to 1.0 second
   e. lasts 10 to 20 seconds

4. Describe working memory. How does it differ from STM?

5. You attempt to remember a phone number by repeating it over and over to yourself. What type of rehearsal are you using?

   a. condensed
   b. permanent
   c. elaborative
   d. maintenance

6. Much memory loss appears to be due to

   a. fading.
   b. disuse.
   c. interference.
   d. poor encoding.

7. Your final exam was a nightmare. All you could remember was the material you had just learned; the older material seemed to have vanished from your memory. This type of memory failure is an example of what kind of interference?

8. Once he has learned the list of items, Kevin's task is to reproduce them in the order in which they were presented. What term do psychologists use for this procedure for measuring memory?

   a. recognition
   b. free recall
   c. serial learning
   d. paired-associate

9. Ted recently moved from New York to Denver, and now he has a new telephone number. When people ask him for his new telephone number, the number he recalls is the old number. What psychological phenomenon is occurring here?

   a. savings
   b. recognition
   c. interference
   d. repression

10. Picking a suspect out of a police lineup is an example of

    a. recall.
    b. recognition.
    c. relearning.
    d. paired-associate learning.

ANSWERS: 1. Nonsense syllables. Nonsense syllables are used to avoid the influence of previous associations on learning. **2.** There is an encoding stage, a storage stage and a retrieval stage in both the information system and human memory. **3. a.** Sensory memory or LTM. **b.** STM. **c.** LTM. **d.** Visual sensory memory. **e.** STM. **4.** Working memory follows the initial 10 to 20 seconds of STM. During working memory, attention and conscious effort are brought to bear on the material. **5. d. 6. c 7.** Retroactive **8. c 9. c 10. b**

OTHER APPROACHES TO MEMORY

Myra volunteered to participate in an experiment involving memory. Her initial task was to read an article in a psychological journal. After reading the article, she was instructed to prepare a brief presentation about the article from the perspective of its author. Finally, Myra took a test that dealt with the content of the article. *What did these procedures have to do with memory?*

Although the stages-of-memory or traditional model makes good sense and has generated a large amount of research activity, it is not the only account of how memory works. In this section we examine several other models of the memory process.

The Levels-of-Processing Model

levels-of-processing model
Theory stating that deeper processing of information increases the likelihood that the information will be recalled

The **levels-of-processing model** proposed by Fergus Craik and Robert Lockhart (1972) represents a radical departure from the stages-of-memory model (Challis, 1993; Challis & Brodbeck, 1992). Craik and Lockhart proposed that there is only one type of memory store and that its capacity is enormous, if not unlimited. Once memories have entered this store, they may be retained there for extremely long periods.

FIGURE 7-8 The levels-of-processing model of memory.

You may be thinking, "One large memory store in which memories last for long periods—that seems simple enough. If that's the way our memory is set up, however, why do we forget some things faster than others?" That question gets to the heart of Craik and Lockhart's view of memory: What really matters is the way we process information. Rehearsal is important, but how we rehearse is even more important. As you can see in Figure 7-8, Craik and Lockhart believe that we can engage in several levels of rehearsal or processing. The maintenance and elaborative rehearsal techniques discussed earlier are only two examples.

A very shallow or simple level might involve processing only the physical characteristics of an object. Thus we might characterize the object in Figure 7-8 as red and rectangular. At a deeper or more complex level of processing, we consider additional characteristics such as the fact that the object has pages. This addition is a form of elaborative rehearsal. Now we are dealing with a red, rectangular book. Adding even more *meaning*—that is, moving to an even deeper level of processing—we now consider what type of book this is and whether it will help us in any of our courses this semester. This last type of processing requires that we examine the book and compare it with other books and with information already stored in memory. Which courses are we taking? Which books are being used in those courses? Will this book help?

We do not automatically progress from one level to another simply because we spend more time processing. If all of our processing time is spent at a very shallow level, our memory will be stored only in terms of shallow cues such as color, shape, or sound. When we want to retrieve this memory, only those shallow cues will be able to access and retrieve it. For example, if we listened only to the sound of a person's name, we might not be able to retrieve it later. The person's physical features, occupation, personality, address, and so forth would be of no help because those cues were not rehearsed when the memory was stored. The sound of the person's name is the only cue that will access the memory of the name. These physical cues are less meaningful; therefore, they do not remain in our memory store as long as more meaningful cues that are rehearsed at deeper levels of processing. In other words, the deeper the level of processing, the greater the likelihood that the information will be stored. Time of processing is not as important as depth of processing.

The instructions given to research participants can have a dramatic effect on what is learned. In one classic study (Hyde & Jenkins, 1969), researchers demonstrated the effects that different types of processing can produce. They instructed four groups of participants to study the same list of words. The specific instructions differed for each group, as shown in Table 7-2. A recall test was then

STUDY TIP

Compare and contrast the stages-of-memory model and levels-of-processing theory. Indicate which makes more sense to you as a model of memory, and why. If your ideal model contains elements of both, describe it.

TABLE 7-2

Instructions Given to Participants in the Hyde and Jenkins (1969) Experiment

Group 1	Count the letters in each word.
Group 2	Mark all the *e*'s in each word.
Group 3	Rate the pleasantness of each word.
Group 4	Memorize the words for a later recall test.

given to all four groups. The test was a surprise for Groups 1, 2, and 3 but not for Group 4.

The results (see Figure 7-9) indicated that the participants in Groups 1 and 2 remembered significantly *fewer* words than did the participants in Groups 3 and 4. Because Groups 3 and 4 did not differ, we can conclude that the surprise value of the test did not produce these results. The groups differed in terms of the level of processing in which they engaged. Groups 1 and 2 never dealt with the words themselves—they just counted letters (Group 1) or marked *e*'s (Group 2). Hence Groups 1 and 2 processed the information at a very shallow level. Because they had to take the words into account, the participants in Group 3 (who rated the pleasantness of the words) and Group 4 (who memorized the words for a test) processed the information at deeper levels and therefore remembered it better.

Consider the memory experiment described at the beginning of this section. What did these procedures have to do with memory? The experiment in which Myra participated was concerned with levels of processing. Unknown to Myra, other participants were required only to read the journal article; they were not required to prepare the brief presentation. When researchers designed the study, they hypothesized that preparing the presentation would require a deeper level of processing and result in better comprehension (Kixmiller, Wann, Weaver, Grover, & Davis, 1987). This prediction was borne out by the experiment's results.

Although many studies have produced results indicating that depth or level of processing influences our memories, this theory has not gone unchallenged. Critics assert that the exact meaning of the term *level of processing* has not been specified (Baddeley, 1998, 2004). Without a clear definition of what a level is or how to measure it objectively, it is difficult to know how many levels there are. Such criticism has encouraged some researchers to view different levels of processing in terms of the amount of cognitive or mental effort expended. In their view, the greater the effort, the deeper the level of processing.

FIGURE 7-9 Mean correct responses on a recall test. Only the participants in Group 4 knew they would be tested. Processing at a deeper level (Group 3) improved memory.

Source: Adapted from Hyde and Jenkins (1969).

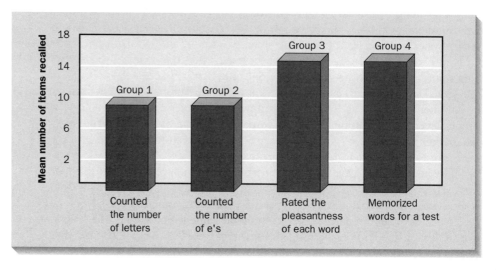

In support of this proposition, several studies have been interpreted as showing that better retention is linked to greater effort. For example, imagine that you are part of an experiment in which the task is to learn words that rhyme. You are presented with a word, such as *cat*, and asked to generate a word, such as *bat*, that rhymes with it. Your task is to memorize the rhyming words that you have generated. Will you remember your rhyming words better than people who were asked only to memorize rhyming words that were presented to them? Because your effort in generating and memorizing the words was greater than their effort in merely memorizing them, the answer is yes.

Finally, the levels-of-processing model assumes that processing occurs through a succession of independent stages; this assumption has yet to be verified. Because of such issues, other approaches have been developed.

Different Types of Long-Term Memory

Recent research has demonstrated that there is more than one type of LTM. We do not just place a memory into LTM (the stages-of-memory model) or simply process at a deeper level (the Craik-Lockhart model). The type of information being processed influences the nature of the stored memory. Four major categories or types of LTM have been proposed: *procedural, semantic, episodic*, and *priming* (or *implicit*). In addition, current research has improved our understanding of encoding, processing, and retrieval strategies. We examine some of these current approaches in the following sections.

Remembering how to rollerblade is an example of procedural memory.

Procedural Memory.   **Procedural memories** are the memories we use in making responses and performing skilled actions (Anderson & Fincham, 1994). Remembering how to rollerblade is an example of procedural memory. Procedural memories are often used at the same time as other types of memory. For example, remembering how to drive a car involves procedural memory. Remembering the traffic laws, however, does not involve the use of motor skills; it involves the memory of general principles. Memory for general principles is known as *semantic memory*.

Semantic Memory.   Our fund of general knowledge is stored in **semantic memory.** Because we are dealing with general knowledge, specific dates and times that pertain to people are not included in our semantic memories. You will find these items in episodic memory. Semantic memory includes concepts, the meanings of words, and facts (Lesch & Pollatsek, 1993; Rohrer, Wixted, Salmon, & Butters, 1995). The following are some examples of items that might be stored in semantic memory:

1. Oil is one of the main ingredients in asphalt.

2. The three branches of government are the executive, legislative, and judicial.

3. In a tennis match, the winner of six games generally wins a set unless the players are tied.

4. Interstate highways that run east and west are given even-number designations.

5. In intercollegiate sports, Division 3 schools do not award athletic scholarships.

Have you ever been asked a question you could not answer immediately, yet you felt the correct response was "on the tip of your tongue"? Such a question produces what is known as the **tip-of-the-tongue (TOT) phenomenon** (Brown &

procedural memory
Memory for making responses and performing skilled actions

semantic memory
Memory for general knowledge

tip-of-the-tongue (TOT) phenomenon
Condition of being almost, but not quite, able to remember something; used to investigate the nature of semantic memory

McNeill, 1966). You know the answer is there, but you cannot retrieve it. In fact, many people who are experiencing TOT may be able to report the first letter of the word, they may know some of the other letters in the word, how many syllables are in the word, and are likely to report related words. The degree of information available during the experience of TOT can be remarkable, especially when you consider that the person cannot report the word itself. For example, the Italian language designates as either masculine or feminine even words that would have no such designations in most languages, including English. In Italian there are two words for stone: *sasso* is masculine and *pietra* is feminine (Caramazza & Miozzo, 1997; Vigliocco, Antonini, & Garrett, 1997). When caught in the TOT dilemma, Italian speakers are often able to report whether the blocked word is masculine or feminine.

Psychological Detective

Let's test your semantic memory. Write down the answer to each of the following questions before reading further.

1. Which ocean is adjacent to California?
2. Which term do we use to describe a car that runs on both gasoline and battery power?
3. What substance found in many foods can lead to clogged arteries?
4. What does a bear do in the winter?
5. Which river separates Indiana from Kentucky?

How many of these questions produced a TOT response? Were you able to search your stored memories and find the correct answer? (The answers can be found at the end of the chapter.) Because most TOT experiences seem to involve semantic memory, they have been studied thoroughly by psychologists who want to learn more about this type of memory and how it is retrieved. Apparently, we are systematic and organized when we search our semantic memories (Reason & Mycielska, 1982). By observing how people search their stored knowledge, we can learn more about the vast network of semantic memories.

Hands On

TOT Phenomenon and Memory

To get a better idea of how the TOT phenomenon is relevant to the study of memory, take the following test. Using strips of cardboard, cover both columns of the letters that follow and write down as many state capitals as you can. Then uncover the columns and see if these alphabetical cues aid your recall for those that were on the tip of your tongue. The answers can be found at the end of the chapter.

State	First Letter of Capital	State	First Letter of Capital
Alabama	M	Maryland	A
Connecticut	H	Massachusetts	B
Florida	T	Mississippi	J
Georgia	A	Nebraska	L
Idaho	B	New Jersey	T
Iowa	D	Oregon	S
Kentucky	F	Texas	A
Louisiana	B	Wyoming	C

Episodic Memory.   Our personal experiences are stored in **episodic memory.** These memories involve events that occurred at certain times with specific people, places, and things (Goldringer, 1996; Levy et al., 1995; Nyberg & Tulving, 1996). The following are some examples of your authors' episodic memories. What episodic memories do you have?

1. Being in Dallas, Texas, the day President John F. Kennedy was assassinated
2. Seeing tornadoes devastate Nashville, Tennessee, in the spring of 1998
3. Watching television coverage of hurricane Katrina in 2005
4. Arriving on campus for the first day of college
5. Watching baseball pitcher Nolan Ryan strike out his 5,000th batter in 1989 and win his 300th major league game in 1990

Just as the TOT phenomenon has been studied to help us learn more about semantic memory, flashbulb memories have been examined to provide information about episodic memory. **Flashbulb memories** are detailed memories of situations that are very arousing, surprising, or emotional. Our memories of such events are often more detailed than our memories of more usual, everyday episodes. For example, Danish people who lived through the Nazi occupation and ultimate liberation had very vivid memories of events from World War II. In fact, their memories for factual questions (such as the weather) were checked against objective records. What's more, members of the resistance movement had more vivid, detailed, and accurate memories than did persons without such participation (Berntsen & Thomsen, 2005). You might think of flashbulb memories as similar to photos taken with a digital camera. Push the button, and in a few seconds you have a perfect re-creation of the scene that you can look at whenever you want. In your mind, the situation is illuminated just as it occurred. Because more effort is expended in the formation of flashbulb memories, such highlighting of details might lead to deeper levels of processing as well as provide more cues for retrieval.

Because flashbulb memories are tied to specific dates, places, and times, it is difficult to give examples that everyone can immediately identify. Some people vividly remember where they were when President Kennedy was assassinated in 1963, but others do not. Other flashbulb memories are the explosion of the space

episodic memory
Memory of one's personal experiences

flashbulb memory
Very detailed memory of an arousing, surprising, or emotional situation

Where were you on September 11, 2001? These images reflect flashbulb memories for many people worldwide.

priming or implicit memory
Unconscious memory processing in which prior exposure to stimulus items may aid subsequent learning

shuttle *Challenger* in 1986, the tearing down of the Berlin Wall in 1989, and the death of Princess Diana in 1997 (Hornstein, Brown, & Mulligan, 2003). The terrorist attacks on the World Trade Center in New York and the Pentagon in Washington, DC, in 2001 are currently flashbulb memories for many people. As new generations grow up, they will not have these flashbulb memories. The strong emotional reactions to events such as those described above seem to provide fertile ground to establish long-lasting memories. On the other hand, evidence indicates that the memories may not be as accurate or consistent as they were once believed to be (Talarico & Rubin, 2003). The emotional component of the memory may lead us to discuss the memory over and over; such repeated rehearsal can at times have the effect of altering the memory, although confidence in the memory often remains quite high.

Priming or Implicit Memory. The recent addition of **priming or implicit memory** to the list of memory types may be one of the most important advances in the study of memory (Poldrack & Cohen, 1998; Schachter & Badgaiyan, 2001). "Priming is a nonconscious form of human memory, which is concerned with perceptual identification of words and objects and which has only recently been recognized as separate from other forms of memory or memory systems" (Tulving & Schachter, 1990, p. 301).

Because priming or implicit memory does not operate on a conscious level, it is difficult to detect and study. The first evidence for priming came from studies of *amnesia*, or memory loss (Warrington & Weiskrantz, 1968). Even though the patients with amnesia had extremely poor memory for recent events, allowing them to study a group of words helped them later when they had to learn those same words. The earlier study period primed or sensitized them to the words they were to learn in the later session. Even though they had no *memory* of the first study session, the *primed* patients with amnesia performed better than other patients with amnesia and normal individuals who had not studied the items earlier. Somehow the earlier study session prepared (primed) the amnesiac patients to recognize the objects they were to learn. Subsequent studies (Schweinberger, 1996) of nonamnesiac individuals examined the timing and production of brain waves to study priming. Priming effects are revealed when appropriate brain waves are shown earlier in primed participants.

Although we still have a great deal to learn, priming appears to facilitate procedural and semantic memory processes by improving our ability to identify perceptual stimuli or objects we encounter (Rajaram & Roediger, 1993). At an unconscious level, priming memory alerts us that we have encountered a particular object previously (Musen & Squire, 1993). This priming effect is better when deeper levels of processing are involved (Hamann & Squire, 1996). The different types of LTM are summarized in the following study chart. Spend a few minutes reviewing it before reading further.

STUDY TIP

In a group of four, each student should briefly study and then describe to the group one of the four types of long-term memory. After a student describes a type, the rest of the group should brainstorm examples of that type.

Retrieval

Last year during spring break, Jennifer paid a surprise visit to her former first-grade teacher. Even though the teacher had not seen Jennifer in 10 years, she immediately said, "Well, Jennifer, how are you? Do you still have Buffy, your pet boa constrictor?" At times we are able to retain and retrieve some remarkable memories. Conversely, sometimes things we should remember seem to be gone forever. For example, are you among the large number of people who seem unable to remember their license plate and telephone numbers?

Study CHART

Types of Long-Term Memory

Type	Description	Examples
Procedural	Memories used in making responses and skilled actions.	Remembering how to ride a bicycle, play tennis, or drive a car.
Semantic	Our store of general knowledge.	Water freezes at 32°F; Texas is the largest of the continental states; metabolism decreases when animals hibernate.
Episodic	Memories of personal events.	Your high school graduation, your first day at college, getting your driver's license.
Implicit (priming)	Nonconscious form of LTM that is related to identification of words and objects.	Allowing amnesia patients to study an object and later finding that learning is enhanced even though they do not remember seeing the object.

Source: GEECH. Reprinted by permission of United Features Syndicate, Inc.

Retrieval from STM.   As mentioned earlier, retrieval is the process by which we locate a memory that has been stored and then bring it into consciousness. Because most people have both extremely good and extremely poor memories, psychologists are interested in studying retrieval.

Psychological Detective

When you read the heading "Retrieval from STM," the following question may have occurred to you: "If the information in STM is already in our consciousness, why would we talk about retrieving it?" Give this question some thought, and write down some possible reasons before reading further.

A series of studies by S. Sternberg (1966, 1975) suggested that retrieval from STM is not instantaneous; we *do* have to scan our STM, locate an item, and process it. Sternberg asked participants to hold a series of letters (such as B, Q, R, D, T, and P) in STM for later recall. But instead of being given the recall test they expected, they were presented with a letter, such as B, and were asked whether it was in the list they were holding in STM. If retrieval was not involved, the participants should have responded almost instantaneously. As it turned out, they did not. What's more, as additional letters were added to the list held in STM, the participants took longer to answer. They were scanning the entire list in STM to match the test letter with those they had stored. The longer the list in STM, the longer the search process required to make a match.

Retrieval from LTM. The process of scanning items in STM to retrieve a specific memory is rather straightforward, but retrieval of long-term memories is a different story. Depending on the situation, various processes may be involved. For example, we have to distinguish between retrieval of memories in recognition tasks and retrieval of memories in recall tasks.

Which type of test would you rather take—a short-answer or essay test in which you have to produce all of the answers, or a multiple-choice test in which you have to recognize the correct answer? Most people prefer the multiple-choice test because it is easier; all you have to do is choose the right answer. Consider the following questions on material from Chapter 4. Which question is easier?

1. Which sleep disorder is characterized by extreme sleepiness, cataplexy, and sleep paralysis?

   a. enuresis
   b. narcolepsy
   c. sleep apnea
   d. somnambulism

2. Which sleep disorder is characterized by extreme sleepiness, cataplexy, and sleep paralysis?

If recognition tasks are easier, perhaps they do not require the same amount or type of retrieval processing. It may be simpler to retrieve memories through recognition. Many researchers supported this view until Tulving and his colleagues demonstrated that in some situations, recall memory is actually superior to recognition memory!

Although one type of memory task is not always easier than the other, perhaps the process of retrieval is the same for both. John Anderson and Gordon Bower (1974) have proposed that recognition and recall use the same retrieval process. Both recall and recognition retrieval have an initial stage during which we search stored memories. This search leads us to a large number of *related* words and phrases. In short, we do not store information as separate bits and pieces; much of it is stored as a semantic network of related items.

Semantic networks are formed by related concepts (called *nodes*) that are linked together (Collins & Loftus, 1975; Collins & Quillian, 1972). For example, mentioning the concept "newspaper" might activate the semantic network shown in Figure 7-10. The process of activating a network constitutes the retrieval process. The length of the lines (called *links*) that connect the various concepts in the newspaper network reflects the strength of the association; shorter links imply stronger associations. For example, the association between "newspaper" and "reporter" is stronger (shorter link) than the association between "newspaper" and "rain" (longer link). Note that in the semantic network every concept is related to the core concept—in this case, "newspaper." In some instances, the relation is direct; in others, it is indirect.

Not all of our stored memories are arranged in semantic networks in which one concept triggers a network of related items. There are numerous occasions when we are required to use a grouping or cluster of knowledge about a sequence of events or an object. Such clusters of knowledge or typical ways of thinking about things are called **schemas** (Ahn, Brewer, & Mooney, 1992; Dopkins, Pollatsek, & Nordlie, 1994). For example, suppose that a friend asked you to tell her about the concert you went to last weekend. Because you have been to several concerts during the past year, you have an organized cluster of knowledge (a schema) about going to concerts. Thus your recall of last weekend's concert will

semantic network
Network of related concepts that are linked together

schema
Grouping or cluster of knowledge about an object or sequence of events

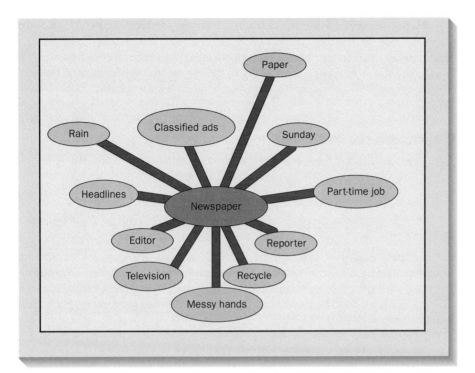

be influenced by your schema for concerts and the specific events that occurred at the concert in question. Similarly, you have schemas for a visit to a doctor, the first day of class, a wedding ceremony, negotiations to buy a new car, and so on.

To get a better idea of the nature of semantic networks and schemas, let's say you have learned a list of words that included the word *horse*. Later in the day you take a recognition test in which you are given a longer list of words and are asked to pick out the ones you have learned. You come to the word *horse*, which serves as a retrieval cue for the semantic network that contains your horse-related memories. Now your job is to determine whether the word *horse* was on the list you learned earlier. Sorting through all of your horse memories could be a rather imposing and confusing task, especially if there are many strong links. On the other hand, the word *aardvark* should be easier to recognize as one of the words you learned because it should activate fewer links than *horse*.

The same process is involved when we retrieve memories under recall conditions. For example, an essay question on your psychology test might ask you to name the four lobes of the cortex. You start scanning your semantic network for items related to the concept "lobes of the cortex." You find a network of related information that includes subcortical structures, stereotaxic surgery, and a group of items that includes the terms *frontal*, *temporal*, *parietal*, and *occipital*—the four cortical lobes you've been looking for.

Consider the next question on the test: "Explain the contributions of Ivan Pavlov". In this case, you need to recall more than just names to answer the question; you need to activate an organized cluster of knowledge, a schema. Your schema for Pavlov contains the information the instructor wants. In fact, it contains even more than you need to recall. Could there be some way to retrieve only the desired memory?

Encoding Specificity. The **encoding specificity** hypothesis states that the effectiveness of memory retrieval is directly related to the similarity of the cues present when the memory was originally encoded to the cues present when the memory is retrieved (Gerrig & McKoon, 2001; Tulving, 1983). In short, specific cues are encoded, and these cues, or very similar ones, should be present when retrieval is attempted.

encoding specificity
Theory stating that the effectiveness of memory retrieval is directly related to the similarity of the cues present when the memory was encoded and when the memory is retrieved

Have you ever had difficulty recalling material you have studied? Part of the problem may be that the studying took place in one location and the testing occurred in a very different place. Most of the effective retrieval cues (those in the room where you studied) were missing in the classroom where you took the test. Hence it was difficult for you to retrieve the needed information.

Psychological Detective

How can you solve this recall problem? Give this issue some thought and write down some possibilities before reading further.

Try to do some studying in the room where the test will be given. The cues in the room will be among those that can help you retrieve the memory. If you cannot study in the room where the test will be given, try varying the locations where you study. This variety will prevent a single set of cues from becoming associated with the memory of the material you are learning. As a result, retrieval of your memories will be tied less directly to a specific set of environmental cues.

Eyewitness Testimony.   One of the most intriguing applications of the encoding specificity hypothesis has been in the area of eyewitness testimony. Such testimony often plays an important part in jury trials.

The possibility that eyewitness reports may be inaccurate has stimulated a large amount of research. One of the most startling findings concerns what can happen to a memory once it has been retrieved. Earlier we saw that when a memory is retrieved from LTM, it appears to be placed in STM for conscious processing. While this memory is in STM, however, it is possible to add new information to it and then *reencode* the modified memory. The next time you retrieve the new memory, your report may not correspond exactly to what actually happened because the new memory now contains the additional information.

This effect was tested in several ingenious experiments conducted by Elizabeth Loftus and her colleagues (Loftus, 1979; Loftus, Miller, & Burns, 1978). The design of one of those experiments is diagrammed in Figure 7-11. In this ex-

FIGURE 7-11 Diagram of the Loftus (1979) experiment on eyewitness accuracy.

Source: Loftus (1979).

One group saw the red sports car approaching a *stop* sign.			
EXPERIMENTAL DESIGN			
STEP 1	*STEP 2*	*STEP 3*	*RESULTS*
See slides of red sports car approaching a *stop* sign.	Answer questions about what they had seen. *Consistent* participants had questions about stop signs. *Inconsistent* participants had questions about yield signs.	View slides and pick those that were seen in Step 1.	Participants who were asked consistent questions in Step 2 were significantly more accurate in picking the slides they had seen than were the inconsistent participants.

The other group saw the red sports car approach a *yield* sign.			
EXPERIMENTAL DESIGN			
STEP 1	*STEP 2*	*STEP 3*	*RESULTS*
See slides of red sports car approaching a *yield* sign.	Answer questions about what they had seen. *Consistent participants* had questions about yield signs. *Inconsistent participants* had questions about stop signs.	View slides and pick those that were seen in Step 1.	Participants who were asked consistent questions in Step 2 were significantly more accurate in picking the slides they had seen than were the inconsistent participants.

periment, two groups of people watched a series of slides that showed an impending collision between a red sports car and another automobile. One group saw the sports car approach a stop sign at an intersection. The second group saw the sports car approach a yield sign at the intersection. After the slide presentation was completed, the participants were asked a series of questions about what they had seen. For half of the participants in each group, the questions were consistent with what they had seen. In other words, if they had seen a stop sign, the questions referred to a stop sign, and if they had seen a yield sign, the questions referred to a yield sign. For the remaining participants in each group, the questions were inconsistent—if they had seen a stop sign, the questions referred to a yield sign, and vice versa. Finally, all participants were shown pairs of slides and asked to pick the one they had actually seen (a recognition test).

As you would expect, a large number (75%) of the participants who were asked consistent questions after seeing the slides picked the slide they had seen. When they were asked inconsistent questions, however, only 40% were able to select the slide they had actually seen. The inconsistent questions altered their memory of the incident. Later, when they retrieved this memory, many participants reported an incorrect memory because they had encoded inaccurate information in their memory after being asked questions that were inconsistent (Ayers & Reder, 1998; Garry & Polaschek, 2000; Porter, Birt, Yuille, & Lehman, 2000). The results of this type of research have significant implications for how police interrogate eyewitnesses. They must be careful in how they formulate questions because suggestive questioning may alter witnesses' memories of an incident (Schacter, 2001).

Eyewitnesses cannot be relied on to provide accurate information. Memory for events can be influenced by many factors, including the questions that are asked after an incident.

In addition to demonstrating the memory-altering effects of questions, research has shown that (a) participants have trouble distinguishing between individuals of other races and (b) violence interferes with memory retrieval (Loftus, 1984). What's more, the correlation between confidence and eyewitness identification accuracy is low, although it can rise and fall as a function of such things as viewing conditions (Loftus, 1984; Wells et al., 2000). Moreover, the false memory effect is exceptionally strong and does not dissipate easily or quickly (Carpenter, 2000). The problems and concerns that such results create for the credibility of eyewitness testimony are obvious.

State-Dependent Learning. For a number of years, psychologists have known that if you learn material under certain special conditions, your retrieval of that material will be successful under the same conditions. For example, Randi drank a lot of coffee while she was studying for her last psychology test. Coffee contains a generous amount of caffeine, a central nervous system stimulant, so Randi was quite alert during her study session. Her physiological state became one of the stimuli that were present when the memories of the material she was studying were encoded. The implication from the encoding specificity hypothesis should be clear: Randi's retrieval will be best when she is tested after drinking a considerable amount of coffee. In other words, material learned in a particular physiological state is recalled best in the same physiological state, a phenomenon known as **state-dependent learning.**

state-dependent learning
Theory stating that when we learn something while in a specific physiological state, our recall of that information will be better when we are in the same physiological state

What you say you saw may not be what actually happened: our memories can be changed. These changes may not be intentional, but the potential for altering eyewitness reports must be recognized and addressed.

Gordon Bower (1981) extended this finding to include mood states, such as being happy or sad. His logic was simple. If you learn material while you are happy (or sad), you should retrieve that material more easily when you are happy (or sad). If the mood state that was present during learning differs from the one present during testing, retrieval should be more difficult (Weaver & McNeill, 1992).

As we saw in Chapter 3, odors can be linked to both emotions and memories. The link between odor and memory has been tested experimentally (Schab, 1990). Students smelled an odor both while they were generating antonyms (opposites) to a set of stimulus words such as *large* and *beautiful* and while they were recalling those antonyms later. These students recalled more antonyms than other students who had smelled an odor only during the learning session or only during the test session. Three very different odors (chocolate, apple-cinnamon scent, and mothball) were used separately to demonstrate that this memory effect was not limited to one specific odor. The results indicated that regardless of the odor type, participants who smelled the same odor during both training and testing remembered antonyms better than participants who smelled an odor only during training or only during testing.

The phenomenon of state-dependent learning indicates that memories acquired under a specific set of circumstances may be difficult to retrieve at another time or under different circumstances. Perhaps we have memories of events that occurred years ago waiting to be triggered.

The Repressed/Recovered Memory Controversy

One of the most dramatic and significant controversies in recent years involves reports of the sudden recall of repressed memories of childhood sexual abuse. For example, a newspaper article carried the headline "Eyewitness Errors Can Doom Innocent" (Associated Press, 2000). Retrieval of such memories has been reported to occur decades after the abuse. The significance of this issue is evident in the fact that the American Psychological Association and the British Psychological Association asked groups of experts to study the issue and write policy statements (Lindsay & Read, 1993). This issue attracted so much professional attention that in 1997 an entire issue of *Current Directions in Psychological Science* was devoted to it. The following cases illustrate the basis for the controversy.

Case 1. While Melody was in the hospital for treatment of depression, her therapist repeatedly suggested that her depression resulted from incest during childhood. After a few sessions, Melody reported that her father had raped her when she was 4 years old. When pressed for details, she wrote pages of her emerging repressed memories, including being molested by her father when she was 1 year old. She confronted her parents and consulted a lawyer about filing charges against her father. After leaving the hospital and consulting new therapists, Melody concluded that the abuse never occurred. She now says that the memories were "a figment of my imagination encouraged by my therapists and the pop psychology books I was reading" (Wartik, 1993, p. 64).

Case 2. Claudia lost more than 100 pounds in a hospital program for treatment of obesity. While in the hospital, she had flashbacks of sexual abuse committed by her brother. After she joined a therapy group for incest survivors, the memories of abuse flooded back. Her brother had died in the Vietnam War more than 15 years before her memories surfaced. Claudia's parents had left his room untouched since his death. She searched his room and found pornographic materials, handcuffs, and a diary in which he had described sexual "experiments" with his sister (Bower, 1993).

Case 3. Nadean Cool, a nurse's aid, sought therapy in 1986 to help her cope with her reaction to a traumatic event experienced by her daughter. Using a variety of techniques, including, hypnosis, a psy-

If you drink a stimulant, such as coffee, while studying, the state-dependent learning phenomenon predicts that you will be better able to retrieve your memories of the material you studied if you drink a stimulant beforehand.

chiatrist "uncovered evidence" that Cool had repressed memories of having been in a satanic cult, of eating babies, of being raped, and of having sex with animals. What's more, she came to believe she had 120 different personalities as a result of the sexual and physical abuse she had experienced. Eventually, Cool realized that false memories had been implanted, and she sued the psychiatrist. In 1997, her case was settled out of court for $2.4 million (Loftus, 1997).

About half of the states in the United States have extended the statute of limitations, allowing people who retrieve memories of abuse to sue alleged perpetrators within 3 to 6 years of the time the memories emerge. A growing number of victims have used these revised laws to file civil and criminal actions.

How are repressed memories retrieved? Psychotherapy (see Chapter 13) is the most common vehicle for the retrieval of memories of childhood abuse (generally incest). Typically, a person (usually a 20- to 30-year-old woman) seeks therapy for any of several problems. Many therapists believe that childhood sexual abuse is associated with a range of problems. Consistent with this belief, some of them ask about the existence of childhood abuse in the first therapy session, and some even insist that such abuse occurred, despite the client's denials.

Many therapists rely on memory-recovery techniques they believe help their patients remember repressed memories of abuse. For example, 83% of a sample of therapists agreed with the statement "Hypnosis seems to counteract the defense mechanism of repression, lifting repressed material into conscious awareness" (Yapko, 1994, p. 57). Unfortunately, memory-recovery techniques (like

Kelly Michaels worked at the Wee Care Day Nursery in Maplewood, New Jersey. As his temperature was being taken at a doctor's office one child said his teacher did the same thing. The accusations against her soon snowballed. Based on repeated interviews with highly suggestive and leading questions, the children said Kelly licked peanut butter off their genitals, forced them to drink urine and eat feces, and assaulted them with objects ranging from silverware to Lego blocks. Despite the absence of forensic evidence to support these accusations, she was convicted of 15 charges and sentenced to 47 years. The case against her was eventually overturned due to a lack of evidence; prosecutors decided that they would not take her to trial again.

hypnosis, imagery, dream interpretation, and journal writing) can also help people create compelling illusory memories (Ceci & Loftus, 1994; Schacter, 2001;
Yapko, 1994). Although there have been impressive successes in using hypnosis
to aid recall, the technique is likely to elicit inaccurate reports. Hypnosis tends to
increase confidence in the memories but has little positive influence on the accuracy of recall. What's more, it may be instrumental in implanting false memories "in individuals through the use of formal hypnotic procedures or even
through simple suggestions, without formal hypnosis" (Yapko, 1994, p. 96).

What is the evidence for repression? The theory that memories can be repressed is a cornerstone of the debate (Arrigo & Pezdek, 1997). Yet, after 70
years of looking, researchers have not found evidence that the process actually
exists (Holmes, 1994). In a typical evaluation of repression, participants learn
groups of words. Then half of the participants are stressed by being told that
they failed a test or that they have some personality defect; the other participants
are either told that they passed the test or they are given neutral personality
comments. When asked to recall the words, participants exposed to stress recall
fewer words. This result seems consistent with the notion that they had been re-
pressing memories associated with stress. Later, when the stressed individuals
are told that they had passed a difficult test or that the earlier test results had
been false, they remember the words as well as the control participants did. Researchers have found that the participants were concentrating on the experience
of the stressful event instead of shutting it out, as repression suggests. Thus participants recalled the words poorly because of the distraction created by concentrating on the stressful event rather than because of repression. Critics argue,
however, that laboratory studies of repression are not relevant to the kinds of
real-life traumas that have been associated with repressed memories.

It seems possible that we can lose contact with memories for long periods of
time; however, repression is an overused explanation of such memory failures. The
more likely explanations are normal forgetting, deliberate avoidance, and *infantile
amnesia*, or the inability to form memories early in life (Ceci & Loftus, 1994). Recall from the first year of life is highly unlikely because the hippocampus is not sufficiently developed to establish long-lasting memories (Loftus, 1997).

There is no evidence that people who report memories of abuse are involved in deliberate deception (Yapko, 1994). On the contrary, it is possible to
create false memories of a childhood event (for example, being lost in a shopping mall) that never happened (Loftus, 1997; Loftus & Ketcham, 1994).
Twenty-four adults read a booklet containing three one-paragraph true stories
of events that had actually happened to them; these events had been recounted
by a parent, an older sibling, or another close relative. A fourth story (the lost-
in-the-mall story) was not true but had believable elements: lost for an extended
period of time, crying, receiving aid and comfort from an elderly woman, and
reunion with the family. After reading the stories, participants wrote what they
remembered about the events. If they did not remember an event, they were
told to write that they did not remember. Two subsequent interviews examined
how much detail they could remember and how their memories compared to
those of their relative. On follow-up interviews, 25% of the participants
claimed to remember the fictitious event. The creation of false memories is not
limited to "memories" of events from childhood. Saul Kassin and his colleagues
found that college students who were falsely accused of having damaged a computer by pressing the wrong key often came to believe and confess to such an
act. A confederate who claimed to have seen the student engage in the act
seemed to lead many participants to confess (Kassin & Kiechel, 1996).

Perhaps the major problem in evaluating memories of childhood sexual abuse
is that there is no way to distinguish true repressed memories from false ones
(Lindsay & Read, 1993; Loftus, 1993, 1997). Ceci and Loftus (1994) write, "The

point is not that suggestive memory techniques unalterably lead to false memory, but merely that they may do so" (p. 359). There is a risk of uncritical acceptance of allegations made by patients: "These activities are bound to lead to an increased likelihood that society in general will disbelieve the genuine cases of childhood sexual abuse that truly deserve our sustained attention" (Loftus, 1993, p. 534).

The problems associated with both hypnosis and the use of suggestive questions (discussed earlier) led researchers to develop new procedures to increase retrieval of accurate information. Listening to numerous tape recordings of police interviews provided researchers with information on traditional police interviews. Typically, the interviewer asked many questions (which often elicited brief responses), usually asked closed-ended questions, and frequently interrupted, thus interfering with the flow of information and making it difficult to establish rapport. One of the most effective new approaches, the *cognitive interview*, is designed to avoid use of suggestive or leading questions and to establish rapport that is likely to elicit narrative descriptions of an incident (Fisher, 1995; Fisher & Geiselman, 1992). In contrast to the traditional interview, the interviewer using the cognitive approach asks fewer questions that are generally open-ended. The interviewee is given plenty of time to respond, so he or she is providing a narrative rather than responding to a series of rapid-fire, closed-ended questions.

The interview begins by asking the person to report everything about a relevant incident (for example, a question is likely to be phrased as "Describe the incident" rather than "What color was the car?"). A second component of the interview requires witnesses to reinstate mentally the context or setting in which the incident occurred. Such reinstatement can enhance memory retrieval. Next, the witness is asked to try to recall events in different temporal orders (beginning to end, end to beginning, and so on). Finally, the witness is asked to take different perspectives on an event such as mentally viewing the event from the perspective of the perpetrator or the victim. Research shows that this technique increases witness recall; generally, there is an increase of 35 to 75% in the amount of information gathered compared to typical police interviews. Although there may be inaccurate information, it tends to be small (Brock, Fisher, & Cutler, 1999; Clifford & Gwyer, 1999; Colwell, Hiscock, & Memon, 2002; Kebell, Milne, & Wagstaff, 1999; Kohnken, Milne, Memom, & Bull, 1999; Memom & Higham, 1999).

Memory Illusions

Clearly, the false-memory research and the repressed-memory controversy have stimulated considerable research. Indeed, a new view of memory may be emerging from this research: "memory is fallible, quirky, and essentially reconstructive in nature" (Lynn & Payne, 1997, p. 55).

Because false memories "occur in many different contexts and can be quite compelling" (Payne, Neuschatz, Lampinen, & Lynn, 1997, p. 56), several investigators view such occurrences as *memory illusions*. (Do you remember some of the visual illusions from Chapter 3? With visual illusions, we see things that don't exist.) In the case of memory illusions, we may remember things that never happened (see Table 7-3).

The strength and believability of memory illusions are shown in studies in which lists of words were learned (Payne, Elie, Blackwell, & Neuschatz, 1996). In these studies, participants claimed that they remembered exactly who said the critical but nonexistent words. What's more, some participants refused to believe that the nonexistent words were not part of the original list, even when they heard a playback of the original tape. Other research clearly indicates that memory

TABLE 7-3
Memory Illusions
Cryptoamnesia: A special type of plagiarism in which we inadvertently forget the actual source of information we read and use the material as if it were our own.
Déjà vu: This term, derived from the French, means "already seen." Déjà vu is the unusual feeling or illusion or having already seen or experienced something that is actually experienced for the first time. The term is widely quoted in the words of former baseball player Yogi Berra, who said, "It's déjà vu all over again."
Paramnesia: A condition in which the proper meaning of words cannot be remembered.
Jamais vu: Essentially the opposite of déjà vu, this condition occurs when a person experiences a scene or situation that is generally part of everyday life yet believes it to be unfamiliar.

illusions are created for very complex situations, such as being hospitalized at a young age (see, for example, Loftus, 1997). Memory illusions are often very strong and believable, and they seem to operate much in the same manner as other normal memory processes.

Even though memory illusions appear to operate similarly to other normal memory processes, there are some differences between them and true memories. Perhaps the most apparent difference concerns the amount of detail that is recalled: Greater detail is recalled with true memories (Mather, Henkel, & Johnson, 1997; Norman & Schachter, 1997).

What part of the brain is involved in creating memory illusions? Daniel Schachter and his colleagues reported data suggesting that the right frontal lobe plays an important role (Schachter, 1997; Schachter, Curran, Galluccio, Milberg, & Bates, 1996). For example, a patient with damage to the right frontal lobe displayed significantly more memory illusions than did people without frontal lobe damage.

Memory illusions are also relevant to eyewitness testimony. However, research has progressed far beyond demonstrating the fallibility of eyewitness testimony to examining specific factors, other than adding misleading questions and planting pieces of misinformation, that can create such memory illusions. For example, Maggie Bruck and Stephen Ceci (1997) demonstrated that interviewer bias is one of the factors leading to memory illusions. Likewise, research on the accuracy of memory recall under hypnosis indicates that such memories are no more accurate than those recalled under nonhypnotized conditions (Erdelyi, 1994). In fact, highly hypnotizable individuals report more memory illusions than do nonhypnotized persons (Lynn, Lock, Myers, & Payne, 1997; Lynn, Myers, & Malinoski, 2000). Although warning people of the possibility of suggestibility before hypnosis reduces the number of memory illusions, it does not eliminate them (Green, Lynn, & Malinoski, 1998).

Clearly, memory illusions are very real and very prevalent. It will be interesting to see what future research will uncover.

TECHNIQUES FOR IMPROVING MEMORY

Brad is an art major who is having difficulty in his U.S. history course. He cannot remember such facts as the major battles of the Civil War. They have no meaning for him. His friends' advice has not helped. Brad is very frustrated and is thinking of dropping the course. Yet he must pass this required course to complete his degree. *What can Brad do to improve his memory?*

mnemonic devices
Procedures for associating new
information with previously stored
memories

TABLE 7-4

Factors That Influence Human Learning and Memory

Factor	Effect
Number of study sessions	The greater the number of study (learning) sessions, the better the learning and memory.
Distribution of study sessions	Study sessions should be spread out. Spaced practice is more effective than massed practice.
Meaningfulness of material	Material that is meaningful will be learned better and remembered longer.
Similarity of items	A group of items of the same general type will be learned better than a group of dissimilar items.
Serial position	Items at the beginning and end of a study session or list will be learned better than items in the middle.

Influential Factors

Psychologists have been trying to answer this question for a long time (Higbee, 1993). As you can see from Table 7-4, they have found several factors that influence learning and memory. Among those factors are number of study sessions, distribution of study sessions, meaningfulness of material, similarity of items, and serial position.

Assuming that Brad really has tried to study, the key to remembering the history assignment is finding some meaning in the material. As long as U.S. history has little meaning or relevance to him, he will have difficulty learning it.

Understanding the factors presented in Table 7-4 also helps us to answer the question "What is the best way to study for a test?" Brad now knows he will do better on his tests if he studies as often as possible (increases the number of sessions) but takes several breaks between study sessions (improves the distribution of sessions). For the best learning to occur, the material he is studying should be meaningful (Moravcsik & Healey, 1995), and he should not try to study several different topics during the same session (maintain similarity of items). Finally, the *serial position effect* indicates that he should give a little extra attention to material he studies during the middle portion of a study session (Baddeley, 2004; Gershberg & Shimamura, 1994; Madigan & O'Hara, 1992). You might want to try these procedures yourself; they could help raise your grades.

Live!
psych   **7.4**

Processing Strategies

Now that you understand how to arrange your study sessions and the type of material that should be studied, you want to know more. Why do some people remember better than others? Do they have special secrets or tricks? This section describes memory techniques that have been shown to work. These active learning devices or methods are called **mnemonic devices;** they are useful because they associate new information with previously stored memories (Ashcraft, 2006). Thus they are forms of elaborative rehearsal and result in deeper processing. To remember new material, you first recall previously learned (familiar) information and then recall the new information that has been associated with it. You can decide whether mnemonic devices really work. As with anything else, some practice is required to learn to use them effectively. Among the most common techniques are imagery, the method of loci, the pegword technique, grouping, and coding.

Imagery.   If you create and use mental pictures or images of the items you are studying, you will remember better (Dewhurst & Conway, 1994; Paivio, 1971). Repeating items over and over again is not an especially effective method to help you remember them; however, visualizing them as you are learning can dramatically increase recall. When we try to remember by using both the words and the images, we have a *dual system* for coding the information, which increases the chances that it will be remembered (Sadoski & Paivio, 2001). For example, if you are learning the components of classical conditioning (see Chapter 5), you should not simply think "CS," "UCS," "UCR," and "CR"; rather, visualize a concrete example of each. The CS might be a noisy buzzer, the UCS a delicious apple pie, and so forth. This process of visualizing items as they are being learned is known as *imagery*.

Beyond this general finding, two more specific techniques for mental imagery have been developed. They are known as the *method of loci* and the *pegword technique*.

Method of Loci.   The method of loci can be traced back to the days of ancient Greek orators who used visual imagery and memorized locations to help them remember speeches or entire epics. *Loci* is the Latin word for "places;" the already stored cues for the **method of loci** are familiar specific places. When using this mnemonic device, you start with a set of familiar locations. For example, if you live on campus, you could list (in order) the major landmarks you see every time you walk from your dormitory room to the student union. Such landmarks could include the door to your room, the staircase to the first floor, the outside door, a tree, a statue, the science hall, and so forth, until you enter the front door of the student union. Then you would assign to each location an item that you want to learn. So if you were trying to learn the parts of the brain, you could pair the medulla with your door, the cerebellum with the staircase to the first floor, and so on. You could imagine an animated medulla hanging on your door. The cerebellum could become the staircase. Some people believe that more bizarre images have a greater effect on improving memory (Hirshman, Whelley, & Palij, 1989). To recall the parts of the brain in order, you would call up the mental image of the things you encounter on the way to the student union and remember the part of the brain associated with each location. This procedure may sound a bit complex, but it has been found to be highly effective.

Psychological Detective

Don, the rock-and-roll expert, can name in order all of the songs on each of the most popular "oldies" rock CDs. Tonight Don is studying for a psychology test. During this study session, he listens to some of his favorite songs. Don hopes that rather than interfering with his studying, listening to music will help him to score higher on the test. He plays one type of music for each section of material he is studying. He studies the first section while Beatles music is playing; during the next section he listens to some Billy Joel, and so it goes for the rest of the evening. How will Don's unusual study session assist him when he takes the test? Write down an answer to this question before reading further.

Pegword Technique.   In the **pegword technique**, which is similar to the method of loci, you start with a list of items that you already know quite well (see Table 7-5). For Don to learn a set of items, all he has to do is assign one item to each song on a particular CD. When he is ready to recall the new information, he simply remembers the song titles and the item associated with each. Don is using the pegword technique to help him remember material for his psychology test. For example, basic learning terms (see Chapter 5) such as *CS, UCS, UCR, CR, reinforcement*, and *extinction* may be associated with the titles on the Beatles CD. Items having to do with states of consciousness (Chapter 4) might be associated with titles on the Billy Joel CD. The main difference between the pegword technique

method of loci
Use of familiar locations as cues to recall items that have been associated with them

pegword technique
Use of familiar words or names as cues to recall items that have been associated with them

TABLE 7-5

The Pegword Mnemonic Technique

Numbered Pegs	Words to Be Learned	Image	
One is bun	Cup		Hamburger bun with a smashed cup
Two is a shoe	Flag		Running shoes with flag
Three is a tree	Horse		Horse stranded in top of tree
Four is a door	Dollar		Dollar bill tacked to front door
Five is a hive	Brush		Queen bee brushing her hair
Six is sticks	Pan		Boiling a pan full of cinnamon sticks
Seven is heaven	Clock		St. Peter checking the clocks at the gates of heaven
Eight is a gate	Pen		A picket fence gate with ballpoint pens as pickets
Nine is a vine	Paper		Honeysuckle vine with newspapers instead of blossoms
Ten is a hen	Shirt		A baked hen in the platter wearing a flannel shirt

Source: Ashcraft (2006).

and the method of loci is that in the method of loci you visualize specific *locations*, whereas in the pegword technique you think of an already established list of items.

Grouping (Chunking).   What is your telephone number? You will answer with a group of numbers, such as 316-555-5800. Since the time of the first experiment on grouping (Bousfield, 1953), psychologists have consistently found that we tend to group or *chunk* items when we recall them. If you must learn material in a certain order, you can group together the first three or four items, the next three or four, and so forth. We use this method of grouping when we learn telephone numbers. If the material does not have to be remembered in a particular order, the possibilities for grouping increase greatly. You can group items according to their type, their ending, their length, or any other way in which they are similar. How would you remember the following words?

> dolphin, green bean, Mickey Mouse, beet, Goofy, carrot,
> minnow, squash, bass, Minnie Mouse, spinach, trout,
> Pluto, salmon, celery, perch, Donald Duck

Study this list for 1 minute; then close the book and write down as many of the words as you can. Did you group the items into three familiar categories—fish, vegetables, and Walt Disney characters? If you did not use those three categories, did you use others? If so, how did they differ from the categories we proposed? Chunking seems to be used most frequently and effectively with STM tasks, such as remembering a phone number or a list of words.

Coding.   Items that are not very meaningful or relevant to the learner are not learned as well or as easily as more meaningful or relevant items. Some people

acronym
A word formed by the initial letter(s) of the items to be remembered

acrostic
A verse or saying in which the first letter(s) of each word stands for a bit of information

STUDY TIP

Make a set of flash cards with the names of the different processing strategies on one side and their definitions on the other. When you are studying material from this or another class, choose a card at random, test yourself on the definition, and then try out that particular strategy with the material you are studying.

create special codes to help them learn material that lacks relevance. They code the less relevant material in a meaningful form and then remember the coded items. It is important, however, to be able to decode the items once they have been learned. For example, the nonsense syllables *cib*, *xos*, and *gip* would be difficult to remember because they do not have high levels of meaning. What if we were to code each by printing it backward? In that case *cib* becomes *bic*, *xos* becomes *sox*, and *gip* becomes *pig*. These coded syllables are high in meaning and therefore are much easier to remember. When we want to recall the coded stimuli, all we have to do is reverse the order of the letters after the familiar words have been recalled.

Acronyms and Acrostics. Acronyms and acrostics are two popular coding techniques. An **acronym** is a word formed by the initial letter(s) of the items to be remembered. To remember the desired information you recall the acronym and then decode it. For example, to help remember the names of the Great Lakes, all you need to do is recall the acronym HOMES and then decode it: H (Lake Huron), O (Lake Ontario), M (Lake Michigan), E (Lake Erie), and S (Lake Superior).

An **acrostic** is a verse or saying (often unusual or humorous) in which the first letter(s) of each word stands for a bit of information. For example, let's say you are assigned the task of remembering the names of the first seven presidents of the United States in order. One approach would be to use rote memorization. On the other hand, you might do better, spend less time, and have more fun if you made up a little phrase such as this: "**W**ashington and **J**efferson **m**ade **m**any **a** **j**oke." The first letter of each word in this saying stands for the last name of a president: George **W**ashington, John **A**dams, Thomas **J**efferson, James **M**adison, James **M**onroe, John Quincy **A**dams, and Andrew **J**ackson. Students frequently create acronyms and acrostics when they study for tests.

Evaluating techniques for improving memory naturally led psychologists to look for the physiological basis of memory. We consider their findings next.

REVIEW SUMMARY

1. Craik and Lockhart proposed only one type of memory. The **level of processing** may determine the permanence of the storage of this memory.

2. There are at least four types of LTM: **procedural, semantic, episodic,** and **priming** (or **implicit**) **memory.** Each serves to store a different kind of information.

3. The **tip-of-the-tongue (TOT) phenomenon** has been used to study the network of semantic memories, whereas the study of **flashbulb memories** has provided information about episodic memory.

4. Research on the retrieval of memories has shown that we scan both STM and LTM to locate an item we wish to recall.

5. **Encoding specificity** has a great deal to do with the ease with which a memory is retrieved. If the cues that were present when a memory was encoded or stored are not present during retrieval, it is difficult to retrieve that memory. Encoding specificity appears to be at work in **state-dependent learning,** which states that we recall information better when we learn and are tested in the same physiological/psychological state. **Schemas** are clusters of knowledge or typical ways of thinking about things. As such, they not only reflect how we

store information, they can also influence how we retrieve information from memory.

6. It has been suggested that memories of childhood sexual abuse may be repressed and recalled during adulthood. Many of these repressed memories appear to have been induced during therapy sessions by suggestions made by the therapist. Psychologists have developed a number of techniques, including the cognitive interview, in order to assist in collecting information from eyewitnesses.

7. The number of sessions, distribution of practice, meaningfulness of items, similarity of items, and *serial position* of items influence human learning. Our memory can be improved by using a **mnemonic device** such as imagery. The **method of loci** and the **pegword technique** are two popular mnemonic devices.

8. Grouping and coding are two other techniques that can be used as memory aids. **Acronyms,** words formed by the first letter(s) of the items to be remembered, and **acrostics,** a verse or saying in which the first letter(s) of each word stands for a bit of information, are two popular forms of coding.

✓ CHECK YOUR PROGRESS

1. If your strategy in studying for a test is to memorize all the material, you may not do as well as someone else who relates the course material to real-life events. Why?

2. What is the main problem with the levels-of-processing approach to the study of memory?

3. How does the Craik-Lockhart model of memory differ from the traditional model of memory?
   a. The second model hypothesizes only one type of LTM.
   b. The second model assumes that retrieval is not an active process in STM.
   c. The first model hypothesizes only one type of memory but different levels of information processing.
   d. The first model uses semantic networking as a core concept in determining what is retained in working memory.

4. What is the most important question for Craik and Lockhart's view of memory?
   a. How long do memories last?
   b. How do we process information?
   c. How are visual memories stored?
   d. How much can we store in memory?

5. Which aspect of golf involves procedural memory?
   a. recalling how to swing the golf club
   b. recalling the time you made a hole-in-one
   c. recalling what type of golf ball you're using
   d. recalling that golf was first played in Scotland

6. The tip-of-the-tongue (TOT) phenomenon is to semantic memory as flashbulb memories are to
   a. implicit memory.
   b. semantic memory.
   c. episodic memory.
   d. procedural memory.

7. Which of the following illustrates a schema?
   a. the definition of the word *mild*
   b. the grocery list you just memorized
   c. your knowledge about going to a play
   d. your memory of a time you played basketball

8. How were psychologists able to implant false memories of a childhood experience of being lost in a mall?
   a. They used hypnosis followed by repeated suggestions that such an event had indeed occurred.
   b. Using specifically created newspaper clippings, they interspersed the reports with other clippings from the same time period.
   c. They collected real memories from family members and asked individuals for their memories of the true memories along with the memory they sought to implant.
   d. Combining sodium amytal treatment with dream imagery, they created an altered state of consciousness that made participants susceptible to suggestive scenes that they were asked to imagine.

9. Psychologists who speak of working memory are referring to a second stage of
   a. STM.
   b. LTM.
   c. episodic memory.
   d. primary memory.

10. What technique did ancient Greek orators use to remember speeches?
    a. coding
    b. transfer
    c. method of loci
    d. state dependence

ANSWERS: 1. You are processing at a very shallow level. The person who relates the material to real-life events is processing at a much deeper level. **2.** The term *level of processing* has never been clearly defined. **3.** c **4.** b **5.** a **6.** c **7.** c **8.** c **9.** a **10.** c

THE PHYSIOLOGICAL BASIS OF LEARNING AND MEMORY

When H.M. was 7 years old, he was struck by a bicycle, fell, and injured his head. Although there appeared to be only minimal damage, several years later he began experiencing minor but intense brain seizures. A major seizure occurred when he was 16. By the time he was 27, the frequency and intensity of the seizures warranted surgery to remove large portions of his hippocampus and amygdala (see Chapter 2). The operation took place in 1953. *What can an operation to control seizures tell us about memory?*

In addition to identifying and studying the processes that occur during learning and memory, psychologists have attempted to isolate the physical changes that accompany those processes. In other words, they have attempted to pinpoint and describe the physiological basis of learning and memory. Their research has focused on patients who suffer memory loss as a result of head injuries or operations like the one just described.

Amnesias

After experiencing a physical or psychological trauma, a person can lose his or her memory of people, places, and things. Such memory losses are called **amnesias.** We discuss amnesias caused by psychological traumas in Chapter 12. The study of amnesias resulting from physical trauma provides insight into the nature of memory. Two types of amnesias have been identified: *anterograde* and *retrograde*.

Anterograde Amnesia and the Hippocampus.   The inability to store new information after a traumatic physical event is known as **anterograde amnesia.** The case of H.M. is a well-known example of anterograde amnesia (Scoville & Milner, 1957). What can this case tell us about memory?

As it turned out, H.M.'s operation, in which large portions of the hippocampus were removed, provided information about the nature of memory. After the operation, H.M. was unable to form new memories; his entire world consisted of memories formed before 1953. He did not remember the names of people he had just met, what he ate for lunch, what was on television last night, or what year it is. In short, his daily experience consisted exclusively of STM, of living from moment to moment, except for his pre-1953 memories.

Psychological Detective

On the basis of this case, you should be able to reach two tentative conclusions. One has to do with the stages-of-memory processing discussed earlier; the second concerns the physiological basis of memory. Spend a few moments reviewing this information; then write down the two conclusions.

If you believe that H.M.'s problem has to do with the memory-storage process, you are correct. For H.M., new information is not reaching long-term storage. Thus we are led to the second conclusion: The hippocampus is involved in the process of storing new memories. Notice we said that this structure is *involved in the process* of storing new memories, not that new memories are stored in this structure. If memories were stored in the hippocampus, H.M.'s operation would have erased memories stored before 1953.

The conclusion that the hippocampus is involved in storing memories is supported by animal research. When the hippocampus is removed from both hemispheres of the brain in laboratory animals, the animals have difficulty holding information about a learning task they have just mastered in STM (Baddeley, 1988).

Retrograde Amnesia and the Consolidation Hypothesis.   Physical trauma may also result in the loss of memory of events that occurred before the trauma. In such cases we are dealing with **retrograde amnesia.** The fact that the greatest memory loss is for events that occurred just before the trauma suggests an interesting and testable hypothesis. Based on the notion that memories must "set" or "consolidate" to be stored in LTM, the **consolidation hypothesis** predicts that memories that are interfered with before they have consolidated will not be stored. This process is analogous to baking a cake: If the oven door is opened, the cake will fall. The blow on the head that produces retrograde amnesia has interrupted the consolidation process for recent memories.

amnesia
Loss of memory that occurs as a result of physical or psychological trauma

anterograde amnesia
Inability to store new memories after a traumatic event

retrograde amnesia
Loss of memories that were stored before a traumatic event

consolidation hypothesis
Hypothesis that memories must be consolidated or set before they can be stored

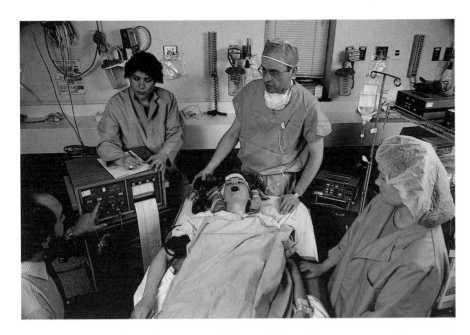

A human patient undergoing ECT may suffer from retrograde amnesia. According to the consolidation hypothesis, this loss of memory occurs because consolidation and transfer to LTM do not take place.

Both human and animal studies have provided evidence to support the consolidation hypothesis. For example, in some cases of severe depression, *electroconvulsive therapy* (*ECT*), also known as *electroshock therapy*, may be used (see Chapter 13). This procedure involves passing an electric current through the patient's brain. In addition to reducing the depression, ECT produces strong retrograde amnesia. Early studies found that the application of electroconvulsive shock (ECS) to animals shortly after a learning task also produced retrograde amnesia, suggesting that it interferes with the formation of a memory. What's more, the longer the delay between completion of the task and the application of ECS, the less the effect of ECS. In the longer delay conditions, we assumed that the memory had more time to consolidate and therefore ECS did not interfere with it as much.

In one study of the effects of ECS (Chorover & Schiller, 1965), rats were placed on small platforms. The normal response of a rat in this situation is to step down from the platform. When the rats stepped down, however, they received an electric shock to their feet. The rats' task was to learn to stay on the platform to avoid a foot shock. Five groups of rats were tested. These groups received ECS (by passing a mild electric current through the brain) either 3, 5, 7, 10, or 30 seconds after stepping off the platform and receiving a foot shock. Figure 7-12 shows that the longer the interval between the learning task and the delivery of ECS, the greater the percentage of animals that stayed on the

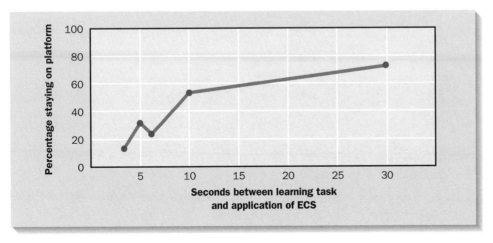

FIGURE 7-12 The longer the delay between original learning and an ECS, the greater the percentage of animals who avoided foot shock by staying on the platform.

Source: Chorover and Schiller (1965).

platform on the next trial. Thus it appears that the memory of receiving the foot shock after stepping off the platform was consolidated more strongly when ECS was applied either 10 or 30 seconds after a foot shock. Although not all animal studies have supported the consolidation hypothesis as well (Maki, 1986), there is no doubt that ECS impairs memory storage.

REVIEW SUMMARY

1. Physical trauma may result in a loss of memory known as **amnesia. Anterograde amnesia** occurs when new information cannot be stored, although old memories remain intact. It can result from damage to the hippocampus. **Retrograde** **amnesia** occurs when memories for events that happened before the traumatic event are lost. It may occur when memories are not allowed to **consolidate** or set.

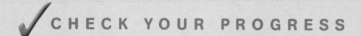

✓ CHECK YOUR PROGRESS

1. Loss of memory owing to a physical trauma is known as
   a. amnesia.
   b. habituation.
   c. consolidation.
   d. long-term potentiation.

2. After a serious car accident, John cannot remember driving in the rain. Nor can he recall skidding and plowing into a truck. This deficit is an example of
   a. retrograde amnesia.
   b. anterograde amnesia.
   c. encoding specificity.
   d. state-dependent learning.

3. What notion is supported by the fact that ECT disrupts memories?

   a. neural circuits
   b. consolidation hypothesis
   c. synaptic changes and memory
   d. protein synthesis and memory

4. Which kind of amnesia results from damage to the hippocampus? Why?

5. Laboratory rats prefer to be in dark places; hence they move readily from a brightly lit chamber to a dark one. Assume that a foot shock is administered when the rats enter the dark compartment. What should the rats learn from this experience? What will happen if they receive an ECS 3 seconds after receiving a foot shock in the dark compartment? What would happen if an ECS was administered 1 hour after the rats received a foot shock in the dark compartment?

ANSWERS: 1. a 2. a 3. b 4. Anterograde amnesia. Damage to the hippocampus results in the inability to form new memories. **5.** The rats should learn not to enter the dark compartment. If an ECS is administered 3 seconds after the shock in the dark compartment, there may be considerable disruption of consolidation. If an ECS is administered 1 hour after the shock in the dark compartment, the memory will have set and an ECS will have no effect.

ANSWERS To Hands-On Exercise

PAGE 301

How many capitals were on the tip of your tongue the first time you went through the list of states? Did the first letter help you recall any additional names?

State	Capital
Alabama	Montgomery
Connecticut	Hartford
Florida	Tallahassee
Georgia	Atlanta
Idaho	Boise
Iowa	Des Moines

State	Capital
Kentucky	Frankfort
Louisiana	Baton Rouge
Maryland	Annapolis
Massachusetts	Boston
Mississippi	Jackson
Nebraska	Lincoln
New Jersey	Trenton
Oregon	Salem
Texas	Austin
Wyoming	Cheyenne

28 How Do Ecosystems Work?

A grizzly bear intercepts a salmon on its spawning journey as it struggles up a
waterfall in an attempt to reach the same streambed where it hatched years earlier.

Reprinted from *Biology: Life On Earth*, Eighth Edition, by Teresa Audesirk, Gerald Audesirk, and Bruce E. Byers (2005),
Prentice-Hall, Inc.

AT A GLANCE

CASE STUDY WHEN THE SALMON RETURN

SOCKEYE SALMON of the Pacific Northwest have a remarkable life cycle. Hatching in shallow depressions in the gravel bed of a swiftly flowing stream, they follow the stream's path into ever-larger rivers that finally enter the ocean. Emerging into estuaries—wetlands where fresh water and salt water mix—the salmon's remarkable physiology allows the fish to adapt to the change to salt water before they reach the sea. The small percentage of young salmon that evade predators grows to adulthood, feeding on crustaceans and smaller fish. Years later, their bodies undergo another transformation. As they reach sexual maturity, a compelling instinctive drive—still poorly understood despite decades of research—lures them back to fresh water, but not any stream or river will do. The salmon swim along the coast (probably navigating by sensing Earth's magnetic field) until the unique scent of their home stream entices them to swim inland. Battling swift currents, leaping up small waterfalls, undulating over shallow sandbars, and evading human traps, they carry their precious cargo of sperm and eggs back home to renew the cycle of life. The fishes' journey back to their birthplace is remarkable in another way. Nutrients almost always flow downstream, carried from the land into the ocean; the salmon, filled with muscle and fat acquired from feeding in the ocean, not only battle against the flow of the current in their upstream journey; they also reverse the usual movement of nutrients. What awaits the salmon at their journey's end? How does their journey affect the web of life upstream?

28.1   WHAT ARE THE PATHWAYS OF ENERGY AND NUTRIENTS?

The activities of life, from the migration of the salmon to active transport of molecules through a cell membrane, are powered by the *energy* of sunlight. The molecules of life are constructed of chemical building blocks that are obtained as *nutrients* from the environment. Solar energy continuously bombards Earth, is used and transformed in the chemical reactions that power life, and is ultimately converted to heat energy that radiates back into space. Chemi-cal nutrients, in contrast, remain on Earth. While they may change in form and distribution, and may even be transported among different ecosystems, nutrients are constantly recycled. Thus, two basic laws underlie ecosystem function. First, energy moves through the communities within ecosystems in a continuous one-way flow, needing constant replenishment from an outside source, the sun. Second, nutrients constantly cycle and recycle within and among ecosystems (**FIG. 28-1**). These laws shape the complex interactions among populations within ecosystems, and between communities and their abiotic environment.

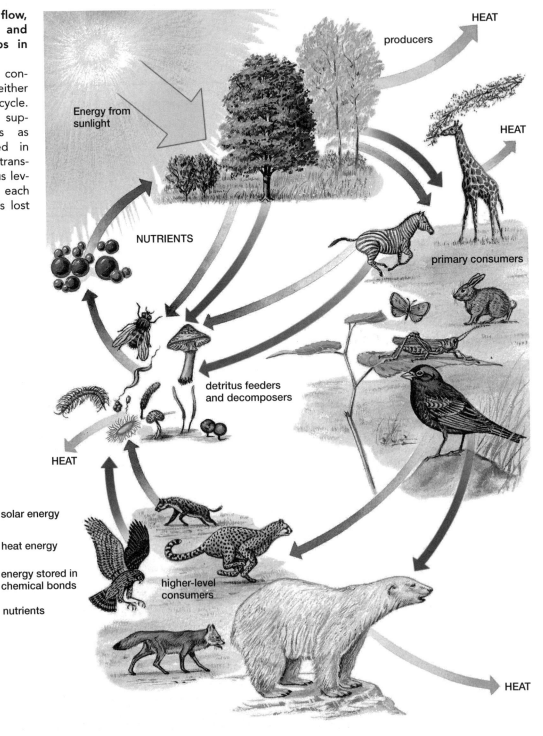

FIGURE 28-1 Energy flow, nutrient cycling, and feeding relationships in ecosystems
Nutrients, which are continuously recycled, neither enter nor leave the cycle. Energy, continuously supplied to producers as sunlight, is captured in chemical bonds and transferred through various levels of organisms. At each level, some energy is lost as heat.

28.2 HOW DOES ENERGY FLOW THROUGH COMMUNITIES?

Energy Enters Communities Through Photosynthesis

Ninety-three million miles away, the sun fuses hydrogen molecules into helium molecules, releasing tremendous quantities of energy. A tiny fraction of this energy reaches Earth in the form of electromagnetic waves, including heat, light, and ultraviolet energy. Of the energy that reaches Earth, much is reflected by the atmosphere, clouds, and Earth's surface. Still more is absorbed as heat by Earth and its atmosphere, leaving only about 1% to power all life. Of this 1%, which reaches Earth's surface as light, green plants and other photosynthetic organisms capture 3% or less. The teeming life on this planet is thus supported by less than 0.03% of the energy reaching Earth from the sun.

During photosynthesis (see Chapter 7), pigments such as chlorophyll absorb specific wavelengths of sunlight. This solar energy is then used in reactions that store energy in chemical bonds, producing sugar and other high-energy molecules (**FIG. 28-2**). Photosynthetic organisms, from mighty oak trees to single-celled diatoms in the ocean, are called **autotrophs** (Greek, "self-feeders") or **producers**, because they produce food for themselves using nonliving nutrients and sunlight. In doing so, they directly or indirectly produce food for nearly all other forms of life as well. Organisms that cannot photosynthesize, called **heterotrophs** (Greek, "other-feeders") or **consumers**, must acquire energy and many of their nutrients prepackaged in the molecules that comprise the bodies of other organisms.

The quantity of life that a particular ecosystem can support is determined by the energy captured by the producers in that ecosystem. The energy that photosynthetic organisms store and make available to other members of the community over a given period is called **net primary productivity**. Net primary productivity can be measured in units of energy (calories) stored by autotrophs in a specified unit of

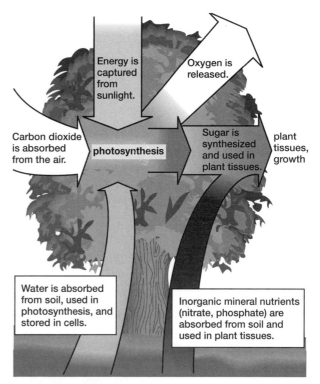

FIGURE 28-2 Primary productivity
Photosynthetic organisms, which capture solar energy and acquire inorganic nutrients from their environment, ultimately provide essentially all of the energy and most of the nutrients for organisms in higher trophic levels.

area (such as square yards, acres, or hectares) during a specified time (often a year). Primary productivity can also be measured as the **biomass**, or dry weight of organic material stored in producers that is added to the ecosystem per unit area during a specified time. The productivity of an ecosystem is influenced by many environmental variables, including the amount of nutrients available to the producers, the amount of sunlight reaching them, the availability of water, and the temperature. In the desert, for example, lack of water limits productivity; in the open ocean, light is a limiting factor in deep water, and lack of nutrients limit productivity in surface water. When resources are abundant, as in estuaries and tropical rain forests, productivity is high. Some average productivity measurements for a variety of ecosystems are shown in **FIGURE 28-3**.

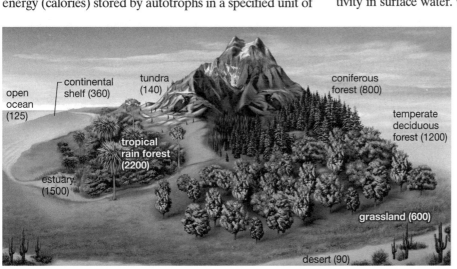

FIGURE 28-3 Ecosystem productivities compared
The average net primary productivity, in grams of organic material per square meter per year, of some terrestrial and aquatic ecosystems is illustrated. Notice the enormous differences. QUESTION What factors contribute to these differences in productivity?

FIGURE 28-4 Food chains
(a) A simple terrestrial food chain. **(b)** A simple marine food chain.

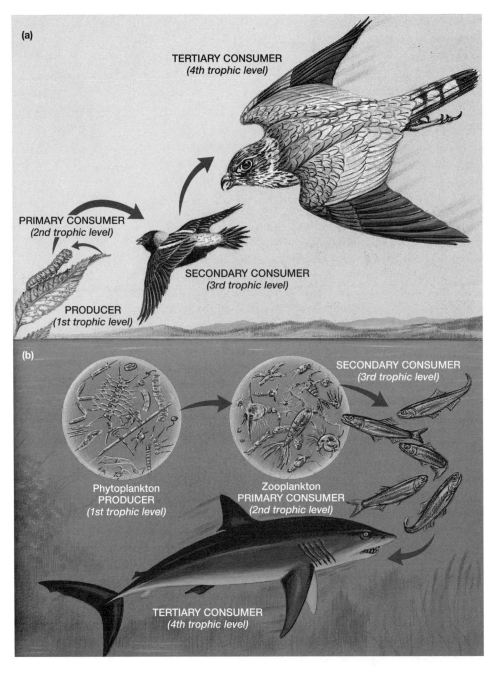

(a)

TERTIARY CONSUMER
(4th trophic level)

PRIMARY CONSUMER
(2nd trophic level)

SECONDARY CONSUMER
(3rd trophic level)

PRODUCER
(1st trophic level)

(b)

SECONDARY CONSUMER
(3rd trophic level)

Phytoplankton
PRODUCER
(1st trophic level)

Zooplankton
PRIMARY CONSUMER
(2nd trophic level)

TERTIARY CONSUMER
(4th trophic level)

Energy Is Passed from One Trophic Level to Another

Energy flows through communities from photosynthetic producers through several levels of consumers. Each category of organisms is called a **trophic level** (literally, "feeding level"). Producers—from redwood trees to cyanobacteria—form the first trophic level, obtaining their energy directly from sunlight (see Fig. 28-1). Consumers occupy several trophic levels. Some consumers feed directly and exclusively on producers, the most abundant living energy source in any ecosystem. These **herbivores** (meaning "plant eaters"), ranging from grasshoppers to giraffes, are also called **primary consumers**; they form the second trophic level. **Carnivores** (meaning "meat eaters")—such as the spider, eagle, and wolf—are predators that feed primarily on primary consumers. Carnivores, also called **secondary consumers**, form the third trophic level. Some

carnivores occasionally eat other carnivores; when doing so, they occupy the fourth trophic level, **tertiary consumers**.

Food Chains and Food Webs Describe the Feeding Relationships Within Communities

To illustrate who feeds on whom in a community, it is common to identify a representative of each trophic level that eats a representative of the level below it. This linear feeding relationship is called a **food chain**. As illustrated in **FIGURE 28-4**, different ecosystems have radically different food chains.

Natural communities, however, rarely contain well-defined groups of primary, secondary, and tertiary consumers. A **food web** shows many interconnecting food chains and more accurately describes the actual feeding relationships within a given community (**FIG. 28-5**).

FIGURE 28-5 A simplified grassland food web

Some animals, such as raccoons, bears, rats, and humans, are **omnivores** (Latin, "eating all")—that is, at different times they act as primary, secondary, and occasionally tertiary (third-level) consumers. Many carnivores will eat either herbivores or other carnivores, thus acting as secondary or tertiary consumers, respectively. An owl, for instance, is a secondary consumer when it eats a mouse, which feeds on plants; but it is a tertiary consumer when it eats a shrew, which feeds on insects. A shrew that eats a carnivorous insect is a tertiary consumer, and the owl that fed on the shrew is then a quaternary (fourth-level) consumer. When it is digesting a spider, a carnivorous plant, such as the sundew, can "tangle the web" hopelessly by serving simultaneously as a photosynthetic producer and a secondary consumer.

Detritus Feeders and Decomposers Release Nutrients for Reuse

Among the most important strands in the food web are *detritus feeders* and *decomposers*. **Detritus feeders** are an army of mostly small and often unnoticed animals that live on the refuse of life: molted exoskeletons, fallen leaves, wastes, and dead bodies (*detritus* means "debris"). The network of detritus feeders is extremely complex and includes earthworms, mites, protists, centipedes, some insects, a land-dwelling crustacean called a pill bug or roly-poly, nematode worms, and even a few large vertebrates such as vultures. They consume dead organic matter, extract some of the energy stored within it, and excrete it in a further decomposed state. Their excretory products serve as food for other detritus feeders and for decomposers. **Decomposers** are primarily fungi and bacteria that digest food outside their bodies by secreting digestive enzymes into the environment. The black or gray fuzz you may notice on tomatoes and bread crusts left too long in your refrigerator are fungal decomposers hard at work. They absorb the nutrients and energy-rich compounds that they need, releasing those that remain.

Through the activities of detritus feeders and decomposers, the bodies and wastes of living organisms are reduced to simple molecules—such as carbon dioxide, water, minerals, and organic molecules—that return to the atmosphere, soil, and water. By liberating nutrients for reuse, detritus feeders and decomposers form a vital link in the nutrient cycles of ecosystems. In some ecosystems, such as deciduous forests, more energy passes through the detritus feeders and decomposers than through the primary, secondary, or tertiary consumers.

What would happen if detritus feeders and decomposers disappeared? This portion of the food web, although inconspicuous, is absolutely essential to life on Earth. Without it, communities would gradually be smothered by accumulated wastes and dead bodies. The nutrients stored in these bodies would be unavailable to enrich the soil. The quality of the soil would become poorer and poorer until plant life could no longer be sustained. With plants eliminated, energy would cease to enter the community; the higher trophic levels, including humans, would disappear as well.

Energy Transfer Through Trophic Levels Is Inefficient

As discussed in Chapter 6, a basic law of thermodynamics is that energy use is never completely efficient. For example, as your car burns gasoline, about 75% of the energy released is lost as heat. This is also true in living systems. For example, splitting the chemical bonds of adenosine triphosphate (ATP) to cause muscular contraction produces heat as a by-product; this is why walking briskly on a cold day will warm you. Small amounts of waste heat are produced by all the biochemical reactions that keep cells alive. Compost piles can achieve internal temperatures of over 130°F (54.4°C) as a result of the heat liberated by decomposer microorganisms.

Energy transfer from one trophic level to the next is also quite inefficient. When a caterpillar (a primary consumer) eats the leaves of a tomato plant (a producer), only some of the solar energy originally trapped by the plant is available to the insect. Some energy was used by the plant for growth and maintenance, and more was lost as heat during these processes. Some energy was converted into the chemical bonds of molecules such as cellulose, which the caterpillar cannot digest. Therefore, only a fraction of the energy captured by the first trophic level is available to organisms in the second trophic level. The energy consumed by the caterpillar is in turn partially used to power crawling and the gnashing of mouthparts. Some is used to construct the indigestible exoskeleton, and much is given off as heat. All this energy is unavailable to the songbird in the third trophic level when it eats the caterpillar. The bird loses energy as body heat, uses more in flight, and converts a considerable amount into indigestible feathers, beak, and bone. All this energy will be unavailable to the hawk that catches it. A simplified model of energy flow through the trophic levels in a deciduous forest ecosystem is illustrated in **FIGURE 28-6**.

Energy Pyramids Illustrate Energy Transfer Between Trophic Levels

Studies of a variety of communities indicate that the net transfer of energy between trophic levels is roughly 10% efficient, although transfer among levels within different communities varies significantly. This means that, in general, the energy stored in primary consumers (herbivores) is only about 10% of the energy stored in the bodies of producers. In turn, the bodies of secondary consumers possess roughly 10% of the energy stored in primary consumers. In other words, for every 100 calories of solar energy captured by grass, only about 10 calories are converted into herbivores, and only 1 calorie is converted into carnivores. This inefficient energy transfer between trophic levels is called the "10% law."

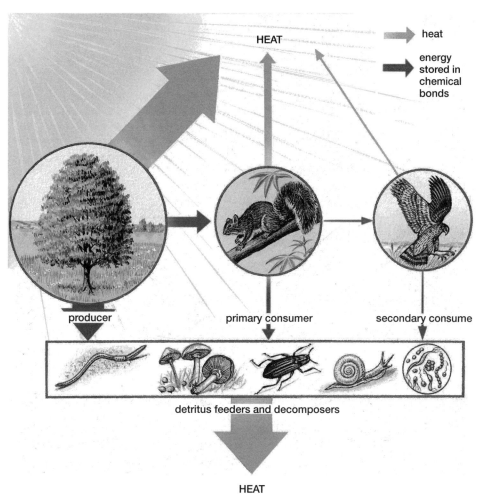

| | heat |
| | energy stored in chemical bonds |

HEAT

producer | primary consumer | secondary consume

detritus feeders and decomposers

HEAT

FIGURE 28-6 Energy transfer and loss

The width of the arrows is roughly proportional to the quantity of energy transferred between trophic levels as chemical energy or lost as heat in a forest community. QUESTION Why is so much energy lost as heat? Explain this effect in terms of the second law of thermodynamics (introduced in Chapter 6), and relate it to the energy pyramid in Figure 28-7.

An **energy pyramid**, which shows maximum energy at the base and steadily diminishing amounts at higher levels, illustrates the energy relationships between trophic levels graphically (**FIG. 28-7**). Ecologists sometimes use biomass as a measure of the energy stored at each trophic level. Because the dry weight of organisms' bodies at each trophic level is roughly proportional to the amount of energy stored in the organisms at that level, a *biomass pyramid* for a given community often has the same general shape as its energy pyramid.

What does this mean for community structure? If you wander through an undisturbed ecosystem, you will notice that the predominant organisms are plants. Plants have the most energy available to them, because they trap it directly from sunlight. The most abundant animals will be those that feed on plants, and carnivores will be relatively rare. The inefficiency of energy transfer also has important implications for human food production. The lower the trophic level we utilize, the more food energy is available to us; in other words, far more people can be fed on grain than on meat.

An unfortunate side effect of the inefficiency of energy transfer, coupled with human production and release of toxic chemicals, is that certain persistent toxic chemicals become concentrated in the bodies of carnivores, including people. This effect is described in "Earth Watch: Food Chains Magnify Toxic Substances."

tertiary consumer
(1 calorie)

secondary consumer
(10 calories)

primary consumer
(100 calories)

producer
(1000 calories)

FIGURE 28-7 An energy pyramid for a prairie ecosystem

The width of each rectangle is proportional to the energy stored at that trophic level. A biomass pyramid for this ecosystem would look quite similar.

EARTH WATCH   Food Chains Magnify Toxic Substances

BIOETHICS

In the 1940s, the properties of the new insecticide DDT seemed close to miraculous. In the Tropics, DDT saved millions of lives by killing the mosquitoes that spread malaria. Increased crop yields resulting from DDT's destruction of insect pests saved millions more from starvation. But DDT was entering food chains and unraveling the complex web of life. In the mid-1950s, the World Health Organization sprayed DDT on the island of Borneo to control malaria. A caterpillar that fed on the thatched roofs of houses was relatively unaffected, but a predatory wasp that fed on the caterpillar was destroyed. Eaten by the burgeoning caterpillar population, thatched roofs collapsed. Gecko lizards that ate poisoned insects accumulated high concentrations of DDT in their bodies. Both they, and the village cats that ate the geckos, died of DDT poisoning. With the cats eliminated, the rat population exploded. Villages were threatened with an outbreak of plague, carried by the uncontrolled rats. The outbreak was avoided by airlifting new cats to the villages.

In the U.S., wildlife biologists during the 1950s and 1960s witnessed an alarming decline in populations of several predatory birds, especially fish-eaters such as bald eagles, cormorants, ospreys, and brown pelicans. The decline pushed some, including the brown pelican and the bald eagle, close to extinction (all have shown significant recovery since the pesticide was banned in the U.S. in 1973). The aquatic ecosystems supporting these birds had been sprayed with relatively low amounts of DDT to control insects. In the tissues of the top predators, scientists found concentrations of DDT up to 1 million times greater than in the water where their fish prey lived. The birds were victims of **biological magnification**, the process by which toxic substances accumulate in increasingly high concentrations in animals occupying higher trophic levels.

DDT and other substances that undergo biological magnification share two properties that make them dangerous. First, decomposer organisms cannot readily break them down into harmless substances—that is, they are not **biodegradable**. Second, they tend to be stored in the body, particularly in fat, accumulating over the years in the bodies of long-lived animals. Exposure to high levels of pesticides and other persistent pollutants has been linked to some types of cancer, infertility, heart disease, suppressed immune function, and neurological damage in children.

Today, mercury contamination is a particular cause for concern. It is an extremely potent neurotoxin that bioaccumulates in muscle as well as fat. Its level in predatory fish consumed by people has become high enough that the U.S. Food and Drug Administration has advised women of childbearing age and young children not to eat swordfish and shark, and to limit their consumption of albacore tuna, because these long-lived ocean predators have accumulated enough mercury to pose a possible health hazard. In the U.S., coal-fired power plants are the largest single source of mercury contamination; but atmospheric mercury can be wafted thousands of miles and be deposited in what should be pristine environments, such as the Arctic. About half the mercury deposited on U.S. soil and water comes from overseas. Researchers have found neurological damage, including lowered IQ, corresponding to elevated mercury levels in mother's hair samples in two different island populations that consume high levels of marine fish and mammals. Inuit natives living north of the Arctic Circle have high levels of mercury and other bioaccumulating pollutants from consuming large quantities of predatory marine mammals and fish.

A class of chemicals called *endocrine disruptors*—including some widely used pesticides, plasticizers (which make plastic flexible), and flame retardants—have become widespread in the environment. Like DDT, they accumulate in fat and either mimic or interfere with the actions of animal hormones. There is compelling evidence that these chemicals are interfering with the reproduction and development of fish (including salmon), fish-eating birds such as cormorants (**FIG. E28-1**), frogs, salamanders, alligators, and many other animals. Endocrine disruptors are also suspected of causing reduced sperm counts in people.

To reduce human health hazards as well as loss of wildlife, we must understand the properties of pollutants and the workings of food webs. When we eat tuna or swordfish, for example, we act as tertiary or even quaternary consumers, and so we are vulnerable to bioaccumulating substances. In addition, the long human life span provides more time for substances stored in our bodies to accumulate to toxic levels.

FIGURE E28-1 The price of pollution
Deformities such as the twisted beak of this double-crested cormorant from Lake Michigan have been linked to bioaccumulating chemicals. Abnormalities of the reproductive and immune systems are also common in many types of organisms exposed to these pollutants. Predatory animals are especially vulnerable owing to biological magnification.

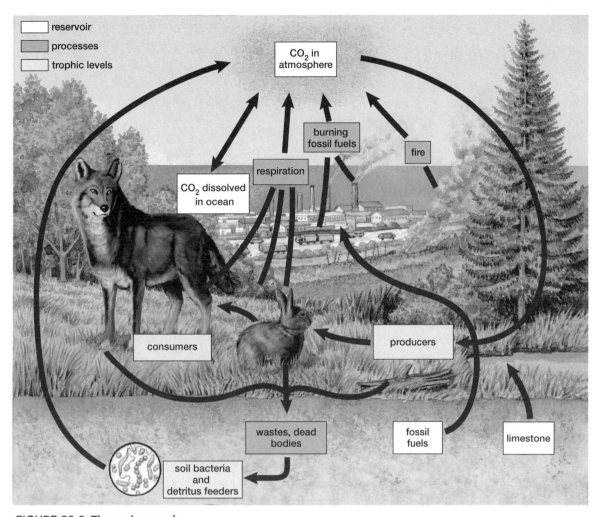

FIGURE 28-8 The carbon cycle

28.3 HOW DO NUTRIENTS MOVE WITHIN AND AMONG ECOSYSTEMS?

In contrast to the energy of sunlight, nutrients do not flow down onto Earth in a steady stream from above. Essentially the same pool of nutrients has been supporting life for more than 3 billion years. *Nutrients* are elements and small molecules that form the chemical building blocks of life. Some, called *macronutrients*, are required by organisms in large quantities. These include water, carbon, hydrogen, oxygen, nitrogen, phosphorus, sulfur, and calcium. *Micronutrients*, including zinc, molybdenum, iron, selenium, and iodine, are required only in trace quantities. **Nutrient cycles**, also called **biogeochemical cycles**, describe the pathways these substances follow as they move from communities to nonliving portions of ecosystems and back again to communities.

The ultimate sources and storage sites of nutrients are called **reservoirs**. The major reservoirs are generally in the nonliving, or abiotic, environment. For example, carbon has several major reservoirs: it is stored as carbon dioxide gas in the atmosphere, in dissolved form in oceans, in rock as limestone, and as fossil fuels underground. In the following sections, we describe the cycles of carbon, nitrogen, phosphorus, and water.

Carbon Cycles Through the Atmosphere, Oceans, and Communities

Chains of carbon atoms form the framework of all organic molecules, the building blocks of life. Carbon enters the living community through capture of carbon dioxide (CO_2) during photosynthesis by producers. On land, producers acquire CO_2 from the atmosphere, where it represents a mere 0.036% of all atmospheric gases. Aquatic producers in the ocean, such as seaweeds and diatoms, find abundant CO_2 for photosynthesis dissolved in the water; in fact, far more CO_2 is stored in the oceans than in the atmosphere. Producers return some CO_2 to the atmosphere and ocean during cellular respiration and incorporate the rest into their bodies. Primary consumers, such as cows, shrimp, or tomato hornworms, eat the producers and acquire the carbon stored in their tissues. These herbivores also release some carbon through respiration and store the rest, which is sometimes consumed by organisms in higher trophic levels. All living things eventually die, and their bodies are broken down by detritus feeders and decomposers. Cellular respiration by these organisms returns CO_2 to the atmosphere and oceans. Carbon dioxide passes freely between these two great reservoirs (**FIG. 28-8**).

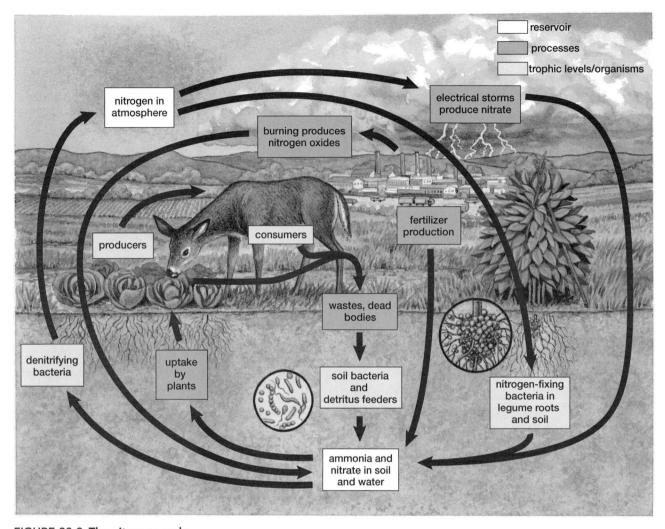

FIGURE 28-9 The nitrogen cycle
QUESTION What incentives caused people to capture nitrogen from the air and pump it into the nitrogen cycle? What are some consequences of human augmentation of the nitrogen cycle?

Some carbon cycles much more slowly. For example, mollusks and microscopic marine organisms extract CO_2 dissolved in water and combine it with calcium to form calcium carbonate ($CaCO_3$) from which they construct their shells. After death, the shells of these organisms collect in undersea deposits, are buried, and may eventually be converted to limestone. Geological events may expose the limestone, which dissolves gradually as water runs over it, making the carbon available to living organisms once again.

Another long-term portion of the carbon cycle is the production of fossil fuels. **Fossil fuels** form from the remains of ancient forms of life. The carbon in the organic molecules of these prehistoric organisms was transformed by high temperatures and pressures over millions of years into coal, oil, and natural gas. The energy of prehistoric sunlight is also trapped in these fossil fuels, captured by ancient autotrophs and then passed upward through various trophic levels before being sequestered in the high-energy hydrocarbons that we burn today. When people burn fossil fuels to use this stored energy, CO_2 is released into the atmosphere. In addition to the burning of fossil fuels, human activities such as cutting and burning Earth's great forests (where much carbon is stored) increase the amount of CO_2 in the atmosphere, as we will discuss later in this chapter.

The Major Reservoir for Nitrogen Is the Atmosphere

The atmosphere contains about 78% nitrogen gas (N_2) and is thus the major reservoir for this important nutrient. Nitrogen is a crucial component of proteins, many vitamins, and the nucleic acids DNA and RNA. Interestingly, neither plants nor animals can extract this gas from the atmosphere. Instead, plants must be supplied with nitrate (NO_3^-) or ammonia (NH_3). But how is atmospheric nitrogen converted to these molecules? Ammonia is synthesized by certain bacteria that live in water and soil. Some have entered a symbiotic association with plants called *legumes* (including alfalfa, soybeans, clover, and peas), upon which the bacteria live in special swellings on the roots. Legumes are extensively planted on farms, where they fertilize the soil. Decomposer bacteria can also produce ammonia from the amino acids and urea found in dead bodies and wastes. Still other bacteria convert ammonia to nitrate.

Nitrogen is also combined with oxygen by nonbiological processes: electrical storms and the combustion of forests and fossil fuels produce nitrogen oxides. Synthetic fertilizers often contain ammonia, nitrate, or both. Plants incorporate the nitrogen from ammonia and nitrate into amino acids, proteins, nucleic acids, and vitamins. These nitrogen-containing molecules from the plant are eventually consumed by primary consumers, detritus feeders, or decomposers. As it is passed through the food web, some of the nitrogen is released in wastes and dead bodies, which decomposer bacteria in soil or water convert back to nitrate and ammonia. This form of nitrogen is available to plants; nitrates and ammonia in soil and water constitute a second reservoir. The nitrogen cycle is completed by a continuous return of nitrogen to the atmosphere by *denitrifying bacteria*. These residents of wet soil, swamps, and estuaries break down nitrate, releasing nitrogen gas back to the atmosphere (FIG. 28-9).

Nitrogen compounds produced by people now dominate the nitrogen cycle, creating serious environmental concerns. When they enter ecosystems, excess nitrogen compounds may change the composition of plant communities by overfertilizing them, or they may destroy forests and freshwater communities by acidifying the environment, as discussed later in this chapter.

The Phosphorus Cycle Has No Atmospheric Component

Phosphorus is a crucial component of biological molecules, including energy transfer molecules (ATP and NADP), nucleic acids, and the phospholipids of cell membranes. It is also a major component of vertebrate teeth and bones. In contrast to the cycles of carbon and nitrogen, the phosphorus cycle has no atmospheric component. The major storage site for phosphorus in ecosystems is rock, where it is bound to oxygen in the form of phosphate. As phosphate-rich rocks are exposed and eroded, rainwater dissolves the phosphate. Dissolved phosphate is readily absorbed through the roots of plants and by other autotrophs, such as photosynthetic protists and cyanobacteria, which incorporate it into biological molecules. From these producers, phosphorus is passed through food webs (FIG. 28-10). At each level, excess phosphate is excreted. Ultimately, detritus feeders and decomposers return the phosphorus that remains in dead bodies back to the soil and water in the form of phosphate. It may then be reabsorbed by autotrophs, or it may become bound to sediment and eventually reincorporated into rock.

Some of the phosphate dissolved in fresh water is carried to the oceans. Although much of this phosphate ends up in marine sediments, some is absorbed by marine producers and eventually incorporated into the

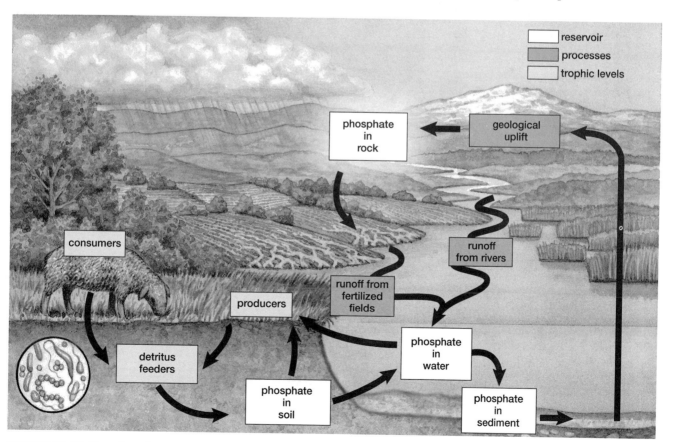

FIGURE 28-10 The phosphorus cycle

bodies of invertebrates and fish. Some of these, in turn, are consumed by seabirds, which excrete large quantities of phosphorus back onto the land. At one time, the guano (droppings) deposited by seabirds along the western coast of South America was mined; it provided a major source of the world's phosphorus. Phosphate-rich rock is also mined, and the phosphate is incorporated into fertilizer. Soil that erodes from fertilized fields carries large quantities of phosphates into lakes, streams, and the ocean, where it stimulates the growth of producers. In lakes, phosphorus-rich runoff from land can stimulate such a rich growth of algae and bacteria that the natural community interactions of the lake are disrupted.

Most Water Remains Chemically Unchanged During the Hydrologic Cycle

The water cycle, or **hydrologic cycle** (FIG. 28-11), differs from most other nutrient cycles in that most water remains in the form of water throughout the cycle and is not used in the synthesis of new molecules. The major reservoir of water is the ocean, which covers about three-quarters of Earth's surface and contains more than 97% of Earth's water. Another 2% is trapped in ice, leaving only 1% as liquid fresh water. The hydrologic cycle is driven by solar energy, which evaporates water, and by gravity, which draws it back to Earth in the form of precipitation (rain, snow, sleet, and dew). Most evaporation occurs from the oceans, and much water returns directly to them as precipitation. Water falling on land takes various paths. Some is evaporated from the soil, lakes, and streams. A portion runs off the land back to the oceans, and a small amount enters underground reservoirs. Because the bodies of living things are roughly 70% water, some of the water in the hydrologic cycle enters the living communities of ecosystems. It is absorbed by the roots of plants; much of this water is evaporated back to the atmosphere from plants' leaves. A small amount is combined with carbon dioxide during photosynthesis to produce high-energy molecules. Eventually these molecules are broken down during cellular respiration, releasing water back to the environment. Consumers get water from their food or by drinking.

Lack of Access to Water for Irrigation and Drinking Is a Growing Human Problem

As the human population has grown, fresh water has become scarce in many regions of the world. Additionally, contaminated, untreated drinking water is a major problem in developing countries, where over 1 billion people drink it. Impure water spreads diseases that kill millions of children each year. In both Africa and India, where water contamination poses significant threats, people are starting to use sunlight to kill disease-causing organisms. They place water in plastic bottles and shake them to increase the oxygen levels in the water. Then they put the bottles in a sunny spot, allowing the combination of oxygen, warmth, and ultraviolet (UV) light to create free radicals that kill bacteria. With no technology other than plastic bottles, these people are generating safe drinking water.

Currently, about 10% of the world's food is grown on cropland irrigated with water drawn from aquifers, which are natural underground reservoirs. Unfortunately, in many areas of the world—including China, India, Northern Africa, and the midwestern United States—this groundwater is being "mined" for agriculture; that is, it is removed faster than it is replenished. Parts of the High Plains aquifer, which extends from the Texas Panhandle north to South Dakota, have been depleted by

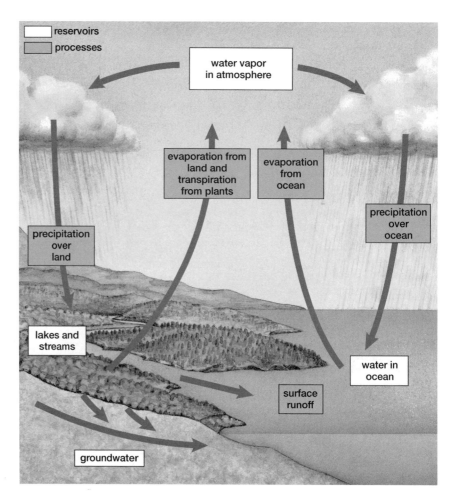

FIGURE 28-11 The hydrologic cycle

about 50%. In India, two-thirds of crops are grown using underground water for irrigation, draining aquifers far faster than they are being replenished. One promising solution is to devise ways of trapping the heavy monsoon rains, whose water usually pours into rivers and eventually into the ocean. People of a village in India have found that by digging a series of holding ponds, they can capture rainwater that would formerly run off. Their system allows the water to percolate down into the soil and helps replenish the underground water supplies. During the dry season, the people can then tap these supplies for irrigation.

28.4 WHAT CAUSES "ACID RAIN"?

Many of the environmental problems that plague modern society have resulted from human interference in ecosystem function. Primitive peoples were sustained solely by the energy flowing from the sun, and they produced wastes that were readily taken back into the nutrient cycles. But as the population grew and technology increased, humans began to act more and more independently of these natural processes. The Industrial Revolution, which began in earnest in the mid-nineteenth century, resulted in a tremendous increase in our reliance on energy from fossil fuels (rather than from sunlight) for heat, light, transportation, industry, and agriculture. In mining and transporting these fuels, we have exposed ecosystems to a variety of substances that are foreign and often toxic to them (**FIG. 28-12**). In the following sections, we describe two environmental problems of global proportion that are primarily a direct result of human reliance on fossil fuels: acid deposition and global warming.

Overloading the Sulfur and Nitrogen Cycles Causes Acid Deposition

Although volcanoes, hot springs, and decomposer organisms all release sulfur dioxide, human industrial activities, primarily burning fossil fuels in which sulfur is trapped, account for about 75% of the sulfur dioxide emissions worldwide. This is far more than natural ecosystems can absorb and recycle. The nitrogen cycle is also being overwhelmed. Although natural processes—such as the activity of nitrogen-fixing bacteria and decomposer organisms, fires, and lightning—produce nitrogen oxides and ammonia, about 60% of the nitrogen that is available to Earth's ecosystems now results from human activities. Burning of fossil fuels combines atmospheric nitrogen with oxygen, producing most of the emissions of nitrogen oxides. On farms, ammonia and nitrate are often supplied by chemical fertilizers produced by using the energy in fossil fuels to convert atmospheric nitrogen into compounds that plants can use.

Excess production of nitrogen oxides and sulfur dioxide was identified in the late 1960s as the cause of a growing environmental threat: *acid rain*, more accurately called **acid deposition**. When combined with water vapor in the atmosphere, nitrogen oxides and sulfur dioxide are converted to nitric acid and sulfuric acid, respectively. Days later, and often hundreds of miles from the source, these acids fall to Earth with rainwater, eating away at statues and buildings (**FIG. 28-13**), damaging trees and crops, and rendering lakes lifeless. Sulfuric acid may form particles that visibly cloud the air, even under dry conditions. In the U.S., the Northeast, Mid-Atlantic, Upper Midwest, and West regions, as well as the state of Florida, are the most vulnerable, because the rocks and soils that predominate there are less able to buffer acids.

Acid Deposition Damages Life in Lakes and Forests

In the Adirondack Mountains, acid rain has made about 25% of all the lakes and ponds too acidic to support fish. But by the time the fish die, much of the food web that sustains them has been destroyed. Clams, snails, crayfish, and insect larvae die first, then amphibians, and finally fish. The result is a crystal-clear lake—beautiful but

FIGURE 28-12 A natural substance out of place
This bald eagle was killed by an oil spill off the coast of Alaska.

FIGURE 28-13 Acid deposition is corrosive
This limestone statue at Rheims Cathedral in France is being dissolved by acid deposition.

FIGURE 28-14 Acid deposition can destroy forests
Acid rain and fog have destroyed this forest atop Mount Mitchell in North Carolina.

The Clean Air Act Has Significantly Reduced Sulfur, but Not Nitrogen, Emissions

In the U.S., amendments to the Clean Air Act in 1990 resulted in substantial reductions in emissions of both sulfur dioxide and nitrogen oxides from power plants. Overall sulfur emissions have decreased considerably throughout the U.S., improving air quality and rain acidity in some regions. Nitrogen oxide and ammonia release is not as strictly limited under the Clean Air Act. Although emissions of nitrogen oxides have dropped in some regions, atmospheric nitrogen compounds have shown a small overall increase, primarily because more gasoline is being burned by automobiles. Release of ammonia (NH_3) mostly from livestock and fertilizers, has increased by about 19% in the U.S. since 1985.

Unfortunately, damaged ecosystems recover slowly. A recent survey of Adirondack lakes found hopeful signs that about 60% of them are becoming less acid, although full recovery is still decades away. Some southeastern soils have become saturated with acid-releasing substances, and in these areas freshwater acid levels are increasing. High-elevation forests remain at risk throughout the U.S. Many scientists believe that considerable additional reductions in emissions, with far stricter controls on nitrogen emissions, will be needed to prevent further deterioration and allow the recovery of damaged ecosystems.

28.5 WHAT CAUSES GLOBAL WARMING?

Interfering with the Carbon Cycle Contributes to Global Warming

Between 345 million and 280 million years ago, huge quantities of carbon were diverted from the carbon cycle when, under the warm, wet conditions of the Car-

dead. The impact is not limited to aquatic organisms. Acid rain also interferes with the growth and yield of many farm crops by leeching out essential nutrients such as calcium and potassium and killing decomposer microorganisms, thus preventing the return of nutrients to the soil. Plants, poisoned and deprived of nutrients, become weak and vulnerable to infection and insect attack. High in the Green Mountains of Vermont, scientists have witnessed the death of about half of the red spruce and beech trees and one-third of the sugar maples since 1965. The snow, rain, and heavy fog that commonly cloak these eastern mountaintops are highly acidic. At a monitoring station atop Mount Mitchell in North Carolina, the pH of fog has been recorded at 2.9—more acidic than vinegar (**FIG. 28-14**).

Acid deposition increases the exposure of organisms to toxic metals, including aluminum, mercury, lead, and cadmium, which are far more soluble in acidified water than in water of neutral pH. Aluminum dissolved from rock may inhibit plant growth and kill fish. The tap water in some households has been found to be dangerously contaminated with lead dissolved by acidic water from lead solder in old pipes. Fish in acidified water often have dangerous levels of mercury in their bodies, because mercury is subject to *biological magnification* as it is passes through trophic levels (see "Earth Watch: Food Chains Magnify Toxic Substances").

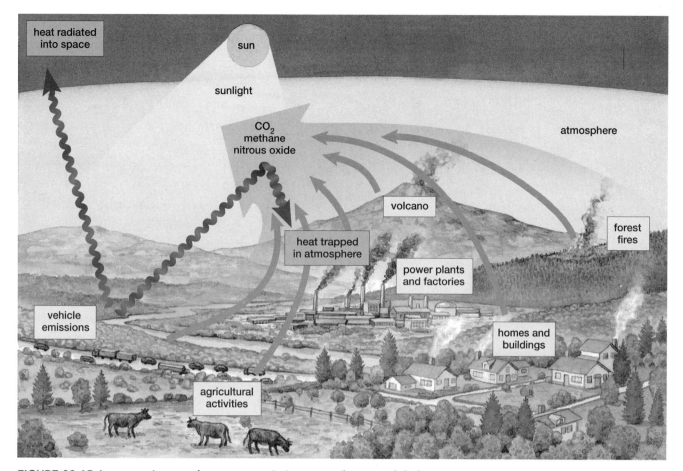

FIGURE 28-15 Increases in greenhouse gas emissions contribute to global warming
Incoming sunlight warms Earth's surface and is radiated back to the atmosphere. Greenhouse gases, released by natural processes but tremendously increased by human activities, absorb some of this heat, trapping it in the atmosphere.

boniferous period, the bodies of prehistoric organisms were buried in sediments, escaping decomposition. Over time, heat and pressure converted their bodies, with their stored energy derived from the sun, into fossil fuels such as coal, oil, and natural gas. Without human intervention, this carbon would have remained underground. Beginning with the Industrial Revolution, however, we have increasingly relied on the energy stored in these fuels. One researcher estimates that a typical gas tank holds the transformed remains of 1000 tons of prehistoric life, largely microscopic phytoplankton. As we burn fossil fuels in our power plants, factories, and cars, we harvest the energy of prehistoric sunlight and release CO_2 into the atmosphere. Since 1850, the CO_2 content of the atmosphere has increased from 280 parts per million (ppm) to 381 ppm, or almost 36%. According to recent analysis of gas bubbles trapped in ancient Antarctic ice, the atmospheric CO_2 content is now about 27% higher than at any time during the past 650,000 years, and CO_2 is increasing at an unprecedented rate of about 1.5 parts per million yearly. Burning fossil fuels accounts for 80–85% of the CO_2 added to the atmosphere each year.

A second source of added atmospheric CO_2 is **deforestation**, which destroys tens of millions of forested acres annually and accounts for 15–20% of CO_2 emissions. Deforestation is occurring principally in the Tropics, where rain forests are rapidly being converted to marginal agricultural land. The carbon stored in the massive trees in these forests returns to the atmosphere (primarily through burning) after they are cut.

Collectively, human activities release almost 7 billion tons of carbon (in the form of CO_2) into the atmosphere each year. About half of this carbon is absorbed into the oceans, plants, and soil, while the remaining 3.5 billion tons remains in the atmosphere, fueling global warming.

Greenhouse Gases Trap Heat in the Atmosphere

Atmospheric CO_2 acts something like the glass in a greenhouse; it allows solar energy to enter, then absorbs and holds that energy once it has been converted to heat (**FIG. 28-15**). Several other **greenhouse gases** share this property, including nitrous oxide (N_2O) and methane (CH_4) which are both released by

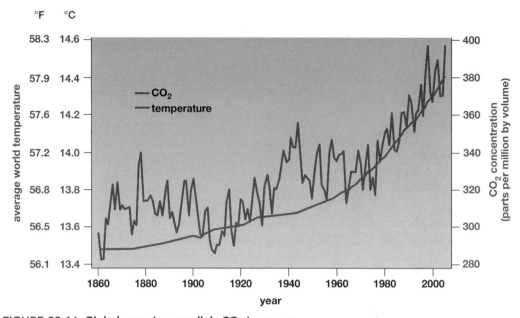

FIGURE 28-16 Global warming parallels CO₂ increases
The CO_2 concentration of the atmosphere (blue line) has increased steadily since 1860. Average global temperatures (red line) have also increased, roughly paralleling the increasing atmospheric CO_2.

agricultural activities, landfills, wastewater treatment, coal mining, and burning fossil fuels. The **greenhouse effect**, which is the ability of greenhouse gases to trap the sun's energy in a planet's atmosphere as heat, is a natural process. By keeping our atmosphere relatively warm, the greenhouse effect allows life on Earth as we know it. However, there is overwhelming consensus among atmospheric scientists that human activities have amplified the natural greenhouse effect, producing a phenomenon called **global warming**.

Historical temperature records have revealed a global temperature increase paralleling the rise in atmospheric CO_2 (**FIG. 28-16**). Nineteen of the twenty hottest years on record have occurred since 1980, and the six hottest years happened between 1998 and 2005, which set an all-time record.

If greenhouse gas emissions are not curtailed, the Intergovernmental Panel on Climate Change (IPCC) predicts that average global temperatures will rise from the current average of about 58°F (14.4°C) to between 61.5°C (16°C) and 66°C (19°C) by the year 2100 (**FIG. 28-17**).

Seemingly small overall temperature changes can have enormous impacts. For example, average air temperatures during the peak of the last Ice Age (20,000 years ago) were only about 5°C lower than at present. The predicted rapid temperature increase is of particular concern because it is likely to exceed the rate at which natural selection can allow most organisms to adapt. The temperature change will not be distributed evenly worldwide; temperatures in both the arctic and parts of the U.S., for example, are predicted to increase considerably faster than the global average.

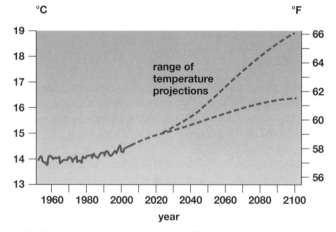

FIGURE 28-17 Projected range of temperature increases

Global Warming Will Have Severe Consequences

As geochemist James White at the University of Colorado quipped, "If the Earth had an operating manual, the chapter on climate might begin with the caveat that the system has been adjusted at the factory for optimum comfort, so don't touch the dials." Earth has begun to experience the consequences of global warming, and all indications are that they will be severe and, in some regions, catastrophic.

A Meltdown Is Occurring

Throughout the world, ice is melting (see "Earth Watch: Poles in Peril"). Worldwide, glaciers are retreating and disappearing (**FIG. 28-18**). In Glacier National Park,

FIGURE 28-18 Glaciers are melting
Photos taken from the same vantage point in 1904 (top) and 2004 (bottom) document the retreat of Carroll Glacier in Glacier Bay, Alaska.

back, in which an outcome of global warming, in this case the release of additional greenhouse gases, accelerates the warming process.

More Extremes in Weather Are Predicted

Many scientists believe that global warming is already affecting our weather. Recent studies have documented that during the past 35 years, both the intensity and duration of hurricanes have increased by 50%, doubling the number in the highest categories of wind speed and destruction (Categories 4 and 5), such as Hurricane Katrina, which devastated New Orleans in 2005. As the world warms, experts predict that droughts will last longer and be more severe, while other regions experience flooding. Scientists at the National Center for Atmospheric Research report that since the 1970s, the area of Earth impacted by severe drought has doubled from about 15% to about 30% as a result of increased temperatures and local decreases in rainfall. Agricultural disruption resulting from such extremes in weather could be disastrous for nations that are barely able to feed themselves.

Wildlife Is Affected

Biologists worldwide are documenting changes in plant and animal wildlife related to warming. The impact of global warming on forests could be profound. Fires, fuelled by drought and overly dense forests resulting from fire suppression in the past, have swept through large areas of the western U.S. and Alaska, releasing still more carbon dioxide into the atmosphere. As the world warms, tree distributions will change, based on their tolerance for heat. For example, sugar maples may disappear from northeastern U.S. forests, while some southeastern forests

where 150 glaciers once graced the mountainsides, only 35 remain, and scientists estimate that these may all disappear within the next 30 years. Greenland's ice sheet is melting at twice the rate of a decade ago, releasing 53 cubic miles (221 cubic kilometers) of water into the Atlantic annually. As polar ice caps and glaciers melt and ocean waters expand in response to atmospheric warming, sea levels will rise, threatening coastal cities and flooding coastal wetlands. Alaskan permafrost is melting, dumping mud into rivers, destroying salmon spawning grounds, and releasing CO_2 into the atmosphere as trapped organic matter decomposes. In Siberia, a region of frozen peat the size of France and Germany combined is melting, creating giant bogs that could release billions of tons of methane (a far more powerful heat-trapping gas than CO_2) into the atmosphere. Permafrost melting provides an example of positive feed-

EARTH WATCH   Poles in Peril

On Earth's opposite poles, Arctic and Antarctic ice is melting. The Antarctic Peninsula is uniquely vulnerable to global warming because its average year-round temperature hovers close to the freezing point of water. Over the past 50 years, the temperature around the peninsula has increased by about 4.5°F (about 2.5°C), far faster than the global average. Since 1995, over 2000 square miles of the ice shelf off the Antarctic Peninsula have disintegrated; based on ice core samples, scientists believe that these shelves had persisted for thousands of years. The loss of floating ice shelves has far-reaching consequences. The sea ice creates conditions that favor abundant growth of phytoplankton and algae. These primary producers provide food for larval krill, shrimplike crustaceans that are a keystone species in the Antarctic food web. Krill comprise a major portion of the diet of seals, penguins, and several species of whales. But over the past 30 years, krill populations in the southwest Atlantic have plummeted by about 80%. Researcher Angus Atkinson of the British Antarctic Survey hypothesizes that the decline is linked to the loss of sea ice. One likely scenario is that as the ice shelves shrink, algae that grows on the underside of the ice dwindles, and the krill that rely on it starve. Researchers are concerned that the impact of the krill loss may reverberate up the food chain, starving whales and seals and perhaps penguins as well. Adélie penguins spend their winters on the Antarctic ice shelves, feeding on krill. Although most Antarctic penguin populations remain healthy, researcher William Fraser, who has been studying Antarctic penguins for 30 years, reports that the Adélie penguin population in the western Antarctic Peninsula has lost about 10,000 breeding pairs since 1975.

At the far end of Earth, arctic temperatures have risen almost twice as rapidly as the world average, causing a 20–30% decrease in late-summer arctic sea ice during the past 30 years. Larger changes are projected for the next century, including temperature increases of about 7°F–14°F (4°C–8°C). In a disturbing example of positive feedback, melting ice will accelerate warming, because ice reflects 80–90% of the solar energy that hits it, but the ocean water exposed when ice disappears absorbs most solar energy, converting it to heat.

Arctic sea ice is critical for polar bears and for ringed seals, their major food source. Complete loss of sea ice, which some scientists predict within the next century, would mean almost certain extinction for polar bears in the wild. In Canada's Hudson Bay, sea ice is breaking up 3 weeks earlier than it did 30 years ago, depriving the bears of a prime opportunity to hunt ringed seals on the ice (**FIG. E28-2**). As a result, Hudson Bay polar bears now start their summers with 15% less weight (150 pounds for an adult male). Leaner females are producing fewer cubs with a lower survival rate, and the local bear population has declined by 22% since 1987. Hungry polar bears are increasingly invading northern Canadian and Alaskan towns, where they are sometimes shot. Polar bears are powerful swimmers; but as the ice floes have retreated, they have now been seen swimming 60 miles offshore, a far greater distance than usual for them. Several bears were spotted floating dead after a storm and are believed to have drowned, being too far out at sea to swim to safety.

The Arctic National Wildlife Refuge is the site of the largest number of onshore polar bear dens in Alaska. In late fall, polar bears congregate along the refuge shoreline. More bears are gathering there as ice retreats farther from the shoreline. Yet there is continuing political pressure in the U.S. to open the refuge to oil drilling. Ironically, polar bears are threatened not only with climate change, but with drilling for yet more oil to fuel the country's voracious appetite for fossil fuels, which will contribute to future global warming.

FIGURE E28-2 Polar bears on thin ice
The loss of arctic sea ice threatens the survival of polar bears.

LINKS TO LIFE Making a Difference

With less than 5% of the world's population, the U.S. is responsible for about 25% of world's greenhouse gases. The total greenhouse gas emissions produced by the U.S. amount to about 6 tons (5 metric tonnes) of carbon per person each year—more than any other country on Earth.

Can one person's actions make a difference? Jonathan Foley of the University of Wisconsin thinks so. He is on the cutting edge of climatological research, having led a team that developed one of the first computer models of global climate change to consider the impact of biological systems and human land use (such as converting forests to cropland) on climate. In 1998 Jon and his wife, Andrea, recognizing that greenhouse gas emissions and the resulting climate change can be significantly impacted by individual decisions and choices, made a choice of their own: to cut their family's energy use and carbon dioxide emissions in half. The Foleys and their young daughter lived in a five-bedroom house 30 miles from their work; Jon and Andrea each used a separate car to commute about 60 miles daily. First, they moved to a smaller house much closer to work. A visitor to the Foleys' new home—warm and cozy in winter and cool in summer—would never realize how little energy it consumes. Cracks have been sealed and the attic insulated. Every appliance has been chosen for energy efficiency. Compact fluorescent bulbs, using 75% less energy than incandescents, shed light throughout. Decorative ceiling fans reduce the need for summer air conditioning. Solar collectors supply over two-thirds of the family's water heating needs, while low-emittance window glass lets sunlight in while reducing heat loss in winter. The Foleys can now ride bicycles or take the bus to work, but they also enjoy their Toyota Prius hybrid gas/electric car—which gets nearly 50 mpg in city driving. Have they reached their goals? Within two years of their resolution, the Foleys, who now have two daughters, cut their energy use by roughly 65%. Foley says:

> Cutting your greenhouse gas emissions doesn't have to be a "sacrifice" at all. We have cut our emissions more than 50%, and we now have lower energy bills, a more comfortable house, more time to spend with our family, and a higher quality of life. Americans have a lot to gain by cutting fossil fuel use: reduced greenhouse gas emissions, improved air quality in our cities, less dependence on foreign oil supplies, and so on. This is a win-win scenario, so why not go for it?

Recently, innovative programs throughout the world (such as Carbonfund.org) are providing additional ways for individuals to "go for it." *Carbon offset* initiatives allow people to help compensate for the carbon they release by investing in projects that encourage energy efficiency, renewable energy use, and reforestation. For example, if your car gets 30 mpg and you drive 12,000 miles/yr, your car will release about 3.5 tons of CO_2 (or about 1 ton of carbon). Carbonfund.org allows you to select projects where your investment will reduce CO_2 emissions for about $5 per ton. This and many other carbon offset initiatives (search "Carbon offsetting" at http://www.ecobusinesslinks.com) provide a great way to augment personal lifestyle choices and further reduce your impact. Can you make a difference? The answer is an unequivocal "Yes!"

---

could be replaced by grasslands. Coral reefs, already stressed by human activities, are likely to suffer further damage from warmer waters, which drive out the symbiotic algae that provide them with energy. Corals are further threatened because, as the oceans absorb more CO_2, their waters are becoming more acidic, making it more difficult for corals to form their limestone skeletons.

Reports of changes keep coming in from throughout the world. The growing season in Europe has increased by more than 10 days over the past 28 years. Mexican Jays in southern Arizona are nesting 10 days earlier than they did in 1971. Many species of butterflies and birds have shifted their ranges northward. In the United Kingdom and the northeastern U.S., spring flowers are blooming earlier. While individual cases could be due to other factors, the cumulative weight of data from diverse sources worldwide provides strong evidence that warming-related biological changes have begun. Global warming is also predicted to increase the range of tropical disease-carrying organisms, such as malaria-transmitting mosquitoes, with negative consequences for human health.

How Are People Responding to the Threat?

Under the landmark Kyoto Treaty, negotiated in 1997 and implemented in 2005, thirty-five industrialized countries have pledged to reduce their collective emissions of greenhouse gases to levels 5.2% below 1990 levels. The treaty exempts developing countries (where most of the world's population resides), whose emissions per person are extremely low, and whose attempts to increase living standards cannot currently be implemented without increases in greenhouse emissions. Although 159 countries have ratified (agreed to implement) the treaty, the U.S.—the world's largest generator of greenhouse gases—has refused (as of this writing) to do so. Encouragingly, several U.S. states (including California) and many city mayors have pledged to adopt Kyoto-type standards independently. Although worldwide efforts are essential, our individual choices, collectively, can also have a big impact, as described in "Links to Life: Making a Difference."

CASE STUDY REVISITED WHEN THE SALMON RETURN

Researchers investigating the sockeye salmon's return to an Alaskan stream witness an awesome sight. Hundreds of brilliant red bodies writhe in water so shallow it barely covers them. A female beats her tail, excavating a shallow depression in the gravel where she releases her coral-colored eggs; meanwhile, a male showers them with sperm. But after their long and strenuous migration, these adult salmon are dying. Their flesh is tattered, their muscles wasted, and the final act of reproduction saps the last of their energy. Soon the stream is clogged with dying, dead, and decomposing bodies—an abundance of nutrients unimaginable at any other time of the year. Eagles, grizzly bears, and gulls gather to gorge themselves on the fleeting bounty. Flies breed in the carcasses, feeding spiders, birds, and trout. The breeding cycles of local mink populations have evolved around the event; females lactate just when the salmon provide them with abundant food. Isotope studies reveal that up to one-fourth of the nitrogen incorporated into the leaves of trees and shrubs near these streams comes from the bodies of salmon. Historically, researchers estimate that 500 million pounds of salmon migrated upstream in the U.S. Pacific Northwest each year, contributing hundreds of thousands of pounds of nitrogen and phosphorus to the Columbia River watershed alone. Now, due to factors including overfishing, river damming, diversion of water for irrigation, runoff from agriculture, and pollution of the estuaries (where several salmon species spend a significant part of their life cycle), migratory salmon populations in the region have declined by over 90% in the past century. The web of life that relied on the mighty annual upstream flow of nutrients has been disrupted.

Consider This Some salmon populations have been so thoroughly depleted that they qualify for protection under the Endangered Species Act. Some people argue that because these salmon are also raised commercially in hatcheries and artificial ponds, they should not be afforded this protection. Meanwhile, researchers studying chinook salmon raised in hatcheries noted a 25% decline in the average size of eggs of hatchery-reared fish over just four generations. These eggs produce smaller juvenile fish. Based on this information, explain why ecologists and conservationists are arguing for protection of wild salmon.

CHAPTER REVIEW

SUMMARY OF KEY CONCEPTS

28.1 What Are the Pathways of Energy and Nutrients?

Ecosystems are sustained by a continuous flow of energy from sunlight and a constant recycling of nutrients.

Web Tutorial 28.1 Energy Flow and Food Webs

28.2 How Does Energy Flow Through Communities?

Energy enters the biotic portion of ecosystems when it is harnessed by autotrophs during photosynthesis. Net primary productivity is the amount of energy that autotrophs store in a given unit of area over a given period of time.

Trophic levels describe feeding relationships in ecosystems. Autotrophs are the producers, the lowest trophic level. Herbivores occupy the second level as primary consumers. Carnivores act as secondary consumers when they prey on herbivores and as tertiary or higher-level consumers when they eat other carnivores. Omnivores, which consume both plants and other animals, occupy multiple trophic levels.

Feeding relationships in which each trophic level is represented by one organism are called *food chains*. In natural ecosystems, feeding relationships are far more complex and are described as food webs. Detritus feeders and decomposers, which digest dead bodies and wastes, use and release the energy stored in these substances and liberate nutrients for recycling. In general, only about 10% of the energy captured by organisms at one trophic level is converted to the bodies of organisms in the next higher level. The higher the trophic level, the less energy is available to sustain it. As a result, plants are more abundant than herbivores, and herbivores are more common than carnivores. The storage of energy at each trophic level is illustrated graphically as an energy pyramid. The energy pyramid leads to biological magnification, the process by which toxic substances accumulate in increasingly high concentrations in progressively higher trophic levels.

28.3 How Do Nutrients Move Within and Among Ecosystems?

A nutrient cycle depicts the movement of a particular nutrient from its reservoir (usually in the abiotic, or nonliving, portion of the ecosystem) through the biotic, or living, portion of the ecosystem and back to its reservoir, where it is again available to producers. Carbon reservoirs include the oceans, atmosphere, and fossil fuels. Carbon enters producers through photosynthesis. From autotrophs it is passed through the food web and released to the atmosphere as CO_2 during cellular respiration.

The major reservoir of nitrogen is the atmosphere. Nitrogen gas is converted by bacteria and human industrial processes into ammonia and nitrate, which can be used by plants. Nitrogen passes from producers to consumers and is returned to the environment through excretion and the activities of detritus feeders and decomposers.

The reservoir of phosphorus is in rocks as phosphate, which dissolves in rainwater. Phosphate is absorbed by photosynthetic organisms, then passed through food webs. Some is excreted, and the rest is returned to the soil and water by decomposers. Some is carried to the oceans, where it is deposited in marine sediments. Humans mine phosphate-rich rock to produce fertilizer.

The major reservoir of water is the oceans. Solar energy evaporates water, which returns to Earth as precipitation. Water flows into lakes and underground reservoirs and in rivers, which flow to the oceans. Water is absorbed directly by plants and animals and is also passed through food webs. A small amount is combined with CO_2 during photosynthesis to form high-energy molecules.

Web Tutorial 28.2 The Carbon Cycle and Global Warming

Web Tutorial 28.3 The Nitrogen Cycle

Web Tutorial 28.4 The Hydrologic Cycle

28.4 What Causes "Acid Rain"?
Environmental disruption occurs when human activities interfere with the natural functioning of ecosystems. Human industrial processes release toxic substances and produce more nutrients than nutrient cycles can efficiently process. Through massive consumption of fossil fuels, we have overloaded the natural cycles of carbon, sulfur, and nitrogen. Fossil fuel combustion releases sulfur dioxide and nitrogen oxides. In the atmosphere, these substances are converted to sulfuric acid and nitric acid, which fall to Earth as acid deposition, including acid rain. Acidification of freshwater ecosystems has substantially reduced their ability to support life, particularly in the eastern U.S. At high elevations, acid deposition has significantly damaged many eastern forests and threatens other forests throughout the U.S.

28.5 What Causes Global Warming?
Burning fossil fuels has substantially increased atmospheric carbon dioxide, a greenhouse gas. This increase is correlated with increased global temperatures, leading nearly all atmospheric scientists to conclude that global warming is due to human industrial activities. Global warming is causing ancient ice to melt and is influencing the distribution and seasonal activities of wildlife. Scientists believe global warming is beginning to have a major impact on precipitation and weather patterns, with unpredictable results.

KEY TERMS

acid deposition   *page 495*
autotroph   *page 485*
biodegradable   *page 490*
biogeochemical cycle
   page 491
biological magnification
   page 490
biomass   *page 485*
carnivore   *page 486*
consumer   *page 485*

decomposer   *page 488*
deforestation   *page 497*
detritus feeder   *page 488*
energy pyramid   *page 489*
food chain   *page 486*
food web   *page 486*
fossil fuel   *page 492*
global warming   *page 498*
greenhouse effect
   page 498

greenhouse gas   *page 497*
herbivore   *page 486*
heterotroph   *page 485*
hydrologic cycle   *page 494*
net primary productivity
   page 485
nutrient cycle   *page 491*
omnivore   *page 488*
primary consumer
   page 486

producer   *page 485*
reservoir   *page 491*
secondary consumer
   page 486
tertiary consumer
   page 486
trophic level   *page 486*

THINKING THROUGH THE CONCEPTS

1. What makes the flow of energy through ecosystems fundamentally different from the flow of nutrients?

2. What is an autotroph? What trophic level does it occupy, and what is its importance in ecosystems?

3. Define *primary productivity*. Would you predict higher productivity in a farm pond or an alpine lake? Defend your answer.

4. List the first three trophic levels. Among the consumers, which are most abundant? Why would you predict that there will be a greater biomass of plants than herbivores in any ecosystem? Relate your answer to the "10% law."

5. How do food chains and food webs differ? Which is the more accurate representation of actual feeding relationships in ecosystems?

6. Define *detritus feeders* and *decomposers*, and explain their importance in ecosystems.

7. Trace the movement of carbon from its reservoir through the biotic community and back to the reservoir. How have human activities altered the carbon cycle, and what are the implications for future climate?

8. Explain how nitrogen gets from air into a plant body.

9. Trace a phosphorus molecule from a phosphate-rich rock into the DNA of a carnivore. What makes the phosphorus cycle fundamentally different from the carbon and nitrogen cycles?

10. Trace the movement of a water molecule from the ocean, through a plant body, and back to the ocean, describing all the intermediate stages and processes.

APPLYING THE CONCEPTS

1. What could your college or university do to reduce its contribution to acid rain and global warming? Be specific and, if possible, offer practical alternatives to current practices.

2. Define and give an example of *biological magnification*. What qualities are present in materials that undergo biological magnification? In which trophic level are the problems worst, and why?

3. Discuss the contribution of population growth to (a) acid rain and (b) global warming.

4. Describe what would happen to a population of deer if all predators were removed and hunting banned. Include effects on vegetation as well as on the deer population itself. Relate your answer to carrying capacity as discussed in Chapter 26.

FOR MORE INFORMATION

Gorman, C. "Global Warming: How It Affects Your Health." *Time*, April 3, 2006. The warming trend may cause more deaths from weather extremes and a possible spread of malaria-carrying mosquitoes.

Kluger, J. "The Turning Point." *Time*, April 3, 2006. Polar ice caps are melting, droughts are increasing, wildlife is vanishing, and the effects of global warming may create positive feedback cycles that further increase the problem.

Krajick, K. "Long-Term Data Show Lingering Effects from Acid Rain." *Science*, April 13, 2001. Acid rain's damaging effects linger, and current control levels are inadequate to restore ecosystem health.

Milius, S. "Decades of Dinner." *Science News*, May 7, 2005. The body of a whale on the seafloor forms the basis of an underwater community.

Moore, K. D., and Moore, J. W. "The Gift of Salmon." *Discover*, May 2003. Salmon migrating upstream to spawn and die reverse the usual travel of nutrients and help replenish nutrients carried downstream during the rest of the year.

Pearce, F. "The Parched Planet." *New Scientist*, February 2006. Drought combined with unsustainable mining of groundwater threatens food production, particularly in developing countries.

Walsh, B. "The Impacts of Asia's Giants." *Time*, April 3, 2006. How India and China develop will have profound impacts on the future of the planet.

Wright, K. "Our Preferred Poison." *Discover*, March 2005. Mercury bioaccumulation threatens animals in the top trophic levels, including people.

Answer Key for Exam on History Textbook Selection

40% Objective

15% Matching

1. D
2. A
3. B
4. E
5. C

Number Correct _____ × 3 = _____

6% True/False

6. F
7. T
8. F

Number Correct _____ × 2 = _____

4% Fill in the blank

9. communes
10. Dow Chemical

Number Correct _____ × 2 = _____

15% Multiple choice

11. C
12. D
13. B
14. B
15. C

Number Correct _____ × 3 = _____

Total Points Objective Portion: _____

60% Essay

Part of Question	*Maximum Points*	*Student's Points*
30 % Question 1:		

Four expressions of frustration
    Possible answers: drug use,
    fragging, slogans, marches
	12 (3 each)	_____

Three problems
    Possible answers: disabilities,
    lack of jobs, drug dependencies,
    psychological problems
	9 (3 each)	_____

Causes of three problems Answers will vary	9 (3 each)	_____
Subtotals	30	_____
30% Question 2:		

Four signs of counter culture
    Possible answers: antiwar protests,
    music, sexual revolution, dress,
    drug use
	8 (2 each)	_____

Description of four signs Answers will vary	12 (3 each)	_____
Attitude toward Vietnam Antiwar, "make love, not war"	10 (5 each)	_____
Subtotals	30	_____

Total Points Essay Portion: _____

Total Points for Exam: _____

Answer Key for Exam on Environmental Selections

40% Objective

15% Matching

1. B
2. A
3. E
4. C
5. D

Number Correct _____ × 3 = _____

6% True/False

6. T
7. F
8. T

Number Correct _____ × 2 = _____

4% Fill in the blank

9. rain forests
10. public libraries

Number Correct _____ × 2 = _____

15% Multiple choice

11. D
12. C
13. C
14. C
15. A

Number Correct _____ × 3 = _____

Total Points Objective Portion: _____

60% Essay

Part of Question	Maximum Points	Student's Points
30% Question 1:		
Definition of global warming	5	_____
Causes?	5	_____
Results?	5	_____
How affect you?	5	_____
How solve problem?	10	_____
Subtotals	30	_____
30% Question 2:		
Durning's 7 items and why they work	10	_____
Two additional good items	4 (2 each)	_____
Their benefits	6 (3 each)	_____
Two harmful items	4 (2 each)	_____
Their harms	6 (3 each)	_____
Subtotals	30	_____

Total Points Essays Portion: _____

Total Points for Example: _____

Glossary

acronym   a word formed by the initial letter(s) of the items to be remembered

acrostic   a verse or saying in which the first letter(s) of each word stands for a bit of information

amnesia   loss of memory that occurs as a result of physical or psychological trauma

analyze (analysis)   to examine the structure of sentences, paragraphs, and sections for ideas; in critical reading and critical thinking, to critically examine written material by understanding such elements as the audience, author's purpose, social context, and evidence

annotation   marginal note made to highlight and organize main ideas and important details

antecedent   word, phrase, or clause that a pronoun refers back to

anterograde amnesia   inability to store new memories after a traumatic event

appeal to needs   appeal to our motivation to acquire what we think we need, such as food, warmth, shelter, sex, security, self-esteem, creativity, or self-expression

appeal to values   appeal to our values, such as honesty, loyalty, creativity, equality, faithfulness, and so on

argument   discourse that deals with controversial subjects that have not yet been settled and that are still open to inquiry and debate

bandwagon appeal   fallacy which claims that if all or most people are doing something, then a particular individual should also do the same

bar graph   plots quantitative information using bars that usually go up and down, but can go sideways, to show comparisons

brainstorming   a method for accessing prior knowledge that involves writing everything, usually in lists, that comes to mind about a topic

cause–effect pattern of organization   a topic is developed by explaining its causes and then its effects; the effects are sometimes explained before the cause

cause–effect reasoning suggests that certain causes inevitably produce certain results

chart organizes a great deal of information in columns under topics to allow comparisons

chronological pattern of organization material is presented as it has occurred over a perod of time

claim states the main point of an argument; types of claims are fact, definition, cause, value, and policy

common ground shared experiences or opinions between the author and the audience

comparison–contrast pattern of organization a topic is developed by showing what it is like or what it is unlike

comprehension monitoring checking your comprehension to make sure you understand the text; includes finding important ideas, rearranging material, and memorizing

conclusion emphasizes the most important or striking idea; usually located at the end of a chapter or article

connotative meaning encompasses all the negative or positive associations most people have with a word

consolidation hypothesis hypothesis that memories must be consolidated or set before they can be stored

context the passage in which a word appears, often can help explain its meaning

context for argument events or conditions that cause issues to surface and come to people's attention

controversy a topic that is arguable or debatable because it invites two or more points of view

Cornell reading notes notes that include marginal annotations and a summary

creative thinking associated with new discoveries, new insights, new combinations of ideas, and new conclusions

critical reading analyzing and evaluating the reading material itself

critical thinking thinking about new ideas that have occurred as the result of critical reading

denotative meaning   the literal, dictionary meaning of a word

diagram   a drawing that is used to show specific types of relationships among ideas

eidetic imagery   a form of memory, often called *photographic memory,* which consists of especially vivid visual recollections of material

either–or   fallacy in which the argument is oversimplified, with only two unsatisfactory possibilities and no alternative choices

elaborative rehearsal   rehearsal in which meaning is added to the material to be remembered

emotional comparison   compares items from different categories that have strong emotional connotations

emotional support   supporting evidence that appeals to emotions, values, and needs

emotionally loaded language   words that appeal to your feelings

encoding   first stage of the memory process; in it information is transformed or coded (a transduction process) into a form that can be processed further and stored

encoding specificity   theory stating that the effectiveness of memory retrieval is directly related to the similarity of the cues present when the memory was encoded and when the memory is retrieved

episodic memory   memory of one's personal experiences

essay exam   test that includes broad questions that ask students to organize and explain what they have learned and thought in well-organized essays

ethos   the Greek word for character; supporting evidence that appeals to ethos suggests that an individual has good character, credibility, admirable accomplishments, and general trustworthiness

evaluate (evaluation)   to differentiate between arguments and evidence that are reliable and convincing and those that are misleading and not convincing

exploratory argument   explains several different views on an issue without taking a particular position

exposition   discourse that informs, describes, explains, and reports facts and ideas that are not controversial

facts   real examples, data, or statistics that can be verified as true

fallacy   faulty type of support that appears to strengthen the argument but which actually weakens it

faulty cause fallacy in which the cause has nothing to do with the effect explained

figurative language language that cannot be taken literally. Reader must supply part of the meaning for it to make sense; examples are idioms and proverbs

flashbulb memory very detailed memory of an arousing, surprising, or emotional situation

flowchart a diagram that presents the sequential steps of a process

format the basic structure of reading material, such as the introduction, body, and conclusion format; textbook format; feature article format; or newspaper article format

free recall learning procedure in which material that has been learned may be repeated in any order

freewriting a method for stimulating thinking after reading; involves writing quickly whatever comes to mind as a result of reading

geographical map a visual representation of a geographical area that shows local, national, or worldwide trends; invites comparisons among geographical locations or emphasizes the special characteristics of particular locations

guilt by association fallacy that suggests that an individual's character can be judged by the character of his or her associates

hasty generalization a fallacy that presents a conclusion based on insufficient evidence

heading and subheading internal titles which divide the reading material into sections

hidden argument a subtle argumentative intent that is sometimes found in what appears on the surface to be informative material, such as that in a textbook, newspaper, or newsmagazine

historical comparison suggests that what happened in the past may also happen again in a similar situation in the present or future

icon objects that are so familiar that they invite an immediate and predictable response, like the flag.

idiom a figurative expression such as "being at the end of one's rope" that is peculiar to a language and that may be confusing to people who have studied only the literal meanings of the words of that language

imply   to leave part of the meaning for the reader to figure out

infer   to supply part of the meaning from one's own prior knowledge

inference   meaning created by the reader who uses prior knowledge to interpret and add to the author's ideas on the page

inferential meaning   the implied or unstated meaning that the author expects the reader to understand

irony   when the actual meaning is the opposite of what the author literally seems to be saying; the purpose is to criticize or ridicule

issue   the general topic of discussion or dispute in an argument

juxtaposition   placing unlike materials next to each other to create new links and associations

key term   important term that is repeated throughout to develop a major concept or idea

level of difficulty   how hard reading material is for a particular reader to read and understand

levels-of-processing model   theory stating that deeper processing of information increases the likelihood that the information will be recalled

line graph   includes a vertical axis, a horizontal axis, and a line or lines plotted on the graph to show trends

listing pattern of organization   material is organized as a list of related items under a descriptive title

literal comparison   shows how items in the same general category are either the same or different

literal meaning   the meaning conveyed by the words themselves without added inferences from the reader

logical support   supporting evidence that appeals to reason and common sense; logical support includes facts, definitions, cause-effect, signs, and comparisons

long-term memory (LTM)   memory stage that has a very large capacity and the capability to store information relatively permanently

main idea   the idea or topic in a paragraph or passage that all additional material further explains or develops

maintenance rehearsal   rehearsal used when we want to save or maintain a memory for a specified period of time

map   a visual representation of ideas and their organization plotted on a diagram composed of circles and lines

media   the various ways in which messages are communicated, from print to video to the Internet

media literacy   the ability to understand, analyze, and evaluate different types of media as well as to create them

memory   system or process by which the products or results of learning are stored for future use

mental connections   relating two or more ideas or sources and identifying what they have in common and how they communicate with each other

mental imaging   creating vivid mental images from reading descriptive passages

metacognition   thinking about how we think in order to improve the thinking process

metaphor   a direct comparison of two unlike things to create new insight and understanding

method of loci   use of familiar locations as cues to recall items that have been associated with them

mixed patterns of organization   combination of two or more patterns of organization in which, typically, a dominant pattern is supported with subpatterns

mnemonic devices   procedures for associating new information with previously stored memories

narration   an anecdote or story used to illustrate and develop a main idea

nonsense syllables   stimuli used to study memory; typically composed of a consonant-vowel-consonant sequence

objective exam   test that includes multiple-choice, true–false, fill-in-the-blank, and matching questions

obvious argument   an author states an issue, takes a position on it, and argues in favor of that position

opinion   statement of personal views or interpretations

organizational chart   describes hierarchies and relationships within an organization

outline   a summary of main ideas and details, with details indented and listed under the main ideas

paired-associate learning   learning procedure in which items to be recalled are learned in pairs. During recall, one member of the pair is presented and the other is to be recalled

paraphrase   rewriting an author's ideas in one's own words

pattern of organization   the order in which information is presented; often follows an established pattern such as chronological, problem–solution, and so on

pegword technique   use of familiar words or names as cues to recall items that have been associated with them

pictograph   composed of sketches of figures set in relation to each other to make abstract ideas more concrete

pie graph   a diagram that looks like a pie cut into pieces to emphasize the various parts and show how they complete the whole

point of view   an author's slant on the subject; indicated by taking a stand, expressing a position, or having a "take" on an issue

positive self-talk   using positive, confidence-building language before and while taking a test to dispel negative feelings and fear of failure

predicting   anticipating the next subject and thinking ahead while reading

prefix   a word part attached to the beginning of a root word that changes its meaning, such as *auto-, trans-,* or *post-*

pre-outline   a sentence, usually found in the introduction, that lists the ideas that will be developed in the coming paragraphs

prereading strategies   activities done before reading to improve concentration and understanding

priming or implicit memory unconscious memory processing in which prior exposure to stimulus items may aid subsequent learning

prior knowledge information about a topic that a reader possesses before beginning to read

proactive interference situation in which previously learned information hinders the recall of information learned more recently

problem–solution pattern of organization a problem is presented along with one or more possible solutions to it

problem solving identifies a problem and tests solutions to it until one solution is found that seems to work best

procedural memory memory for making responses and performing skilled actions

process pattern of organization identifies and explains the steps needed to complete a project

proverb a saying that conveys meaning different from its literal meaning, such as "the early bird catches the worm"

psycholinguistic reading theory theory of reading that emphasizes that the mind of the reader interacting with the language on the page enables people to read and understand in their own unique ways

purpose for reading varies with the specific reading assignment and the reader's reason for reading; may include reading to understand and learn or reading to analyze, evaluate, and come up with new ideas of one's own

purpose sentence states what a chapter or essay will be about, often found in the introductory paragraph

quantitative exam test that involves mathematics and problem solving, usually in math and science classes

reading process describes what readers do when they read; often divided into activities for prereading, reading, and postreading

reading strategy a conscious procedure that a reader uses to understand and think about reading material

recite to repeat ideas aloud or to write them down to help commit them to memory; one of the "3 R's" for exam study

recognition test test in which retention is measured by the ability to pick out previously learned items from a list that also contains unfamiliar items

red herring fallacy in which evidence is introduced to support a claim that is actually unrelated and has nothing to do with the claim

reduce to simplify difficult sentences and paragraphs by writing them in familiar language that helps the reader understand them better; one of the "3 R's" for exam study

reflect to pause and think about what was read in order to understand and remember it

refutation to identify the opposing positions in argument and demonstrate what is wrong with them

relearning test test of retention that compares the time or trials required to learn material a second time with the time or trials required to learn the material the first time

retrieval third stage of the memory process; in it stored memories are brought into consciousness

retroactive interference situation in which information learned more recently hinders the recall of information learned previously

retrograde amnesia loss of memories that were stored before a traumatic event

review to read through previously studied material in an effort to commit it to memory; one of the "3 R's" for exam study

root the base or stem of a word, to which prefixes and suffixes can be added to change its meaning

sarcasm saying the opposite of what is true, but with the intent to ridicule or make fun of

savings score difference between the time or trials originally required to learn material and the time or trials required to relearn the material; also known as *relearning score*

scanning looking through reading material for a specific bit of information that is likely to be there; used to locate particular bits of information very quickly

schema grouping or cluster of knowledge about an object or sequence of events

section of material usually several paragraphs that develop one of a few major ideas in a chapter or essay

semantic memory memory for general knowledge

semantic network network of related concepts that are linked together

sensory memory very brief (0.5 to 1.0 second for visual stimuli and 2 to 3 seconds for auditory stimuli) but extensive memory for sensory events

serial learning learning procedure in which material that has been learned must be repeated in the order in which it was presented; also known as *ordered recall*

serial position effect tendency for items at the beginning and end of a list to be learned better than items in the middle

short-term memory (STM) memory stage in which information is held in consciousness for 10 to 20 seconds

sign used in an argument to prove that the existence of one thing indicates that something else is true; for example, ragged clothes are a sign of poverty

sign of bias clue that the author has strong opinions, even though they may not be directly stated

simile a comparison of two things, using *like* or *as*, to create a vivid mental picture

skimming involves reading the first and last paragraphs and the intervening sentences and words that carry the most meaning; the objective is to locate the subject, the most important ideas, and enough details to identify the subject and determine what the author is saying about it

slippery slope fallacy in which the suggestion is made that if one thing is allowed to happen, many other things just like it will inevitably happen as well

spatial pattern of organization material is described as it is located and arranged within a space or area

specialized vocabulary the vocabulary associated with a particular field of study

stacked (stacking) evidence when an author selects evidence to support only one side of an issue and ignores others

state-dependent learning theory stating that when we learn something while in a specific physiological state, our recall of that information will be better when we are in the same physiological state

storage second stage of the memory process; in it information is placed in the memory system. This stage may involve either brief or long-term storage of memories

straw man fallacy that attributes an argument to an opponent that the opponent never made, and then refutes it

study reading   emphasizes what the reader knows as a result of reading; reading to understand and learn

study sheet   organizes information from several sources according to major topics; used to learn information for exams

suffix   a word part attached to the end of a root word that changes its meaning, such as *er, able,* or *ly.*

summary   restates the main ideas and is usually found at the end of a chapter or essay

supporting detail   develops and explains the main idea; details may include examples, explanations, comparisons and contrasts, statistics and facts, quotations, and description

surveying   a procedure that enables a reader to identify the subject of a text, find some of the main ideas, study how the ideas are organized, and locate some of the key terms

survey map   a graphic representation of the most obvious main ideas that a reader has located by surveying

symbol   an object that calls up association with past experience, knowledge, and feelings and invites applications to the new object.

synthesis   involves drawing ideas and materials from a variety of sources and putting them together to form new combinations or new wholes

table of figures   presents summaries of numerical data that are usually explained more fully in the text

test anxiety   nervous feelings before an exam that, without treatment, can be debilitating

test taking strategies   a method or procedure used to improve test performance

tip-of-the-tongue (TOT) phenomenon   condition of being almost, but not quite, able to remember something; used to investigate the nature of semantic memory

topic sentence   the sentence in a paragraph that introduces and states the main idea; usually found at or near the beginning of the paragraph

transition   word, phrase, sentence, or paragraph that helps the reader move mentally from one idea to another; also emphasizes main ideas to show how they relate to each other

UAS process   a text marking process that involves Underlining, Annotating, and Summarizing

unconscious argument occurs when an author is unable to remain neutral on a topic and allows bias to creep in without realizing it

visual argument visual materials, from charts and graphs to photographs and drawings that express opinions on controversial issues.

visual material photographs, illustrations, charts, graphs, cartoons, diagrams, and maps that make written explanations clearer, more interesting, and more memorable

whole into parts pattern of organization a broad subject is divided into subtopics or subcategories; each subtopic is then discussed individually

word family words grouped together according to a common root

working memory second stage of short-term memory; in it attention and conscious effort are brought to bear on material

writing convention the rules and customs that writers follow as they write that also help readers anticipate and predict as they read, such as paragraph construction or the use of titles and introductions

writing to learn helps readers clarify and condense material in the form of reading notes, summaries, lists, maps, vocabulary sheets, and outlines

writing to think helps readers analyze, think, react, work out, and express positions and original ideas in the form of summary response papers, reaction papers, and freewriting

Credits

P. 18, *New York Times* editorial, "Teaching Johnny to Read" from *The New York Times* (January 25, 1997). Copyright © 1997 by The New York Times Company. Reprinted with the permission of The New York Times. P. 19, Aziza Davis, "My Father, the Graduate" from *Tools for Life from Tripod*, Vol. 1 (Fall 1996). Copyright © 1996. Reprinted by permission. P. 21, Malcolm X, excerpts from "Learning to Read" from *The Autobiography of Malcolm X*, by Malcolm X with the assistance of Alex Haley. Copyright © 1964 by Alex Haley and Malcolm X. Copyright © 1965 by Alex Haley and Malcolm X. Copyright © 1965 by Alex Haley and Betty Shabazz. Reprinted with the permission of Random House, Inc. P. 25, Gerald Graff, excerpts from *Beyond the Culture Wars: How Teaching the Conflicts Can Revitalize American Education.* Copyright © 1992 by Gerald Graff. Reprinted with the permission of W. W. Norton & Company, Inc. P. 29, Michael Ryan, "Join the Incredible Reading Rally" from *Parade* magazine (January 5, 1997). Copyright © 1997 by Michael Ryan. Reprinted with the permission of Scovil Chichak Galen Literary Agency, Inc.

Pp. 58, 84, 172, 240, 241, 247–254, 329, John Mack Faragher, Mari Jo Buhle, Daniel Czitrom, and Susan H. Armitage, excerpts (including Figure 6-12) from *Out of Many: A History of the American People*, Second Edition. Copyright © 1997. Reprinted with the permission of Prentice-Hall, Inc., Upper Saddle River, NJ.

Pp. 75, 86, 161, Charles G. Morris, excerpts (including Figures 6-7, 6-15, 6-17, and 6-19) from *Psychology: An Introduction*, Ninth Edition. Copyright © 1996. Reprinted with the permission of Prentice-Hall, Inc., Upper Saddle River, NJ. P. 76, Definition for "comply" from *The Random House College Dictionary*, Revised Edition. Copyright © 1984 by Random House, Inc. Reprinted with the permission of the publishers. P. 77, Pp. 78, 85, 103, 133, 171, 266, 278, 431, John J. Macionis, excerpts from *Sociology*, Sixth Edition. Copyright © 1997. Reprinted with the permission of Prentice-Hall, Inc., Upper Saddle River, NJ. Pp. 82, 171, 195, James M. Burns, J. W. Peltason, Thomas E. Cronin, and David B. Magleby, excerpts (including Figure 6-3) from *Government by the People*, Second Edition. Copyright © 1997. Reprinted with the permission of Prentice-Hall, Inc., Upper Saddle River, NJ. P. 83, Tarbuck Lutgens, excerpts from *Earth Science*, Eighth Edition. Copyright © 1997. Reprinted with the permission of Prentice-Hall, Inc., Upper Saddle River, NJ. Pp. 85, 157–158, 163, 173, 182, 194, 226, 329, Teresa Audesirk and Gerald Audesirk, excerpts (including Figures 6-1, 6-29, and 6-30). Copyright © 1997. Reprinted with the permission of Prentice-Hall, Inc., Upper Saddle River, NJ. Pp. 87, 99, 196, 213, Ricky W. Griffin and Ronald J. Ebert, excerpts (including Figures 6-3, 6-4) from *Business*, Fourth Edition. Copyright © 1996. Reprinted with the permission of Prentice-Hall, Inc., Upper Saddle River, NJ. Pp. 87, 162, 163, 176, 264–265, Thomas I. White, excerpts from *Discovering Philosophy.* Copyright © 1991. Reprinted with the permission of Prentice-Hall, Inc., Upper Saddle River, NJ.

Pp. 122, 123, 124, 125–126, 174–175, 263 Louis Giannetti and Scott Eyman, excerpts from *Flashback: A Brief History of Film*, Third Edition. Copyright © 1996. Reprinted with the permission of Prentice-Hall, Inc., Upper Saddle River, NJ. Pp. 139, 170, 329, 331, 391, Stephen F. Davis and Joseph J. Palladino, excerpts from *Psychology.* Copyright © 1995. Reprinted with the permission of Prentice-Hall, Inc., Upper Saddle River, NJ. P. 144, Alex Kozinski, excerpts from "Tinkering with Death" from *The New Yorker* (February 10, 1997). Copyright © 1997 by Alex Kozinski. Reprinted with the permission of the author.

Pp. 155, 440–412, Richard P. Feynman, excerpts from *"Surely You're Joking, Mr. Feynman!": Adventures of a Curious Character*, Copyright © 1985 by Richard P. Feynman. Reprinted with the permission of W. W. Norton & Company, Inc. Pp. 158, 172, 281, Philip Kotler and Gary Armstrong, excerpts (including Figure 6-2) from *Marketing: An Introduction*, Fourth Edition. Copyright © 1997. Reprinted with the permission of Prentice-Hall, Inc., Upper Saddle River, NJ. Pp. 165–166, George McMichael and Edgar M. Glenn, "Who Wrote the Works of Shakespeare?" adapted from *Shakespeare and His Rivals: A Casebook on the Authorship Controversy* (New York: The Odyssey Press, 1962). Copyright © 1962 and renewed 1990 by George McMichael and Edgar M. Glenn. Reprinted with the permission of the authors. P. 168, Nancy V. Wood, "Twelve Clues to Main Ideas" from *College Reading and Study Skills*, Fifth Edition. Copyright © 1996 by Holt, Rinehart and Winston, Inc. Reprinted with the permission of the publishers.

P. 194, Figure 6-1: "Relative Sizes" from Teresa Audesirk and Gerald Audesirk, Life on Earth. Copyright © 1997. Reprinted with the permission of Prentice-Hall, Inc., Upper Saddle River, NJ. P. 200, Figure 6-10: "How Is the United Nations Doing?" from the Gallup Organization (1996). Reprinted with permission of The Gallup Organization. P. 209, Figure 6-16: Jim Morin cartoon, "Revenge of the Environment" (March 23, 1989). Copyright © 1989 by The Miami Herald. Reprinted with the permission of King Features Syndicate. P. 213, Figure 6-22: "Percentage of children in different child-care arrangements in the United States" adapted from Sandra L. Hofferth, April Brayfield, Sharon Deich, and Pamela Holcomb, *National Child Care Survey*, 1990. Reprinted with the permission of The Urban Institute Press. P. 214, Figure 6-23: "The Behavioral Effects of Blood Alcohol Levels" based on data from Oakey Ray, *Drugs, Society and Human Behavior*, Third Edition. Copyright © 1983 by Mosby-Year Book, Inc. Reprinted with permission. Pp. 220–222, Conrad P. Kottak, "Television and Cultural Behavior" in *Common Culture*, Michael F. Petracca and Madeleine Sorapure, eds. (Englewood Cliffs: Prentice Hall, 1995). Reprinted with permission of Prentice-Hall, Inc. P. 221, Kevin Sack, "Symbols of Old South Feed a New Bitterness" from *The New York Times* (February 8, 1997). Copyright © 1997 by The New York Times Company. Reprinted with the permission of The New York Times. P. 222, illustration of "Carry Me Back to Old Virginny": Joyce Dopkeen/NYT Pictures. P. 223, photographs of Franklin, Tenn. Confederate statue: Christopher Berkey/NY Times Pictures. P. 249, Bob Dylan, excerpt from "The Times They Are A Changin'." Copyright © 1963 by Warner Bros., Inc.; renewed 1991 by Special Rider Music. All rights reserved and administered by Special Rider Music, New York.

P. 262, H. W. Janson and Anthony F. Janson, excerpt from *A Basic History of Art*, Fifth Edition. Copyright © 1997. Reprinted with the permission of Prentice-Hall, Inc., Upper Saddle River, NJ. Pp. 265–266, 393, Harvey Blatt, excerpts from *Our Geologic*

Subject Index

A

Academic disciplines, critical thinking in, 417–18
Acid deposition, 495–96
Acid rain, 495–96
Acronyms, 476
Acrostics, 476
Adenosine triphosphate, 488
Adirondack lakes, acid rain and, 495–96
Amino acids, 493
Ammonia, 492–93, 496
Amnesias, 478–80
Annotating, 169–71
  See also Underlining, annotating, and summarizing (UAS) method
Antecedents, 156
Anterograde amnesia, 478
Argument, 5, 259–326
  the author, 268
  claim identification, 273–74
  claims of cause, 271
  claims of definition, 270–71
  claims of fact, 270
  claims of policy, 272
  claims of value, 271–72
  common ground and, 274
  the conclusion, 304–08, 311
  context for, 269, 274
  defined, 261–66
  emotional support, 293, 301–03
  exploratory, 267–68
  forming an issue question, 273
  hidden, 267
  logical reasons, 295
  logical support, 293, 295–99, 305–08, 310–11
  obvious, 267
  opinions, 299–300, 311
  personal credibility, 293, 300, 311
  point of view, 260, 268–69, 274
  purpose and, 260
  recognizing a biased point of view, 308–10
  refutation, 303–08, 311
  source of, 269
  the subject, 268
  unconscious, 267
  See also Inferences; Media literacy; Visual argument
Articles
  surveying, 41–42, 45–46
  survey sheets for, 56–57
Association-based model of memory, 445
Atmosphere, nitrogen in, 492–93
Attitude, 37
Auditory memory (echoic sensory memory), 449
Autotrophs, 485

B

Bandwagon appeal, 382
Bar graphs, 200–201
Beliefs. *See* Values and beliefs; Inferences
Bias, 308–10
  analyzing, 310
  signs of, 309
Bioaccumulating chemicals, 490
Biodegradable, 490
Biogeochemical cycles (nutrient cycles), 484, 491
Biological magnification, 490
Biomass, 485
Biomass pyramid, 489
Body format, 114–15
Books
  surveying, 41, 44–45
  survey sheets for, 55–56
Brainstorming, 420, 423

C

Calcium carbonate, 492
Calories, 485
Carbon cycles, global warming and, 496–97
Carbon dioxide, 491–92
  global warming and, 497–98
Carbonfund.org, 501
Carnivores, 486
Cause-effect pattern, 119–20
  map for, 125
Cause-effect reasoning, 296
Center for Media Literacy website, 366
Chapters
  formats and, 127
  surveying, 41–42, 45–46
  survey sheets for, 56–57
  textbook, 115
Charts, 193–94, 378
  See also Visual materials
Chronological pattern, 117–18
  map for, 123
Chunking (grouping), 450–51, 475
Claims, 270–72
  of cause, 271
  of definition, 270–71
  of fact, 270
  identifying, 273–74
  of policy, 272
  of value, 271–72
Clean Air Act, 496
Closed-ended questions, 471
Clusters of knowledge, 464–65
Coding, improving memory and, 475–76
Cognitive interviews, 471
Collaborating, 6–7, 9
College reading
  defined, 3–4
  See also Critical reading; Critical thinking; Study reading
Common ground, 274
  visual argument and, 371, 373, 385
Comparison-contrasts, for supporting details, 160
Comparison-contrast pattern, 120
  map for, 125
Comparisons, 296
  emotional, 301–02
Compost piles, 488
Comprehension monitoring, 8
Concluding paragraphs. *See* Summary paragraphs
Conclusion format, 115
Conclusions, 304–08
  analyzing, 305–08
  evaluating, 311
  values and beliefs and, 340
  visual materials and, 208
Connective words, 38
Connotative meaning, 301
Consolidation hypothesis, 478–80
Consumers (heterotrophs), 485, 486–88
Context, 6
  argument and, 269, 274
  words and, 74–75
Cornell reading notes, 49–51, 122, 126–27
Creative thinking, 415–16
  questions for, 422–23
  See also Critical thinking
Critical reading, 259
  after reading, 410
  before reading, 409
  inferences and, 334–36
  questions that guide, 407–08
  while reading, 409
  See also Argument
Critical reading and thinking, 8–9
  defined, 8
  integrating with study reading, 9
  See also Argument
Critical thinking, 410–23
  in the academic disciplines, 417–18
  brainstorming and, 420, 423
  creative thinking and, 415–16, 422–23
  defined, 410–12
  freewriting, 423
  metacognition and, 419–20
  problem solving, 413–15, 422
  questions for, 421–23
  setting a thinking goal, 420
  strategies for, 412–13
  synthesizing and making mental connections, 418–19
  visual argument and, 377–79
Cryptoamnesia, 472
Cynobacteria, 486

D

DDT (insecticide), 490
Decomposers, 488, 491–93
Definitions, 296
Deja vu, 472
Denitrifying bacteria, 493
Denotative meaning, 301
Density of material, 38
Descriptions, 160
Details. *See* Supporting details
Detritus feeders, 488, 491
Diagrams, 204–05
Diatoms, 485
Dictionaries, 76–77
Difficulty level in reading, 36–39
  identifying, 37–38
  See also Efficient reading
Directed forgetting, 452–53
Distributed practice, 443–44
Drinking water, 494–95

E

Ebbinghaus, Hermann, 199, 441–43
Echoic sensory memory (auditory), 449
Ecosystems, 482–504
  acid rain, 495–96
  energy flow through communities, 485–90
  global warming, 496–501
  nutrients in, 491–95
  pathways of energy and nutrients, 484

T

Table of contents, 127
Table of figures, 201–02, 378–79
Tactile (touch) sensory memory, 449
10 % law, 488
Take-home exams, 242
Teacher-made tests, 7
Technical article format, 116
Tertiary consumers, 486–88
Test anxiety, 243
Tests
    standardized, 7
    strategies for taking, 242–43
    teacher-made, 7
    See also Exams
Texasminutemen.org, 387
Textbook chapters, 115
Textbook format, 115
Textbooks
    studying for exams, 232, 239
    theshadowlands.net, 387
    writing reading notes in, 166
Thinking, reading and, 4
Three R's (reduce, review, and recite), 237
Time Analysis Sheet, 34
Time limits, for reading, 43–44
Tip-of-the-tongue phenomenon, 459–60
Topic sentences, 157–59, 161
    See also Main ideas
Traditional model of memory.
    See Stages-of-memory model
Transitional paragraphs, 163
Transitional words and phrases, 157, 161
Trophic levels, 486–90

U

UAS. *See* Underlining, annotating, and summarizing method

Unconscious argument, 267
Underlining, 169–71
    See also Underlining, annotating, and summarizing (UAS) method
Underlining, annotating, and summarizing (UAS) method, 155, 169–71
    example of, 170–71
Urea, 493

V

Values
    appeals to, 302
    media messages and, 367, 383
Values and beliefs, 336–37, 340
    conclusions and, 340
    See also Inferences
Visual argument, 369–74
    emotional response, 371–72, 373, 385
    icons, 372, 373, 385
    immediacy and tangibility of, 371, 373, 385
    interpreting, 372–73, 385
    juxtaposition and, 372, 373, 385
    personal identification (common ground) and, 371, 373, 385
    recognizing and analyzing, 370–71, 385
    selectiveness and, 372, 373, 385
    symbols, 372, 373, 385
    See also Fallacies; Media literacy; Visual materials
Visual materials, 192–231
    bar graphs, 20–201
    creating, 205, 208
    diagrams, 204–05
    drawing conclusions, 208
    example of information-packed chart, 193–94

five questions for reading visuals, 206–07
flowcharts, 196
geographical maps with legends, 202–03
importance of studying, 192–93
line graphs, 198–99
organizational charts, 197
as part of reading process, 205–06
pie charts, 195
summarizing, 208
table of figures, 201–02
tracing or redrawing, 208
    See also Visual argument
Vocabulary improvement, 70–110
    for biology, 85
    for business, 87–88
    circling words and writing their meanings in the margins, 78
    context of words, 74–75
    determining meaning of words, 74–77
    dictionaries, 76–77
    for earth science, 83–84
    for history, 84
    locating and learning new words, 73–74
    Malcolm X and, 70
    memorizing words, 77, 81
    motivation for, 70–71
    past development, 71
    for philosophy, 88–89
    for political science, 82
    prefixes, 75–76, 89–94
    for psychology, 86–87
    roots, 75–76, 89–90, 95–98
    for sociology, 85
    specialized vocabulary, 73–74
    suffixes, 75–76, 89–90, 98–99
    using lists or maps, 80
    vocabulary cards, 72–73, 80
    vocabulary sheets, 78–80

W

Water, 494–95
Weather extremes, 499
Web-based materials
    evaluating, 374–77, 386–87
    See also Internet; Media literacy
Web sites
    Center for Media Literacy, 366
    evaluating, 374–77, 386–87
    Media Awareness Network, 368
    MSNBC.com, 387
    New Mexico Media Literacy Project, 367
    Texasminutemen.org, 387
    theshadowlands.net, 387
    See also Internet; Media literacy
Whole into parts pattern, 116
    map for, 122
Wildlife, global warming and, 499–501
Word families, 98
Words
    connotative meaning, 301
    denotative meaning, 301
    lists and, 80
    maps and, 80–81
    memorizing, 81
    parts of, 75–76
    related, 156
    repetition of key words, 157
    transitional, 157
    See also Vocabulary improvement
Working memory, 451
Writing, 128–29
    while reading, 13
Writing conventions, 6
Writing process, 9–10
Writing to think, 261

Reading Index